A Practical Guide to Civil Litigation

Thi.
sel

A Practical Guide to Civil Litigation

Second edition

District Judge Robert Hill

*Scarborough District Registry and County Court;
Recorder; Regional Costs Judge on the North-Eastern
Circuit; Visiting Professor of Law, Leeds Metropolitan
University; former Principal of the College of Law, York*

District Judge Helen Wood

Harrogate County Court

Suzanne Fine, Barrister, Solicitor

*Head of Legal Training, Lovells;
Visiting Professor of Law, Nottingham Law School*

JORDANS

2005

Published by Jordan Publishing Limited
21 St Thomas Street
Bristol BS1 6JS

© Jordan Publishing Limited 2005
First edition 2003
Reprinted June 2004; second reprint November 2004

British Library Cataloguing-in-Publication Data

A catalogue record for this book is available
from the British Library.

ISBN 0 85308 990 6

Typeset by Etica Press Ltd, Malvern
Printed and bound in Great Britain by Antony Rowe Ltd, Chippenham, Wilts

Foreword to the first edition

The implementation of the Civil Procedure Rules 1998 and the accompanying Practice Directions represents a dramatic shift in litigation culture. The institutionally slow and expensive procedure that ultimately served to impede the objectives of justice has been swept away and replaced by a fresh approach whose two principal characteristics are fairness and efficiency. Gone are the uncertainties of procedure that allowed practitioners to polarise the parties' positions. Also disappeared are the surprise tactics and turf wars on procedural technicalities that bedevilled litigation. The court's duty of active case management, married to its wide powers to monitor and regulate the progress of a case, promote expeditious dispute resolution. Underpinning those powers is the concept of proportionality so that parties now can expect an intensity of treatment that is proportionate to the complexity of the legal issues and the amount of money involved.

Newly qualified lawyers are now trained in the basic concepts and idiom of the CPR. Detail in abundance they will find in the White Book, but they are at risk of finding themselves floundering in the trees and unable to make out the form of the wood. What they need is a guide which explains in clear language how the rules work, what they are intended to achieve and how to make use of them. This is just what the authors of *A Practical Guide to Civil Litigation* have achieved. Practical it certainly is. It maps out the course of dispute resolution from the first step – funding, through pre-action protocols and consideration of ADR, case management, preparation for trial, the trial itself, appeal, and ends with what is often the most critical, and least regarded, aspect of the whole enterprise – enforcement. But this guide is no mere route map. It contains valuable advice on tactics and strategy at every stage of the journey.

The authors are to be congratulated for identifying a gap in the young practitioner's bookshelf and filling this most admirably, save that this is not a volume which will spend much time on the litigator's shelf – it is likely to be in almost constant use.

THE RIGHT HONOURABLE THE LORD PHILLIPS,
MASTER OF THE ROLLS
December 2002

Foreword to the first edition

Preface

Following the warm welcome given to our first edition we are pleased to offer this second edition. Our aims and objectives are unchanged. A second edition is required merely because changes in procedural law have rendered much of the first edition out of date.

Although written mainly for the newly qualified lawyer the book does, of course, have a wider readership. The Civil Procedure Rules 1998 are '... a new procedural code ...' (see rule 1.1) but given that they have been in force now since April 1999 there are already a significant number of lawyers who never knew the old rules which the CPR replaced. Unfortunately, the old rules cannot be ignored, for many reasons including the simple fact that some of them are still in force. The CPR, as is so often the case with modern legislation, were brought out in too much of a hurry. The Civil Procedure Rules Committee (constituted under the Civil Procedure Act 1997) had not finished its task and fudged doing so by including in Schedule 1 to the CPR unchanged rules from the Rules of the Supreme Court 1965 and in Schedule 2 rules from the County Court Rules 1984. These Schedules are now much reduced in size, but frankly ought not to be there at all. The Committee seems to have lost its sense of urgency and it is to be hoped that by the time the third edition of this work appears the Committee will have finished this task and that Schedules 1 and 2, suitably updated, have been incorporated into the main body of the CPR.

Acknowledgements

Chapters 3, 9–13, 33 and 35 in this book draw on materials developed by Nottingham Law School and the National Institute for Trial Advocacy (NITA (UK)). The authors would like to take this opportunity to express their gratitude to both institutions for granting permission to use these materials. In particular the authors would like to mention the following members of the Nottingham Law School:

Professor Peter Jones;
Professor Phil Knott;
Professor Ian McLachlan;
Jane Ching;
Susan Luke.

The authors would like to thank Richard Holt of BPP Law School for his assistance in revising these chapters for the second edition.

Thanks also are due to the Lovells Library Information Service for advice on Chapter 10, and to His Honour Michael Cook for casting his expert eye over the chapters dealing with Costs and Funding.

Contents

Chapter 4 – FUNDING OF LITIGATION

Chapter 5 – LIMITATION OF ACTIONS

Chapter 6 – PRE-ACTION PROTOCOLS

Chapter 7 – CHANGE OF SOLICITOR

Chapter 8 – INTEREST

PART II – CIVIL LITIGATION SKILLS

Chapter 9 – INTERVIEWING

Chapter 10 – LEGAL RESEARCH

Chapter 11 – DRAFTING

Chapter 12 – ADVOCACY

Chapter 13 – NEGOTIATION

PART III – COMMENCEMENT

Chapter 14 – COMMENCING PROCEEDINGS UNDER PART 7 OF THE CIVIL PROCEDURE RULES 1998

Chapter 15 – COMMENCING PROCEEDINGS – OTHER THAN UNDER PART 7 OF THE CIVIL PROCEDURE RULES 1998

Chapter 16 – COUNTERCLAIMS AND OTHER ADDITIONAL CLAIMS (PART 20)

Chapter 17 – SERVICE

PART IV – DETERMINATION OF A CASE WITHOUT TRIAL

Chapter 18 – JUDGMENT IN DEFAULT

Chapter 19 – ADMISSIONS

Chapter 20 – SUMMARY JUDGMENT

Chapter 21 – DISPOSALS

PART V – CASE MANAGEMENT

Chapter 22 – ALLOCATION

Chapter 23 – CASE MANAGEMENT

Chapter 24 – THE SMALL CLAIMS TRACK

Chapter 25 – THE FAST TRACK

Chapter 26 – THE MULTI-TRACK

PART VI – EVIDENCE

Chapter 27 – DISCLOSURE

Chapter 36 – TRIAL

PART VIII – COSTS

Chapter 37 – PART 36 OFFERS AND PAYMENTS

Chapter 38 – SECURITY FOR COSTS

Chapter 39 – COSTS

PART IX – POST-TRIAL ISSUES

Chapter 40 – APPEAL

Chapter 41 – ENFORCEMENT OF JUDGMENTS

PART X – OTHER PROCEEDINGS

Chapter 42 – RECOVERY OF LAND

Chapter 43 – MISCELLANEOUS PRACTICE DIRECTIONS

TABLE OF CASES

References are to page number.

TABLE OF STATUTES

References are to page number. Page numbers in bold indicate where an Act is set out in full or in part.

TABLE OF STATUTORY INSTRUMENTS

References are to page number. Page numbers in bold indicate where an SI is set out in full or in part.

TABLE OF EUROPEAN MATERIALS

References are to page number. Page numbers in bold indicate where material is set out in full or in part.

TABLE OF OTHER MATERIALS

References are to page number.

TABLE OF FORMS

References are to page number.

TABLE OF ABBREVIATIONS

ACAS	Advisory, Conciliation and Arbitration Service
ADR	Alternative Dispute Resolution
ATE	After-the-event insurance
BATNA	Best Alternative to a Negotiated Agreement
CCA 1984	County Courts Act 1984
CD	Civil Division
CEA 1995	Civil Evidence Act 1995
CFA	Conditional Fee Agreement
CJJA	Civil Jurisdiction and Judgments Act 1982/91
CMC(s)	Case Management Conference(s)
COA 1979	Charging Orders Act 1979
CPR	Civil Procedure Rules 1998
DCJ	Designated Civil Judge
EC	European Community
EFTA	European Free Trade Association
FILEx	Fellows of the Institute of Legal Executives
JA 1838	Judgments Act 1838
LCD, June 1995	Access to Justice – Interim Report
LSC 2000	Legal Service Costs
RCJ	Royal Courts of Justice
RSC	Rules of the Supreme Court 1965
RTA	Road Traffic Accident
SCA 1981	Supreme Court Act 1981

Part I

PRELIMINARY MATTERS

Chapter 1

INTRODUCTION TO THE CIVIL COURTS

GENERAL

This book is primarily aimed at the newly qualified lawyer. The training received by law students today has never been better. In particular, the Legal Practice Course undertaken by solicitors and the Bar Vocational Course by barristers prepare the modern generation of lawyers for practice far better than was the case for earlier generations. Yet the volume of material to be absorbed is daunting. The student manuals, specifically designed and written for the courses, are of necessity confined to an irreducible minimum. It is right that lawyers should learn the basics first. When things go badly wrong, it is not because a minor point of detail has been overlooked; it is because some fundamental principle has been misunderstood, forgotten or, even worse, never grasped in the first place. Thus, the newly qualified lawyer has to make a rapid transition from the excellent law student manuals to the books used on a daily basis by judges and practitioners alike. Such a transition can be daunting. This book aims to smooth the transition and act as a link.

In the field of civil litigation, the longest established and most widely used book is *Civil Procedure* (Sweet & Maxwell), usually known as 'the White Book'. This is a comprehensive two-volume work with supplements. For practitioners who prefer a one-volume work, the *Civil Court Service* (Jordans) ('the Brown Book') is by far and away the best of the available texts. This book does not seek to compete with either of those. On the contrary, it encourages its readers to make the transition to the practitioner works as soon as possible, but seeks to re-emphasise the irreducible minimum acquired at the professional stage of training and expand and explain further, where necessary.

The book is, therefore, for newly qualified solicitors, newly qualified barristers, newly qualified legal executives and other paralegals, the law student who wants to go beyond the basics of the professional course, lawyers changing specialisms or returning to practice, or indeed any lawyer who wants a quick-reference, short volume to consult prior to referring to the more detailed practitioner works.

THE CIVIL COURTS

The main civil courts are the High Court and the county courts. The bulk of civil work is undertaken in county courts. County courts were created by the County Courts Act 1846, in one of the main reforms of law and procedure of the nineteenth century. The current statute is the County Courts Act 1984 (CCA 1984), as subsequently amended. There is no longer a logical reason for having different courts. It is submitted that, whatever it might be called, it would be better to have just one civil court with an appropriate number of Divisions. The proposed reform has the support of most judges and is likely before too long.

The High Court, in its modern form, was also created by nineteenth-century reforms, principally the Judicature Act 1873. The modern statute is the Supreme Court Act 1981 (SCA 1981), as subsequently amended. The High Court comprises three Divisions:

(1)   the Queen's Bench Division (which includes the Admiralty Court and the Commercial Court);
(2)   the Chancery Division (which includes the Companies Court and the Patents Court); and
(3)   the Family Division.

All three Divisions have equal jurisdiction but business is allocated to an appropriate Division as an administrative convenience. Cases should be commenced in the correct Division (see SCA 1981, s 61) but can be transferred to another Division if it is felt to be more appropriate.

In London, the High Court has a separate building – the very imposing building in The Strand known as 'The Royal Courts of Justice'. County courts are established throughout London in less grand premises. This is not the case out of London, where county courts and High Courts share the same building and the same staff. Outside London, the various High Court offices are known as 'district registries'.

Just as cases can be transferred between Divisions of the High Court, so cases can be transferred between county courts and, indeed, between the High Court and a county court (CCA 1984, s 40). The jurisdiction of the High Court is virtually unlimited. In so far as it is limited, this is invariably because a particular statute (eg the Consumer Credit Act 1974), or a particular rule (eg the Civil Procedure Rules 1998 (CPR) Part 55) gives exclusive jurisdiction to the county court. Claims for damages for personal injuries must be commenced in the county court, unless the claim is for £50,000 or more, in which case the claim can be issued in either the High Court or a county court. A non-personal injury claim must be commenced in a county court unless the claim exceeds £15,000 in which case it can be issued in either the High Court or a county court. County courts have unlimited jurisdiction in contract and tort cases (the exception is defamation: see CCA 1984, s15). Apart from equity claims (where the limit is £30,000: see the High Court and County Court Jurisdiction Order 1991, SI 1991/724, Art 2(3)) there is no upper limit on the jurisdiction of a county court. Although county courts are not formally organised into Divisions, there are, in practice, specialist areas, in particular the 'Technology and Construction Court', in which only specially trained and nominated judges sit. There is also a Patents County Court and, in London, the Central London County Court has a 'Mercantile Court' and deals with cases similar to those which, in the High Court, would be dealt with by the Commercial Court. The Commercial Court is in London, but each circuit has a 'Mercantile Court' for similar cases. (See CPR Parts 58 and 59.)

THE JUDICIARY

There are three levels of judge trying cases at first instance: High Court judges, circuit judges and district judges. Obviously, High Court judges (who are addressed as 'My Lord' or 'My Lady', as appropriate) sit only in High Court cases. It does not follow, however, that all High Court cases are tried by High Court judges. Many are tried by circuit judges, appointed to sit in the High Court under SCA 1981, s 9 (often simply known as 'a section 9 judge'). However, the main work of the circuit judge (who is addressed as 'Your Honour') is trying the weightier cases of the county court. District judges (who are addressed as 'Sir' or 'Madam', as appropriate) try county court cases allocated to the fast track or the small claims track. In certain circumstances, they can also try cases allocated to the multi-track. (See Chapter 2 for details of these tracks.) District judges are also concerned with case management. Outside London, many county court district judges are also district judges of the High Court, and sit in their local district registry. This is, of course, in practice, the same building and the same courtroom as that in which they undertake county court work. In London, the system is different: district judges of the county court do not also sit at the Royal Courts of Justice. District judges are appointed in the Family Division, but the Chancery Division and the Queen's Bench Division in London still retain the long-established, but now rather quaint, title of 'Master'. The modern system also makes extensive use of part-time judges, who are known as recorders, deputy district judges and deputy masters. Some recorders are authorised to sit in the High Court.

In addition to the judiciary, there are many formal or administrative acts performed by court clerks. It has to be decided from the context whether 'the court' means the building, a court clerk or a judge. By CPR r 2.3(3):

> 'where the context requires, a reference to "the court" means a reference to a particular county court, a district registry or the Royal Courts of Justice.'

By CPR r 2.4:

> 'where [the CPR] provide for the court to perform any act then, except where an enactment, rule or practice direction provides otherwise, that act may be performed:
>
> (a) in relation to proceedings in the High Court, by any judge, master or district judge of that court; and
>
> (b) in relation to proceedings in a county court by any judge or district judge.'

CPR r 2.5 specifically provides for an act of a formal or administrative character to be performed by a court officer. Article 6 of the European Convention for the Protection of Human Rights and Fundamental Freedoms 1950 (ECHR), which is incorporated into English law (see Sch 1 to the Human Rights Act 1998 (HRA 1998)), provides for civil hearings to be in 'public'. This is the general rule provided for by CPR Part 39, although there are, of course, exceptions.

CIVIL PROCEDURE RULES 1998

As a result of Lord Woolf's 5-year-long 'Access to Justice' inquiry, the CPR 1998 (made under the authority of the Civil Procedure Act 1997) came into force on 26 April 1999. There is thus just one set of rules governing both the High Court and the county court. Prior to this, there were different rules governing the High Court and county courts, indeed using different terminology. Much of this was sterile and has been swept away. The complete rewriting of the civil rules is still not complete. Consequently, CPR Sch 1 contains rules that were formerly in the Rules of the Supreme Court 1965 (RSC), and CPR Sch 2 contains rules formerly in the County Court Rules 1981 (CCR). The task of updating these and incorporating them into the main body of the CPR has still not been completed and is continuing. However, for the first time, there is one set of rules governing civil procedure. The next chapter outlines these rules (see also Appendix A).

Chapter 2

INTRODUCTION TO THE
CIVIL PROCEDURE RULES 1998

THE OVERRIDING OBJECTIVE

Rule 1.1(1) of the CPR provides 'these rules are a new procedural code with the overriding objective of enabling the court to deal with cases justly'. The importance of the overriding objective as the bedrock of the CPR cannot be overemphasised. Rather than just launching into the details of the rules, the overriding objective defines what the rules are all about. The answer to any problem arising under the CPR can be found by applying the overriding objective. (Note the use of the term 'overriding'.)

The use of the words 'a new procedural code' emphasises that, as far as possible, the provisions of old rules and authorities on the interpretation of those old rules are not to be taken into consideration (*Biguzzi v Rank Leisure plc* [1999] 1 WLR 1926). Although the past can never be regarded as irrelevant (*DEG – Deutsche Investitions und Entwicklungsgesellschaft mbH v Koshy and others* [2000] TLR 29), there is a clear attempt to break with the past and start again with a clean sheet of paper.

The CPR are in plain, modern, straightforward English and do not use any Latin words. Consequently, in many instances, the text of the rule itself requires no elaboration. For example, r 1.1(2) provides:

'Dealing with a case justly includes, so far as practicable –

    (a)   ensuring that the parties are on an equal footing;
    (b)   saving expense;
    (c)   dealing with the case in ways which are proportionate –

        (i)   to the amount of money involved
        (ii)   to the importance of the case
        (iii)   to the complexity of the issues, and,
        (iv)   to the financial position of each party;

    (d)   ensuring that it is dealt with expeditiously and fairly; and,
    (e)   allotting to it an appropriate share of the court's resources, while taking into account the need to allot resources to other cases.'

By r 1.2, the court must seek to give effect to the overriding objective when it exercises any power given to it by any rule or interprets any rule. Further, r 1.3 is entitled 'Duty of the Parties', and provides that 'the parties are required to help the court to further the overriding objective'.

Of course, even an overriding objective has limitations. It cannot be relied upon to override the specific provision of another rule of the CPR. (See, eg, *Godwin v Swindon Borough Council* [2001] 4 All ER 641, strictly applying the rules of service.)

The crucial difference between the CPR and its predecessor's rules is that the new rules mean what they say and say what they mean. Unfortunately, due to lax interpretation, the old RSC and CCR had become little more than pious expressions of hope. Time-limits were ignored and no sanctions were imposed. Cases moved at a slow pace and delaying tactics were common. Tactical interlocutory applications were common. Some cases drifted and took years.

There must be no doubt that it is intended that the CPR should be complied with. Where they are not, sanctions will follow and, at the very least, the defaulting party can be expected to pay – and pay immediately – costs unnecessarily incurred by any delay and/or costs of any necessary steps taken to ensure compliance with the rules. Obviously, sanctions must be proportionate, but the ultimate sanction is for the court to strike out a party's case and give judgment to the other party. (See further, CPR Part 3, in particular rr 3.8 and 3.9.)

CASE MANAGEMENT

To some extent, the CPR in 1998 took litigation out of the hands of the parties. Under the old rules, the parties themselves controlled the pace of litigation. This is no longer so.

By r 1.4(5), the court must further the overriding objective by actively managing cases. Put simply, this means that the court (usually the district judge) decides what needs to be done to get the case concluded and sets a timetable for doing it. The majority of cases settle without a trial. The judge bears in mind, therefore, that usually he is case managing settlement negotiations rather than managing a case destined for trial and allows for this when giving directions.

By r 1.4(2), active case management includes:

'(a) encouraging the parties to co-operate with each other in the conduct of the proceedings;
(b) identifying the issues at an early stage;
(c) deciding promptly which issues need full investigation and trial and accordingly disposing summarily of the others;
(d) deciding the order in which issues are to be resolved;
(e) encouraging the parties to use an alternative dispute resolution procedure if the court considers that appropriate and facilitating the use of such procedure;

(f)   helping the parties to settle the whole or part of the case;

(g)   fixing timetables or otherwise controlling the progress of the case;

(h)   considering whether the likely benefits of taking a particular step justify the cost of taking it;

(i)   dealing with as many aspects of the case as it can on the same occasion;

(j)   dealing with the case without the parties needing to attend at court;

(k)   making use of technology; and,

(l)   giving directions to ensure that the trial of the case proceeds quickly and efficiently.'

One immediate impact of these provisions is the increasingly common use of hearings being conducted by telephone, without solicitors having to attend court. (See further, CPR PD 23, para 6.)

TRACKING

Once a case has become defended, the court's first and important task is to allocate the case to the appropriate track. (See Part 26 – Case Management: Preliminary Stage, Part 27 – The Small Claims Track, Part 28 – The Fast Track and Part 29 – The Multi-track.) Claims of under £5,000 (and personal injury claims of under £1,000) are allocated to the small claims track. On allocation, the district judge usually gives appropriate case management directions and a trial date. Thus, the parties only have to come to court for the trial itself. The fast track (an innovation of the CPR) is for claims not exceeding £15,000 (including claims for damages for personal injuries that exceed £1,000). Once again, the district judge fixes a trial date or, more usually, a trial window of not more than 3 weeks and commencing not more than 27 weeks ahead. The intention is that all fast track cases should be concluded within 30 weeks of allocation. Directions will also be given within that time frame. Thus, usually, the parties and their lawyers only have to come to court for the trial itself. Multi-track cases are for cases which cannot be allocated to the small claims or fast track, and generally will exceed £15,000. In the more simple multi-track cases, directions along the lines of those for fast track cases can be given and the case can proceed to trial. In other cases, a case management conference will be held at some stage between allocation and trial. As part of its allocation and case management directions, the court will give either a trial date or trial window, or a date for a case management conference. One of the main purposes of that case management conference will then be to fix the trial date or trial window. In a more complex case, a date for another case management conference may be appropriate. The intention is that the majority of multi-track cases should be concluded within 50 weeks of allocation.

As already noted, it is intended that the directions given by the court should be complied with, and sanctions must be expected if they are not. However, the rules are an aid to achieving justice and not an end in themselves. It is possible for parties to agree variations to the timetable and they should do so where appropriate, rather than requiring one party to apply to the court for an extension. Rule 2.11 is entitled 'Time limits may be varied by parties' and provides that 'Unless these rules or a practice direction provide otherwise or the court orders otherwise, the time specified by a rule or by the court for a person to do any act may be varied by the written agreement of the parties'. The rules provide that certain milestone dates cannot be changed. It is never possible to vary by consent the date of trial, a trial window or the date of a case management conference or the date for filing a pre-trial checklist (listing questionnaire). Only the court can change these dates. (See, further, Part V of this book – Case Management.)

Chapter 3

ALTERNATIVE DISPUTE RESOLUTION

WHAT IS ADR?

Alternative dispute resolution (ADR) is a generic term for a number of different processes by which disputes can be settled without recourse to the court. They can, however, be divided into two broad categories defined below.

Alternative adjudication

This method involves a decision-maker being appointed who decides how the dispute should be resolved.

Assisted settlement

This method allows the parties to reach agreement themselves with the aid of a third party. Here the decision is not imposed *by* the third party.

COMPARISON OF ADR WITH OTHER FORMS OF DISPUTE RESOLUTION

Litigation

Although this is a voluntary process for the claimant it might be described as an involuntary process for the defendant. It is difficult for either party to extricate themselves once litigation is in progress. However, a judgment obtained in litigation is binding, whereas generally the result in ADR is not binding.

Negotiation

This is a voluntary process similar to ADR, and its outcome is not binding (unless it results in a contract). However, unlike in mainstream ADR, no third party is involved.

REFERENCE TO ADR IN THE CIVIL PROCEDURE RULES 1998

Mention of ADR is specifically made in the following contexts.

The overriding objective and active case management

See for example, CPR r 1.1(2), but in particular CPR r 1.4(2), which explicitly requires the court to encourage the use of ADR.

Protocols

Eight pre-action protocols have been introduced to date. (These are discussed in detail in Chapter 6.) The personal injury protocol stresses that litigation should be the last resort. The clinical negligence protocol suggests that the parties should consider the full range of ADR options, and the protocol contains a whole section (section 5) on an alternative approach to settling disputes.

The construction and engineering protocol demands a pre-action meeting between the parties during the course of which the parties must consider whether the dispute (or individual parts of the dispute) can be resolved by ADR and if so, by which form.

The defamation protocol (in section 3.7) says that both parties will be expected by the court to provide *evidence* that they have considered alternative means of resolving the dispute.

Staying proceedings

CPR Part 3 allows the court to stay proceedings until a specific date on its own initiative. CPR r 26.4 in the allocation questionnaire asks the parties whether they want a stay.

Costs

CPR PD Protocols itself provides potential costs implications for failure to comply with the protocols. However, or in addition, CPR Part 44 provides that the court, on making orders as to costs, will take account of the conduct of the parties including efforts made before and during the course of proceedings to try to resolve the dispute. Parties will be expected to seek to resolve the dispute by ADR unless it is unreasonable to do so (*Halsey v Milton Keynes General NHS Trust* [2004] EWCA 576, CA).

MEANS OF ARRIVING AT ADR

The parties may be referred to ADR by means of a joint decision through court referral or by prior agreement.

Joint decision

The parties may reach a joint decision to engage in ADR as a result of legal advice, possibly because both parties applied in their allocation questionnaires for a stay.

Court referral

Parties may be referred to ADR by the court, for example, under the Commercial Court scheme. However, any court can impose a stay under CPR Part 3. What the court cannot do in this jurisdiction (unlike in some others, for example Florida) is insist that the parties actually begin mediating in good faith or even attend the mediation. The court might, however, on the expiry of a stay, ask how far the parties have got by way of ADR and why the dispute has not yet been resolved.

Prior agreement

There may be an arbitration clause in the contract, for example: if there is a clause in the contract between A and B submitting a dispute arising from that contract to arbitration, but despite this A issues court proceedings, B can apply for the court proceedings to be stayed so that the matter can be dealt with by arbitration, *provided* B has not taken a step in the court action (by, for example, serving a defence). The defendant should acknowledge service but then immediately make an application to stay the court proceedings.

It is vitally important to check at the outset of any contractual case whether there is an arbitration clause in the contract in order to avoid inadvertently depriving the client of his right to go to arbitration. For a relevant case, see *Halki Shipping Corporation v Sopex Oils Limited* [1998] 1 WLR 726.

See further:

–   Arbitration Act 1950, s 4(1);
–   Arbitration Act 1996, s 9; and
–   CPR Part 62 for some general provisions about the link between arbitration and court proceedings.

SUMMARY OF THE ADVANTAGES AND DISADVANTAGES OF ADR

Advantages	*Disadvantages*
Speed	Not suitable for all disputes or all clients
Cost	May be perceived as a sign of weakness
Confidential	Result may not be binding
Less stressful	Result may not be enforceable
Allows commercial relationships to be maintained	
Client-centred	
Allows flexible/creative solutions	

FORMS OF ADR

Arbitration

Many lawyers would not regard arbitration as being a true form of ADR since it is adversarial.

The arbitrator is chosen by the parties to a dispute. The choice may be made in advance and reflected in an arbitration clause in the contract between the parties.

The arbitrator decides according to the law and the outcome is legally binding and can be enforced through the courts. It is enforceable like a judgment and is binding on the parties. Arbitration can be cheaper and quicker than litigation.

However, the rules (now contained in the Arbitration Act 1996) are complex. Arbitration is a variation of the court process rather than an alternative.

Expert determination

An expert is selected by the parties to decide the case. The procedure is not as complex or as detailed as arbitration, and the expert does not have powers equivalent to those of an arbitrator.

The outcome cannot be enforced.

Ombudsman

An ombudsman is involved mainly in alleged cases of maladministration by a government body: for example, there is a local government ombudsman, a legal services ombudsman and, for disputes with banks and similar organisations, a banking ombudsman and an insurance ombudsman.

An ombudsman's powers are limited. The ombudsman may only be able to make a recommendation. However, there is not usually any fee for using an ombudsman so it can sometimes be a cheaper alternative for, say, a client having a dispute with his or her bank.

Early neutral evaluation

Each party summarises their case to a neutral third party (usually an experienced lawyer) who provides an opinion on its strengths and weaknesses.

No decision is imposed; the idea is that views are expressed and this may lead to a productive negotiation.

Mediation

The neutral third party helps the parties to the dispute to reach an agreement that both or all of them consider acceptable.

Any agreement is reduced to writing and forms a binding contract unless the parties agree that they do not want a binding result. Otherwise, a successful outcome is enshrined in a contract which can then be enforced if necessary.

FEATURES OF ADR

Independent third party

An independent third party may be employed either as a decision-maker or a mediator.

Less costly if successful

If a settlement is achieved then ADR will be much cheaper than going through the litigation process to trial. However, if ADR is unsuccessful and the parties then have to resolve their dispute through litigation, it will add to the costs.

Speed

The procedures themselves tend to be quicker than litigation. However, whether a result is reached earlier than the proposed trial date depends on the stage at which ADR is engaged in.

Private and confidential

The dispute and/or details of the dispute can be kept confidential as between the parties.

Simple and flexible

Other than with arbitration, there are generally in ADR no procedural complexities such as interim hearings.

Less stressful

Clients find ADR less intimidating. The fact that costs are not normally recoverable may also alleviate some of a client's concerns.

Preservation of commercial relationship

Other than with adversarial arbitration, ADR does not generally involve any public loss of face. The parties may be able to achieve a result that benefits both of them: a win:win situation.

Creative solutions

Other than with arbitration, the neutral third party may suggest outcomes other than payment of money – such as an apology, a new joint venture, a new contract, and so on.

Client participation

Clients in litigation often complain that control of the process is taken away from them. In ADR the clients are fully involved (so, for example, in mediation it is compulsory that the clients attend but not that their lawyers do).

Non-binding referral

At present, although the court can give very strong hints and stay litigation for ADR, the parties cannot be compelled to participate.

However, in the present climate, the human rights aspects of forcing parties to undertake ADR should also be considered.

Agreement not enforceable

Arbitration awards are enforceable through the courts. However, the outcome of other forms of ADR, if successful, is a binding contract. Failure to comply with the terms of the settlement is then actionable as a breach of contract.

Chapter 4

FUNDING OF LITIGATION

In the last decade, the funding of civil litigation has changed markedly. It has become a complex area and what follows can be no more than a brief summary of what is available.

COURTS AND LEGAL SERVICES ACT 1990

Before the Courts and Legal Services Act 1990, there was a prohibition against solicitors having any form of financial interest in the outcome of litigation. Most personal injury claims were funded from the Legal Aid Fund and by trade unions.

The Courts and Legal Services Act 1990 introduced the concept of the Conditional Fee Agreement (CFA), defined as an agreement providing that a client's 'fees and expenses, or any part of them, are to be payable only in specified circumstances'.

CONDITIONAL FEE AGREEMENTS

CFAs became lawful in 1995. They now enable lawyers to provide legal services in civil litigation for which, in return for substantially funding the litigation themselves, they may be able to recover more by way of costs if successful than would otherwise be the case.

There are, broadly speaking, two types of CFA. One provides for a success fee. The other, often referred to as a *Thai Trading* agreement, after the case of *Thai Trading Co v Taylor* [1998] 3 All ER 65, does not but, instead, provides for payment of all or part of the fees and expenses only in specified circumstances. If the case is successful, the solicitor is entitled to charge his or her usual fees but, if the case is not successful, there may be an agreement to pay a reduced fee or nothing at all ('no win, no fee').

Conditional fees are not to be confused with contingency fees. Contingency fees, which provide for the lawyer to receive a percentage of the proceeds of the litigation, are not lawful in this jurisdiction (except in Employment Tribunals, which are classified as contentious business), although they are widely used in the USA.

AFTER-THE-EVENT INSURANCE

The Courts and Legal Services Act 1990 also permitted after-the-event (ATE) insurance to cover the risk in litigation of having to pay an opponent's costs. ATE insurance goes hand in hand with CFAs to provide a scheme that enables litigants to pursue or defend cases whilst limiting their exposure not only to payment of their own costs but also those of their opponent. Before-the-event insurance, or legal expenses insurance, had already been in use for several years (see below).

ACCESS TO JUSTICE ACT 1999

The Access to Justice Act 1999 (AJA 1999) extended the scope of CFAs by enabling any ATE insurance premium and percentage increase to be recovered from an unsuccessful opponent. Hitherto, the CFA had been strictly between the lawyer and the client, except to the extent of the operation of the indemnity principle (see Chapter 37). However, there has already been litigation that has successfully challenged the extent to which ATE insurance premiums and success fees are recoverable from an opponent on assessment. (See Chapter 39.)

In relation to the ATE insurance premium, in *Re Claims Direct Test Cases* [2002] All ER (D) 76, the Senior Costs Judge, Chief Master Hurst, agreed with the defendants that the proportion of the premium that related to claims handling services was not recoverable. The premium charged by Claims Direct was £1250 plus tax of £62.50. A total of £621.13 was allowed. The judge also held that in general it would be disproportionate and unreasonable to take out ATE insurance cover in a minor road traffic claim in which liability had been accepted at the outset, unless there were complicating features, for example an argument on causation.

The question of the recoverability of the success fee was considered in *Callery v Gray, Russell v Pal Pak Corrugated Limited* [2001] 3 All ER 833, and then in *Halloran v Delaney* [2002] All ER (D) 30. In the latter case, although allowing a 20% success fee consistent with *Callery*, the court held that for CFAs entered into after 1 August 2001 (after *Callery* was heard in the Court of Appeal) the appropriate success fee for simple cases settling in the protocol period should ordinarily be 5%. The court made express reference to Lord Woolf's judgment in *Callery* which drew attention to the availability of two-stage success fees where an uplift of, say, 100% would be discounted to 5% if the claim settled before the issue of proceedings. By way of additional guidance, the court was content that the CFA also embraced the costs-only proceedings which followed, but asked that any future redraft of the Law Society model agreement should make this abundantly clear.

Funding arrangements

Following the AJA 1999, CFAs are but one of three types of funding arrangement. The other funding arrangements are ATE insurance and an agreement with a membership organisation, for example a trade union, to meet legal costs. Funding arrangements are not restricted to claimants and any party to litigation, including incorporated bodies, may have a funding arrangement with their lawyers.

Regulation of conditional fee agreements

Currently, CFAs are regulated by the Conditional Fee Agreements Regulations 2000, SI 2000/692 (CFA Regulations 2000). These provide what is to be contained in an agreement and the information that clients must have before the agreement is made. Breach of the Regulations may render a CFA unenforceable. This would leave a solicitor unable to recover his costs from his own client, and as a result of the operation of the indemnity principle, those costs could not be recovered from the paying party. This led initially to much satellite litigation with paying parties trying to avoid their liability to pay by taking points about technical breaches of the CFA. It was hoped that this was effectively brought to an end by the decision of the Court of Appeal in *Hollins v Russell* [2003] 4 All ER 590. In that case the court said that:

> '... a CFA will only be unenforceable if in the circumstances of the particular case the conditions applicable to it by virtue of s 58 CLSA 1990 have not been sufficiently complied with in the light of their statutory purposes. Costs judges should ask themselves the following question: has the particular departure from a regulation or requirement in s 58, either on its own or in conjunction with any other such departure in this case, had a materially adverse effect either upon the protection afforded to the client or upon the proper administration of justice?'

Even applying the approach of *Hollins,* CFAs have continued to be held to be invalid and therefore the costs awarded not recoverable. In *Spencer v Wood* [2004] EWCA Civ 352 failure to specify how much of the success fee related to postponement of payment (and therefore not recoverable – see p 354) was held to be a material defect, while in *Samonini v London General Transport Services Ltd* [2005] EWHC 90001 (Costs) 19 January the senior costs judge held it to be a material defect for the solicitors not to have properly enquired about the existence of legal expenses insurance – even though the client did not in fact have any! In a further attempt to prevent parties being deprived of their costs by technical breaches, the CFA regulations are to be revoked with effect from 1 November 2005 and their provisions incorporated in Solicitors Practice Rule 15 and the Solicitors Costs Information and Client Care Code.

Public funding of litigation

The AJA 1999 significantly extended the options that are available to solicitors to assist clients in paying for their services whilst, at the same time, making changes to what was then known as the Legal Aid Scheme, thereby reducing the extent to which litigation is publicly funded.

The Legal Services Commission replaced the Legal Aid Board and is responsible for the Community Legal Service Fund. This is available to provide legal advice, services and representation on a very limited, means-tested basis.

Changes to public funding brought about by the AJA 1999 mean that most personal injury claims will be excluded from public funding and so, whereas previously the majority of personal injury claims would be publicly funded, now they will be the subject of a funding arrangement.

Notwithstanding the severe limitations on the availability of public funding, a solicitor has a duty in litigation to keep a client's eligibility for public funding under review.

Legal expenses insurance

Before-the-event (or legal expenses) insurance has been in widespread use in Europe for decades, and, since the late 1980s, has increasingly become a part of the insurance market in this country. For a relatively small premium, insurance cover against the cost of litigation may be provided.

Commonly, legal expenses insurance is sold alongside motor and household policies. In relation to motor policies, it will typically enable the policy-holder to have legal representation at no cost in any claim for recovery of losses falling outside the general motor policy, for example hire charges, recovery of any policy excess, and personal injury. It will usually be a condition of provision of legal representation that there are good prospects of success in the claim. The cover will normally include any liability to pay the opponent's costs.

Many people have legal expenses insurance without realising it. The premium is usually added to the renewal notice they receive from their insurance broker, without much further explanation. It is always important when advising clients about funding litigation to consider this possibility (see *Sarwar v Alam* [2001] 4 All ER 541).

Privately paying clients

The various funding options that are available do not, of course, prevent a solicitor and client from reaching an agreement that the client will pay the solicitor's charges from his or her own funds. This is, of course, subject to the solicitor's duty to advise about the availability of public funding, and to investigate whether there is any insurance in place that may be available to fund the costs, or other means of funding, for example through a trade union or other membership organisation.

The solicitor also has a duty to advise about ATE insurance that may be taken out to insure against the risk of paying an opponent's costs. Advice about insurance must include an indication of the client's likely exposure so that the appropriate level of risk is covered.

The retainer

Whenever a solicitor accepts instructions to act for a client, a contractual relationship, known as a retainer, arises. The retainer may arise by written or oral agreement, or by implication. In view of Practice Rule 15, which requires compliance with the Solicitors' Costs Information and Client Care Code, it will be ill-advised for a solicitor to agree to carry out work for a client unless the terms of the retainer, including provisions as to charges, are in writing and signed by the client.

A clear agreement in writing between solicitor and client in relation to payment of fees for litigation, which may include a funding arrangement, together with other aspects of the retainer, is called a contentious business agreement and is governed by s 59(1) of the Solicitors Act 1974. In practice, this will generally take the form of a letter that sets out the information required by the Solicitors' Costs Information and Client Care Code.

SOLICITORS' COSTS INFORMATION AND CLIENT CARE CODE

This revised code came into effect on 3 September 1999, and sets out in detail what is expected of solicitors in relation to the information and advice they are required to give about charges and complaints handling. The code applies to publicly funded clients and to those who have entered into a funding arrangement, as well as to clients who are paying from their own funds. As far as charges are concerned, the object of the code is to ensure that, at every stage of the proceedings, the client is fully aware of his or her likely liability for costs. The basis of charging must be entirely transparent. Every solicitor in private practice must have a procedure for handling complaints and this must be fully explained to the client.

Failure to comply with the code in any respect may lead to disciplinary proceedings, a complaint to the Office for the Supervision of Solicitors, leading to a possible finding of inadequate legal services, or failure by the solicitor to recover all or part of the fees.

COUNSEL AND CONDITIONAL FEE ARRANGEMENTS

Members of the Bar are prevented by their Code of Conduct from accepting instructions directly from members of the public. There are a few limited exceptions. For the most part, therefore, a barrister will be instructed by a solicitor, and the obligation to pay the fee will be that of the solicitor. There is nothing to prevent solicitor and counsel negotiating a CFA, although, in practice, they are not much favoured by the Bar.

Chapter 5

LIMITATION OF ACTIONS

OVERVIEW

After many turbulent years, the law on limitation has finally settled down. The relevant statute is now the Limitation Act 1980, a consolidating statute which has been amended several times. This is an important area of substantive law and, arguably, has no place in a procedural textbook. However, the fact is that a working knowledge of the law on limitation is essential for every litigation lawyer – hence this summary.

The purpose of the law on limitation can be simply stated: defendants should not be faced with stale claims, possibly brought many years after relevant events. Claimants should be given a reasonable period of time in which to bring proceedings and, if they do not do so, the cause of action, though not extinguished as a matter of law, is barred. It is thus of the utmost importance for a lawyer to ensure that a client's case does not become statute barred. Equally, defence lawyers should ensure that a limitation defence is taken whenever it is appropriate to do so.

It is, of course, a matter for Parliament to decide what is a 'reasonable time' for the purpose of bringing proceedings. Parliament has prescribed different periods for different causes of action. Similarly, it is for Parliament to authorise the circumstances in which an extension of the limitation period can be obtained and the conditions that must be satisfied in order to do so. Arguments on the relevant statutory provisions regularly come before the courts.

When a case gives rise to a limitation point, it is always for consideration whether that issue should be tried as a preliminary issue. No hard and fast rule can be stated here. Cost is a key factor. Although there is always a risk of increasing costs whenever there is a trial of a preliminary issue, in many cases, resolution of the preliminary issue is the key to resolution of the whole case and, although the risk cannot be eliminated, it is minimal.

Every litigation lawyer needs to be able to answer all of the following questions: What is the relevant limitation period? From when does the period start to run? What must a claimant do to avoid being statute barred? Is any extension to the limitation period possible? What must a defendant do if sued on a statute-barred claim? How do the limitation rules affect amendments? How does a limitation issue affect the conduct of the whole case?

WHAT MUST A CLAIMANT DO TO AVOID BECOMING STATUTE BARRED?

This is, of course, a purely procedural question and it is thus appropriate that we answer this one first. All that a claimant must do to prevent a claim becoming statute barred is to issue the claim form before the relevant limitation period expires. Proceedings are started when the court issues a claim form at the request of the claimant. By r 7.2(2), a claim form is issued on the date entered on the form by the court.

A claimant needs at least three copies of the claim form: one for the claimant, one for the court and one for service on each defendant. Having prepared the claim form (which does not, even at this stage, have to include the particulars of claim (see further, Chapter 14, Commencing Proceedings under Part 7 of the Civil Procedure Rules 1998)), the claimant must send or take this to the relevant court office and pay the appropriate court fee to issue the proceedings. Obviously, in an ideal world, the court will immediately issue the claim form and this ensures that the claimant cannot become statute barred. What if the court is so busy, understaffed and behind with its work that the claim form is merely put to one side, to be attended to later? This should never happen, but the fact is that it does and, somewhat pragmatically, the situation is provided for by CPR PD 7, para 5.1. Proceedings are started when the court issues a claim form at the request of the claimant but, where the claim form was received by the court office on a date earlier than the date on which it was issued by the court, the claim is 'brought', for the purposes of the Limitation Act 1980 and any other relevant statute, on that earlier date.

The date on which the claim form is received by the court will be recorded by a date stamp, usually on the claim form retained on the court file. Parties proposing to start a claim which is approaching the expiry of the limitation period should recognise the potential importance of establishing the date on which the claim form was received by the court and should themselves make arrangements to record the date. Thus, in practice, where a claim form is to be issued towards the end of the limitation period, whether it is posted or hand-delivered to the court, it should be accompanied by a letter asking the court to immediately note the date (and preferably the time) on which the claim form has been received. Of course, parties using the post do so at their own risk and it is better, therefore, to make arrangements for the claim form to be hand-delivered. It may be possible to start some claims online (see CPR PD 7E) and, ultimately, it will be possible to issue all claims online, thus minimising the problem here discussed.

WHAT MUST A DEFENDANT DO IF SUED ON A STATUTE-BARRED CLAIM?

A defendant who wishes to argue that the claim issued against him or her is statute barred must specifically plead the point in his or her defence. Statutes of limitation are included in the small number of statutes of which judges do not take judicial notice. Thus, if the defendant does not take the limitation point, the court will not do so. CPR PD 16, para 13.1 requires a defendant to give details of the expiry of any relevant limitation period relied on. This links in with para 13.3, whereby parties may refer, in their statement of case, to any point of law on which their defence is based. This is not an invitation to mount a detailed legal argument in a statement of case. What is sought here is a reference to the point of law relied on, not an exposition of it.

AMENDMENTS

Can a party amend a statement of case after the expiry of a limitation period? The basic law is contained in s 35 of the Limitation Act 1980. For the purposes of that Act, any new claim made in the course of any action shall be deemed to be a separate action and to have been commenced on the same date as the original action (save in the case of a new claim made in or by way of Part 20 – proceedings against a third party which are commenced on the date on which the Part 20 proceedings were commenced). A new claim means any claim by way of set-off or counterclaim and any claim involving either the addition or substitution of a new cause of action or the addition or substitution of a new party.

Neither the High Court nor the county court can allow a new claim, other than an original set-off or counterclaim, to be made in the course of any action after the expiry of any time-limit under the Act. A claim is an original set-off or an original counterclaim if it is a claim made by way of set-off or (as the case may be) by way of counterclaim by a party who has not previously made any claim in the action. (For the meaning of 'new claim', see *Yorkshire Regional Health Authority v Fairclough Building Ltd* [1996] 1 All ER 519.)

The section specifically authorises rules of court to allow for a new claim, but only if the conditions mentioned in s 35(5) are satisfied and 'subject to any further restrictions the rules may impose'. The relevant rules are r 17.4 – amendments to statements of case after the end of a relevant limitation period – and r 19.5 – special provisions about adding or substituting parties after the end of a relevant limitation period.

Rule 17.4 applies where a party wants to amend his or her statement of case after a period of limitation has expired. The court may allow an amendment, the effect of which will be to add or substitute a new claim, but only if the new claim arises out of the same facts, or substantially the same facts, as a claim in respect of which the party applying for permission has already claimed a remedy in the proceedings.

The court will allow an amendment to correct a mistake as to the name of a party, but only where the mistake was genuine and not one that would cause reasonable doubt as to the identity of the party in question.

The court may allow an amendment to alter the capacity in which a party claims if the new capacity is one which that party had when the proceedings started or has since acquired.

This is one area in which pre-CPR cases remain authoritative. (See *Welsh Development Agency v Redpath Dorman Long Ltd* [1995] 1 WLR 1409 for the correct approach.) It remains impermissible to amend or to add a cause of action that was not in existence at the date on which the original proceedings were issued (*Eshelby v Federated European Bank Ltd* [1932] 1 KB 254). What is involved is a comparison between the essential facts alleged in the statement of case before and after the proposed amendment, not the issues that might arise (*Savings and Investment Bank (in liquidation) v Fincken* [2001] EWCA Civ 1639, (2001) 98 (48) LSG 29).

Rule 19.5 applies to a change of parties after the end of a period of limitation. The court may add or substitute a party only if the relevant limitation period was current when the proceedings were started and the addition or substitution is necessary. By r 19.5(3), the addition or substitution of a party is necessary only if the court is satisfied that:

'(a)   the new party is to be substituted for a party who was named in the claim form in mistake for the new party;

(b)   the claim cannot properly be carried on by or against the original party unless the new party is added or substituted as claimant or defendant; or

(c)   the original party has died or had a bankruptcy order made against him and his interest or liability has passed to the new party.'

Rule 19.5 applies when the application is to substitute a new party where the wrong person was named on the claim form. Rule 17.4 applies where the intended party was named in the claim form but there was a genuine mistake in giving his or her name and no one was misled. There is no conflict or inconsistency between the two rules (*International Distillers and Vintners Ltd v JF Hillebrand (UK) Ltd* [2000] TLR 40).

These rules repeat the provisions of s 35(5) of the Limitation Act 1980.

PERSONAL INJURY CASES

Personal injury cases are, of course, a species of negligence claim and negligence itself is one of many torts. However, they merit special mention here because personal injury cases are subject to special limitation rules and form a significant part of the business of the courts.

Personal injury cases have been subjected to special rules because of the injustice to claimants by strict application of the ordinary time-limit (see, eg, the House of Lords' decision in *Cartledge v Jopling* [1963] AC 758). The special time-limit for actions in respect of personal injuries is provided for by s 11 of the Limitation Act 1980. The period is 3 years, which starts from the date on which the cause of action accrued or the date of knowledge (if later) of the person injured.

A cause of action in tort accrues when the elements of the tort are complete. Thus, in *Cartledge v Jopling* (above) the claimant's cause of action had accrued and become statute barred before he knew anything about it! Hence, the alternative 'date of knowledge' provision is now included in Limitation Act 1980, s 11.

There is usually no problem at all in ascertaining the date of accrual of the cause of action in road-traffic accidents nor in many other types of personal injury claims. Sometimes, however, there can be immense problems in cases of industrial disease and clinical negligence. These issues are regularly before the courts.

The definition of 'date of knowledge' for the purposes of s 11 of the Limitation Act 1980 is contained in s 14 of that Act and the section itself needs to be studied, together with the many reported decisions. The leading cases are *Nash v Ely Lilly and Co* [1993] 1 WLR 782, *Dobbie v Medway Health Authority* [1984] 1 WLR 1234 and *Forbes v Wandsworth Health Authority* [1997] QB 402.

By Limitation Act 1980, s 14, references to a person's date of knowledge are references to the date on which he or she first had knowledge of the following facts:

(1)   that the injury in question was significant; and,
(2)   that the injury was attributable in whole or in part to the act of omission which is alleged to constitute negligence, nuisance or breach of duty; and,
(3)   the identity of the defendant; and,
(4)   if it is alleged that the act or omission was that of a person other than the defendant, the identity of that person, and the additional facts supporting the bringing of an action against the defendant; and,
(5)   the knowledge that any acts or omissions did or did not as a matter of law involve negligence, nuisance or breach of duty is irrelevant.

Where an argument as to date of knowledge arises and there is clearly a risk that the decision will not go in the claimant's favour, the claimant should also consider asking the court to exercise its discretion under s 33.

Section 33 of the Limitation Act 1980 gives the court the discretion to exclude the basic time-limit in actions in respect of personal injuries or death. This is another important section, widely relied on in practice and regularly before the courts, the scope of which is not of general application but confined to personal injury and death cases.

Section 33(1) of the above Act provides:

'If it appears to the court that it would be equitable to allow an action to proceed having regard to the degree to which:

(a)   the provisions of section 11 or 11A or 12 of this Act prejudice the claimant or any person whom he represents, and,

(b)   any decision of the court under this sub-section would prejudice the defendant or any person whom he represents;

the court may direct that those provisions shall not apply to the action or shall not apply to any specified cause of action to which the action relates.'

Thus, the court has a discretionary power to override the basic time-limit in actions for personal injuries or death.

Despite the fact that this has been the law for over 20 years and that there are very many cases in which the section has been applied, the precise scope of the section is still not entirely free from doubt. There is a 'narrow view' and a 'wide view'. The narrow view is that the discretionary power under s 33 is limited and restricted in its operation and derives from the House of Lords' decision in *Walkley v Precision Forgings Ltd* [1979] 1 WLR 606. The wide view is that the section confers a wide, unfettered discretion on the court that is based, at least in part, on the decision of Lord Denning MR in *Firman v Ellis* [1978] QB 886 (but see also *Simpson v Norwest Holst Southern Ltd* [1980] 1 WLR 968). In our opinion, the wide view is to be preferred and is more in keeping with the modern civil procedure regime. This view seems to be finding increased favour with the courts (see, eg, *Shapland v Palmer* [1999] 1 WLR 2968, distinguishing *Walkley v Precision Forgings Ltd*) but, as *Walkley* is a House of Lords case, only the House of Lords can definitively rule on the matter.

Cases in which the claimant seeks to persuade the court to exercise its discretion under s 33 are usually suitable for that point to be decided as a preliminary issue. The judge deciding the issue is required to systematically go through the factors listed in s 33(3), which provides:

'In acting under this section the court shall have regard to all the circumstances of the case and in particular to:

(a)   the length of and the reasons for the delay on the part of the claimant;

(b)   the extent to which, in regard to the delay, the evidence adduced or likely to be adduced by the claimant or the defendant is or is likely to be less cogent than if the action had been brought within the time allowed by section 11, by section 11A or (as the case may be) by section 12;

(c)   the conduct of the defendant after the cause of action arose, including the extent, if any, to which he responded to requests reasonably made by the claimant for information or inspection for the purpose of ascertaining facts which were or might be relevant to the claimant's cause of action against the defendant;

(d)   the duration of any disability of the claimant arising after the date of the accrual of the cause of action;

(e)   the extent to which the claimant acted promptly and reasonably once he knew whether or not the act or omission of the defendant to which the injury was attributable might be capable at that time of giving rise to an action for damages;

(f)   the steps if any taken by the claimant to obtain medical, legal or other expert advice and the nature of any such advice he may have received.'

Preliminary issues arising under s 33 may be suitable for trial by the district judge. However, they will often be tried by a circuit or High Court judge, especially if the application arises out of a clinical negligence claim.

LIMITATION ACT 1980 – A SUMMARY

For the reasons set out in the first section of this chapter, every litigation lawyer needs a working knowledge of the Limitation Act 1980. The Act itself, set out in full together with a detailed commentary thereon, can be found at section 8 of Vol 2 of The White Book. What follows is a summary of the main provisions of the Act, to aid further research.

Main provisions of the Limitation Act 1980

Section 2 – time-limits for actions founded on tort. This provides an ordinary time-limit of 6 years from the date on which the cause of action accrued in tort actions.

Section 4A – time-limit for actions for defamation or malicious falsehood. The normal time-limit under s 2 does not apply to actions for libel, slander, slander of title, slander of goods or other malicious falsehoods. Instead, there is a limitation period of one year from the date on which the cause of action accrued.

Section 5 – time-limits for actions founded on simple contract. The basic period is 6 years.

Section 6 – special time-limit for actions in respect of certain loans. This section applies to loans which do not provide for repayment of the debt on or before a particular date – typically, informal loans between family members. The 6-year period runs from the date of a demand for payment.

Section 7 – time-limit for actions to enforce certain awards.

Section 8 – time-limit for actions on a speciality. The basic period is 12 years.

Section 9 – time-limit for actions for sums recoverable by statute. The basic period is 6 years.

Section 10 – special time-limit for claiming contribution. This section applies to claims for contribution under the Civil Liability (Contribution) Act 1978. The period is 2 years, which runs from the date of the relevant judgment.

Section 11 – special time-limit for actions in respect of personal injuries. This is discussed above, in the previous section of this chapter.

Section 11A – actions in respect of defective products. This applies to an action for damages by virtue of the Consumer Protection Act 1987.

Section 12 – special time-limit for actions under fatal-accidents legislation. This section provides a special time-limit for actions brought under the Fatal Accidents Act 1976. No action shall be brought after the expiration of 3 years from the date of death or the date of knowledge of the person for whose benefit the action is brought, whichever is later.

Section 13 – operation of time-limit under s 12 in relation to different dependants. Provides for s 12 to be applied separately to each dependant for whose benefit an action is brought under the Fatal Accidents Act 1976.

Section 14 – definition of date of knowledge for the purposes of ss 11 and 12. This is a very important section, discussed in the previous section of this chapter.

Section 14A – special time-limit for negligence actions where facts relevant to the cause of action are not known at date of accrual. This section was inserted by the Latent Damage Act 1986 and provides for a period of 6 years from either the date on which the cause of action accrued or 3 years from the starting date, as defined in s 14A(5).

Section 14B – overriding time-limit for negligence actions not involving personal injuries. Inserted by the Latent Damage Act 1986, this section provides for a long stop period of 15 years.

Section 15 – time-limit for actions to recover land. The basic period is 12 years.

Section 19 – time-limit for actions to recover rent. The basic period is 6 years.

Section 20 – time-limit for actions to recover money secured by a mortgage or charge, or to recover proceeds of the sale of land. The basic period is 12 years.

Section 24 – time-limit for actions to enforce judgments. This section provides that an action shall not be brought upon any judgment after the expiration of 6 years from the date on which the judgment became enforceable and that no arrears of interest in respect of any judgment debt shall be recovered after the expiration of 6 years from the date on which the interest became due.

Section 28 – extension of limitation period in cases of disability. This provides that limitation periods do not begin to run against a child until the child dies or attains majority. Limitation periods do not begin to run against a patient until the patient dies or recovers.

Section 28A – extension for cases where the limitation period is the period under s 14A(4)(b).

Section 29 – fresh accrual of action on acknowledgement or part payment.

Section 32 – postponement of limitation period in cases of fraud, concealment or mistake. In cases where the action is based on fraud by the defendant or any fact relevant to the claimant's right of action has been deliberately concealed by the defendant or the action is for relief from the consequences of a mistake, the period of limitation does not begin to run until the claimant has discovered the fraud, concealment or mistake or could, with reasonable diligence, have done so.

Section 32A – discretionary exclusion of time-limit for actions for defamation or malicious falsehood. This gives the court discretion to override the basic one-year limitation period in s 4A.

Section 33 – discretionary exclusion of time-limit for actions in respect of personal injuries or death. A very important section, which is considered above in the context of personal injury cases.

Section 35 – new claims in pending actions: rules of court. An important section, considered above under the heading 'Amendments'.

Section 36 – equitable jurisdiction and remedies. This section provides that certain time-limits (ss 2, 4A, 5, 7, 8, 9 and 24) shall not apply to a claim for specific performance of a contract or for an injunction or for other equitable relief, except in so far as any such time-limit may be applied by the court by analogy.

Chapter 6

PRE-ACTION PROTOCOLS

BACKGROUND

In his Access to Justice reports (*Access to Justice – Interim Report* (LCD, June 1995) and *Access to Justice – Final Report* (LCD, July 1996)), Lord Woolf recognised that one obstacle to affordable justice was the tendency for lawyers to regard the issue of proceedings as the first resort, rather than the last resort. The introduction of pre-action protocols serves to emphasise that litigation is a process to be avoided altogether, if possible, with parties being encouraged to exchange information and begin negotiations at an early stage with a view to reaching agreed terms of settlement.

To date, eight pre-action protocols are in use, and they, together with the Practice Direction that applies to them, are contained in Section C of Vol 1 of the White Book and Section 4 of the Brown Book. The existing pre-action protocols relate to:

– personal injury claims;
– the resolution of clinical disputes;
– construction and engineering disputes;
– defamation;
– professional negligence;
– judicial review;
– disease and illness claims;
– housing disrepair.

In cases in which a pre-action protocol applies, if proceedings have to be issued, the court will expect the parties to have complied with the protocol, and may impose sanctions on any party who has failed to do so if the non-compliance has led to the issue of proceedings or to costs being incurred which compliance may have avoided. Although the court will disregard minor breaches of the protocol, as indeed should the parties themselves, the standards set in the protocols will be regarded by the court as the normal, reasonable approach to the conduct of a claim.

Where there is no relevant protocol, the court will still expect the parties to act reasonably to avoid the need for proceedings.

CPR PD Protocols sets out the objectives of pre-action protocols at para 1.4:

'(a) to encourage the exchange of early and full information about the prospective legal claim,

(b) to enable parties to avoid litigation by agreeing a settlement of the claim before the commencement of proceedings,

(c) to support the efficient management of proceedings where litigation cannot be avoided.'

An introduction to each of the protocols that will be most commonly used follows. For the protocols for defamation and judicial review, reference should be made to Section C of Vol 1 of the White Book or Section 4 of the Brown Book.

Each protocol has its own particular approach, but what they have in common is the emphasis on:

– putting the cards on the table;
– communication with the other party;
– keeping the number of experts involved to a minimum;
– looking at alternatives to litigation.

PROTOCOL FOR PERSONAL INJURY CLAIMS

The protocol is intended to apply to all aspects of claims that include a claim for personal injury, save for industrial disease claims and clinical negligence claims, but is principally intended to cover straightforward road traffic accidents, tripping and slipping on the highway, and accident at work cases that could be expected to be allocated to the fast track. It is essential to the efficient operation of the fast track, in which there should be no more than 30 weeks from allocation to trial, that the case is more or less fully prepared before proceedings are issued.

The essential features of the personal injury protocol are:

– early notification of the claim;
– letter of claim in standard format;
– defendant's response;
– early disclosure of documents;
– consultation over choice of experts;
– encouragement to negotiate/settle.

Part 3 of the protocol sets out the detailed procedure to be followed at each stage.

Letter of claim

The letter should follow the format of the example at Annex A of the protocol (reproduced here at p 38 below) but should in any event contain the following information:

– a clear summary of the facts giving rise to the claim so that the defendant can assess liability and estimate the likely size of the claim;

– the nature of the injuries;

– any financial losses;

– in road traffic accident (RTA) cases, the name of any treating hospital and the claimant's hospital number.

If the claimant knows the identity of the defendant's insurer, a copy of the letter should be sent to the insurer. If not, the letter should be sent to the defendant in duplicate, with a request for details of the defendant's insurer and a request that the defendant forward the second copy to the insurer. Ordinarily, once the letter of claim is sent, no further steps should be taken to investigate liability until the defendant has responded and indicated whether or not liability is in issue.

Defendant's response

The defendant should reply within 21 days (42 days if the defendant and/or the site of the accident is outside England and Wales) from the date of posting of the letter of claim. The response should provide details of any insurers, if requested. If there is no response, the claimant will be entitled to issue proceedings.

Defendant's investigations

The defendant, or his insurers, is allowed 3 months (6 months if the defendant and/or the site of the accident is outside England and Wales) from the date of the letter of response in which to investigate the claim and notify the claimant whether liability is in dispute.

If liability is in issue, reasons must be given, and the defendant must disclose with his letter of reply copies of all documents which are material to the issues between the parties and which would form part of the standard disclosure if ordered by the court. Annex B to the protocol (reproduced here at p 39) contains lists of the documents which are likely to be material in different types of claim, namely RTA cases, highway tripping cases and claims arising out of accidents at work. These are not necessarily exhaustive, but each provides a very helpful checklist.

If liability is admitted, the presumption is that the defendant will be bound by this admission for all claims up to a total value of £15,000. In other words, if the claim ultimately proves to be worth considerably more, the defendant will have an opportunity to reconsider his position.

If primary liability is admitted, but contributory negligence on the part of the claimant is alleged, the defendant should give reasons and support these with documents where available.

The claimant should respond to any allegations of contributory negligence before issuing proceedings.

Statement of financial loss

The claimant should send a statement of financial loss, or special damages, to the defendant, along with supporting documents, as soon as possible.

Experts

Before any party instructs an expert, he or she should give the other party the name(s) of one or more chosen experts in the relevant speciality.

The other party must indicate any objections within 14 days, and the party wishing to instruct the expert should choose the expert from those that the other party will agree to.

In the event that the other party cannot agree any of the experts put forward, both parties may instruct experts of their choice.

Annex C to the protocol (reproduced here at p 44) contains a specimen letter of instruction to a medical expert.

Where the other party does not object to the instructing party's choice of expert, he or she may not then rely on his or her own expert evidence unless the opponent agrees, the court so directs, or the first report has been amended and there is a refusal to disclose the original report.

Ordinarily, a report obtained by one party under the terms of the protocol does not have to be disclosed if the party who obtained it does not wish to rely upon it. However, where the defendant admits liability in whole or in part before the issue of proceedings, a medical report obtained from an agreed expert under the terms of the protocol should be disclosed to the other party. Furthermore, the claimant should wait for 21 days after disclosure of the report before issuing proceedings in order to attempt settlement.

Avoiding litigation

Before proceedings are begun, the parties should consider whether it is appropriate to make a Part 36 offer to settle. (See further Chapter 37.)

Where a defendant admits liability in whole or in part before the issue of proceedings, any medical reports that are relied upon by the claimant and that have been obtained under the protocol should be disclosed to the defendant, and the issue of proceedings should be delayed for 21 days from disclosure of the medical evidence in order for the parties to consider whether a negotiated settlement is possible.

Rehabilitation

A recent addition to the aims of the protocol is the duty of the parties to consider as early as possible the provisions of medical or rehabilitation treatment to meet the needs of the claimant. This applies to all claims, not just to those of high value. Reference should be made to the Rehabilitation Code which appears as Annex D to the protocol. The main aim of the code is to promote the use of rehabilitation and early intervention in the claims process so that the injured person makes the best and quickest possible medical, social and psychological recovery. It is a joint initiative between lawyers and insurers.

Annexes to the protocol

ANNEX A
LETTER OF CLAIM

To

Defendant

Dear Sirs

Re: Claimant's full name
Claimant's full address
Claimant's Clock or Works Number
Claimant's Employer (name and address)

We are instructed by the above named to claim damages in connection with *an accident at work/road traffic accident/tripping accident* on *(day)* of *(year)* at *(place of accident which must be sufficiently detailed to establish location)*.

Please confirm the identity of your insurers. Please note that the insurers will need to see this letter as soon as possible and it may affect your insurance cover and/or the conduct of any subsequent legal proceedings if you do not send this letter to them.

The circumstances of the accident are:
(brief outline)

The reason why we are alleging fault is:
(simple explanation eg defective machine, broken ground)

A description of our clients' injuries is as follows:
(brief outline)

(In cases of road traffic accidents)
Our client *(state hospital reference number)* received treatment for the injuries at *(name and address of hospital)*.

He is employed as *(occupation)* and has had the following time off work *(dates of absence)*. His approximate weekly income is *(insert if known)*.

If you are our client's employers, please provide us with the usual earnings details which will enable us to calculate his financial loss.

We are obtaining a police report and will let you have a copy of the same upon your undertaking to meet half the fee.

We have also sent a letter of claim to *(name and address)* and a copy of that letter is attached. We understand their insurers are *(name, address and claims number if known)*.

At this stage of our enquiries we would expect the documents contained in parts *(insert appropriate parts of standard disclosure list)* to be relevant to this action.

A copy of this letter is attached for you to send to your insurers. Finally we expect an acknowledgement of this letter within 21 days by yourselves or your insurers.

Yours faithfully

ANNEX B
STANDARD DISCLOSURE LISTS

PRE-ACTION PERSONAL INJURY PROTOCOL

FAST TRACK DISCLOSURE

RTA CASES

SECTION A

In all cases where liability is at issue –

(i) Documents identifying nature, extent and location of damage to defendant's vehicle where there is any dispute about point of impact.

(ii) MOT certificate where relevant.

(iii) Maintenance records where vehicle defect is alleged or it is alleged by defendant that there was an unforeseen defect which caused or contributed to the accident.

SECTION B

Accident involving commercial vehicle as potential defendant –

(i) Tachograph charts or entry from individual control book.

(ii) Maintenance and repair records required for operators' licence where vehicle defect is alleged or it is alleged by defendants that there was an unforeseen defect which caused or contributed to the accident.

SECTION C

Cases against local authorities where highway design defect is alleged –

(i) Documents produced to comply with Section 39 of the Road Traffic Act 1988 in respect of the duty designed to promote road safety to include studies into road accidents in the relevant area and documents relating to measures recommended to prevent accidents in the relevant area.

HIGHWAY TRIPPING CLAIMS

Documents from Highway Authority for a period of 12 months prior to the accident –

(i) Records of inspection for the relevant stretch of highway.

(ii) Maintenance records including records of independent contractors working in relevant area.

(iii) Records of the minutes of Highway Authority meetings where maintenance or repair policy has been discussed or decided.

(iv) Records of complaints about the state of highways.

(v) Records of other accidents which have occurred on the relevant stretch of highway.

WORKPLACE CLAIMS

(i) Accident book entry.

(ii) First aider report.

(iii) Surgery record.

(iv) Foreman/supervisor accident report.

(v) Safety representatives accident report.

(vi) RIDDOR report to HSE.

(vii) Other communications between defendants and HSE.

(viii) Minutes of Health and Safety Committee meeting(s) where accident/matter considered.

(ix) Report to DSS.

(x) Documents listed above relative to any previous accident/matter identified by the claimant and relied upon as proof of negligence.

(xi) Earnings information where defendant is employer.

Documents produced to comply with requirements of the Management of Health and Safety at Work Regulations 1992 –

(i) Pre-accident Risk Assessment required by Regulation 3.

(ii) Post-accident Re-Assessment required by Regulation 3.

(iii) Accident Investigation Report prepared in implementing the requirements of Regulations 4, 6 and 9.

(iv) Health Surveillance Records in appropriate cases required by Regulation 5.

(v) Information provided to employees under Regulation 8.

(vi) Documents relating to the employees health and safety training required by Regulation 11.

WORKPLACE CLAIMS – DISCLOSURE WHERE SPECIFIC REGULATIONS APPLY

SECTION A – WORKPLACE (HEALTH SAFETY AND WELFARE) REGULATIONS 1992

(i) Repair and maintenance records required by Regulation 5.

(ii) Housekeeping records to comply with the requirements of Regulation 9.

(iii) Hazard warning signs or notices to comply with Regulation 17 (Traffic Routes).

SECTION B – PROVISION AND USE OF WORK EQUIPMENT REGULATIONS 1992

(i) Manufacturers' specifications and instructions in respect of relevant work equipment establishing its suitability to comply with Regulation 5.

(ii) Maintenance log/maintenance records required to comply with Regulation 6.

(iii) Documents providing information and instructions to employees to comply with Regulation 8.

(iv) Documents provided to the employee in respect of training for use to comply with Regulation 9.

(v) Any notice, sign or document relied upon as a defence to alleged breaches of Regulations 14 to 18 dealing with controls and control systems.

(vi) Instruction/training documents issued to comply with the requirements of Regulation 22 insofar as it deals with maintenance operations where the machinery is not shut down.

(vii) Copies of markings required to comply with Regulation 23.

(viii) Copies of warnings required to comply with Regulation 24.

SECTION C – PERSONAL PROTECTIVE EQUIPMENT AT WORK REGULATIONS 1992

(i) Documents relating to the assessment of the Personal Protective Equipment to comply with Regulation 6.

(ii) Documents relating to the maintenance and replacement of Personal Protective Equipment to comply with Regulation 7.

(iii) Record of maintenance procedures for Personal Protective Equipment to comply with Regulation 7.

(iv) Records of tests and examinations of Personal Protective Equipment to comply with Regulation 7.

(v) Documents providing information, instruction and training in relation to the Personal Protective Equipment to comply with Regulation 9.

(vi) Instructions for use of Personal Protective Equipment to include the manufacturers' instructions to comply with Regulation 10.

SECTION D – MANUAL HANDLING OPERATIONS REGULATIONS 1992

(i) Manual Handling Risk Assessment carried out to comply with the requirements of Regulation 4(1)(b)(i).

(ii) Re-assessment carried out post-accident to comply with requirements of Regulation 4(1)(b)(i).

(iii) Documents showing the information provided to the employee to give general indications related to the load and precise indications on the weight of the load and the heaviest side of the load if the centre of gravity was not positioned centrally to comply with Regulation 4(1)(b)(iii).

(iv) Documents relating to training in respect of manual handling operations and training records.

SECTION E – HEALTH AND SAFETY (DISPLAY SCREEN EQUIPMENT) REGULATIONS 1992

(i) Analysis of work stations to assess and reduce risks carried out to comply with the requirements of Regulation 2.

(ii) Re-assessment of analysis of work stations to assess and reduce risks following development of symptoms by the claimant.

(iii) Documents detailing the provision of training including training records to comply with the requirements of Regulation 6.

(iv) Documents providing information to employees to comply with the requirements of Regulation 7.

SECTION F – CONTROL OF SUBSTANCES HAZARDOUS TO HEALTH REGULATIONS 1988

(i) Risk assessment carried out to comply with the requirements of Regulation 6.

(ii) Reviewed risk assessment carried out to comply with the requirements of Regulation 6.

(iii) Copy labels from containers used for storage handling and disposal of carcinogenics to comply with the requirements of Regulation 7(2A)(h).

(iv) Warning signs identifying designation of areas and installations which may be contaminated by carcinogenics to comply with the requirements of Regulation 7(2A)(h).

(v) Documents relating to the assessment of the Personal Protective Equipment to comply with Regulation 7(3A).

(vi) Documents relating to the maintenance and replacement of Personal Protective Equipment to comply with Regulation 7(3A).

(vii) Record of maintenance procedures for Personal Protective Equipment to comply with Regulation 7(3A).

(viii) Records of tests and examinations of Personal Protective Equipment to comply with Regulation 7(3A).

(ix) Documents providing information, instruction and training in relation to the Personal Protective Equipment to comply with Regulation 7(3A).

(x) Instructions for use of Personal Protective Equipment to include the manufacturers' instructions to comply with Regulation 7(3A).

(xi) Air monitoring records for substances assigned a maximum exposure limit or occupational exposure standard to comply with the requirements of Regulation 7.

(xii) Maintenance examination and test of control measures records to comply with Regulation 9.

(xiii) Monitoring records to comply with the requirements of Regulation 10.

(xiv) Health surveillance records to comply with the requirements of Regulation 11.

(xv) Documents detailing information, instruction and training including training records for employees to comply with the requirements of Regulation 12.

(xvi) Labels and Health and Safety data sheets supplied to the employers to comply with the CHIP Regulations.

SECTION G – CONSTRUCTION (DESIGN AND MANAGEMENT) REGULATIONS 1994

(i) Notification of a project form (HSE F10) to comply with the requirements of Regulation 7.

(ii) Health and Safety Plan to comply with requirements of Regulation 15.

(iii) Health and Safety file to comply with the requirements of Regulations 12 and 14.

(iv) Information and training records provided to comply with the requirements of Regulation 17.

(v) Records of advice from and views of persons at work to comply with the requirements of Regulation 18.

SECTION H – PRESSURE SYSTEMS AND TRANSPORTABLE GAS CONTAINERS REGULATIONS 1989

(i) Information and specimen markings provided to comply with the requirements of Regulation 5.

(ii) Written statements specifying the safe operating limits of a system to comply with the requirements of Regulation 7.

(iii) Copy of the written scheme of examination required to comply with the requirements of Regulation 8.

(iv) Examination records required to comply with the requirements of Regulation 9.

(v) Instructions provided for the use of operator to comply with Regulation 11.

(vi) Records kept to comply with the requirements of Regulation 13.

(vii) Records kept to comply with the requirements of Regulation 22.

SECTION I – LIFTING PLANT AND EQUIPMENT (RECORDS OF TEST AND EXAMINATION ETC) REGULATIONS 1992

(i) Record kept to comply with the requirements of Regulation 6.

SECTION J – THE NOISE AT WORK REGULATIONS 1989

(i) Any risk assessment records required to comply with the requirements of Regulations 4 and 5.

(ii) Manufacturers' literature in respect of all ear protection made available to claimant to comply with the requirements of Regulation 8.

(iii) All documents provided to the employee for the provision of information to comply with Regulation 11.

SECTION K – CONSTRUCTION (HEAD PROTECTION) REGULATIONS 1989

(i) Pre-accident assessment of head protection required to comply with Regulation 3(4).

(ii) Post-accident re-assessment required to comply with Regulation 3(5).

SECTION L – THE CONSTRUCTION (GENERAL PROVISIONS) REGULATIONS 1961

(i) Report prepared following inspections and examinations of excavations etc. to comply with the requirements of Regulation 9.

(ii) Report prepared following inspections and examinations of work in cofferdams and caissons to comply with the requirements of Regulations 17 and 18.

NB Further Standard Discovery lists will be required prior to full implementation.

ANNEX C
LETTER OF INSTRUCTION TO MEDICAL EXPERT

Dear Sir

Re: *(Name and address)*

D.O.B.

Telephone No.

Date of Accident

We are acting for the above named in connection with injuries received in an accident which occurred on the above date. The main injuries appear to have been *(main injuries)*.

We should be obliged if you would examine our Client and let us have a full and detailed report dealing with any relevant pre-accident medical history, the injuries sustained, treatment received and present condition, dealing in particular with the capacity for work and giving a prognosis.

It is central to our assessment of the extent of our Client's injuries to establish the extent and duration of any continuing disability. Accordingly, in the prognosis section we would ask you to specifically comment on any areas of continuing complaint or disability or impact on daily living. If there is such continuing disability you should comment upon the level of suffering or inconvenience caused and, if you are able, give your view as to when or if the complaint or disability is likely to resolve.

Please send our Client an appointment direct for this purpose. Should you be able to offer a cancellation appointment please contact our Client direct. We confirm we will be responsible for your reasonable fees.

We are obtaining the notes and records from our Client's GP and Hospitals attended and will forward them to you when they are to hand/or please request the GP and Hospital records direct and advise that any invoice for the provision of these records should be forwarded to us.

In order to comply with Court Rules we would be grateful if you would insert above your signature a statement that the contents are true to the best of your knowledge and belief.

In order to avoid further correspondence we can confirm that on the evidence we have there is no reason to suspect we may be pursuing a claim against the hospital or its staff.

We look forward to receiving your report within _____ weeks. If you will not be able to prepare your report within this period please telephone us upon receipt of these instructions.

When acknowledging these instructions it would assist if you could give an estimate as to the likely time scale for the provision of your report and also an indication as to your fee.

Yours faithfully

PROTOCOL FOR THE RESOLUTION OF CLINICAL DISPUTES

The summary to the protocol sets out its purpose:

–   to encourage a climate of openness when something has 'gone wrong' with a patient's treatment or the patient is dissatisfied with that treatment and/or the outcome;
–   to provide general guidance on how this more open culture might be achieved when disputes arise;
–   to recommend a timed sequence of steps for patients and healthcare providers, and their advisers, to follow when a dispute arises; and so
–   to facilitate and speed up the exchange of relevant information and increase the prospect of the dispute being resolved without resort to legal action.

It is emphasised that the protocol attempts to set out a code for good practice, and not to provide a comprehensive procedure governing all the steps in clinical disputes, which by their very nature will be varied and complex.

Annex A to the protocol

Set out as Annex A to the protocol is the following useful illustrative flowchart of the likely sequence of events in a typical situation that may give rise to a clinical claim.

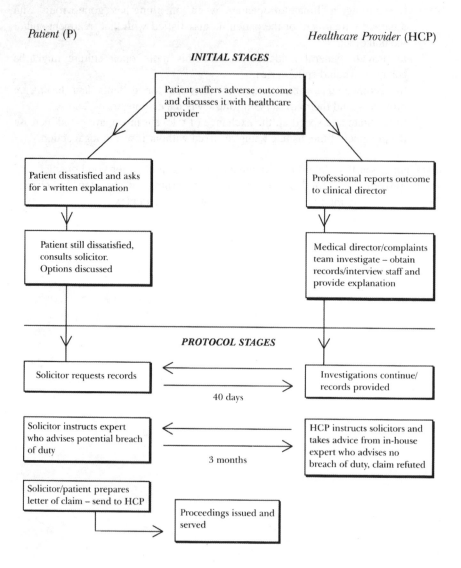

Patient (P)   *Healthcare Provider* (HCP)

INITIAL STAGES

Patient suffers adverse outcome and discusses it with healthcare provider

Patient dissatisfied and asks for a written explanation

Professional reports outcome to clinical director

Patient still dissatisfied, consults solicitor. Options discussed

Medical director/complaints team investigate – obtain records/interview staff and provide explanation

PROTOCOL STAGES

Solicitor requests records

Investigations continue/ records provided

40 days

Solicitor instructs expert who advises potential breach of duty

HCP instructs solicitors and takes advice from in-house expert who advises no breach of duty, claim refuted

3 months

Solicitor/patient prepares letter of claim – send to HCP

Proceedings issued and served

Obtaining the clinical records

If discussions with the healthcare professionals do not produce a satisfactory outcome following an adverse clinical incident, the first formal step will usually be to obtain the patient's records.

Requests for copies of the clinical records should be made using the approved form that is set out in Annex B to the protocol.

The records should be provided within 40 days of the request. The charge should not exceed that prescribed by the Access to Health Records Act 1990, which currently is a maximum of £10 plus photocopying and postage costs.

If the records are not provided within the time allowed, and there is no good excuse, the patient may apply to the court for an order for pre-action disclosure.

Letter of claim

If an assessment of the case after perusal of the clinical records indicates that a claim should proceed, a letter of claim should be sent as soon as possible to the proposed defendant.

Annex C1 to the protocol sets out a template for a letter of claim which can be adapted to suit the particular requirements of each case. However, the following information must be included so that the proposed defendant is in a position to begin investigations and will have some idea of the potential value of the claim:

–   a clear summary of the facts upon which the claim is based;
–   the main allegations of negligence;
–   the patient's injuries, present condition and prognosis;
–   financial losses incurred to date;
–   likely heads of future financial loss, with an estimate of the likely sums involved;
–   a chronology of relevant events;
–   relevant documents.

Response to the claim

There should be an acknowledgement of the letter of claim within 14 days of receipt, and an indication should be given of who will be handling the matter.

There will then be a period of no more than 3 months when investigations may be carried out. By the end of that time, a reasoned answer to the letter of claim should be provided.

The answer will deal with any admissions in clear terms, and any denials of liability with a detailed response to the allegations.

Proceedings should not be issued within the 3-month period unless a response has been received.

Experts

The role of experts in a clinical dispute is more complex than in other areas. A variety of experts may be required to deal with the liability aspects, the patient's condition and prognosis, and to assist in assessing the amount of the claim. It may be appropriate for each party to instruct his or her own expert to deal with the more contentious issues of breach of duty and causation, but for the other issues to be dealt with by a single joint expert. However, there can be no hard and fast rules in this field, and the protocol is not prescriptive as to the instruction of experts in the way that, for example, the personal injury protocol is.

Avoiding litigation

As with all protocols, the aim is to avoid litigation if this is at all possible. This protocol concludes with a reminder of the alternatives to litigation, which include face-to-face meetings for discussion and negotiation, mediation, and the use of any of the ADR services. In some cases, a patient may be seeking no more than an explanation or an apology, and in this case, the NHS Complaints Procedure may be followed.

PROTOCOL FOR CONSTRUCTION AND ENGINEERING DISPUTES

This protocol is intended to apply to all construction and engineering disputes, including professional negligence claims against the associated professions.

The general aim of the protocol is stated to be:

'to ensure that before court proceedings commence:

(i)   the claimant and the defendant have provided sufficient information for each party to know the nature of the other's case;

(ii)   each party has had an opportunity to consider the other's case, and to accept or reject all or any part of the case made against him at the earliest possible stage;

(iii)   there is more pre-action contact between the parties;

(iv)   better and earlier exchange of information occurs;

(v)   there is better pre-action investigation by the parties;

(vi)   the parties have met formally on at least one occasion with a view to:
   – defining and agreeing the issues between them, and
   – exploring possible ways by which the claim may be resolved;

(vii)   the parties are in a position where they may be able to settle cases early and fairly without recourse to litigation; and

(viii) proceedings will be conducted efficiently if litigation does become necessary.'

Letter of claim

The contents of the letter of claim in construction and engineering disputes are clearly prescribed by the protocol that states that the letter must contain the following information:

(i)   the claimant's full name and address;

(ii)   the full name and address of each proposed defendant;

(iii)   a clear summary of the facts upon which each claim is based;

(iv)   the basis upon which each claim is made, identifying the principal contractual terms and statutory provisions relied on;

(v)   the nature of the relief claimed: if damages are claimed, a breakdown showing how the damages have been quantified; if a sum is claimed pursuant to a contract, how it has been calculated; if an extension of time is claimed, the period claimed;

(vi)   where a claim has been made previously and rejected by a defendant, and the claimant is able to identify the reason(s) for such rejection, the claimant's grounds of belief as to why the claim was wrongly rejected;

(vii)   the names of any experts already instructed by the claimant on whose evidence he or she intends to rely, identifying the issues to which that evidence will be directed.

The defendant's response

The defendant is required to acknowledge the letter of claim in writing within 14 days of receipt, and may give details of any insurers.

If no acknowledgement is received, the claimant is entitled to commence proceedings.

Pre-action meeting

A meeting should be arranged between the parties as soon as possible after the defendant's response to the claim or, if there is a counterclaim, following the claimant's response to the counterclaim.

The protocol suggests that, as well as the parties and their legal advisers, a representative from any insurer involved and any other party with a contractual interest in the claim may also be in attendance.

According to the protocol, the purpose of the meeting will be to identify the main issues in the case and decide whether there is an alternative to litigation. The protocol specifically says that the parties should consider ADR. More than one meeting may be necessary to achieve these objectives.

Although the content of the meeting cannot be disclosed, any party who attended the meeting may tell the court when the meeting took place, who attended, who refused to attend and why, and any agreements that were concluded at the meeting.

If the parties cannot agree on a course other than litigation, they should take steps to ensure that the litigation will be conducted in accordance with the overriding objective. This will include making provision for the following:

–   agreeing which issues will require expert evidence and, where appropriate, identifying a single joint expert to instruct;

–   agreeing to what extent disclosure will be necessary, in the interests of saving costs;

–   agreeing how the litigation will be conducted in order to save costs and
      reduce delay.

PROTOCOL FOR PROFESSIONAL NEGLIGENCE

This protocol will apply where a claim against a professional is proposed arising
out of allegations of negligence and/or breach of contract or fiduciary duty. This
protocol should not be used for claims against healthcare professionals or
construction professionals to whom the clinical disputes and construction and
engineering protocols will respectively apply. It is not intended that the protocol
should replace any other forms of pre-action dispute resolution that may be
available through a professional body.

The stated aim of this protocol is:

> 'to establish a framework in which there is an early exchange of information so that
> the claim can be fully investigated and, if possible, resolved without the need for
> litigation. This includes:
>
> > (a)   ensuring that the parties are on an equal footing;
> > (b)   saving expense;
> > (c)   dealing with the dispute in ways which are proportionate:
> > > (i)   to the importance of the case;
> > > (ii)   to the complexity of the issues;
> > > (iii)   to the financial position of each party;
> >
> > (d)   ensuring that it is dealt with expeditiously and fairly.'

The protocol sets out the likely pre-action stages of a claim.

Preliminary notice

This should be in the form of a letter sent to the professional concerned as soon as
there is a reasonable chance that a claim will be brought. The letter should briefly
outline the basis of the complaint and give an idea of the likely size of the claim.
The letter should ask the proposed defendant to notify any professional indemnity
insurers of the situation immediately.

The professional should acknowledge the letter within 21 days of its receipt.

Letter of claim

As soon as the claimant has decided that there are grounds to bring a claim, he or
she should write a detailed letter of claim to the proposed defendant.

This will usually be an open letter (ie it should not be headed 'without prejudice')
which should include the following:

–   a chronology of the facts upon which the claim is based;
–   copies of the key documents in support of the claim;

  – details of the allegations (what has the professional done wrong, or omitted to do?);
  – an explanation of how the alleged error has caused the loss claimed;
  – an estimate of the financial loss incurred with documentary evidence in support;
  – details of any other person involved in the dispute, or in a related dispute;
  – details of any expert who has been instructed;
  – a request that the letter of claim be forwarded to the relevant insurers.

Letter of acknowledgement

This letter should be acknowledged by the professional within 21 days of its receipt.

Investigations

The professional will have 3 months from the date of the letter of acknowledgement, or such longer period as he or she may reasonably require, to investigate the claim.

The early exchange of information and documents is critical to the successful operation of the protocol. However, it should be noted that a party is required to disclose only those documents that a court could order as part of an order for pre-action disclosure.

When the investigations have been completed, the professional should be in a position to send the claimant either a letter of response or a letter of settlement, or both.

Letter of response

This should be an open letter setting out a reasoned answer to the claimant's allegations. In particular, it should deal with any admissions that are made, and give reasons for any denials of liability. If there is an issue over the value of the claim, the professional should say what he or she believes the claim to be worth, and why. Copies of any supporting documents should also be supplied.

Letter of settlement

If the professional has an offer of settlement to make at this stage, this will be set out in a 'without prejudice' letter of settlement. If he or she has not also sent a letter of response, it will be necessary to set out his or her position in relation to each of the issues in order that the offer may be fully understood.

If the letter of response makes no admissions, and there is no letter of settlement, the claimant is entitled to issue the claim. Otherwise, the parties should begin negotiations with a view to concluding them no later than 6 months from the date of the letter of acknowledgement. The parties may agree an extension to the time for negotiations, failing which, once the parties have agreed which issues remain in dispute, the claimant may start the proceedings.

Where possible, 14 days' notice should be given of the claimant's intention to start proceedings, giving details of the court in which it is proposed to issue.

Experts

Expert evidence will not always be necessary. Some issues of professional negligence will be purely factual, for example whether or not a particular procedural step was taken or a crucial piece of advice given. Other issues may require the court to have an expert view, or a range of expert opinion.

Where there is an issue that requires expert evidence to resolve it then, if the parties have not already instructed their own experts, they are encouraged by the protocol to agree on a single joint expert. The protocol recognises that the use that is made of expert evidence will vary from case to case, and so it does not attempt to set down a standard approach.

Alternative dispute resolution

The protocol enables the parties to agree at any time that the claim, or any issue in it, is suitable for some method of ADR, and for the operation of the protocol to be suspended or modified accordingly.

PROTOCOL FOR DISEASE AND ILLNESS CLAIMS

This protocol will apply instead of the personal injury protocol to claims arising out of disease and illness. These claims are often more complex than other personal injury claims even though their value may be within the fast track limit.

The main differences from the personal injury protocol are that the claimant may obtain medical evidence before sending a letter of claim, and the letter of claim must include a chronology of events relating to the claimant's employment/exposure history and the illness. It is also recognised that the role of the expert is different, and that, for example, an opinion on causation may be needed before a claim is started.

The objectives of the protocol are to encourage openness in the notification of the possibility of a work-related illness, or similar problem arising out of the occupation of land or premises, or use or consumption of a product, and timeliness in the investigation and resolution of claims.

Unlike the more prescriptive personal injury protocol, the disease and illness protocol aims to provide a code of good practice to be followed in the conduct of these claims.

Obtaining occupational and health records

The protocol permits a potential claimant to request records before a letter of claim is sent and the records must be provided within 40 days of the request. The request should provide sufficient information to alert the potential defendant to the nature of the possible claim. If the requested documents are not provided, the potential claimant may then apply to the court for an order for pre-action disclosure under r 31.16.

Letter of claim

A template for a letter of claim appears at Annex B to the protocol (reproduced below). If this template is followed it will ensure that all relevant information is made available to the defendant. The letter of claim is very detailed, but the protocol suggests that no point should be taken by the defendant in the event that if proceedings are issued the statement of case differs from the case set out in the letter of claim. The protocol recognises that during the course of investigating a claim it may change in some respects.

ANNEX B
TEMPLATE FOR LETTER OF CLAIM

To: – Defendant

Dear Sirs

Re: Claimant's full name
      Claimant's full address
      Claimant's National Insurance Number
      Claimant's Date of Birth
      Claimant's Clock or Works Number
      Claimant's Employer (name and address)

We are instructed by the above named to claim damages in connection with a claim for: –

Specify occupational disease

We are writing this letter in accordance with the pre-action protocol for disease and illness claims.

Please confirm the identity of your insurers. Please note that your insurers will need to see this letter as soon as possible and it may affect your insurance cover if you do not send this to them.

The Claimant was employed by you (*if the claim arises out of public or occupiers' liability give appropriate details*) as job description from date to date .During the relevant period of his employment he worked: –

description of precisely where the Claimant worked and what he did to include a description of any machines used and details of any exposure to noise or substances

The circumstances leading to the development of this condition are as follows: –

Give chronology of events

The reason why we are alleging fault is: –

Details should be given of contemporary and comparable employees who have suffered from similar problems if known; any protective equipment provided; complaints; the supervisors concerned, if known.

Our client's employment history is attached.

We have also made a claim against: –

Insert details

Their insurers' details are: –

Insert if known

We have the following documents in support of our client's claim and will disclose these in confidence to your nominated insurance manager or solicitor when we receive their acknowledgement letter.

eg Occupational health notes; GP notes

We have obtained a medical report from (name) and will disclose this when we receive your acknowledgement of this letter.

(This is optional at this stage)

From the information we presently have: –

(i)   the Claimant first became aware of symptoms on (*insert approximate date*)

(ii)   the Claimant first received medical advice about those symptoms on (*insert date*)
(*give details of advice given if appropriate*)

(iii)   the Claimant first believed that those symptoms might be due to exposure leading to
this claim on (*insert approximate date*)

A description of our client's condition is as follows:-

This should be sufficiently detailed to allow the Defendant to put a broad value on the claim

He has the following time off work: –

Insert dates

He is presently employed as a *job description* and his average net weekly income is £

If you are our client's employers, please provide us with the usual earnings details, which will enable us to calculate his financial loss.

Please note that we have entered into a conditional fee agreement with our client dated in relation to this claim which provides for a success fee within the meaning of section 58(2) of the Courts and Legal Services Act 1990.Our client has taken out an insurance policy dated with (name of insurance company) to which section 29 of the Access to Justice Act 1999 applies in respect of this claim.

A copy of this letter is attached for you to send to your insurers. Finally we expect an acknowledgement of this letter within 21 days by yourselves or your insurers.

Yours faithfully

Defendant's response

The defendant should acknowledge the letter of claim within 21 days the claimant is entitled to issue proceedings.

Within 3 months of the date of the acknowledgement, the defendant should provide a reasoned answer to the letter of claim. Any admissions should be made in clear terms. Any defence to the whole or part of the claim should be set out with an explanation and disclosure of relevant documentary evidence.

Unless there is a limitation problem, the claimant should not issue proceedings until 3 months have passed from the date of the acknowledgement.

Special damage

The claimant will supply the defendant with full details of special damages, with documents in support, as soon as practicable.

Experts

The protocol recognises that different considerations may apply in disease and illness claims than in more straightforward personal injury claims, and the approach to expert evidence is intended to be flexible in order to accommodate this.

Where the parties agree that a single joint expert should be instructed there is provision for the parties to try to agree on the expert.

PROTOCOL FOR HOUSING DISREPAIR

As with other protocols, the emphasis is on the early exchange of information with a view to achieving an early resolution.

The protocol is intended to cover all claims arising from the condition of residential property occupied by tenants. These claims are generally well within the fast track limit and one of the aims of the protocol is to keep the costs proportionate to the size of the claim.

The Guidance Notes in Part 4 of the protocol highlight the importance of attempting to resolve the dispute before using the protocol, by direct negotiation or alternative dispute resolution.

If this does not bring about a settlement, the protocol provides a framework within which further discussions and negotiation may take place.

Early notification letter

The landlord should be given notice of the claim as soon as possible. If a matter is urgent and it is not possible to send a detailed letter of claim, an early notification letter may be sent to alert the landlord to the problem. A specimen letter is included in the protocol at Annex A (reproduced here at p 58 below).

Letter of claim

This should be sent to the landlord as soon as possible. It should contain full details of the claim and it is advisable to follow the specimen letter that appears at Annex B of the protocol (reproduced here at p 61 below).

Landlord's response

The landlord should respond to the first notification from the tenant within 20 working days of receiving the letter.

In the case of an early notification letter, the landlord should give disclosure of the documents requested by the tenant pursuant to the protocol, and indicate his position on the instruction of an expert.

In response to a letter of claim, the landlord should say whether or not liability is admitted, and to the extent that it is not, provide reasons. The landlord should also state his own case in relation to the repair claim, and set out any offers in respect of compensation and costs.

Failure by the landlord to respond is a breach of the protocol and the court may impose sanctions.

Experts

The protocol offers guidance on the instruction of experts. Expert evidence will not always be necessary. Photographs and video evidence may suffice to illustrate a tenant's own evidence.

Where expert evidence is necessary, the use of a single joint expert is encouraged, and there is provision for the parties to try to agree on the expert to be used.

Annex C to the protocol contains a specimen letter of instruction to an expert (reproduced here at p 64 below).

Special damage form and schedule of disrepair

Annexes E and G contain a specimen special damages form and schedule of disrepair, respectively. In the interests of conformity and consistency it is helpful to use these as the basis for your own schedules.

ANNEX A
EARLY NOTIFICATION LETTER

(i) LETTER FROM SOLICITOR

To Landlord

Dear Sirs,

RE: TENANT'S NAME AND ADDRESS OF PROPERTY

We are instructed by your above named tenant. (*Include a sentence stating how the case is being funded.*) We are using the Housing Disrepair Protocol. *We enclose a copy of the Protocol for your information.**

Repairs

Your tenant complains of the following defects at the property (*set out nature of defects*).

We enclose a schedule, which sets out the disrepair in each room.*

You received notice of the defects as follows: (*list details of notice relied on*).

Please arrange to inspect the property as soon as possible. Access will be available on the following dates and times:– (*list dates and times as appropriate*)

Please let us know what repairs you propose to carry out and the anticipated date for completion of the works.

Disclosure

Please also provide within 20 working days of receipt of this letter, the following:–

All relevant records or documents including:–

(i)   copy of tenancy agreement including tenancy conditions
(ii)   documents or computerised records relating to notice given, disrepair reported, inspection reports or repair works to the property.

We enclose a signed authority from our clients for you to release this information to ourselves.

We also enclose copies of the following relevant documents from our client:–

Expert

If agreement is not reached about the carrying out of repairs within 20 working days of this letter, we propose to jointly instruct a single joint expert (*insert expert's name and address*) to carry out an inspection of the property and provide a report. We enclose a copy of their CV, plus a draft letter of instruction.

Please let us know if you agree to his/her appointment. If you object, please let us know your reasons within 20 working days. If you do not object to the expert being instructed as a single joint expert, but wish to provide your own instructions, you should send those directly to (*insert expert's name*) within 20 working days of this letter. Please send to ourselves a copy of your letter of instruction. If you do not agree to a single joint expert, we will instruct (*insert expert's name*) to inspect the property in any event. In those circumstances, if you wish to instruct your expert to attend at the same time, please let ourselves and (*insert expert's name*) know within 20 working days of this letter.

Claim

Our client's disrepair claim requires further investigation. We will write to you as soon as possible with further details of the history of the defects and of notice relied on, along with details of our client's claim for general and special damages.

Yours faithfully,

* Delete as appropriate

(ii)   LETTER FROM TENANT

To Landlord

Dear

RE: YOUR NAME AND ADDRESS OF PROPERTY

I write regarding disrepair at the above address. I am using the Housing Disrepair Protocol. *I enclose a copy of the Protocol for your information.**

Repairs

The following defects exist at the property (*set out nature of defects*).

I enclose a schedule which sets out the disrepair in each room.*

Please arrange to inspect the property as soon as possible. Access will be available on the following dates and times:– (*list dates and time as appropriate*)

You received notice of the defects as follows: (*list details of notice relied on*).

Please let me know what repairs you propose to carry out and the anticipated date for completion of the works.

Disclosure

Please also provide within 20 working days of receipt of this letter, the following:–

All relevant records or documents including:–

(i)   copy of tenancy agreement including tenancy conditions
(ii)   documents or computerised records relating to notice given, disrepair reported, inspection reports or repair works to the property.

I also enclose copies of the following relevant documents:– (*list documents enclosed*)

Expert

If agreement is not reached about the carrying out of repairs within 20 working days, I propose that we jointly instruct a single joint expert (*insert expert's name and address*) to carry out an inspection of the property and provide a report. I enclose a copy of their CV, plus a draft letter of instruction. Please let me know if you agree to his/her appointment. If you object, please let me know your reasons within 20 working days.

If you do not object to the expert being appointed as a single joint expert but wish to provide your own instructions, you should send those directly to (*insert expert's name*) within 20 working days. Please send a copy of your letter of instruction to me. If you do not agree to a single joint expert I will instruct (*insert expert's name*) to inspect the property in any event. In those circumstances if you wish your expert to attend at the same time, please let me and (*insert expert's name*) know within 20 working days.

<u>Claim</u>

I will write to you as soon as possible with further details of the history of the defects and of notice relied on, along with details of my claim for general and special damages.

Yours sincerely,

* *Delete as appropriate*

ANNEX B
LETTER OF CLAIM

(a) For use where an Early Notification Letter has been sent (as set out in Annex A).

(i) LETTER FROM SOLICITOR

To Landlord

Dear Sirs,

RE: TENANT'S NAME AND ADDRESS OF PROPERTY

We write further to our letter of (*insert date*) regarding our client's housing disrepair claim. We have now taken full instructions from our client.

Repairs

The history of the disrepair is as follows:– (*set out history of defects*).

I enclose a schedule which sets out the disrepair in each room.*

You received notice of the defects as follows (*list details of notice relied on*).

The defects at the property are causing (*set out the effects of the disrepair on the client and their family, including any personal injury element. Specify if there will be any other additional claimant*).

Please forward to us within 20 working days of receipt of this letter a full schedule of works together with the anticipated date for completion of the works proposed.

Claim

We take the view that you are in breach of your repairing obligations. Please provide us with your proposals for compensation. (*Alternatively, set out suggestions for general damages ie £x for x years.*) *Our client also requires compensation for special damages, and we attach a schedule of the special damages claimed.**

Yours faithfully,

* *Delete as appropriate*

(ii) LETTER FROM TENANT

To Landlord

Dear

RE: YOUR NAME AND ADDRESS OF PROPERTY

I write further to my letter of (*insert date*) regarding my housing disrepair claim. I am now able to provide you with further details.

Repairs

The history of the disrepair is as follows:– (*set out history of defects*).

You received notice of the defects as follows (*list details of notice relied on*).

The defects at the property are causing (*set out the effects of the disrepair on you and your family, including any personal injury element. Specify if there will be any other additional claimant*).

Please forward to me within 20 working days of receipt of this letter a full schedule of works together with the anticipated date for completion of the works proposed.

Claim

I take the view that you are in breach of your repairing obligations. Please provide me with your proposals for compensation. (*Alternatively, set out suggestions for general damages ie £x for x years*). *I also require compensation for special damages, and I attach a schedule of the special damages claimed.* *

Yours sincerely,

* *Delete as appropriate*

(b) For use where an Early Notification Letter has <u>NOT</u> been sent.

(i) LETTER FROM SOLICITOR

To Landlord

Dear Sirs,

RE: TENANT'S NAME AND ADDRESS OF PROPERTY

We are instructed by your above named tenant. (*Insert a sentence stating how the case is being funded.*) We are using the Housing Disrepair Protocol. *We enclose a copy of the Protocol for your information.* *

Repairs

Your tenant complains of the following defects at the property (*set out nature and history of defects*).

We enclose a schedule which sets out the disrepair in each room.*

You received notice of the defects as follows (*list details of notice relied on*).

The defects at the property are causing (*set out the effects of the disrepair on the client and their family, including any personal injury element, specifying if there are any additional claimants*).

Disclosure

Please provide within 20 working days of receipt of this letter a full schedule of the works you propose to carry out to remedy the above defects and the anticipated date for completion of the works.

Please also provide within 20 working days of this letter the following:–

All relevant records or documents including:–

(i)   copy of tenancy agreement including tenancy conditions

(ii)   tenancy file

(iii)   documents relating to notice given, disrepair reported, inspection reports or repair works to the property

(iv)   computerised records.

We enclose a signed authority from our clients for you to release this information to ourselves.

We also enclose copies of the following relevant documents:– (*list documents enclosed*)

Expert

If agreement is not reached about the carrying out of repairs within 20 working days of receipt of this letter, we propose to jointly instruct a single joint expert (*insert expert's name and address*) to carry out an inspection of the property and provide a report. We enclose a copy of their CV, plus a draft letter of instruction. Please let me know if you agree to his/her appointment. If you object, please let me know your reasons within 20 working days.

If you do not object to the expert being instructed a single joint expert, but wish to provide your own instructions, you should send those directly to (*insert expert's name*) within 20 working days. Please send to ourselves a copy of your letter of instruction to ourselves. If you do not agree to a single joint expert, we will instruct (*insert expert's name*) to inspect the property in any event. In those circumstances, if you wish to instruct your expert to attend at the same time please let ourselves and (*insert expert's name*) know within 20 working days.

Claim

We take the view that you are in breach of your repairing obligations. Please provide us with your proposals for compensation. (*Alternatively, set out suggestions for general damages ie £x for x years.*) *Our client also requires compensation for the special damages, and we attach a schedule of the special damages claimed.**

Yours faithfully,

* *Delete as appropriate*

(ii) LETTER FROM TENANT

To Landlord

Dear

RE: YOUR NAME AND ADDRESS OF PROPERTY

I write regarding the disrepair at the above address. I am using the Housing Disrepair Protocol. *I enclose a copy of the Protocol for your information.**

Repairs

The property has the following defects (*set out nature and history of defects*).

*I enclose a schedule which sets out the disrepair in each room.**

You received notice of the defects as follows (*list details of notice relied on*).

The defects at the property are causing (*set out the effects of the disrepair on you and your family, including any personal injury element, specifying if there are any additional claimants*).

Please provide within 20 working days of receipt of this letter a full schedule of the works you propose to carry out to remedy the above defects and the anticipated date for completion of the works.

Disclosure

Please also provide within 20 working days of receipt of this letter the following:–

All relevant records or documents including:–

(i)   copy of tenancy agreement including tenancy conditions
(ii)   tenancy file

(iii)   documents relating to notice given, disrepair reported, inspection reports or repair works to the property

(iv)   computerised records.

I also enclose copies of the following relevant documents:– (*list documents enclosed*).

Expert

If agreement is not reached about the carrying out of repairs within 20 working days of receipt of this letter, I propose that we jointly instruct a single joint expert (*insert expert's name and address*) to carry out an inspection of the property and provide a report. I enclose a copy of their CV, plus a draft letter of instruction. Please let me know if you agree to his/her appointment. If you object, please let me know your reasons within 20 working days.

If you do not object to the expert being instructed as a single joint expert, but wish to provide your own instructions, you should send those directly to (*insert expert's name*) within 20 working days. Please also send a copy of the letter of instruction to me. If you do not agree to a single joint expert, I will instruct (*insert expert's name*) to inspect the property in any event. In those circumstances, if you wish to instruct your expert to attend at the same time please let me and (*insert expert's name*) know within 20 working days.

Claim

I take the view that you are in breach of your repairing obligations. Please provide me with your proposals for compensation. (*Alternatively, set out suggestions for general damages ie £x for x years.*) *I also require compensation for special damages, and I attach a schedule of the special damages claimed.**

Yours sincerely,

* *Delete as appropriate*

ANNEX C
LETTER OF INSTRUCTION TO EXPERT

(i)   LETTER FROM SOLICITOR

Dear

RE: TENANT 'S NAME AND ADDRESS OF PROPERTY

We act for the above named in connection with a housing disrepair claim at the above property. We are using the Housing Disrepair Protocol. *We enclose a copy of the Protocol for your information.**

Please carry out an inspection of the above property by (*date*)** and provide a report covering the following points:–

(a)   whether you agree that the defects are as claimed

(b)   whether any of the defects is structural

(c)   the cause of the defect(s)

(d)   the age, character and prospective life of the property.

Access will be available on the following dates and times:– (*list dates and times as appropriate*)

*You are instructed as a single joint expert / The landlord is (landlord's name and details) / The landlord will be providing you with their own instructions direct / The landlord will contact you to confirm that their expert will attend at the same time as you to carry out a joint inspection.**

Please provide the report within 10 working days of the inspection. Please contact us immediately if there are any works which require an interim injunction.

If the case proceeds to court, the report may be used in evidence. In order to comply with court rules we would be grateful if you would insert above your signature a statement that the contents are true to the best of your knowledge and belief. We refer you to part 35 of the Civil Procedure Rules which specifies experts' responsibilities, the contents of any report, and the statements experts must sign.

Insert details as to cost and payment.

Yours sincerely,

* *Delete as appropriate*

** *The date to be inserted should be 20 working days from the date of the letter, in accordance with paragraph 3.6(f) of the Protocol.*

(ii) LETTER FROM TENANT

Dear

RE: YOUR NAME AND ADDRESS OF PROPERTY

I am currently in dispute with my landlord about disrepair at the above property. I am using the Housing Disrepair Protocol. *I enclose a copy of the Protocol for your information.**

Please carry out an inspection of the above property by (*date*)** and provide a report covering the following points:–

(a) whether you agree that the defects are as claimed
(b) whether any of the defects is structural
(c) the cause of the defect(s)
(d) the age, character and prospective life of the property.

Access will be available on the following dates and times:– (*list dates and times as appropriate*)

You are instructed as a single joint expert / The landlord is (landlord's name and details) / The landlord will be providing you with their own instructions direct / The landlord will contact you to confirm that their expert will attend at the same time as you to carry out a joint inspection.*

Please provide the report within 10 working days of the inspection. Please contact me immediately if there are any works which require an interim injunction.

If the case proceeds to court, the report may be used in evidence. In order to comply with court rules I would be grateful if you would insert above your signature a statement that the contents are true to the best of your knowledge and belief. I refer you to part 35 of the Civil Procedure Rules which specifies experts' responsibilities, the contents of any report, and the statements experts must sign.

Insert details as to cost and payment.

Yours sincerely,

* *Delete as appropriate*

** *The date to be inserted should be 20 working days from the date of the letter, in accordance with paragraph 3.6(f) of the Protocol.*

Chapter 7

CHANGE OF SOLICITOR

ADDRESS FOR SERVICE

Every party to proceedings must have an address for service. This is the address to which the court itself, and other parties to the proceedings, will serve documents, including notices, applications and court orders.

CPR Part 6 contains detailed provisions about the address for service. The rules in Part 6 differentiate between parties represented by solicitors and those who are not. Rule 6.5(2) provides that a party must give an address for service within the jurisdiction. Rule 6.5(5) provides that, where a solicitor is acting for a party and the document to be served is not the claim form, that party's address for service is the business address of his or her solicitor. Rule 6.13 relates to service of the claim form: the defendant's address for service of the claim form may be the address of his or her solicitor but only where the solicitor has been authorised to accept service on the defendant's behalf.

It can be seen from these rules that, where a party employs a solicitor, the solicitor's business address will be the address for service. All documents served by the court or another party are properly served at that address. If, for any reason, a party changes solicitor, CPR Part 42 – Change of Solicitor – must be complied with.

'ON THE RECORD'

A solicitor who has given his or her address as a party's address for service is said to be 'on the record'. The court and other parties must now communicate with that solicitor and it is improper to do otherwise, unless the court has specifically ordered it. Thus, for example, if the court makes an order, the proper place to serve that order on a party is at the address of the solicitor on the record. Exceptionally, however, the court may, in addition, require personal service on the party, but this would be specifically ordered. A party who knows that his or her opponent is represented by a solicitor must deal with that solicitor and not with the party directly.

By being on the record, a solicitor not only provides an address for service for his or her client, but also indicates that that client will be making a claim for solicitors' costs in the proceedings. The phrase 'on the record' is not found in the CPR but is still used and accurately summarises the position.

Once a solicitor is on the record, the address for service of the party is the business address of his or her solicitor. The solicitor will be considered to be acting for that party until the provisions of Part 42 have been complied with (r 42.1). If, for any reason, a party changes solicitor, it is of the utmost importance that the new solicitor complies with Part 42 immediately.

NOTICE OF CHANGE OF SOLICITOR

There are three distinct situations where notice of change of solicitor is required. All are dealt with in CPR r 42.2.

Notice of change is required where:

(1)   a party for whom a solicitor is acting wants to change his or her solicitor;
(2)   a party, after having conducted the claim in person, appoints a solicitor to act on his or her behalf (except where the solicitor is appointed only to act as an advocate for a hearing);
(3)   a party, after having conducted the claim by a solicitor, intends to act in person.

In the first two cases, the new solicitor should give notice of the change as soon as instructed. In the third situation, it is, of course, the responsibility of the party personally to give the requisite notice, but the reality is that he or she will need to be advised to do this – and its urgency emphasised – by the former solicitor. Notice is given in Form N434.

In these three situations, the solicitor (if acting) or the party must file notice of the change and serve notice of the change on every other party and, in the first and third situations above, also on the former solicitor.

The notice must, of course, give the party's new address for service, and the notice filed at court must state that the notice has been served as required.

Where a party has changed his or her solicitor, or intends to act in person, the former solicitor will be considered to be the party's solicitor unless and until notice is served in accordance with r 42.2 or the court makes an order under r 42.3 and the order is served as required by that rule.

The notice should be given to the appropriate court, ie the county court office or district registry. If the claim is proceeding in the Royal Courts of Justice, CPR PD 42, para 2.6 requires the notice to be filed in the Action Department of the Central Office for Queen's Bench Division cases; in Chancery Chambers for Chancery Division cases; in the Administrative Court Office for a claim proceeding in the

Administrative Court; in the Admiralty and Commercial Registry for cases proceeding there; and in the Registry of the Technology and Construction Court for cases proceeding in that court. The notice should also be filed in the Civil Appeals Office if the claim is subject to an appeal to the Court of Appeal.

APPLICATION FOR ORDER THAT SOLICITOR HAS CEASED TO ACT

If r 42.2 was properly complied with in all situations, then an application for an order under r 42.3 would never be necessary. The above paragraphs emphasise the importance of the address for service and the fact that a solicitor on the record remains on the record until removed by notice or order.

As already noted, if a client withdraws instructions to a solicitor expressly or by implication (eg by leaving a solicitor without instructions), the client needs to be advised of his or her duty to give notice under r 42.2. As noted, the solicitor is still on the record, and the court and other parties will still be communicating with him or her. If the client does not comply with the requirements of r 42.2 and give the necessary instructions, then a solicitor may apply under r 42.3 for an order declaring that he or she has ceased to be the solicitor acting for the party.

An application for an order that a solicitor has ceased to act differs from other applications. Notice of the application must be given to the party for whom the solicitor is acting (unless the court otherwise directs) but is not to be given to the other parties to the proceedings. The application is made in accordance with CPR Part 23 and must be supported by evidence. It is the party for whom the solicitor acted who is the respondent to the application.

The court may well be prepared to make an order without a hearing, provided the evidence is sufficient, and the court has been given all necessary information. (See *Miller v Allied Sainif (UK)* [2000] TLR 757.) However, the reality is that it is often necessary for the solicitor to attend court, and there are two situations in which the solicitor must always attend, namely where the case is complex or unusual, and where a trial date is imminent. Further, of course, the court cannot make an order unless it is satisfied that the application has been properly served, and the court will require evidence of this.

Although not a requirement of the rule, courts, when removing a solicitor from the record, frequently specify, in the order declaring that the solicitor has ceased to act, a new address for service for the party concerned. This is good practice and it is surprising that the rule does not actually require it. If it is not done, then the party's new address for service will be determined in accordance with r 6.5.

Where the court makes an order that a solicitor has ceased to act, a copy of the order must be served on every party to the proceedings. The order does not take effect until it is served (CPR PD 42, para 3.3).

NOTICE OF DISCHARGE/REVOCATION OF PUBLIC FUNDING

Since 1 April 2000, the Legal Services Commission has been responsible for funding legal services under the Community Legal Service Fund, established by the AJA 1999. Prior to that date, public funding was in the hands of the Legal Aid Board.

Where the certificate of a publicly funded client is revoked or discharged, the solicitor who acted for that person will cease to be the solicitor acting in the case as soon as his or her retainer is determined. This applies both under the Community Legal Service (Costs) Regulations 2000, SI 2000/441, and the Civil Legal Aid (General) Regulations 1989, SI 1989/339.

A solicitor will come off the record simply by filing notice of revocation or discharge with the court. No further notice is required (see r 42.2(6)).

A solicitor's retainer, where the client was publicly funded, ends upon receipt by the solicitor of the notice of revocation or discharge of the certificate. It is important, therefore, that the court and all other parties are notified of this immediately, for, as previously noted, that solicitor's business address continues to be the address for service of the former client until CPR Part 42 has been complied with. CPR PD 42, para 2.2 requires that notice of the change (which, in this situation, means revocation or discharge) must give the last-known address of the former assisted party. That address will now become the new address for service of the party who formerly was publicly funded.

If that person wishes to continue the proceedings notwithstanding revocation or discharge of his or her public funding, then he or she will do so either as a litigant in person or by appointing a solicitor to act privately. If he or she appoints a new solicitor (or even re-appoints the same solicitor who previously acted when he or she was publicly funded), the new solicitor is obliged to give notice of change in accordance with r 42.2. If the party continues as litigant in person, then he or she is also required to give notice and must provide an address for service (r 42.2(6)).

REMOVAL OF SOLICITOR

For the sake of completeness, r 42.4 provides for the removal of a solicitor who has ceased to act on the application of another party. This is unusual, as it applies only where a solicitor who has acted for the party has died, become bankrupt, ceased to practise or cannot be found, and all these situations are extremely unusual. (See the rule itself and CPR PD 42, para 4.)

THE COURT'S DISCRETION

The court has a discretion as to whether or not to grant an application to come off the record. Invariably, the application will be granted, except in the one situation in which it is likely to be refused, namely where the trial itself is imminent. The court has to do justice to all the parties involved in the case and is loath to grant adjournments of trials. A solicitor who applies to come off record the week before the date fixed for trial is likely to find that the district judge or master will refuse the application outright or, alternatively, adjourn it to the trial judge. The fact that this may happen further emphasises the importance of complying with Part 42 promptly. The court may well require the party concerned to attend the hearing of the application so as to inform the court whether the case (or defence) is to be abandoned or whether he or she is to continue to act in person or intends to appoint a new solicitor. The court cannot order a party to appoint new solicitors (*SMC Engineering (Bristol) Limited v Fraser* [2001] CP Rep 76).

Chapter 8

INTEREST

INTRODUCTION

The entitlement to claim interest on damages or a debt derives from a number of sources.

Whenever interest is claimed, full particulars must be given in the claim form. CPR r 16.4(2) provides that the claimant must specify on what basis interest is claimed, ie under a contract, under a statute or on some other basis, and if the claim is for a specified sum of money, the following must be stated:

- the rate of interest claimed;
- the date from which it is claimed;
- the date to which it is calculated, being a date no later than the date of issue of the claim form;
- the total amount of interest claimed to that date;
- the daily rate at which interest accrues after that date.

CONTRACTUAL INTEREST

A contract may provide for interest to be payable in default of payment of the contract sum on the due date. This is payable as of right provided that the agreement is not found by the court to have been an 'extortionate credit bargain' under the Consumer Credit Act 1974.

STATUTORY INTEREST

Certain statutes and statutory instruments allow for interest to be recovered on debts or other demands for a specific sum. For example, solicitors are entitled to claim interest on an unpaid bill for non-contentious work under the Solicitors (Non-Contentious Business) Remuneration Order 1994, SI 1994/2616, and interest can be claimed on certain late payments of commercial debts under the Late Payment of Commercial Debts (Interest) Act 1998. Again, this is an absolute entitlement.

INTEREST IN THE DISCRETION OF THE COURT

Section 35A of the SCA 1981 and s 69 of the CCA 1984 give the court a discretionary power to award interest on damages. However, interest must be awarded to a claimant who recovers more than £200 for personal injury or death unless the court considers that there are special reasons why interest should not be awarded.

The purpose of awarding interest is to compensate the claimant for being kept out of his or her money from the date when it would otherwise have been due. If a claimant has been unduly dilatory in the prosecution of the claim this may be a reason for the judge to decide that an award of interest is inappropriate.

The court's discretion extends to the rate of interest and the period for which it should be paid, and of course the court may decide that there should be no liability to pay interest.

As to the rate of interest, the court will generally award interest either at what is known as the special account rate or at the rate payable under the Judgments Act 1838 (JA 1838). The special account rate is the rate at which interest is earned on money in court, and the rates are reviewed periodically and published. The rate from 1 February 2002 is 6%. The rate payable under the JA 1838 is that applied to default judgments and, since 3 April 1993, it has been 8%.

In appropriate cases, however, there is nothing to prevent a court from awarding interest at a more commercial rate, for example a percentage over base rate, nor indeed such other rate as is deemed fair in the circumstances. If you wish to try to persuade the judge to award interest at a rate other than the Judgments Act rate or special account rate, you should produce evidence of the rate you are asking to be applied. In a commercial matter, you may be able to argue successfully that it would be unjust to award interest at any figure less than the bank is charging the claimant on overdraft (which will have been increased by the amount owed by the defendant), since by not paying the claimant, the defendant has in effect had the use of that money at a preferential rate, and certainly less than the defendant's own bankers would charge.

Interest will usually be claimed 'until judgment or earlier payment'. The date from which interest will begin to run will be a matter of discretion but, as a general rule, in the case of a debt, interest will run from the date by which the money should have been paid. For any other financial loss, the date will usually be the date on which the loss was incurred. For non-financial loss such as damages for personal injury, the date that is customarily used is the date of service of the claim form.

When calculating interest payments that have accrued over a period of time, you will have to take into account any fluctuations in the rate. The most straightforward way to deal with this is to obtain a figure for the average rate over the period from one of the conversion tables that appear in the *Law Society Gazette* or *Kemp and*

Kemp: The Quantum of Damages (Sweet & Maxwell, looseleaf), the leading textbook on personal injury damages.

There are special principles concerning payment of interest in personal injury claims for general damages and financial loss that will be applied in all cases, except where to do so would result in substantial injustice. These derive from the Court of Appeal decisions in *Jefford v Gee* [1970] 2 QB 130 and *Birkett v Hayes* [1982] 2 All ER 710.

When the court is considering the question of interest in a personal injury case, it is required to put the various heads of damage as found by the judge into one of three categories:

(1)   the claimant's actual financial loss up to the date of trial, eg lost earnings;
(2)   the claimant's financial losses from the date of trial, eg future loss of earnings;
(3)   damages for pain and suffering and loss of amenity (usually called 'general damages').

No interest will be awarded on future financial losses. This is because the principle behind awarding interest is to compensate the claimant for being kept out of his or her money. In relation to future losses, the claimant has not yet incurred the loss, and, indeed, is having the benefit of receiving compensation before the loss is even incurred.

Interest on financial losses to the date of the trial (such losses are also referred to as 'special damages') will usually be awarded from the date of the accident until the date of trial at half the appropriate rate of interest. This broad-brush approach takes into account that not all the financial losses will have been incurred on the date of the accident, without the need to make precise calculations of each and every item.

Interest on general damages is always awarded at 2% from the date of issue of the claim form until the date of trial. It is arguable that to align the date from which interest is to run with the date of issue of the claim form may encourage litigation and be contrary to the spirit of the civil procedure reforms. However, the interest rate applied will rarely make much difference to the size of the ultimate award.

Similar general principles apply to interest on awards of damages under the Fatal Accidents Act 1976. The items of loss as found by the judge are put into one of three categories:

(1)   financial losses incurred from the date of death to the date of trial, on which interest will be applied from the date of death until the date of trial at half the special account rate;
(2)   damages for bereavement, which will have interest applied at the full special account rate;
(3)   financial losses from the date of trial, on which no interest is allowed.

INTEREST UNDER THE COURT'S EQUITABLE JURISDICTION

The court has power to award interest when it gives equitable relief.

INTEREST ON DEFAULT JUDGMENT

Where judgment is entered in default in a claim for a specified amount of money, a calculation of interest to the date of judgment may be included in the judgment debt, provided that interest was properly claimed in the claim form. (See further CPR r 12.6.)

INTEREST ON JUDGMENT DEBTS

Interest on damages is not to be confused with interest on judgments which applies to all unsatisfied judgments in the High Court (JA 1838, s 17) and on unsatisfied judgments of £5,000 or more in the county court (CCA 1984, s 74). An unsatisfied award of damages which includes an element of interest may therefore attract interest at the judgment debt rate from the date of judgment at the current rate. However, interest is not recoverable on the same sum for the same period both under the JA 1838 and under the interest provisions applied by the court to the judgment debt.

The rate of interest on judgment debts is currently 8% as set by the Judgment Debts (Rate of Interest) Order 1993 (SI 1993/564).

INTEREST AND OFFERS TO SETTLE

The court is given the power by CPR r 36.21 to award interest at a punitive rate not exceeding 10% above base rate as a sanction for failure by a defendant to accept a claimant's proposal for settlement, when the claimant does better than his or her proposal at trial. This is a separate power from the discretionary power given to the court under SCA 1981, s 35A and CCA 1984, s 69.

Part II

CIVIL LITIGATION SKILLS

Chapter 9

INTERVIEWING

Interviewing a client is an important skill. Often the first meeting with a client will establish rapport and enable the lawyer to understand the full story. It is most likely that a meeting will take place with a new client once the documents have been received and reviewed. At interview, you will want to extract from the client the important facts to substantiate the case. The facts you glean from the interview will in due course be used by you to draft the client's witness statement. It is therefore useful to have analysed in advance of the interview the facts that you need to gather for this purpose.

PREPARATION FOR THE INTERVIEW

Unless you are assisting at a law centre or law clinic, it is likely that you will have some advance information about the client and the nature of the client's problem. This may be as little as a telephone note, or as much as a letter of explanation and a copy of the client's file. Does anyone else in the office have regular dealings with this client: can they give you some background on the client and on the client's business?

Use whatever information you have to plan the interview in advance if possible. Think about the areas you want to question your client about. Think about possible resolutions to the client's problem. Carry out some initial research on the legal issues involved. Can you identify a provisional case theory? What possible pathways might be available?

Think about practicalities, for example sending the client a map showing how to reach your office (if you are meeting there), booking a room in which you will not be interrupted, arranging refreshments, and considering how you are going to take notes.

STRUCTURE

Some individuals and some firms use very precise checklists for interviews. However you decide to structure your interview, consider including the following.

An introduction

Let the client know who you are and what you plan to do in the interview. If specific arrangements have been made for the funding of the interview (see Chapter 4), clarify these.

An overview

Let the client tell you about the problem at an early stage. The client may well be very emotionally involved with the problem and desperate to get it off his or her chest. If you let the client tell you about the problem without interrupting, you may discover that your initial analysis of the problem was incorrect or incomplete. The client may also give you some clues about his or her goals in seeking legal advice and any underlying concerns. If you have no clear initial idea about goals and concerns, consider simply asking the client what he or she wants to achieve.

Questioning

You will need to ask questions to refine what your client has already told you and to get down to details. Try using open questions first (eg 'Tell me more about ...', 'How ...?', 'What ...?', etc) and then 'funnel' down into more detailed and specific questions ('Have you got a copy of the will?', 'What is the name of the witness?'). Try to avoid leading questions, ie questions that suggest their answer ('You confirmed all that in writing, of course?'). The questioning of a client or witness in interview is not unlike the process involved in examination-in-chief (see Chapter 35 below).

Structure your questioning around one topic at a time. This will assist both you and your client by concentrating on each topic separately. Headline your topics (eg 'Now I'd like to move on to what happened on the 16th ...') so that both you and your client know where you are.

Bring out the bad points as well as the good.

If your client uses technical expressions that you do not understand, consider asking your client to explain them: ultimately, the meaning of such terms may have to be made clear to a judge, arbitrator or mediator.

Think about how you can make notes most effectively. Do you need to transcribe everything (the closer the statement to the client's actual words the more credible it will be)? What do you need to make notes of? Can you use a brief checklist of topics that you are likely to have to cover? Having a third party present at the interview helps to encourage:

(a)   better behaviour, and
(b)   protection for the solicitor in the future.

Avoid writing down too many specific questions in advance; consider identifying areas of questioning instead.

Consider questions which go beyond the basic facts and explore the client's goals and underlying concerns.

In summary, when conducting the interview, you should try:

– to establish rapport; listen to the client; and conclude the interview appropriately (if you do not, this will prejudice the co-operation of the client);

– to allow the client an opportunity to tell his or her story before asking questions. This should be done by asking the client to tell the story in his or her own words;

– to structure your questioning so that the client is properly directed as to what to concentrate on;

– to use simple questions which do not confuse the client. Try not to include more than one point in each question.

You should try to avoid:

– leading the client, as this prevents new information emerging and means that notes will not record the client's own words. Your questions should be open and not attempt to put words into the client's mouth;

– interrupting the client;

– allowing the client's opinions and conclusions to stand without probing for the facts behind them (opinion is, of course, inadmissible, and detail and facts are, in any event, more credible and persuasive. So, for example, 'He was drunk' would be an opinion, and not as persuasive as, 'He was staggering, his eyes were glazed, and his breath smelt of alcohol', etc);

– asking very detailed questions too soon.

At the end of the questions, you should have:

– your client's name, address and telephone number;

– the names and addresses of any witnesses;

– details of the relevant times, dates and places (make sure the claim is not statute-barred);

– details of the amounts of money involved (consider whether the claim should be brought, if at all, on the small claims track);

– some idea of the relative finances of both parties;

– some idea of what documents exist;

– some idea of how far your client has already gone in an attempt to resolve the problem (for instance, he or she might already have tried and failed to negotiate);

– some idea about what is really important to your client (eg resolving the problem quickly, or cheaply, or with no publicity).

LISTENING

Listen to what your client is saying, especially when he or she is answering your questions. Unexpected answers may take your questioning into areas you had not anticipated but which may turn out to be very important. If you have all your questions pre-planned in advance you may lose this opportunity by simply going on to the next question without responding fully to your client's previous answer (which may indicate an entirely new line of enquiry).

Show your client that you are listening. Try non-invasive prompts (eg 'yes', 'really', 'and then ...'). Make eye contact with your client.

ADVICE

You may not be able to give definitive legal advice on the basis of what you have been told during the interview. You should, however, be able to give the client some idea of the legal issues involved and a preliminary idea of your views, even if this is with the caveat of, 'On the basis of what you have told me'. You may prefer to deal with the uncertainty by identifying the risks (eg 'The risks are that the court believes her rather than you, and because there is no evidence in writing of what the contract was ...'). Your client will probably, however, if not in the interview itself, at least shortly afterwards, expect written advice, including an assessment of the chances of success and the risks involved.

Set out the legal issues involved, even if very simply (for instance: 'If it was a term of the contract that they should have insured the goods and they did not do so, you will be able to claim compensation in court for that breach of contract').

Even at a very early stage, you can set out some potential solutions to the client. The fact that you may wish to give further thought to the chances of success in litigation and that your client will certainly want to think about whether or not to get involved in litigation, does not of itself invalidate litigation as a *potential* way forward.

Does your client need to take any action at all? Perhaps the problem is a threat which may or may not materialise.

Is paying up, giving in and putting it all down to experience a potential way forward?

Consider both the advantages and the disadvantages of potential solutions. Consider these in the light of your client's expressed concerns (eg 'Since you are concerned about how quickly this can be resolved, let me set out the possible options on a scale of speed ...').

Conclusion

It may be impossible for the client to make a definitive decision about the most appropriate option immediately. That decision may be dependent on further research, decisions by the client's board of management, an opportunity to consider the written advice, and so on. However, it is important to finish the interview with a clear idea of what is going to happen next and when.

If you are instructed to take any further action, make sure you know what it involves and whether you need the client to do anything first. Does the client need to do anything independently (for example, find documents, locate witnesses, etc)? What arrangements have you made about costs? Are you going to write to the client? Are you going to meet again, and, if so, within what time scale?

ISSUES OF PROFESSIONAL CONDUCT

Look out for conflicts of interest, especially if you are being instructed on behalf of a group of people. Consider, when being instructed by one of a number of partners or directors, whether you should ask for the authority of all the parties or a decision of the board.

On the face of it, everything you are told by a client in interview is confidential, until matters reach the public domain if proceedings are commenced.

Courtesy and interpersonal skills

In interviewing a client or a witness, you are representing your firm. Think about the impression you are giving.

Surveys have suggested that clients:

–   look for creative solutions not just statements of law;
–   identify with lawyers who are technically competent and understand their business and the deal;
–   expect their solicitor to differentiate between the mountains and the molehills;
–   are comforted by lawyers who listen;
–   look for clear communication even in a crisis;
–   expect their solicitor to anticipate and not just to react;
–   expect their solicitor to take an interest in their business;
–   assume that their solicitor will treat deadlines as if his or her livelihood depended on it;
–   can react positively to the word 'no';
–   expect 'quality' service;
–   do not want their solicitor to promise more than he or she can deliver.

Chapter 10

LEGAL RESEARCH

INTRODUCTION

Legal research is vital in analysing a case. It is part and parcel of preparing for litigation.

Practical legal research requires you to carry out the following steps.

1   **Identifying and analysing the problem:**
   – finding out the facts and isolating the issues;
   – identifying assumptions;
   – thinking of keywords and phrases.

2   **Locating relevant information to solve the problem:**
   – being aware of materials available, both paper-based and electronic;
   – knowing their content, general effect and worth;
   – locating information within these materials;
   – ensuring that up-to-date materials are being used.

3   **Interpreting the information and reporting back the results clearly:**
   – understanding the meaning and effect of cases/statutory provisions, etc;
   – knowing the principles of interpretation;
   – applying the law to the facts of your problem;
   – recording the research you have undertaken, citing sources correctly;
   – providing clear, concise conclusions or client-friendly advice.

Focused and unfocused problems

A client's problem can be said to be focused if the issue involved is clear and you can condense the problem into a simple question. By finding the answer to that question, you will put yourself into the position where you can give advice.

If the problem is unfocused, you will usually have been presented with a set of facts from which you must first *identify* the issue(s) and/or problems arising from the facts. This in itself may involve an element of problem solving. Having done this, you should then be able to deal with the matter and advise as you would with a focused problem.

* * * * *

Consider the following sets of facts and decide whether they present you with focused or unfocused problems.

(a)   You are due to interview a client who has been the victim of an 'off the ball' incident during a football match. You need to establish whether anyone has been successful in bringing a claim for damages following a similar incident.

(b)   Your accountant client informs you that he is about to distribute funds to creditors of an insolvent company to which he was appointed liquidator. He tells you that he has not called a meeting of creditors at which to announce the amount for distribution. He has not received in all the funds which he expects to receive from debtors. He asks for advice.

* * * * *

HOW TO CARRY OUT PRACTICAL LEGAL RESEARCH

1   Isolate and classify the issues

If the problem is unfocused, you will have to isolate the relevant issues from the series of facts with which you are presented by the client or your supervisor. If you have a good knowledge of the relevant area of law, the issues may be immediately apparent. If this is not the case, then you may need to make educated hypotheses (or guesses) as to what the issues may be. Do not worry if you go down blind alleys: it could be that the issues will not become wholly apparent until you have undertaken practical research. You will usually find that, where this is the case, the answer to the problem will become apparent at the same time as the issues emerge or shortly thereafter.

Once you have isolated the issues which you have to deal with, you should attempt to classify the *type of problem(s)* you have to solve and the *area(s) of law* which you think applicable to the facts, eg the problem involves regulations and their interpretation in the area of employment law.

2   Key words and phrases

Another useful process to follow to assist in preparing a research strategy is to think of key words and phrases which you might use when consulting indexes, citators, digests, and so on.

It may be useful to adopt a 'thesaurus' approach when noting useful key words and phrases, as different texts and authors may use different terminology for one particular subject. In addition, this may prevent the scope of your practical research from being too confined. For example, if you were trying to solve a problem involving prisons and prisoners, the words 'custody', 'custodial', 'governor', 'imprisonment', 'prison service' and 'jail' might assist.

* * * * *

What key words or phrases could be used in addition to the following:

(a) 'matrimonial'?
'marriage', 'wedding', 'nuptials', 'family'

(b) 'employment'?
'job', 'career', 'work', 'profession'

* * * * *

3   Planning a practical research strategy

In addition to carrying out the above stages, you must have an awareness of legal sources and materials. You will need:

– to locate suitable sources of information (this will include practitioner texts, journals and online sources);
– to ensure that the information is up to date.

WHERE TO LOOK

The following list is a suggestion of sources for research.

Primary materials

Primary materials include statutes, statutory instruments and case-law.

BAILII
http://www.bailii.org/
The British and Irish Legal Information Institute website is a good general resource.

BAILII aims to provide a single access point to free primary legal sources on the internet. Databases include statutes, statutory instruments and case-law.

Statutes

Halsbury's Statutes of England & Wales
Gives the current text of statutes still in force. Use the main volumes, together with the annual Cumulative Supplement and the latest volume of the Noter-up Service.

Public General Acts/HMSO
The Stationery Office publishes the definitive text but note that this will not be updated. Copies of Acts from 1988 are also available on the Stationery Office website: *http://www.legislation.hmso.gov.uk/acts.htm*

Current Law Statutes Annotated
Includes useful annotations which set out the legislative history, including details of relevant Green Papers, White Papers and parliamentary debates.

Butterworths LexisNexis Direct – Legislation Direct
http://www.butterworths.com
Subscription service. Providing the current text of statutes still in force. Updated within 3 to 4 working days.

Lawtel UK
http://www.lawtel.co.uk/
Subscription service. Full-text versions of statutes, as enacted, are available from 1984. Details of amendments are provided via a table.

Westlaw
http://www.westlaw.co.uk
Subscription service offering the current text of statutes still in force as well as historical versions back to 1991.

Justis
http://www.justis.com
Subscription service providing access to the full text of both current and repealed Acts.

Statutory instruments

Halsbury's Statutory Instruments of England & Wales
Details, summaries and (for the more important instruments) the full text of statutory instruments still in force. Use the main volumes, together with the annual Cumulative Supplement and the Monthly Survey.

Office of Public Sector Information
http://www.opsi.gov.uk/legislation/index.htm
The Office of Public Sector Information (OPSI) (formerly Her Majesty's Stationery Office) publishes the definitive text, but note that this is not updated. Copies of statutory instruments are also available on their website from 1987. Electronic versions of draft statutory instruments date back to 1997.

Butterworths LexisNexis Direct – Legislation Direct
http://www.butterworths.com
Subscription service. Providing the current text of statutory instruments still in force. Updated within 3 to 4 working days.

Lawtel UK
http://www.lawtel.co.uk/
Subscription service. Full-text versions of statutes, as enacted, are available from 1984. Details of amendments are provided via a table.

Westlaw
http://www.westlaw.co.uk
Subscription service offering the current text of statutes still in force as well as historical versions back to 1991.

Case-law

The Law Reports
Published by the Incorporated Council of Law Reporting, the Law Reports are deemed to be the 'official' version and are preferred by the courts. The Law Reports date back to 1865. Electronic versions are available via subscription services such as Butterworths.

Weekly Law Reports
Also published by the Incorporated Council of Law Reporting. More significant cases will also appear in the Law Reports. Electronic versions are available via Justis (see above).

All England Law Reports
A weekly series published by Butterworths. Similar coverage to that of the Weekly Law Reports.

House of Lords judgments
http://www.publications.parliament.uk/pa/ld199697/ldjudgmt/ldjudgmt.htm
Available in full-text versions on the House of Lords website from November 1996.

Butterworths Lexis-Nexis Direct – All England Direct
http://www.butterworths.com
Subscription service, providing access to a complete archive of the All England Law Reports. The All England Law Reporter provides next-day/same-day case summaries with links to transcripts of judgments.

Lawtel UK
http://www.lawtel.co.uk/
Subscription service providing access to summaries of cases dating back to 1980. Copies of transcripts are also available.

Westlaw
http://www.westlaw.co.uk
Subscription service including full-text versions of Lloyd's, the Law Reports and many of Sweet & Maxwell's specialist series.

Secondary materials

Encyclopaedias

Halsbury's Laws of England

Summarises the whole of English law. It provides a useful starting-point for legal research. The main work is updated by annual Cumulative Supplement and a monthly Noter-up Service.

Butterworths LEXIS direct

Halsbury's Laws Direct website.

Journals

Legal Journals Index

A subscription service from Sweet & Maxwell offering access to an index of articles published in all UK legal journals from 1986. Many full-text articles are available from document supply services such as Sweet & Maxwell's DocDel. Legal Journals index is also available on Westlaw.

Index to Legal Periodicals

Published by HW Wilson, Index to Legal Periodicals covers all the main UK journals as well as many US titles. The service is also available on Lexis.

Lawtel

http://www.lawtel.co.uk/

Subscription service offering access to an index of articles dating back to 1998. Full-text copies are available via Lawtel.

Practitioners' materials

The Encyclopaedia of Forms and Precedents (Sweet & Maxwell).

Civil Procedure Rules 1998

Although there are paper-based versions of the CPR 1998, it is recommended that you use the internet to ensure that you are consulting the most up-to-date version of the Rules, as numerous changes are still appearing. The Rules can be found on the Department of Constitutional Affairs (DCA) website.

Chapter 11

DRAFTING

INTRODUCTION

Drafting the statements of case becomes easy once you have worked on your case analysis and case theory (this is covered in detail under 'Case preparation' in Chapter 12). Your drafting should be an extension of your case theory, ie it should be the clear and simple statement of your case, whether you are making or defending a claim, in a logical form, simply expressed. Your statement of case should tell the story clearly. There is usually no absolute right or wrong way to draft statements of case. Your own style should prevail, subject to a few technical rules which are dealt with below.

Consistency makes statements of case easy to read. Avoid using a variety of terms to refer to the same thing, eg 'the house', 'the premises', 'the demise' etc. Use either 'the House' or 'the Premises' throughout. (Initial capitals should be used for any previously defined terms.) Always think of your audience: the judge; the opponent; and your client.

DRAFTING THE PARTICULARS OF CLAIM – GENERAL POINTS

Layout of heading

Make sure that you set out the heading correctly, for example:

[Claim No]

<u>IN THE HIGH COURT OF JUSTICE</u>
<u>QUEEN'S BENCH DIVISION</u>
<u>ROYAL COURTS OF JUSTICE</u>
B E T W E E N:

[CLAIMANT'S NAME]

<u>Claimant</u>

– and –

[DEFENDANT'S NAME]

<u>Defendant</u>

If proceedings are taking place in the county court, the heading should state:

<u>'IN THE X COUNTY COURT'</u>

or if not in the Central Office in London but in the High Court elsewhere:

<u>'IN THE HIGH COURT OF JUSTICE</u>
<u>QUEEN'S BENCH DIVISION</u>
<u>X DISTRICT REGISTRY'</u>

The claim

Set out the claim, ensuring that you *properly and appropriately* include the following.

(a)   An introduction to the parties if appropriate (see 'Suggestions of useful phrases for drafting particulars of claims' below).

(b)   All the 'essential elements' of the claim: the consequences of failing properly to include all of the essential elements are that the claim may be struck out or there may be a request for further information.

(c)   All material facts to support the claim:
   –   CPR r 16.4 requires the claimant to put in his particulars of claim 'a concise statement of the facts on which the claimant relies'. Avoid unnecessary allegations thrown in to give spurious weight which simply invite a request for further information;
   –   CPR PD 16, para 13.3(3) permits evidence to be attached. Points of law may also be put in the Particulars of Claim (para 13.3(1)) and the names of witnesses may be stated (para 13.3(2));
   –   it is also important that the facts stated accurately reflect your client's story as set out in your papers.

(d)   All necessary particulars: for example, if a breach of contract is alleged, the way in which the contract has been breached will need to be particularised.

(e)   Any other necessary matters:

– any criminal convictions, if relevant. These are often encountered in road traffic accident cases;

– details of any breaches of the HRA 1998 (CPR PD 16, para 15);

– a party's knowledge, if relevant (for example, of a liquidated damages clause imposed upon A by C where A is suing B and wishes to recover the amount paid out to C).

(f) A claim for interest if appropriate.

(g) Names of witnesses you intend to call (although this is optional).

Ending

Set out the ending correctly:

(a) the 'Prayer' should commence '**AND the Claimant claims** ...' and should constitute:

    (i) the appropriate remedy/ies; and

    (ii) interest, if and as appropriate;

(b) the statement of case should be signed. The name of a solicitor's firm or counsel must appear at the foot of any statement of case which a solicitor or counsel has drafted. Where statements of case are drafted on a word processor, this is simply printed;

(c) the Particulars of Claim must be verified by a statement of truth (see CPR PD 16, para 3.4 and CPR Part 22);

(d) the claimant's address for service must be endorsed at the end;

(e) any documents must be attached to your Particulars of Claim in accordance with CPR PD 16.

Main points to consider in drafting the Particulars of Claim

Remember the cardinal rules:

(1) structure the statement of case logically;

(2) be precise;

(3) be concise;

(4) use correct, plain and professional English; and

(5) set out your client's claim completely, clearly and persuasively.

If you adhere to the following recommended steps, your drafting is likely to improve.

– Thoroughly plan your statement of case before starting to draft.

– Set out a draft framework for your statement of case.

– Draft your statement of case.

– As you go along, try to refine and improve what you have written.

– Finally, thoroughly check your completed statement of case (paragraph by paragraph and as a whole document). Can it be further refined or improved:

    (i) Is it complete?

    (ii) Can its structure be improved?

    (iii) What about your terminology?

    (iv) Is it clear and persuasive?

Use of precedents

Old copies of precedent books do not incorporate the Woolf reforms (or, if they do, may not incorporate the most recent version), so should be used with extreme care. In any event, using a precedent often results in having to 'dovetail' the facts to the template being used, which is rather like the 'tail wagging the dog'.

DRAFTING CLAIMS FOR DAMAGES FOR BREACH OF CONTRACT

Basic structure of claim

A claim for damages for breach of contract should include the following details:

(1)   the contract;
(2)   the relevant term(s) of the contract;
(3)   details of the breach of the term(s) of the contract;
(4)   loss and damage *and* causation.

If any one of these essential elements is missing from the claim, the consequence, at best, will be a need to amend, which could be embarrassing and costly, but, ultimately, at worst, the claim could be struck out under CPR r 3.4.

1   The contract

Set out the material facts:

– specify whether the contract was oral or written and list the details and/or documents required by CPR PD 16, paras 7.3, 7.4 and 7.5;
– give the date when the contract was made;
– name the parties (ie the claimant and the defendant);
– give a *brief* description of the subject-matter of the contract;
– state the consideration for the contract (although there is no need to use the word 'consideration').

Additional 'material facts' to be given in relation to oral contracts
Specify the contractual words used and state by whom, to whom, when and where they were spoken. (If either the claimant or defendant made the contract through an agent or employee, that agent's name should also be stated.)

Additional 'material facts' to be given in relation to written contracts
– A description of the contractual document(s), sufficient to identify it/them, should be supplied.
– A copy of the contractual documents should be attached to or served with the Particulars of Claim (unless they are bulky, in which case relevant extracts will suffice).

2   The relevant term(s) of the contract

Set out only the term(s) that you will later rely on as having been breached.

Identify the term(s) as express and/or implied.

In describing each term, utilise the language of the contract (refer to the statute or case-law if an implied term). State any preconditions necessary for the implication of an implied term (eg it was a sale in the course of a business).

3   Details of the breach of the term(s) by the defendant

'Particularise' (detail) the defendant's breach(es).

–   Identify precisely what the defendant has not done which he or she ought to have done, or vice versa.
–   Deal with one breach at a time.

A specific term may be breached in a single way; a more general term may be breached in various ways.

If there are more than one or two 'particulars', you should list them under a subheading, for example:

PARTICULARS OF BREACH

(a)

(b)

4   Damage and causation

Two distinct elements must be set out:

–   the *damage* suffered by the claimant;
–   the fact that this was *caused* by the defendant's breach(es).

Measuring damages for breach of contract
The basic principle is to put the claimant in the same position as if the defendant had properly performed the contract.

The damage must not be too remote. (See *Hadley v Baxendale* (1854) 9 Exch 341, [1843–60] All ER Rep 461: knowledge (imputed or actual) is required if the damage would otherwise be too remote.)

Setting out loss and damage
'Particularise' (detail) the loss and damage:

–   briefly identify each 'head of loss' separately;
–   briefly explain how the loss was incurred;
–   state the amount claimed (if applicable, show the means of calculation);
–   if property has been damaged, state ownership;
–   state knowledge of remote losses, if applicable.

Setting out causation
Matters of causation are conventionally put alongside 'loss and damage'.

Further matters
The following matters should also be stated:

–   any claim for interest on financial claims for special damages;
–   relief sought;
–   damages;
–   interest (if sought).

DRAFTING CLAIMS FOR DAMAGES IN NEGLIGENCE

Basic structure of a claim

A claim for damages in negligence should proceed as follows:

(1)   duty of care;
(2)   breach of the duty;
(3)   causation;
(4)   loss and damage.

The consequence of any one of these essential elements missing from the claim is the same as in a claim for breach of contract: if you are lucky, you will be granted an application to amend but, ultimately, you are at risk of having your claim struck out (CPR r 3.4).

1   Duty of care

Was there a duty of care owed to this claimant by this defendant?

–   If the duty arose under statute, state this, referring to the specific provision.
–   Specify how the duty arose, giving details of the relationship between the parties.
–   List the material facts, ie 'tell the story' so far as material so that the subsequent allegations of breach are in context.

Additional 'material facts'
If the negligent act was committed in the course of the employee's/agent's employment/agency, the fact of the employment/agency and that the employee/agent was acting in the course of his or her employment/agency must be stated.

If there is a claim for trespass to land, state ownership of the land.

Knowledge is another matter that may have to be stated, but only when relevant. For example, where, but for knowledge of particular circumstances, it would not be reasonably foreseeable that the consequences of an act or omission would lead to damage, knowledge of those circumstances is necessary and must be stated.

2   Breach of the duty of care by the defendant

'Particularise' (detail) the defendant's breach(es) (the particulars should be very concise):

–   identify precisely what the defendant has not done which he or she ought to have done, or vice versa;
–   deal with one breach at a time.

A duty may be breached in a number of ways. You need to identify specific duties that were breached. At trial, you will need evidence to establish the stated breaches.

If there are more than one or two 'particulars', you should list them under a subheading, for example:

PARTICULARS OF NEGLIGENCE

(a)

(b)

3   Causation and damage

There are two distinct elements:

–   the fact that the breach caused the claimant's loss and damage; and
–   the damage suffered by the claimant.

The factual causal connection between the defendant's wrongful conduct and the alleged loss is for the claimant to prove and must be stated.

Measuring loss and damage

The basic principle is to put the claimant in the same position as he or she would have been in had the tort not been committed.

The damage must not be too remote. The test is reasonable foreseeability.

Setting out loss and damage

(a)   General damages (to be assessed by the court)

Do not attempt to quantify general damages, but instead set out the factual basis of the injuries. In a personal injury case, note the requirement to include a description of the injuries, and the claimant's date of birth, and to attach a medical report (CPR PD 16, para 4). A statement of special damages should also be appended.

(b)   Special damages (capable of mathematical calculation by the claimant)

Particularise (detail) the loss and damage:

–   briefly identify each 'head of loss' separately;
–   briefly explain how the loss was incurred;
–   state the amount claimed (if not possible, state 'Damages to be assessed' or leave a blank space for the figure);
–   if applicable, show the means of calculation.

Further matters

The following matters should also be stated:

–   any claim for interest on financial claims for special damages;
–   relief sought;
–   damages;
–   interest (if sought).

SUGGESTIONS OF USEFUL PHRASES FOR DRAFTING PARTICULARS OF CLAIMS

'At all material times ...'/'At all relevant times ...'

This can be a more convenient and concise way of saying, for example, 'At the time the parties entered into the contract ...' or 'At the time of the accident ...', etc. It can also assist if you are not sure precisely when an event took place or in circumstances where the event was/is continuing. This phrase could also prevent your client from being restricted to relying only on the precise timings, etc, that you might otherwise have stated.

'... and/or ...'

This is a useful term for connecting clauses as it offers two options rather than restricting you to one or the other.

'Further or alternatively ...'

This phrase may be employed where a paragraph is included or an allegation is made either in addition to or as an alternative to a preceding paragraph or allegation. In these circumstances, if you do not use this phrase, you may be limited to arguing one or the other rather than both.

'[By reason of/As a result of] the Defendant's [breach/negligence etc], the Claimant has suffered [pain and injury,] loss and damage'

This is an example of how to plead *causation* and *damage*. Both are essential in order to succeed at court. Note that the nature and extent of the damages sought must also be detailed underneath the heading:

'PARTICULARS OF [PAIN AND INJURY,] LOSS AND DAMAGE'

'Failed, adequately or at all …'

In appropriate circumstances, this phrase can be a useful introduction to allegations within the particulars of breach or negligence.

'The Claimant claims interest pursuant to [section 69 of the County Courts Act 1984/section 35A of the Supreme Court Act 1981] at such rate and for such period as the court deems fit'

This is a reasonably standard phrase for claiming interest on a money claim for an unspecified amount.

'The Claimant claims interest pursuant to [section 69 of the County Courts Act 1984/section 35A of the Supreme Court Act 1981] at the rate of 8% per annum, being £[*amount*] until today's date and continuing at a daily rate of £[*amount*]'

This is a reasonably standard phrase for claiming interest on a money claim for a specified amount.

DRAFTING THE DEFENCE

Layout of heading

Set out the heading correctly (see under 'Drafting the Particulars of Claim' above).

Response

An appropriate response should be made to all allegations in the Particulars of Claim (see CPR r 16.5). In a personal injury case, note the specific requirement to respond to the medical report and the schedule of special damages (CPR PD 16, para 12).

A defendant may respond in one of four ways to any allegation contained in the Particulars of Claim. He or she may:

(1)   admit it, ie concede the allegation;

(2)   not admit it: where the defendant is unable to admit or deny an allegation and he or she requires the claimant to prove it (eg because it is something peculiarly within the knowledge of the other party);

(3)   deny it: if a defendant denies an allegation he or she must state his or her reason for doing so and state his or her own version of events if it is different from the claimant's version;

(4)   admit it, but with some stated qualification.

Do not respond to 'particulars' (ie detailed lists of breaches) except:

–   when a 'material fact' (as opposed to a generalised allegation) has been alleged in the particulars with which you positively disagree; or

–   where you wish to allege that:
    –   the claimant has not mitigated his or her loss; and/or
    –   the head of damage is too remote.

Ignore the claim for interest and the prayer.

What should be included in the response

Additional material facts in support of your client's case
Where you will seek to rely at trial on a positive story which contradicts that of the claimant, the material parts of that story must be stated.

All necessary particulars
Some matters in a defence should be fully particularised. These include particulars of:

–   contributory negligence;
–   remoteness of damage;
–   failure to mitigate.

Any other necessary matters
You should specifically state any matter which:

–   is required to be stated by CPR PD 16, paras 13–15;
–   makes the claimant's claim (or part of it) unsustainable;
–   if not specifically stated, would take the claimant by surprise;
–   raises issues of fact not arising out of the Particulars of Claim;
–   is an allegation of contributory negligence;
–   relates to:
    –   knowledge;
    –   relevant criminal convictions;
    –   limitation; or
    –   waiver.

Statement of truth

Remember to include a statement of truth at the end of the Defence. (Witnesses' names may also be inserted and evidence attached, as with a Particulars of Claim.)

Main points to consider in drafting a Defence

Your Defence is likely to be greatly improved if you follow these recommended steps.

–   Preparation should consist of:
    –   understanding the facts of the case;
    –   ascertaining the defendant's objectives;
    –   analysing the Particulars of Claim.
–   Break the claim down, paragraph by paragraph, into its constituent essential elements. For example, in a negligence claim, these would be:
    –   the duty of care;
    –   the factual details of the negligent act;
    –   breach;
    –   causation; and
    –   injury, loss and damage.
–   Compare the factual allegations with your client's version of events: where/how do they differ (if at all)?
–   Decide what you will admit, what you are not prepared to admit and what you will deny.
–   Deal with every component of the claim, including causation.
–   Consider whether you should allege contributory negligence.
–   Draw up a framework plan of your defence.
–   Draft the body of the defence.
–   Adopt a style and stick with it throughout the defence.
–   Do not use personal pronouns.
–   Be concise.
–   Check your draft.

SUGGESTIONS OF USEFUL PHRASES FOR DRAFTING DEFENCES

'Paragraph [*number*] is [denied/not admitted/admitted]'

This is a simple, straightforward means of dealing with the entire contents of a paragraph.

'If, which is [denied/not admitted], …'

This is useful where you are stating an alternative defence/point: you are therefore saying to the claimant, 'I do not accept your point, you will have to prove it. Furthermore, even if you do, I will then argue …'.

'[Except/Save] [that/for] …, it is [denied/not admitted] that …'

This is a useful phrase where part of a paragraph is accepted and part is not.

'… whether as alleged or at all'

This is a good method of dealing with the *substance* of an allegation rather than merely the specific wording. This is useful when you are denying breach of duty (negligence, statutory or contract) or other general allegations.

'… and/or …', 'Further or alternatively …'

See under 'Suggestions of useful phrases for drafting Particulars of Claim'.

'Further or alternatively, the accident was caused or contributed to by the Claimant's negligence [*then particularise the allegations of negligence*]'

This is a standard paragraph to allege contributory negligence.

'In particular, but without prejudice to the generality of the foregoing …'

This can be useful, for example, where you have just stated a general denial of negligence but also wish to deal specifically with one of the particulars of negligence. In these circumstances, this phrase makes it absolutely clear that, just because you are only specifically dealing with one of the particulars, you still (generally) deny the remainder.

'In the circumstances, it is denied that the Claimant is entitled to the relief claimed or any relief, for the reasons alleged or at all'

This paragraph is entirely optional. Some lawyers will argue that it is perhaps an exception to the general rule that you only state what is necessary and that this statement 'rounds off' what would otherwise be an abruptly ending defence, making the defence as a whole appear more complete and eloquent. Alternatively, you may think that it is completely superfluous and should not be used. This is a matter of personal choice.

DRAFTING A COUNTERCLAIM

A counterclaim is a claim being made by the defendant against the claimant in the proceedings brought by the claimant. There are therefore two claims being made within the same action.

The Defence and Counterclaim should normally form one document with the Counterclaim following on from the Defence (CPR Part 20).

Layout of the heading

Where a defendant makes a counterclaim against the claimant, the title of the Defence and Counterclaim should be as follows:

[AB]
Claimant/Part 20 Defendant

– and –

[CD]
Defendant/Part 20 Claimant

Set-off as distinguished from mere counterclaim

A set-off must amount to a defence (or part defence) to the claimant's claim.

A set-off arises *only* in the following circumstances:

–   where there are mutual (liquidated) debts;
–   under Sale of Goods Act 1979, s 53(1);
–   where the claim relates to the price of services in respect of poor workmanship; and
–   in cases of equitable set-off.

To be used as a defence (or partial defence) to the claimant's claim, a set-off must therefore be put as a paragraph within the Defence, although it may also be put as a counterclaim (ie a set-off can always be a counterclaim, but not vice versa).

If the set-off is to form part of the Defence, add a paragraph at the end, such as:

'If necessary the Defendant will rely on his Counterclaim in this action by way of set-off in extinction or diminution of the Claimant's claim.'

If the set-off is also to be pleaded as a Counterclaim, at the end of the Defence (after the above paragraph), add a centred subheading 'COUNTERCLAIM' and state the claim fully. (See CPR PD 15, para 3.1.)

Cross-referencing

For example, where paragraphs 1, 2 and 3 of the Particulars of Claim need to be stated in the Counterclaim (ie as essential elements/material facts), and paragraphs 1 and 2 of the Defence deal with those paragraphs, the beginning of the Counterclaim section might start as follows:

'1.   Paragraphs 1 and 2 of the Defence are repeated.'

The Counterclaim

Plead the counterclaim in a similar way as you would when drafting a claim.

Prayer for relief

At the end of the Counterclaim insert:

> 'And the Defendant counterclaims:
>
> 1   Damages;
> 2   [Interest, etc]'

as appropriate.

Statement of truth

Remember to put in a statement of truth (CPR Part 22 and PD 15, para 2.1) and an address for service (if not already endorsed on the acknowledgement of service form previously filed).

Chapter 12

ADVOCACY

INTRODUCTION

There are seven initial duties that you should reflect on before any court appearance. These are of paramount importance and should take precedence over 'winning' the case.

(1)   You should always try to assist the judge in reaching a decision.
(2)   You should never mislead the court and always be accurate when providing information.
(3)   You should do the best you can for your client.
(4)   You should not allow personal opinions to influence you and should never voice personal opinions in court.
(5)   You should adhere to the Codes of Conduct for Solicitors, Solicitor Advocates or the Bar, whichever is appropriate.
(6)   You should always guard against sacrificing your good reputation in the courtroom. Your client's case will always benefit if you are polite and courteous to the judge, your opponent and other court personnel.
(7)   You should be prepared to take personal responsibility for the conduct of a case.

CASE PREPARATION

Case analysis and case theory

When you are preparing a case, you should always analyse the facts from the very outset before making strategic decisions and considering the prospects of success. Often, lawyers will sort the facts of a case in a rather haphazard manner, which can lead to an incomplete or unhelpful result. A more structured method of analysis leading to the formulation of a case theory is suggested below. This enhances the benefits of the analysis and leads to more effective litigation and dispute resolution. Careful analysis will allow the lawyer to:

–   have a sound grasp of the case;
–   focus on the essentials of the case;
–   identify the evidence required to succeed should the case reach trial;

–   keep a record of the case analysis which assists in the later development of
     the matter.

If full analysis is carried out at the commencement of the litigation you will
develop an ability to 'think trial' from the outset, so that you are familiar with the
strengths and weaknesses of the case, how the facts can be proved and what
additional evidence may be required.

Method of case analysis

The method suggested below is one easy-to-use method of analysis. However, it is
not the only possible way of analysing a case and you may already have an
alternative. This method of case analysis comprises five stages.

(1)   Identify the proposition(s) that need to be established in order to succeed.
(2)   Brainstorm each of the propositions, using the 'good facts/bad facts'
       approach.
(3)   Analyse the outcome of the brainstorm.
(4)   Formulate a working case theory, bearing in mind your instructions.
(5)   Fact investigation and case management.

Stage 1 – Identify the proposition(s) that need to be established in order to succeed

Your analysis should focus on the core propositions that will be in contention.
Normally, these will be the elements of the cause of action.

For example, in a breach of contract case, the cause of action includes the terms of
the contract, the breach and any loss or damage caused by the breach. If a
particular term of the contract is alleged by your client and denied by the other side
(eg that the goods were to be delivered by 8 August) then you would take the
proposition as 'it was a term of the contract that the goods were to be delivered by
8 August'. Using this proposition you would then move on to Stage 2.

Stage 2 – Brainstorm each of the propositions, using the 'good facts/bad facts' approach

Write the proposition you have selected at the top of a sheet of paper. Underneath,
draw a vertical line down the centre of the page. Head one column 'good facts' and
the other column 'bad facts'. The aim of the process used in this type of brainstorm
is to focus your mind on the essentials of the case. You should end up with a list of
'good facts', which are those facts that support your client's case, and a list of 'bad
facts' which are those facts that damage your case or support the other side's story.
Irrelevant facts, rumours and assumptions should not appear on either list.
Brainstorming, carried out in this way, is an effective 'quick fire' approach to
analysis. It can be undertaken by one person or a team of people working in the
office (or on a training course). Where the brainstorm is being carried out by a
team, one person should be responsible for writing down the team's ideas and
keeping to the rules of brainstorming. With the full facts of your instructions in
your mind, you should then note all possible facts on either side of the vertical line,

as either a 'good fact' or a 'bad fact'. There should at this stage be no discussion of any points raised and no debate or criticism of any fact recorded. Any fact that is thought to be both 'good' and 'bad' should be noted on both sides of the vertical line and can be analysed later, at Stage 3. You should only allow yourself a certain maximum length of time for the brainstorming stage (eg 5 minutes). This will depend on the complexity of the case and the number of people conducting the brainstorm.

Stage 3 – Analyse the outcome of the brainstorm

Following Stage 2, you will have a lot of recorded information that now needs to be further analysed. During the brainstorm, points were not discussed or debated; now is the time to look at each one in turn and decide whether the item is a useful fact (whether it is 'good' (helpful to your client's case) or 'bad' (supportive of the other side's case)). If the item is evidence to support a fact, rumour, or assumption, then this should be discarded at this stage. You should then aim to prioritise the facts so that you can identify which of them is most important to proving your client's case or supporting the other side's case.

Stage 4 – Formulate a working case theory, bearing in mind your instructions

Your case theory will be the best explanation on the information available which indicates that your client should succeed. You should try to make your case theory simple and short. It will help you to focus on the central issues of the case and, if you revise the case theory whenever new information comes to light, it will keep you focused on these issues at every stage of the litigation including the trial.

Start formulating your case theory by identifying the two strongest facts for each proposition. Then consider whether you would succeed if you could prove these. Your case theory might commence with the words, 'My client should succeed because ...'. So, for example, a case theory might be: 'My client should succeed because the Defendant breached the contract by not delivering the goods by 8 August, causing a loss of profits of £20,000'.

To succeed, your theory of the case should:

– correspond with your instructions from your client;
– be persuasive, bearing in mind the nature of the eventual tribunal (eg judge/tribunal);
– be simple;
– be easy to believe;
– be based on common sense and be logical;
– take into account all undisputed and undeniable facts;
– be based on admissible evidence and credible witnesses;
– remember that rules of conduct require that your assertions should derive from actual evidence;
– ignore facts which cannot be established by admissible evidence;
– deal with the legal elements of the case that must be satisfied to entitle your client to the relief sought.

If your case theory takes more than two sentences then it is probably too long and you should simplify it.

If a matter reaches trial, advanced case analysis might lead you to develop a theme from the case theory. The theme might be contained in a single idea or phrase. It is a central unifying concept of the case and is a thread which runs through and links all the facts. The idea of a theme will be resumed later when looking at opening and closing speeches and witness examination in the context of advocacy at the trial. An oft-quoted example of a theme is in relation to the story of Little Red Riding Hood, where the theme could be said to be 'good triumphs over evil'.

Stage 5 – Fact investigation and case management

The development of case analysis and a workable case theory is a continuing process. As new facts emerge you need to conduct further analysis and amend your case theory accordingly. In addition you need to consider what further information may be available or whether an expert needs to be instructed.

Part of case analysis is investigation of the facts. At this stage, you need to consider:

– what additional information is required;
– which witnesses can support the factual issues;
– which witnesses can support the legal issues;
– the admissibility of potential evidence;
– that the contents of a statement may differ from the evidence that a witness might give in the witness box;
– methods of analysis; good facts/bad facts, chronologies, flow charts, consideration of how different facts affect each other;
– ask the question 'why': why is this fact important?; why did this happen?, etc;
– fact inferences: facts, propositions and fact inferences are available to you. Your proposition may be that C must be the explanation and that facts A and B would only have occurred or make sense if proposition C is correct: this is a fact inference.

STRUCTURE, DELIVERY AND WORD CHOICE

When deciding on issues of structure, delivery and word choice, the advocate should consider the tribunal before which he or she is to appear. This will influence the choices that are made. The approach to a judge sitting alone and to a judge and jury will require different considerations.

Structure

Whether it is an oral or written presentation, any reasonable structure is appropriate as long as it is simple and easily understood. Whether you are presenting an opening statement, conducting witness examination or making a closing speech you should have structured the content or the order in which you ask the questions. It is advisable to start and end with a favourable and strong point.

Delivery

You should be confident and sincere in what you say and reflect a belief in the merits of your case. You should also show interest in your case and use an energetic and enthusiastic manner but not a dramatic one.

Appropriate use of gestures can make what you say more interesting. You should aim for gestures that are natural, firm and purposeful, and not awkward or wild hand movements.

Vocal control and pace are important, as they will affect the listeners' ability to concentrate and absorb what you say. Dull monotone and dramatic presentations are equally ineffective. Use of transitions and sentences which introduce the next issue or topic, can greatly aid the effectiveness of what is said. Transitions are excellent times to use techniques such as:

– pauses or silence;
– increasing or decreasing the volume of your voice;
– gestures; and
– movement (so far as the confines of the court allow).

Be mindful of the judge as a note-taker and the needs of a jury considering sometimes complex facts in a strange environment.

Word choice

Simple language
Clarity of expression is important. Do not use overly simplistic words but aim for words that are readily and quickly understood. You are not showing the breadth of your vocabulary but communicating with words that make it easy for the listener. Particularly, keep it simple for a jury but you can afford to use more complicated or technical language for a civil trial.

Factual words
Facts and not conclusions should be presented.

Impact phrases
Descriptive words are useful in emphasising an important fact. However, you should not over-use impact words or you will lose their impact, and care should be taken to select words that are accurate and do not exaggerate the evidence.

CONDUCT CONSIDERATIONS

Where a solicitor has been acting for a client and then takes on the role of advocate, remember to take account of the specific conduct considerations for the advocate. The solicitor advocate must become familiar with the sections of the *Law Society's Guide to the Professional Conduct of Solicitors* which relate to litigation and advocacy and any additional guidance that is issued by the Law Society. Barristers must take account of the Bar Code of Conduct issued by the Bar Council.

The solicitor in civil proceedings, whether or not he or she also acts as advocate, should remember that his or her duty is to help the court achieve the overriding objective in Part 1 of the Civil Procedure Rules 1998. The solicitor in criminal proceedings should be mindful of the different conduct considerations for prosecution and defence.

The Law Society's Code for Advocacy covers such matters as:

–   Fundamental Principles, for example, the advocate's duty to the Court, their client, the circumstances in which the advocate can decline to accept instructions.
–   Organisation of the Advocate's Practice.
–   The Decision to Appear as the Advocate.
–   Withdrawal from a Case.
–   Conduct of Work.
–   Communications with Clients.

MODES OF ADDRESS

The following are the modes of address to be used in open court and in chambers. When present in a private room at court with any person sitting as a judge, the correct form of address is 'Judge'. The correct forms of address in correspondence and socially are different.

House of Lords

Lord of Appeal in Ordinary:	My Lord/My Lady
	Your Lordship/Your Ladyship

Court of Appeal

Lord Justice of Appeal and	My Lord/My Lady
Lady Justice of Appeal:	Your Lordship/Your Ladyship

High Court

Judge:	My Lord/My Lady
	Your Lordship/Your Ladyship
Master:	Master

Crown Court

High Court judge	My Lord/My Lady
Circuit judge:	Your Honour
Central Criminal Court Judge:	My Lord/My Lady
Recorder/Assistant Recorder:	Your Honour

County court

Circuit judge:	Your Honour
Recorder:	Your Honour
District judge:	Sir/Madam

Tribunal/arbitration

Chairman:	Sir/Madam
Other members:	Your colleagues

SKELETON ARGUMENTS

The role of skeleton arguments in civil cases

In civil proceedings, the use of the skeleton argument is always relevant. In criminal proceedings, the advocate should be aware when a skeleton is compulsory and when it is optional. Where the criminal advocate has a choice he or she should consider using a skeleton argument to assist in any complex submissions.

Where a skeleton argument is to be used, the following issues may guide your preparation.

Some advocates produce massively long documents which purport to be skeleton arguments. A skeleton argument is intended to be a shortcut to the case, summarising the issues and the law. Brief skeleton arguments are often the most cogent.

Does the content and drafting of your skeleton argument assist you as an advocate and will it assist the judge? Consider the differences between how you talk and how you write, as this will influence how you draft your skeleton argument.

Only submit a skeleton argument if you intend to use it. All too often skeletons are submitted and then not used or the advocate does not refer to the skeleton save in passing, eg 'I take it, My Lord, you have read my skeleton ...' Both are unhelpful and unpersuasive. Judges who take the trouble to read the skeleton argument beforehand are annoyed if the oral advocacy is merely a repetition of what they have read or if it bears no relation to what they have read.

The key is submitting concise skeletons which identify what is being sought, what the issues are, and some *brief* exposition of the contentions: all of this should leave room for persuasive argument using the skeleton argument as the launch pad.

Preparation of skeleton arguments

There are variations in the style adopted for skeleton arguments. However, there are several common factors reflected in good skeleton arguments. A good skeleton argument:

–   is drafted in a way that is consistent with the manner in which it will be
      stated orally;
–   is not a script for the advocate's address to the court;
–   should be useful to supplement the oral argument. It should in itself be
      persuasive and assist the delivery of oral argument rather than stifle it;
–   will become a part of the case preparation and court preparation and not an
      add-on that is ignored in court;
–   gets to the heart of the matter;
–   summarises the issues;
–   is concise;
–   includes references citing precise paragraph numbers or page numbers, etc.

The content of a skeleton argument will be dictated by the party the advocate
represents and the purpose for which it is being prepared. For example, a skeleton
argument in criminal proceedings to support a submission to the judge will be
more narrowly drafted than a skeleton by the claimant in civil proceedings. In civil
matters it is generally accepted that the claimant sets out the dramatis personae and
a chronology of events.

CIVIL INTERIM APPLICATIONS AND CASE MANAGEMENT CONFERENCES

Introduction

The subject matter and the relative informality of applications and case
management conferences (CMCs) bring different considerations for the skills of
the advocate. When these take place seated then this requires the advocate to
consider different presentation issues to trial advocacy.

Note that throughout the following pages on interim advocacy, all references to a
judge should be taken to also refer to a master or district judge where relevant.

General preparation for applications and CMCs

As with any court appearance, the need for thorough preparation is vital. If you
adopt a method of preparation that incorporates organisation and retention of notes
then the time spent in preparation for an interim application will pay dividends
thereafter, whatever the outcome of the application.

Perhaps because the appointments are brief and less formal than a full court
hearing there is sometimes a tendency to view them as less important. The reality
is that the outcomes of these applications have a major effect on the case.
Therefore, they should not be taken lightly.

Points to consider
Ensure that you know:

(1)   your case theory and propositions that must be established based on your case analysis;

(2)   the orders and directions you want the court to make but always have a fall-back position;

(3)   all of the facts of the case;

(4)   where all the evidence can be found in the witness statements, and documents filed with the court;

(5)   the arguments that you want to put forward;

(6)   the conclusions that you want the judge to make;

(7)   what the position is with regard to costs so you can make the appropriate representations (including any schedules filed in anticipation of summary assessment of costs at the end of the hearing itself);

(8)   in what circumstances it would be appropriate to appeal.

Consider the information the judge needs in order to decide the application in your client's favour.

Consider whether your application has any feature that makes it unusual and therefore requires you to give additional information or outline the law.

Consider what arguments the advocate for the other party is likely to advance and prepare an argument to counter these.

Prepare a skeleton argument, except where the case is extremely straightforward (if in doubt it is better to prepare a skeleton). Provide the judge and your opponent with a copy. This guidance holds true in most applications. However, part of knowing your tribunal is to be aware of when to deviate from general guidance.

In addition to a skeleton argument in a complex case, you may need to prepare a chronology and dramatis personae. Many advocates include these in their skeleton argument. If they are prepared separately the judge and your opponent should again be provided with copies.

Presentation for applications and CMCs

General preparation
As with any piece of advocacy, to be persuasive and authoritative you should not *read* from notes. However, notes outlining the essential points aid your preparation, quickly re-focus your thoughts when you go back to the file and act as a guide during your submissions. Do not prepare long-hand submissions: it is best to use headings and keywords.

You should be so well prepared that interruptions and questions do not fluster or confuse you. Be prepared for questions from the judge and always answer in a manner that is helpful and respectful.

Structure your submissions and arguments. Preface your argument with a brief outline of what will be covered and in your first submission, unless it is clear that the judge already knows, you should outline what your client is seeking at *this* application.

Develop a system for organising facts so that they are readily accessible when addressing the court. Make notes of references to documents, and use 'post-it' tabs, notes and other methods that will assist you and make you feel comfortable and confident.

Delivery

Speak clearly and at a pace that makes it easy for the judge to follow and to take notes. This does not *just* mean avoiding speaking too quickly. It means that you should make use of pauses. Pause between sentences, between topic areas and pause where you can see that the judge is making a note. Pauses that seem to last a long time to the advocate will hardly be noticed by those listening except to the extent that they will find it easier to follow what the advocate is saying.

Pausing is particularly relevant when referring to documents. Pause to ensure the judge has the relevant document, page and paragraph.

As with all advocacy, you should use persuasive language. This is not a debate and at all times you must be an advocate.

The majority of interim advocacy is conducted seated and so the advocate must develop the skill of effective and persuasive body language when seated. Remember that you are 'on show' throughout, not just when you are speaking. Sitting erect, using small gestures when appropriate, eye contact and generally using your physical presence to be persuasive as you would if you were on your feet are important.

One of the dangers of advocacy, which is particularly evident in interim advocacy, is that insufficient attention is given to the judge. Advocates can become so engaged in what they have prepared or in arguing with the other advocate that they fail to concentrate on the most important person who will make the decision on the outcome of the application. You should always focus your attention on the judge and not debate with the other side's advocate.

Avoid fidgeting, especially with pens and rings. Mannerisms that distract should be avoided. Be careful not to slouch or sink down in your seat. Concentrate on presenting your case clearly without creating distractions.

Maintain good eye contact with the judge. You may find that the judge is not looking at you but continue to look at the judge. This ensures that when the judge does look up you make eye contact. In addition voice projection and quality are greatly improved if you are looking up even if the judge is not looking in your direction.

Address all submissions to the judge and do not talk directly to the other advocate.

You should not interrupt the advocate who is representing the other party. The only exception to this would be where the other advocate has, in your opinion, put forward facts incorrectly. Even in these circumstances, be slow to interrupt, but if you do intervene you should confine yourself to indicating politely that you believe there is a mistake. If the judge wishes you to comment at that stage, proceed. Otherwise make a note and comment on it when it is next appropriate for you to address the judge.

Questions during applications and CMCs

Welcome any questions from the judge. They are an opportunity to gauge the way the judge is viewing the case. They are also an opportunity to deal with issues that the judge views as important or which need clarification.

Deal effectively with the judge's questions when he or she asks them. Always give a direct answer.

Be polite and courteous to the judge and your opponent. Avoid becoming frustrated or irritated.

Respond to the judge's questions in a concise and clear manner reflecting a thorough knowledge of the case and your own lines of argument.

Where appropriate, be prepared to argue your point but also be ready to concede to the judge's view where this is sensible.

Chapter 13

NEGOTIATION

INTRODUCTION

The skill of negotiation is not as difficult as many people assume. It is really a question of being properly prepared and being aware of what you are doing. If you plan and prepare for a negotiation, you will be better able to deal with different types of negotiator, crisis points, gains and concessions and opportunities which open up during a negotiation for lasting, effective settlements.

A pervasive belief is that a person is born to be a good negotiator but, in fact, there are very few 'natural' negotiators. Good negotiators are not born; they are self-made. Effective negotiation, like other skills, requires practice. The problem is that most people do not get an opportunity to develop effective negotiation skills in a disciplined fashion, but, rather, have to learn them on the job.

Negotiators need not take risks. There are many films and books in which the protagonist gambles on what appear to be incredibly small odds and manages to come out ahead, giving the message that good negotiators take risks, defy the odds, and step out on a limb. Whereas this works in the movies, it does not lead to success in real negotiations. Effective negotiators do not take risks – they know how to evaluate a situation where a decision is required and make an optimal choice given the information that is available to them. In some instances, it may be wise to choose a risky course of action; but in other instances, sticking with the status quo or a less risky alternative is wiser. The key is to know how to evaluate different courses of action and to choose wisely among them so as to maximise one's outcomes. What would the client feel about you taking risks with his or her money?

Preparation is the key to an effective negotiation strategy.

Commonly held views of the purpose of negotiation

Any of the following might be legitimate reasons for entering into a negotiation:

- fact-finding;
- listening to a proposal;

–   responding to an offer;
–   making an offer;
–   seeking a settlement;
–   problem-solving;
–   risk management;
–   avoiding litigation;
–   meeting your client's interests.

PREPARATION

In preparing for a negotiation you will first need to carry out a careful analysis of the case together with an evaluation, which will lead you to determining the issues in the case. A fuller treatment of case analysis is given in Chapter 12 but the essential components are the theory of the case and the theme of the case, which are outlined below.

Theory of the case – an explanation of the facts

Every case needs to be analysed from the outset and this is something which solicitors and barristers do either explicitly or implicitly when they are weighing up a case and considering the prospects of success. A more structured method of analysis which leads to the formulation of a case theory enhances the benefit of the analysis and produces more effective litigation and dispute resolution.

The theory of the case which emerges from analysis is the best explanation of the information available which indicates that the party you represent should succeed. A workable theory can be developed from the start but must, of course, be revised whenever new information becomes available. You should try to keep your theory of the case simple and short. This will help you to focus on the real issues in the case.

For example, if you were representing the claimant in the famous case of *Donoghue v Stevenson* [1932] AC 562, your theory might be: 'My best explanation is that since Stevenson knew my client would drink the ginger beer, he owed her an absolute duty not to hurt her, which was breached because there was a snail in the bottle, the sight of which caused my client to be ill'.

Theme of the case – a persuasive element of the argument

The theme of the case is a particularly persuasive element of the case which is consistent with your case theory. The theme is a central unifying concept of the case and is a thread which runs through and links all the facts. The theme of the case can be presented and reinforced throughout a trial, or any interim hearing, by use of key words, phrases and images.

NEGOTIATION STYLES AND STRATEGIES

Every litigator has an individual approach to the skill of negotiation. This will be the result of a process of 'natural selection': those techniques which seem to work best, as acquired by observation or just bitter experience.

Types of negotiating strategy

The competitive strategy
The characteristics of the 'Competitive Negotiator' are that he or she:

–   treats the opponent as an adversary and plans to win;
–   pressurises;
–   makes threats and creates false issues;
–   will not give ground; demands concessions from the opponent, without making any concessions in return;
–   misleads about the bottom line.

The advantage of the competitive strategy is that it avoids the risk of exploitation. The risks of this strategy are that the increased tension will lead to a likelihood of mistrust and the breakdown of the negotiation. The competitive reputation of the lawyer could lead to a loss of credibility and might influence the outcome of other cases.

The principled negotiation strategy
The characteristics of the 'Principled Negotiator' are that he or she:

–   understands that negotiators are people first;
–   focuses on the parties' interests, not their stated positions;
–   invents options for mutual gain: 'makes the cake bigger';
–   insists on using objective criteria.

The advantage of this strategy is that the outcome is based on objective standards. Furthermore, the parties' relationship is not endangered. The one risk of this strategy is that you might be viewed as being 'holier than thou'.

The co-operative strategy
The characteristics of the 'Co-operative Negotiator' are that he or she:

–   tends to be friendly;
–   will try to avoid contest;
–   is willing to make unilateral concessions to reach agreement;
–   is willing to disclose the bottom line at the right time;
–   sees the goal as reaching an agreement acceptable to both parties.

The advantages of the co-operative strategy are that there is higher joint benefit and, in repeat situations, higher individual benefit. The risks of this type of strategy are that unilateral concessions may not generate agreement. The negotiator may be vulnerable to exploitation and may not recognise it when it happens. Also, he or she may be regarded by the client as not fighting the client's corner. The typical negotiator using this type of strategy can react emotionally to competitive negotiation with resultant loss of face.

Research has shown that competitive negotiators are less effective negotiators in the long term. Research also shows that 75% of lawyers see themselves as co-operative, and that lawyers see between 70% and 90% of those that they negotiate with as competitive.

STAGES IN THE NEGOTIATION

(a)   Preparation

The essential questions are:

–   What are your client's interests?
–   What are the issues?

To determine the issues, consider what questions you can ask your opponent to elicit information about his or her client's interests and weaknesses. Try to devise as many options as possible.

Fisher and Ury in *Getting to Yes* (Century Business Books, 1991) suggest that you consider your BATNA (Best Alternative To a Negotiated Agreement), but that you should then negotiate as if it did not exist.

How do you reach your BATNA? Normally, you negotiate because you think that by doing so you may obtain a better result for your client than by not negotiating. (Sometimes you may negotiate for other reasons, eg to delay or to use the negotiation solely to obtain information.) To negotiate in the hope of getting a better result than you would get otherwise, you need to know what to compare your eventual result with.

You need to select the alternatives to negotiation, and their implications for your client. Then you should decide which of these alternatives your client would pursue *if the negotiation breaks down*. This will be the *alternative to negotiation* that appears to be best. If you cannot improve on it in the negotiation you are better off not negotiating. If you can achieve a better option in the negotiation, you should negotiate a settlement.

It follows that the *best alternative* may not be wonderfully attractive, but it informs your thinking in relation to the negotiation process.

*   *   *   *   *

Example
You act for a Housing Authority which has dismissed an employee for gross incompetence in the collection of rents. The employee issues proceedings in the employment tribunal seeking compensation only.

What are your alternatives to negotiation?
(a)   To pay compensation now.
(b)   To go to a hearing.

What is your BATNA?
(a) is not acceptable; the employee's demand is excessive (enquiries through ACAS reveal that he will not settle for less than a maximum award); he will crow over his victory and upset your client.

(b) is your BATNA. However, you have to consider the implications of your BATNA and this involves risk assessment. The risk assessment will be of non-legal as well as legal risks. You might win the case, avoid paying compensation and send a message to the rest of the staff, and the public, that incompetence will not be tolerated. You might lose the case, send a message to the rest of the staff, and the public, that staff can get away with incompetence and the employer has to pay for it. Alternatively, the employee may win but be found to have contributed to his dismissal. In any event, there may be publicity for your client. Even if the authority wins, there may be adverse comment that your client runs an inefficient organisation and that the incompetence should have been dealt with at an earlier stage.

Bear in mind that the opponent too runs risks; you should have as clear a picture of these as is possible before you enter a negotiation.

Your approach to settlement will be informed by your view of the BATNA, together with a view as to what is important for your client: the amount of money involved, the internal and external relationships (ie your client's real interests).

*   *   *   *   *

The table overleaf shows those areas which most commonly are done well or badly during negotiations.

Good Practice	Bad Practice
set agenda	no agenda
comprehends facts of the case	ill prepared
planned and justified opening offer	ill-considered opening offer
planned strategy for negotiation	no strategy
staged concessions	unjustified and large concessions
questions to seek weaknesses/strengths	failure to seek new information
listening for clues	talking but not listening
being prepared to advance and accept options	adopting set position
using and defending against tactics effectively	using no tactics; intimidated by tactics
client focused	negotiator focused
stability of agreement considered	stability of agreement not considered

(b)   Opening stage

This stage will include:

–   agenda setting;
–   questioning;
–   listening;
–   a justified opening offer.

(c)   Bargaining stage

(d)   The crisis

As the deadline approaches, the parties look for a mutually acceptable deal which will protect their own interests as far as possible.

(e)   Conclusion

Either the parties will reach agreement or negotiations will break down. Do you need to take your client's instructions before final agreement?

NEGOTIATION PLAN

You may find it useful to plan your negotiation using the following format.

* * * * *

1 Identify: Your client's underlying interests:

_____

_____

2 Identify: Your client's strengths: highlight *two* of your client's strengths (or your opponent's weaknesses).

(a) _____

_____

(b) _____

_____

3 Identify: Your client's weaknesses: highlight <u>two</u> of your client's weaknesses and your strategies for dealing with them.

(a) _____

_____

(b) _____

_____

4 Identify: Areas for questioning: draft questions to ask your opponent which will highlight his or her strengths or weaknesses and throw light on his or her negotiating position.

_____

_____

_____

5 Identify: What information (if any) you would consider withholding from your opponent, and why.

_____

_____

_____

6 Identify: Your *overall strategy* and state why it is in your client's interests for you to adopt it. State what you estimate your opponent's client's *interests* to be (not his or her position).

_____

_____

---

7 Justify: An opening offer.

_____

_____

_____

8 List: Two settlement options that may meet both your client's interests and the interests of your opponent's client.

(a) _____

_____

(b) _____

_____

---

* * * * *

Finally, plan your tactics.

Opponent's tactic	What would your response be?
large demand	
false demand	
take it or leave it	
delay	
silence	
claims lack of authority	
raise client's irrationality	
'slicing the salami' – giving a little at a time	

Aggressive opponent's tactic	
anger	
threats	
personal attacks	

Part III

COMMENCEMENT

Chapter 14

COMMENCING PROCEEDINGS UNDER PART 7 OF THE CIVIL PROCEDURE RULES 1998

HOW TO START PROCEEDINGS

The same form is now used whether the proceedings are issued in the High Court or in a county court. Prior to the introduction of the CPR 1998, proceedings in the High Court were commenced by issuing a 'writ' (newspapers and the media generally still tend to use this obsolete term) and in the county court by issuing a 'summons'. Neither of these old terms is now used in the context of issuing a claim. The procedure now is to issue a 'claim form'. See Form N1 – Part 7 (general) Claim Form. The claimant or his or her solicitor must prepare enough copies of the claim form, which will be a minimum of three: one for the court, one personal copy, and one for service on each defendant.

Completion of the claim form

The claim form must be headed with the title of the proceedings. The title should state:

(1)   the number of the proceedings (this will be given by the court on issue);
(2)   the court (and Division of the High Court if necessary) in which they are proceeding;
(3)   the full name of each party;
(4)   the status in the proceedings of each party (eg claimant/defendant).

Where there is more than one claimant and/or more than one defendant, the parties should be described as follows:

(1)   AB
(2)   CD
(3)   EF

Claimants

– and –

(1)   GH
(2)   I J
(3)   KL

Defendants

(See CPR PD7, para 4.2.)

The particulars of claim may be endorsed on the claim form itself or contained in a separate document. If it can be conveniently done, it is better to endorse the particulars of claim on the claim form itself. However, if the case cannot be so summarised, a separate document must be used, and this can be served on the defendant either with the claim form or subsequently. In any event, particulars of the claim must be served no later than the latest time for serving a claim form (see rr 7.4 and 7.5).

The claim form must:

(a)   contain a concise statement of the nature of the claim;
(b)   specify the remedy which the claimant seeks;
(c)   where the claimant is making a claim for money, contain a statement of value in accordance with r 16.3; and
(d)   contain such other matters as may be set out in a practice direction (see r 16.2 and PD 16).

Date of issue of claim form

Proceedings are started when the court issues a claim form at the request of the claimant (r 7.2). A claim form is issued on the date entered on the form by the court. Ideally, all courts should deal with all correspondence on the day it is received, whether received by post or personal delivery. Unfortunately, recent experience shows that this is not happening, and some county courts are considerably behind with the issuing of process. Although this will always be frustrating for the claimant who wants to get on with his or her case, a few days' delay is usually not significant. However, it could be extremely significant where the limitation period is about to expire. The wording of r 7.2(2) does seek to protect claimants by specifically stating that the claim form is issued 'on the date entered on the form by the court'. Thus, even in a case where the court is badly behind with its correspondence, it should be able at the very least to date-stamp receipt of the claim form so as to ensure that it has been issued. It may be a few days before the court completes the issuing process and effects service, but as the claim has been issued, the claimant cannot now become statute-barred due to lack of prompt attention in the court office. Nevertheless, where a particular time-limit is about to expire and the date of issue may well be significant, it is as well to draw this fact to the attention of the issuing clerk so as to ensure that the document will be appropriately dated. See further CPR PD 7, para 5.1.

SERVICE OF THE CLAIM FORM

Once the claim form has been issued the general rule is that it must be served upon the defendant within 4 months after the date of issue. The time for service is extended to 6 months where service is to be effected outside England & Wales. For details of the rules as to service see CPR r 6.5 and Chapter 17 below.

EXTENSION OF TIME FOR SERVING THE CLAIM FORM

In certain circumstances it may not be possible to effect valid service of the claim form within the time limit prescribed by the Rules. It will therefore be necessary to apply to the court to extend the time for service under CPR 7.6.

It is preferable to make the application before the initial period for serving the claim form expires. If you fail to do so and have to make the application after the time has expired, the court's discretion to extend the time for service of the claim form is very limited.

In either case the application must be made in Form N244 and must be supported by evidence. It will usually be made without notice.

If you are applying to extend the time for service of the claim form after the expiry of the initial period of validity the court may make an order only if the application is made promptly and either the court has been unable to serve the claim form, or the claimant has taken all reasonable steps to serve the claim form but has been unable to do so.

The circumstances in which the court has failed to serve the claim form will often amount to the court overlooking to do so when service by the court has been requested. Unfortunately such indulgence is not extended to solicitors. If you have overlooked serving the claim form this will be classed as incompetence for which there is no relief available under r 7.6. The authorities clearly show that the courts will not exercise the discretion to extend the time for service of the claim form unless it can be shown that all reasonable steps have been taken to serve the claim form.

Even if you are applying to extend the time for service of the claim form within the initial period of validity, you will still have to provide the court with evidence of your attempts to serve and an explanation as to why service has not taken place. In *Hashtroodi v Hancock* [2004] EWCA Civ 652 the claimant made an application one day before the end of the 4 month period. Although the reason for the failure to serve was largely the incompetence of the claimant's solicitors an extension of time was granted. The defendant applied to set aside the order. His application was refused and he appealed. The Court of Appeal allowed the appeal and gave guidance on how the court's discretion under r 7.6(2) should be exercised:

> '... it cannot have been intended that r 7.6(2) should be construed as being subject to a condition that a "good reason" must be shown for failure to serve within the specified period [as under the pre-CPR interpretation of the equivalent provision] ... In the absence of any such condition ... the power must be exercised in accordance with the overriding objective ... We have no doubt that it will always be *relevant* for the court to determine and evaluate the reason why the claimant did not serve the claim form within the specified period ... If there is a very good reason for the failure to serve the claim form ... then an extension of time will usually be granted ... The weaker the reason, the more likely the court will be to refuse to grant the extension. If the reason why the claimant has not served the claim form within the specified period is that he (or his legal representative) simply overlooked the matter, that will be a strong reason for the court refusing to grant an extension of time for service.'

The court went on to say the following:

> 'One of the important aims of the Woolf reforms was to introduce more discipline into the conduct of civil litigation. One of the ways of achieving this is to insist that time limits be adhered to unless there is a good reason for a departure.'

The clear message from the authorities, therefore, is that the court will not exercise its discretion to assist you if through inadvertence you have failed to have regard to time limits.

WHERE TO START PROCEEDINGS

A claim must be issued in the High Court or a county court if an enactment so requires. Thus, for example, claims under the Consumer Credit Act 1974 must be in the county court. Certain possession proceedings must also be in the county court (see, eg, *Yorkshire Bank plc v Hall* [1999] 1 All ER 878, where the Court of Appeal held that the High Court had had no jurisdiction to make a possession order in a case which should have been in the county court). The county court only has jurisdiction in libel and slander by consent (CCA 1984, s 15). Therefore, it is always advisable to check the relevant statute under which proceedings are brought, the CCA 1984 and the particular provisions of the CPR, before deciding whether to issue in the High Court or the county court. CPR Part 54 requires claims for judicial review to be in the High Court.

In the majority of cases, it will be found that the High Court and the county court have concurrent jurisdiction and the question of which court is appropriate should be determined by the amount of the claim and the issues in the proceedings.

CPR PD 7, para 2.4 provides the claim should be started in the High Court if by reason of:

(1)   the financial value of the claim and the amount in dispute; and/or

(2)   the complexity of the facts, legal issues, remedies or procedures involved; and/or

(3)   the importance of the outcome of the claim to the public in general,

the claimant believes that the claim ought to be dealt with by a High Court judge.

Proceedings may not be started in the High Court unless the claim is for more than £15,000 (a figure which is far too low and which ought to be at least £100,000). In practice – save in unusual cases where the dispute is not really about money – a claim for a sum in only five figures will not be dealt with by a High Court judge. As the claimant is issuing proceedings he or she has the choice of court but, if the case becomes defended and has to be case managed by the court, one of the first things the court will consider is whether the case is in the right level of court – and indeed the right court geographically.

Most cases can in fact be issued in any county court, any district registry or the central office (ie the Royal Courts of Justice). However, there are certain rules that require certain types of proceedings to be issued in a particular county court. Thus, for example, CPR Part 55 – possession claims – specifically requires that the claim must be started 'in the county court for the district in which the land is situated ...' (r 55.3).

Where the defendant is an individual and the claim is for a specified sum of money, if the case is defended it will automatically be transferred to the 'defendant's home court' (see r 2.3(1)). In any event, it is always open to the defendant – or indeed the claimant – to apply to transfer to a different court either for case management or trial. As a general rule, however, a claimant has nothing to lose by starting proceedings in the court which he or she finds most convenient, usually the local county court.

Production centre

The 'production centre' (formerly called the 'bulk issue centre') has existed for over 10 years to cater for the needs of certain claimants who have many hundreds of claims to issue and the nature of whose business justifies a streamlined service making more use of modern technology – in particular communication by computer – than is current for – other litigation. Thus, for example, utility companies, mail order companies and the like have made arrangements to issue proceedings online through the production centre. The production centre is no more than an administrative convenience which, for any particular case, is deemed to be part of the county court where proceedings would have to be issued if it did not exist. It happens to be based in Northampton, but this is of no particular significance. It is provided for by CPR r 7.10 and PD 7C – Production Centre. The centre applies to county court cases only and cannot be used where the claim exceeds £100,000. Only an authorised 'centre user' can make use of the facility and that user must agree to be bound by the relevant code of practice. See further the relevant rule and practice direction. Because the centre deals with cases only in electronic form, certain modifications to the normal rules are made.

If a production centre case becomes defended it is transferred to the appropriate county court (usually the defendant's 'home court') and it is that court which will give case management directions and try the case.

Money Claim Online

Eventually it will be possible for any person to deal with the court online instead of having to telephone, visit or write. This will include issuing of all types of claim.

Money Claim Online began as a pilot scheme but such has been its success that it now issues more civil cases than any county court. Provision is made in rr 7.12 and 7EPD.1 for the continuation of the scheme.

It is possible to issue a county court claim online if the claim is for a specified sum of less than £100,000 against not more than two defendants who both have a postal address for service in England and Wales. Court fees must be paid by credit or debit card. In addition to issuing the claim form, it is also possible to obtain judgment by default or on an admission, and to issue warrants of execution. The relevant address is *www.courtservice.gov.uk/mcol* and the customer helpdesk telephone number is 0845 6015935. The Court Service will issue and serve (by post) the claim within 48 hours.

Chapter 15

COMMENCING PROCEEDINGS – OTHER THAN UNDER PART 7 OF THE CIVIL PROCEDURE RULES 1998

WHY MORE THAN ONE METHOD?

Why is there more than one method of commencing proceedings? Why, indeed? One of the inadequacies of the CPR is that they have failed to achieve just one simple form of issuing process, regardless of the matters to be decided by the court. Historically, there were several different methods of issuing proceedings, and it was one of the intentions of the 'Access to Justice' inquiry to have just one method. This aim has not been achieved.

PART 8 CLAIMS

Part 8 of the CPR is entitled 'Alternative procedure for claims'. A claimant may use the Part 8 procedure where he or she seeks the court's decision on a question which is unlikely to involve a substantial dispute of fact (r 8.1(2)) or where a rule or practice direction may, in relation to a specified type of proceedings, require or permit the use of the procedure (r 8.1(6)). The majority of cases do involve disputes of fact and thus must be commenced under Part 7. Part 8 disapplies many of the usual rules of the CPR and is mainly intended for claims which can be disposed of without a statement of case, disclosure or expert evidence. The lack of any real factual disputes means that these steps are not necessary. Thus, most Part 8 cases concern purely a question of law or construction of a document.

The 'claim form' (the same term is used) in a Part 8 case is Form N208. The claim form must state (see r 8.2):

(a)   that Part 8 applies;
(b)   (i)   the question which the claimant wants the court to decide; or
       (ii)   the remedy which the claimant is seeking and the legal basis for the claim to that remedy;
(c)   if the claim is being made under an enactment, what that enactment is;

(d)   if the claimant is claiming in a representative capacity, what that capacity is; and

(e)   if the defendant is sued in a representative capacity, what that capacity is.

The claim form, as with any claim form, must be verified by a statement of truth (Part 22). The evidence on which the claimant relies must be filed with the claim form (r 8.5).

MODIFICATIONS TO THE GENERAL RULES

First, it is necessary to state that many of the general rules do apply to Part 8 claims. Thus, for example, the defendant is required to file an acknowledgement of service (r 8.3).

The following is a list of the main modifications made either by Part 8 itself or by PD 8 to the main body of rules.

(a)   The content of the claim form must state the matters required by r 8.2.

(b)   The court may fix the date for hearing when the Part 8 claim form is issued (PD 8, para 4.1).

(c)   A claimant must file and serve his written evidence at the same time as he files and serves the claim form (r 8.5(1), (2) and PD 8, paras 5.1, 5.2).

(d)   A claimant may not obtain a default judgment under Part 12 (r 8.1(5)).

(e)   A defendant must file an acknowledgement of service which is in a different form and will include a statement of truth (see r 8.3(1)(a), Form N210 and r 22.1(1)).

(f)   The defendant himself must serve the acknowledgement of service (r 8.3(1)(b)). However, a defendant may apparently respond informally by, eg, a letter rather than by using Form N210 (PD 8, para 3.2).

(g)   A defendant who fails to file an acknowledgement of service in time may not take part in the hearing unless the court gives permission (r 8.4(2)), save where Section B of PD 8B applies.

(h)   Disputing the court's jurisdiction under Part 11 is modified (r 8.3(4)).

(i)   A claimant does not serve either a form of defence or a form of admission on the defendant (r 8.9).

(j)   A defendant must file and serve any written evidence on which he intends to rely at the same time he files and serves his acknowledgement of service (r 8.5).

(k)   Part 16 (Statements of Case) does not apply (r 8.9).

(l)   Part 15 (Defence and Reply) does not apply (r 8.9).

(m)   A claimant may not obtain judgment by request on an admission (r 8.9).

(n)   While the parties may agree in writing on an extension of time for filing and serving evidence, the extensions are limited by PD 8. A Part 20 claim may only be made with the court's permission (r 8.7).

(o)   A Part 8 claim is treated as allocated to the multi-track (r 8.9).

(See also section B of PD 8B.)

(p)   If a hearing date was not fixed when the claim was issued, judicial case management is triggered by the filing of the defendant's acknowledgement of service and evidence or by the expiry of the time for doing so (r 8.8(2) and PD 8, para 4.2).

(q)   Neither party may file an allocation questionnaire.

(r)   Part 32, which deals with evidence, is modified by r 8.6. Part 8 may itself be disapplied or modified by rule or practice direction (r 8.1(6)(b)); see, for instance, PD 8B.

MAIN USES OF PART 8

PD 8 describes the types of claim in which a Part 8 procedure may be used, which include:

(1)   a claim by or against a child or patient which has been settled before the commencement of proceedings and the sole purpose of which is to obtain the approval of the court to the settlement;

(2)   a claim for provisional damages which has been settled before the commencement of proceedings and the sole purpose of the claim is to obtain a consent judgment;

(3)   a claim under r 44.12A, where the parties have settled the case before the commencement of proceedings but cannot agree costs.

CPR PD 8, para 1.5 provides:

> 'where it appears to a court officer that a claimant is using the Part 8 procedure inappropriately, he may refer the claim to a judge for the judge to consider the point.'

Rule 8.1(3) provides: 'The court may at any stage order the claim to continue as if the claimant had not used the Part 8 procedure and, if it does so, the court may give any directions it considers appropriate'. Such directions will include allocation to track.

There are two Practice Directions supplementing Part 8, namely PD 8 and PD 8B. Part 8 itself was drafted shortly before the CPR came into force and seems to have been done in something of a rush and without the care and forethought that went into the main body of the CPR. This is, no doubt, due to the fact that it had been the original intention to have just one method of commencing proceedings, no matter what those proceedings were about; however, at a very late stage, that simple aim was, unfortunately, abandoned and the mish-mash that is Part 8 was inserted into the rules. In its original form, Part 8 included possession proceedings but the CPR were subsequently amended to add Part 55 – Possession Claims, which is a self-contained Part, and thus Part 8 itself no longer applies to possession proceedings.

An example of appalling drafting is provided by CPR PD 8B, Section A. It includes the words, 'Section A applies if ... before 26 April 1999, a claim or application in the High Court would have been brought by originating summons ...'. The 'originating summons' was, prior to 26 April 1999, one method of commencing proceedings in the High Court and was mainly used in the Chancery Division. Although it is an over-simplification to say so, it may nevertheless be helpful to say that, in the High Court, claims that used to be commenced by writ are now commenced under Part 7, and claims that used to be commenced by originating summons are now commenced under Part 8. Thus, Part 7 applies mainly in the Queen's Bench Division and Part 8 mainly in the Chancery Division. In the county court, claims that used to be commenced by summons are now brought under Part 7, and claims that used to be brought by originating application are now brought under Part 8. It is worth restating that Part 8 is mainly for cases that do not involve disputes of fact.

PART 55 – POSSESSION CLAIMS

A possession claim means a claim for the recovery of possession of land (including buildings or parts of buildings). Such a claim must generally be started in the county court for the district in which the land is situated. It may be issued elsewhere if an enactment provides otherwise, and claims may be started in the High Court if the claimant files with his or her claim form a certificate stating the reasons for bringing the claim in that court and verifies it with a statement of truth. CPR PD 55, para 1.3 sets out circumstances that may, in an appropriate case, justify starting a claim in the High Court. Such cases are rare, however, and the vast majority of possession actions are in the county court. (See further, Part 55 and PD 55.) Note, in particular, however, that different claim forms are used in possession actions (r 55.3(5) and PD 55, para 1.5). (See further, Part 4 – Forms, and PD 4.) The claim form itself will include the date of trial which, in possession claims, is usually 8 weeks from issue.

PART 23 APPLICATIONS

Part 23 is entitled 'General Rules about Applications for Court Orders'. The circumstances in which a person may make an application for a court order are many and varied. 'Application' is not a term of art. Most applications to the court are made in the course of proceedings already commenced, usually by claim form, issued pursuant to Part 7. Thus, Part 23 is mainly concerned with interlocutory applications during the course of pending proceedings. However, Part 23 is not restricted to such applications and sometimes Part 23 can be used to originate process.

As previously stated in the context of Part 8, it was originally an objective of the reformed rules of court to provide for just one form of application to the court ('claim form'), regardless of what that claim was about. That aim has not been achieved. Hence, in addition to Part 7, there is also the alternative procedure under Part 8 and the specialist procedure required by certain other rules, in particular Part 55. It is a further complication that some rules provide for an application to the court to be made under Part 23, even though the court is not seized of any pending proceedings. Do not be surprised, therefore, if a rule requires you to do this. See, for example, r 25.4 – 'Application for interim remedy where there is no related claim'.

Chapter 16

COUNTERCLAIMS AND OTHER ADDITIONAL CLAIMS (PART 20)

OVERVIEW

The Rule Committee has accepted the criticism that we made in the first edition (we were not alone, of course) and has changed the title of Part 20 to re-introduce the former, but accurate and helpful, term 'counterclaim'.

Part 20 of the CPR serves an extremely important purpose. A Part 20 claim is, as r 20.2 puts it: 'Any claim other than a claim by a claimant against a defendant'. A 'Part 20 claimant' means a person who makes a Part 20 claim. It follows that a 'Part 20 defendant' is anyone against whom a Part 20 claim is made. This has the consequence that parties can have more than one title. In a straightforward case, where a claimant claims against a defendant and the defendant counterclaims through Part 20 proceedings against the claimant, it means that the defendant is not only the defendant but also a Part 20 claimant. In fact, this is all very simple but the rules unfortunately make it seem a little more complex than it actually is.

Essentially, Part 20 is concerned with five different situations:

(1)   counterclaim by a defendant against a claimant (r 20.4);
(2)   counterclaim by a defendant against someone other than a claimant (r 20.5);
(3)   co-defendants claiming contribution and/or indemnity against each other (r 20.6);
(4)   claims by a defendant against a non-party (a 'third party');
(5)   claims by a third party against a fourth party, etc.

The purpose of Part 20 is to enable Part 20 claims to be managed in the most convenient and effective manner.

A Part 20 claim is treated as if it were a claim for the purposes of the CPR, except that certain rules are expressly disapplied. Thus, by r 20.3, the following rules do not apply to Part 20 claims:

(1)   rr 7.5 and 7.6 (time within which a claim form may be served);

(2)   r 16.3(5) (statement of value where a claim is to be issued in the High Court);

(3)   Part 26 (case management – preliminary stage).

Further, Part 12 (Default judgment) applies only to counterclaims but not to other Part 20 claims. Similarly, Part 14 (Admissions) applies to a counterclaim but not to other Part 20 claims, save that rr 14.1(1), (2) (which provide that a party may admit the truth of another party's case in writing) and 14.3(1) (admission by notice in writing, application for judgment) apply to all Part 20 claims. Part 20 is, of course, supplemented by PD 20, which is short and helpful.

Is permission required to make a Part 20 claim or may a defendant do so without permission? Put simply, if it is done at the right time and in the right way, permission is not required if the claim is proceeding under Part 7. Permission is always required if the claim is proceeding under Part 8.

Rules 20.4(2)(b), 20.5(1) and 20.7(3)(b) set out the circumstances in which the court's permission is needed to make a Part 20 claim. Where an application is made for permission, the application notice should be filed together with a copy of the proposed Part 20 claim (PD 20, para 1.2).

A defendant may make a counterclaim against a claimant by filing particulars of the counterclaim and may do so without the court's permission if he or she files it *with* the defence (r 20.4(2)).

A defendant needs the court's permission to make a Part 20 claim if:

(1)   the defendant wishes to counterclaim against the claimant after filing the defence;

(2)   a defendant wishes to claim against a third party after filing the defence in the main action;

(3)   a defendant wishes to claim against a co-defendant for any remedy other than contribution and/or indemnity.

Further, permission is needed for any other Part 20 claim, eg a 'third party' wishes to claim against a 'fourth party'.

PART 20 COUNTERCLAIMS (RULE 20.4)

A defendant may make a counterclaim against a claimant by filing particulars of the counterclaim. The subject matter of the counterclaim need not be related to the claim itself. Thus, the defendant can add any cause of action to the proceedings and claim any appropriate relief or remedy.

The claim is a separate claim and it will be a case management decision as to whether the claim and counterclaim will be tried together or separately. For example, in a road traffic accident, where a claimant sues the defendant for damages for personal injuries and for damages to his motor vehicle, the defendant may not only deny liability but counterclaim against the claimant for his or her own personal injuries and damage to the motor vehicle. Clearly, there is just one incident, and it is convenient to have both claim and counterclaim tried together. If, in addition, it so happened that the claimant owed the defendant money for the price of goods sold and delivered, there is nothing in law or the rules of procedure to prevent the defendant adding a counterclaim for the price of those goods. It is most unlikely, however, that that claim would be tried with the road traffic accident claim.

A counterclaim is, of course, a 'statement of case' and is drafted as such. Permission to issue a counterclaim is not needed if the counterclaim is filed with the defence. It is convenient to include both the defence and counterclaim as a single document.

It is possible for a defendant who brings a counterclaim to obtain a default judgment. Accordingly, a claimant who is also a Part 20 defendant to a counterclaim must file a defence to the counterclaim. A defendant who wishes to counterclaim against a person other than the claimant must apply to the court for permission to do so. If permission is granted, that person is then added as a defendant to the counterclaim and becomes a 'Part 20 defendant'. The defendant can make application without notice to the claimant but the court can direct that notice be given, and usually does so, save in an obvious case. The rules do not set out the circumstances in which it is appropriate for someone other than the claimant to be joined in the proceedings by the defendant as a Part 20 defendant. This is no doubt deliberate policy, to prevent rules being over-complex and prescriptive, thus leaving the issue as a case management matter to be decided by the district judge. Usually, permission will be given if the proposed counterclaim is connected in some way with the main claim. By r 20.9, the court must have regard to:

(1)   the connection between the Part 20 claim and the claim made by claimant against the defendant;

(2)   whether the Part 20 claimant is seeking substantially the same remedy which some other party is claiming from him or her; and

(3)   whether the Part 20 claimant wants the court to decide any question connected with the subject matter of the proceedings (a) not only between existing parties but also between existing parties and a person who is not already a party, or (b) against an existing party, not only in the capacity in which he or she is already a party but also in some further capacity.

As already noted, the terminology of Part 20 can be confusing. It is important to appreciate that r 20.5 is concerned with counterclaims by a defendant against the claimant and another party, and is not the same as r 20.7, which applies where a defendant wishes to claim not against the claimant but only against some other person ('a third party').

To avoid confusion in the title of the proceedings, see PD 20, para 7. Thus, for example, where a defendant does counterclaim against the claimant and someone else, the title of the case should be as follows:

AB	Claimant/Part 20 Defendant,
CD	Defendant/Part 20 Claimant,
XY	Part 20 Defendant

For an example of a case which would now be entitled as such, see *Montgomery v Foy, Morgan & Co* [1895] 2 QB 321.

For the comparatively rare situation in which a defendant wishes to counterclaim against the claimant and another person together with someone else, it would be necessary to consider also the provisions of Part 19.

PART 20 – CONTRIBUTION AND/OR INDEMNITY CLAIMS BETWEEN CO-DEFENDANTS (RULE 20.6)

By the Civil Liability (Contribution) Act 1978, where two or more defendants are held liable for the same damage (whether liability is in tort, contract, breach of trust or otherwise), the trial court has power to apportion liability between them. There is no prescribed form of application for seeking a contribution and/or indemnity. Nevertheless, as a matter of common sense, courts can only be expected to adjudicate on matters placed before the judge for adjudication. Thus, any defendant who does wish to seek contribution or indemnity from a co-defendant must make this clear in the statement of case.

The glossary to the CPR defines 'contribution' as 'a right of someone to recover from a third person all or part of the amount which he himself is liable to pay' and defines 'indemnity' as 'a right of someone to recover from a third party the whole amount which he himself is liable to pay'.

By r 20.6, a defendant who has filed an acknowledgement of service or a defence may make a Part 20 claim for contribution or indemnity against another defendant by:

'(a)   filing a notice containing a statement of the nature and grounds of his claim; and
(b)   serving that notice on the other defendant.'

As already noted, there is in fact no prescribed form of 'notice'. The important point is, of course, that the court and all parties should know what the claim is all about, hence the need to give that notice.

A defendant may file and serve a contribution notice under r 20.6 without the court's permission if he or she files and serves it with the defence (or if the claim is against a defendant added to the claim later, within 28 days after that defendant files his or her defence). At any other time the court's permission is required (see r 20.6(2)).

'THIRD PARTY' PROCEEDINGS/OTHER PART 20 CLAIMS (RULE 20.7)

This section is concerned with situations where the defendant wishes to make a claim, not against the claimant (and not against the claimant joined with any other person), but against someone else who is not yet a party to the proceedings. These used to be called 'third party proceedings', and this is a rare example of where the old terminology is more meaningful than the new.

A typical situation is where the claimant sues a contractor and the contractor defendant wishes, in turn, to sue a sub-contractor. The claimant has no contract with the sub-contractor and cannot claim direct (even if he or she wished to do so) in contract. However, the defendant will have a contract with the sub-contractor.

Another example would be where the claimant sues the defendant and the defendant claims on his or her insurance policy but the insurer argues that the loss is not covered by the terms of the policy. The defendant may wish to add his or her insurer as a party. In effect, the defendant is saying to the third party, 'If the claimant proves this claim against me, I am seeking contribution or indemnity from you'.

The title of the proceedings will be:

AB	Claimant
CD	Defendant/Part 20 Claimant,
EF	Part 20 Defendant

The defendant will make the claim by issuing a Part 20 claim form (Form N211). Permission is not required if it is issued before or at the same time as the defendant filed the defence. Particulars of the Part 20 claim must be contained on the Part 20 claim form or served with it (not later). A Part 20 claim is treated as if it were a claim (r 20.3) and, thus, it is served in exactly the same way as a claim form, with notes for guidance and a form of acknowledgement of service.

In the type of scenario discussed in this section, there are, of course, two claims, but the rules work on the assumption that it is more convenient for the claims to be dealt with together. Usually, this assumption will be correct but, as part of its case management powers, the court could always order separate trials in a rare case where it would be more appropriate to do so. Usually, although there are technically two separate claims, they are tried together.

A defendant who is able to compromise the claim brought against him or her by the claimant is entitled to proceed with his or her claim against the Part 20 defendant. However, the Part 20 defendant will not be bound by any admissions or concessions made by the defendant to the claimant, unless the Part 20 defendant is also a party to that compromise.

Just as the defendant can add a third party, so a third party can add a fourth party. Such cases are most likely to arise in the Commercial/Mercantile Court or in the Technology and Construction Court. Care must be taken with the title of the proceedings to avoid confusion. A claim may, for example, have to be entitled as follows:

AB   Claimant and Part 20 Defendant (Second Claim)

CD   Defendant and Part 20 Claimant (First Claim)

EF   Part 20 Defendant (First Claim) and Part 20 Claimant (Second Claim)

GH   Part 20 Defendant (Second Claim)

Where the full name of a party is lengthy, it must appear in the title, but thereafter, in the statement of case, it may be identified by an abbreviation, such as initials or a recognised shortened name. Where a party to the proceedings has more than one status (eg AB, CD and EF in the above example), the combined status must appear in the title to the proceedings but, thereafter, it is more convenient to refer to the party by name, eg Mr Smith, or by initials or a shortened name.

Of course, the more parties there are, the more expensive the case will be. Cases with multiple parties require careful case management. In particular, the court will consider whether to use its powers under Part 1 to try issues separately rather than all together. Often, it is possible, in a multi-party case, to identify one key issue that will lead to a resolution of the main point or several points.

Chapter 17

SERVICE

OVERVIEW

Notice must be given to all parties at the commencement of proceedings and whenever steps are taken in the proceedings. This is achieved by the service of the relevant documents in accordance with CPR Part 6. Generally, until a party has been served, the court has no jurisdiction over that party.

Part 6 is divided into three parts, dealing with:

(1)   general rules about service;
(2)   special provisions about service of the claim form; and
(3)   special provisions about service outside England and Wales.

The rules in CPR Part 6 do not apply when:

(1)   any other rule, practice direction or enactment makes different provision, for example different rules apply to the service of possession claims (see CPR Part 55); or
(2)   the court orders otherwise.

WHO IS TO SERVE?

The general rule is that the court will effect service. Thus, on issue, the court will have to be provided with a copy of the documents for each party to be served – one to be returned to the issuing party and a copy to be retained on the court file.

Service by a party

Sometimes, a party may have to make his or her own arrangements to effect service, either because the court so orders because a rule or practice direction so provides, or because the court has failed to serve and has issued a notice of non-service. There will also be occasions when a party chooses to make his or her own arrangements for service. In such a case, the court must be notified of that intention (r 6.3(1)(b)), otherwise it will effect service itself in accordance with the general rule.

Service on another party

The address at which a party may be served will depend upon the legal capacity of that party.

Capacity of party to be served	Address for service
Individual	Usual or last known address
Individual with a solicitor acting for him or her who is authorised to accept service of the proceedings	Business address of solicitor (Note: service of the claim form may only be effected by this means if the defendant's solicitor is authorised to accept service)
Individual who is under 18 years of age	The claim form, or an application for an order appointing a litigation friend, must be served on a parent or guardian, or, if there is neither, upon the person with whom the child lives or in whose care he or she is. Any other document must be served on the litigation friend
Patient (ie a person who, by reason of mental disorder within the meaning of the Mental Health Act 1983 (MHA 1983), is incapable of managing and administering his or her own affairs)	The claim form and any application for an order appointing a litigation friend must be served on any person authorised by the MHA 1983 to conduct proceedings on his or her behalf, and, if no person is so authorised, the person with whom the patient lives or in whose care he or she is. Any other document must be served on the litigation friend
Proprietor of a business	Usual or last known residence, place of business or last known place of business
Individual who is suing or being sued in the name of a firm (Mr X trading as X Products) or partners sued in the name of a partnership	Usual or last known residence, place of business or last known place of business
Corporation incorporated in England and Wales, other than a company	Principal office of the corporation or any place within England and Wales where the corporation carries on its activities *and* has a real connection with the claim

Capacity of party to be served	Address for service
Company registered in England and Wales	Principal office of the company or any place within England and Wales where the company carries on its activities *and* has a real connection with the claim (Note: this is an alternative to the procedure prescribed in the Companies Act 1985, s 725 and will not be conclusive as to service in cases in which the court cannot be satisfied that the proceedings have come to the attention of the company. In doubtful cases, it would be safer to use the method of service set out in the Companies Act 1985 (service of documents by leaving, sending or posting to the company's registered office))

METHODS OF SERVICE

Service will usually be effected by one of the following means:

(1)   first-class post or Special Delivery to the address for service;
(2)   leaving the document at the address for service;
(3)   document exchange (see CPR PD 6, para 2);
(4)   fax (see CPR PD 6, para 3.1);
(5)   other electronic means (see CPR PD 6, para 3.3); or
(6)   personal service.

The general rule is that the court will effect service, and the method used by the court will usually be either first-class post or document exchange. When a party is to be responsible for effecting service, any means of service may be chosen, but, because of the expense, personal service will usually be confined to cases where there is a degree of urgency, or where there is a risk that the defendant will try to dispute receipt of the papers in order to cause delay.

Personal service

Personal service on an individual means that the papers are left with that individual. The person serving the papers will have to provide a statement of service to that effect, and should set out the means by which the person served was identified. A company or corporation can be personally served with a document by leaving it with a person holding a senior position within the company or corporation. In the case of a partnership, personal service is effected by leaving it either with a partner or a person who, at the time of service, has the control or management of the partnership business at its principal place of business. Personal service may not be used where the party to be served has instructed solicitors who have notified the party serving the proceedings that they are authorised to accept service.

Contractually agreed method

Sometimes, a contract between parties will contain a term that provides for the method of service of a claim form in the event of a dispute between them. If the claim form relates only to the subject-matter of that contract, then it will be deemed served if it is served by the method set out in the contract. If the contract provides for service outside England and Wales, the permission of the court may be required, as it would be for any other claim. (See below, 'Service out of the jurisdiction'.)

Service by an alternative method

It is not always possible to effect service by any of the means already mentioned, usually because the party to be served is evading service, or quite simply, because the party serving does not have details of an address for service. In these circumstances, an application may be made to the court for an order that there be service by an alternative method. This could include, in the case of an individual, service at an employer's address or at the address of a relative, service on another person who is known to be in regular contact with the party to be served, or, where appropriate, the party's insurers. For obvious reasons, giving notice of the application is not necessary, but a formal application must be made and evidence filed in support. This will take the form of a witness statement, setting out what steps have been taken to effect service by other means and why service by an alternative method is the only way forward.

Generally, an enquiry agent's report, detailing efforts to find the party to be served and indicating that, if a particular method of service were used, the proceedings would come to the attention of the party, will be helpful evidence to be annexed to the witness statement. Details of the alternative method proposed should be given. You will need to satisfy the court that every other option for service has been exhausted or is impracticable and that the method proposed is the best that can be done to bring the proceedings to the attention of the party concerned. Recent Court of Appeal authority makes it clear that gaining a tactical advantage over another party is not a good reason for ordering service by an alternative method (*Knauf UK GmbH v British Gypsum Ltd* [2001] EWCA Civ 1570, [2002] 1 WLR 907). If the court makes an order, the order will state the method of service to be used and the date on which the document will be deemed to be served. It is not possible to obtain an order for service by an alternative method retrospectively.

DISPENSING WITH SERVICE

The court has a general power to dispense with service of a document. This is likely to be used only where the party to be served is already aware of the document. For example, where an application is made for amendment to a statement of case, the draft of which is annexed to the application which has been served, the court may consider it unnecessary for the amended document to be formally served, and make an order dispensing with service. It must be emphasised that the court will not be persuaded to use this power to avoid the need for service where difficulties have arisen (*Godwin v Swindon Borough Council* [2001] EWCA Civ 1478, [2002] 1 WLR 997, disapproving *Infantino v Maclean* [2001] 3 All ER 802. However, subsequent decisions of the Court of Appeal suggest that in very exceptional cases service may be deemed to have been effected where the proceedings have come to the notice of the defendant within the time allowed for service although technically service has not been effected in accordance with the Rules (*Anderton v Clwyd County Council* [2002] EWCA Civ 933; *McManus v Sharif* [2003] EWCA Civ 656).

WHEN IS A DOCUMENT DEEMED TO BE SERVED?

It is important to know the date on which a document is deemed to be served because of time-limits imposed by the CPR or by the terms of any order. The deemed date of service will depend upon the method of service that has been used.

Method of service	Deemed served
First-class post	The second day after posting
Document exchange	The second day after it was left at the document exchange
Fax transmitted before 4 pm	The same day
Fax transmitted after 4 pm	The next day
Other electronic means	The second day after transmission
Delivering or leaving at address for service	The day after it was left/delivered

(Note: in relation to all of the above, if the deemed day of service is not a 'business day', ie if it falls on a Saturday, Sunday or Bank Holiday (which includes Good Friday, Easter Monday, Christmas Day, Boxing Day and New Year's Day), service will be deemed to have taken place on the next business day, eg if a document is served by first-class post on Christmas Eve, it will be deemed served on the second business day after Boxing Day)

Personal service	On the day it was left with the party, *except* when this was after 5 pm, or at any time on a Saturday, Sunday or Bank Holiday (which includes Good Friday, Easter Monday, Christmas Day, Boxing Day and New Year's Day), when it will be deemed served on the next business day, eg a document served at 3 pm on Good Friday will be deemed served on the Tuesday after Easter Monday
Contractually agreed method	As set out in the contract
Service by an alternative method	The date specified by the court in the order

The question arises as to whether the rules as to deemed service contained in CPR r 6.7(1) are absolute, or whether it is possible to use other evidence to prove that service in fact took place on another date. In *Godwin v Swindon Borough Council* [2001] EWCA Civ 1478 (above), the Court of Appeal said that r 6.7(1) did not create a rebuttable presumption. The court took the view that, whilst not altogether satisfactory, the deemed dates of service provided in the Rules did at least create certainty. This might operate to the disadvantage of a defendant who, in fact, receives a claim form after the deemed date and has default judgment entered against him or her. In those circumstances, the remedy would be to apply under CPR r 13.3 to have the judgment set aside.

PROOF OF SERVICE

If the party served does not respond, the court may require you to prove service. You will do this by filing at court a certificate of service. In the case of service of a claim form, you must file a certificate of service within 7 days of service and you will not be able to obtain judgment in default until you have done so. A certificate of service must state, first, that the document has not been returned undelivered, and secondly, the date on which the document was posted, left at the document exchange, delivered, transmitted electronically, or handed to the party, depending upon the method of service used.

SOLICITORS INSTRUCTED TO ACCEPT SERVICE

Where a party authorises solicitors to accept service, the claimant must serve those solicitors with the proceedings. It will not be valid service under CPR r 6.5(5) if the defendant is served direct when the claimant is aware that solicitors have been instructed to accept service. However, it is not sufficient simply for the defendant to have solicitors acting for him. The claimant must have been notified of the solicitors' authority to accept service (*Maggs v Marshall & another* [2005] EWHC 200 (QB)).

SERVICE AT THE USUAL OR LAST KNOWN ADDRESS

It is sufficient for there to be good service under CPR that a document has not been returned undelivered when served at the usual or last known address of an individual or the proprietor of a business. This remains the case even if the defendant does not in fact receive the document. In *Akram v Adam* [2005] 1 All ER 741 a claim form for possession was served on the defendant at his usual address but it went astray and he did not learn about the proceedings until about 3 months later. By this time a possession order had been made and a warrant issued. The district judge hearing the defendant's application to set aside the judgment found that the claim form had not been delivered to the defendant at his address and concluded that there had not been good service. The possession order was set aside. The claimant appealed. The Court of Appeal held that the circuit judge hearing the claimant's successful appeal was correct to apply a literal interpretation of r 6.5(6):

'The rule does not say that it is not good service if the defendant does not in fact receive the document ... The rule is intended to provide a clear and straightforward mechanism for effecting service where the two conditions precedent ... are satisfied.'

There had been no finding that the claim form had been returned undelivered nor any finding that the claimant had deliberately hidden the claim form from the defendant. In these circumstances there had been good service and the only remedy for the defendant was to apply to set aside the judgment under CPR 13.3. This is a discretionary remedy and the implications of Article 6 ECHR in terms of the defendant's right of access to the court were considered by the court:

> '[CPR] gives a defendant access to a court if for some reason the prescribed method of service does not draw the proceedings to his attention before the judgment is entered. So long as the claimant has complied with the rules, the judgment is a regular one, but if the defendant can show that he has a real (and not merely fanciful) prospect of successfully defending the claim or that there is some other good reason why the court should intervene, the court is empowered to set aside the judgment, so long as the application is made promptly, after the defendant has become aware of the proceedings.'

USUAL OR LAST KNOWN ADDRESS

As we have seen from the decision in *Akram v Adam* it is not necessary for the court to be satisfied as to service that documents served at the usual or last known address have come to the attention of the addressee. In *Mersey Docks Property Holdings & Others v Kilgour* [2004] EWHC 1638 (TCC) it was held that 'last known place of business' meant the last place of business known to a claimant. This, however, required a claimant to take reasonable steps to ascertain the current place of business, or the last known place of business. In that case the court held that there had not been valid service on an architect at an address he had left some years before. A search through yellow pages, or in the directory of his professional association would have easily produced his current address and the claimant should have taken these steps before attempting service.

SERVICE ON A COMPANY USING COMPANIES ACT 1985, S 725

As an alternative to the method under CPR, service may be effected on a company by using the procedure prescribed in the Companies Act 1985, s 725. This requires the document to be served by leaving it at, or by sending it by post to, the company's registered office. This will be good service even if the document has not come to the attention of an officer of the company, as long as the document is not returned undelivered.

In *Murphy v Staples UK Ltd* [2003] EWCA Civ 656 the Court of Appeal confirmed that service under the Companies Act 1985, s 725 was a true alternative to service by one of the methods permitted by CPR. In that case the defendant's solicitors were instructed to accept service of proceedings. In these circumstances, in order to be valid service under CPR the proceedings would have to be served upon the solicitors, and not upon the defendant direct. The claimant in fact served the proceedings on the defendant direct at its registered office address. It was held that in the absence of a binding agreement to serve at the solicitors' address the claimant could rely upon service under s 725.

SERVICE OUT OF THE JURISDICTION

The general rule is that, if you wish to serve a claim form on a party that does not have an address for service in England and Wales, then you must have the permission of the court. However, where the party is in Northern Ireland or Scotland, which are part of the United Kingdom but with separate legal systems, or in a country of the European Community (EC) or the European Free Trade Association (EFTA), the provisions of the Civil Jurisdiction and Judgments Act 1991 (CJJA 1991) apply and, subject to certain conditions, the court's permission is not required. Currently, the relevant countries are the United Kingdom, Austria, Belgium, Denmark, Finland, France, Germany, Greece, Iceland, the Republic of Ireland, Italy, Luxembourg, the Netherlands, Norway, Portugal, Spain, Sweden, and Switzerland.

The conditions to be satisfied are that:

(1)   each claim is one which, by virtue of the CJJA 1991, the court has power to hear and determine; *and*
(2)   each claim is made in proceedings to which the following conditions apply:
    (a)   there are no proceedings about the same subject-matter in any other court in the United Kingdom or another Convention country; *and*
    (b)   either the defendant is domiciled in the United Kingdom or another Convention country, or the claim is one in which Art 16 gives exclusive jurisdiction to the court of a particular Convention country, or the claim is one in which, under Art 17, the contracting parties have agreed to the courts of a nominated Convention country having exclusive jurisdiction; *or*
(3)   it is a claim which the court has power to determine under any other enactment, even though either the defendant is outside England and Wales, or there is no connection between England and Wales and the subject-matter of the claim.

If the CJJA 1991 does not apply, an application must be made for permission to serve the claim form out of the jurisdiction. The application must be supported by written evidence that sets out the following:

(1)   the grounds on which the application is made, and the paragraph(s) of r 6.20 relied upon. You will have to refer to that rule, decide which part(s) apply to your claim and give the details in your witness statement;
(2)   that the claimant believes that the claim has a real prospect of success; and
(3)   the defendant's address, or, if not known, in which place or country the defendant is believed to be.

In the unlikely event that you are faced with an application to serve outside the jurisdiction, it is recommended that you read carefully the detailed notes to r 6.21 that appear in the White Book or the Brown Book.

Part IV

DETERMINATION OF A CASE
WITHOUT TRIAL

Chapter 18

JUDGMENT IN DEFAULT

OVERVIEW

The vast majority of civil cases do not go to trial. There are many ways in which cases can be concluded without the delay and expense of a trial, for example by compromise (which may or may not involve a consent order and may or may not arise because of the Part 36 procedure), by striking out or by summary judgment. This chapter considers one of the most common ways in which cases are brought to a conclusion without the need for a trial and sometimes without the need for any judicial input whatsoever. This is governed by CPR Part 12 and PD 12, and is known as 'default judgment'. Put simply, all this means is that where a defendant is in default, the claimant can obtain a judgment in his or her favour.

There are two stages at which it is possible for the claimant to seek default judgment, and both are governed by Part 12. Rule 12.1 provides that 'default judgment' means judgment without trial where a defendant:

(1)   has failed to file an acknowledgement of service; or
(2)   has failed to file a defence.

CPR PD 12, para 1 adds: 'for this purpose a defence includes any document purporting to be a defence'. What this means is that, if a defendant returns the relevant version of Form N9 (which will have been served on him or her with the claim form), duly completed, saying anything (even if it is not a defence in law and even if it is in fact gibberish), the claimant cannot obtain a default judgment. However, what happens in practice in this situation is that a court clerk will refer the matter to the district judge for directions (if, for any reason, this does not happen, then the claimant should request it) and the district judge will then normally exercise the power to strike out under r 3.4(2). The district judge will then either give judgment to the claimant or give the defendant a further opportunity to file a meaningful defence, depending on the nature of the case. It is a feature of the modern case management system that each case receives individual attention and an appropriate order. Clearly, this particular provision in CPR PD 12 is intended to benefit litigants in person, not those advised by lawyers who are expected to do a proper job with the defence.

Procedures used to differ between the High Court and county court, but now, of course, under the CPR, the same rules apply to both. It will be recalled that the claimant has the choice of either putting the 'particulars of claim' on the claim form itself or, alternatively, in a separate document, which can then be served with the claim form or subsequently. A common mistake is to assume that the rules require the defendant to acknowledge service of the claim form – they do not. The defendant is required to acknowledge service of the Particulars of Claim (see r 9.1(2) and Part 10).

There are two ways of obtaining a default judgment and the relevant rule sets out which way applies in a particular case: 'by request' or 'by application'. The former does not involve any court hearing at all, whereas the latter does.

There are two different types of default judgment, again depending on the nature of the case. If the claim is for a specified sum of money, the claimant enters judgment for that sum (less, of course, anything paid in the meantime) and fixed costs, and that concludes the case. The term 'a specified amount of money' (see r 12.4(1)) is a much wider term than the former term 'liquidated sum', which appeared in the pre-CPR rules. It covers any case where the claimant puts a figure on the amount of his or her claim. If a claimant chooses to put a value on the claim, he or she can take advantage of the rules applying to such claims where the defendant is in default.

The second main type of default judgment is for 'an amount of money to be decided by the court'. Typically, this is a claim for damages which will need a hearing to assess them (whether at a disposal or trial). Such a judgment is final on the issue of liability, but, of course, leaves the payment amount to be decided subsequently. Some practitioners still refer to this type of judgment by its pre-CPR title of 'interlocutory judgment', but it is technically wrong to do so and that expression should now be avoided. Although a judgment for an amount to be decided by a court fixes liability, it does not prevent the defendant from raising points as to quantum arising from acts or omissions claimed (see *Lunnun v Singh* [1999] CPLR 587).

JUDGMENT IN DEFAULT OF ACKNOWLEDGEMENT OF SERVICE OR DEFENCE (RULE 12.3(1) AND (2))

A defendant must respond to service of the Particulars of Claim upon him or her within 14 days. Part 10 and Part 15 encourage a defendant to miss out the acknowledgement stage and go straight to the filing of a defence. If the defendant does this, the defence must be filed within the 14 days following service. However, as r 10.1 puts it, 'A defendant may file an acknowledgement of service if he is unable to file a defence within the period specified in rule 15.4'. Thus, instead of a defence, but within the same 14-day period, the defendant can acknowledge service of the Particulars of Claim. Accordingly, a claimant may obtain judgment in default of an acknowledgement of service if the defendant fails to file that document, or a defence, and the relevant time for doing so has expired.

If a defendant does file an acknowledgement of service, this allows another period of 14 days in which to file his or her defence. If the defendant thus does file an acknowledgement of service but then fails to file a defence, the claimant can obtain judgment in default of defence.

Obviously, the claimant knows the date of service if he or she has effected service, but, normally, service is effected by post by the court and the court will send a notice telling the claimant of the date on which the claim form was served. If the particulars of the claim are endorsed on the claim form or served with it, the claimant should enter the relevant date in his or her diary and then enter default judgment, if appropriate. For example, if a claim form is posted by the court on Monday, 1 April, it will be deemed to be served on Wednesday, 3 April, and the defendant has 14 days, ie until Wednesday, 17 April, to acknowledge service. If this has not been done, the earliest date on which the claimant can enter a default judgment is Thursday, 18 April. Does it matter if the claimant is late? Not usually. If an acknowledgement of service or defence is filed late, the court will always accept it, unless a default judgment has already been obtained. However, r 15.11 provides:

> 'where at least 6 months have expired since the end of the period for filing a defence ...; no defendant has filed or served an admission or filed a defence or counterclaim; and the claimant has not entered or applied for judgment under Part 12 (default judgment) or Part 24 (summary judgment), the claim shall be stayed.'

Note that it is an automatic stay – not an automatic strike-out. Any party may apply for the stay to be lifted (r 15.11(2)).

DEFAULT JUDGMENT ON REQUEST (RULE 12.4)

A claimant may obtain a default judgment by filing a request in the relevant practice form where the claim is for:

(1) a specified amount of money;
(2) an amount of money to be decided by the court;
(3) delivery of goods where the claim form gives the defendant the alternative of paying their value (but note that this does not apply to cases governed by the Consumer Credit Act 1974); or
(4) any combination of these remedies.

The relevant practice forms are Form N205A for a specified sum of money, Form N205B for an amount to be decided by the court, and Form N255 for delivery of goods with an option to pay the value of the goods.

Most default judgments concern cases for a specified sum of money. In addition to the specified sum, the claimant can obtain interest down to the date of judgment, provided it has been properly pleaded in accordance with SCA 1981, s 35A or CCA 1984, s 69.

What form will such a judgment take? Is it for the full amount to be paid forthwith or is it to be paid by instalments? This is for the claimant to decide. Whichever is chosen, to a large extent, depends on how the claimant intends to enforce the judgment if it is not promptly paid. Some claimants will take the pragmatic view that payment by instalments that the defendant can meet and is likely to pay is better than a forthwith judgment which will be ignored. On the other hand, if, for example, the claimant intends to apply for a charging order or has some other specific form of enforcement in mind, then the claimant is more likely to prefer a forthwith judgment. (As to charging orders and other methods of enforcement, see Chapter 41.)

Whatever form the judgment takes, it will generally be drawn up by the court and served (see rr 40.3 and 40.4). The claimant will also be entitled to fixed costs (see Part 45). As for judgments for an amount of money to be decided by the court, see further, Chapter 21, Disposals.

DEFAULT JUDGMENT ON APPLICATION (RULE 12.10)

A claimant must make an application in accordance with Part 23 if he or she wishes to obtain default judgment where the claim is against a child or patient, or is in tort by one spouse against the other, or is against the Crown. (A proposed Part 66 will remove the requirement in claims against the Crown.)

It has never been possible to obtain a default judgment against a child or patient (defined in Part 21) merely by request. By CPR PD 12, para 4.2, on an application against a child or patient, a litigation friend to act on behalf of the child or patient must be appointed by the court before judgment can be obtained. Further, the claimant must satisfy the court by evidence that he or she is entitled to the judgment claimed.

The Law Reform (Husband and Wife) Act 1962 required the court to consider a stay of proceedings between husband and wife in an action in tort. Although that no longer applies (as a result of amendments made by the Civil Procedure (Modification of Enactments) Order 1998, SI 1998/2940), r 12.10(a)(ii) now requires an application. Claims by the Crown are governed by the Crown Proceedings Act 1947 and, currently, CPR Sch 1, RSC Ord 77, which exempts the Crown from many rules of procedure that apply to the subjects of the Crown. Of course, in modern society, 'the Crown' means a government department – not Her Majesty personally. A new Part 66 is intended to repeal and replace Sch 1 RSC Ord 77 with more modern provisions removing most of the Crown's procedural privileges.

In addition to the three situations just noted, there are a further five cases where the claimant must make an application in order to obtain a default judgment. These are cases:

(1)   against a defendant who has been served with the claim out of the jurisdiction under r 6.19(1) (service without leave under the Civil Jurisdiction and Judgments Act 1982);

(2)   against a defendant domiciled in Scotland or Northern Ireland or in any other Convention territory;

(3)   against a State;

(4)   against a diplomatic agent who enjoys immunity from civil jurisdiction by virtue of the Diplomatic Privileges Act 1964;

(5)   against persons or organisations who enjoy immunity from civil jurisdiction pursuant to the provisions of the International Organisations Acts 1968 and 1981.

(See further, CPR PD 12, para 4.)

CLAIMS AGAINST MORE THAN ONE DEFENDANT (RULE 12.8)

What if there are two or more defendants, but not all of them are in default? The basic rule is that the claimant can obtain a default judgment against the defendant who is in default. (See further, r 12.8.)

DEFAULT JUDGMENT FOR COSTS ONLY (RULE 12.9)

It not infrequently happens that a claimant, having lost patience with the defendant's failure to pay, commences proceedings, only to be met with payment, immediately or shortly afterwards, of the debt but leaving costs unpaid. There was a time when a claimant would be pleased to receive payment and would write off the costs incurred as a collection cost. Such benevolence is rare, given the size of court fees nowadays.

The pre-CPR rules were deficient in failing to provide a clear procedure to deal with 'costs only' disputes, but the CPR contain several provisions dealing with such disputes and the relevant one for default-judgment purposes is r 12.9. If the claim is for fixed costs, the claimant may obtain default judgment by filing the request in the relevant practice form. If the claim is for any other type of costs, the claimant must make an application in accordance with Part 23. Part 45 sets out when the claimant is entitled to fixed costs.

CASES IN WHICH DEFAULT JUDGMENT CANNOT BE OBTAINED (RULES 12.2 AND 12.3, AND PD 12)

A claimant may not obtain a default judgment:

(1)   on a claim for delivery of goods subject to an agreement regulated by the Consumer Credit Act 1974;

(2)   where the Part 8 procedure has been used;

(3)   on mortgage claims governed by Part 55;

(4)   on specialist proceedings governed by Part 49;

(5)   on admiralty proceedings (Part 61);

(6)   on arbitration proceedings (Part 62);

(7)   on contentious probate proceedings;

(8)   on claims for provisional damages;

(9)   where the defendant has filed or served an admission of the claim and has requested time to pay (see Chapter 18);

(10)   where the defendant has made an application, either for summary judgment or to strike out the claimant's claim, and that application has not yet been decided;

(11)   where the defendant has satisfied the whole claim, including any claim for costs.

PART 20 CLAIMS AND DEFAULT JUDGMENT

By r 20.3(3), 'Part 12 (default judgment) applies to a Part 20 claim only if it is a counterclaim'. Thus, where the defendant has served a counterclaim (and is thus a Part 20 claimant) against the claimant (who is now also a Part 20 defendant), a Part 20 defendant must file a defence to the counterclaim to prevent entry of a default judgment. For the special provisions relating to a default judgment on a Part 20 claim other than a counterclaim or a contribution or indemnity notice, see r 20.11. (See Chapter 16 for Part 20 claims.)

Default judgments cannot be obtained on claims for a contribution or indemnity.

SETTING ASIDE OR VARYING A DEFAULT JUDGMENT (PART 13)

Default judgment can be contrasted with summary judgment (Part 24) and judgment following a trial. Both of these have involved a judicial decision on the merits, and cannot be set aside, but can be subject to appeal. There is no provision for appealing a default judgment. Instead, the appropriate procedure is to apply to set aside or vary the default judgment in accordance with Part 13.

By r 13.2, the court *must* set aside a judgment entered under Part 12 if judgment was wrongly entered because:

'(a)   in the case of a judgment in default of an acknowledgement of service, any of the conditions in rule 12.3(1) and 12.3(3) was not satisfied;

(b)   in the case of a judgment in default of a defence, any of the conditions in rule 12.3(2) and 12.3(3) was not satisfied; or

(c)   the whole of the claim was satisfied before judgment was entered.'

This rule is self-explanatory and requires little elaboration – an error has resulted in a judgment which is irregular and which should not have been obtained. No more is required. The court must set it aside.

By r 13.3, in any other case, the court may set aside or vary a judgment entered under Part 12 if:

'(a) the defendant has a real prospect of successfully defending the claim; or
(b) it appears to the court that there is some other good reason why:
    (i)   the judgment should be set aside or varied, or
    (ii) the defendant should be allowed to defend the claim.'

In considering whether to set aside or vary a default judgment, the court will take into account whether the person seeking to set aside the judgment has done so promptly (r 13.3(2)).

The phrase 'real prospect of success' is based on the pre-CPR decision of the Court of Appeal in *Alpine Bulk Transport Co Inc v Saudi Eagle Shipping Co Inc, the Saudi Eagle* [1986] 2 Lloyd's Rep 221. This was a summary judgment case (now governed by Part 24). Under r 13.3, the court may set aside if 'the defendant has a real prospect of successfully defending the claim' (ie it is for the defendant to show this). This mirrors the modern test for summary judgment in r 24.2, where the claimant applies for summary judgment (see further, Chapter 19) on the grounds that 'the defendant has no real prospect of successfully defending the claim ...' (ie it is for the claimant to show this). It is not enough for a defendant to show that he or she has an 'arguable defence'. To set aside a default judgment, the defendant must show that he or she has 'a real prospect of successfully defending the claim'.

An application under r 13.3 must be supported by evidence (r 13.4(3)). The evidence should be in the form of a witness statement, although, if a party's statement of case or application notice is verified by a statement of truth, this can be used as evidence (r 32.6). The evidence should set out the explanation of the failure to respond to the Particulars of Claim in time and then go on to show that the defendant has a real prospect of successfully defending the claim.

It is good practice to accompany the application to set aside with a draft of the defence which it is proposed to file and serve, should the application be successful. Each and every allegation made in the Particulars of Claim must be addressed and the proposed defence should, of course, contain a statement of truth. In an appropriate case, relevant documents should be exhibited, either to the application itself or to the draft defence.

Generally, the witness statement should be drafted by someone with direct knowledge of the case, ie by the defendant (if a company, an appropriate senior person) and not by solicitor for the defendant merely repeating instructions in a hearsay form. (See further, Chapter 20, Summary judgment, and, in particular, the judgment of Lord Woolf MR in *Swain v Hillman* [2001] 1 All ER 91.)

AUTOMATIC TRANSFER

In any case, the issues of selecting the appropriate court to manage the case and the appropriate court for trial arise. The claimant has the choice of court when issuing proceedings but there are several rules which provide for automatic transfer, one of which is r 13.4. Where:

(1)   the claim is for a specified amount of money (not, for example, a claim for damages to be decided by the court);

(2)   the judgment was obtained in a court which is not the defendant's home court (defined in r 2.3(1));

(3)   the claim has not already been transferred to another defendant's home court under r 14.12 or r 26.2;

(4)   the defendant is an individual (not, for example, a limited company or partnership); and

(5)   the claim has not been commenced in a specialist list,

then, where the defendant makes an application under Part 13 to set aside or vary a judgment, the court automatically transfers that application to the defendant's home court to be heard.

By r 2.3(1), 'defendant's home court' means, in county court cases, the county court for the district in which the defendant resides or carries on business and, in High Court cases, the district registry for the district in which the defendant resides or carries on business or, where there is no such registry, the Royal Courts of Justice.

VARIATION OF PAYMENT

Either the judgment creditor or judgment debtor (as the parties are now called, following the conclusion of the case) can apply to vary the rate of payment by increasing or decreasing the figure in the default judgment (which will have been chosen by the judgment creditor on requesting judgment and not fixed by a judicial decision). Similarly, a judgment creditor may apply in writing, without notice, for an order that a money judgment, if payable in one sum, be paid at a later date or by instalments. (See further, CPR Sch 2, CCR Ord 22, r 10.)

EFFECT OF SETTING ASIDE JUDGMENT

If a judgment is set aside, the judgment is, of course, cancelled, as will be any registration of the judgment in the Registry of County Court Judgments. What happens next? The district judge who sets aside judgment will give case management directions to progress the case. Judgment can be set aside in whole or in part.

Default judgment is not available in all types of situation and, if the claimant abandoned a claim in order to take advantage of Part 12 and obtain judgment, such an abandoned claim is, by r 13.6, automatically restored when the default judgment is set aside.

Chapter 19

ADMISSIONS

OVERVIEW

Part 14 and its accompanying practice directions deal with admissions. Rules 14.1 and 14.2 deal with the manner in which a defendant may make an admission of a claim or part of a claim. Rules 14.3 to 14.7 set out how judgment may be obtained on a written admission. It is pointless, and merely increases costs, to deny matters that are known to be true.

It is part of the philosophy of the CPR to make litigation less adversarial and to require the parties to co-operate in ascertaining the real issues which require decision by a trial judge (see, for example, CPR Part 1). There is something to be admitted in virtually every case.

In deciding what order to make about costs, r 44.3(4) requires the court to have regard to all the circumstances, including 'the conduct of all the parties'. Rule 44.3(5) provides that 'the conduct of the parties' includes:

'(a) conduct before, as well as during, the proceedings and in particular the extent to which the parties followed any relevant pre-action protocol;
(b) whether it was reasonable for a party to raise, pursue or contest a particular allegation or issue;
(c) the manner in which a party has pursued or defended his case or a particular allegation or issue; and
(d) whether a claimant who has succeeded in his claim, in whole or in part, exaggerated his claim.'

The parties should co-operate in defining the real issues to be tried by the court and this necessarily involves some admissions.

Put simply, Part 14 governs two distinct situations: formal admissions in damages cases, to reduce or define the issues to be litigated, and, secondly, a debtor's admission of liability when sued for a specific sum of money. The two situations are rather different but have been lumped together in Part 14. However, a debtor's admission of liability, usually accompanied by an offer to pay, is very straightforward and causes little difficulty in practice.

MAKING AN ADMISSION

The first opportunity to make admissions arises pre-action, when the parties comply with the pre-action protocols. Further, r 14.1 provides that a party may admit the truth of the whole or any part of another party's case by giving notice in writing (such as in a statement of case or by letter).

Where the only remedy that the claimant seeks is the payment of money, the defendant may also make an admission in accordance with:

(1)   r 14.4 (admission of the whole claim for a specified amount of money);
(2)   r 14.5 (admission of part of the claim for a specified amount of money);
(3)   r 14.6 (admission of liability to pay the whole of the claim for an unspecified amount of money); or
(4)   r 14.7 (admission of liability to pay the claim for an unspecified amount of money where the defendant offers a sum in satisfaction of the claim).

Where the defendant makes any of these admissions, the claimant has a right to enter judgment, except, of course, where either party is a child or patient (r 21.10 provides that approval of the court will be required).

Formal admissions pursuant to Part 14 should be distinguished from informal admissions which, although admissible in evidence, are not governed by Part 14. For example, one party may say: 'I am sorry'. If, by that, the speaker intended to admit liability and still does so, then, of course, an admission should be made in accordance with Part 14. However, the mere fact that someone apologises is not conclusive of liability. The courts distinguish between an expression of regret that an accident has occurred and a formal admission of liability. Part 14 is concerned with the latter. It depends on the facts of the case, as established by the other evidence, whether the apology is an admission or not and, even if it is, whether or not it assists the other party.

By r 14.3, where a party makes an admission in writing, any other party may apply for judgment on that admission. Thus, for example, if, in a damages action, the defendant admits the claim, judgment can be obtained 'for an amount to be decided by the court'. Judgment on an admission 'shall be such judgment as it appears to the court that the applicant is entitled to on the admission' (r 14.3(2)). In a negligence claim, the defendant must admit not only that he or she was negligent, but also that the claimant thereby suffered damage, for, without damage, the elements of the tort are not complete and it does not amount to a full admission of liability (see *Rankine v Garton Sons and Co* [1979] 2 All ER 1185 and cases cited therein).

Whenever the court enters judgment for an amount to be decided by the court, it will, if appropriate (as it usually is), allocate to track and give case management directions. Thus, when requesting judgment, you should give the court sufficient information to enable the district judge to give such directions. If this is not done, the court will have little option but to list for directions or disposal, the costs of which may not always be recoverable.

Many cases are, of course, concluded by compromise, even without formal admission. If, say, as a result of without prejudice discussions, a compromise is reached, a simpler course of action is to submit a consent judgment for approval by the court.

REQUEST FOR TIME TO PAY

For many reasons, including redundancy, marriage breakdown or simply bad financial management, debtors may find themselves in a situation where they cannot afford to pay the debt, even though it is not disputed. If a claimant has resorted to court proceedings to recover the debt, it is better for the defendant to respond to the claim form by admitting the debt (on the form provided by the court in the 'response pack' served on the defendant with the claim form) and then, also, pursuant to r 14.9, requesting time to pay. The most common form of admission in practice is pursuant to r 14.4 ('admission of whole claim for specified amount of money'), which, by r 14.4(2), must be made by returning to the claimant an admission in the relevant practice form (contrast admissions under rr 14.5 and 14.7, which must be filed with the court). The request for time to pay accompanies the admission.

If the claimant accepts the defendant's request, he or she may obtain judgment by filing the relevant practice form. If the claimant does not accept the defendant's proposals for payment, he or she will again file notice in the relevant practice form (r 14.10). The rate of payment is then, as a general rule, determined by a court officer, pursuant to r 14.11, although there is provision in rr 14.12 and 14.13 for determination or re-determination by a judge.

If a defendant admits only part of the claim, then, under r 14.5, the court will serve notice of this on the claimant, requiring the claimant to state whether he or she accepts the amount admitted in satisfaction of the claim or does not accept the amount admitted and wishes to continue the proceedings.

WITHDRAWING AN ADMISSION

Withdrawal of an admission is rare, but r 14.1(5) does provide that 'the court may allow a party to amend or withdraw an admission'. The court, when doing so, may impose conditions, including a payment into court (r 3.1(3)) or a costs sanction (r 44.3). The court will, of course, be concerned to further the overriding objective (r 1.1) and to identify the issues between the parties (r 1.4). A party may wish to withdraw an admission where new evidence has come to light. For example, in a road traffic accident case, the defendant may admit liability and that the claimant's car was damaged. Later, it is discovered that the claimant had been in an earlier accident and that the major damage to his vehicle was caused by the earlier accident – not the later one involving the defendant. Faced with such new evidence, the court will undoubtedly permit the defendant to withdraw the admission and let the case proceed to trial. There are few reported cases on this topic and none post-CPR. For pre-CPR cases, see *Hollis v Burton* [1892] 3 Ch D 226, *Bird v Birds Eye Walls Limited* (1987) *The Times*, July 24, and *Gale v Superdrug Stores plc* [1996] 1 WLR 1089.

Chapter 20

SUMMARY JUDGMENT

OVERVIEW

All civil procedure codes need to have a system for weeding out claims which cannot succeed and defences which cannot succeed without subjecting a party who is bound to succeed to the delay and expense of a full trial. CPR Part 24 sets out a procedure by which a court may decide a claim or a particular issue without a trial. This procedure is known as 'summary judgment'.

By r 24.2, the court may give summary judgment against a claimant or defendant on the whole of a claim or on a particular issue if:

'(a) it considers that:
  (i)   the claimant has no real prospect of succeeding on the claim or issue, or
  (ii) the defendant has no real prospect of successfully defending the claim or issue; and
(b) there is no other compelling reason why the case or issue should be disposed of at trial.'

The hearing of an application for summary judgment is not a summary trial. The proper disposal of a case or issue under Part 24 does not involve the court conducting a trial – not even a mini-trial (see *per* Lord Woolf MR in *Swain v Hillman* [2001] 1 All ER 91). Part 24 enables the court to dispose summarily of both claims and defences that have no real prospect of succeeding. The words 'no real prospect of succeeding' are clear enough. The word 'real' distinguishes fanciful prospects of success and directs the court to the need to see whether there is a realistic prospect of success, as opposed to a mere fanciful prospect.

What might constitute a 'compelling reason' why the case or issue should be disposed of at trial? In the pre-CPR case of *Miles v Bull* [1969] 1 QB 258, Megarry J said: 'Order 14 [which was the RSC's predecessor to Part 24] is for the plain and straightforward not for the devious and crafty. There is here a case for investigation and so not for summary decision'. The defendant's husband had sold the matrimonial home in which she was living to the claimant, who now sued for possession and sought summary judgment. It was refused. However, it is important to bear in mind that an unsuccessful applicant for summary judgment may well still succeed at the trial itself. The claimant did, in fact, ultimately succeed (see *Miles v*

Bull (No 2) [1969] 3 All ER 1585), following the full investigation at trial that Megarry J had held was necessary. More recently, in *Merchantbridge & Co Ltd v Safron General Partner I Ltd* [2005] EWCA Civ 158 the Court of Appeal warned against giving summary judgment where the issue in dispute arises out of an oral agreement. Such cases need to be determined following oral evidence at a full trial.

Although the rule does not expressly exclude applications for summary judgment in defamation cases, it is important to remember that the respondent to the application may have a right to trial by jury (CCA 1984, s 66; SCA 1981, s 69). The right to jury trial is not a matter of mere procedure and the CPR do not override it (*Safeway Stores Plc v Tate* [2001] 2 WLR 1377).

OVERLAP WITH RULE 3.4 – POWER TO STRIKE OUT A STATEMENT OF CASE

Under r 3.4(2), the court may strike out a statement of case if it appears to the court:

> '(a) that the statement of case discloses no reasonable grounds for bringing or defending the claim;
> (b) that the statement of case is an abuse of the court's process or is otherwise likely to obstruct the just disposal of the proceedings; or
> (c) that there has been a failure to comply with a rule, practice direction or court order.'

'Statement of case' means 'a claim form, particulars of claim where these are not included in the claim form, defence, Part 20 claim or reply to a defence' (r 2.3(1)). 'Striking out' means the court ordering written material to be deleted so that it may no longer be relied upon.

Some claims are so obviously misconceived or abusive of the court process that they may be struck out before proceedings have even been served. A court clerk faced with someone who wishes to issue such a claim will, in fact, issue in the appropriate way, but will then refer the case to a district judge for directions. In an appropriate case, the district judge can strike out, before the proceedings have been served, under r 3.4 as part of the court's duty to case manage. If this has not happened in an obviously misconceived case, then it may be that a letter from the aggrieved party or that party's solicitor to the district judge would be sufficient to enable the district judge to strike out pursuant to r 3.4 (likewise, in the case of a defence which is gibberish, is not a defence in law or is said to be an abuse, etc).

Alternatively, it may by necessary for a party to issue an application to strike out. This is best done as soon as possible and before the case has been allocated to a track. In an appropriate case, the application can be under both r 3.4 and Part 24. There is clearly an overlap but there are also differences which need to be noted. Rule 3.4 is concerned only with statements of case (not part of a case) and is not suitable to dispose of a preliminary issue. There are no specified procedural requirements for r 3.4 but the specific rules of Part 24 must be complied with in an application for summary judgment. Powers of the court under Part 24 and the grounds are wider than those contained in r 3.4.

BURDEN OF PROOF

It is submitted that the test which has to be satisfied on an application for summary judgment is the same as that which has to be satisfied on an application to set aside judgment under Part 13, and is based on the decision in *Alpine Bulk Transport Co Inc v Saudi Eagle Shipping Co Inc, the Saudi Eagle* [1986] 2 Lloyd's Rep 221.

The test which has to be satisfied is clear from the wording of the rule itself. There is no 'reverse burden of proof'. The court can give summary judgment in favour of a claimant if satisfied that the defendant has no real prospects of successfully defending the claim and it is for the claimant to establish this. Similarly, the court can give summary judgment in favour of a defendant if it considers that the claimant has no real prospect of succeeding on the claim or issue and it is for the defendant to establish that.

Thus, the burden of proof placed upon the applicant is indicated by the actual wording of r 24.2 and by para 2(3) of the Practice Direction supplementing Part 24. The applicant must establish his assertion that the respondent has no real prospect of success (*ED & F Man Liquid Products Ltd v Patel* [2003] EWCA Civ 472).

The respondent has the burden of proving some real prospect of success or some other reason for trial but the standard of proof required is not high. The leading case is *Swain v Hillman* [2001] 1 All ER 91, but see also *Glaxo Group Limited v Dowelhurst Limited* [1999] All ER (D) 1288 and the pre-CPR case of *National Westminster Bank Plc v Daniel* [1993] 1 WLR 1453.

In order that applications for summary judgment succeed where a strike-out application would not succeed, three conditions must be satisfied:

(1)   all substantial facts relevant to the claimant's case that are reasonably capable of being before the court must be before the court;
(2)   those facts must be undisputed or there must be no reasonable prospect of successfully disputing them;
(3)   there must be no real prospect of oral evidence affecting the court's assessment of the facts (*S v Gloucestershire County Council* [2001] Fam 313).

It is important that a judge in an appropriate case should make use of the powers contained in Part 24. In doing so, he or she gives effect to the overriding objective in Part 1: it saves expense; it achieves expedition; it avoids the court's resources being used up on cases where this serves no purpose; and it is in the interests of justice. If a claimant has a case which is bound to fail, then it is in the claimant's interest to know this as soon as possible. Likewise, if a claim is bound to succeed, a defendant should know that as soon as possible.

EFFECT OF SET-OFF OR COUNTERCLAIM

Rule 16.6 is entitled 'Defence of Set-Off' and provides that:

'where a defendant:

(a) contends he is entitled to money from the claimant; and
(b) relies on this as a defence to the whole or part of the claim,

the contention may be concluded in the defence and set off against the claim, whether or not it is also a Part 20 claim.'

The glossary to the CPR defines counterclaim as 'a claim brought by a defendant in response to the claimant's claim, which is included in the same proceedings as the claimant's claim'. Rule 20.2 provides that a Part 20 claim is any claim other than a claim by a claimant against a defendant, and includes a counterclaim by a defendant against a claimant or against the claimant and some other person.

The question which arises for consideration here is whether the respondent to an application for summary judgment can defeat that application by relying on set-off or counterclaim. It is not easy to discern any principle from reported cases – both pre- and post-CPR – save to say that each case must turn on its own facts. In some cases, the court has refused to give summary judgment requiring the case to proceed to full trial (it is submitted that under the CPR this approach will be avoided if at all possible), whereas in other cases, the court has granted summary judgment but subjected it to a stay on enforcement proceedings, pending trial of the set-off or counterclaim (see, eg, *Hanak v Green* [1958] 2 QB 9). In exceptional cases, the claimant obtained summary judgment and was permitted to enforce it, notwithstanding that the defendant was permitted to continue with a counterclaim. In particular, in a claim based on a dishonoured cheque, the claimant will be entitled to judgment for the amount of his or her claim without a stay of execution. 'We have repeatedly said in this court that a bill of exchange or a promissory note is to be treated as cash. It is to be honoured unless there is some good reason to the contrary' (*per* Lord Denning MR in *Fielding and Platt Limited v Selim Najjar* [1969] 1 WLR 357). (See also *Nova (Jersey) Knit Limited v Kammgarn Spimmereo GmbH* [1977] 1 WLR 713.) The point is that a seller can choose to sell for cash or for credit. If he or she sells for cash, the cheque will be treated as being the equivalent of cash. Even if the goods purchased are defective, that is no excuse for dishonouring the cheque (it is worth reflecting on the terminology – 'dishonour' – used here) and, if sued on a dishonoured cheque, a defendant would not be permitted to defeat an application for summary judgment, or even obtain a stay of execution, merely by alleging defective goods. The defendant must do what he or she would have had to do if in fact cash had been paid, ie commence his or her own proceedings (which he or she will be allowed to do by continuing with the counterclaim).

English law does not allow cross-claims or defences in claims based on a dishonoured cheque. Exceptional circumstances required to permit a defendant to defend a claim on a dishonoured cheque or bill of exchange would have to be based on fraud (eg that the cheque is a forgery or has been altered in some way or obtained by fraud), or that the cheque was paid in respect of a debt which is irrecoverable as a matter of law (eg a gambling debt).

The special rules that apply to bills of exchange and cheques were extended in *Esso Petroleum Co. Limited v Milton* [1997] 1 WLR 938 to apply to a direct debit mandate, the court observing that these have often taken the place of cheques in modern commerce.

TYPES OF PROCEEDINGS IN WHICH SUMMARY JUDGMENT IS AVAILABLE

By r 24.3(2), the court can give summary judgment against the claimant in any type of proceedings, except:

'(a)   proceedings for possession of residential premises against:
(i)   a mortgagor; or
(ii)   a tenant or a person holding over after the end of his tenancy whose occupancy is protected within the meaning of the Rent Act 1977 or the Housing Act 1988, and
(b)   proceedings for an admiralty claim in rem.'

Note, however, that, in some cases, there might be a right to jury trial (see *Safeway Stores Plc v Tate* [2001] 2 WLR 1377). Further, by r 53.2, an application for summary judgment may not be made if an application for summary disposal under the Defamation Act 1996, ss 8 and 9 has been made and not yet disposed of, or summary leave under the Defamation Act 1996, s 9 has been granted. Further, CPR Sch 1, RSC Ord 77, r 7 currently prohibits an application in proceedings 'against' the Crown (though a new Part 66 is likely to change this).

Note that there is no bar on applications for summary judgment in claims issued under the Part 8 procedure. However, such applications should rarely be necessary, as Part 8 itself is intended to provide a simple and expeditious means of determining appropriate cases. If a remedy sought by a claimant in his or her claim form includes, or necessarily involves, taking an account or making an inquiry, an application can be made under Part 24 by any party to the proceedings for an order directing any necessary accounts or inquiries to be taken or made (PD 24, para 6).

If a remedy sought by a claimant includes a claim for specific performance of an agreement for the sale, purchase, exchange, mortgage or charge of any property, or for the grant or assignment of a lease of tenancy of any property (with or without an alternative claim for damages), or for recission of such an agreement, or for the forfeiture or return of any deposit made under such an agreement, then the claimant can apply under Part 24 for judgment. The procedure in such specific performance cases is slightly modified (PD 24, para 7).

HOW TO APPLY

The procedure for an application for summary judgment is governed by r 24.4. A claimant may not apply for summary judgment until the defendant has filed an acknowledgement of service or a defence, unless the court gives permission or the Practice Direction provides otherwise. (If a claimant applies for summary judgment before the defendant has filed a defence, that defendant need not file a defence before the hearing.)

Ideally, a party intending to apply for summary judgment should do so as soon as possible and, preferably, before or at the same time as filing the allocation questionnaire. The court would then list the application for hearing and would not allocate the case to track at that stage. This means, for example, that a claimant can avoid the limited costs regime of the small claims track by applying promptly, before the claim has been allocated to that track.

It will be remembered that the time-limit for filing an acknowledgement of service and a defence runs from the date of service of the claimant's Particulars of Claim. It follows that the claimant must have served his or her own statement of case in order to be able to apply for summary judgment.

A defendant can apply for summary judgment on the claimant's claim at any time – there is no requirement to acknowledge service or file a defence first. Of course, the defendant must always take care to comply with appropriate time-limits to avoid a default judgment.

The application notice must be completed and filed in accordance with Part 23. The application notice must include a statement that it is an application for summary judgment made under Part 24 (PD 24, para 2).

The application should be on Practice Form N244 and should be completed in accordance with the requirements of both Parts 23 and 24. Thus, in addition to making it clear that it is an application under Part 24, the application must comply with the formal requirements set out in PD 23, para 2, state what order the applicant is seeking and why (r 23.6), identify the written evidence on which the applicant relies (PD 24, para 2(4)) and draw the attention of the respondent to r 24.5 (see below).

Applications are normally heard before a district judge or, in the High Court in London, a master. As, however, the jurisdiction of district judges and masters to grant injunctions is limited (see PD 25 – Interim injunctions) such applications will be listed for hearing before the High Court judge or, in the county court, the circuit judge.

Applicants cannot rely on oral evidence when applying for summary judgment. However, an applicant may rely on written evidence set out on the claim form, statement of case, application notice or in a witness statement, provided that each is properly verified by a statement of truth (see Part 22 and PD 22).

The applicant for summary judgment will be required to give a time estimate, and experience has shown that these estimates are often inadequate. If the applicant expects that it will take 30 minutes to make the application, then bear in mind that the respondent is likely to require a similar period of time, the court itself will require a similar period of time to give judgment, and there will then need to be further time taken to deal with any costs application and to give case management directions if the whole case has not been concluded by the result of the application for summary judgment. In this example, therefore, a proper time estimate would be 2 hours, and certainly not the 30 minutes which the applicant expects his or her own case to take. It is better practice to make time estimates too long rather than too short. Judges cannot deal with the case properly if there is inadequate time and the judge may well refuse to hear the application at all if it is manifestly obvious that insufficient time has been estimated for the hearing, thus necessitating an adjournment and further delay.

All applications are important but it is submitted that an application for summary judgment is of particular importance because, by making the application, the applicant is saying that the other side's case is so hopeless that it does not merit a trial. In other words, the applicant seeks to deprive a respondent of a full trial to which he or she would normally be entitled. Such applications cannot be rushed and demand careful preparation, presentation and consideration. Properly used, however, Part 24 is undoubtedly one of the most useful provisions in the CPR.

EVIDENCE

As noted in the preceding section (How to apply), the applicant cannot rely on oral evidence and must serve written evidence with the application.

Rule 24.4(3) provides that a respondent to an application must be given at least 14 days' notice. The application must specifically direct the respondent's attention to r 24.5.

Rule 24.5(1) requires the respondent to an application for summary judgment, who wishes to rely on written evidence at the hearing, to file the witness statement and serve copies on every other party to the application, at least 7 days before the summary judgment hearing.

If the applicant wishes to rely on a witness statement in reply to the respondent's evidence, he or she must file the written evidence and serve a copy on the respondent at least 3 days before the summary judgment hearing (r 24.5(2)).

COURT'S POWERS AND CONSEQUENTIAL ORDERS

The orders that the court may make on an application under Part 24 include:

(1)   judgment on the claim;
(2)   the striking-out or dismissal of the claim;

(3)   the dismissal of the application; and

(4)   a conditional order.

It will be recalled that, under r 24.2, the court may give summary judgment if it considers that the claimant has no real prospect of succeeding on the claim or issue, or the defendant has no real prospect of successfully defending the claim or issue and there is no other compelling reason why the case or issue should be disposed of at trial. (See further, 'Burden of Proof', above.) What if it appears possible to the court that a claim or defence may succeed, but it is improbable that it will do so? By PD 24, para 4, the court, in such a situation, may make a conditional order.

A conditional order is an order which requires a party to pay a sum of money into court or to take a specified step in relation to his or her claim or defence, as the case may be, and provides that that party's claim will be dismissed or the statement of claim will be struck out if he or she does not comply. In practice, the most common condition imposed by the court is one requiring a defendant to pay the amount of the claim into court. If the defendant is, in reality, putting forward a sham defence in an attempt to delay payment or as a negotiating ploy to reduce the sum payable, then, by forcing the defendant to pay the amount into court, the ruse has failed. Of course, if the court were entirely satisfied that the defence was a sham, it would be giving summary judgment for the claimant. The court has, instead, come to the conclusion that the defence may succeed but it is improbable that it will. So, by ordering payment into court, it gives some security to the claimant, whilst not depriving the defendant of a full trial. The money is, of course, returned to the defendant if, in fact, the defence does succeed (together with accrued interest) but will be ordered to be paid out to the claimant should the claimant succeed. There is nothing wrong in the court finding that a defendant has a real prospect of success (so as to deny summary judgment to the claimant) but that success is nevertheless improbable and ordering a payment in under a conditional order: *Jordan Grand Prix Ltd v Tiger Telematics Inc* [2005] EWHC 76.

If the whole case has not been disposed of by the result of the summary judgment application, then the court must proceed to give directions as to filing and service of a defence, if this has not already been done, and give further directions about the management of the case (r 24.6).

The court will also have to deal with the costs of the application for summary judgment. Fixed costs may be applicable under Part 45.

Chapter 21

DISPOSALS

OVERVIEW

Disposals are a useful innovation of the CPR. (The term was used in a different, but obsolete, sense in the former CCR.) Yet, no part of the CPR is entitled 'Disposals'. Disposals are in fact governed by para 12 of the Practice Direction which supplements Part 26 – Case Management.

Paragraph 12 is entitled 'Determining the amount to be paid under a judgment or order', and para 12.4 is entitled 'Disposal hearings'.

Disposals are designed to deal with a fairly common situation. A defendant admits liability to compensate the claimant but disputes the amount claimed or wishes to make submissions on the quantum of the claim.

The most common situations in practice arise out of personal injury claims after a road traffic accident or based on employer's liability where a defendant concedes liability, but is not in a position to concede the amount of the claim, or disputes the sum being claimed.

SCOPE

By CPR PD 26, para 12.4(1) a disposal hearing is a hearing which will not normally last longer than 30 minutes and at which the court will not normally hear oral evidence.

At a disposal hearing the court may either decide the amount payable under the relevant order and give judgment for that amount, or give directions as to the future conduct of the proceedings. Typically, such directions would include the obtaining of medical evidence in the form of expert reports.

By CPR PD 26, para 12.1, a 'relevant order' means an order or judgment of the court that requires the amount of money to be paid by one party to another to be decided by the court.

A relevant order may have been obtained by a judgment in default under Part 12; by a judgment on an admission under Part 14; on the striking out of a statement of case under Part 3; on a summary judgment under Part 24; on the determination of a preliminary issue; at a split trial as to liability only; or at a full trial.

A relevant order includes an order for an amount of damages or interest to be decided by the court, an order for the taking of an account or the making of an inquiry as to any sum due and any similar order. However, a relevant order does not include an order for the assessment of costs, except where the court has made an order for the assessment of costs payable under a contract other than a contract between a solicitor and client for legal services.

Typically, therefore, the defendant would have admitted liability and the claimant would have entered judgment for 'an amount of money to be decided by the court'. A disposal is the basic procedure for deciding that amount.

Where a claimant obtains judgment by default under Part 12 without a hearing, then, on entry of the judgment, the court will list a disposal hearing. Where a relevant order is a judgment entered without a hearing under Part 14 (admissions), the court will give directions and may, in particular, direct a disposal hearing.

Where a relevant order is made by a judge at a hearing, the judge should, at the same time, give directions to enable the case to progress to assessment of damages.

It is submitted that PD 26, para 12 is somewhat loosely drafted. When a judge is seized of a case at a hearing, it is perfectly sensible for him or her to go on, with the benefit of the party's representatives or the parties, to give appropriate directions. However, it is submitted that there should be a requirement that a party obtaining judgment in default or judgment on an admission should, at the same time, suggest appropriate directions. Unfortunately, there is not. Thus, a lacuna in the Practice Direction is exposed. It frequently – and unfortunately – happens that a claimant obtains a default judgment and invites the court to list the case for disposal. The court, however, has no idea how long that disposal is likely to take and whether or not, for example, there is agreed or disputed medical evidence. Although not a requirement of the CPR nor of PD 26, it is respectfully submitted that solicitors should not leave the court to guess what directions might be required. Until such time as CPR PD 26, para 12 is amended to require this information, it is still good practice for solicitors to give the court some basic information about the case and, at the very least, suggest appropriate directions and give a time estimate bearing in mind that a disposal hearing 'will not normally last longer than 30 minutes' (see above). Other than in claims allocated to the small claims track, the court will not exercise its power to assess damages unless any written evidence on which the claimant relies has been served on the defendant at least 3 days before the disposal hearing (para 12.4(5)). In straightforward cases the evidence will be in the form of a medical report which will have been annexed to the particulars or claim and thus already served.

JURISDICTION OF MASTERS AND DISTRICT JUDGES

By CPR PD 26, district judges and masters may decide the amount payable under a relevant order irrespective of the value of the claim or the track to which the claim has been allocated.

ALLOCATION AND DIRECTIONS

Where, as is often the case, a claim has not been allocated to track at the time that a relevant order is made, the court will not normally consider it to be appropriate to allocate it to a track (other than the small claims track) unless the amount payable appears to be genuinely disputed on grounds which appear to be substantial.

If the financial value of the claim (determined in accordance with Part 26) is such that the claim would, if defended, be allocated to the small claims track, the court will normally allocate it to that track and may treat a disposal hearing as a final hearing, in accordance with Part 27.

Allocation of appropriate disposals to the small claims track ensures that a defendant who admits liability or submits to judgment is not in a worse position than if he or she had defended the claim, because, of course, cases allocated to the small claims track are subjected to a very limited costs regime.

In addition to allocating to track, where considered necessary, the court can give all necessary directions to enable the judge to assess the quantum of the claim. Directions may have to include exchange of witness statements, disclosure and, in particular, permission to rely on expert evidence and whether it is to be confined to a written report or whether oral expert evidence is required.

The court will also have to consider the level of judge before whom a hearing or further hearing will take place. Unless the court otherwise directs, a master or district judge may decide the amount payable under a relevant order, irrespective of the financial value of the claim and of the track to which the claim may have been allocated (PD 26, para 12.6). However, solicitors should assist the court in deciding which level of judge ought to deal with the case and, where a personal injury case involves substantial damages, it is generally inappropriate for a district judge to assess those damages (*Sandry v Jones* [2000] TLR 595).

DISPOSAL HEARINGS

A disposal hearing does not usually take longer than 30 minutes so unless, for good reason, a party has requested longer, it will not be given more than 30 minutes (see PD 26, para 12.4).

At a disposal hearing, the court may give directions or decide the amount payable in accordance with PD 26, para 12.4. The court may order the amount payable to be decided there and then, without allocating the claim to a track, but can only exercise those powers if any written evidence on which the claimant relies has been served on the defendant at least 3 days before the disposal hearing (para 12.4(3)).

Thus, if there appears to be no real dispute about the amount payable, the court can direct the case to be listed for a disposal hearing and, at that hearing, can either:

(1)   decide the amount payable straight away;
(2)   allocate to the small claims track and then treat the disposal hearing as a final hearing; or
(3)   allocate to track and give directions.

There are differences between a disposal hearing and a hearing following allocation to track. Unless the judge allocates the matter to a track, evidence is not given orally, but by witness statements (para 12.4(1)). Thus, a party wishing to cross-examine a witness at a disposal hearing must first apply to the court for a direction to that effect.

Despite the rather vague and inadequate wording of PD 26, para 12, disposals are working well in practice in straightforward cases. However, more complicated cases require directions and a full trial, albeit with that trial being limited to the issue of damages only.

COSTS

Costs will normally be dealt with at the conclusion of the hearing, by way of summary assessment. (See further, para 12.5.)

Part V

CASE MANAGEMENT

Chapter 22

ALLOCATION

THE ALLOCATION QUESTIONNAIRE

Once a claim has become defended, the court's first task is to allocate the claim to the appropriate track and then give necessary case management directions. Your task in completing the allocation questionnaire is to assist the court in allocating the case to the appropriate track, to give all the necessary case management directions that you seek and to avoid an allocation hearing. The court will send an allocation questionnaire in Form N150 and your task is to complete it appropriately.

One of the key aims of the CPR is to make litigation less confrontational. The parties are required to help the court to further the overriding objective (r 1.3). In the context of allocation, CPR PD 26, para 4.1 provides:

> 'The Civil Procedure Rules lay down the overriding objective, the powers and duties of the court and the factors to which it must have regard in exercising them. The court will expect to exercise its powers so far as possible in co-operation with the parties and their legal representatives so as to deal with the case justly in accordance with that objective.'

Paragraph 2.3 of PD 26 requires parties to consult one another and co-operate in the completion of allocation questionnaires and giving other information to the court. This needs to be done promptly, for the process of consultation must not delay the filing of the allocation questionnaires. In particular, parties should try to agree the case management directions which they will invite the court to make. If such directions (which will, of course, include allocation to the appropriate track) are agreed, all parties should submit a draft consent order for approval with the allocation questionnaire. If it is not possible for you to agree a draft order with the other side, then you should submit a draft of your own proposed order, and you should do this whether you act for the claimant or the defendant.

The court will expect to have enough information from the statements of case and allocation questionnaires to be able to allocate the claim to a track and to give case management directions.

ALLOCATION HEARINGS

The court will hold an allocation hearing on its own initiative only if it considers that it is necessary to do so. In practice, the most common reason for having an allocation hearing is that both parties have failed to give the court adequate information. If one party has given full information and, in particular, if that party has provided a draft order of necessary case management directions which seems to the court to be appropriate, then the court is likely to allocate and give directions in accordance with that draft order, without having an allocation hearing.

Sometimes, however, an allocation hearing is necessary, even where all solicitors have given adequate information – for example, parties who request allocation to the multi-track of a case in which the financial limit would suggest it ought to be allocated to the fast track, because the parties consider that the case cannot conclude within the maximum 5 hours allowed for a fast-track trial. The court will be anxious to ensure, whenever possible, that a claim is not allocated to a higher track than necessary and may well wish to explore with the parties whether, by ordering a split trial and trying the issue of liability first, an allocation to the fast track would still be possible.

Allocation hearings are relatively rare, and usually an unwarranted expense, and your aim should be to avoid them wherever possible. It is always possible to apply for re-allocation at a later stage.

A legal representative who attends an allocation hearing should, if possible, be the person responsible for the case, and must, in any event, be familiar with the case, be able to provide the court with the information that it is likely to need in order to make its decisions about allocation and case management, and have sufficient authority to deal with any issues that are likely to arise (PD 26, para 6.5).

THE THREE TRACKS

Every defended case is allocated to the small claims track, the fast track or the multi-track. Put simply (but see below), the small claims track is for cases valued up to £5,000; the fast track is for cases valued at more than £5,000 but not more than £15,000; and the multi-track is for cases valued at over £15,000.

The small claims track

As a working rule, it is fair to say that the small claims track is for claims valued at not more than £5,000. However, there are important exceptions to this, particularly in the case of claims for personal injuries and claims by a tenant of residential premises against a landlord.

By r 26.6, the small claims track is the normal track for a claim for personal injuries where the financial value of the claim is not more than £5,000 *and* the financial value of any claim for damages for personal injuries is not more than

£1,000. In this context, 'damages for personal injuries' means damages for pain, suffering and loss of amenity only – not other damages, such as lost earnings.

The sum of £1,000 is a very modest figure for damages for pain, suffering and loss of amenity, and it is important to note, therefore, that it is only where the damages are under that figure and the total of the claim is less than £5,000 (when including other damages, such as lost earnings) that the claim will be allocated to the small claims track. In practice, this means that there are very few personal injury claims indeed allocated to the small claims track. Personal injury claims form a very significant part of litigation before the courts and, because of this low limit on general damages, the majority of them are allocated to the fast track. (Whether this low figure of £1,000 should be increased is one of several issues currently under consideration.)

The small claims track is the normal track for any claim which includes a claim by a tenant of residential premises against his or her landlord where the tenant is seeking an order requiring the landlord to carry out repairs or other work to the premises (whether or not the tenant is also seeking some other remedy), the cost of the repairs or other work to the premises is estimated to be no more than £1,000, and the financial value of any other claim for damages is no more than £1,000.

Subject to the special rules mentioned above for personal injury claims and certain claims by tenants against landlords, the small claims track is the normal track for any claim which has a financial value of not more than £5,000. The small claims track is dealt with in Part 27.

The fast track

The fast track has proved to be an extremely valuable and popular innovation of the CPR. For many years, it was obvious that something rather more than the informal trial procedure which now exists for cases allocated to the small claims track (and which, pre-CPR, existed in a slightly different form) and the full procedure given to cases allocated to the multi-track (and which, pre-CPR, applied to all cases) was needed. The fast track is a necessary intermediate track.

Unfortunately, although the fast track has been a huge success, there is one major deficiency which still persists over the failure to implement Lord Woolf's recommendation for a fixed-costs regime for fast-track cases. It is said that this necessary reform is still being considered.

The fast track is the normal track for any claim for which the small claims track is not the normal track and which has a financial value of not more than £15,000. In practice, it has proved to be the most common track for personal injury claims.

However, the fast track is the normal track for claims of not more than £15,000 only if the court considers that the trial is likely to last for no longer than one day (which means 5 hours of court hearing time). There is, in fact, a conflict between r 26.6(5)(b) and r 35.5(2), but this has proved not to be problematic in practice. Rule 26.6(5)(b) provides that:

'oral expert evidence at trial will be limited to:

    (i)   one expert per party in relation to any expert field; and,

    (ii)   expert evidence in two expert fields.'

Rule 35.5 provides:

'(1) Expert evidence is to be given in a written report unless the court otherwise directs.

(2) If a claim is on the fast track, the court will not direct an expert to attend a hearing unless it is necessary to do so in the interests of justice.'

Fortunately, this is an area in which solicitors have entered into the spirit of the CPR. Compliance with the pre-action protocol for personal injury claims (and it is crucial that this pre-action protocol is complied with) ensures that medical disputes are much less common than was the case pre-CPR. It is now rare for oral expert evidence to be necessary in a fast-track case. Provisions for agreeing choice of expert and clarifying reports by questions are invariably adequate.

The essence of the fast track is that, on allocation, the case will be given a trial window of not more than 3 weeks and commencing not more than 27 weeks from allocation with the intention that fast-track trials should be concluded within 30 weeks of allocation. The court will direct only the minimum necessary pre-trial steps, which will usually be confined to standard disclosure, exchange of witness statements, and directions for written expert evidence and for the filing of pre-trial checklists.

The fast track is governed by CPR Part 28.

The multi-track

By r 26.6(6), the multi-track is the normal track for any claim for which the small claims track or the fast track is not the normal track. The multi-track is governed by CPR Part 29.

FINANCIAL VALUE

It is for the court to assess the financial value of a claim (r 26.8(2)), although, obviously, in doing so, it is guided by the information provided by the parties, both in their statements of case and the allocation questionnaires.

In assessing the financial value, the court will disregard any amount not in dispute, any claim for interest, contributory negligence, and costs.

CPR PD 26, para 7.4 elaborates on the meaning of 'any amount not in dispute'. In deciding, for the purposes of r 26.8(2), whether an amount is in dispute, the court applies the following principles:

'(1) Any amount for which the defendant does not admit liability is in dispute.

(2) Any sum in respect of an item forming part of the claim for which judgment has been entered (for example a summary judgment) is not in dispute.

(3) Any specific sum claimed as a distinct item and which the defendant admits he is liable to pay is not in dispute.

(4) Any sum offered by the defendant which has been accepted by the claimant in satisfaction of any item which forms a distinct part of the claim is not in dispute.'

It follows from these provisions that if, in relation to a claim, the value of which is above the small claims track limit of £5,000, the defendant makes, before allocation, an admission that reduces the amount in dispute to a figure below £5,000, the normal track for the claim will be the small claims track. As to recovery of pre-allocation costs, the claimant can, before allocation, apply for judgment with costs on the amount of the claim that has been admitted. (See r 14.3, and para 15.1(3) of PD Costs, under which the court has a discretion to allow pre-allocation costs.)

The court will treat the views of the parties as an important factor, but the allocation decision is one for the court, to be taken in the light of all the circumstances, and the court will not be bound by any agreement or common view of the parties. The court is astute in preventing agreements to allocate to a higher track without justification.

By r 26.8(3), where two or more claimants have started a claim against the same defendant, using the same claim form, and each claimant has a claim against a defendant separate from the other claimants, the court will consider the claim of each claimant separately when it assesses financial value for the purpose of allocation.

There is no point in inflating the claim in an attempt to secure allocation to a higher track. In particular, in a personal injury case, it should be clear enough whether the claim does or does not exceed £1,000. (See p 187.)

By r 26.5(3), before deciding the track to which to allocate proceedings or deciding whether to give directions for an allocation hearing to be fixed, the court may order a party to provide further information about his or her case. The court is likely to make an order under this rule, directing the claimant to justify the amount claimed if the court believes that the amount sought exceeds what the claimant may reasonably be expected to recover. If the court is still not satisfied following receipt of the further information, it is likely to convene an allocation hearing.

The court cannot allocate a claim to a track if the financial value exceeds the limit for that track, unless all parties consent. In practice, consent is rare between parties represented by solicitors, but consent may be appropriate with litigants in person. Experience has shown that litigants in person often have difficulty in complying with directions given on the fast track, even though the court keeps such directions to a minimum. Further, as litigants in person, as a general rule, prefer the informal trial of the small claims track, where both parties act in person the court may well invite the parties to consent to a case being allocated to the small claims track, even though the financial value is such that it would merit allocation to the fast track.

MATTERS RELEVANT TO ALLOCATION

The matters relevant to allocation to a track are specified in r 26.8(1). In addition to the financial value of the claim (see above), the court also has regard to the factors listed in the rule, which include the nature of the remedy sought, the likely complexity of the law, facts or evidence, and the number of parties or likely parties.

In fact, allocation has proved to be a very straightforward task for district judges. First and foremost, the financial value of the claim is decisive in the vast majority of cases. Areas of dispute about allocation centre on whether a claim is or is not worth more than the small claims track limit (in particular, the £1,000 limit for personal injury claims) and whether or not a fast-track case can be concluded within a day. (See further, PD 26, para 9.)

Where a claim has no financial value – for example, a claim for an injunction – the court will allocate the claim to the track which it considers most suitable, having regard to the factors mentioned in r 26.8. Few injunction cases will be suitable for informal trial on the small claims track.

NOTICE OF ALLOCATION

Having decided the track to which the case is to be allocated, the court will then give the appropriate case management directions. In small claims track cases, these directions are likely to include the actual trial date together with the limited steps which parties must take to prepare. In a fast-track case, the directions will include the fixing of a trial window and an order for the filing of pre-trial checklists, upon receipt of which the court will fix the trial date. In multi-track cases, the directions will probably include provision for a case management conference. (If the order does not so provide, then it would, instead, as in a fast-track case, fix a trial window and provide for the filing of pre-trial checklists.)

By r 26.9, where the court serves notice of allocation on a party, it will also serve a copy of the allocation questionnaires filed by the other parties and a copy of any further information provided by another party about his or her case. Parties are required to file allocation questionnaires with the court and need not serve them on other parties, as the court does this with notice of allocation.

RE-ALLOCATION

By r 26.10, the court may subsequently re-allocate a claim to a different track. If a claim is initially allocated to the small claims track and it is re-allocated to a different track, the cost limitations that apply in small claims cases cease to apply as from re-allocation (see r 27.15). It is not possible to allocate different parts of the same case to different tracks. The whole case proceeds on the relevant track.

There has been an increase in the number of split trials under the CPR as compared with the old rules. This is particularly common in a case which, if tried on liability only, would conclude within 5 hours and thus would be suitable for allocation to the fast track. If, at the conclusion of such a split trial, the claimant has succeeded but, in the intervening period, it has become apparent that the injuries are more significant than at first thought, then, following the split trial, the quantum issue could be re-allocated to the multi-track.

If a solicitor feels that the court has made the wrong decision and allocated a case to the wrong track, he or she should consider appealing or applying for re-allocation (PD 26, para 11). If the allocation decision was made on paper, then the solicitor should make an application to the court for re-allocation, either immediately or later. If the allocation decision was taken at a hearing at which the solicitor received due notice, then (PD 26, para 11.1(2)) he or she should appeal. In fact, appeals against allocation are not mentioned anywhere in the Rules themselves and are extremely rare in practice. Nonetheless, the facility is there for use in an exceptional case. (For appeals, see Part 52, and Chapter 40 of this book.) Often, however, it will be better to complete pre-trial preparation and, if still of the view that the claim is on the wrong track, apply for re-allocation at a later stage. The court can re-allocate where there has been a change in circumstances or where new evidence makes re-allocation appropriate.

As mentioned at the beginning of this chapter, it is your aim to complete the allocation questionnaire in such a way that allocation to the appropriate track is secured without a hearing. The allocation questionnaire is a very straightforward form indeed, which solicitors should have no trouble completing. The majority of trials are of cases proceeding on the small claims track, with parties representing themselves. Litigants in person rarely have difficulty in properly completing the allocation questionnaire, and there can be no excuse whatsoever for a solicitor's failure to do so.

Allocation is the first and main (often the only) stage in the proceedings, when the court gives case management directions.

Chapter 23

CASE MANAGEMENT

OVERVIEW

Prior to the CPR, parties (or rather their solicitors) controlled the pace of litigation. This is no longer the case. Courts now manage cases.

This has had a profound effect on the way litigation is conducted. There is far more 'front loading' than before. Considerable pre-action work now has to be undertaken. Gone are the days when proceedings could be commenced and the case then drifted at a leisurely pace resulting some years later in a trial or compromise. Once proceedings are commenced, the court will in a small claims track case fix the trial date, in a fast-track case fix a trial window, and in a multi-track case either fix a date for a case management conference or fix a trial window, or both. Time-limits set by the court will be realistic but tight.

It is, of course, essential to comply with any relevant pre-action protocol and, even if there is no relevant pre-action protocol, the court will expect the parties, in accordance with the overriding objective and the matters referred to in r 1.1(2)(a), (b) and (c), to act reasonably in exchanging information and documents relevant to the claim and generally in trying to avoid the necessity of starting proceedings (PD Protocols, para 4). The issue of proceedings should now be regarded as the last resort not as a first option. Once proceedings have been issued, parties must be ready to comply with the court's case management directions.

Rule 1.4 provides that the court must further the overriding objective (see r 1.1) by actively managing cases.

Active case management includes:

(a)   encouraging the parties to co-operate with each other in the conduct of proceedings;
(b)   identifying the issues at an early stage;
(c)   deciding properly which issues need full investigation and trial and accordingly disposing summarily of the others;
(d)   deciding the order in which issues are to be resolved;

(e)   encouraging the parties to use an alternative dispute resolution procedure
        (see Chapter 3) if the court considers that to be appropriate and facilitating
        the use of such procedure;
(f)   helping the parties to settle the whole or part of the case;
(g)   fixing timetables or otherwise controlling the progress of the case;
(h)   considering whether the likely benefits of taking a particular step justify the
        cost of taking it;
(i)   dealing with as many aspects of the case as it can on the same occasion;
(j)   dealing with the case without needing to attend at court;
(k)   making use of technology, and;
(l)   giving directions to ensure that the trial of the case proceeds quickly and
        efficiently.

The court having given case management directions, parties must comply with
them. The court has power to impose sanctions (which could include the striking
out of the case or defence) if its orders are not complied with. At the very least,
costs sanctions will be imposed for failure to comply. (See further Chapter 34.)

The introduction of case management by the court was a major innovation of the
CPR. Accordingly, the topic of case management is dealt with at considerable
length both in the CPR and in Practice Directions. In addition to Part 1 –
Overriding Objective, see: Part 3 – The Court's Case Management Powers, PD 3
and PD 3B; Part 26 – Case Management – Preliminary Stage, and PD 26; Part 27 –
The Small Claims Track, and PD 27; Part 28 – The Fast Track, and PD 28; and
Part 29 – The Multi-track, and PD 29. Particular topics dealt with as part of case
management by the court also have specific Parts, eg Part 31 – Disclosure and
Inspection of Documents, Part 32 – Evidence, and Part 35 – Experts and Assessors.
Although no specific Part deals with witness statements, see, in particular: Part 22
– Statements of Truth and PD 22; Part 32 – Evidence, and PD 32; Part 33
Miscellaneous Rules about Evidence, and PD 33; and Part 34 – Depositions and
Court Attendance by Witnesses, and PD 34.

Case management is undertaken by district judges and masters but can, of course,
also be undertaken by circuit judges in the county court and by a High Court judge
in High Court cases. All county courts have a circuit judge who is also the
'Designated Civil Judge' (DCJ) whose duties include case management of
appropriate cases which, in practice, are likely to be the more complex multi-track
cases. However, even a DCJ cannot case manage a High Court case unless it has
been specifically released to him or her by a High Court judge pursuant to SCA
1981, s 9. In fact, such release is common for trials but rare for case management
purposes, with the result that the vast bulk of case management decisions are taken
by district judges.

ALLOCATION

The court's first case management decision will be to allocate the defended case to
its appropriate track. Many cases conclude without reference to a judge at all (eg

by a default judgment) and generally the court cannot begin its case management unless and until the case is defended.

Allocation as such is considered in Chapter 22. In addition to allocating a case to track, the court will also give case management directions.

SMALL CLAIMS TRACK – CASE MANAGEMENT

The small claims track is intended to provide a proportionate procedure by which most straightforward claims with a financial value of not more than £5,000 can be decided without the need for substantial pre-hearing preparation and the formalities of a traditional trial and without incurring high legal costs (note the lower financial value in certain cases, in particular personal injury cases, provided by r 26.6).

The procedure laid down in Part 27 for the preparation of the case is designed to make it possible for litigants to prepare and conduct their own case without legal representation if they so wish. Cases suitable for the small claims track include consumer disputes, accident claims, disputes about the ownership of goods and disputes between a landlord and tenant other than claims for possession.

The court will not normally allow more than one day for the hearing of small claims. Most are dealt with in an hour or so.

Directions for case management of small claims will be given on allocation. Rule 27.4 contains provisions about directions and PD 27 sets out the standard directions which the court will usually give. The Appendix to PD 27 contains six forms of directions which have proved to be suitable for virtually all small claims. They are:

–   Form A – the standard directions;
–   Form B – standard directions for use in claims arising out of road accidents;
–   Form C – standard directions for use in claims arising out of building disputes, vehicle repairs and similar contractual claims;
–   Form D – tenants' claims for the return of deposits/landlords' claims for damage caused;
–   Form E – holiday and wedding claims;
–   Form F – some special directions.

Experience has shown that these standard forms are sufficient for nearly all cases.

Thus, case management is considered without attendance by the parties, and on one occasion only by the district judge. The district judge allocates the case to track, gives the appropriate directions (which will always be kept to the absolute minimum necessary) and gives a time estimate for the trial. Relying on that estimate, the court staff will then fix the trial date which will be about 8 weeks ahead. The parties thus receive from the court notice of allocation, all necessary directions and the trial date and time. The parties only have to visit court once and that is for the trial itself.

FAST TRACK – CASE MANAGEMENT

Directions for case management of claims allocated to the fast track will be given at the allocation stage. Further directions (intended to be no more than fine-tuning) can be given at listing stage when the parties have filed their pre-trial checklist (listing questionnaire). If necessary (usually it is not), directions can be given at other times.

PD 28 contains further provisions about case management and standard directions which the court may give.

Paragraph 3.12 of PD 28 contains a typical timetable which the court may give for the preparation of a fast-track case. It is as follows:

Disclosure	4 weeks
Exchange of witness statements	10 weeks
Exchange of experts' reports	14 weeks
Sending of listing questionnaires by the court	20 weeks
Filing of completed listing questionnaires	22 weeks
Hearing	30 weeks

These periods will run from the date of the notice of allocation.

In fact, experience of the fast track has shown that even these directions can be simplified. The majority of personal injury claims are on the fast track. Compliance with the personal injury pre-action protocol will have ensured that a suitable medical expert – possibly a joint expert – has been chosen prior to the issue of proceedings. The medical report will be annexed to the claimant's Particulars of Claim. It is not usually necessary in the majority of fast-track cases for defendants to go to the expense of instructing their own expert. Defendants are better advised to co-operate in assisting the claimant to choose an acceptable expert or, alternatively, instructing a single joint expert with the claimant. Thus, in practice, 'exchange of experts' reports' is not usually necessary so far as medical evidence is concerned. Instead of ordering exchange of such reports, the court gives permission for parties to ask questions of the expert within a period of 4 weeks from allocation with such questions to be answered 3 weeks thereafter.

Where it considers that some or all the steps in the above specimen timetable are not necessary, the court will omit them or vary them as explained and will, if possible, direct an earlier trial. This may happen where the court is informed that a pre-action protocol has been complied with and that steps which it would otherwise have ordered have already been taken. Rather than fix a trial date, the court usually fixes a trial window, not exceeding 3 weeks, within which the trial is to take place pursuant to r 28.2. The standard period between the giving of directions and the trial for a fast-track case is not more than 30 weeks and a trial window will not exceed 3 weeks. It is not usually possible to give a trial date that far ahead and the actual trial date, within the window, will be given when the court has considered the pre-trial checklists (listing questionnaires) which the parties will be ordered to file. It is often possible to give a trial window less than 30 weeks ahead, but although the court is anxious to assist the parties with a swift resolution of the dispute, there are disadvantages in listing cases too quickly. Experience has shown that the settlement rate of cases allocated to the fast track is extremely high, and it is in no one's interests to rush to trial a case which otherwise could have settled by negotiation.

As with cases allocated to the small claims track, the aim of case management of fast-track cases is for the court to give all necessary directions on paper without requiring the attendance of the parties. The parties should have to attend court only once and that is for the trial itself.

Directions required in fast-track cases are usually so obvious that disputes are rare. However, where a party is dissatisfied with a direction given by the court, that party should take steps to vary it as soon as possible. This can be done either by agreement with the other side pursuant to r 2.11, or by application to the court. By r 2.11, unless the CPR or a Practice Direction specifically provides otherwise, the time specified by a rule or by the court for a person to do any act may be varied by the written agreement of the parties. However, by r 28.4, a party must apply to the court if he or she wishes to vary the date which a court has fixed for the return of the pre-trial checklists (listing questionnaires) or for trial or as a trial window.

The court will assume for the purposes of any later application that a party who did not appeal a case management decision and who made no application to vary within 14 days of service of the order containing the directions was content that these directions were correct in the circumstances then existing. The proper procedure is to agree a variation with the other side if permitted and, if not, to make application to the court. An appeal is necessary only if an application is not successful and the party considers that the decision is wrong. An application to reconsider is, if possible, heard by the judge who gave the directions and, if this is not possible, by another judge of the same level. An appeal is, of course, to a higher judge, which means in practice, in county court cases that the appeal is from the district judge to the circuit judge and, in High Court cases, from the district judge or master to the High Court judge.

Where a party fails to comply with a direction given by the court, any other party may apply for an order to enforce compliance or for a sanction to be imposed or both. A party entitled to apply for such an order must do so without delay but should first warn the other party of this intention (see further PD 28, para 5).

Once fixed, the trial window must be considered sacrosanct. (Hence the need to inform the court of any relevant absences, eg holidays, in the allocation questionnaire. It is too late to leave this until the pre-trial checklist.) Paragraph 5.4(1) of PD 28 states: 'The court will not allow a failure to comply with directions to lead to the postponement of the trial unless the circumstances of the case are exceptional'. If it is practicable to do so the court will exercise its powers in a manner that enables the case to come on for trial on the date or within the period previously set. In particular, the court will assess what steps each party should take to prepare the case for trial, direct that those steps are taken in the shortest possible time and impose a sanction for non-compliance. Such a sanction may, for example, deprive a party of the right to raise or contest an issue or to rely on evidence to which the direction relates. For example, if a claimant has failed to serve and update his or her schedule of special damages, the court would not permit this to be done late and would require the claimant to rely on the original schedule. If a defendant has failed to serve a counter-schedule, he or she may not be permitted to do so.

At the very least, all costs of all parties incurred in connection with any application to adjourn will be ordered to be paid by the party in default. The court will usually summarily assess such costs and order them to be paid forthwith.

Litigants and their lawyers must be in no doubt that the court will regard the postponement of a trial as an order of last resort. The court usually exercises its power to require parties as well as their legal representatives to attend court at a hearing where such an order is to be sought.

In a fast-track case, the pre-trial checklist provides an opportunity for fine-tuning the directions. In practice, usually the court needs to do no more than fix a trial date within the trial window, fix a trial timetable and order preparation of the trial bundle.

Fast-track standard directions are set out in the Appendix to PD 28.

MULTI-TRACK – CASE MANAGEMENT

A High Court case proceeding in London will be case managed at the Royal Courts of Justice by a master; if proceeding in a district registry it will be case managed at that registry by a district judge. Not all county courts, however, case manage multi-track cases. The case management of a claim allocated to the multi-track would normally be dealt with at a 'civil trial centre'. A county court which is not a civil trial centre (often referred to as a satellite court or, as para 10 of PD 26 puts it, a 'feeder court') will have a designated civil trial centre. Where a judge sitting in a feeder court decides that the claim should be dealt with on the multi-track, he or she will normally make an order allocating the claim to the multi-track, giving case management directions and transferring the claim to a civil trial centre. However, a judge sitting in a feeder court may, rather than making an allocation order himself, transfer the claim to a civil trial centre for the decision to be taken there. There is provision in para 10.2 of PD 26 for certain multi-track cases to be case managed at the feeder court with the agreement of the designated civil judge.

If the claim has been issued in, or automatically transferred to, a civil trial centre it will, of course, be allocated and case managed there.

The hallmarks of the multi-track are the ability of the court to deal with cases of widely differing values and complexity, and the flexibility given to the court in the way it manages a case appropriate to its particular needs. Unlike the small claims track and the fast track, neither the CPR nor any Practice Direction contains specimen directions for use in multi-track cases.

On allocating a claim to the multi-track, the court may give directions without a hearing, including fixing a trial date or a trial window. Alternatively, and whether or not it fixes a trial window, it may either give directions for certain steps to be taken and fix a date for a case management conference or simply fix a date for a case management conference. Wherever appropriate, the court will give such directions as it can to enable some progress to be made in pre-trial preparation prior to a case management conference.

The court will seek to tailor its directions to the needs of the case and the steps which the parties have already taken and of which the court has been informed (this should be done by careful completion of the allocation questionnaire).

By r 29.4, if the parties agree proposals for the management of the proceedings (including a proposed trial window) and the court considers the proposals to be suitable, it may approve them without a hearing and give directions in the terms proposed. Every effort should be made to take advantage of this rule. Bear in mind that the parties have a duty to assist the court in furthering the overriding objective (r 1.3) and are encouraged to try to agree directions (PD 29, para 4.6). Directions agreed by the parties should address the following issues:

(1)   filing and service of any reply or amended statement of case that may be required;
(2)   dates for the service of any request for further information under PD 18 and of questions to experts under rule 35.6;
(3)   disclosure;
(4)   exchange of witness statements;
(5)   the use of a single joint expert wherever possible and, in cases where it is not possible, the exchange of expert evidence (including whether exchange is to be simultaneous or sequential) and for without prejudice discussions between experts. As ever, efforts must be made to limit the use of expert evidence but the court recognises that in multi-track cases it will invariably be appropriate for each party to instruct an expert on the main issue of dispute. For example, if the main area of dispute in a personal injury claim concerns orthopaedic injuries it will be appropriate for each party to have permission to rely on the medical evidence of a consultant orthopaedic surgeon. However, joint medical experts may still be appropriate for secondary issues. Thus psychiatrists, neurologists, radiologists or any other expert could be instructed jointly on these secondary issues. It is extremely unlikely that the court will give all parties permission to instruct their own experts in all disciplines;
(6)   fixing a date for a case management conference and/or a trial window and the filing of pre-trial checklists (listing questionnaires).

By para 4.7 of PD 29, to obtain the court's approval, the agreed directions must set out a timetable by reference to calendar dates. The court will scrutinise the timetable carefully and will be concerned to see that any proposed trial date, trial window and case management conference is no later than is reasonably necessary.

CASE MANAGEMENT CONFERENCES

Whilst not all multi-track cases have a case management conference, the majority do and some have more than one.

At any case management conference, the court will review the steps which the parties have taken in the preparation of the case (and in particular their compliance with any directions that the court has already given); decide and give directions about the steps to be taken to secure the progress of the case in accordance with the overriding objective; and ensure, as far as it can, that all agreements that can be reached between the parties about the matters in issue and the conduct of the claim are made and recorded.

By r 29.3, if a party has a legal representative, who is familiar with the case and who has sufficient authority to deal with any issues that are likely to arise, that representative must attend a case management conference. (Where the inadequacy of the person attending or of his or her instructions leads to the adjournment of the conference, the court will expect to make a wasted costs order – see PD 29, para 5.2.) Prior to a case management conference, the claimant should prepare a case summary designed to assist the court to understand the issues in the case and deal with questions arising. Case summaries should set out a brief chronology of the claim, the issues of fact which are agreed or in dispute, and the evidence needed to decide them. It should not exceed 500 words in length and should be agreed with the other parties if possible.

Parties should also seek to agree directions that will be required at a case management conference and file these with the court prior to that conference. If proposed directions cannot be agreed, both sides should file a draft of the order which they will be inviting the court to make.

Paragraph 5.8 of PD 29 requires a party who wishes to obtain an order not routinely made at a case management conference and who believes that the application will be opposed, to issue and serve the application in time for it to be heard at the case management conference.

Experience has shown that one of the most common issues arising at a case management conference is the use of expert evidence. The court will not give permission to use expert evidence unless it can identify each expert by name or field in its order. The court will say, if possible, whether the evidence is to be given orally, or in the form of a written report, or may have to defer that decision to a later case management conference. Parties should not obtain expert evidence without discussions with the other side. As noted above, it is particularly important, wherever possible, to make use of the provisions in Part 35 for joint single experts. 'A party who obtains expert evidence before obtaining a direction about it, does so at his own risk as to costs, except where he obtains that evidence in compliance with a pre-action protocol' (PD 29, para 5.5(2)).

Use of expert evidence prior to the CPR was becoming a growth industry, and one of the key aims of the CPR is to limit expert evidence to that which is necessary to decide the case. Certain types of expert, eg so-called 'accident reconstruction experts', have all but disappeared since the introduction of the CPR.

It is now the court's job actively to manage cases and, therefore, legal representatives attending a case management conference should expect the district judge to take a full part in the conference. The judge does not simply sit and listen and give a decision at the end. The judge will have read the case summary and chronology (and where possible the full file) prior to the case management conference and will have considerable experience in the sort of directions required in the type of case under consideration. The judge will be concerned to ensure adequate but not excessive preparation and to allow adequate but not excessive time for this.

In furtherance of the court's duty to 'make use of technology', many case management conferences are held by telephone, thus saving expense.

A party dissatisfied with a decision given at a case management conference can appeal. However, courts are anxious to discourage such appeals and they are rarely successful. The court is anxious to try the case itself and avoid satellite disputes.

A final matter that has to be considered at a case management conference is the appropriate venue for trial and level of the trial judge. Should a case proceeding in the High Court be transferred to the county court pursuant to CCA 1984, s 40? Should a county court case be transferred to the High Court?

If the case is to be tried at a different place from that where it is being managed it should preferably be transferred to that other court for final case management there. A decision on whether a High Court case can be released to be tried by a circuit judge pursuant to SCA 1981, s 9 can be made only by a High Court judge. However, the district judge managing the case often assists the High Court judge in making that decision.

There can be no standard format for a case management conference for it is of the essence of the multi-track that each case receives tailor-made directions. Thus consider carefully all other matters. For example, if liability is no longer an issue, has an interim payment been agreed? Or even if liability is an issue, is it a case where interim payment can still be obtained? Is it a case where evidence can be given by video link? Is it a case where a deposition needs to be taken?

Case management conferences, as already noted, should be attended by a legal representative fully conversant with the case. It is, of course, permissible to brief counsel but this is rarely necessary. The solicitor conducting the case is usually the best person to conduct the case management conference.

A court will usually allow about half an hour for a case management conference. But longer should be sought if necessary, in particular if any application (which must be made in accordance with Part 23) is to be made and to be heard at the same time as the case management conference.

As a case management conference is an integral part of modern procedure, the usual costs order is 'costs in the case', although of course a different order can be made if a party is in default.

Chapter 24

THE SMALL CLAIMS TRACK

Parties to a small claim are very rarely legally represented, but you may find that you are instructed in a small claim, and that your client is prepared to pay your costs, although there is very little prospect of those costs being recovered, even if the client is successful. Sometimes, your client may wish you to prepare the case for the hearing but, to save costs, will conduct the case in person, and, on occasions, you may find yourself instructed at the very last minute by a litigant in person who cannot, after all, face attending the hearing without a legal representative. Whatever the circumstances, small claims are a useful way of gaining experience of handling claims and advocacy.

Preparing for a claim that is worth less than £5,000 can take as long, and require as much thought, as a claim on the fast track. The reality is that it is not cost-effective, except as a training exercise, for a fee-earner, however junior, to be engaged for any longer than is strictly necessary on work of this kind. This often leads to very shoddy preparation and presentation, which is not helpful to the district judge who deals with the case. However, if a proper analysis of the issues in the case is carried out, and thought given to what evidence is required, a small claim can be effectively prepared within a reasonable time and presented well.

DIRECTIONS

In the majority of cases that are allocated to the small claims track, directions will be given by the district judge on paper and a hearing date fixed. Specimen standard directions that the district judge may issue are to be found in the Appendix to CPR Part 26, which contains the rules and Practice Directions that govern the small claims track. In certain cases, the district judge will find it necessary to issue a special direction, and some examples of special directions are also set out in the Appendix. The court may make further directions, or vary or revoke existing directions, at any time.

CLARIFICATION OF A PARTY'S CASE

The statements of case in a small claim are usually very informal. In a case where litigants appear in person, statement of case are invariably handwritten, and much is left to the imagination. There is no formal procedure on the small claims track for one party to request further information from another and, in practice, it is the district judge on allocation who will give directions in order to obtain clarification of what a party's case is, or to require him or her to file and serve documents upon which the case appears to turn. If the district judge considers that there is no cause of action, or no defence with a real prospect of success, the statement of case will generally be struck out before or at the allocation stage. Sometimes the district judge will give the party a further opportunity to set out the case properly within a prescribed time-limit.

PRELIMINARY HEARING

Very occasionally, it may be necessary for the district judge to direct that there be a preliminary hearing. This may be because there are special directions that are needed which are best explained to the parties in person, for example concerning the instruction of an expert witness. Alternatively, the district judge may consider that either party has no real prospect of success and may wish to dispose of the matter as soon as possible. If there is a preliminary hearing, then, unless the parties agree, the district judge cannot make a final order at that stage and a final hearing will have to be fixed.

DISCLOSURE OF DOCUMENTS

Unlike the other tracks, there is no provision for formal disclosure and inspection on the small claims track. The standard direction will be for the filing and exchange of documents, including witness statements, by a certain date, or no later than 14 days before the hearing, with the originals to be brought to the hearing. There is no requirement for a list of documents or a disclosure statement.

In practice, documents are often seen for the first time on the day of the hearing, and it is not only litigants in person who routinely fail to comply with the direction for disclosure. Quite often, litigants in person will urge the district judge to penalise solicitors who have failed to comply! It is very unhelpful to all concerned if documents are not filed and served before the hearing, and the court can decide not to take a document or a witness's evidence into account or to adjourn the hearing if the direction has not been complied with.

However, generally speaking, the district judge will be concerned to proceed with the hearing and to ensure that all the available evidence is taken into account, as long as this does not cause prejudice to the party objecting. If there are many new documents to consider, or the documents raise new matters which the other party is not prepared for, then, if standing the case down for a short while will not solve the problem, the district judge will usually give the defaulting party the option of paying at least the other party's expenses in attending court if there has to be an adjournment, or proceeding without the evidence that is objected to.

WITNESS STATEMENTS

The requirements of CPR Part 32 relating to evidence do not apply to small claims, save that the court retains the power to restrict evidence. However, it is a fundamental part of a fair hearing that the evidence upon which a party intends to rely is disclosed in advance so that a party is not taken by surprise. Very often, the evidence that a witness will give has already been rehearsed in correspondence, and so the absence of a formal witness statement is not critical, but this is not always the case.

Witness statements are usually overlooked by litigants in person, and very often overlooked by solicitors. The directions will invariably provide for them to be disclosed at the same time as the other documents in the case and the parties are warned that, if a witness statement is not disclosed in accordance with the directions, the court may not take account of the witness's evidence. As with directions for disclosure of documents, failure to serve witness statements is a common source of objection by a party affected. Again, the district judge will take a pragmatic and not a technical approach, preferring not to adjourn the case unless there is a real risk of injustice if the hearing is not adjourned. If there does have to be an adjournment, the party in default will be expected to pay any expenses incurred by the other party in attending court.

EXPERTS

Although most of CPR Part 35 that relates to experts and assessors does not apply to small claims, the court's powers to restrict expert evidence to that which is reasonably required to resolve the proceedings and to direct the appointment of a single joint expert do apply, as does the provision that an expert's overriding duty is to the court and not to the party or parties instructing him or her. The definition of 'an expert' for small claims purposes is much looser than it might be for a claim of greater value, thus enabling useful technical evidence to be given to the court by suitable people who may not be in the same league as the experts used on the other tracks. Cost is a consideration in this, since the most that a successful party can recover towards the cost of instructing an expert is £200, which includes the preparation of the report and any court attendance.

Reliance on experts on the small claims track will usually be limited, and, in any event, permission has to be given by the court if an expert witness is to be used. Although the parties will have expressed their views about the need for expert evidence on the allocation questionnaire, the district judge will look at the statements of case and any other documents on the court file, identify the issues, and decide whether expert evidence will be necessary for the case to be decided properly. For example, where a building dispute turns on what the parties agreed would be done for the agreed price, this will be a question of fact for the judge to decide on the basis of the evidence of the contracting parties. However, if the dispute is about a technical building or engineering matter that is not simply a question of cosmetic appearance, then it is likely that the district judge will order the parties to jointly instruct an appropriate expert to deal with the relevant issues.

If the district judge gives a direction for expert evidence, this will usually provide for how the cost of the report is to be shared, and will state the date by which the report must be filed. When a joint expert is involved, it is sensible to take the opportunity to try to promote a settlement between the parties, or, at the very least, narrow the issues between them. In cases in which a joint expert's report is obtained, it should not be necessary for the author of the report to attend court to give evidence – the conclusions in the report should be clear enough for the district judge to make a decision. Indeed, if the report's conclusions are clear, it should be possible to conclude the matter without the need for a hearing. It is sometimes difficult for parties to agree on a suitable expert. If you are in this position, you should write immediately to the district judge for further directions and, if there is likely to be a delay, ask for the hearing date to be put back.

Occasionally, one or both of the parties will have obtained their own expert's report, usually before proceedings are begun. Each will want permission to use the report, but, as the reports' conclusions will generally be different, in order to decide which expert evidence he or she prefers, the judge will almost certainly need to hear oral evidence. This will be an expensive exercise, and it may be more cost effective simply to obtain a joint report from a new expert.

PHOTOGRAPHS/VIDEOS/SKETCH PLANS

There will be cases when it will be of great assistance at the hearing to have photographs or a sketch plan available. The obvious example is a road traffic case, when it will usually be helpful for the district judge to know the layout of the accident scene. In some road traffic cases, it may be important that the judge is aware of road widths and relative distances, but, all too often, this is overlooked when sketch plans are prepared.

The court will usually direct photographs and a sketch plan in a road traffic case, but if you consider that they may be helpful in another case, provided that you have sent copies to the other party, the district judge will generally be pleased to see anything that will assist him or her to understand the case, even if this has not been specifically directed. If you are referring to photographs, you should ensure that good colour copies are available for all parties and the district judge, and that they are numbered. You may wish to use video footage, for example in a holiday claim. If you do, you must supply a copy in advance to the other party, and you must notify the court so that arrangements may be made for viewing the video at the hearing.

AGREEING THE COST OF RECTIFICATION OR REPAIR

The standard directions will usually provide for the issues to be narrowed by the parties attempting to agree the cost of repair or remedial work, or other financial loss, subject to liability.

SUMMARY JUDGMENT

This is available on the small claims track, but, in practice, if the district judge has not already struck out a statement of case that fails to contain reasonable grounds for bringing or defending a claim, or listed the matter for a preliminary hearing because there are no real prospects of success, it will usually be as quick to wait for the final hearing date as to make an application for summary judgment, which will, of course, attract a fee. However, if an application for summary judgment is made before a case is allocated (eg simultaneously with filing the allocation questionnaire) and is successful, the limited costs regime of the small claims track will not apply as the case will not have reached the stage of being allocated. Instead, fixed costs will be awarded in accordance with CPR Part 45. (See 'Costs on the small claims track' below and Chapter 39, Costs.)

DECISION ON PAPER

When considering the papers on allocation, the district judge may decide that the matter is straightforward enough to dispose of on paper, ie without the need for a hearing. If this is the view the district judge takes, notice of this has to be given to the parties, and they have an opportunity to object or agree within the time allowed by the court. If the parties agree, the district judge will deal finally with the matter on paper and send out a short, written decision. If the parties object, the district judge will give directions leading to a hearing.

CONDUCT OF THE HEARING

Although referred to as a 'small claims hearing', it is, nonetheless, a trial, and the judge has to decide the factual issues in the case on the basis of the evidence that is presented by the parties, apply the relevant law and give a reasoned decision or judgment. However, many of the provisions relating to fast-track and multi-track trials do not apply to the small claims track.

Rule 27.8 provides that:

(1)   the court may adopt any method of proceeding at a hearing that it considers to be fair;

(2)   hearings will be informal;

(3)   the strict rules of evidence do not apply;

(4)   the court need not take evidence on oath;

(5)   the court may limit cross-examination; and

(6)   the court must give reasons for its decision.

Small claims hearings are public hearings, but are usually held in the district judge's chambers and very rarely in open court like other trials because they are intended to be informal and they usually follow a less rigid structure. Where appropriate, the district judge may hear the claim in a party's home, for example if it concerns a dispute over carpet fitting, or such other place that may be relevant to the subject matter of the dispute, if to do so would assist.

The district judge will have read the papers before the hearing begins. Styles of conducting hearings vary, but most district judges adopt an interventionist approach, and so you need to be prepared to have your carefully honed opening dispensed with entirely. It is unlikely that the district judge will expect a witness to take the oath. Unlike a more formal trial on the other tracks, when the judge will usually only ask questions at the end of a witness's evidence, you will find that district judges will quite often ask questions of a witness either before or during the course of the evidence as well. Do not be put off by this – simply wait until the judge has indicated that you may continue with your examination of a witness. The judge has power to limit cross-examination and to take the evidence in any order that he or she may wish, provided, of course, that the hearing is still conducted fairly. You will become used to the way small claims hearings are dealt with in your local courts, you will also learn that there is no substitute for knowing all the facts of your case, and being able to put your hand on relevant documents quickly.

THE RULES OF EVIDENCE

It is said that the rules of evidence are not strictly applied to hearings on the small claims track. This means that the district judge is not going to be interested in technical objections to the use of hearsay evidence, or the use of statements from witnesses who do not attend to be cross-examined about their evidence. However, the relaxation of the rules of evidence is very much a matter for the district judge concerned, and it would be foolish to imagine that he or she will give much weight to the written statement of a witness who is not at court if this is contradicted by oral evidence from a witness, present at the hearing, who the district judge considers to be reliable. When you are deciding how to present your evidence it is a question of balancing what is proportionate with what is necessary to prove the case.

SETTLING BEFORE THE HEARING

Many small claims settle before the final hearing. You should always inform the court if a case settles. If you are able to give reasonable notice, the time may be re-allocated. Many courts overlist small claims to accommodate some cases settling at short notice, but any notice that you can give is better than no notice at all, as the district judge will then know at the beginning of the day how much time he or she has available to deal with the hearings that will be proceeding.

SUBMITTING A CASE IN WRITING

There is a facility for a party who does not wish to attend the hearing to ask the court to consider written and other documentary submissions in his or her absence. CPR r 27.9(1) provides that he or she must give at least 7 days' notice in writing to the court of that intention. If a party who has given notice under r 27.9(1) does not attend court for the hearing, the district judge will prepare a written note of his or her decision, which will be sent to the parties. If you have a client whose case is proceeding in a court some distance away, and the sums at stake hardly merit the trouble and expense of attending the hearing in person, in a straightforward case, you may advise your client to make written representations under r 27.9(1).

NON-ATTENDANCE AT THE HEARING

If a claimant fails to give notice to the court that he or she wishes his or her case to be considered on paper and does not attend the court, the judge will usually strike out the claim, unless there appears to be some reason why it would be better to adjourn the hearing to another day. If a defendant fails to appear and the claimant does appear or has given notice under r 27.9(1), the court may decide the claim on the basis of the claimant's evidence alone. If neither party appears, the claim and any counterclaim will usually be struck out.

If a party who has failed to attend and has failed to give notice under r 27.9(1) wishes to challenge the decision made in his or her absence, an application may be made for the order to be set aside and for there to be another hearing. The application will be to the district judge, and will be granted only if there is a good reason for the failure to attend and reasonable prospects of success if there were to be another hearing. A good reason for failing to attend may be a sudden emergency, failure to receive notice of the hearing date, or a genuine case of forgetfulness. Some district judges may require corroborating evidence where this is available.

COSTS ON THE SMALL CLAIMS TRACK

The special provisions relating to costs in small claims are effective from the time that a claim is allocated to the small claims track. If judgment is entered before allocation, then the special provisions do not apply, unless the district judge allocates to the small claims track for disposal. This is often the preferred course, as it upholds the principle of proportionality. Where a case is allocated to the small claims track, this will not affect any orders for costs made before allocation. A case may be allocated to the small claims track by consent, even though the value of the claim exceeds the limit for the small claims track. In this type of case, it will be treated as if it were proceeding on the fast track for costs purposes, save that the court may award trial costs that are lower than those allowed on the fast track.

One often hears of the 'no costs' rule applying to small claims. However, it is not accurate to say that there are no costs implications on the small claims track. Whether to award costs, and how much to award, is, as with most aspects of costs on the other tracks, a question of discretion for the judge. However, on the small claims track, the general rule is that there are limits to the amounts that can be awarded. These will be the prescribed fixed costs on issue, and these will only arise where a claimant's solicitor has issued the claim.

In addition to any fixed costs on issue, the court may order a party to pay all or any of the following:

(1)   all or part of the court fees paid by another party, for example on issue of the claim or counterclaim and on filing of the allocation questionnaire (a fee is payable only where the amount claimed exceeds £1,000);

(2)   a sum not exceeding £50 to each party or witness, for lost earnings owing to attendance at the hearing or staying away from home in order to attend the hearing;

(3)   expenses that a party or witness has reasonably incurred in travelling to and from the hearing or staying away from home for the purposes of attending the hearing. There is no upper limit on the amount recoverable, save that the expenses must have been reasonably incurred. It will not usually be reasonable to make the paying party meet the costs of lavish accommodation or dining, and the district judge will make a judgment about what might be a reasonable cost in the particular circumstances;

(4)   a sum not exceeding £200 for each expert's fee. This will include preparation of the report and any attendance at court.

The rules do not provide for the cost of photocopying, preparation of plans, photographs, videos or other out-of-pocket expenses to be recovered from the unsuccessful party.

UNREASONABLE BEHAVIOUR

In cases in which a party is found to have behaved unreasonably, the court may make an order for that party to pay costs which the judge will summarily assess. The question arises as to what may be regarded as unreasonable behaviour, sufficient to persuade the district judge to make a substantive order for costs. CPR Part 36, relating to payment into court and offers to settle, does not apply to small claims, but this does not mean that parties should not attempt to settle their dispute without a hearing. It is arguable that, if an open offer to settle is made, and this is not beaten at the final hearing, the party refusing the offer has behaved unreasonably and costs consequences should follow. Similarly, any party who deliberately persists in making or defending a claim that he or she knows or ought to know has no prospect of success could be found to be behaving unreasonably.

District judges will be reluctant to erode the general principle that the small claims procedure should be available without penalty, even to those who are misguided in their belief in the strength of their case, but, equally, they will wish to mark any attempt to abuse the system by an unscrupulous party.

If you wish to pursue an order for costs on the basis that your opponent has behaved unreasonably, you should file and serve a statement of costs in the prescribed form because, if you are successful, the district judge will carry out a summary assessment. It will also be advantageous to forewarn your opponent so that you are not defeated by an argument that it was not fair to spring your application on him or her at the hearing.

If your application for a summary assessment of your costs is successful, you will need to bear in mind that, as well as looking to see that the costs claimed are reasonable in amount and reasonably incurred, the district judge will also want to be satisfied that they are proportionate. In a small claim, it is possible that even your reasonable costs are well in excess of the amount in issue, and most district judges will be reluctant to make an award that is disproportionate to the amount of money involved, the importance of the case, the complexity of the issues and the relative financial positions of the parties. You must, therefore, accept any reduction in your costs with good grace.

APPEALS

The CPR brought the rules relating to appeals in small claims in line with the other tracks. CPR Part 52 will, therefore, apply.

Chapter 25

THE FAST TRACK

CPR Part 28 sets out the general provisions that apply to the management of cases allocated to the fast track. The key objectives on the fast track are economy, expedition and proportionality.

CASE MANAGEMENT DIRECTIONS

Case management by the court is at the heart of the CPR. In Chapter 24 it was shown how on the small claims track the conduct of the claim was determined at the outset by the directions made by the district judge. The same applies to the fast track, and indeed the multi-track.

Once allocation questionnaires have been completed, the file is put before the district judge who will consider the allocation questionnaires, the statements of case, reports and any other documents on the court file. If you wish the district judge to consider any further documents that you may send with the allocation questionnaire, PD 28, para 3.4 requires you to confirm either that the contents have been agreed by every other party, or whether the documents have been sent to them, and if so, when.

If the claim is allocated to the fast track in accordance with the criteria for allocation, the district judge will give directions and fix a timetable leading to trial.

Specimen standard directions that the district judge may issue are to be found in the Appendix to Part 28. It will be clear that there is an emphasis on keeping pre-trial preparation to the minimum, in accordance with the overriding objective.

The district judge will do his or her best to issue directions on the basis of the information on the file, in particular the allocation questionnaire, and any proposed or agreed directions submitted by the parties. However, if he or she does not have sufficient information to give meaningful directions, or there is a matter that requires clarification, the district judge will direct that a case management hearing be listed.

On the fast track it is preferable for the expense of case management hearings to be avoided, and this points to the need to give careful thought to the completion of the allocation questionnaire and to provide the court with as much additional information as possible. One area that frequently prevents the district judge from issuing standard directions is ambiguity in the allocation questionnaires concerning the expert evidence. The district judge cannot give directions about expert evidence if it is not clear whether the claimant's expert evidence is disputed, and if so whether the defendant has already obtained a report or has only recently instructed an expert to provide a report.

It is, of course, open to the district judge to impose costs sanctions on any party whose inadequate completion of the allocation questionnaire makes a case management conference necessary.

AGREED DIRECTIONS

The court recognises that the solicitors having the conduct of the case are usually in the best position to know what directions may be necessary, and the time scale within which they can comply with them. It is for this reason that solicitors are encouraged to submit a draft of any agreed directions, or any directions sought even if they are not agreed, with the allocation questionnaire. However, the court will not simply rubber stamp the directions without considering the papers on the file, and the district judge will substitute his or her own directions for any of those that are – proposed that he or she considers to be unnecessary or inappropriate. PD 28, paras 3.6 and 3.7 set out guidelines to be followed if you wish to submit agreed directions for approval. The experience of many district judges is that, in a number of cases, agreed directions submitted for approval indicate that the solicitors have failed to take full notice of the Practice Direction. For example, there will be reference to 'disclosure by list in 4 weeks' when the Practice Direction makes it clear that the proposed directions must set out a timetable by reference to calendar dates, or in some cases important directions will have been omitted altogether. If, when drafting agreed or proposed directions, you bear in mind that the court will base its orders on the specimen directions contained in the Appendix to Part 28, and make sure that you follow the Practice Direction (PD 28, paras 3.6 and 3.7), you will find that the district judge will be more likely to approve your proposals.

CASE MANAGEMENT HEARINGS

Even if the parties are local, case management hearings are most efficiently dealt with by telephone. If the judge has not directed that the hearing take place by telephone, it is open to the parties to agree on this and request the court's approval, which is likely to be forthcoming.

It must be stressed that, on the fast track, case management hearings should not usually be necessary if the parties have given all relevant information on the filing of the allocation questionnaire.

TIMETABLE

It is a requirement of the rules that when a case is allocated to the fast track, as well as giving case management directions, the district judge will set a timetable for each step to be taken until trial (r 28.2(1)). A trial date or a trial period of up to 3 weeks (often referred to as a 'trial window') will appear in the notice of allocation that is sent by the court to the parties, and this will be no more than 30 weeks hence. A typical timetable is set out in PD 28, para 3.12.

When you have notice of the trial window it is up to you to notify all your witnesses. In the allocation questionnaire you should have noted any dates on which you, an expert or an essential witness would be unable to attend court for the trial. If you have failed to do so, and you discover that a vital witness has had a holiday booked in the trial window for some time, you will have some explaining to do to the court. All the same, the sooner any potential problems are notified to the court the better. You are more likely to persuade a judge to alter the trial window when it is 28 weeks away than when it is only 4 weeks away.

VARYING THE TIMETABLE

It is by no means uncommon for the court's timetable to slip, and for the parties to agree between themselves in writing revised dates for disclosure and exchange of evidence. This is acknowledged in the Rules. Rule 2.11 states that, unless the Rules or a Practice Direction provides otherwise or the court orders otherwise, the time specified by a rule or by the court for a person to do any act may be varied by the written agreement of the parties. However, it is important to note that the Rules do not allow the parties to agree to vary the date that the court has fixed for the return of the pre-trial checklist under r 28.5 or the trial date or trial window, nor the dates by which other steps should be taken if to do so would have the effect of delaying the trial (r 28.4). It is the cornerstone of the efficient conduct of proceedings on the fast track that the trial date is not moved unless there is a very good reason for it.

If a party wishes to vary the timetable in a way that will affect the trial, application must be made to the court but it must be understood that trial dates will not be moved lightly or without stringent enquiry by the court. Even if a party succeeds in the application, costs sanctions will usually follow.

DISCLOSURE OF DOCUMENTS

The standard directions issued by the court will contain provision for disclosure of documents. Disclosure will be ordered either by list, or by serving copies with a disclosure statement. It will be standard disclosure, unless the court orders otherwise, and the direction may limit it further, for example to documents relating to damage or, where there is to be a split trial, to documents relating to the issue of liability. The allocation questionnaire may have disclosed that one party has requested essential documents from the other which have not been provided, and the district judge may then specifically direct that those documents be provided as part of the disclosure process. Likewise, if the allocation questionnaires reveal that disclosure has already taken place, or that for some other reason disclosure is not necessary, the court may issue a direction that no disclosure of documents is required.

As with all directions that are given by the court, the date and time for compliance will form part of the order. Generally this will be at least 4 weeks from the date of the order for directions.

WITNESS STATEMENTS

The court will direct the exchange of witness statements, usually 4 to 6 weeks from the date for disclosure of documents. Invariably, the order will be for simultaneous exchange. There will only be very limited circumstances in which the sequential disclosure of witness statements will be appropriate.

The direction will usually provide that unless the statement of an intended witness is served within the time specified then the evidence of that witness will not be received at trial unless the trial judge gives permission. This is, of course, subject to the ability of the parties to agree in writing to vary certain time-limits.

On occasions it will be appropriate for there to be a direction that the evidence of a witness be limited to a particular issue of the case. Rule 32.1(1) gives the court the power to control evidence in this way.

EXPERTS

The court will have to give directions as to service of experts' reports. The court's permission is always required if a party wishes to use expert evidence. Rule 26.6(5) provides that, on the fast track, oral expert evidence at trial will be limited to one expert per party in relation to any expert field, and expert evidence in two fields only. However, even with a potential maximum of four experts giving oral evidence, the trial would be in danger of exceeding the one day that is generally allowed on the fast track. It is doubtless for this reason that r 35.5 provides that, in fast-track cases, the court will not direct an expert to attend a hearing unless it is necessary to do so in the interests of justice. There are obvious costs benefits as well if experts are not required to attend the trial, and the district judge will give other directions that are intended to limit the unnecessary involvement of experts. For example, where one party has indicated that expert evidence is in dispute and that he or she wishes to instruct his or her own expert, the district judge may order that the expert be required to answer questions that are put to him or her in an attempt to reduce or eliminate the areas in issue. Where each party has an expert in a particular field, the court will invariably direct that the experts confer in order that they may identify the issues between them and reach agreement if possible, and then prepare a statement for the court setting out the issues on which they agree and those on which they disagree, with their reasons. The district judge will be relying upon the parties to give a clear picture in their allocation questionnaires of the position in relation to expert evidence. In a personal injury claim, the court file will contain the medical report that was attached to the claim form, but this may not be up to date. Unless the parties tell the court whether further medical evidence has been obtained or is proposed to be obtained, and by whom, and whether there is a dispute about any aspect of the medical evidence, the district judge will either have to make assumptions that may not be valid, or direct that there be a case management conference in order to clear up any uncertainty. This is unsatisfactory because it increases the costs.

STATEMENT OF FINANCIAL LOSS

In cases in which there is an ongoing claim for financial loss, for example a claim for lost earnings, the court will usually direct that an up-to-date statement of past and future financial loss is served, with documentation in support, usually near to the trial window. Provision will also be made for the defendant to file a counter-statement.

SPLIT TRIALS

The timetable from allocation to trial on the fast track is tight and all too often it proves impossible to accommodate expert witnesses who are generally booked up many months ahead. The solution in many of the less straightforward cases is for there to be a split trial: that is, for liability to be tried first, and then, if necessary, for there to be a trial to decide the amount of damages.

Take as an example a claim arising out of a road traffic accident where there is a dispute on both liability and amount. The claimant has suffered a whiplash injury the symptoms from which he claims have persisted for 3 years since the accident. The defendant believes that the claimant's symptoms beyond 6 months to be constitutional and/or psychological, and requires further evidence. The parties are poles apart, and the medical evidence will not be available before the end of the trial window. This situation clearly points to a direction for a split trial. If the claimant is not successful in establishing liability, the matter ends there before the expense of medical experts attending trial has been incurred. If the claimant is successful on liability, experience shows that the arguments on amount are generally resolved without the need for a further hearing, but, of course, if necessary there will be a further trial to decide the amount of damages.

Split trials can also be used to dispose of any decisive factual issues at an early stage.

Before ordering a split trial, the district judge will need to be satisfied that to do so will result in a saving of time and/or costs and thus be in accordance with the overriding objective. This will usually be the case.

PRE-TRIAL CHECKLIST

The court's directions will include provision for pre-trial checklists to be filed by a certain date. This will be no later than 4 weeks before the start of the trial window. The pre-trial checklist is a vital document that is used by the Diary Manager at the Trial Centre to allocate trials between courts and judges. See further Chapter 31.

DIRECTIONS ON LISTING

The pre-trial checklist is also a vital document to the district judge. As soon as the pre-trial checklists are filed, the court file will be put before the district judge. From looking at the pre-trial checklist, it can be seen whether the timetable has been adhered to, and if not, whether he or she needs to give further directions or to call a case management conference in an attempt to put the case back on track.

If you have a specific application to make (eg to serve a further witness statement) you should make the application in accordance with CPR Part 23. It is incorrect practice to attempt to make an application under cover of the pre-trial checklist.

If the case is ready for trial, the district judge will give directions about the filing of a trial bundle and case summary, and may also give directions for the timetable to be followed at trial if he or she is to be the trial judge, but in practice this will often be left until the day of the trial itself. It will be sensible for you to try to agree a timetable with your opponent to present to the judge. Remember to make provision for reading time for the judge and time for considering the evidence and submissions as well as for giving judgment.

LISTING FOR TRIAL

If the district judge considers that there is nothing in the pre-trial checklists to suggest that the case will not be ready for trial within the trial window, he will order that the case be listed. The file will then be passed to the Diary Manager's office at the Trial Centre when a fixed date will be allocated. If the Diary Manager encounters any difficulty with this, the file will be referred back to the district judge, or to the trial judge for directions. The parties will receive at least 3 weeks' notice of the trial date unless they have agreed to accept shorter notice.

THE TRIAL

Trials on the fast track are intended to occupy the court for no longer than one day, which in court time is 5 hours. Every effort will have been made by careful case management to ensure that where evidence can be restricted to fit the time constraints it will be, rather than re-allocate the case to the multi-track.

The management of cases continues throughout the trial, with the trial judge setting a timetable for the various stages. The judge will have read the papers, and a direction may have been given either at the allocation or listing stage for the filing of an agreed case summary, usually limited to 250 words, which will mean that an opening may be dispensed with. Submissions will be strictly limited, and the time allowed for examination of witnesses will be restricted to that which is absolutely necessary. Witness statements will invariably stand as the evidence-in-chief, and to what extent supplementary questions will be allowed will depend upon the judge.

At the end of the trial, the trial judge should carry out a summary assessment of the costs so that all matters are concluded on that day.

CHALLENGING A DIRECTION MADE ON THE COURT'S INITIATIVE

As explained above, most of the directions made on the fast track will be made without the attendance of the parties at a hearing. The first that the parties or their solicitors will know about the order that the district judge has made will be when they receive the Notice of Allocation from the court with the directions set out.

It is important to look carefully at the directions and make sure that you can comply with each within the time scale allowed. If there is a good reason why you may not be able to comply by the given date then, as long as the delay will not affect the trial date, you may try to agree a longer time with your opponent. If your opponent will not agree to extend the time then you will have to apply to the court to vary the timetable. If you do not have either your opponent's or the court's agreement to the variation, then when you fail to comply with the direction you risk being faced with an application to enforce compliance and/or for a sanction to be imposed. It will catch you on the back foot and leave you in a tactically poor position.

If you wish to challenge one of the court's directions for another reason, for example because you do not agree with the district judge's decision about the expert evidence you will be allowed to use, you must act quickly. PD 28, para 4.2(2) provides that, unless a dissatisfied party applies within 14 days of service of the order for directions for the order to be varied, it will be assumed that he or she considered the order acceptable at the time it was made. In other words, it will be a much harder job to persuade the court that the direction is inappropriate if you do not challenge it with alacrity. There is no place on the fast track for a dilatory approach.

If the decision to be challenged was made at a hearing at which the party was present, the challenge is made by way of an appeal. Permission to appeal should have been requested at the hearing, but may be requested subsequently.

In any other case, the dissatisfied party should apply to the court to reconsider its decision. Quite often, the same judge will look at the grounds for the challenge and, if satisfied that they are valid, will vary the direction. This may be done without a hearing.

FAILURE TO COMPLY WITH CASE MANAGEMENT DIRECTIONS

The importance of complying with the time-limits set by the court is nowhere more evident than on the fast track. The time scale is short and the entire system depends for its success upon the willingness of the parties to co-operate with each other and with the court in moving cases on to trial in an efficient manner. Regrettably, there are still some practitioners who have not been able to adjust to this ethos or to the change in pace that the CPR have brought to the conduct of civil litigation. The court's case management powers are such that nobody can be in any doubt that it is not the parties who control the litigation as once was the case, but the court. You can be sure that you will receive scant sympathy from the court if you fail to comply with directions and further compound that failure by omitting to apply to vary a direction when you know that you will not be able to comply with it.

If you are able to comply without delaying the trial, you may escape with a costs sanction and an unless order. If the trial date is at risk because of your failure to comply you may find, for example, that you will not be able to rely on the evidence as yet undisclosed.

The vast majority of judges have been busy practitioners themselves and understand the pressures that lawyers are under. Nonetheless, they have a duty to further the overriding objective, and in the context of the fast track, this means to view the postponement of a trial as a last resort.

Chapter 26

THE MULTI-TRACK

CPR Part 29 sets out the procedure to be followed for the management of cases that are allocated to the multi-track.

A case will be allocated to the multi-track if it has a financial value exceeding £15,000, or if, although the value is less than £15,000, it is expected that the trial will last for longer than one day or involve more than one expert witness giving oral evidence. In addition, all claims that proceed under Part 8 will be allocated to the multi-track.

It is self-evident that all claims that are not suitable for allocation to either the small claims track or fast track will be allocated to the multi-track.

CASE MANAGEMENT DIRECTIONS

As with claims on the small claims track and fast track, case management by the court is central to the CPR. Even with cases of greater value and complexity, it is considered essential that the court keeps control by means of a timetable and case management leading to trial, in order to ensure that the overriding objective is met. This necessarily requires flexibility if the individual requirements of cases on the multi-track are to be taken into account.

It will be an important part of the judge's role when managing a case on the multi-track to ensure that the issues are carefully defined at the outset, and for the issues to be narrowed, if at all possible. Consideration may need to be given as to whether an issue may be disposed of by trial as a preliminary issue or whether a split hearing may be necessary.

It is particularly important with a case on the multi-track that the fee earner who has conduct of the matter is responsible for completing the allocation questionnaire, putting forward agreed or suggested directions, and attending case management hearings.

Depending upon the practice in any particular group of courts, case management of a case on the multi-track will take place either at the trial centre, where it may be dealt with by a district judge or the trial judge, or at one of the feeder courts, where it will be dealt with by the district judge.

Unlike on the small claims track and fast track, there are no specimen directions that are routinely used by the court. This is because cases on the multi-track will usually require tailor-made directions. However, the court has to consider the questions of disclosure, evidence and all steps leading to trial and, very often, the directions will be - similar to those given on the fast track.

Following allocation to the multi-track, the court must give directions and fix a timetable leading to trial. This can be done wholly or in part on consideration of the papers alone, or at a case management conference. In practice, the court will usually give directions after consideration of the papers, including the allocation questionnaires and any suggested directions.

AGREED DIRECTIONS

The parties are encouraged by r 29.4 to agree a timetable and directions for approval by the court. Even if the directions are not approved, they will assist the judge in considering what directions may be appropriate and may avoid the need for a case management conference.

CASE MANAGEMENT HEARINGS

A case management conference will be called only if there are any areas about which the judge is uncertain, for example the scope of any expert evidence that may be necessary, or the prognosis for any injuries that may affect the trial date. It is preferable, however, that the judge be provided with sufficient information to answer any queries that he or she may have and, thus, avoid the need for a case management conference and the attendant cost. Where a case management conference is unavoidable, it will be directed to be held by telephone wherever practicable, in order to save costs. Even if not specifically directed by the court, it is helpful if the parties ensure that the judge dealing with the telephone hearing has copies of all the documents that will be referred to by them on the court file and a brief case summary.

TIMETABLE

Unlike the fast track, there is no prescribed period within which the proceedings should be concluded. This would be impossible in most multi-track cases in which the issues may be far from straightforward, and there may be problems of delay associated with an uncertain medical prognosis.

Nonetheless, the court will be mindful of the overriding objective and will endeavour to set a timetable that enables the case to be brought on for trial at the earliest convenient date. There will be some cases when it will not be possible to achieve this at the allocation stage, but r 29.2(2) recognises this and provides that the court must place the case within a trial window or fix a trial date as soon as is practicable.

VARYING THE TIMETABLE

If the parties agree to a variation of the directions, including the timetable, they may do so without the court's involvement, except where the variation will require the date of any case management hearing or the trial itself to be altered. In such a case, CPR PD 29, para 6.5(2) provides that the parties must file a draft of the order that they seek and an agreed statement of the reasons why the variation is sought.

DISCLOSURE OF DOCUMENTS

There is no difference between disclosure for a multi-track case and disclosure for a fast-track case (see Chapter 25). However, in a complex case, standard disclosure may not be sufficient and an application for specific disclosure may be necessary.

EXPERTS

The fact that a case is proceeding on the multi-track does not mean that the provisions of Part 35 relating to the limiting of expert evidence and the requirement for the court's permission to rely upon it do not apply.

There is no reason why a single joint expert may not be appropriate in a multi-track case, but, unlike on the fast track, there is no presumption that this is how the expert evidence will be dealt with. What is important is that the court has available to it the expert evidence that it reasonably needs to decide the issue. For example, in a clinical negligence claim, this may mean that a single joint expert is instructed to report on the result of the allegedly negligent treatment, with the parties obtaining their own expert evidence on what is likely to be the more contentious issue of whether the treatment was indeed negligent.

In Chapter 29, Experts, it will be seen that CPR PD 35, para 5 enables the court to give permission for one expert in a particular discipline, who may refer to other experts in connected but subsidiary fields, to prepare a report. This is a direction that is more likely to be given on the multi-track than the fast track.

Whatever direction is made for expert evidence, it is important that the name and discipline of the expert are referred to in the order.

SPLIT TRIALS

Similar considerations apply as to cases on the fast track (see Chapter 25). However, there may be more reason for the judge to direct a trial of a preliminary issue in order to narrow down what is in dispute.

PRE-TRIAL CHECKLIST

The court's directions may include provision for a pre-trial checklist to be filed by a certain date. However, as there may have been one or more case management hearings or a pre-trial review when there will have been an opportunity to provide information about availability, the court may dispense with it.

PRE-TRIAL REVIEW

In a heavy multi-track case, the court may decide to fix a pre-trial review, usually before the trial judge, which the advocates, who are instructed for the trial, will attend. This may be up to 2 months before the start of the trial. The object will be to explore whether there is any scope for settlement, or, at the very least, the narrowing of issues, and to ensure that any steps are taken to ensure that the trial will be ready to proceed. The trial judge may take the opportunity to fix a timetable for the trial at this stage.

FAILURE TO COMPLY WITH DIRECTIONS

The most important consideration on the multi-track is to ensure that the case is ready for trial on the date that has been fixed and the court will not hesitate to impose sanctions where necessary to achieve this end. It is not easy to find alternative dates for a trial with a time estimate that may run into days or even weeks, as some cases on the multi-track will.

The court's approach to the imposition of sanctions on the multi-track is set out in PD 29, para 7. This underlines the principle that the postponement of the trial because of a failure to comply with case management directions will be ordered only if the circumstances are exceptional and that every effort will be made to avoid doing so.

THE TRIAL

The trial will usually take place at a Civil Trial Centre but the needs or convenience of the parties and the court's resources may result in the trial taking place at another court.

If a timetable for the trial has not been fixed at any pre-trial review, the judge will usually begin by dealing with this. The provisions of Part 32 as to the control of evidence apply as they do to a case on the fast track.

Part VI

EVIDENCE

Chapter 27

DISCLOSURE

HISTORICAL INTRODUCTION

In order to understand fully the modern law of disclosure, a brief historical introduction is necessary to explain how the law arrived at its present state.

Strange though this now seems to modern ears, the common law rule was that a party could not be a witness in his own case. Thus, the persons now called 'claimant' and 'defendant' were not competent witnesses! Cases had to be proved by independent evidence from non-parties.

As time moved on and both ordinary life and commercial life became more complex, documents became of increasing importance. A party may well have wished to produce documents to the court to prove his case or to help disprove the opponent's case. If such documents were in the hands of a witness, there was no difficulty. A *subpoena duces tecum* (now called a witness summons – see CPR Part 34) could be issued and served on the relevant witness. Whereas the *subpoena ad testificandum* merely required the witness to attend court to give evidence, the *subpoena duces tecum* required the witness to attend court and produce documents. However, given that the opponent was not a competent witness, it followed that a *subpoena* could not be served on the opponent to require him to come to court, either to give evidence or to produce documents. If the opponent had documents which were clearly of relevance to the case, an injustice was all too obvious. Accordingly, the Chancery Court evolved the process known as 'discovery'.

Discovery became a very important weapon in litigation. A party to litigation was obliged to give discovery of all documents in his possession, custody or power. The obligation was obviously mutual and thus, through this process of discovery, relevant documents were obtainable and could be put in evidence before the court. As was so often the case, the harshness of the common law was mitigated by a rule of equity.

As long ago as 1852, parties became competent witnesses but the discovery process continued to evolve. Pre-CPR, the leading case on discovery was 'Peruvian Guano' (*Cie Financière et Commerciale du Pacifique v Peruvian Guano Co* (1883) 11 QBD 55). This decision required each party to carry out a thorough search of all documents relevant to the issues of the case, including all documents which *may* lead to a *train of inquiry* enabling a party to advance his own case or damage that of his opponent. This may well have been a sensible and proportionate decision in the nineteenth century but, as life became more complex and documentation became more common, it eventually led to a preposterously onerous burden being placed on parties. The process of discovery was a cause of major expense in all litigation. (For an example of this highly onerous obligation, see *Procon (Great Britain) Ltd v Provincial Building Co Ltd* [1984] 1 WLR 557 where, as a result of the obligation of discovery, over 5 million documents had to be made available; the costs to both parties can easily be imagined!) Whilst the process and the aims of discovery were laudable and just, in practice it had become disproportionately expensive and capable of working an injustice. Huge numbers of documents had to be searched for and disclosed (because they may have led the opponent to a train of inquiry) but, in practice, usually only a modest number turned out to be significant.

The 'Access to Justice' inquiry concluded that discovery must be retained as a part of the modern litigation process, but its scope must be limited.

CPR Part 31 is designed to achieve those aims. To emphasise the break with the past, the similar but different word 'disclosure' was deliberately chosen to replace the former term of 'discovery'.

Previous rules had imposed automatic obligations on parties. The CPR do not. As part of the case management process, the court will decide what disclosure is required in each particular case and will be concerned to limit disclosure to the minimum necessary to further the overriding objective.

As part of the modernisation process, disclosure is even more limited on the small claims track, and Part 31 does not apply to a claim on the small claims track (r 31.1(2)).

MEANING OF 'DISCLOSURE'

By r 31.2, a party discloses a document by stating that the document exists or has existed. Obviously, if that were all there was to it, it would be a rather pointless process. The key to it is in r 31.3, which provides:

'(1) A party to whom a document has been disclosed has a right to inspect that document except where:

    (a) the document is no longer in the control of the party who disclosed it,

    (b) the party disclosing the document has a right or a duty to withhold inspection of it, or,

    (c) paragraph (2) applies.

(2) Where a party considers that it would be disproportionate to the issues in the case to permit inspection of documents within a category or class of document disclosed under rule 31.6(b):

(a) he is not required to permit inspection of documents within that category or class; but

(b) he must state in his disclosure statement that inspection of those documents will not be permitted on the grounds that to do so would be disproportionate.'

Thus, in summary, where the court so orders, the rule imposed is an obligation on a party to disclose documents and then gives a right, subject to exceptions, to the opponent to inspect that document.

INSPECTION

Inspection is dealt with in r 31.15. The party who has a right to inspect a document must give the party who disclosed it written notice of his or her wish to inspect it, and the party who disclosed it must permit inspection not more than 7 days after the date on which he or she received that notice. Further, a party may request a copy of a disclosed document and, if he or she also undertakes to pay reasonable copying costs, the party who disclosed the document must supply him or her with a copy, not more than 7 days after the date on which the request was received.

The appropriate place of inspection is the office of the solicitor for the party who disclosed the document, but, of course, the parties can agree that inspection should be elsewhere. However, it should never be necessary to bring to court a dispute as to the appropriate place of inspection. Such disputes did happen in the nineteenth century (*Lesley v Cave* [1886] WN 162) but have no place in the modern system, where parties have a duty to further the overriding objective in Part 1. The court retains a discretion to order inspection at any place, including adopting the old Chancery practice, which required documents to be deposited in the court for inspection to take place there.

MEANING OF 'DOCUMENT'

By r 31.4, 'document' means anything in which information of any description is recorded and 'copy', in relation to a document, means anything onto which information recorded in the document has been copied, by whatever means and whether directly or indirectly. Thus, 'document' is not restricted to a written paper – it includes tape recordings, video films and computer databases (*Derby and Co Ltd v Weldon (No 9)* [1991] 1 WLR 652).

Thus, for example, in a personal injury case, where a claimant is alleging that, as a result of an accident, he or she has certain disabilities so that he or she has difficulty walking and cannot indulge in his or her pre-accident hobbies but the defendant has, through an inquiry agent, obtained a videotape of the claimant jogging and playing football for the local team, the videotape is a 'document' and is subject to the process of disclosure. (See, eg, *Rall v Hume* [2001] EWCA Civ 146, [2001] 3 All ER 248 and *Jones v University of Warwick* [2003] EWCA Civ 151, [2003] 1 WLR 954.)

STANDARD DISCLOSURE

In a deliberate attempt to limit the scope of disclosure, the CPR have, by r 31.5, created the concept of 'standard disclosure'. This replaces the obligations in the pre-CPR rules, imposed by such cases as *Peruvian Guano* (see above). An order to give disclosure is, unless the court otherwise directs, an order to give standard disclosure only. Even then, the court has power to dispense with or limit standard disclosure, and parties may agree in writing to dispense with or limit disclosure.

By r 31.6:

'Standard disclosure requires a party to disclose only:

    (a)   the documents on which he relies; and

    (b)   the documents which:

        (i)   adversely affect his own case;

        (ii)   adversely affect another party's case; or

        (iii) support another party's case; and

    (c)   the documents which he is required to disclose by a relevant practice direction.'

In practice, there is likely to be little difference between r 31.6(a) (documents on which a party relies) and r 31.6(b)(ii) (documents which adversely affect another party's case). Almost certainly, a party would wish to rely on a document that adversely affects his opponent's case!

The true obligation of disclosure is, in reality, contained in r 31.6(b)(i) and, to a lesser extent, r 31.6(b)(iii). A party to litigation is under an obligation under the CPR to disclose to his or her opponent any document which 'adversely affects his own case'. The origin of the modern rule can clearly be traced back to the former Chancery Court practice of discovery (see 'Historical Introduction', above).

DUTY OF SOLICITOR

It is the duty of a solicitor to advise clients, at an early stage, of the obligation of disclosure. (See, for example, the House of Lords' decision in *Myers v Elman* [1940] AC 282.) The extent of the obligation of disclosure may well come as a surprise and a disappointment to clients. For example, a solicitor may have received instructions from a client's head office. On the client's file is an internal memorandum from regional office to head office, complaining that a branch office has made a complete mess of the specification for the task in hand, which has led to the litigation. This internal memorandum is hardly a document on which the client would wish to rely to advance his or her own case, but it is clearly a document which adversely affects the client's own case and thus is disclosable. A client may not like it, but it is the solicitor's duty to advise about it (*Rockwell Machine Tool Co Ltd v EP Barrus (Concessionaires) Ltd* [1968] 1 WLR 693) and to ensure that the obligation to give disclosure is carried out. After all, if this client is being sued for bad workmanship, this internal memorandum strongly suggests that a claimant's case may have some merit! When viewed in the context of the overriding objective, the rule makes perfect sense.

When giving standard disclosure, a party is required to make a reasonable search for documents falling within r 31.6(b) or (c) (see r 31.7). What is a reasonable search? The factors relevant in deciding the reasonableness of the search include the following:

(1)   the number of documents involved;
(2)   the nature and complexity of the proceedings;
(3)   the ease and expense of retrieval of any particular document; and
(4)   the significance of any document which is likely to be located during the search.

Where a party has not searched for a category or class of document, on the grounds that to do so would be unreasonable, he or she must state this in his or her disclosure statement and identify the category or class of document concerned.

The extent of the search that must be made will depend upon the circumstances of the case. Parties must bear in mind the overriding principle of proportionality. It may, for example, be reasonable to decide not to search for documents coming into existence before a particular date or to limit the search for documents in some particular place or places, or to documents falling into particular categories. Disclosure is an onerous obligation and it is reasonable for a party to limit the scope of it. The courts are very mindful of the fact that, under the pre-CPR Rules, huge numbers of hours were spent on discovery, which, in the event, often added little or nothing to the case. The new Rules have successfully reduced expense in this particular aspect of litigation.

PROCEDURE FOR STANDARD DISCLOSURE

How does a party actually undertake the obligation of disclosure? The court will have ordered, as part of its case management directions, the extent to which disclosure should take place and the date by which it must be given. The usual order will be for 'standard disclosure'.

The procedure for standard disclosure is that each party must make and serve on every other party a list of documents in the relevant practice form (r 31.10). The relevant form is N265. The list must identify the documents in a convenient order and manner, and as concisely as possible. It will normally be necessary to list documents in date order, to number them consecutively and to give each a concise description (eg 'letter – claimant to defendant'). Where there is a large number of documents, all falling into a particular category, the disclosing party may list those documents as a category rather than individually (eg 50 bank statements relating to account number 123456 at the Harrogate branch of the Royal Bank of Scotland from 1 January 2005 to date).

A party must list and number documents in his or her control that he or she does not object to being inspected.

If a party is obliged to give disclosure of a document but has a valid reason for not permitting all of it to be inspected, then the relevant part can be blanked out. The list would say, for example, 'the claimant's medical records from her date of birth to date save for entries which have been blanked out'. (See, eg, *GE Capital Corporate Finance Group v Bankers Trust Co* [1995] 1 WLR 172.) The general rule is that medical records are disclosed to both medical and legal advisers. (See *McIvor v Southern Health and Social Services Board* [1978] 1 WLR 757, where the House of Lords overruled cases limiting disclosure of medical reports to medical advisers only.) In the majority of cases, claimants are content for all their medical records to be disclosed to the defendant. This is normally regarded as an essential part of the process, not only of valuing the claim itself, but also of proving that the claimant's present complaints were caused by the incident complained of and not pre-existing. However, by their nature, medical records are confidential. Everyone has a right to respect for his or her private and family life, his or her home and correspondence. (See ECHR, Art 8 in Sch 1 to the HRA 1998.) Thus, it must be permissible for a claimant to delete wholly irrelevant but possibly embarrassing entries in medical records. If a claimant complains of neck and shoulder injuries, how can it be relevant that he or she had a sexually transmitted disease 10 years ago? It is suggested that, before medical records are sent to the other side, they should be considered in conjunction with the client to confirm that there are no entries which are irrelevant to the litigation and which the client wishes to keep confidential.

In addition to listing and numbering documents which a party does not object to being inspected, the list must indicate (r 31.10(4)):

> '(a) those documents in respect of which the party claims a right or duty to withhold inspection; and
> (b) (i) those documents which are no longer in the party's control; and
> (ii) what has happened to those documents.'

All lists must include a disclosure statement. The form of the disclosure statement is contained in the annex to CPR PD 31 and reads:

> 'I, the above named claimant [or defendant] [if party making disclosure is a company, firm or other organisation, identify here who the person making the disclosure statement is and why he or she is the appropriate person to make it] state that I have carried out a reasonable and proportionate search to locate all the documents which I am required to disclose under the order made by the court on ___ day of ___. I did not search:
>
> (i) for documents predating ...
> (ii) for documents located elsewhere than ...
> (iii) for documents in categories other than ...
>
> I certify that I understand the duty of disclosure and to the best of my knowledge I have carried out that duty. I certify that the list above is a complete list of all

documents which are or have been in my control and which I am obliged under the said order to disclose.'

By r 31.8, a party's duty to disclose documents is limited to documents which are, or have been, in his or her control. For this purpose, a party has or has had a document in his or her control if it is or was in his or her physical possession; he or she has or has had a right to possession of it; or he or she has or has had a right to inspect or take copies of it. The rule thus gives a very wide meaning to the term 'control'.

A party need not disclose more than one copy of the document. However, a copy of a document which contains a modification, obliteration or other marking or feature and on which a party intends to rely or which adversely affects his or her own or the other party's case is to be treated as a separate document (r 31.9).

It has long been the rule that a party has a right to inspect a document referred to by another party. The modern rule is contained in r 31.14. A party may inspect a document mentioned in a statement of case, a witness statement, a witness summary or an affidavit. Further, and subject to r 35.10(4), a party may apply for an order for inspection of any document mentioned in an expert's report which has not already been disclosed. As ever, the proper procedure is to request inspection before applying to the court for an order.

CONTINUING DUTY

As is evident from what has already been said, the obligation to give disclosure is an onerous one. However, it is important to bear in mind that it is not a one-off duty. The duty continues until the proceedings are concluded (r 31.11). If documents to which the duty extends come to a party's notice at any time during the proceedings, but after disclosure has been given, that party must immediately notify every other party. The appropriate procedure is to serve a supplemental list. There is no prescribed form of supplemental list, but it would be appropriate to use Form N265 again in a suitably amended form.

LEGAL PROFESSIONAL PRIVILEGE

It is a fundamental principle of English law that a client must be able to consult his or her lawyer in confidence, in the sure knowledge that whatever he or she tells his or her lawyer in confidence will never be revealed without his or her consent. It is more than a rule of evidence; it is a fundamental condition on which the administration of justice rests. (See *R v Derby Magistrates' Court ex parte B* [1996] AC 487.) It is such a fundamental principle of English law that its limitation or abrogation could only be effected by an Act of Parliament. Thus, a provision in the CPR purporting to undermine the principle was held to be *ultra vires* in *General Mediterranean Holdings v Patel* [2000] 1 WLR 272 (the offending rule was subsequently changed).

An authoritative summary of the law on legal professional privilege is given by Sir Richard Scott VC (as he then was) in *Secretary of State for Trade and Industry v Baker* [1998] Ch 356.

There is a conflict between disclosure and legal professional privilege. As the review of the authorities in *Seabrook v British Transport Commission* [1959] I WLR 509 shows, one approach is to confine privilege to communications made solely for the use of legal practitioners. Another approach is to extend privilege to a document where one purpose of bringing it into existence is to obtain legal advice. In *Waugh v British Railways Board* [1980] AC 521 the House of Lords committed itself to the dominant purpose test. That test gives legal professional privilege a wider scope. According to the dominant purpose test, legal professional privilege protects a communication from disclosure if the communication is dominantly, even if not solely, for a legal practitioner's use.

Legal advice privilege extends to advice given as to what should or should not be prudently and sensibly done in a relevant legal context and is not confined to advice concerning legal rights and obligations (*Three Rivers District Council v Governor and Company of the Bank of England (No 6)* [2004] UKHL 48; [2004] 3 WLR 1274).

Subject to the dominant purpose test, a communication with a solicitor for the purpose of existing or anticipated litigation is privileged (*Anderson v Bank of British Columbia* (1876) 2 Ch D 644). This is important because it protects a solicitor's communications with third parties for the purposes of litigation. Experts' reports, for example, are privileged and case management rules which require disclosure are confined to reports which the litigant wishes to use in evidence (or has agreed to disclose thus waiving privilege): see eg *Hajigeorgiou v Vasiliou* [2005] EWCA Civ 236. Privilege arises when a party has a reasonable apprehension of being sued, even before the cause of action fully accrues (*Alfred Crompton Amusement Machines Ltd v Customs and Excise Commissioners (No 2)* [1974] AC 405).

INADVERTENT DISCLOSURE

In recent years, there have been several cases (far too many) where documents which are privileged have been inadvertently copied and sent to the other side. The fact that this has happened is a lesson itself for solicitors. Disclosure is an onerous and serious step, which should be managed by the solicitor who is conducting the case. It is neither sensible nor appropriate for this vital task to be wholly delegated to a junior (see, eg, *Woods v Martins Bank* [1959] 1 QB 55).

What is a solicitor to do if he or she receives privileged documents from the other side? Documents which have been sent as a result of 'an obvious mistake' should be immediately returned unread. This would include, for example, the other side's brief to counsel which has clearly been sent to you in error. However, a solicitor does not have a duty, in the face of a mistake which was less than obvious, to enquire. (See *IBM v Phoenix International (Computers) Ltd* [1995] 1 All ER 413.)

A party is always free to waive privilege and, if a solicitor has exhibited to an affidavit over 400 pages, including over 100 for which a claim of privilege could have been made, it is a reasonable assumption that privilege has been deliberately waived and far from being a case of obvious mistake.

It is now provided by r 31.20 that, where a party inadvertently allows a privileged document to be inspected, the party who has inspected the document may use it or its contents only with the permission of the court. The rule goes some way towards resolving difficulties caused by inadvertent disclosure, but leaves open, and subject to case-law, the circumstances in which permission will be given (*Breeze v John Stacy and Sons Ltd* (1999) 96 (28) LSG 27).

The only solution in practice is for solicitors to have adequate in-house procedures to ensure that such mistakes are not made.

SPECIFIC DISCLOSURE

Orders for specific disclosure are now rare. Standard disclosure is adequate for nearly all cases. However, r 31.12 enables the court to make an order for specific disclosure or specific inspection. An order for specific disclosure is an order that a party must do one or more of the following things:

(1)   disclose documents or classes of documents specified in the order;
(2)   carry out a search to the extent stated in the order;
(3)   disclose any documents located as a result of that search.

An order for specific inspection is an order that a party permits inspection of a document referred to in r 31.3(2) (the rule which allows a party to state in his or her disclosure statement that he or she will not permit inspection of a document on the grounds that it would be disproportionate to do so).

The procedure for making an application for specific disclosure and the test to be applied are set out in PD 31, para 5. The onus is on the party who is applying to satisfy the court, on evidence, that there has not been adequate compliance with an order. The application must specify the order that the applicant intends to ask the court to make and state the ground on which the order is sought.

In deciding whether or not to make an order for specific disclosure, the court will take into account all the circumstances of the case and, in particular, the overriding objective.

Whereas pre-CPR applications for specific discovery (as it then was) were common, under the CPR applications for specific disclosure are rare. This is as a consequence both of the change of culture which the rules set out to achieve and of the improved wording of the present rules. Solicitors should make every effort to avoid disputes about disclosure coming before the courts. Bear in mind that the unsuccessful party to the application will not only have to pay the costs of it but will also find, as a general rule, that such costs will be summarily assessed and ordered to be paid immediately.

DISCLOSURE OTHERWISE THAN BETWEEN PARTIES

Hitherto, this chapter has been concerned with disclosure between parties to proceedings before the court. Originally, of course, disclosure and its predecessor were so limited. However, by statute and by extensions of the common law, there are three situations in which disclosure may be obtained otherwise than between parties to proceedings. These are:

(1)   where an Act permits disclosure before proceedings. This is governed by r 31.16. Such an application is permitted, by SCA 1981, s 33 and CCA 1984, s 52, between likely parties to subsequent proceedings. For example, see *Bermuda International Securities Ltd v KPMG* [2001] EWCA Civ 269, [2001] CP Rep 73. The general rule is that the applicant will have to bear the respondent's costs of the application. However, in that case, the judge refused so to order, on the grounds that the pre-action disclosure had been unreasonably resisted. See also *Rose v Lynx Express Ltd* [2004] EWCA Civ 447: it is normally sufficient to found an application under r 31.16 for the proposed substantive claim to be properly arguable and the court should not in the application embark upon any substantive determination;

(2)   where an Act permits disclosure against a non-party during proceedings. This is governed by r 31.17. It is permitted by SCA 1981, s 34 and CCA 1984, s 53. Rule 31.17 is very widely drawn. See, for example, *Re Howglen Ltd* [2001] 1 All ER 376 and *Frankson v Secretary of State for the Home Department* [2003] EWCA Civ 655; [2003] 1 WLR 1952.

(3)   in certain other, well-established situations, such as under the principles set out in *Norwich Pharmacal Co v Customs and Excise Commissioners* [1974] AC 133: search orders (formerly *Anton Pillar* orders) and freezing orders (formerly *Mareva* injunctions). For a recent example, see *Ashworth Security Hospital v MGN Ltd* [2001] 1 WLR 515. The wide powers under r 31.17 now usually make consideration of the principles in *Norwich Pharmacal* unnecessary.

SUBSEQUENT USE OF DISCLOSED DOCUMENTS

A party to whom a document has been disclosed may use the document only for the purpose of the proceedings in which it is disclosed. The only exceptions are where: the document has been read to or by the court or referred to at a hearing which has been held in public; the court gives permission; or the party who disclosed the document and the person to whom the document belongs agree (r 31.22).

The court may make an order restricting or prohibiting use of a document which has been disclosed, even in cases where the document has been read to or by the court or referred to at a hearing which has been held in public.

FALSE DISCLOSURE STATEMENTS

Disclosure is a key and fundamental aspect of the modern system of civil procedure. The heavy onus this places on parties and solicitors has already been referred to. Rule 31.23 underlines the importance of the obligation by authorising proceedings for contempt of court to be brought against a person who makes or causes to be made a false disclosure statement without an honest belief in its truth.

Chapter 28

EVIDENCE

OVERVIEW

Evidence is no more than the means employed for the purpose of proving a disputed fact. Evidence is direct where the fact proved by it ('the evidentiary fact') is the fact required to be proved, for example where, at a trial following a road traffic accident, a witness gives evidence that he or she saw the defendant drive through a red traffic light. Indirect evidence is where the existence of the fact in issue is inferred from the evidentiary fact and is often called 'circumstantial evidence'.

The facts which have to be proved in any given case are established by the relevant substantive law. The facts which a claimant has to prove to succeed in a claim in the tort of negligence depend upon the law of negligence and are not matters of practice or procedure. *How* facts are proved is determined by a combination of the law of evidence and the rules of procedure. The law of evidence specifies which party must prove the facts in issue and the types of evidence that can be used to prove them. The CPR prescribe ways in which evidence may or may not be placed before the court.

This chapter is concerned mainly with the procedural aspects of the law of evidence. The very important topic of expert evidence merits its own chapter and is considered separately.

Put simply, there are four types of evidence that can be placed before the court, namely witness evidence, documentary evidence, real evidence and demonstrative evidence. Each of these is considered separately. It is important to bear in mind the category in which any item of evidence belongs. Inexperienced lawyers sometimes make the mistake of confusing witness evidence with documentary evidence, largely because of the modern practice of all witness evidence being in the form of written statements. A witness statement is not documentary evidence. A witness statement is no more than an indication of what the evidence of the witness will be when that witness comes to testify. It does not, in fact, become evidence until the witness enters the witness-box, takes the oath and confirms that the statement represents his or her evidence in the case. However, in certain circumstances, the witness statement itself can be evidence, but this is still categorised as witness evidence and not as documentary evidence. If the witness does not give the evidence, but instead a statement is admitted (permissible in certain circumstances), this is categorised as hearsay evidence, that is, second-hand, not first-hand, witness evidence.

BURDEN OF PROOF

A party who asserts a fact has the burden of proving it. This is known as 'the legal burden of proof'.

The legal burden of proof can be distinguished from the evidential burden of proof, which imposes a burden of producing some evidence, failing which, the claim (or defence, as the case may be) must fail. For example, if a claimant gives evidence that his car was parked at the side of the road when the defendant drove into collision with him, then, if the defendant calls no evidence, the defendant has failed to discharge an evidential burden and the defence must fail. If the defendant does give evidence that she was parked by the side of the road when the claimant reversed into her, then there is a conflict of evidence, and the trial judge must decide whether or not the claimant has discharged the legal burden of proof. If there is no other evidence either way, the judge will have to decide which evidence he or she believes and which he or she does not. It would be somewhat unusual if a judge were not able to make such a decision, but, if that were the case, the claimant must fail because, as stated, it is the claimant who has the legal burden of proof. A party who alleges a fact must prove it.

STANDARD OF PROOF

In civil cases, the relevant standard of proof is 'on the balance of probabilities'. When assessing probabilities, the court will have in mind as a factor, to whatever extent is appropriate in the particular case, that the more serious the allegation, the less likely it is that the event occurred and, hence, the stronger should be the evidence before the court concludes that the allegation is established on the balance of probabilities. In recent years, cases on the burden of proof tend to occur in the field of family law, especially in cases concerning children. (See, eg, the House of Lords' decision in *Re H (Minors) (Sexual Abuse: Standard of Proof)* [1996] AC 563, [1996] 1 FLR 80.) As a matter of common sense, where there is a strong allegation, the court requires strong evidence to prove it. Fraud is less common than negligence, but to prove fraud does not require a higher standard of proof than to prove negligence. However, the standard of proof is 'the balance of probabilities' and the court must weigh the probabilities in deciding whether or not it is proved that the events alleged did in fact occur. The more improbable the event, the stronger must be the evidence that it did occur before, on the balance of probabilities, its occurrence will be established.

RELEVANCE AND ADMISSIBILITY

The primary rule of admissibility of evidence is relevance. Evidence can be put before the court only if it is relevant to the facts in issue, that is if it helps to establish (or disprove), as a matter of logic, the matter which is to be proved.

Evidence which is relevant is admissible, unless excluded by a particular rule of court, by agreement between the parties (eg 'without prejudice' correspondence) or by a rule of law, such as legal professional privilege or public interest immunity.

COURT'S CONTROL OF EVIDENCE

The main Parts of the CPR concerning evidence are Parts 32, 33, 34 and 35.

By r 32.1:

'(1) The court may control the evidence by giving directions as to:

(a) the issues on which it requires evidence;
(b) the nature of the evidence which it requires to decide those issues; and
(c) the way in which the evidence is to be placed before the court.

(2) The court may use its powers under this rule to exclude evidence that would otherwise be admissible.

(3) The court may limit cross-examination.'

Directions on evidence will be given initially by the court, when the case is allocated to track. In the small claims track, the fast track and for some multi-track cases, those directions will be the only directions given. Most multi-track cases, however, have a case management conference, and one of the main purposes of a case management conference is to give directions as to which evidence will, and which will not, be admissible. As part of its active case management, the court must identify the issues at an early stage and, where appropriate, direct the trial of a preliminary issue. At the trial of a preliminary issue, it is for the trial judge to determine the extent of the evidence to be admitted (*GKR Karate (UK) Ltd v Yorkshire Post Newspapers Ltd* [2000] 1 WLR 2571). The court noted that, in libel cases, novel and imaginative case management was called for and that admissible and relevant evidence and cross-examination could be excluded where it was disproportionately expensive or time-consuming, provided that the order was made in accordance with the overriding objective.

WITNESS STATEMENTS

By r 32.2, the general rule is that any fact which needs to be proved by the evidence of witnesses is to be proved at trial by their oral evidence given in public and, at any other hearing, by their evidence in writing. Thus, witness statements are adduced as evidence in their own right at hearings other than the trial itself (eg an application for summary judgment or for an interim payment).

For the trial itself, as we shall see, rules require witness statements to be served before trial, but, as r 32.2 makes clear, the evidence is given by the witness, and the witness statement does not become evidence as such until the witness has taken the oath and confirmed that it represents his or her evidence. By r 32.4, a witness statement is a written statement, signed by a person, which contains the evidence that that person would be allowed to give orally.

As part of case management (and pursuant to r 32.4(2)), the court always orders a party to serve on the other parties any witness statement of the oral evidence which the party serving the statement intends to rely on in relation to any issues of fact to be decided at the trial.

The timing and form of the order giving directions for exchange of witness statements are not dealt with in Part 32, but in Parts 28 and 29, save that r 32.4(3) specifically enables the court to give directions as to the order in which witness statements are to be served and whether or not the witness statements are to be filed. The most common order in practice, made on allocation, is for witness statements to be mutually exchanged 10 weeks from allocation.

PRACTICE DIRECTION – WRITTEN EVIDENCE (CPR PD 32)

The Practice Direction which supplements Part 32 does not deal with evidence generally but is specifically entitled 'Written evidence'. Because written evidence is now so common, this Practice Direction is extremely important and it is necessary to acquire familiarity with it. It contains, for example, details on the format of affidavits. Paragraphs 17–25 are concerned with witness statements.

The witness statement should be headed with the title of the proceedings and appropriately marked in the top, right-hand corner of the first page (see para 17.2). The witness statement must, if practicable, be in the intended witness's own words. The statement should be expressed in the first person and should state:

(1)   the full name of the witness;
(2)   his or her place of residence or, if he or she is making a statement in his or her professional, business or other occupational capacity, the address at which he or she works, the position he or she holds and the name of his or her firm or employer;
(3)   his or her occupation or, if none, his or her description; and
(4)   the fact that he or she is a party to the proceedings or is the employee of such a party, if it be the case.

The statement must indicate which of the statements in it are made from the witness's own knowledge and which are matters of information and belief, and the source of any matters of information or belief.

The drafting of a witness statement is now one of the most important tasks that solicitors undertake. (See further, Chapter 9, Interviewing.) Bear in mind that, in civil trials, the judge will have pre-read the witness statements. The witness, when called, enters the witness-box and takes the oath (or affirms) and confirms his or her name and address. The advocate who has called the witness will then refer the witness to the trial bundle and ask him or her to turn to the relevant page on which his or her statement begins. The witness will then be asked to confirm that the signature at the end is his or her own signature and then that the statement is true to the best of his or her information and belief. The witness will confirm that it is. The witness (unlike in a criminal trial) is not expected to repeat the evidence from memory to the court nor (unlike at a planning inquiry) to read his or her statement to the court.

A witness giving oral evidence may, with the permission of the court, amplify his or her witness statement and give evidence in relation to new matters which have arisen since the witness statement was served on the other parties (r 32.5(3)). 'Amplify' means no more than clarifying any apparent ambiguity or filling in minor gaps. Judges are relaxed about giving permission to do this. Doing so often helps the witness to settle down in a strange environment, and the judge knows that the witness is about to face cross-examination. However, judges do not normally permit significant further evidence to be produced. If, in the interests of the overriding objective, the judge felt obliged to give such permission, there would certainly be, at the very least, adverse costs consequences for the party making the application (or his or her lawyers).

SERVICE OF WITNESS STATEMENTS

The court will give directions as to when witness statements are to be exchanged. Mutual exchange is still the general rule, although sequential exchange can be ordered (see r 32.4(3) and the observations of Lord Woolf MR in *McPhilemy v The Times* [1999] 3 All ER 775). When the deadline is approaching for exchange of witness statements, it is appropriate for solicitors to arrange a date for this, and the normal practice is for solicitors to undertake to put all witness statements in the DX system or in the post on a specific date.

You should make every effort to ensure that the witness statements are exchanged by the date given in the court's order. To this end, first seek a realistic period of time in which to do so. A period of 10 weeks from allocation is normally regarded as the minimum, but longer can be given in an appropriate multi-track case. Although parties cannot, by consent, vary 'milestone' dates (dates for the filing of pre-trial checklists, the trial date or a trial window), parties can agree in writing to vary the time for other directions so long as the milestone dates are not affected (r 2.11). Thus, try to agree an extension of time with other solicitors, if necessary. This agreement must be in writing. If, however, this cannot be achieved, an application to the court will be necessary.

Similarly, you should agree a reasonable extension with an opponent, if requested.

Should you serve your witness statements even if the opponent is not in a position to do so by the relevant deadline? Usually, no disadvantage is secured by doing so, but this must depend on the nature of the case. It is for the party in default to seek an extension, but, if your opponent does not do so, then you should apply to the court on a 'without notice' application in accordance with Part 23, for an order requiring the opponent to exchange witness statements by a certain date or be debarred from producing such evidence. The court would normally make an 'unless' order on such an application, thus placing the onus on the defaulting party to comply with the terms of the 'unless' order or make their own application.

What if your opponent is acting in person? Again, usually, no disadvantage is secured by complying with the court's orders yourself, but, if it is a case where it is felt that the opponent might tailor his or her own evidence having had the benefit of reading your client's evidence first, then, once again, an application should be made to the court. The application should make it clear that you have prepared your witness statements and are ready, willing and able to exchange but that the opponent has failed to agree a date to do so. The judge is likely to make an 'unless' order.

Witness statements are usually ordered to be exchanged some weeks in advance of the trial. This is necessary to enable all parties to prepare for trial. Even in a fast-track case, witness statements will be exchanged at about 10 weeks after allocation, whereas the trial date is up to 30 weeks after allocation. What if a new witness is discovered or comes forward after witness statements have been exchanged? The first thing to do is to explain to the opponent what has happened and ask if he or she will agree to the service of a late witness statement. If agreement is not forthcoming, you will have to make an application to the court for permission to serve further statements. The court is always loathe to lose a trial date or trial window and, if that would be necessary, it may be that permission would be refused. It is the court's task to control evidence. On the other hand, no hard and fast rule can be laid down, as the court will apply the rule and the overriding objective to each individual case and, at the end of the day, is concerned to achieve justice between the parties.

Similar comments apply if it is not a question of a new witness but of supplemental evidence from an existing witness. Do not assume that the witness will be allowed to 'amplify' his or her statement at trial. Instead, agreement or permission of the court should be sought to serve a supplemental statement.

In significant multi-track cases, a pre-trial review is held before the trial judge, and it is possible to request a pre-trial review in other cases. Late applications are better dealt with by the judge who will have to try the case and courts do make every effort to list a pre-trial review before the trial judge.

Rule 32.5 deals with use at trial of witness statements which have been served. As already stated, if a party who has served a witness statement wishes to rely on the evidence of the witness who made the statement, he or she must call the witness to give oral evidence, unless the court otherwise orders that statement to be put in as hearsay evidence.

If a party who has served a witness statement does not call the witness to give evidence at trial or put the witness statement in as hearsay evidence, any other party may put the witness statement in as hearsay evidence. This provision (in r 32.5(5)) was an innovation of the CPR, but is not likely to be used very often in practice. It is unlikely that a statement prepared by the opposing party, albeit for a witness that he or she now chooses not to rely upon, will be of assistance in your case. In any event, the court retains its power to control evidence. The court would not, for example, allow a claimant to put in evidence a witness statement served by the defendant which conflicts substantially with the claimant's case, for the purpose of inviting a libel jury to conclude that the statement was not true (*McPhilemy v The Times Newspapers (No 2)* [2000] 1 WLR 1732).

WITNESS SUMMARIES

Sometimes, a witness has useful evidence to give but does not wish to 'get involved'. Such a witness can be served with a witness summons to require him or her to attend trial. However, how are you to comply with a requirement to serve a witness statement when he or she will not give you one?

Sometimes a witness is ready, willing and able to give evidence and it is known that he or she will be available during the trial window, but a witness statement cannot be taken straight away because the witness is working, say, in the Middle East, and it is impossible to make arrangements to take the statement. How can you comply with the court order to serve a witness statement?

The answer to both these questions is contained in r 32.9, which provides for 'witness summaries'. A party who is required to serve a witness statement for use at trial but is unable to obtain one may apply, without notice, for permission to serve a witness summary instead.

A witness summary is a summary of the evidence, if known, which would otherwise be included in a witness statement or, if the evidence is not known, the matters about which the party serving the witness summary proposes to question the witness. The witness summary must include the name and address of the intended witness, unless the court orders otherwise, and is to be served within the period in which a witness statement would have had to be served. So far as is practicable, the form of the witness summary should comply with CPR PD 32 – Written Evidence.

HEARSAY EVIDENCE

Rule 33.1 defines 'hearsay' as 'a statement made otherwise than by a person while giving oral evidence in proceedings which is tendered as evidence of the matters stated'. References to hearsay include hearsay of whatever degree. The definition is a direct quotation from Civil Evidence Act 1995, s 1. In practice, in a civil case, hearsay evidence often means no more than relying upon a witness statement of a witness who is not called to give oral evidence at trial.

At common law, hearsay evidence was not admissible (subject to limited but well-defined exceptions). That rule has gone in civil cases. The principle statute now is the Civil Evidence Act 1995 (sections of the Evidence Act 1938, Civil Evidence Act 1968 and Civil Evidence Act 1972 remain in force).

By Civil Evidence Act 1995, s 1, in civil proceedings, evidence shall not be excluded on the ground that it is hearsay. Hearsay evidence can thus be admitted in all civil cases, subject only to complying with the appropriate procedure. In certain circumstances, notice is required and, in others, it is not.

Although the most common example in practice of hearsay evidence is that of a witness statement of a person not called to give evidence, there are, of course, other situations. It may well be, for example, that you wish to call a witness who has overheard something. You wish the witness to tell the court what he or she overheard and invite the court to believe that what he or she overheard was true. An example might be where a former employee of your client's firm was heard complaining about the very piece of equipment that caused your client's injury. The witness who complained cannot be traced but the person who overheard the witness can. It is hearsay evidence but, as we have seen, hearsay evidence is now admissible; it is a question of deciding whether the case falls under r 33.2 (notice of intention to rely on hearsay evidence) or r 33.3 (circumstances in which notice of intention to rely on hearsay evidence is not required).

Hearsay notice (rule 33.2)

By r 33.2, where a party intends to rely on hearsay evidence at trial and either that evidence is to be given by a witness giving oral evidence or that evidence is contained in a witness statement of a person who is not being called to give oral evidence, that party complies with Civil Evidence Act 1995, s 2(1)(a) (which requires notice) by serving a witness statement on the other parties in accordance with the court's order.

The party intending to rely on the hearsay evidence must, when he or she serves the witness statement, inform the other parties that the witness is not being called to give oral evidence (if that be the case) and give the reason why the witness will not be called.

In all other cases where a party intends to rely on hearsay evidence at trial, it is necessary to serve a notice which:

(1)   identifies the hearsay evidence;
(2)   states that the parties serving the notice propose to rely on the hearsay evidence at trial; and
(3)   gives the reason why the witness will not be called.

The party proposing to rely on the hearsay evidence must serve the notice no later than the latest date for serving witness statements and, if the hearsay evidence is to be in a document, supply a copy to any party who requests him or her to do so.

Hearsay – notice not required (rule 33.3)

Civil Evidence Act 1995, s 2(1) (duty to give notice of intention to rely on hearsay evidence) does not apply:

(1)   to evidence in hearings other than trials;
(2)   to an affidavit or witness statement which is to be used at trial but which does not contain hearsay evidence;
(3)   to a statement which a party to a probate action wishes to put in evidence which is alleged to have been made by the person whose estate is the subject of the proceedings;
(4)   where the requirement is excluded by a Practice Direction (as yet there is no such Practice Direction).

EVIDENCE BY VIDEO LINK

By r 32.3, the court may allow a witness to give evidence through a video link or by other means. This practice is well established in certain other common law jurisdictions, for example, Western Australia – consider the vast distances that would have to be travelled, even within Australia, if such a facility were not available. Unfortunately, such facilities are still in their infancy in England, but the use of video can be expected to grow and practitioners are encouraged to seek its use in an appropriate case where it will effect a saving in costs.

The former 'Video Conferencing Protocol' of the Royal Courts of Justice (referred to in both the Chancery Guide at para 14.14 and the Queen's Bench Guide at para 2.7.7) has been superseded by Annex 3 to PD32 – 'Video Conferencing Guidance'. It is based on the protocol of the Federal Court of Australia and is the same as the document appended to the Admiralty and Commercial Courts Guide (for details of these various Guides, see Chapter 43). Annex 3 is comprehensive and is found in all the practitioner manuals. The use of a video link for taking evidence of an overseas witness can achieve a material saving in costs. The issue of evidence being given by way of video link should be raised with the other side and the court as soon as it becomes clear that its use is desirable. Leaving it to a pre-trial review may well be too late.

In *Polanski v Condé Nast Publications Ltd* [2005] UKHL 10 the House of Lords made an order permitting the claimant to give evidence by video link in his action for defamation (which, at trial, succeeded).

Ultimately, it must be anticipated that video link will be the rule rather than the exception. Consider, for example, the enormous saving in expert witness time if this were done. Most NHS hospitals already have video links. A medical expert would be able to give evidence over a video link at a predetermined date and time, thus, perhaps interrupting his or her normal day's work for only a couple of hours instead of having to lose a whole day at court (and possibly longer with travel time, etc). Unfortunately, this development is still some way off. Nevertheless, always consider whether a video link can be used in your case.

DEPOSITIONS

Depositions are provided for by Part 34. If a witness cannot attend trial, it may be possible to obtain an order under r 34.8 for the examination of the witness. The witness gives evidence before an 'examiner', as if the examination were the trial itself. There is, thus, the opportunity for full cross-examination. The evidence is reduced to writing, and the resulting deposition is then admitted in evidence at the trial.

In practice, depositions are now extremely rare. Alternatives should be explored. It is not cheap to obtain evidence in this way and, with current low-cost air fares, it is often cheaper to fly a witness in to give evidence than to seek to obtain a deposition, especially if the deposition has to be taken in Europe. Alternatively, is it possible for the witness to give evidence by video link (see above)? Finally, is it really necessary for the witness to be there? Can the witness's evidence be admitted as hearsay in his or her absence (see above)? If the evidence is strongly disputed and controversial, obviously it is better for the witness to be there rather than for you to have to rely on hearsay evidence, but, if the evidence is, say, merely confirmatory of evidence that is to be given in any event by another witness in person, then you may consider that hearsay would be sufficient. For the rare case in which evidence is to be taken on deposition, see further, Part 34 and PD 34.

Exceptionally, if it is desirable, there is nothing to prevent the trial judge appointing himself as examiner and travelling to the country where the witness resides. Langley J has recently so appointed himself after an intended video link with the witness in Cuba had failed (*Peer International Corpn v Termidor Music Publishers Ltd* [2005] EWHC 1048).

OPINION EVIDENCE

The general rule is that only an expert can give opinion evidence to the court. Indeed, the usual reason for calling expert evidence is so that the court can benefit from the expert's opinion. This aspect is considered in Chapter 29.

Admissibility of non-expert opinion is governed by Civil Evidence Act 1972, s 3(2). The subsection provides:

'It is hereby declared that where a person is called as a witness in any civil proceedings, the statement of opinion by him on any relevant matter on which he is not qualified to give expert evidence, if made as a way of conveying relevant facts personally perceived by him, is admissible as evidence of what he perceived.'

The law is recognising, in a common-sense way, that all of us express opinions as part of normal daily life, as a way of explaining what we have seen – a car was driven 'too fast', 'the youths who approached me were drunk'. It would be preposterous if such statements were excluded from evidence because they are 'opinion'. However, when drafting the witness statement, do not go too far. The witness can say, for example, that the driver was 'drunk' or was driving 'too fast', but it is very easy to add 'and the accident was entirely his fault', and because the latter statement is the very issue to be decided by the trial judge, it is not admissible. The point is that we all know what 'too fast' and 'drunk' mean. However, the issue to be decided at trial (eg negligence) is the province of the trial judge.

DOCUMENTARY EVIDENCE

Documentary evidence rarely causes problems in practice. The importance of disclosure and inspection has already been considered. In practice, solicitors for all parties should agree which documents they wish to place before the court and these should form part of a bundle (or bundles, suitably divided if voluminous). The documents are thus placed before the court as agreed documents.

Obviously, photocopies should be of good quality and legible, but there should be little difficulty, given the quality of equipment these days. The former rule that the court would not look at a copy, only the original, is long since dead. Formal proof of authenticity is rarely required.

By r 32.19, a party is deemed to admit the authenticity of a document disclosed to him or her under Part 31 (disclosure), unless he or she served notice that he or she wishes the document to be proved at trial. A notice to prove a document must be served by the latest date for serving witness statements, or within 7 days of disclosure of the document, whichever is the later. The prescribed form of notice is Form N268 – notice to prove documents at trial. In practice, such a notice is rarely required, but the need for one must not be overlooked if it is indeed intended to dispute the authenticity of a document which has been disclosed to you.

REAL EVIDENCE

'Real evidence' consists of things viewed by the court itself, for example an island where mining operations have taken place (*Tito v Waddell (No 2)* [1977] Ch 106), the knife with which the claimant was stabbed or the machine which injured the claimant.

Most cases do not have any evidence categorised as real evidence as such. If, for example, there is some dispute concerning the machine which caused an accident, it is usually sufficient for this to be inspected by an appropriate expert and for the relevant evidence to be given to the court in the form of the expert's report, rather than for the court to have to view the machine itself. If necessary, a video of the machine in operation could be obtained and played to the court; in addition, or alternatively, photographs or a brochure could be produced. It would be rare for the court to have to look at the machine itself, but, if it did, the evidence would be categorised as real evidence. In *Regina (0) v Coventry Magistrates Court* (2004) *The Times*, April 22, a computer printout recording successful and unsuccessful attempts to enter a website was admissible as real evidence.

DEMONSTRATIVE EVIDENCE

'Demonstrative evidence' is the modern term used to describe evidence which demonstrates facts to the court, for example a working model or video reconstruction. The relevant rule is r 33.6, entitled 'Use of plans, photographs and models as evidence':

> 'The rule applies to evidence (such as a plan, photograph or model) which is not:
>
> (a)   contained in a witness statement, affidavit or expert's report;
> (b)   to be given orally at trial; or,
> (c)   evidence of which prior notice must be given under rule 33.2 (hearsay).'

Unless the court orders otherwise, the evidence is not receivable at trial unless the party intending to put it in evidence has given notice to the other parties, in accordance with the rule. Notice must be given not later than the latest date for serving witness statements.

Where a party has given notice that he or she intends to put in the evidence, he or she must give every other party an opportunity to inspect it and to agree to its admission without further proof.

Disputes as to the admissibility of such evidence will, of course, be resolved by the district judge or master, as part of the case management process, bearing in mind the court's duty to control evidence but to do so in a way consistent with the overriding objective.

Chapter 29

EXPERTS

The use of expert witnesses is an area in which the civil procedure reforms have had a noticeable impact. This was identified by Lord Woolf in his Access to Justice reports as being responsible for considerable delay and expense in litigation and in need of radical reform. It is now no longer the norm for each party to instruct his or her own expert and for the experts to give oral evidence in court. On the fast track, there is a presumption in favour of expert evidence taking the form of the written report of a single joint expert. Even on the multi-track, every effort will be made to keep expert evidence to a minimum. In all cases, the experts instructed will owe their duty not to the parties, but to the court.

There has been a complete change of culture in relation to expert evidence, from a culture in which one's hand was shown as late as possible to one in which the cards are on the table more or less from the start.

WHAT IS AN EXPERT?

An expert is a person who is qualified to give an opinion on a particular matter, within his or her own field of expertise. The role of the expert witness is to assist the court by bringing his or her technical knowledge to bear on the relevant issues in the case. The judge is not bound to accept an expert's evidence if there are good reasons for not doing so, but the judge may not substitute his or her own opinion about a technical matter for that of an expert.

SELECTION OF AN EXPERT

Very often, your firm or chambers will have a database of tried and tested experts who are instructed regularly. You will also come across the experts that are used by another party, or hear from discussion with fellow professionals which experts are recognised as being good in a particular field. However, from time to time, you may be completely in the dark when it comes to instructing an expert. Many people will put themselves forward as experts on all manner of subjects. As well as being members of their own professional bodies, for example the Royal Institute of Chartered Surveyors, many expert witnesses will also belong to one of the organisations that have developed in response to the civil procedure reforms, such as the Expert Witness Institute (*www.ewi.org.uk*) or the Society of Expert Witnesses. There are also registers of experts. Membership of these bodies may give some guarantee of minimum standards, but it is clearly impossible to judge from simply looking at a directory whether a particular expert will be appropriate for your case. These sources should be regarded as a starting point from which to compile a shortlist of those who might be suitable. You should then make contact with each expert and make your own assessment. Apart from the technical skill of the witness, you will also need to establish whether his or her area of specialism is the right one for the issues in the cases, and, of course, his or her availability to provide a report and attend court, and the cost of doing so.

INSTRUCTING AN EXPERT

Most lawyers do not have the detailed technical knowledge that may be necessary to advise a client about the prospects of success in, say, a building dispute. They may be able to see that there is clearly something wrong with the construction of the building, but they cannot necessarily say what it is that the architect, surveyor or builder has done or omitted to do that has caused the problem. Even if they could, they would not be qualified to give evidence to the court. It is for this reason that an expert has to be instructed. A note of caution, however – do not instruct an expert simply to express an opinion about something that is obvious. If the judge does not see any benefit from an expert witness then the costs of instructing him or her will not be allowed.

The next question is, at what stage should an expert become involved? Your client will want to know as early as possible whether or not he or she has a good case. It may be that there is some urgency – because, if you do not act quickly, you may be overtaken by events. However, as a general rule, you will want to carry out some preliminary investigations, and take witness statements so that you present as full a case as possible to the expert. It is always a good idea to have a preliminary discussion with your chosen expert, to find out whether there is any particular information or documents that it will be helpful to include in the instructions.

Where a pre-action protocol applies, you will need to be aware that, if you do not follow the relevant terms of the protocol as to the instructing of an expert witness, you may find that you have a report that the court will not allow you to use, the cost of which, therefore, will not be recoverable from the other side. Similarly, in a fast-track case, if your own expert's report is not agreed, the judge giving directions may order expert evidence to be given by a different expert, instructed on a joint basis. You will, therefore, need to think very carefully, and advise your client as to the risks, before instructing an expert without either obtaining the consent of the other side or agreeing a joint instruction.

There will be some straightforward cases in which it will be obvious that the best course is to agree a single joint expert. The conclusions in the report may be so clear as to bring an end to the dispute, or at least to narrow the issues and enable the parties to reach a compromise. This is, after all, part of the overriding objective of the CPR.

In some cases in which a single joint expert has been instructed, usually on the court's direction, it is not uncommon for one or both parties to instruct another expert to advise them on any areas of weakness or deficiency in the joint report. Such experts may, for example, assist in the drafting of questions to be put to the joint expert. It is more than likely that the existence of these so-called 'shadow' experts will be unknown to the other side or the court. The cost of instructing such an expert will not be recoverable, and their use does seem to run counter to the spirit of the civil justice reforms.

You will find the 'Code of Guidance on Expert Evidence: A Guide for experts and those instructing them for the purpose of court proceedings', which is located at the end of CPR Part 35 in the White Book, indispensable to you, whether or not you have reached the stage of proceedings. The Code sets out in clear terms what the court expects of experts and what experts can expect from those who instruct them. In your dealings with an expert, the court will expect you:

(1) to keep him or her informed regularly about any deadlines that affect him or her;

(2) to advise him or her as to the court timetable and any changes to it – 35PD 6A now makes provision for any order that requires an act to be done by an expert, or otherwise affects an expert to be served on the expert by the party instructing him, or in the case of a joint expert, by the claimant;

(3) without delay, to provide further or updated instructions, as the progress of the case requires;

(4) to provide him or her with any order that makes provision for expert evidence;

(5) to advise whether, and, if so, when, his or her report will be disclosed to the other party; and

(6) to give him or her the opportunity to consider and comment upon other reports which deal with the same issues.

EXPERTS AND THE PRE-ACTION PROTOCOLS

As discussed in Chapter 7, the pre-action protocols encourage a less adversarial approach to the use of experts. The personal injury protocol, in particular, is clear in requiring any party who wishes to instruct an expert first to give the other party the opportunity to object to the choice of expert. Failure to comply with the protocol may result in costs sanctions.

EXPERTS AND THE COURT

CPR Part 35 applies whenever an expert is instructed to provide written or oral evidence for the court, subject to the limited application of Part 35 to small claims. It has already been mentioned that an expert witness has a duty to assist the court, which overrides any obligations to the party giving instructions or paying the fees (r 35.3).

Rule 35.4 gives the court complete control over the use of expert evidence at trial and, indeed, the court has a duty to restrict the evidence 'to that which is reasonably required to resolve the proceedings' (r 35.1). This was underlined by Evans-Lombe J in *Barings plc v Coopers & Lybrand (No 2)* [2001] Lloyd's Rep Bank 85 in which he said that admissible expert evidence:

'may still be excluded by the court if the court takes the view that calling it will not be helpful to the court in resolving any issue in the case justly. Such evidence will not be helpful where the issue to be decided is one of law or is otherwise one on which the court is able to come to a fully informed decision without hearing such evidence.'

Expert evidence can only be used at trial if the court has given permission and there is a presumption that this will be in written form (r 35.5(1)). The direction should specify the name and discipline of the expert. It is also a prerequisite for the use of expert evidence that it has been disclosed to the other party in accordance with the court's directions. The court will not allow any expert evidence to be used that is disclosed late, unless, in the particular circumstances, it would be plainly unjust not to allow it to be relied upon (r 35.13).

THE FORMALITIES OF AN EXPERT'S REPORT

CPR r 35.10 and PD 35 set out the formal requirements of an expert's report. In particular, the report must be addressed to the court and not to the party by whom the expert was instructed. It must be verified by a statement of truth, which, as well as giving full details of the expert's qualifications and acknowledging that the expert has complied with his or her overriding duty to the court, must contain the information set out in PD 35, para 1.2. You need to check that the expert has not overlooked the important requirement to summarise the range of opinion and give reasons for his or her own opinion. The expert you instruct should be aware of what is required, but it will be your duty to check the report and make sure that he or she has complied before the report is filed at court. Remember when you instruct an expert that he or she is obliged to set out the substance of the instructions given, whether written or oral. Professional privilege will not therefore attach to the instructions.

EXPERTS ON THE FAST TRACK

Since most cases that proceed on the fast track will have a value of less than £15,000, proportionality will dictate that the involvement of experts is kept to a minimum. The instruction of no more than two single joint experts to provide written evidence will be the norm. Oral evidence from experts is not allowed on the fast track, unless this is necessary in the interests of justice.

EXPERTS ON THE MULTI-TRACK

The presumption in favour of a single joint expert on the fast track does not apply to cases on the multi-track. The wide diversity of cases that are allocated to the multi-track means that the court has to have a greater degree of flexibility in case management. This is not to say that there will not be cases on the multi-track for which it will be appropriate for there to be a direction for written evidence from a single joint expert – many straightforward cases are allocated to the multi-track only because the value of the claim is in excess of £15,000. However, in a more complex case with multiple issues, the court is more likely to be assisted by hearing a range of opinion, at least on the crucial issues. There is nothing to prevent the court from giving permission for oral evidence from both parties' experts on the main issue, and directing a single joint expert on the secondary issues.

In heavier cases, in which there might otherwise be an overabundance of overlapping experts, PD 35, para 5 allows the court to direct that one of the experts (usually the leading expert among them) should be responsible for co-ordinating the preparation of one report, for which he or she will seek the contributions of the other experts, as required. In a large personal injury claim, for example, this may enable evidence that might otherwise necessitate reports on the cost of care, aids and equipment, and accommodation requirements all to be dealt with in one report.

SINGLE JOINT EXPERTS

It will generally be at the stage of allocation and directions that the court will first make provision for the use of expert evidence. It will be unusual, except in personal injury claims, for any expert evidence to be on the court file at that stage.

In a personal injury claim, there will be a medical report attached to the claim form, and the allocation questionnaires should indicate whether the defendant is content for that report to be relied upon, or whether another report has been or is to be obtained. In what appears from the papers to be a straightforward case, the district judge is unlikely, at that stage, to give permission for another report. It is more likely that the defendant will be given an opportunity to put written questions to the claimant's expert in the expectation that this will clear up any misgivings that the defendant has about the report. If the defendant has already obtained a report and wants permission to use it, the court may take the view that it makes sense, in terms of both time and expense, for both parties to have their own experts, provided that the issues can be narrowed by requiring the experts to have discussions and prepare a statement of what they can and cannot agree upon. If there does appear to be a good reason why the report is not capable of agreement by the defendant, rather than allowing the defendant to instruct his or her own expert, a direction may be given for the parties jointly to instruct a single expert.

Before the court gives a direction for an expert to be instructed, whether jointly or otherwise, the judge will need to be satisfied that the area of specialisation of the proposed expert is relevant to the issues, that he or she is willing to accept instructions and that the length of time that the expert will take to prepare the report can be accommodated within the court timetable. The expert will also have to be available within the trial window if he or she is to give oral evidence. You will, therefore, have to ensure that you are in a position to satisfy the court about these matters if you are asking for a direction for expert evidence.

WHAT IF YOU WANT ANOTHER REPORT?

Sometimes, one or both parties will be dissatisfied with a report prepared by the single joint expert instructed and may ask the court's permission to instruct another expert. This is what happened in *Daniels v Walker* [2000] 1 WLR 1382, a case in which the claimant had suffered serious personal injuries and would require some form of care for the rest of his life. The parties had agreed to obtain a joint report from an expert about the cost of care. The defendants were unhappy with the joint report because, in their experience, the figure given for the care regime was excessive and they wished to instruct their own expert to prepare another report. The claimant refused to allow the defendants' nominated expert facilities to interview the claimant and his family for the purposes of the report and so the defendants applied to the court for permission. This was refused and the defendants appealed. In the Court of Appeal, permission was given, and Lord Woolf helpfully summarised the court's approach:

'Where a party sensibly agrees to a joint report and the report is obtained as a result of joint instructions ... the fact that a party has agreed to adopt that course does not prevent that party being allowed facilities to obtain a report from another expert ....

In a substantial case such as this, the correct approach is to regard the instruction of an expert jointly by the parties as the first step in obtaining expert evidence on a particular issue. It is to be hoped that in the majority of cases it will not only be the first step but the last step.

If, having obtained a joint expert's report, a party, for reasons which are not fanciful, wishes to obtain further information before making a decision as to whether or not there is a particular part (or indeed the whole) of the expert's report which he or she may wish to challenge, then they should, subject to the discretion of the court, be permitted to obtain that evidence ....

It may be said in a case where there is a modest amount involved that it would be disproportionate to obtain a second report in any circumstances. At most what should be allowed is merely to put a question to the expert who has already prepared a report.

However, in this case a substantial sum of money depended on the issue as to whether full-time or part-time care was required. In those circumstances it was perfectly reasonable for the defendant [to obtain a second report].

In a case where there is a substantial sum involved one starts ... from the position that, wherever possible, a joint report is obtained. If there is a disagreement on that report, then there would be an issue as to whether to ask questions or whether to get your own expert's report. If questions do not resolve the matter and a party, or both parties, obtain their own expert's reports then that will result in a decision having to be reached as to what evidence should be called. That decision should not be taken until there has been a meeting between the experts involved. It may be that agreement could then be reached; it may be that agreement is reached as a result of asking the appropriate questions.

It is only as a last resort that you accept that it is necessary for oral evidence to be given by the experts before the court. The cross-examination of expert witnesses at the hearing, even in substantial cases, can be very expensive.'

GIVING JOINT INSTRUCTIONS

First, agreement must be reached on which expert is to be instructed. If agreement cannot be reached, then the court will usually select an expert from a list of experts who would be acceptable to both parties, or, failing agreement even to that limited extent, by selecting an expert through the relevant professional body (r 35.7(3)).

There is, in theory, nothing to prevent both parties from writing separate letters of instruction to a joint expert (r 35.8(1)), although the letters would have to be exchanged. In practice, it is preferable for the parties to agree a joint letter of instruction, and the judge may well direct that you do exactly this. In a complicated case, the judge may wish to see your agreed draft before it is sent, and, in any event, will usually direct that a copy of the letter be filed at court. If one letter in agreed terms is sent to the expert, the instructions will be clear to all concerned, not least to the expert, who could otherwise be left wondering whether the case that the claimant has instructed him or her on is, in fact, the same as that on which he or she has received instructions from the defendant.

LIABILITY FOR FEES

Unless the court makes any other direction, parties jointly instructing an expert will be jointly and severally liable to the expert for the fees. In any event, as solicitors giving instructions to an expert, you will be contractually bound to pay. There is power for the court to restrict the amount of fees and expenses that an expert may be paid (r 35.8(4)). This rule is most likely to be used to put a ceiling on the fees that one party, with boundless financial resources, may incur, in order not to disadvantage a party whose resources are limited, rather than in an attempt to limit the expert's fees generally. An expert's fees will, in any case, have to withstand the scrutiny of the assessment process (see Chapter 39).

WRITTEN QUESTIONS TO AN EXPERT

When a direction is made for expert evidence in a particular field to be given by a single joint expert, or where only one party has obtained a report which is not agreed by the other, the court will usually make provision for written questions to be put to the expert, in an attempt to clear up any concerns so that it will not be necessary for another expert to be instructed. The usual direction will be for questions to be put within 28 days of service of the report, with written replies to be given within 28 days thereafter. However, r 35.6 enables a party, on one occasion only, to put written questions about the report to a single joint expert, or the other party's expert, without an order of the court. The Rule requires the questions to be put within 28 days of service of the report, and that they must be for the sole purpose of clarification of the report. In other words, the questions should be confined to issues dealt with in the report and should not take the form of cross-examination by correspondence.

If you send the questions directly to the expert, PD 35, para 4.2 requires you to send a copy of them to the other party's solicitor.

The Rules do not prescribe a time within which the expert should reply to the questions, but, in most circumstances, 28 days will be considered a reasonable time. If an expert does not answer a question that is put to him or her under r 35.6, then the court may make an order that his or her evidence may not be used at trial, and/or that the party instructing the expert may not recover the expert's fees.

In the first instance, the party putting the questions to the expert must pay his or her fees for answering them. The expert's answers will be treated as part of his or her report.

DISCUSSIONS BETWEEN EXPERTS

Whenever more than one expert of a particular discipline is instructed, the court will invariably direct that they shall have discussions in order to prepare a statement, setting out what they can agree and what remains in dispute, with their reasons. The importance of this was emphasised in *Hubbard v Lambeth, Southwark and Lewisham Health Authority* [2001] EWCA Civ 1455, [2001] TLR 562, in which the Court of Appeal held that, as discussions between experts assist in narrowing the issues, even in a very complex case, there has to be a very good reason not to order a meeting, and, furthermore, a meeting can be ordered, even if one or both parties object. It is a matter for the experts involved whether they hold their discussions by meeting face to face or by telephone or video link, as long as the objective is achieved. It will not generally be necessary for the parties' legal representatives to attend but there is nothing in the Rules to prevent it. However, if such attendance was regarded by the court as unnecessary, the cost may not be recoverable.

It is important to note that any matters discussed between experts will not be referred to at trial unless the parties agree, and an agreement reached between experts in the course of their discussions does not bind the parties, unless they have expressly agreed to be bound. In narrowing the issues in this way before the trial begins, the time that experts may have to spend at court will be reduced, and possibly eliminated altogether.

WHEN THE EXPERT REQUIRES DIRECTIONS FROM THE COURT

From time to time, an expert may find difficulty in complying with a direction of the court. This may be simply an inability to meet a deadline imposed by the court, or it may be more substantial. Rule 35.14 gives an expert the right to ask the court for directions. However, the expert is not permitted to write to the court without first sending to both parties a copy of what he or she proposes to send to the court.

EXPERTS WHO DO NOT COMPLY

Ultimately, it is the responsibility of the person instructing the expert to ensure that he or she complies with the court's requirements, both as to the formalities of his or her report, and the time scale within which it is produced. If expert evidence is not disclosed in accordance with the court's directions, the court has power to order that the evidence may not be used. This does not assist the party on whose behalf the expert was instructed, but there may be some justification in refusing to pay his or her fees. In *Stevens v Gullis* [2000] 1 All ER 527, the Court of Appeal upheld a decision to debar an expert witness from giving evidence when it was clear that he had no conception of his responsibilities to the court under Part 35. More recently, in *Phillips v Symes* [2004] TLR 5 November it was decided that an expert witness can be joined as a party to proceedings for the purposes of making a wasted costs order. However, the circumstances in which this step would be taken would be exceptional, and would require evidence of gross and reckless disregard for his duty as an expert.

Part VII

TRIAL

Chapter 30

APPLICATIONS TO THE COURT

OVERVIEW

Part 23 is entitled 'General rules about applications for court orders' and is supplemented by CPR PD 23. Before making any application to the court, it is necessary to consider Part 23 in conjunction with the relevant Part of the CPR under which the application is made, for example: Part 6, if applying to serve the claim form outside the jurisdiction; r 7.5, if applying for extension of time for serving a claim form; Part 24, if applying for summary judgment; Part 25, if applying for an interim remedy; and so on. Thus, consider first of all what it is you are applying for and then how the application is to be made, pursuant to Part 23.

Is your application one which will require evidence in support? If so, what form will that evidence take? Will the statement of case and the application form itself be sufficient or is further evidence in the form of a witness statement required? Is your application governed by one of the few rules which insist on affidavit evidence?

Draft the order which you will be asking the court to make. Rule 23.6 requires an application notice to state what order the applicant is seeking and, briefly, why the applicant is seeking the order. It is good discipline to draft verbatim the order which you will be asking the court to make. If this can be conveniently and briefly stated in the application notice itself, all well and good, but, if it cannot, annex the draft order to the application notice and refer to it. Any judge is entitled to ask the applicant what order is being sought (and usually does so) and this must be answered in specific, not general, terms – hence the need to be clear about this and draft the order sought in advance. Do not forget to include any costs order being sought.

We will now consider the four different ways in which applications can come before the court, pursuant to Part 23. Although Part 23 is primarily concerned with applications made after proceedings have been commenced but before trial, there are certain situations in which applications must be made, pursuant to Part 23, before proceedings have been issued (rather than by using a claim form under either Part 7 or Part 8). This includes an application for pre-action disclosure, for example.

APPLICATION ON NOTICE WITH A HEARING

Most applications are dealt with in this manner. A copy of the application notice must be served as soon as is practical after it has been filed and, unless the rule or Practice Direction specifies a different time-limit, must be served at least 3 days before the court is to deal with the application (r 23.7). It can be served by the court (r 23.7(2)). When a copy of an application notice is served, it must be accompanied by a copy of any witness statement or affidavit in support and a copy of any draft order which the applicant has attached to his or her application form. However, the rule does not require written evidence to be filed if it has already been filed, or to be served on a party on whom it has already been served (r 23.7(5)). (See further, PD 23, para 9 – Evidence.)

If a respondent to an application wishes to rely on evidence which has not yet been served, he or she should serve it as soon as possible and, in any event, in accordance with any directions the court may have given (PD 23, para 9.4). The rule under which the application is made may well contain other specific provisions. (See, for example, r 24.5 in connection with respondent's evidence opposing an application for summary judgment.) If it is necessary for the applicant to serve any evidence in reply, it should be served as soon as possible and, in any event, in accordance with any directions the court may have given (PD 23, para 9.5). The contents of an application notice may be used as evidence (otherwise than at trial), provided the contents have been verified by a statement of truth (see Part 22).

Even where there is no specific requirement to provide evidence, it should be borne in mind, as a practical matter, that the court will often need to be satisfied by evidence of the facts that are relied on in support of (or for opposing) the application.

The application will be heard by the level of judge indicated on the application form and will have been given a time-estimate, based on that requested in the application notice. When giving a time-estimate, ensure that you have allowed sufficient time, not only to make the application, but also for the court to hear the other side and then for the judge to give judgment and deal with costs. If you consider, for example, that your application will take only 10 minutes, it is likely that the other side will also need 10 minutes and then so will the judge to give judgment, etc. Thus, your time-estimate should be 30 minutes – not 10 minutes. If insufficient time has been allowed, the application may have to be adjourned, possibly at the expense of the solicitor who gave the inadequate time-estimate. Always make your time-estimates too long rather than too short. Bear in mind that, if the hearing does 'go short', the district judge will have plenty of paperwork to be getting on with and will be glad of the opportunity to do so.

Applications that require a hearing should, wherever possible, be made so that they can be dealt with at any other hearing for which a date has already been fixed, or for which a date is about to be fixed. This is particularly so in relation to case management conferences, allocation hearings, listing hearings and pre-trial reviews

(PD 23, para 2.8). Where the court has already listed an application for, say, a case management conference and given it 30 minutes and you now wish to make an application which you estimate will take one hour, this should immediately be drawn to the attention of the court so that the court can consider whether it is possible to allow more time at the case management conference or, alternatively, whether the case management conference should be adjourned to a later date, to be dealt with concurrently with your application. The latter course is the more likely, as having two separate hearings increases costs unnecessarily and, in any event, the case management directions may well be affected by the results of your application.

The general rule is that all hearings – and this will include the hearing of your application – are held in public (r 39.2). This rule was introduced when the CPR came into force in April 1999, no doubt with an eye to the ECHR, Art 6. However, although courts which have been built since that date (of which there are very few) are built to a new design which provides more public access, the vast majority of hearings before district judges and masters take place in hearing rooms (formerly known as chambers) which are not large enough to accommodate more than a very few members of the public. Rule 39.2(2) does not require the court to make special arrangements for accommodating members of the public and, thus, the reality is that members of the public and press are not usually present for the hearing of applications.

There are, of course, exceptions, set out in CPR PD 39, to the general rule that a hearing is to be in public (see paras 1.4A and 1.5 of PD 39).

The court may order that an application, or part of an application, be dealt with by a telephone hearing. The applicant should indicate on his application notice if he or she seeks an order for this to happen (see PD 23, para 6.1A). Consent of all parties is required.

Either both parties should be physically present or should attend by telephone. No representative of a party to an application being heard by telephone may attend the judge in person while the application is being heard, unless the other party to the application has agreed that he or she may do so (PD 23, para 6.4).

One advantage of a telephone hearing – quite apart from the saving in costs – is that it is automatically recorded and a transcript is provided. The applicant's legal representative must arrange for this to be done. (See further, PD 23, para 6.)

PD 23, para 7 enables parties who wish to use video conferencing, where those facilities are available, to apply to the master or district judge for directions. At the moment, very few courts have such facilities.

Who should attend to conduct the hearing of the application? Generally, the solicitor having the conduct of the case or a suitably briefed member of staff. It is, of course, possible to brief counsel. Bear in mind that your application may well be heard alongside another hearing, for example a case management conference, where the court will be dealing with other matters. In any event, parties must anticipate that, at any hearing of any application, the court may wish to review the conduct of the case as a whole and give any necessary case management directions. Accordingly, advocates must be ready to assist the court in doing so and to answer any questions the court may ask for this purpose (PD 23, para 2.9).

Try to avoid the need for applications to be dealt with separately if they relate to purely interlocutory matters (such as disclosure or applications to serve further witness statements). In contrast, an application for summary judgment is likely to require a separate hearing.

If the court has already fixed a date for a hearing and a party wishes to make an application at that hearing but does not have time to serve an application notice, he or she should, in accordance with PD 23, para 2.10, inform the other party and the court (if possible, in writing), as soon as he or she can, of the nature of the application and the reason for it. He or she should then make the application formally at the hearing. The court will deal with it if there is time to do so.

APPLICATION ON NOTICE WITHOUT A HEARING

In comparison with applications which require a hearing, there are very few applications on notice which do not. Rule 23.8 enables the court to deal with an application without a hearing if:

> '(a) the parties agree as to the terms of the order sought;
> (b) the parties agree that the court should dispose of the application without a hearing; or,
> (c) the court does not consider that a hearing would be appropriate.'

The most common situation arising in practice is where an application has been made anticipating a hearing but then, following negotiation, an appropriate order is agreed, thus bringing the case within r 23.8(a). (See further, PD 23, para 10, which is entitled 'Consent orders'.) The court should be informed as soon as possible (it may be able to make use of the time saved for other matters). Even if the matter is not totally agreed – but much of it has been – the case might fall within r 23.8(b) or (c) quoted above. For example, the parties' solicitors may have agreed the substance of the application and agreed that the respondent will pay the applicant's costs, but may not have agreed the amount of those costs. To save yet further expense, the parties could agree that the court should dispose of the application without a hearing and carry out a summary assessment of costs based on written representations of the parties, rather than incur yet more costs in attending.

APPLICATION WITHOUT NOTICE WITH A HEARING

An application without notice but with a hearing is the usual way of obtaining an urgent injunction. Thus, in this context, Part 23 has to be read in conjunction with

Part 25 and, in particular, PD 25. By PD 23, para 3, an application may be made without serving an application notice only:

(1)   where there is exceptional urgency;
(2)   where the overriding objective is best furthered by doing so;
(3)   by consent of all the parties;
(4)   with the permission of the court;
(5)   where para 2.10 applies (considered above);
(6)   where a court order, rule or Practice Direction permits.

An application for a 'freezing injunction' thus falls within (1), (2) and (6) (permitted under PD 25) above.

The appropriate procedure is to telephone the court and explain that there is an urgent, without notice application. If the telephone call is made during normal court office hours, the court will find a suitable judge to hear the application at the local court, if possible, but, if not, at the nearest convenient court. If the telephone call is made out of hours to the urgent business officer, he or she will make specific arrangements and telephone you back, telling you where and when the application will be heard.

By r 23.9(3), the order must contain a statement of the right to make an application to set aside or vary the order under r 23.10.

The court draws up most orders and serves them (rr 40.3 and 40.4). However, applicants are required to draft injunctions and the like.

In addition to the order itself, r 23.9 requires that where the court makes an order, whether granting *or dismissing* the application, a copy of the application notice and any evidence in support be served with the order on any party or other person against whom the order was made and against whom the order was sought (unless the court otherwise orders).

APPLICATION WITHOUT NOTICE WITHOUT A HEARING

Applications invariably fall within this category because, although a judicial decision is required, the relevant rule is clear, all the evidence or submissions are in writing and there is, as yet, no opponent to be served. This category will include, typically, applications under r 6.8 for service by an alternative method; an application under r 6.21 for permission to serve the claim form out of the jurisdiction; an application under r 7.6 for an extension of time for serving a claim form. There will be other applications where, although there is an opponent, the rules expressly permit such applications, for example in the context of enforcement, an application for a third party debt order under r 72.4, or an application for an interim charging order under r 73.4.

They are, of course, also governed by PD 23, para 3, and r 23.8 (both set out above).

APPLICATION NOTICE

CPR PD 23, para 2.1 provides that practice form N244 may be used (there are specific, prescribed forms for enforcement purposes, eg third party debt orders and charging orders, mentioned above). The paragraph also provides that the application, in addition to matters set out in r 23.6 (set out above), be signed and include:

(1)   the title of the claim;
(2)   the reference number of the claim;
(3)   the full name of the applicant;
(4)   where the applicant is not already a party, his or her address for service; and
(5)   either a request for a hearing or a request that the application be dealt with without a hearing.

The practice form also includes provision for specifying the level of judge who you wish to hear the application and for a time-estimate.

On receipt of an application notice containing a request that the application be dealt with without a hearing, the application notice is referred to a master or district judge, who must decide whether the application is suitable for consideration without a hearing and, if it is, whether or not to make the order requested. If the master or district judge does not agree that the application is suitable for consideration without a hearing, the court will notify the applicant and the respondent of the time, date and place for the hearing of the application and may, if appropriate, give directions as to the filing of evidence.

There are some applications for which an application form may not be necessary and a letter to the court will be sufficient. This will include, for example, an application to the court to correct a court order which has been incorrectly drawn under the 'slip rule' (r 40.12), or an application to extend a stay under r 26.4.

COSTS

At the end of the hearing of any application, if it is one not governed by fixed costs (as to which, see Part 45), it must be anticipated that the costs of the application will be summarily assessed if they are to be ordered to be paid by one party to the other. If, however, the application is part of the routine management and progress of the case, then the usual order will be 'costs in the case'.

When making an application, consider what the appropriate order for costs should be and include it in the application. If your opponent has made an application, consider whether it is appropriate to consent to it or oppose it and consider separately whether to consent to or oppose the costs order being sought in the application.

Even if your application succeeds, it may be appropriate for you to concede that you should pay the other side's costs. For example, if a client with a good defence has failed to instruct you in time for you either to serve the defence in accordance with the requirements of the rules or to obtain an extension from the opponent or the court and, as a consequence, the claimant has obtained a default judgment, even though you may successfully make an application under Part 13 for judgment to be set aside, the extra costs incurred have been incurred as a result of the defendant's default and, thus, it ought to be conceded that, in any event, the defendant should pay the claimant's costs of the application to set aside judgment. It must be anticipated that the costs will be summarily assessed and ordered to be paid immediately.

The court needs the necessary information in order to carry out a summary assessment of costs. Accordingly, all parties must file and serve a statement of costs in Form N260 not less than 24 hours before the hearing at which summary assessment will take place (see further Section 13 of PD44 – Costs).

Chapter 31

PRE-TRIAL CHECKLIST
(LISTING QUESTIONNAIRE)

The pre-trial checklist is used on the fast track and multi-track, but not on the small claims track. Its purpose is to provide a means of checking that all is on course for trial and to alert the court to any matters that may need attention to ensure that the trial will be ready to proceed in the time allocated.

DIRECTIONS FOR FILING

At the allocation stage in a fast-track case, and either at that stage or later on the multi-track, the court will give a direction for the filing of a pre-trial checklist by each party by a certain date. That date will be no later than 8 weeks before the trial date or the start of the trial window, and the court will send out a pre-trial checklist in the prescribed form to each party at least 14 days before the date for filing.

PD Costs, Section 6 requires a costs estimate to be filed with the pre-trial checklist and served on the other party. The costs estimate should follow the format of Costs Precedent H (see PD Costs, Sections 6 and 18). When preparing your costs estimate, you should bear in mind that it may be produced at a later stage if there is an issue as to costs.

It is a good idea to agree with the other party that you will exchange pre-trial checklists before sending them to the court so that you ensure that the court is not given conflicting information. Indeed, the questions that are asked in Section E of Form N170 about whether the case is ready for trial encourage you to speak to the other party and agree a timetable and time estimate for the trial.

INFORMATION SOUGHT

The purpose of the pre-trial checklist is to confirm to the court whether or not the case will be ready for trial on the date or in the window that has already been fixed.

The revised Form N170 asks for the following information.

A Directions: whether the court's directions have been complied with, and whether there are any matters outstanding that need to be dealt with before the case is ready for trial. This information was requested in the original listing questionnaire. However, the revised Form N170 makes it clear that if additional directions are necessary before the trial, a separate application must be made in accordance with Part 23 and attached to the pre-trial checklist, together with the fee and a draft order. The application should include all directions needed to enable the case to be tried on the date fixed or within the existing trial window. In other words, it is not envisaged that at this stage you will be seeking directions that will result in the trial date or window being vacated.

B Witnesses: the number of lay witnesses to be called, and whether there are any dates that are not convenient for them to attend the trial. If this is the case, the name of the witness and the reason for avoiding these dates must be supplied. If any special facilities are required for a witness, eg an interpreter or wheelchair access, these must be set out.

C Experts: if the court has given permission for the use of oral and/or written expert evidence, details of each expert and the field of expertise must be supplied. It must be specified if the expert is a joint expert and whether the evidence has been agreed. It must also be stated whether or not there has been any discussion between the experts and whether they have signed a joint statement. Directions will usually have been given for this on allocation. Form N170 asks for confirmation as to whether or not permission has been given for oral evidence, and if an expert is giving oral evidence and the trial date has not been fixed, any dates within the trial window that are to be avoided, with the reason, must be given. The provision in the original listing questionnaire that gave an opportunity for a party to ask the court for permission for an expert to give oral evidence at trial has been removed in the revised form. Clearly, leaving such an application to the stage of the pre-trial checklist is late in the day, and any such application should, in any event, be made separately and not under cover of the Form N170.

D Legal representation: details are requested of who will be presenting the case at trial and for any non-availability of that person, again giving reasons.

E The trial: you are asked to say whether the original time estimate for the trial has changed, and if so, what the time estimate is now. Before supplying this information, the revised Form N170 encourages you to discuss with the other party or parties how much time is required for the trial and attempt to agree a time estimate. You will also have to discuss a timetable for the trial, which is to be attached to the pre-trial checklist and agreed if possible. Finally, in a fast-track case, you are asked whether you are prepared to accept shorter notice than the 3 weeks that is normally allowed.

F Document and fee checklist: the revised form helpfully sets out the documents that must accompany the pre-trial checklist. These are as follows:

–   an estimate of costs;
–   a proposed timetable for trial;

– any application and fee for additional directions, if appropriate; and
– a draft order.

In addition, the listing fee must accompany the Form N170.

COURT ACTION ON RECEIPT OF CHECKLISTS

When the pre-trial checklists are received by the court, the file is put before the district judge, who will be concerned to see whether there is any risk that the trial may not be ready to proceed on the date fixed or within the trial window.

Any applications for further directions that accompany the pre-trial checklist will be considered. Orders may be made without a hearing if the parties consent and the district judge approves the terms, or under the court's general case management powers. The pre-trial checklist does not contemplate an application at that stage for directions that would result in the removal of the case from the list and, if that were to be the situation, the court would direct an urgent case management hearing or pre-trial review.

Non-receipt by due date

In view of the importance to the court of the information requested in the pre-trial checklist, if a party fails to file his pre-trial checklist by the due date this will be viewed very seriously. Depending upon the circumstances, the judge may decide to list the case on the basis of any pre-trial checklist filed by another party, make an unless order to secure compliance, or call a listing hearing which will almost certainly result in the party in default paying the costs of that hearing.

Availability of witnesses and experts

You will have notified your witnesses and experts of the trial window when you received the allocation notice, and the pre-trial checklist gives you the opportunity to inform the court of any dates within the trial period when a witness, expert or representative will not be available. You are now required to give reasons for any non-availability.

The court recognises that not all the witnesses will be available for the entire period of the trial window, and that some juggling will have to be done. However, this is not the time to present the court with non-availability that means that there is no prospect of listing the trial within the trial window. It is your responsibility to keep an eye on witness availability and to flag up any potential problems at an early stage.

Directions on listing

The court is required to fix the trial date or week, give a time estimate and specify in which court the trial will take place (PD 28, para 7.1(1); PD 29, para 9.1).

In addition the district judge may give other directions. However, you should be clear that any directions that you consider necessary must form the subject of a separate application and must not be requested under cover of the pre-trial checklist.

Directions to secure compliance

Very often, the pre-trial checklist will disclose that certain directions have not been complied with, although there is space on Form N170 for you to indicate the date by which you will have complied. In an effort to ensure that there is no further slippage in the timetable, the judge may make an unless order requiring a party in default to comply by a certain date or, for example, have his or her statement of case struck out. If the trial date is at risk, the judge may decide to call a case management hearing to establish the reasons for non-compliance and try to salvage the situation. The party in default can expect to pay the costs of that hearing.

Trial timetable and time estimate

Using the information in the pre-trial checklist, the court will confirm or vary the provisional time estimate given at the allocation stage. It is important to give a realistic time estimate for the trial. This is best achieved by conferring with the other party over the timetable for the trial that now has to accompany the pre-trial checklist, and reaching agreement if possible. This will assist the Diary Manager, whose job it is to make best use of court time so that delays in cases coming for trial are minimised.

Chapter 32

COMPROMISE BEFORE TRIAL

The whole thrust of the new civil procedure is that litigation should be a last resort, and, even after proceedings have commenced, all avenues for settlement should be actively pursued.

It has already been seen that settlement may be achieved by means of Part 36 offers and payments, in which case, the proceedings are brought to an end by service of a formal notice of acceptance and specified costs consequences follow.

Where an agreement is negotiated without any formal steps being taken, it is necessary to achieve finality by seeking an order from the court.

CONSENT ORDERS

Generally, the parties will agree the wording of an order, which will be endorsed with the consent of each party and sent to the court with a request that the judge should make an order in the agreed terms.

There is no basis upon which a judge may interfere with the settlement terms agreed, unless one of the parties is a child or a patient, in which case the court's approval of the terms must always be obtained. However, a judge may consider that the wording of the proposed consent order is inappropriate, beyond what is within the court's power to direct, or ineffective to achieve the desired result, and a consent order may be refused on this basis.

If the terms that have been agreed between the parties are no more than for payment of an agreed figure and costs, the order will simply provide that judgment is entered for the sum agreed and an order made for payment of costs, to be assessed if not agreed. It is incorrect to submit a consent order for approval that requires a party to accept a specified sum in satisfaction of his or her claim: this is not within the court's power to direct.

TOMLIN ORDERS

Sometimes, the terms that have been negotiated will not be straightforward. They may involve matters that are completely outside the scope of the proceedings. In these cases, an order in the form of a *Tomlin* order (named after the case in which it was first used) is the best way to conclude matters. A *Tomlin* order provides for the proceedings to be stayed on the basis that the parties have agreed terms that are recorded in a schedule to the order.

The basic framework of a *Tomlin* order is as follows:

> 'BY CONSENT
>
> IT IS ORDERED THAT all further proceedings herein be stayed upon the terms set out in the schedule to this order save for the purpose of enforcing the terms set out in the schedule for which purpose permission is given to apply to the court:
>
> AND IT IS FURTHER ORDERED THAT
>
> [include here orders for assessment of costs or for payment out of court]
>
> SCHEDULE
>
> [the agreed terms]
>
> **DATED this   day of   200 .**
>
> [signatures of the parties/their solicitors]'

Many practitioners are confused about the terms that may be included in the schedule and those that must appear as part of the order, and an unsatisfactory hybrid very often results.

The schedule

The parties are free to agree the terms for the schedule and, as has been noted above, these may include matters that are unconnected with the proceedings. However, the terms in the schedule cannot be directly enforced as the terms of an order may. Before schedule terms may be enforced, an application must be made to the court for an order for specific performance or an injunction. This is why permission is given in the body of the order to apply to the court.

It is important to bear in mind when drafting the agreed terms for the schedule that they may have to be the subject of such an application, and that to have a chance of being successful, the terms must be clear and unambiguous, and capable of performance.

The order

Any agreed terms that may need to be enforced as an order must be contained within the body of the order (see above), and not in the schedule. Generally, this will include orders for the assessment of costs by the court, or for payment out of court.

It is important that any matters that appear in the body of the order are matters that the court has jurisdiction to order, otherwise the order will be refused.

SETTLEMENT WHEN A TRIAL DATE/WINDOW IS FIXED

CPR PD 39, para 4.1 sets out the procedure to be followed if a claim is settled or discontinued after a trial date has been fixed. This provides for the listing officer for the trial court to be notified immediately and for a sealed copy of the order giving effect to the settlement or notice of discontinuance to be filed with the listing officer.

COMPROMISE ON BEHALF OF A CHILD OR PATIENT

As previously discussed, any settlement reached on behalf of a child or a patient, including by way of a payment into court, can be accepted only with the court's approval. Rule 21.10 and PD 21, para 6 set out the procedure to be followed.

If settlement has been achieved without proceedings, a claim must be made under Part 8, requesting the court's approval to the settlement. The claim form must set out full details of the claim, as well as the proposed terms of settlement and a draft order in Form N292.

Whether there are proceedings or not, the court will need the information set out in PD 21, para 6.2 before it can consider what is proposed:

(1)   whether and to what extent the defendant admits liability;
(2)   the age and any occupation of the child or patient;
(3)   that the compromise is approved by the litigation friend;
(4)   in a personal injury claim arising out of an accident, details of the circumstances of the accident, any medical reports, and a schedule of any past and future financial losses;
(5)   except in very clear cases, there should be an opinion from counsel as to the merits of the compromise proposed.

At the hearing, you will be required to produce Form CFO 320 and, in the case of a child, the child's birth certificate.

Chapter 33

PREPARATION FOR TRIAL

TERMINATION WITHOUT TRIAL

There are several ways in which a matter can end without actually going to trial. These include:

–   summary judgment (CPR Part 24) (Chapter 20);
–   strike out (CPR r 3.4);
–   default judgment (CPR Part 12) (Chapter 18);
–   discontinuance (CPR Part 38) and withdrawal;
–   compromise (Chapter 32).

PREPARATION FOR TRIAL

If a matter proceeds to trial, the following steps will have been taken.

–   The parties will have investigated their cases.
–   The claim will have been issued and a defence filed (Chapter 14).
–   Directions will have been given (Chapter 23).
–   Disclosure will have taken place (Chapter 27).
–   Witness statements will have been exchanged (Chapter 28).
–   Expert evidence will have been dealt with according to the directions (Chapter 29).
–   Any interim applications should have been made by now, eg for summary judgment or interim payment (Chapter 30).
–   Part 36 offers or Part 36 payments may have been made (Chapter 37).

The pre-trial checklist will be completed and the trial date will be fixed. You will have arranged witnesses of fact and any experts required.

DOCUMENTS ('THE TRIAL BUNDLE')

The trial bundle should contain:

- an index;
- all statements of case;
- case summary and/or chronology;
- all requests for further information under CPR Part 18 and the answers;
- witness statements and witness summaries;
- any hearsay notices;
- any notices of intention to rely on plans and/or photographs;
- expert reports and responses to questions;
- documents relied on in evidence (including translations where necessary);
- any order giving trial directions;
- any other necessary documents (but not any Part 36 correspondence);
- if the documents contain legal authorities, a certificate that *Practice Direction (Citation of Authorities)* [2001] 1 WLR 1001, [2001] 2 All ER 510, CA, has been complied with.

You will also need to prepare:

- costs schedules for summary assessment of costs of trial (see PD 29, para 10.5; PD Costs, Section 13);
- a list of witnesses;
- original documents;
- copies of any interim orders not in the trial bundle;
- a note of the name and address of the trial advocates;
- Part 36 details;
- skeleton arguments.

(See Chapter 36 for further discussion.)

WHO WILL CONDUCT THE ADVOCACY AT THE TRIAL?

You may decide to instruct counsel at various stages, for example:

- prior to commencement to see whether or not you have a case or a defence;
- as part of the team throughout the case;
- for specific tasks such as trial advocacy or drafting complex statements of case;
- just for a 'second opinion' on the evidence;
- towards the end of the case if and when it heads towards trial; or
- not at all.

If your case is in the county court, either solicitor or counsel may represent the client at trial. In the High Court, either counsel or a solicitor–advocate may appear. For guidance, see Principle 7.02 note 4, and The Law Society Model Anti-discrimination Policy, Section C. See also The Law Society's Code for Advocacy and Principles 21.02, 21.03, 21.06, 21.17 and 21.21.

See also Principles 20.06 and 20.07 for guidance on counsel's fees. Note that individual counsel may be prepared to represent clients under a conditional fee arrangement.

There are obligations on a solicitor when instructing counsel with regard to maintaining a professional relationship and conduct. In particular, these include:

–   sending the right materials and in sufficient time (Principle 20.03; see also Principle 21.08);
–   attending the advocate whilst in court (Principle 20.04);
–   choosing appropriate counsel and taking responsibility (Principle 20.05).

Typical tasks undertaken by counsel might include:

–   drafting (or 'settling') documents such as statements of case;
–   preparing an Opinion;
–   giving advice on evidence;
–   attending the case management conference;
–   advising the client in conference (junior counsel) or in consultation (leading counsel)
–   preparing skeleton arguments;
–   advocacy.

Note that, particularly in a case where counsel has been involved from the outset, it may not be necessary to send formal instructions or briefs, and a letter or even a telephone call may be sufficient. In all cases (save where the client is publicly funded) counsel's fee should be agreed in advance with counsel's clerk.

OTHER ISSUES

Other issues that you might wish to consider at this stage, before commencing trial, include the following.

Interest on damages after judgment

Interest will generally continue to run on any damages after the judgment has been given (except in the county court on judgments under £5,000). The interest rate will be 8% – or the contract rate if applicable.

Part 36 issues

Only after judgment will the trial judge be notified of any Part 36 payments or offers.

The cost consequences will then be taken into account.

Costs

Costs are always at the discretion of the court. Generally, costs follow the event (ie the loser is ordered to pay most of the winning party's costs).

However, the court will take into account factors such as failure to comply with pre-action protocols, the general conduct of the parties in pursuing the litigation, wasted costs orders, the outcome of interlocutory applications and any Part 36 consequences.

Detailed assessment of costs

If the costs are not immediately summarily assessed by the judge after the trial there will be an order for detailed assessment (see further, Chapter 39). Usually, the parties negotiate and agree the precise amount of costs to be paid by the loser following judgment. However, if they are unable to agree, there is a further hearing before a costs judge who decides upon the precise figure.

Stay of execution

If judgment has been awarded, a defendant may ask for a stay of execution if the defendant:

–   wishes to appeal; or
–   wishes to apply for an order permitting payment by installments.

A CHECKLIST

The following checklist shows the time-scale for the procedural stages leading up to trial.

TIMESCALE	ACTIVITY	CPR RULE/ PRACTICE DIRECTION
FIXING OF TRIAL DATE		
REACTING TO WITNESS STATEMENTS/EXPERTS' REPORTS	CEA 1995, s 2 particulars of hearsay?	
		r 33.4
		r 33.5
		r 35.12
		r 35.6; PD 35, para 4.5
	Advice on evidence from counsel?	
NOT LESS THAN 10 WEEKS BEFORE TRIAL	Receive pre-trial checklist from court.	r 29.6(1)
NOT LESS THAN 8 WEEKS BEFORE TRIAL	Return pre-trial checklist within 14 days of receipt	r 29.6(2); PD 29, paras 8.1(5), 9.2
		r 29.6(3); PD 29, para 8.3
		PD Costs, para 6.4(2)
COURT'S RESPONSE TO RECEIPT OF PRE-TRIAL CHECKLIST	Court may convene a listing hearing if parties are in default.	r 29.6(3); PD 29, para 8.4
	Court may convene a pre-trial review or cancel one already fixed.	r 29.7; PD 29, para 8.5
		r 29.3(2); PD 29, para 5.2
		r 29.8; PD 29, para 9.1
		PD 39, para 4.1
		PD 29, para 9.2
	As soon as trial date and place fixed, notify witnesses and advocate.	
NOT LESS THAN 21 DAYS BEFORE	Notice to Admit facts	r 32.18

TIMESCALE	ACTIVITY	CPR RULE/ PRACTICE DIRECTION
TRIAL	Notice of intention to rely on plans, photos, etc, not already dealt with.	r 33.6
NOT LESS THAN 7 DAYS BEFORE TRIAL	Witness summons	rr 34.3–34.7
	If you settle within the 7 days before trial, the listing fee will not be returned.	
NOT LESS THAN 3 DAYS BEFORE TRIAL	Claimant to file trial bundles not more than 7 days and not less than 3 days before trial.	r 39.5; PD 39, para 3.1
		PD 39, para 3.9
		PD 39, para 3.2
NOT LESS THAN 24 HOURS BEFORE TRIAL (IF TRIAL TO LAST LESS THAN ONE DAY)	Prepare and file costs schedule for summary assessment of costs at end of trial.	PD 29, para 10.5 PD Costs, para 13
AT TRIAL	Have original documents and any other court orders.	PD 39, para 3.3
	Hand up to judge details of advocates.	PD 39, para 5.1

THE SKELETON ARGUMENT

Skeleton arguments are an essential part of preparation for trial (see Chapter 12). They set out the parties to the action and the main issues in the case for the court to decide. There follows an example of a skeleton argument on behalf of a claimant which demonstrates an appropriate layout and style.

Claim No HQ 07564

IN THE HIGH COURT OF JUSTICE
QUEEN'S BENCH DIVISION
ROYAL COURTS OF JUSTICE
B E T W E E N:

ARNOLD ROBINSON

Claimant

– and –

CASTLETON DELIVERIES PLC

Defendant

SKELETON ARGUMENT ON BEHALF OF THE CLAIMANT

DRAMATIS PERSONAE

NAME	DESCRIPTION	ABBREVIATION
Jocelyn Bailey	Credit Controller of the Defendant.	Ms Bailey
Castleton Deliveries plc	The Defendant, a company engaged in the supply of goods by mail order.	Defendant
Castleton Deliveries (Wales) Limited	A subsidiary of the Defendant.	Castleton Wales
Devereux Hatfield	Solicitors for the Claimant.	Devereux
Peter Elias	Expert witness instructed by the Claimant on heating and air conditioning issues.	Mr Elias
James Boyd & Partners	Solicitors for the Defendant.	Boyd
Cynthia Harbin	Administrative Director of the Defendant.	Mrs Harbin
Microclimates.com plc	Specialist contractor employed by the Defendant to install heating and air conditioning equipment. Now in insolvent liquidation.	Microclimates
Hugh Morrison	Expert witness instructed by the Defendant on heating and air conditioning issues.	Prof Morrison
Anne Penfold	Chartered accountant, expert witness instructed by the parties jointly on quantum issues.	Ms Penfold
Arnold Robinson	The Claimant, a self-employed heating and air conditioning consultant.	Claimant

CHRONOLOGY

DATE	EVENT	PAGE
September 2002	Claimant is approached by Mrs Harbin.	
October 2002	Initial planning meeting between Claimant and Mrs Harbin.	
20 January 2003	Claimant contracts with Defendant to provide consultancy services ('the Contract').	
21 January 2003	Review meeting. Claimant begins work.	
10 February 2003	Board meeting at which Microclimates system is discussed.	
16 February 2003	Heating and air conditioning system is delivered to Defendant by Microclimates.	
17 February 2003	Claimant is informed of Defendant's purchase of Microclimates system.	
8 June 2003	Review meeting at which snagging list is discussed.	
20 September 2003	Microclimates goes into insolvent liquidation.	
10 October 2003	Mrs Harbin goes on maternity leave.	
8 January 2004	Further review meeting at which Claimant recommends purchase of additional equipment.	
27 February 2004	Further review meeting.	
28 February 2004	System is signed off.	
24 March 2004	Claimant's invoice.	
6 April 2004	Claimant's letter of claim.	
3 May 2004	Issue of claim form and particulars of claim.	
14 May 2004	Acknowledgement of service.	
16 July 2004	Hearing of Claimant's application for summary judgment which is unsuccessful.	
1 July 2004	Defence and counterclaim.	
12 July 2004	Reply and defence to counterclaim.	
21 September 2004	Allocation.	
16 October 2004	Case management conference.	
26 October 2004	Claimant's list of documents.	
28 October 2004	Defendant's list of documents.	
6 February 2005	Mutual exchange of witness statements.	
12 October 2005	Trial date.	

THE ISSUES

1   Whether or not the Claimant acted with reasonable skill and care in performing his obligations under the Contract.

2   Whether or not under the terms of the Contract and in the factual circumstances surrounding the project, the Claimant completed his obligations within a reasonable time.

3   Quantum.

THE CLAIMANT'S CASE

The first issue – reasonable skill and care

1   There was an implied term in the Contract under s 13 of the Supply of Goods and Services Act 1982 that the Claimant should provide his services with reasonable skill and care.

2   By analogy with *Wilsher v Essex Area Health Authority* [1987] QB 730, the standard of the obligation referred to in 1 above is that which a member of the public would expect from a person in the Claimant's position.[1]

3   The Claimant had limited information prior to entering into the Contract about the Defendant's premises or the nature of its activities.

4   The Claimant did not become aware until February 2000 of the existence of Castleton Wales. The Claimant did not become aware until after that date of the nature of the activities of Castleton Wales, those activities rendering the Contract more difficult to complete.

5   The Defendant purchased the Microclimates system without the knowledge and/or recommendation of the Claimant. The Claimant had merely used the Microclimates system as an illustration during a presentation and had made no formal recommendation in respect of it. Further, as appears from the reports of both Mr Elias and Prof Morrison, the system purchased was a standard system not tailored to the Defendant's specific requirements.

6   The Claimant experienced difficulties both technically and in obtaining the co-operation of Mrs Harbin and of the Defendant generally in remedying the problems arising from the purchase of the Microclimates system.

7   Consequently, in all the circumstances, the Claimant complied with his contractual obligations with reasonable skill and care and is entitled to payment of his invoice.

The second issue – completion within a reasonable time

1   As the time for completion of the Contract was not fixed by the Contract, but left to be fixed in a manner agreed by the Contract or determined by the course of dealing between the parties, there was an implied term under

---

[1]   See *Practice Direction (Citation of Authorities)* [2001] 1 WLR 1001, [2001] 2 All ER 510, CA.

s 14(1) of the Supply of Goods and Services Act 1982 that the services would be carried out within a reasonable time.

2   Further, under s 14(2) of the Supply of Goods and Services Act 1982, what is a reasonable time is a question of fact.

3   The Claimant made no representations to Mrs Harbin or otherwise as to the length of time it would take him to complete the Contract.

4   The Claimant had limited information prior to entering into the Contract about the Defendant's premises or the nature of its activities.

5   The Defendant has an internal structure requiring all specifications to be approved by a full meeting of the Defendant's board. Such meetings are held infrequently.

6   The Claimant did not become aware until February 2000 of the existence of Castleton Wales. The Claimant did not become aware until after that date of the nature of the activities of Castleton Wales, those activities rendering the Contract more difficult to complete.

7   The Defendant purchased the Microclimates system without the knowledge and/or recommendation of the Claimant.

8   The Claimant experienced difficulties both technically and in obtaining the co-operation of Mrs Harbin and of the Defendant generally in remedying the problems arising from the purchase of the Microclimates system.

9   The Contract was completed in February 2001. In the circumstances this was the earliest practicable time at which completion could have taken place.

10   Consequently the Claimant is not in breach of contract and is entitled to payment of his invoice.

Quantum

1   If the Claimant is successful, he is entitled to judgment in the sum of £58,750 together with interest.

2   If the Defendant is successful in its counterclaim, it is agreed that it is entitled to the sum set out in the report of Mrs Penfold.

Chapter 34

SANCTIONS

THE 'NEW CULTURE' REQUIRED BY CASE MANAGEMENT

The importance of complying with court orders, rules of court, practice directions and pre-action protocols cannot be over-emphasised. Prior to the CPR – and already it seems strange to recollect that this was so – there were no pre-action protocols. Litigation was in the hands of the parties. The parties themselves controlled the litigation and its pace. Although both the RSC and the CCR imposed time-limits, these were frequently ignored. Save for extreme delay (ie years rather than months), the reality was that no effective sanctions were imposed. Parties were ordered to take certain steps (eg exchange experts' reports) by a specified date; yet if neither did, nothing was done about it. Ultimately, a case could be struck out for 'want of prosecution' (this term is now obsolete), but only where the delay was measured in years. Even then, courts were reluctant to strike out a claim that was still within the limitation period. This was part of the unsatisfactory background to Lord Woolf's 'Access to Justice' inquiry. Under the CPR, the court (not the parties) controls the pace of litigation, what is to be done and the time by which it must be done.

This has been a huge change for lawyers who were in practice prior to the introduction of the CPR. However, it is generally accepted that one of the successes of the CPR is the fact that the required change of culture has largely been achieved. This change of culture does not apply only after proceedings have been issued. On the contrary, the pre-action protocols are a vital aspect of the current procedural regime (see further, Chapter 6). Parties are required to help the court to further the overriding objective (r 1.3) and the court must do this by actively managing cases (r 1.4).

Time-limits

As part of the case management regime, the court will insist that its orders are complied with. The court will set realistic time-limits, which must be honoured. In short, court orders and the rules say what they mean and mean what they say.

One of your early tasks is to assist the court in setting realistic time-limits for directions, which will have to be complied with. One reason for the failure of the RSC and CCR is that the time-limits imposed by those rules were preposterously short.

Parties were required to take steps within 14 days or a month, when the reality was that they could not be done in such a limited time-scale. Thus, the rules came to be ignored. Time-limits imposed by the CPR and by court orders are meant to be tight, but realistic and achievable. (Consider, for example, the specimen directions given in a fast track case – see Chapter 24. Typical time-limits are 4 weeks, 10 weeks, 16 weeks and so on, rather than 7, 14 or 21 days.) If, in a particular case, you know that, for a particular reason, a step will take longer than usual (eg because a key witness is ill), this should be explained to the court at allocation stage (or some other suitable stage) to assist the court in setting an appropriate time-scale.

The vital point is that, once the timetable has been set, it must be complied with. Time-limits in the CPR, Practice Directions and court orders are there to be obeyed and are not just targets to be aimed at. Therefore, if a party has not complied with a court order, rule or Practice Direction and has thereby caused delay or put the opponent to expense it is likely that the court will impose a sanction.

If you cannot comply with a time-limit

What should you do if you find yourself in a position whereby you cannot, for some reason, comply with a time-limit? Bear in mind that the courts look upon adjournment of a trial as something to be avoided and very much as a last resort (see, eg, CPR PD 29, para 7). You will have extreme difficulty in persuading the court that a trial should be adjourned. However, at the end of the day, the court's task is to further the overriding objective and justice must be done. Thus, if, in an exceptional case, the trial is adjourned, it is virtually certain that a sanction will be imposed on the defaulting party.

By r 2.11, unless the Rules or a Practice Direction provide otherwise, or the court orders otherwise, the time specified by a rule or by the court for a person to do any act may be varied by the written agreement of the parties. (The dates that cannot be varied by agreement are the 'milestone dates', such as the trial date, the trial window and the date for filing pre-trial checklists (listing questionnaires).) If you cannot comply with a rule, etc, it may be possible to agree a different timetable with the opponent, pursuant to r 2.11. When this is not possible, you must make an application to the court. The one thing you must not do is simply to ignore the time-limit.

Where a rule, Practice Direction or court order has given a time-limit, the onus is now on the defaulting party to apply for an extension of that time-limit if it cannot be met. The onus is not on the other party to apply for an order. It is very important to keep this in mind. In summary, all court orders, rules and Practice Directions must be complied with. If, for any reason, they cannot be, see if a new timetable can be agreed pursuant to r 2.11 and, if not, make an application to the court.

If your opponent has not complied with a time-limit

What do you do if your opponent has not complied and has neither approached you pursuant to r 2.11 nor applied to the court? The first step is to remind the opponent of the imminent or actual default. If no satisfactory response is received, then you can apply to the court (warning your opponent that you will do so) for a suitable order, which invariably will include a sanction.

Avoiding sanctions for default

Before the introduction of the CPR, striking-out for want of prosecution was regarded as a drastic remedy that the courts were reluctant to impose. Yet there were no other effective sanctions. All of that has now changed. The ultimate sanction of striking-out (of a claim or defence) remains, but the court now has another range of less serious – but effective – sanctions, which can be applied in proportion to the default in question. Your aim must be to avoid any sanctions being applied against your client or yourself. As you are required to further the overriding objective (r 1.3), you should accept reasonable requests from the other side and agree a new timetable, pursuant to r 2.11.

As mentioned in Chapter 22, if the court has given case management directions with which you are dissatisfied, it is essential to take steps to apply to vary them (or to appeal) as soon as possible. The court will assume, for the purposes of any later application, that a party who did not make an application to vary (or appeal) within 14 days of service of the relevant order for directions, was content that the directions were correct in the circumstances then existing. If the direction was given on paper (eg on allocation), then an application to vary is appropriate; if the direction was given at a hearing at which the party, or his lawyer, was present (eg at a case management conference), then a dissatisfied party must appeal (see further, PD 28, para 4 (fast track) and PD 29, para 6 (multi-track)).

SANCTIONS IMPOSED BY THE RULES

Rule 3.7 imposes sanctions for non-payment of certain fees. A fee is required not only to issue a claim but also at various other stages, including, for example, when filing an allocation questionnaire or pre-trial checklist (listing questionnaire). If the relevant fee is not paid, the court will impose a time-limit within which the fee is to be paid. If the claimant does not comply, the claim will be struck out (see further, r 3.7, which is self-explanatory).

Various other rules, although not using the term 'sanctions', have consequences which are extremely serious if not complied with. For example, a claim form must be served within the time prescribed in r 7.5, and extensions of time for serving a claim form can only be obtained pursuant to r 7.6. However, generally, sanctions are imposed by court order to deal with a particular situation that has arisen in a particular case, rather than by the Rules themselves.

If a party fails to file an allocation questionnaire, PD 26, para 2.5 applies. If neither party has filed one, the case is referred to the district judge for directions. The judge will usually make an 'unless order', that is, an order that, unless the allocation questionnaire is filed within 3 days of service of that order, the claim and any counterclaim will be struck out. Where one party files the allocation questionnaire but the other party does not, the court may either allocate to track and give directions based solely on the statements of case and the one allocation questionnaire filed, or order an allocation hearing. The costs of that hearing will invariably be summarily assessed and ordered to be paid immediately by the party in default.

Pre-trial checklists (listing questionnaires) are not required in cases allocated to the small claims track. In a fast-track case, if one party fails to file a pre-trial checklist by the date specified in the court order, the court will give such directions as it thinks appropriate. This could be the fixing of the trial date based on the information provided in the filed pre-trial checklist. Alternatively (and particularly if neither party has filed a pre-trial checklist), the court could order a listing hearing. The costs of that hearing are likely to be summarily assessed and ordered to be paid immediately by the party in default. If both were in default, the court is likely to make 'no order for costs'.

In practice, the most common reason for failing to file a pre-trial checklist is that the parties have compromised the case but failed to so inform the court. Do not make this elementary mistake. Cases cannot remain in limbo. One way to conclude a compromised case is with a consent order (see r 40.6).

In multi-track cases, pre-trial checklists are dealt with in CPR PD 29, para 8. If neither party has filed a pre-trial checklist by the required date, the court will normally make an order that, if no pre-trial checklist is filed by any party within 3 days of service of the order, the claim and any counterclaim will be struck out. Where only one party files the pre-trial checklist, the court will fix a listing hearing. The costs of that hearing are likely to be summarily assessed and ordered to be paid immediately by the party in default.

By now, it is hoped that the message of this chapter is clear. For the avoidance of any lingering doubt, the message is that the relevant pre-action protocol, all court orders, rules and Practice Directions must be complied with. If they are not, sanctions must be expected.

WHAT SANCTIONS ARE AVAILABLE?

As part of its duty to case manage and to further the overriding objective, the court is concerned to protect a party from being put to additional expense or delay by the opponent. Sanctions imposed must be proportionate to the default but adequate both to compensate the party who has been put to delay and/or expense and to encourage the party in default (and others) to a better appreciation of the obligations imposed by the current civil procedure regime. Tactical manoeuvrings and dubious applications, which so disfigured the pre-CPR regime, belong to history. To be fair, as noted, the legal profession has adapted well to the culture of the CPR, but the court will deal with any lapses by lawyers or their clients. It is, thus, part of the lawyer's duty to impress upon the client the duties and obligations which the client undertakes when involved in court proceedings.

In accordance with the overriding objective, the court is to deal with cases justly. Litigants are entitled to have their cases resolved with reasonable expedition. Non-compliance with time-limits can cause prejudice to more than one of the parties. In addition, the adjournment of the date of trial prejudices other litigants and disrupts the administration of justice. Accordingly, the court will strive to impose an appropriate sanction, which is proportionate. It is, thus, not practical to give a list of all possible sanctions. The court will impose the most appropriate sanction for the particular default in the particular case. This does not necessarily mean that the court will impose the most minor appropriate sanction. Although it is not possible to give an exhaustive list of all sanctions that can be imposed, the following sanctions are among the most common that will be considered whenever the imposition of a sanction is in issue.

Striking-out

Striking out a party's statement of case for failure to comply with a rule, Practice Direction or court order is the ultimate sanction. Pursuant to r 3.4(2)(c), the court has power to strike out a statement of case if there has been failure to comply with a rule, practice direction or court order. Where the court does strike out a statement of case, it may make any consequential order which it considers appropriate and, thus, for example, the party whose statement of case has been struck out is likely to be ordered to pay the costs of the other party. If there is one, the court will give directions concerning a Part 20 claim.

To strike out is such a serious sanction – in effect, it brings the case to an end – that the court will consider whether it is proportionate and necessary. Arguably, to strike out a claim solely on the ground of the claimant's delay may be a breach of ECHR, Art 6, at least in a case where it appears that the claimant has reasonable prospects of success (*Annodeus Entertainment Ltd v Gibson* [2000] TLR 160). Thus, the court will always consider whether a lesser sanction than striking-out can be imposed and whether it is proportionate to strike out. The court may well strike out if there has been a history of default. It is unlikely to strike out for the first default, as, inevitably, a lesser sanction will be appropriate and proportionate.

A claimant whose case has been struck out will not be able to commence fresh proceedings raising the same case, even if the claim is still not statute barred (see Chapter 5, 'Limitation of Actions'). A litigant now has no right to commence a second claim, even within the limitation period, where an earlier claim has been struck out for delay or abuse of process. The claimant's wish to try again has to be considered in the context of the overriding objective and, in particular, r 1.2(2)(e) – appropriate share of the court's resources. (See *Securum Finance Ltd v Ashton* [2001] Ch 291 (sounding the death knell for the oft-cited pre-CPR case of *Birkett v James* [1978] AC 297).) This second striking-out would be pursuant to r 3.4(2)(b) – abuse of the court's process.

Rule 3.4(2)(c) gives the court an unqualified power to strike out a statement of case where there has been a failure to comply with a rule, Practice Direction or court order. The leading case is *Biguzzi v Rank Leisure Plc* [1999] 1 WLR 1926, where Lord Woolf MR gave the leading judgment. For guidance on the relationship between the power to strike out and the power to give summary judgment, see the judgment of May LJ in *S v Gloucestershire County Council* [2000] 3 All ER 346.

In practice, the court has no option but to strike out if it reaches the conclusion that the delay is such that the court can no longer hold a fair trial.

For striking out a statement of case generally, see also r 3.4, and PD 3, which is entitled 'Striking out a statement of case'.

No order for costs

At the opposite end of the scale to striking-out, the court could, as a sanction, simply deprive a party of costs. (This is not, of course, the same thing as ordering the party to pay the other party's costs.) As a sanction, no order for costs could be made in a situation where a party would normally have expected to have his or her costs paid by the other party.

Further, for example, if both parties failed to file a pre-trial checklist (listing questionnaire) by the ordered date and the court therefore convened a listing hearing, it is likely to be appropriate to make no order for costs in respect of that hearing. Thus, neither party can recover the costs of that hearing from the other.

The court makes 'no order for costs', either by using those words or by saying nothing at all about costs (r 44.13).

Costs

Forcing a party in default to pay the other party's costs is a very common sanction and often the first sanction to be considered by the court. A defaulting party can expect to have costs of the application summarily assessed and ordered to be paid immediately. If, for example, a party has been ordered to exchange witness statements by a certain date but has not done so and did not respond to letters from the other side, thus necessitating the opponent's making an application to the court for an 'unless order' (see below), then, whatever order is made at the hearing of that application, the defaulting party must expect to pay the costs of it. The court will normally summarily assess those costs and order them to be paid within 14 days.

What do you do if you are on the receiving end of such an application?
The answer depends on who has been in default. If it is, in fact, your fault because you have overlooked the matter, then the sensible thing to do is to acknowledge your default, attempt to agree a suitable order with the other side (subject to the court's approval) and agree to pay the other side's costs. You may well feel honour-bound to pay those costs personally. If you are in default, and not the client, how can such costs justifiably be passed on to the client? On the other hand, if it is in fact the client's fault because, for example, you have not been given documents which you have requested and have been pressing for, then the client will no doubt have been warned of the possible consequences and will now have to face them.

Rule 44.2(1) requires a solicitor to notify a client in writing, within 7 days of receiving the order, of any costs order made against the client if the client was not present when the order was made.

Other, more specific, costs orders

The court's powers on costs are discretionary and incredibly wide and varied (see generally, Part 44). In the context of sanctions, it is not just a question of summarily assessing costs and ordering them to be paid immediately. There are many other possible orders which the court can make, according to the particular facts of the particular case (see r 44.3(6)). The court could refuse to award any costs after a specific date (or before a specific date), or of a particular issue. A costs sanction is the most common sanction imposed, whether it is imposed alone or in conjunction with any other sanction. It is no longer a question of 'winner takes all'. Partial orders for costs are often appropriate. (See generally, r 44.3 and *AEI Rediffusion Music Ltd v Phonographic Performance Ltd* [1999] 1 WLR 1507.)

When deciding what order (if any) to make about costs, the court must have regard to all the circumstances, including the conduct of the parties. Conduct includes conduct before, as well as during, the proceedings and, in particular, the extent to which the parties followed any relevant pre-action protocol.

In the context of the sanctions, an appropriate order for costs – especially if summarily assessed and ordered to be paid immediately – is often all that is required.

Wasted costs orders

The court can make a 'wasted costs' order against any legal representative (*Brown v Bennett* [2002] 1 WLR 713). The power derives from SCA 1981, s 51, and the procedure is governed by r 48.7. It has become an important topic, and the courts are now anxious to control costly satellite litigation which is in danger of occupying significant court time. As the general principle is that applications for a wasted costs order should be sought after the trial, an application for such an order at the interlocutory stage should be made only in exceptional and clear circumstances. The whole topic is considered in considerable detail in the White Book's commentary to r 48.7.

Indemnity costs

There are only two bases of costs: the standard basis and the indemnity basis. As a sanction, the party in default can be ordered to pay costs on the indemnity basis rather than the standard basis.

Interest

If the party at fault is a claimant in whose favour an order for the payment of damages or some specified sum is subsequently made, as a sanction, the court can make an order depriving that party of interest on such sum and in respect of such period as may be specified and/or award interest at a lower rate than that at which interest would otherwise have been awarded. Thus, for example, where a claimant's default has caused an adjournment, the court could order that interest stops running as from the date on which the original trial should have taken place, or could deprive the claimant of interest altogether.

If the party at fault is a defendant and an order for the payment of damages or some specified sum is subsequently made in favour of the claimant, the court can award interest on such sum and in respect of such period as may be specified, at a higher rate (not exceeding 10% above base rate) than the rate at which interest would otherwise have been awarded. (See PD Protocols, para 2.3(4); *Biguzzi v Rank Leisure Plc* [1999] 1 WLR 1926, and compare with the similar, but different, power in r 36.21(2)).

Cut-off dates

The court usually makes a sanctions order in the form of an 'unless order' with a cut-off date. An example of such an order would be:

> 'Unless the claimant serve an updated schedule of special damages by 18 December 2005, he shall be debarred from doing so and entitled to rely only on the schedule of special damages annexed to the Particulars of Claim.'

Another example would be:

> 'Time for exchanging witness statements is extended to 31 January 2006. Only witnesses whose statements have been so exchanged will be permitted to give evidence at trial.'

An order such as this, as the wording makes clear, would be a second order, where the relevant party had failed to exchange witness statements by an earlier specified date.

As already noted, it is impossible to give a list of all possible sanctions orders. The court will do what is right in the instant case, bearing in mind the criteria set out above.

'Unless orders'

An 'unless order' is an order giving a defaulting party a final opportunity to put right the default by a specified date. Unless the party does so, a specified sanction will take effect (see examples in above paragraph, 'Cut-off dates'). Additionally, the defaulting party is usually required to pay the costs of the application which caused the court to make the 'unless order'.

Payment into court

CPR Part 3 deals with the court's case management powers. Rule 3.1(5) provides that the court may order a party to pay a sum of money into court if that party has, without good reason, failed to comply with a rule, Practice Direction or a relevant pre-action protocol. The court must have regard to the amount in dispute and the costs which the parties have incurred and which they may incur. Although r 3.1(5) does not mention court orders, r 3.1(3) provides that, where the court makes an order, it may:

> '(a) make it subject to conditions, including a condition to pay a sum of money into court, and,
> (b) specify the consequences of failure to comply with the order or a condition.'

Ordering a payment into court is, in fact, a very effective sanction. Such an order thwarts a party who is really trying just to delay payment. However, in practice, it is not always available. If a party is publicly funded (ie receiving legal aid), he or she may not have any money, and an order would be disproportionate. In *Chapple v Williams* [1999] CPLR 731, the Court of Appeal said that an order requiring an impecunious defendant to pay money into court should not have been made. However, if a company has no assets and has ceased trading, a conditional order can still be made if there is evidence that it is able to raise funds when needed (*Foot and Bowden v Anglo Europe Corp Ltd* (unreported) 17 February 2000, CA).

An order requiring a defendant to pay into court (which, in effect, is equivalent to ordering security) may be appropriate where there is a history of repeated breaches of timetables and court orders or where conduct is such as to raise suspicions of not being bona fide so that the other party should have protection (see eg *Mealey Horgan Plc v Horgan* [1999] STC 711 and *Olatawura v Abiloye* [2002] EWCA Civ 988; [2003] 1 WLR 275).

Multiple sanctions

The court need not impose only one sanction at a time. Where appropriate, more than one sanction can be imposed simultaneously. A costs sanction is often imposed in addition to another.

SANCTIONS HAVE EFFECT UNLESS DEFAULTING PARTY OBTAINS RELIEF

By r 3.8, where a party has failed to comply with a rule, Practice Direction or court order, any sanction for failure to comply imposed by the rule, Practice Direction or court order has effect, unless the party in default applies for and obtains relief from the court. Where the sanction is the payment of costs, the party in default may only obtain relief from the sanction by appealing the order for costs.

Where a rule, Practice Direction or court order requires a party to do something within a specified time *and specifies the consequences of failure to comply*, the time for doing the act in question may not be extended by agreement between the parties. Thus, for example, if the court has ordered written statements to be exchanged by a certain date, parties could agree a different date in writing, pursuant to r 2.11. Where, however, the court has said: 'The time for exchange of witness statements is extended to 31 January 2006 and only witnesses whose statements have been so exchanged shall be permitted to give evidence at trial', the order specifies the consequences of a failure to comply and, thus, pursuant to r 3.8(3), the time for doing the action in question cannot be extended by agreement between the parties, and an application to the court would be required for relief from that sanction.

Bear in mind that r 2.11 does permit time-limits to be varied by parties in certain circumstances, but this is a limited rule, intended for minor matters only. A delay of a week or so may not matter, and parties can agree minor extensions in writing. By r 2.11, unless the Rules or a Practice Direction provide otherwise, or the court orders otherwise, the time specified by a rule or by the court for a person to do any act may be varied by the written agreement of the parties. Several rules do, of course, provide otherwise, including r 3.8 (above), r 28.4 (variation of case management timetable – fast track), r 29.5 (variation of case management timetable – multi-track), and r 52.6 (appeals). This list is not exhaustive.

RELIEF FROM SANCTIONS (RULE 3.9)

On an application for relief from any sanction imposed for a failure to comply with any rule, Practice Direction or court order, the court will consider all the circumstances, including:

(1)   the interests of the administration of justice;
(2)   whether the application for relief has been made promptly;
(3)   whether the failure to comply was intentional;
(4)   whether there is a good explanation for the failure;
(5)   the extent to which the party in default has complied with other rules, Practice Directions, court orders and any relevant pre-action protocol;
(6)   whether the failure to comply was caused by the party or his legal representative;
(7)   whether the trial date or the likely trial date can still be met if relief is granted;
(8)   the effect which the failure to comply has on each party; and
(9)   the effect which the granting of relief would have on each party.

An application for relief must be supported by evidence. In particular, the court will need evidence as to the explanation for the failure and who was responsible. However, the evidence – which will usually be in the form of a witness statement from either the party or the solicitor – must address each of the factors listed above, as the court will consider all of them in turn. Any other relevant matters must be mentioned, for the rule is not exhaustive and the court can consider 'all the circumstances'. The court will consider the statements of case. For example, if a defendant is applying for relief, the court can consider the merits of the defence (*Chapple v Williams* [1999] CPLR 731, CA).

Although r 3.9 is concerned with relief from sanctions, the court will also consider the matters set out in this rule to assist in deciding an order appropriate to the default when imposing a sanction (*Keith v CPM Field Marketing* [2001] CP Rep 35).

On an application for relief from sanctions the judge must systematically in his/her judgment consider in turn each of the factors listed in r 3.9. If the judge does not do so it is virtually certain that the decision will be overturned on appeal: see eg *Primus Telecommunications Netherlands BV v Pan European Ltd and others* [2005] EWCA Civ 273.

CONCLUSION

The purpose of imposing sanctions is to discourage both deliberate and inadvertent ignoring of court orders, rules and Practice Directions, and to maintain the momentum of judicial case management. Parties are encouraged to resolve disputes without coming to court but, when a case does come to court, the court is in charge.

Chapter 35

TRIAL ADVOCACY

OPENING SPEECHES

The opening speech sets the scene and outlines why your client's case should succeed. It needs to present the court with an easily understood and cohesive description of the case. It should be succinct.

In some civil trials, there will not be an opening speech but instead the judge will rely on the advocate's skeleton arguments.

Even with the use of skeleton arguments, the importance of the opening speech, when the opportunity for this is available, should not be underestimated. Skeleton arguments identify the issues and submissions in relation to those issues. They form the skeleton of the case. The opening speech begins to add flesh to the bones. There is no excuse for a poor opening speech as it can, and should, be prepared well in advance of the hearing.

An opening speech should include:

– a brief statement of the nature of the case;
– a brief statement of the issues of the case; also set out the matters that are agreed between the parties as this helps the judge to distinguish the matters that are in issue;
– a cohesive, succinct, persuasive and confident summary of the evidence you intend to present, avoiding overstatement;
– a brief statement of why, on the law and the facts, your client should succeed.

An opening speech should *not* include:

– reference to evidence the availability or admissibility of which is doubtful;
– explicit coverage of anticipated defences or the other party's evidence;
– argument, as this should be reserved for the closing speech when all the evidence is before the court.

In your opening speech, it is also best to avoid:

–   inappropriate use of the witness-by-witness approach as this can be very tedious and can lack impact. There is a place for the witness-by-witness approach, but in most instances if you want to refer to the evidence of a particular witness you can insert this into your opening speech when covering a specific issue. The other danger of the witness-by-witness approach is that it can lead you into overstating what a witness will say;

–   inappropriate use of the chronology approach. Again this has its place, but all too often it leads to long, less structured openings. Deal with the issues and supporting facts and use chronologies only where the timing of a series of incidents is important. If your skeleton argument contains a chronology then this is already available to assist the judge.

Making an opening speech is a skill that can be mastered with practice more readily than any other advocacy skill, using the following general guidelines.

–   Practise, rehearse, try out, and listen to your opening speeches before you make them. Get a partner, colleague or friend to listen.

–   Recognise the opening speech for what it is: a persuasive statement of what the evidence *will* prove but avoiding overstatement.

–   Recognise the opening speech for what it is not: it is not an argument. This is not a time to infer, plead or fulminate. It is a time to tell the court what the case is about and what you expect your evidence to be.

–   Although witness statements are usually accepted as evidence-in-chief, additional oral evidence may not proceed quite as expected. Therefore it is wise not to overstate your case and it is safer slightly to understate the evidence.

–   Most importantly, remember that this is your first opportunity to be helpful to the judge and give the assistance that the judge wants rather than only what you think he or she should have. Be flexible and welcome questions from the judge and deal with them immediately.

Preparation of an opening speech

Consider the following:

–   review your case theory;
–   review the documents;
–   check that what you intend to put forward and the evidence fits with the statements of case;
–   check that what you intend to say in your opening speech is supported by evidence;
–   organise and structure the evidence;
–   decide how you will use your skeleton argument and how it will fit with the your oral delivery;
–   consider what you will want to say in your closing speech;
–   start on a strong point;
–   conclude on a strong point;
–   prepare and rehearse;
–   prepare notes that:

- do not contain sentences;
- are as brief as possible while maintaining your confidence;
- make it easy for you to find your point quickly by use of highlighting, capitalisation, and space;
- are free from deletions and insertions.

Specifically in relation to delivery:

- use clear, simple language;
- do not overstate your case;
- avoid over-use of notes;
- maintain eye contact;
- vary the volume and tone of your voice;
- vary the pace of delivery and make use of pauses;
- use transitions or sub-headings to introduce the next topic or incident;
- use lists where they can be short.

LEGAL / EVIDENTIAL SUBMISSIONS

The main difference between the techniques and content of opening speeches and submissions is one of focus. The submission will be concerned with one aspect of the case. You should ensure that you keep to the point and do not stray into the wider issues of the case that are not relevant at this time. The techniques of delivery and structure remain the same as for other addresses to the judge.

Ensure that from the outset you make it clear to the judge what you are asking the judge to decide. Welcome questions from the judge and deal with them immediately. Judicial interventions will focus your attention on the matters with which the judge requires your assistance.

WITNESS EXAMINATION

General considerations

During witness examination it is all too easy for the advocate to allow the process to become a two-way affair and thereby ignore the judge. You should ensure that you involve the judge and that the witness primarily addresses his or her answers to the judge.

One difference between examination-in-chief and cross-examination is the balance of the amount of talking done by the advocate and the witness. With examination-in-chief it is the witness who should be doing most of the talking. This is because this will be more persuasive. By contrast, in cross-examination it is the advocate who does most of the talking.

You need to feel confident in the use of non-leading and leading questions. Non-leading questions do not suggest the answer, and even when they require a short answer they should elicit more than a 'yes' or 'no' response. As a general rule during examination-in-chief, advocates are not allowed to lead their witnesses.

Non-leading questions are likely to be expressed in the form, eg:

Who ... ?

What ... ?

Where ... ?

When ... ?

Why ... ?

How ... ?

Please describe ...

Please explain ..., etc.

Leading questions are allowed in cross-examination, and full advantage of this should be taken. A leading question suggests an answer often and requires just a short 'yes' or 'no' response. Consider the question, 'When did you go to the off-licence?' If it has already been established that the witness has been to the off-licence, it is *not* a leading question: it is a classic 'when' question designed to keep the examination moving at a reasonable pace. But if it has not already been established that the witness has been to the off-licence then, by assuming a fact not yet in evidence, it *is* a leading question and should not be asked during examination-in-chief. In fact in cross-examination the question is more likely to be 'You went to the off-licence, didn't you?' (do not say 'I put it to you that you went to the off-licence').

As with any skill, practice is the only sure way of achievement. The practice should be conducted with some guidelines in mind:

–   the purpose of any witness examination is to elicit information;
–   the information elicited should be what you need for your closing speech;
–   the basic format is an interrogative dialogue;
–   the lay witness is probably insecure. The witness is appearing in a strange environment and is expected to perform under strange rules. This is a handicap which you must overcome in examination-in-chief and an advantage you have in cross-examination;
–   your questions should be short, simple and easily understood by the witness and the judge in both examination-in-chief and cross-examination;
–   always make sure that what you are asking truly is a question;
–   maintain an appropriate speed for the judge (and others) to take a note;
–   relevance – know and be prepared to explain the relevance of a question;

- obey the rules of evidence;
- if the witness puts a question to the advocate, this should not be answered;
- be prepared to adapt your approach according to the witness and his or her demeanour;
- keep to an appropriate volume for you and for the witness;
- give an impression of confidence in your questioning;
- typically, a good approach is not to script every question, but to identify topics, and what you wish to achieve within each topic;
- discipline your reaction to answers, particularly so that you do not obviously betray your feelings when a witness's response has been unfavourable to your case;
- be realistic and recognise when you have achieved all you can.

A vital but often difficult consideration is what to include in your witness examination. With examination-in-chief you need to include sufficient of the surrounding facts in order for the judge to make sense of the important aspects of the evidence. However, you need to avoid including so much that the essential facts are obscured. With cross-examination there is even more of a danger of covering too much ground.

The key to knowing what to include is first to have used a good method of case analysis. Secondly, consider all the evidence that each witness could give. Now go through a process of excluding:

- unnecessary facts;
- those which cannot be proven;
- those which are not persuasive or do not add to your case; and
- those which open a door to your opponent.

Finally, you should go through what remains and check that, with this information, you are likely to succeed and can satisfy the elements of your case. Additionally, check that you are not misleading the court by omission.

If you have weaknesses in your case that you are afraid to reveal, remember not only your duty not to mislead but also that if *you* are the person to reveal your weaknesses you can do so in a better light than the other parties will.

Examination-in-chief

In civil proceedings there is the advantage of exchange of witness statements. However, there may be little or no opportunity for examination-in-chief at the trial. Where examination-in-chief is allowed it is important to have the skill to question effectively and to control and structure the examination-in-chief. A knowledge of what examination-in-chief can achieve improves the drafting of witness statements as well as improving the skill of conducting an examination-in-chief when the opportunity is given to do so at trial.

Remember:

–   as a general proposition, you may not lead during examination-in-chief except as to preliminary matters or non-contentious matters with the agreement of the other advocates and the judge;
–   in any event, on examination-in-chief, leading questions and the perfunctory answers they elicit are not persuasive: the evidence needs to come from the witness.

However, when deciding if you will lead on matters where you are allowed to do so bear in mind that these are usually easy questions for the witness to answer and it may be advisable to use these to help settle the witness and make him or her more confident.

Consider the following:

–   establishing qualifications and background;
–   starting with some easy questions to relax your witness;
–   avoiding very open questions;
–   keeping in mind the admissibility of the evidence you are seeking to elicit;
–   setting the scene;
–   knowing your objectives with the witness;
–   eliciting a clear and detailed picture – this will best withstand cross-examination;
–   confining the scope of your questions to matters within the witness's knowledge;
–   describing the action;
–   using non-leading questions, ie questions that begin who, what, why, where, when, how, please describe, please explain;
–   when examining a witness who keeps notes as part of his or her job –for example a police officer, a social worker, medical staff – be aware of the potential for reference to contemporaneous notes and know how to lay the evidential basis for this;
–   when examining character witnesses, keep in mind the limits to the matters about which they can properly speak;
–   starting on a strong point and ending on a strong point;
–   avoiding interrupting your witness: let him or her finish then seek the detail or clarification, etc, that made you want to interrupt;
–   using transitions/introductory sentences as this will help to guide your witness, eg 'I am now going to ask you about what happened prior to that first contract';
–   if you know that the cross-examination of your witness will disclose unfavourable information, consider the possible advantage of eliciting it during examination-in-chief.

Cross-examination

Remember:

- during cross-examination you may lead and you should do so. Control of the witness on cross-examination is imperative;
- ensure that you put disputed matters to the relevant witness(es);
- do not conduct a cross-examination:
  - that does nothing other than afford the witness an opportunity to repeat the evidence given in examination-in-chief;
  - if there is nothing to be gained by cross-examination (but remember that you should make it clear if evidence is not accepted, although this does not mean you have to repeat all that you disagree with).

Consider the following:

- controlling the witness by use of leading questions;
- viewing cross-examination as a time for gathering points for your closing speech but not for winning those points *during* the cross-examination;
- aiming to expose the weaknesses/inconsistencies in the witness's account;
- avoiding asking questions that require the witness to give a conclusion. Elicit the answers that mean you can make conclusions in your closing speech. Do not expect the witness to give you helpful conclusions;
- only asking questions to which you know the answer or do not care what the answer is, as it cannot be damaging;
- avoiding argument with the witness;
- listening to the witness's answers;
- avoiding questions that allow witnesses the opportunity to explain themselves in terms helpful to them;
- challenging all material parts of evidence not agreed with; if you do not do this the judge may refuse to allow you to challenge the evidence in your closing speech;
- when challenging, avoiding the use stock phrases such as, 'I put it to you';
- avoiding asking witnesses for answers to questions with which they cannot deal, for example asking a witness to comment on other witnesses' evidence or to engage in speculation, hypothetical propositions or matters of opinion for an expert;
- staying alive to the reaction of the judge and being guided by it;
- ending on a strong point.

Impeachment of a witness

Cross-examination frequently includes exposing inaccuracies or rebutting evidence given by the witness but not discrediting him or her overall. The purpose of impeaching a witness is to discredit him or her so that he or she is considered by the tribunal of fact to be an unreliable witness. If you attempt to impeach a witness on unimportant, trivial or petty inconsistencies then you will not succeed in discrediting the witness and are in danger of undermining your own standing before the court.

Do not impeach a witness unless you are sure of the following:

–   where the witness can give you some useful information, that you are not
       losing more than you gain if you impeach;
–   that you are confident of success;
–   that there is a true inconsistency, poor character or personal interest by
       which to impeach.

There are two main sources for impeachment.

(1)   The witness has made a prior statement, action or omission, which differs
       from his or her present evidence, and the inconsistency is significant enough
       to warrant impeachment.
(2)   The witness has some personal interest in the case, eg he or she would gain
       by a particular outcome or he or she is prejudiced against one of the parties.

Impeachment using a prior inconsistent statement
A four-stage process is the best method by which to impeach.

(1)   Confirming with the witness his or her evidence that is before the court. The
       advocate 'plays-back' the relevant part of the evidence: 'You have said in
       evidence that, when you entered his office, Mr Jones was lying on the
       floor?'; 'You said he was in his socks and underpants?'. Do not ask the
       witness to repeat the point as he or she may reword the point and take away
       the impact. If you do not read out verbatim what the witness has said, then
       be careful that your wording accurately reflects what he or she said or the
       witness may deny having said it. You need to consider how your opponent
       could re-examine on this and take care that you have not omitted some
       additional fact or statement which alters the meaning of what you are asking
       the witness to confirm that he or she said.
(2)   Confirming that he or she made a previous statement. At this stage do not
       put the previous statement to the witness but have him or her merely
       confirm that he or she did make a previous statement: 'You gave a written
       statement to your employer about the incident with Mr Jones?'.
(3)   Confirming the accuracy of the previous statement. If you put the previous
       inconsistent statement to the witness now you would gain something.
       However, by emphasising the accuracy and honesty of the previous
       statement the impact is greater and the likelihood of discrediting the witness
       is increased. You may emphasise the accuracy of the previous statement by
       showing that the witness had a reason to be accurate, knew the importance
       of accuracy, or was under a duty by his or her employment, or that the facts
       were fresh in his or her mind. You might need to ask a series of questions,
       eg 'When you wrote the statement for your employer you knew it was
       important?'; 'You knew that Mr Jones had been accused of assaulting Miss
       Smith?'; 'You wanted to be accurate?'; 'You made the statement the
       following morning while the events were still fresh in your mind?'.
(4)   Confronting the witness with the prior statement. Putting the previous
       statement to the witness and getting him or her to confirm that he or she
       said it is usually sufficient, for example: 'Would you look at the statement
       you made to your employers at the top of the second page?'; 'In your

statement you have said that when you went into the room Mr Jones was fully clothed and sitting at his desk?'. Any further use of the impeachment can be made in your closing speech. The danger of saying too much at the fourth stage is that if you do more than have the witness confirm what he or she said you give the witness an opportunity to reason away the difference or otherwise undermine your point.

Impeachment on personal interest

If there is a personal reason why the witness may be less than candid or be biased in some way then this can be brought out with the same notes of caution as outlined above, for example: 'You have a brother named John?'; 'He used to work for the same firm as you do?'; 'John no longer works for the firm?'; 'John is currently unemployed?'; 'He lost his job as a result of an argument with Mr Jones?'.

General considerations

Bear in mind the following:

– the significance of the testimony compared with the gravity of challenge;
– the relevance of the impeachment to the case;
– the alternatives: the witness may be mistaken, or his or her memory may have faded;
– the best time tactically to impeach.

Re-examination

The purpose of re-examination is two-fold: first, to repair any damage done in cross-examination if that is achievable; and secondly, to ask that next question that was deliberately not asked during cross-examination. If, during cross-examination the other side's advocate avoided asking 'one question too many' or seeking an explanation, then you can now ask those questions but only if you know the answers and they will assist your case.

The potential scope of re-examination is limited to those matters that were raised during cross-examination. You will still be restricted to using non-leading questions but can base your questions on the matters already spoken of by the witness.

CLOSING SPEECHES

In civil proceedings, the defendant's or defendants' advocate(s), followed by the claimant's or claimants' advocate(s), address the judge with closing speeches.

This is your last chance to persuade the tribunal of fact to favour your client's case. Although it is important to give a clear and persuasive summary of the arguments and the relevant evidence, it is unlikely that you can snatch victory from the jaws of defeat by the brilliance of a closing speech. The opening arguments, written and oral evidence and the manner in which the advocates have handled these will inevitably have the main impact. However, if the judge has not fully decided, then the closing speech can assist the judge and help your client's case. A poor closing speech or one that is defensive or misleading can certainly damage your client's case.

In your closing, your main aim is to advance points that assist your case. You cannot, however, ignore evidence that has been detrimental. You must cover damaging evidence and deal with it in the best way possible. If you ignore damaging evidence you give the other side's advocate an advantage as the only interpretation put on that evidence will be from your opponent's perspective. In addition, if you omit unfavourable evidence you may be misleading the judge and you are certainly not assisting the judge, if he or she is inclined to find in your favour, as he or she will need to deal with this evidence in the judgment. In structuring your closing speech, you should start and finish with a strong favourable point.

You should not go through all the evidence that has been heard but refer in brief outline only to those parts with which it is necessary for you to deal, either because the evidence supports your theory of the case or because it is detrimental as described above.

In civil proceedings, think of your closing speech as 'writing the judge's judgment'.

Presentation of closing speeches

If you incorporate key words and themes into your closing speech, you will maximise the impact and enhance the persuasive quality of what you say. The judge hears your closing speech once only so you need to keep it clear, concise and simple.

Preparation

Think about the structure and likely content of your closing speech in advance of the case. This helps to concentrate your attention on the essential elements of your case and case theory and the evidence of all the parties. You will hope that you do not have to rewrite much of your closing speech in the light of the evidence that is given.

General considerations in preparing your closing speech

–   Be selective.
–   Merge your theory of the case with supporting evidence.
–   Cover relevant evidence and quote verbatim where this assists and is relevant.
–   Be brief.
–   Be accurate in your submissions and do not mislead.

- Deal with selected points that are against you as well as those in your favour, especially if you can do something positive with them or you can at least put your client's perspective.
- Where there are several advocates do not go over the same ground unless you are making a separate point.
- The advocate should avoid putting forward personal submissions and should use phrases such as 'I submit' or 'I would ask you to conclude' and not 'I think' or 'I feel that'.
- Cover those matters that the judge is likely to have to deal with in the judgment.
- Include what you want to find in the judgment to assist you and the judge.
- Remember this is a closing speech and not an emotional plea.
- Be prepared to amend your closing speech in the light of the evidence that emerges at the trial and in the light of views expressed by the judge.

USUAL ORDER IN A CIVIL TRIAL

1   Introducing yourself and your opponent

The judge will indicate when the advocate for the claimant is to start. You should introduce yourself and the other advocates to the judge: 'My Lord, I appear on behalf of the Claimant company BMI; my friend/learned friend Mr White appears for the Defendant company Maxicom'. Do not use your own or others' first names during these introductions.

2   Opening speech

The judge has the discretion not to allow an opening speech. Where there is an opening speech it is the claimant's advocate who will address the court. If the defendant is adducing evidence he or she may, although it is rare, address the court before calling witnesses.

3   Referring to authorities

Consider whether you need to refer to any authorities. If you do, make sure that you refer the court only to authorities which are directly relevant to the point in issue. Inform the court and the advocate for the other party of the authorities to which you intend to refer. If you are unable to inform the court or the other parties of the authorities you intend to use in reasonable time you must take to court sufficient copies of the entire report and be prepared to explain why you were not able to inform the court and other parties in time.

Remember that as an officer of the court you have a duty to inform the court of authorities that are against you as well as those that support your case. Therefore, if you know of a relevant authority that is against your case, and the other party does not refer the judge to that authority, you must do so. If possible, distinguish the case from the instant case.

When referring the court to authorities, be careful not to commit 'overkill' by citing several authorities when in fact one authority makes the point perfectly well. Sometimes it can be useful to cite two cases on the same point, but only if you are in a different or unfamiliar area of law, or if the facts of your case do not fit precisely into either case.

Judges become irritated if you cite an authority to them on what they regard as 'trite' law. If, therefore, you feel that the judge may be familiar with this area of law, it is often sensible to ask him or her before you launch into the case whether he or she would like to see the authority you have brought along.

It is usually a good idea, before taking the judge to the specific passage in a case upon which you rely, to read the headnote or, if the judge prefers, allow him or her to read it. Then refer the judge to the relevant passages by reference to the page number and letter on the page.

Avoid, if possible, reading out huge chunks of largely irrelevant judgments. Often, the shorter the passage to which you refer, the more effective it is.

4 Claimant witnesses

Each witness who is to give oral evidence will confirm his or her witness statement, be examined-in-chief if the judge allows, cross-examined and then re-examined.

5 Defendant witnesses

Although rare, the defendant's advocate could address the court with his or her opening speech or, even more rarely, submit that there is no case to answer. Each witness who is to give oral evidence will confirm his or her witness statement, be examined-in-chief if the judge allows, cross-examined and then re-examined.

6 Closing speeches

In civil trials, the defendant's advocate addresses the court with his or her closing speech first. The claimant's advocate makes the final closing speech.

7 Judgment

The judge will give judgment. Make sure you take as detailed a note as possible of the judgment. If the case goes to appeal, you may decide to have your notes of the judge's judgment typed up and approved by him or her, so that it can be shown to the appeal judge. All judgments are recorded unless the judge has directed otherwise (para 6.1 PD39) and the judge may insist on an official transcript but the advocate's note is invaluable if, for any reason, the official transcript is incomplete.

Chapter 36

TRIAL

GENERAL

The majority of civil cases do not go to trial. Most cases will have ended by default judgment, summary judgment or compromise. The settlement rate of cases allocated to the fast track is astonishingly high. In contrast, the settlement rate for cases allocated to the small claims track is very low (no doubt because both parties are usually litigants in person, each believing that he or she is right). Of course, cases allocated to the small claims track proceed to trial very quickly, usually without any interlocutory hearings. Without the benefit of a lawyer's input, settlement is often not even broached. The reality is that, because of the limited costs regime for cases on the small claims track, the incentive to settle is not so great. However, costs of cases on the fast track usually exceed the amount of the claim, and the incentive to avoid such costs is very high.

All judges giving case management directions are mindful of the fact that they are both giving directions to prepare for trial and dealing with the equally important (if not more important) task of case managing settlement negotiations.

If your case is one of the minority that is proceeding to a final trial, it is necessary to pause and consider why. Is there room for compromise after all? Generally, a trial results in a successful party and an unsuccessful party. To put it bluntly, half the people who come to court lose. Is your case to be one of those? Is there a fatal weakness in your case which has not yet been spotted? If you have a strong case, why have you failed to persuade the other side of this?

Your aim as a solicitor is to avoid the case going to trial. If that aim cannot be achieved, then your secondary aim is to prepare the case for trial in such a way that the advocate will win it.

TRIAL OR HEARING?

The only Part of the CPR with an unhelpful title is Part 39 – Miscellaneous Provisions Relating to Hearings. It, in fact, contains some very important rules concerning trials.

Is there a difference between a hearing and a trial? Neither is defined in the CPR, and r 39.1 simply states: 'In this Part, reference to a hearing includes a reference to the trial'. In practice, in civil cases, the final hearing is usually referred to as the trial. There can, of course, be an order for a 'split trial', typically involving the issue of liability being tried first and separately from the issue of quantum. In such cases, if the claimant succeeds on liability and the case is not then compromised on quantum, there will, of course, be two trials, but each will deal with separate issues. Trial of issues is very common in the Commercial Court.

The trial in a High Court case will take place before a High Court judge or will have been released under SCA 1981, s 9 to a circuit judge or recorder; county court multi-track cases are tried by the circuit judge, a recorder or a district judge; fast-track cases are tried by a circuit judge, a recorder, a district judge or deputy district judge; and small claims cases by a district judge or a deputy district judge.

Apart from the final hearing, known as the trial, all other hearings before the judge are, in contrast, known as 'hearings' rather than as 'trials'.

PUBLIC HEARINGS

By r 39.2, the general rule is that all hearings are to be in public. Indeed, Art 6 of the ECHR (incorporated into English law – see the HRA 1998 and, for the Convention itself, Sch 1 to that Act) provides:

> 'In the determination of his civil rights and obligations ... everyone is entitled to a fair and public hearing within a reasonable time by an independent and impartial tribunal established by law. Judgment shall be pronounced publicly but the press and public may be excluded from all or part of the trial in the interests of morals, public order or national security in a democratic society, where the interests or juveniles or the protection of the private life of the parties so require, or to the extent strictly necessary in the opinion of the court in special circumstances where publicity would prejudice the interests of justice.'

Part 39 reflects the principles of the Article.

The requirement for the hearing to be in public does not require the court to make special arrangement for accommodating members of the public. In practice, for trials which will attract wide public interest, courts do make special arrangements, particularly for the press. If you have such a case, you will wish to ensure that it proceeds smoothly and should make appropriate arrangements, through the court manager, in good time.

Rule 39.2(3) specifies hearings which may be in private. This may be the whole or part of any hearing or trial. Reasons are if:

(1)   publicity would defeat the object of the hearing;
(2)   it involves matters relating to national security;

(3)   it involves confidential information (including information relating to personal financial matters) and publicity would damage that confidentiality;

(4)   a private hearing is necessary to protect the interests of any child or patient;

(5)   it is a hearing of an application made without notice and it would be unjust to any respondent for there to be a public hearing;

(6)   it involves non-contentious matters, arising in the administration of the trusts on the administration of a deceased person's estate;

(7)   the court considers this to be necessary in the interests of justice.

Further, by PD 39, para 1.5, the following types of hearings shall be listed in the first instance by the court as hearings in private:

(1)   a claim by a mortgagee against one or more individuals for an order for possession of land;

(2)   a claim by a landlord against one or more tenants or former tenants for repossession of a dwelling-house based on the non-payment of rent;

(3)   an application to suspend a warrant of execution or a warrant of possession where the court is being invited to consider the ability of a party to make payments to another party;

(4)   a re-determination under r 14.13 or an application to vary or suspend the payment of a judgment debt by instalments;

(5)   an application for a charging order (including an application to enforce a charging order), third party debt order, attachment of earnings order, administration order, or the appointment of a receiver;

(6)   an order to attend court for questioning;

(7)   the determination of the liability of an LSC-funded client under Community Legal Service (Costs) Regulations 2000, regs 9 and 10, or of an assisted person's liability for costs under Civil Legal Aid (General) Regulations 1989, reg 127;

(8)   an application for security for costs under the Companies Act 1985, s 726(1);

(9)   proceedings brought under the Consumer Credit Act 1974, the Inheritance (Provision for Family and Dependants) Act 1975 or the Protection from Harassment Act 1997;

(10)   an application by a trustee or personal representative for directions as to the bringing or defending of legal proceedings.

TRIAL BUNDLE

Trial bundles are required by virtue of r 39.5. In practice, as a reminder, courts often order bundles to be prepared and filed not more than 7 days and not less than 3 days before the start of the trial, but, in fact, a trial bundle is required even if the court has not ordered it. This vital part of final preparation for trial is considered in Chapter 32. (See also, PD 39 para 3.)

As required by PD 39, the first page of a trial bundle should be a case summary. Although there is a court file in fast-track and multi-track cases, the trial judge does not have it and, instead, has only the trial bundle. The case summary is the first thing that the trial judge will read. The trial judge will then proceed to read the statements of case, witness statements and experts' reports and anything else in the bundle which is clearly significant. This can involve a considerable amount of pre-trial reading.

TRIAL TIMETABLE

In fast-track and multi-track cases, the trial will proceed according to a pre-determined trial timetable. The timetable for a fast-track trial tends to follow a standard format, as such trials cannot take more than 5 hours. The timetable is usually given when final directions are given, after filing of pre-trial checklists, and with the trial date. The 5-hour maximum allowed for a fast-track trial does not include the judge's reading time, which is additional. A typical trial timetable on a fast-track case will be as follows:

Opening statement(s)	15 minutes
Cross-examination of claimant's witnesses	75 minutes
Re-examination of claimant's witnesses	15 minutes
Cross-examination of defendant's witnesses	75 minutes
Re-examination of defendant's witnesses	15 minutes
Defendant's closing submissions	20 minutes
Claimant's closing submissions	20 minutes
Judge's preparation time and delivery of judgment	30 minutes
Summary assessment of costs and consequential orders	30 minutes

The opening speech is usually restricted to that of the claimant, but the judge may take the opportunity to ask the defendant's advocate if there is anything to add. Alternatively, given that, by their very nature, fast-track trials are short and the trial bundle will not be voluminous, the trial judge may decide to dispense with opening speeches altogether and proceed straight on with the evidence. (As to the lack of any time allocated for examination-in-chief, see below.)

In a multi-track case (by r 29.8), as soon as is practicable after each party has filed a pre-trial checklist, or after a listing hearing or pre-trial review, if there is one, the court will set a timetable for the trial (if this has not already been done), unless the court considers that it would be inappropriate to do so. By r 28.9, unless the trial judge otherwise directs, the trial will be conducted in accordance with any order previously made.

A trial timetable is of some importance and is fixed in consultation with the parties. However, the conduct of the trial remains under the control of the trial judge. Thus, in a long case, it is important that the pre-trial review should be before the trial judge, if only for the purpose of fixing the trial timetable. Although, conventionally, the court hears all of the claimant's evidence and then all of the defendant's evidence, this is not necessarily the best way to proceed in every case. It is very common, for example, for issues to be tried in a specific order in Commercial Court cases. Thus, all evidence on one issue, both claimant's and defendant's, is given before proceeding to the next issue. This can be of some importance where expert evidence is in dispute and there will be a series of experts giving oral evidence to the court. In a long case, it is normally regarded as far too expensive for all experts to be at court for the whole of the trial. The trial timetable is, therefore, fixed in such a way as to ensure that the attendance of experts is only required for a specific part of the whole trial. In a clinical negligence case, for example, evidence of gynaecologists could be taken at one stage (all parties), psychiatric evidence at another stage, and so on. It follows that the trial judge should not alter the trial timetable without very good reason (which will have to be given), as the parties will have made preparations based on the trial timetable.

If, for practical reasons, it is not possible to arrange a pre-trial review before the trial judge (and this happens frequently outside London) and the trial timetable has to be fixed by a district judge, it is standard practice for the district judge to submit a proposed draft timetable to the trial judge (if already identified) for final approval, before it is issued to all parties in the form of an order.

The court sets a trial timetable unless it 'considers that it would be inappropriate to do so' (r 29.8(c)(i)). It may be inappropriate to do so in a jury case. Claims for defamation, malicious prosecution or false imprisonment will be tried by a judge sitting with a jury, unless the court otherwise orders.

EVIDENCE-IN-CHIEF

Evidence is dealt with in Part 32. The general rule is that any fact which needs to be proved by the evidence of a witness is to be proved at trial by their oral evidence, given in public (r 32.2). However, r 32.4 imposes a requirement to serve witness statements for use at trial, and directions will have been given by the court as part of its case management.

Where a witness is called to give oral evidence, his or her witness statement 'shall stand as his or her evidence-in-chief unless the court orders otherwise' (r 32.5(2)). A witness giving oral evidence at trial may, with the permission of the court, amplify his or her witness statement or give evidence in relation to new matters which have arisen since the witness statement was served. The court will give permission only if it considers that there is good reason not to confine the evidence of the witness to the contents of his or her witness statement.

These rules explain the absence of any time allocated for examination-in-chief in the above specimen trial timetable. Obviously, it takes a few moments, but it is not necessary to make specific provision for it.

If a party has served a witness statement and wishes to rely at trial on the evidence of the witness who made the statement, he or she must call the witness to give oral evidence (unless the court orders otherwise or the evidence is put in as hearsay evidence).

The court will have been supplied with two identical copies of the trial bundle (obviously, all advocates and solicitors and the clients will have one each, too). Of the two bundles supplied to the court, one is for the use of the trial judge and the other for the use of witnesses and is placed in the witness-box.

When the time comes for the witness to give evidence, the advocate who wishes to call him or her will simply say: 'I call the claimant' or 'I call John Smith', or whatever. The court usher (if necessary, after repeating the call) then guides the witness into the witness-box and administers the oath (or affirmation). The advocate will then ask the witness his or her name, address and, if relevant, occupation, and then invite the witness to turn to a specific page of the relevant trial bundle, which will be page 1 of that witness's statement. He or she will then invite the witness to turn to the last page of the statement, which will contain the witness's signature, and ask the witness to confirm that it is his or her signature and that it was signed on the date given on the statement. The advocate then usually adds a further question – something like: 'You signed the statement on 14 November 2004 – have you had the opportunity to read it again since then?'. The answer should be: 'Yes'. (The witness is entitled to – and should – read the statement again, before going into the witness-box.) Although not necessary, strictly speaking, advocates often add a further question, such as: 'Do you invite the court to accept that statement as your evidence in this case?', to which, of course, the witness will answer: 'Yes'.

Judges recognise that it is often daunting for an ordinary person to have to come to court to give evidence and they are anxious to help the witness to relax so far as possible and feel comfortable when giving evidence. Accordingly, many modern judges at this point will turn to the witness and say something like: 'Mr Smith, as I'm sure your lawyers have told you, under the modern practice witness statements stand as evidence and I would like to confirm to you that I have read your evidence before coming into court and I am familiar with it'.

Examination-in-chief these days proceeds very quickly and, in no time at all, the witness will be cross-examined. (For trial advocacy generally, see further, Chapter 35.)

SUPPORTING THE TRIAL ADVOCATE

The brief to counsel (or to a solicitor–advocate) will have been delivered in good time for the trial. Do solicitors leave the conduct of the trial to the advocate or do they have a role at trial? It used to be always regarded as professionally improper for a barrister to appear in court without his or her instructing solicitor (or solicitor's representative, such as a legal executive or other clerk). However, this 'double manning' rule has been relaxed following considerable criticism. Barristers nowadays conduct both small claims and fast-track trials without a solicitor. However, in many fast-track trials, it will be appropriate for the solicitor (or representative) to attend court with a claimant, and the cost rules recognise this.

In multi-track cases, there is no question and, obviously, a solicitor should attend, as well as the trial advocate. What does the solicitor do? The first task is to ensure that everyone has got to court at the right time and then to introduce the client to the counsel who will be conducting the case (or re-introduce them if they have already met at a conference). The client and witnesses should be given the opportunity to re-read their statements and extra copies should be brought along to the trial for this purpose. Former rules preventing barristers discussing cases with witnesses have been relaxed. In fact, barristers have always been able to talk to their lay client and expert witnesses.

Get to court early and, if possible, show the client and witnesses the courtroom and explain what is going to happen. In civil cases, there is no reason why all witnesses should not remain in court for the whole of the case. Unlike a criminal case, a witness is not required to wait outside until called to give evidence. Explain to the client what to call the judge – district judges are addressed as 'Sir' or 'Madam', as appropriate; circuit judges and recorders sitting in the county court are addressed as 'Your Honour'; any judge sitting in the High Court is addressed as 'My Lord' or 'My Lady', as appropriate. Witnesses generally like to get this right and it takes only a few moments to help them to do so.

Take a note of what is going on, particularly when your advocate is cross-examining the other side's witnesses and is unable to take his or her own notes. It may be necessary later on to read back precisely the words used by a witness. The judge will also be taking notes.

All trials are now recorded. At all hearings, whether in the High Court or the county court, oral evidence and the judgment (or summing-up, where the case is being decided by a jury) will be recorded (see PD 39, para 6). No party or member of the public may use unofficial recording equipment in any court or judge's room without the permission of the court, and to do so without permission constitutes a contempt of court.

Any party *or person* may require a transcript of the recording of any trial to be supplied on payment of the appropriate authorised charge. Where any hearing takes place in public, members of the public may obtain a transcript of any judgment given or a copy of any order made, subject to payment of the appropriate fee (PD 39, para 1.11). This contrasts with judgments and orders made in private – for which, although a party can obtain a transcript, any member of the public who is not a party must seek the permission of the judge who gave the judgment or made the order before he or she can receive a copy of the judgment or order.

CONDUCT OF SMALL CLAIMS TRIALS

Conduct of small claims trials is governed by r 27.8. The court may adopt any method of proceeding that it considers to be fair. In particular, hearings will be informal, the strict rules of evidence do not apply, the court need not take evidence on oath, and the court may limit cross-examination. At the conclusion of the case, the judge must given reasons for the decision.

The procedure for small claims trials is intended to be simple and straightforward, so that parties can represent themselves without having to employ a lawyer. Judges usually begin the trial by explaining to the parties the procedure that will be adopted. (See further, PD 27, para 4.)

Parties can, of course, employ lawyers at their own expense to represent them at small claims trials, if they wish. In fact, in the majority of small claims trials arising out of road traffic accidents, parties tend to be represented by a barrister (present without a solicitor), instructed with the benefit of relevant insurance.

In practice, something akin to a normal trial process is followed. The claimant will give evidence and the judge will ask questions and invite the defendant to do so. The process is then repeated with the claimant's witnesses. Then, the defendant gives evidence, and the same process is repeated. The judge will have pre-read the papers and will often begin by explaining to the parties what he or she understands the issues to be. Opening speeches are rare. However, at the conclusion of the evidence, the judge can invite first the defendant and then the claimant to make a closing speech, if they wish to do so. The judge will then proceed to give judgment and, after having done so, will deal with costs. There is, of course, a limited costs regime. (See further, r 27.14.)

FAILURE TO ATTEND THE TRIAL

Failure to attend a trial is rare but does happen. In the case of fast-track and multi-track trials, r 39.3 applies. The court may proceed with the trial in the absence of a party. If the claimant does not attend, the court will strike out his or her claim and any defence to counterclaim. If a defendant does not attend, it may strike-out his or her defence or counterclaim, or both. If no party attends, the court will strike out the whole of the proceedings. The point of striking out is that proceedings struck out can be restored. Where a party does not attend and the court gives judgment or makes an order against him, that party may apply for the judgment or order to be set aside (see r 39.3(2) and (3)). Any application to restore or set aside must be supported by evidence. The court can grant an application to restore or set aside only if the three conditions of r 39.3(5) are satisfied: that is, only if the applicant:

> '(a)   acted promptly when he found out that the court had exercised its power to strike out or to enter judgment or make an order against him;
> (b)   had a good reason for not attending the trial; and
> (c)   has a reasonable prospect of success.'

The application must be made in accordance with Part 23.

The requirements of r 39.3(5) are stringent and pre-CPR cases on the former more relaxed provision can no longer be regarded as a useful guide. The court has no residual discretion and can set aside a regular judgment only if the party can satisfy all the requirements of the rule (*Barclays Bank Plc v Ellis* [2001] CP Rep 50. However, the test is similar to that set out in *Alpine Bulk Transport Co Inc v Saudi*

Eagle Shipping Co Inc, the Saudi Eagle [1986] 2 Lloyd's Rep 221 (see pp 163 and 173 above where this case is discussed).

It is particularly important to act promptly. The question is whether the applicant has acted with reasonable celerity in the circumstances (*Regency Rolls Ltd v Carnall* [2000] All ER(D) 1417 (Oct), noted in *Civil Procedure News*, 23 April 2001). A defendant who knows of proceedings against him is not entitled to have an order made against him set aside as of right simply because he was not notified of a new trial date (*Hackney London Borough Council v Driscoll* [2003] EWCA Civ 1037, [2003] 1WLR 2602). In *National Westminster Bank v Aaronson* [2004] EWHC 618, [2004] All ER (D) 178 Royce J refused to set aside judgment given in the absence of the defendant where he knew of the trial date and had failed to obtain an adjournment.

FAILURE TO ATTEND A SMALL CLAIMS TRIAL

Failure to attend a small claims trial is far more common than in trials allocated to other tracks. A party may decide on the day that the claim or defence is not worth pursuing, or find that he or she has more profitable business to attend to. However, the court has allocated time for the case and will be reluctant to do so again. In fact, r 27.9 specifically provides for the non-attendance of parties at a final hearing. If a party gives written notice at least 7 days before the date of hearing that he or she will not attend, and has, in that notice, requested the court to decide the claim in his or her absence, the court will take into account that party's statement of case and any other documents he or she has filed when it decides the claim.

If a claimant does not attend the hearing and has not given notice pursuant to r 27.9, the court may strike out the claim. If a defendant does not attend the hearing and has not given notice pursuant to r 27.9, and the claimant either does attend or has given notice, the court may decide the claim on the basis of the evidence of the claimant alone. If neither party attends, or gives r 27.9 notice, the court may strike out the claim and any counterclaim. Notice in accordance with the rule need not be formal – a letter will suffice.

In practice, district judges often take the initiative – especially if a case can clearly be decided on documents and the parties are some distance away from court – and invite the parties to proceed in this way. Rule 21.10 provides that the court may, if all parties agree, deal with the claim without a hearing.

The setting aside of judgments in small claims cases is dealt with by r 27.11. A party who was neither present nor represented at the hearing (and who had not given written notice under r 27.9) may apply for an order that the judgment be set aside and the claim reheard. A party who applies for an order setting aside a judgment under r 27.11 must make the application not more than 14 days after the day on which notice of the judgment was served on him. The court can grant the application only if the applicant:

(1)   had a good reason for not attending or being represented at the hearing or giving written notice to the court under r 27.9; and

(2)   has a reasonable prospect of success at the hearing.

In *Shocked v Goldschmidt* [1998] 1 All ER 372 (a pre-CPR case), the Court of Appeal held that 'a party who has deliberately chosen to be absent from a hearing is not entitled to a re-hearing even if the party has a good claim or defence'. Under the CPR, such a party would not be able to persuade the court that there was a good reason for not attending. The test of 'a reasonable prospect of success' is similar to the pre-CPR case of *Alpine Bulk Transport Co Inc v Saudi Eagle Shipping Co* [1986] 2 Lloyd's Rep 221 (see pp 163 and 173 above where this case is discussed).

JUDGMENTS AND ORDERS (PART 40)

At the conclusion of the trial, the judge will give a reasoned judgment, which will be recorded. A transcript can be obtained on payment of the appropriate fee. (An unsuccessful party may wish to obtain one so that an appeal can be considered.) Once the judge has delivered judgment, it is necessary for the appropriate order to be drawn up.

In a claim which has resulted in an award of a sum of money, the question of interest arises. It is normal practice for the judgment to record separately the amount awarded by the judge and any interest, so the calculation should be done immediately by the advocate (or instructing solicitor) and stated.

An appropriate order for costs must be sought. Any advocate representing a party whose case has been financed out of public funds will need to apply for a detailed assessment of the costs payable out of the community legal service fund. In the case of all trials that have lasted less than one day (and this would necessarily include all fast-track trials), the usual procedure is for costs to be summarily assessed immediately. If, for any reason, this cannot be done, the summary assessment can be adjourned to a different day (but not to a different judge). Alternatively, the judge could order a detailed assessment. In a case where there is a conditional fee agreement, the judge has the option of summarily assessing the whole costs, summarily assessing the base costs and referring the additional liability for detailed assessment, or ordering detailed assessment of the entire costs. In any case in which a detailed assessment is ordered, the court should also order an immediate payment on account of costs, pursuant to r 44.3(8). An order for detailed assessment should not be sought or made merely as a means of delaying payment. In *Mars UK Ltd v Teknowledge (No 2)* [1999] 2 Costs LR 44, (1999) *The Times*, July 8, it was held that the court should normally order the minimum sum that the successful party would be likely to recover on detailed assessment. A similar approach was taken in *Mabey and Johnson Ltd v Ecclesiastical Insurance Office Plc (Costs)* [2000] CLC 1570. (If, for any reason, payment on account was not ordered under r 44.3(8), or the payment later seems inadequate, an interim costs certificate can be sought, pursuant to r 47.15.)

Where a Part 36 payment into court has been made, there will need to be an order for payment out of the money and any accrued interest thereon.

The order itself will be drawn up by the court (r 40.3) unless:

'(a)   the court orders a party to draw it up,
(b)   a party, with the permission of the court, agrees to draw it up,
(c)   the court dispenses with the need to draw it up, or,
(d)   it is a consent order under rule 40.6.'

Part 40 – Judgments and Orders is supplemented by four Practice Directions. (See, in particular, PD 40B – Judgments and Orders.)

Part VIII

COSTS

Chapter 37

PART 36 OFFERS AND PAYMENTS

The ethos of the CPR is one of settlement. It will not always be possible for the parties to reach agreement by negotiation and so the Rules provide for either party to force the other to consider acceptance of its own compromise terms.

Before the new procedural rules came into effect, there was provision for payment into court by a defendant as a means to try to force a claimant's hand, but there was no similar procedure available to claimants.

CPR Part 36 introduced the concept of offers to settle by both claimant and defendant, as well as retaining payment into court as an option for defendants. Costs and interest penalties apply as an incentive to settlement if reasonable offers are not made and accepted.

As was the case before the CPR, the parties are free to make offers to settle in the course of their negotiations right up until the end of the trial, but unless offers are made in accordance with the provisions of Part 36, such offers will not carry the costs and interest consequences.

Although *Calderbank* offers are largely redundant as a result of Part 36, there will be circumstances in which they may still be used, and the court has a discretion to take them into account on the question of costs. A *Calderbank* letter is one that contains settlement proposals, but expresses them to be *without prejudice save as to costs*.

In relation to a defendant's offer to settle a money claim, r 36.3 requires a Part 36 payment.

However, r 44.3(4) provides that, in deciding whether to make an order for costs, the court shall have regard to any offer, whether it has been made in accordance with Part 36 or not. In *Trustees of Stokes Pension Fund v Western Power Distribution (South West) plc* EWCA 11July 2005 the Court of Appeal held that CPR gave the court the discretion to order that an offer by a defendant was to have the same costs consequences as a Part 36 payment into court. The guidance given was that the court might reasonably conclude that an offer to settle a money claim should be treated as having the same effect as a payment into court if the offer was expressed in clear terms, was open for acceptance for at least 21 days, was a genuine offer and the defendant was able to pay the sum offered when the offer was made. In practice, therefore, it will be unwise to ignore offers that are made even if they are not made strictly in accordance with Part 36.

Part 36 does not apply to claims on the small claims track. This does not mean that offers to settle should not be made and, if made, that they should not be given serious consideration. Failure to accept a reasonable offer may be sufficient for the court to conclude that there has been unreasonable behaviour and that a substantive costs order should follow (r 27.14(2)(d)). (See also Chapter 24, The Small Claims Track.)

WHEN OFFERS AND PAYMENTS MAY BE MADE

A Part 36 offer or payment may be made at any time after proceedings have begun. However, r 36.10 provides that, if a party makes an offer to settle before proceedings have begun, and that offer complies with Part 36, the court will take it into account when making a costs order. Any offer or payment made pursuant to Part 36 must state as much and must be signed by the party making the offer, or that party's legal representative.

CONTENTS OF A PART 36 OFFER

A Part 36 offer to settle may be made by any party and must be in writing. There is no prescribed form, but it must contain the following information:

(1)   it must state whether the offer relates to the whole of the claim, or, if relating to only a part of the claim, or a particular issue, which part and which issue;

(2)   it must state whether it takes into account any counterclaim;

(3)   if the offer does not include interest, it must say so, otherwise interest will be deemed to be included. If interest is not included in the sum offered, the offer must state whether interest is offered or not, and, if it is, the amount offered, and the rate(s) and period(s) covered;

(4)   if it is made no less than 21 days before the start of the trial, it must be expressed to remain open for acceptance for 21 days and provide that if the offer is not accepted within that time, it may only be accepted either with the court's permission, or if the parties agree the liability for costs; and

(5)   if it is made less than 21 days before the start of the trial, it must state that it may only be accepted either with the court's permission, or if the parties agree the liability for costs.

CONTENTS OF A PART 36 PAYMENT NOTICE

When a defendant makes a payment into court, a notice must be filed that sets out the following information:

(1)   the amount of the payment;

(2)   whether the payment relates to the whole of the claim, or, if relating to only a part of the claim, or a particular issue, which part and which issue;

(3)   whether the payment takes into account any counterclaim;

(4)   whether the payment takes into account any interim payment that may have been made;

(5)   if the payment does not include interest, it must say so, otherwise interest will be deemed to be included. If interest is not included in the payment, the notice must state whether interest is offered or not, and, if it is, the amount offered, and the rate(s) and period(s) covered;

(6)   where benefit is recoverable under the Social Security (Recovery of Benefits) Act 1997, the amount of gross compensation must be stated, the amounts of each benefit by which the gross compensation is reduced, and that the sum paid or offered is the net amount after deduction of benefit;

(7)   if it is made no less than 21 days before the start of the trial, it must be expressed to remain open for acceptance for 21 days and provide that, if the payment is not accepted within that time, it may only be accepted either with the court's permission, or if the parties agree the liability for costs; and

(8)   if it is made less than 21 days before the start of the trial, it must state that it may only be accepted either with the court's permission, or if the parties agree the liability for costs.

TIME FOR ACCEPTANCE

If an offer or payment is made more than 21 days before the start of the trial, the general rule is that the party to whom the offer is made has 21 days in which to accept, without requiring the permission of the court. An offer or payment made less than 21 days before the start of the trial cannot be accepted without the court's permission, unless the parties can agree on what the costs consequences will be.

In *Scammell and Others v Dicker* [2001] 1 WLR 631, the Court of Appeal held that, although an offer to settle may be expressed to be open for acceptance for 21 days, the offer could be withdrawn within that period. A payment into court, however, may only be withdrawn with the court's permission (r 36.6(5)).

COSTS CONSEQUENCES OF ACCEPTANCE OF A DEFENDANT'S PART 36 OFFER OR PART 36 PAYMENT

The costs consequences of acceptance by a claimant of a Part 36 offer or payment will depend upon whether notice of acceptance is served within 21 days of the offer or payment being made. The 21-day period begins to run from the date the offer is received in the case of a Part 36 offer, and from the date written notice of the payment into court is served in the case of a Part 36 payment. If notice of acceptance is served within the 21-day period, the claimant will be entitled to his or her costs up to the date of service of the notice of acceptance. This also applies where a claimant accepts an offer or payment that relates to part of the claim, only if, at the same time, the balance of the claim is abandoned. If there is a counterclaim which the defendant has taken into account in making the offer or payment, the claimant's costs will include those incurred in relation to the counterclaim. The claimant's costs will be subject to a detailed assessment on the standard basis, if not agreed.

ACCEPTANCE OF PART 36 OFFERS OR PAYMENTS BY MULTIPLE DEFENDANTS

If a claimant wishes to accept offers or payments made by all of the defendants to a claim, the procedure is as set out above. However, if not all of the offers or payments are acceptable, the procedure will depend upon whether the defendants are either sued jointly or in the alternative, or severally. If the defendants are sued jointly or in the alternative, the claimant may accept the offer of one or more of the defendants if the claim against the remaining defendants is discontinued and those defendants consent in writing to the acceptance of the offer or payment made by their co-defendant(s). If the claimant alleges that each defendant has several liability to him or her, the claimant may accept the offer(s) or payment(s) made and continue the claim against the remaining defendants.

COSTS CONSEQUENCES OF ACCEPTANCE OF A CLAIMANT'S PART 36 OFFER

Where a defendant accepts a claimant's Part 36 offer within the 21-day period allowed, the claimant will be entitled to the costs of the proceedings up to the date upon which the defendant serves notice of acceptance.

WHAT HAPPENS IF THE CLAIMANT FAILS TO BEAT A PART 36 OFFER OR PAYMENT?

Rule 36.20 sets out the consequences of the failure of a claimant to do better at trial than any Part 36 offer or payment made. Unless the court considers that it would be unjust, the claimant will be ordered to pay the defendant's costs from the last day of the 21-day period for acceptance.

When the court is considering whether it would be unjust to make such an order, it will consider all the circumstances of the case, which will include what information the claimant had when the Part 36 offer or payment was made and the conduct of the parties in relation to the provision of information for the purposes of enabling the offer or payment to be evaluated. The court will not penalise a claimant in costs if the defendant failed to supply information that the claimant needed in order to properly assess whether the payment or offer should be accepted.

WHAT HAPPENS IF THE CLAIMANT DOES BETTER THAN HIS OR HER PART 36 OFFER?

If the defendant fails at trial to beat the claimant's own Part 36 offer, there are two financial penalties that the court has to impose, unless it would be unjust to do so:

(1)   the court may award interest on the whole or part of any sum awarded to the claimant, excluding interest, at a rate not exceeding 10% above base rate for some or all of the period, starting with the twenty-first day after the claimant's Part 36 offer was made; and

(2)   the court may order the defendant to pay the claimant's costs, assessed on an indemnity basis.

The presumption in favour of imposing penalties may be dislodged if it would be unjust, and, in considering whether it would be unjust, the court has to take into account all the circumstances of the case, including the matters set out in r 36.21(5):

(1)   the terms of any Part 36 offer;

(2)   the stage in the proceedings when any Part 36 offer or Part 36 payment was made;

(3)   the information available to the parties at the time that the Part 36 offer or Part 36 payment was made; and

(4)   the conduct of the parties with regard to the giving or refusing to give information for the purposes of enabling the offer or payment into court to be made or evaluated.

The court clearly has a very wide discretion and is encouraged to take a pragmatic and common-sense approach, in order to achieve justice between the parties.

Chapter 38

SECURITY FOR COSTS

The object of an order to give security for costs is to prevent injustice where the applicant is placed in a position by another party of incurring costs in the litigation when there is a risk that, if the applicant is successful, there will be no prospect of enforcing any order for costs against that party. The order will typically require the respondent to pay a certain sum into court, which will then be available as a fund against which to enforce any subsequent order for costs. The proceedings will generally be stayed until compliance.

Such applications will usually be made by a defendant to a claim which is regarded as being speculative, or of having limited prospects of success, and where the defendant is not confident that any order for costs against the claimant will be satisfied. Rules 25.12 and 25.13 apply in these circumstances.

There is also provision in r 25.14 for the court to make an order for security for costs against someone other than a claimant (including a Part 20 claimant), where there is evidence that there is an agreement between such a person and a claimant that has the result of either making an impecunious claimant a nominee or assignee of the person who is the true claimant, or providing funding for an impecunious claimant in exchange for a share of the fruits of the litigation. In either case, the intention of the agreement must be to defeat any costs order.

In addition to the court's powers to order security for costs under Part 25, the court may, as part of its general powers of management under r 3.1, order any party to pay a sum of money into court as security for any sum payable to another party in the proceedings. The power arises where a party has, without good reason, failed to comply with any procedural requirement.

In *Olatawura v Abiloye* [2002] EWCA Civ 998, [2002] All ER (D) 253, the Court of Appeal upheld the decision of a district judge to make an order for a claimant to provide security for costs on the defendants' unsuccessful application for summary judgment. The rationale for the decision was that, although the claimant's prospects of success were limited, the court could not be satisfied that the claimant had no real prospect of success. In that case, the Court of Appeal said that r 3.13 gave the court the power to make an order subject to a condition that a party pays a sum of money into court, and PD 24 specifically applied that to applications for summary judgment made under Part 24.

However, it was emphasised that the power to make such orders should be exercised sparingly.

SECURITY FOR COSTS AGAINST A CLAIMANT

This will be the most common application for security for costs. The rules extend to applications by defendants to Part 20 claims and respondents to appeals.

Rule 25.13 sets out the conditions to be satisfied. To begin with, the claimant must fall into one or more of the categories set out in r 25.13(2):

(1)   an individual or a company or incorporated body ordinarily resident outside England and Wales and not subject to the enforcement procedures available under the CJJA 1982;

(2)   any company or other body about which there is reason to believe it will be unable to pay any order for the defendant's costs;

(3)   a claimant who has changed his or her address since the claim was issued, with a view to avoiding the consequences of the litigation;

(4)   a claimant who, in the claim form, failed to give his or her address, or gave a false address;

(5)   a claimant who is a nominal claimant where there is reason to believe that he or she will be unable to pay any order for the defendant's costs; and/or

(6)   a claimant who has taken steps to put his or her assets out of reach.

If one or more of those conditions is satisfied, the court will then have regard to all the circumstances of the case, and only if satisfied that it is just to make an order will an order be made. This can be a very fine balancing exercise. On the one hand, the court will wish to prevent any injustice to a defendant who may ultimately be considerably out of pocket in the event that a claimant is unable to pay any order for costs. Equally, the court will be mindful of the implications, under the ECHR and otherwise, of making an order for an impecunious claimant to give security for costs. Without going into the merits in great detail, the claimant's prospects of success will be a factor that the court will consider, as will any evidence of the defendant's view of the claim, for example any offers made to settle or payments into court. The stage in the proceedings at which the defendant makes the application will also have a bearing. The longer a claim has been progressing, the harder it will be for a defendant to persuade the court that an order for security for costs would be just. The claimant may have already invested considerable sums in the litigation and may not be in a position to raise any extra funds to meet an order without prejudicing his or her ability to continue to fund the claim. The court may also take the view that it would be unjust at a later stage in the proceedings to introduce a potential difficulty for the claimant, when the defendant could and should have made the application at an early stage, before the claimant had committed to the litigation.

SECURITY FOR COSTS AGAINST NON-PARTIES

Although most applications for security for costs will be against claimants, there are two circumstances in which an application may be appropriate against a person who is not a party to the claim at all. Provision is made in r 25.14. There are two categories of respondent identified by the rule:

(1)   a person who has assigned the right to the claim to the claimant, with a view to avoiding the possibility of a costs order being made against him or her; and

(2)   a person who has contributed or agreed to contribute to the claimant's costs in return for a share of any money or property that the claimant may recover in the proceedings.

In both cases, the implication is that the claimant has no personal funds from which to meet any order for costs against him or her, but has financial backing for his or her own legal costs from a person who is not a party to the proceedings. This is a situation that would clearly cause prejudice to a successful defendant and in which it would be proper to ask the court to make an order for security to be given for costs.

Any application for an order against a person who is not a party to the proceedings must be coupled with an application to join that party (see r 19.3). If the court is satisfied that either or both of these situations applies, it may make an order if, having regard to all the circumstances, it would be just to do so. Clearly, any evidence of bad faith or abuse of process on behalf of a claimant will be influential in the court's decision.

PROCEDURE FOR APPLICATIONS UNDER RULE 25

Applications will be made on notice and must be supported by written evidence, ie a witness statement. The witness statement should set out:

(1)   the conditions in r 25.13(2) relied upon;
(2)   an estimate of the costs incurred to date, and likely to be incurred;
(3)   the amount of security required; and
(4)   any other evidence in support of the application.

SECURITY FOR COSTS UNDER RULE 3.1

The court may make an order against any party to the proceedings in the course of exercising its case management powers. It is, in effect, a penalty for failing, without good reason, to comply with any rule, Practice Direction or a relevant pre-action protocol. An order may be made on the court's own initiative or on the application of another party to the proceedings. When exercising its power under this rule, the court must have regard to the amount in dispute and the costs which the parties have incurred or which they may incur. There are plainly implications for rights of access to the court if the court is considering making an order against a party who would not have the means to satisfy such an order, for example a publicly funded party.

Chapter 39

COSTS

CPR Parts 44 to 48 inclusive deal with the practice and procedure relating to contentious costs. The accompanying Costs Practice Direction is long and detailed. Annexed to the Practice Direction are costs precedents. Between them, they have introduced a significantly different costs regime from that in operation before the CPR were introduced. Before the CPR, the procedure for the assessment of costs was known as 'taxation' and, although it was possible for a judge to make a summary assessment of costs, it was by no means the cornerstone of the costs system that it is now.

As discussed in Chapter 4, there are a number of options for the funding of litigation which are essentially matters between lawyer and client. This chapter deals with the court's powers to make orders for costs against another party and the procedural steps that have to be taken to assess the amount that is payable.

ORDERS FOR COSTS

The court may make an order for costs at any stage in the proceedings. The order will either provide for a party's costs to be summarily assessed, in which case the summary assessment will be carried out by the judge conducting the hearing and will almost always take place there and then, or will provide for there to be a detailed assessment at a later date by district or costs judge.

Orders for costs that are made before the end of the proceedings may be expressed in a number of different ways, depending upon what the costs order is intended to achieve. Section 8.5 of PD Costs sets out some of the commonly made costs orders.

Term	Effect
Costs Costs in any event	The party in whose favour the order is made is entitled to the costs in respect of the part of the proceedings to which the order relates, whatever other costs orders are made in the proceedings.
Costs in the case Costs in the application	The party in whose favour the court makes an order for costs at the end of the proceedings is entitled to his costs of the part of the proceedings to which the order relates.
Costs reserved	The decision about costs is deferred to a later occasion, but if no later order is made the costs will be costs in the case.
Claimant's/defendant's costs in the case/application	If the party in whose favour the costs order is made is awarded costs at the end of the proceedings, that party is entitled to his costs of the part of the proceedings to which the order relates. If any other party is awarded costs at the end of the proceedings, the party in whose favour the final costs order is made is not liable to pay the costs of any other party in respect of the part of the proceedings to which the order relates.
Costs thrown away	Where, for example, a judgment or order is set aside, the party in whose favour the costs order is made is entitled to the costs which have been incurred as a consequence. This includes the costs of – (a) preparing for and attending any hearing at which the judgment or order which has been set aside was made; (b) preparing for and attending any hearing to set aside the judgment or order in question; (c) preparing for and attending any hearing at which the court orders the proceedings or the part in question to be adjourned; (d) any steps taken to enforce a judgment or order which has subsequently been set aside.
Costs of and caused by	Where, for example, the court makes this order on an application to amend a statement of case, the party in whose favour the costs order is made is entitled to the costs of preparing for and attending the application and the costs of any consequential amendment to his own statement of case.
Costs here and below	The party in whose favour the costs order is made is entitled not only to his costs in respect of the proceedings in which the court makes the order but also to his costs of the proceedings in any lower court. In the case of an appeal from a Divisional Court the party is not entitled to any costs incurred in any court below the Divisional Court.

Term	Effect
No order as to costs Each party to pay his own costs	Each party is to bear his own costs of the part of the proceedings to which the order relates whatever costs order the court makes at the end of the proceedings.

If the order does not mention costs, this will generally mean that no party is entitled to costs. However, in the case of a mortgagee in a possession claim, this will not prevent the recovery of costs under the terms of the mortgage deed. (See also Chapter 42.)

BASIS OF ASSESSMENT

As well as providing for which party is to pay the costs, the costs order may also specify the basis of assessment. There are two bases of assessment: standard and indemnity. The default position is the standard basis and so, if the order is silent as to which basis is to apply, it will be the standard basis. If an order purports to use some basis for assessment other than standard or indemnity, for example 'costs on the solicitor and own client basis', the assessment will be on the standard basis.

From time to time, however, the court may make an order for costs on the indemnity basis. Indemnity costs will generally be awarded – on one of two grounds. First, if there has been an element of improper or unreasonable conduct on the part of the paying party which the court considers should not go unmarked. Secondly, if a claimant has offered to settle for an amount not more than the amount awarded by the court, the defendant may be ordered to pay costs on an indemnity basis. However, an order for costs on the indemnity basis is not the same as saying that the paying party must pay all the costs of the receiving party. Costs must always be reasonably incurred and reasonable in amount.

There are two main differences between an assessment on the standard basis and an assessment on the indemnity basis. First, if the costs judge is unsure whether the costs were reasonably incurred and reasonable in amount, on an assessment on the standard basis, he or she will give the benefit of the doubt to the paying party, and, on an assessment on the indemnity basis, to the receiving party.

Secondly, on the standard basis, costs must be either proportionate to the matters in issue, or necessary.

EXERCISE OF THE COURT'S DISCRETION WHEN ASSESSING COSTS

The court will approach the assessment of costs slightly differently, depending upon whether costs are being assessed on the standard basis or on the indemnity basis.

Rule 44.5(1) provides that the court must, in either case, have regard to all the circumstances, but if the costs are being assessed on the standard basis the court is looking to ensure that the costs are *proportionately and reasonably incurred, or were proportionate and reasonable in amount.*

If the costs are being assessed on the indemnity basis, the court will look at whether the costs were *unreasonably incurred or unreasonable in amount.*

The court will not allow costs that were unreasonable in amount or unreasonably incurred, whichever basis for assessment is used, and the distinction between the two bases is that if there is any doubt about whether costs are unreasonable, the benefit of the doubt goes to the paying party on the standard basis and to the receiving party on the indemnity basis. Also, indemnity costs do not have to pass the test of proportionality.

The Rules also provide that the court must have regard to a number of additional factors when assessing the amount of costs. These are set out in r 44.5(3):

> '(a)   the conduct of the parties, including in particular –
> >   (i)   conduct before, as well as during, the proceedings; and
> >   (ii)   the efforts made, if any, before and during the proceedings in order to try to resolve the dispute;
> (b)   the amount or value of any money property involved;
> (c)   the importance of the matter to all the parties;
> (d)   the particular complexity of the matter or the difficulty or novelty of the questions raised;
> (e)   the skill, effort, specialised knowledge and responsibility involved;
> (f)   the time spent on the case; and
> (g)   the place where and the circumstances in which work or any part of it was done.'

THE COURT'S DISCRETION TO MAKE AN ORDER FOR COSTS

Whether or not an order for costs is made, and the terms of any order, are entirely at the discretion of the court. The general rule, however, is that costs will 'follow the event'. In other words, the party who has not been successful will pay the costs of the successful party. Having said that, the court has complete flexibility. It is not always the case that one party is wholly successful, and there may be considerations arising from the making of offers or a party's conduct that will affect the court's decision. It is open to the court to make an order that reflects these matters.

CPR r 44.3(4) sets out what the court should have in mind when deciding whether to make an order for costs and, if so, in what terms:

> 'the court must have regard to all the circumstances including:
> > (a)   the conduct of the parties;

(b) whether a party has succeeded on part of his case, even if he has not been wholly successful; and

(c) any payment into court or offer to settle made by a party which is drawn to the court's attention (whether or not made in accordance with Part 36).

(5) The conduct of the parties includes:

(a) conduct before, as well as during, the proceedings, and in particular the extent to which the parties followed any relevant pre-action protocol;

(b) whether it was reasonable for a party to raise, pursue or contest a particular allegation or issue;

(c) the manner in which a party has pursued or defended his case or a particular allegation or issue;

(d) whether a claimant who has succeeded in his claim, in whole or in part, exaggerated his claim.'

It is clear from this that the court is required to take a pragmatic, issues-based approach to costs and this is reflected in the different orders that CPR r 44.3(6) suggests, ie that the court may make:

'(a) a proportion of another party's costs;

(b) a stated amount in respect of another party's costs;

(c) costs from or until a certain date only;

(d) costs incurred before proceedings have begun;

(e) costs relating to particular steps taken in the proceedings;

(f) costs relating to a distinct part of the proceedings;

(g) interest on costs from or until a certain date, including a date before judgment.'

THE PROCEDURE FOR ASSESSMENT OF COSTS

When an order for costs has been made, the amount to be paid has to be assessed. This will either be by way of summary assessment or a detailed assessment. Whichever procedure is used, the principles applied by the court will be the same.

SUMMARY ASSESSMENT

The general rule is that the court will make a summary assessment of costs at the end of a fast-track trial or any other hearing lasting no longer than a day, unless there is a good reason for not doing so (PD Costs, para 13.2). A good reason may be a significant dispute over the sums claimed, or an issue about the indemnity principle that cannot be resolved without more detailed investigation. Similarly, if there is insufficient time to complete a summary assessment at the end of a hearing, the judge may either adjourn to another day, or order a detailed assessment.

There can be no summary assessment of costs when the receiving party is a child, a patient or a party who is publicly funded. In those circumstances, costs must be assessed by the detailed assessment procedure. However, a summary assessment may be made where any of those parties is the paying party.

It is not possible for the judge who made the order for costs to adjourn a summary assessment of costs to another judge – a summary assessment must be carried out by the judge who dealt with the hearing. A detailed assessment will be dealt with by a district judge or a costs judge and there is no requirement that the trial judge should deal with it.

STATEMENT OF COSTS

A summary assessment of costs is carried out on the basis of a statement of costs.

PD Costs, para 13.5(4) provides that each party should file at court, and serve on any party against which it will, if appropriate, seek a costs order, a statement of costs. This should be filed and served as soon as possible, and, in any event, no later than 24 hours before the date of the hearing.

Most people interpret this rule incorrectly and serve a statement of costs the day before the hearing, when the rule in fact requires service no later than the day before that. So, for example, for a hearing on a Friday, the statement of costs should be served by close of business on the Wednesday.

In practice, the distinction matters little. Most judges take the view that, even if the statement of costs has only been served on the day of the hearing, the paying party can be given a short time to consider it and the summary assessment may then proceed. Some judges will mark late filing and service of statements of costs by making a reduction in the costs allowed; others may adjourn the summary assessment and order the party in default to pay the costs thrown away. However, since the decision in *MacDonald v Taree Holdings Limited* [2001] CPLR 439, there is no question of costs being wholly disallowed if the receiving party fails to file a statement of costs in time, or, indeed, at all.

It will fall to the advocates to address the judge on the statement of costs filed by the receiving party. If counsel has been instructed, it is unlikely that he or she will have anything useful to say, unless full instructions have been given by the fee earner with the conduct of the matter. You will not be aware when you brief counsel whether you will be the paying party or the receiving party. It follows, therefore, that you should include instructions that will enable counsel to justify your own costs, as well as to challenge your opponent's costs.

Preparation of the statement of costs

The statement of costs should be prepared in Form N260, which is set out below. It can be found also in The Supreme Court Costs Office, *Guide to the Summary Assessment of Costs*, as well as in the Forms volume of the White Book.

There are essentially five components to the statement of costs:

(1)   a record of the work carried out;

(2)   the grade(s) of fee earner who carried out the work. Four grades of fee earner are specified, as follows:

(a)   solicitors with 8 years' post-qualification experience, including at least 8 years' experience in litigation;

(b)   solicitors and Fellows of the Institute of Legal Executives (FILEx) with over 4 years' experience, including at least 4 years' experience in litigation;

(c)   other solicitors, FILEx and fee earners of equivalent experience to FILEx, ie a minimum of 6 years';

(d)   trainee solicitors, para-legals and other fee earners.

These are the only grades of fee earner that are recognised;

(3)   the hourly rate applied. All groups of courts make available their guideline hourly rates. These have been arrived at following consultation between the designated civil judges, district judges and local law societies. They are designed to reflect the actual cost of providing legal services in different locations. A composite summary of the guideline rates in four bands is published in the *Guide to the Summary Assessment of Costs* and is revised every 2 years. The rates promulgated locally will be more precise and probably more up-to-date than those in the Guide. Courts will always use the guideline rates as a starting point, and very often as a finishing point, but they are only guidelines and, in appropriate cases, the judge may depart from the rates, in either direction;

(4)   a statement that the indemnity principle has not been breached. The principle is that the receiving party is not entitled to receive more from the paying party than he or she is contractually bound to pay his or her solicitor. So, for example, if a solicitor is acting for a friend at a special rate or for no fee at all, it will not be possible to claim costs from the other side, on the basis of the solicitor's usual charging rate. In order that the paying party and the court may be satisfied that the indemnity principle has not been breached, the statement of costs must contain the following declaration: *'The costs estimated above do not exceed the costs which the [party] is liable to pay in respect of the work which this estimate covers'*. If the costs statement is signed by a solicitor, this will usually be sufficient to satisfy the court that the indemnity principle has not been breached. The future of the indemnity principle is uncertain, following Government recommendations, but it is likely that it will eventually cease to apply to the assessment of costs;

(5)   the statement must be signed by the party or his or her legal representative.

CONDUCT OF THE SUMMARY ASSESSMENT

At the conclusion of the hearing, when an order for costs for summary assessment has been made, the judge will ascertain whether a statement of costs has been served and filed by the receiving party, allowing any short adjournment necessary for procedural defaults to be remedied. The representative of the paying party will usually be asked to bring to the attention of the judge any items to be challenged, and the representative of the receiving party will have an opportunity to reply.

When a summary assessment is being carried out, the court will not have a detailed bill setting out the background information about the work that has been done. It is of particular importance, therefore, to make sure, if there are special circumstances, including those set out in r 44.5(3), which the court should be asked to take into account, that the advocate is adequately briefed to deal with them.

The paying party may take issue with the charging rate applied if it is higher than the guideline hourly rate and the time spent. There may also be scope for challenging the grade of fee earner: a straightforward case may not justify being dealt with by a grade A fee earner. If counsel's fees are greater than the fee paid to the paying party's counsel, this is an obvious point to make to the judge in an effort to achieve a reduction (but note that fixed trial costs apply on the fast track – see 'Fast-track trial costs' below). However, it is not unknown for the judge to make comparison between the parties' statements of costs in the assessment process, and so there is nothing to be gained by arguing that the costs of the receiving party are too high if your costs as the paying party are the same or even more. Even if the judge does not notice, the receiving party is bound to point it out.

As well as listening to the arguments on both sides, the judge will bring his or her own knowledge and experience to bear. He or she will also have in mind the principle of proportionality, and may reduce costs to ensure that those awarded are not disproportionate to the sums at issue. Once the costs have been summarily assessed, the judge will make an order for the sum to be paid. If a date is not specified, payment is due within 14 days of the order for costs.

DETAILED ASSESSMENT

All cases in which costs are payable and have not been dealt with either by fixed costs or by summary assessment will be subject to detailed assessment.

Procedure for detailed assessment

Rule 47 sets out the procedure for detailed assessment.

Once an order for costs has been made for detailed assessment, the receiving party must prepare a bill of costs. The bill must then be served on the paying party, together with a notice of commencement in Form N252. Copies of fee notes of counsel and experts, and written evidence of any other disbursements exceeding £250, must also accompany the bill.

The time allowed for commencing the assessment proceedings is 3 months from the date of the order for assessment or other event giving rise to the assessment, for example acceptance of a Part 36 offer (see below, 'When costs orders are deemed to have been made'). The receiving party is not prevented from commencing the assessment process outside the 3-month period, and the court's permission is not required; however, a sum in respect of costs, interest or both may be disallowed from the bill because of the delay. The parties may agree between themselves to extend or reduce the 3-month period, and either party may apply to the court for an order in either terms.

On receipt of the bill and notice of commencement, the paying party has 21 days in which to respond. Unless the paying party agrees to pay the costs claimed in the bill, points of dispute must be served on the receiving party. PD Costs, Section 35 sets out in detail the form and content of the points of dispute. A precedent for points of dispute can be found at G in the Schedule of Costs Precedents annexed to the Practice Direction, and this should be followed as closely as possible. Points of dispute must set out each item in the bill that is disputed and state clearly and concisely why objection is taken. Woolly generalisations are not acceptable. Where it is possible to do so, the paying party should put forward a suggestion as to what should be allowed.

If no points of dispute are served within 21 days from the date of service of the notice of commencement, the receiving party may apply to the court on Form N254 for a default costs certificate, which will order the paying party to pay the sum claimed in the bill. If points of dispute are served out of time, the paying party will need the court's permission to be heard and there is nothing to prevent the court from issuing a default costs certificate. However, there are certain circumstances in which the court must, and may, set aside a default costs certificate. The court *must* set aside a default costs certificate if the receiving party was not entitled to it, and the court *may* set aside a default costs certificate if it appears that there is some good reason why the detailed assessment proceedings should continue.

Where points of dispute are served, the paying party may serve a reply. It is good practice to do so in an effort to narrow the issues, and failure to do so may result in a costs penalty.

If agreement cannot be reached between the parties, it is up to the receiving party to file at court a request in Form N258 for a detailed assessment. This must, in any event, be filed within 3 months of the end of the 3-month period allowed for the commencement of the detailed assessment proceedings. In other words, no more than 6 months should elapse from the date of the order for detailed assessment and the request for a detailed assessment hearing.

If the paying party either fails to commence the detailed assessment proceedings or fails to request a hearing for a detailed assessment within the period specified, the receiving party may apply to the court. This is likely to result in an order that, unless the receiving party complies with the Rules by a given date, all or part of the costs will be disallowed. Even if the paying party does not take any steps to enforce compliance, late compliance by the receiving party can be met by the court's disallowing all or any part of the interest that may otherwise be payable.

Conduct of the detailed assessment hearing

The detailed assessment will be dealt with by a district judge, sitting as a costs officer or, in the RCJ, by a costs judge.

The key documents will be the bill itself, and also the points of dispute and any reply. Unless permission is given, the issues to be dealt with at the detailed assessment will be confined to those in the points of dispute.

If you are the receiving party, it will be important to take your file of papers to the hearing, or at least those parts of it that are relevant. For example, if there is a dispute about the number of letters written, and whether they were necessary, the judge may wish to see them. It will be helpful to you and to the judge if the relevant correspondence or documents are flagged or otherwise organised so that they are readily at hand.

The judge will hear from both sides on the points in dispute and give a decision on each. You should make a careful note of each item, as, when the assessment has been concluded, the judge will almost certainly expect you and your opponent to make a calculation of the amount due, which will then be endorsed on the bill. If you are in any doubt as to what was allowed or disallowed, and why, ask the judge as each item is dealt with, so that you have a clear record in case you wish to appeal.

COSTS OF THE ASSESSMENT PROCEEDINGS

As with any other hearing, the court has the power to make an order for costs at the conclusion of the assessment hearing. The starting point is that the receiving party is entitled to the costs of the assessment proceedings. However, the court may make a different order. When deciding whether to do so, r 47.18(2) sets out the criteria to be applied in the exercise of the court's discretion:

> '... the court must have regard to all the circumstances, including –
>
> (a)   the conduct of all the parties;
> (b)   the amount, if any, by which the bill of costs has been reduced; and
> (c)   whether it was reasonable for a party to claim the costs of a particular item or to dispute that item.'

In order to achieve some protection from a costs order on the assessment hearing, either party may make a written offer to settle the costs of the substantive proceedings that is expressed to be *without prejudice, save as to the costs of the detailed assessment proceedings* (a *Calderbank* letter). The fact that offers to settle may have been made must not be referred to until the conclusion of the assessment hearing, when, if appropriate, any offer letters will be shown to the judge, who will take them into account when deciding where the liability for the costs of the assessment proceedings should lie.

Detailed assessment of costs of a publicly funded client

Slightly different provisions apply in the case of a detailed assessment where the costs will be paid only from the Community Legal Service Fund.

The detailed assessment proceedings are begun by the solicitor's filing the bill of costs, together with a request in Form N258A. Three months is allowed from the date of the order for an assessment, or other event giving rise to the right to an assessment, for example the discharge of the public funding certificate. Before the bill can be considered, the court must be satisfied either that the client has no financial interest in the assessment, or that the client has a financial interest, has been served with a copy of the bill, and does not wish to be heard. This is dealt with by a certificate attached to the bill and signed by the person authorised to sign the bill.

If the client does not wish to be heard on the assessment, the district judge will usually carry out a provisional assessment, without the attendance of the solicitor. Sums may be disallowed on the provisional assessment. The solicitor will have the option of either accepting the provisional assessment, in which case a costs certificate will be issued in that sum, or requesting a hearing, at which he or she will seek to justify the sums disallowed.

If the bill is lengthy and/or complex, a hearing may be fixed, when the solicitor will attend.

If a publicly funded client has a financial interest in the bill and wishes to be heard, a hearing will be fixed, which will be attended by the solicitor and the client. The judge will then hear from the client which aspects of the bill he or she objects to, and, having heard from the solicitor, make a decision about whether or not to allow them, as claimed.

LIMITATIONS ON THE COURT'S DISCRETION AS TO ASSESSMENT

In certain cases, the court's otherwise broad discretion about the amount of costs to be allowed is fettered. These cases include the following:

(1)   where fixed costs apply;
(2)   cases on the small claims track (see Chapter 24);
(3)   fast-track trial costs.

Fixed costs

In specified circumstances, fixed costs will apply, unless the court orders otherwise. These circumstances are set out in Part 45 and include where judgment is obtained in default, summary judgment under Part 24, and similar situations in which the proceedings come to an end at an early stage.

Fast-track trial costs

Only in very exceptional cases will the costs of claims on the fast track be dealt with other than by summary assessment. At the end of a fast-track trial, the judge may ask to see any previous costs statements in order to gain an impression of the costs of the claim as a whole, to ensure that they are proportionate.

On the fast track, the costs that can be allowed for the trial itself are fixed. The prescribed amounts are set out in r 46, which deals solely with fast-track trial costs. The amount varies, depending upon the value of the claim. For a claim in which the claimant has recovered up to £3,000, the trial costs are £350. Where the claimant recovers more than £3,000 but not more than £10,000, the trial costs are £500, and where more than £10,000 is recovered, the trial costs are £750. The trial costs include the advocate's preparation for and conduct of the trial, and all travelling time and costs, and they cannot be increased if the trial lasts longer than a day, nor reduced if the hearing goes short. However, it is irrelevant if counsel's brief fee is less than the sum prescribed for the trial costs. That is entirely a matter between counsel and the instructing solicitors.

In the following, limited circumstances, the court may depart from the prescribed amount, either upwards or downwards:

(1)   where no fast-track costs are awarded;
(2)   where a party's legal representative attends the trial with the advocate and the court considers that it was necessary to assist the advocate, an additional £250 may be awarded. In general, there is no provision for a fee earner to attend court with the advocate. The Law Society has published guidance on when a solicitor should or need not attend;
(3)   where the court awards a sum representing an additional liability (see below, 'Assessment of costs where additional liability';
(4)   where there has been improper or unreasonable conduct during the trial on the part of the receiving party, the court may reduce the costs allowed;
(5)   where the paying party is guilty of improper or unreasonable conduct during the trial, the costs allowed to the receiving party may be increased; and
(6)   where the court has directed a separate trial of an issue, costs may be allowed, but only on the basis of a maximum of two-thirds of the prescribed rate allowed for the value of the claim and a minimum of £350 (eg for a claim worth £11,000, a figure of between £350 and £500).

SPECIAL RULES FOR LITIGANTS IN PERSON

Litigants in person are those who represent themselves in court. A barrister, solicitor or other legal representative acting for himself or herself is regarded as a litigant in person, as is a company that is not legally represented.

If an order for costs is made in favour of a litigant in person, other than a solicitor, the amount to be allowed will depend upon whether or not the litigant in person can prove financial loss as a result of preparing the case and attending the trial.

Financial loss will usually mean lost earnings or loss of profit for a self-employed person. Provided a solicitor has conducted the litigation through his firm he will be able to charge as a solicitor and not as a litigant in person.

Following a change to CPR r 48.6, the costs that may be allowed for work carried out before 2 December 2002 by a litigant in person who can prove financial loss will be treated differently from those for work carried out after that date.

For work carried out before 2 December 2002, where financial loss can be proved, the costs awarded will be a maximum of two-thirds of the amount that would be have been awarded to a legal representative and a minimum of the actual financial loss sustained (r 48.6(4)(a)).

Where financial loss cannot be proved the position after 2 December 2002 remains the same. The court will allow the time reasonably spent by the litigant in person preparing the case and attending the trial at a specified rate, currently £9.25 per hour.

For work carried out by a litigant in person after 2 December 2002, the following amended paragraphs of r 48.6 apply:

'(3) The litigant in person shall be allowed:

    (a)   costs for the same categories of:
        (i)   work; and
        (ii)   disbursements,
        which would have been allowed if the work had been done or the disbursements had been made by a legal representative on the litigant in person's behalf;
    (b)   the payments reasonably made by him for legal services relating to the conduct of the proceedings; and
    (c)   the costs of obtaining expert assistance in addressing the costs claim.

(The costs practice direction deals with who may be an expert for the purpose of paragraph (3)(c)).

(4) The amount of costs to be allowed to the litigant in person for any item of work claimed shall be:

    (a)   where the litigant can prove financial loss, the amount that he can prove he has lost for time reasonably spent on doing the work; or
    (b)   where the litigant cannot prove financial loss, an amount for the time reasonably spent on doing the work at the rate set out in the practice direction.'

The amended rule removes the anomaly that enabled a litigant in person who could prove any financial loss, however small, to recover up to two-thirds of what a solicitor would have charged for all the work done regardless of whether all the work had caused financial loss.

In addition, litigants in person may claim the following costs, whether they were incurred before or after 2 December 2002:

(1)   disbursements, if they are reasonable in amount and reasonably incurred;
(2)   any legal costs reasonably incurred relating to the conduct of the proceedings;
(3)   the costs of taking expert advice (eg from a costs draftsman) on the assessment procedure.

COSTS-ONLY PROCEEDINGS

It will often be the case that a claim is settled for the payment of damages and costs before proceedings are begun. The amount of damages will be agreed and, if costs are not agreed at that stage, the settlement will be concluded on the basis that costs will be negotiated. If it proves impossible to agree the amount of the costs that are to be paid, either party may make an application to the court for an order for the costs to be assessed.

The procedure is for a Part 8 claim to be made. The claim form should have annexed to it proof of the agreement to pay costs. This will usually consist of correspondence between the parties that sets out the agreement reached. The claim form will be served on the respondent. After the time for acknowledging service has passed, the claim and any acknowledgement will be referred to a district judge. If the application is not opposed and he or she is satisfied that there is an agreement to pay costs, an order for costs will be made. Such an order for costs will always be the subject of a detailed assessment. If the claim form does not satisfy the district judge that there is an agreement, or the application is opposed, the application will be dismissed, and proceedings will have to be issued to enforce the alleged agreed.

FIXED COSTS IN COSTS ONLY PROCEEDINGS IN CLAIMS ARISING OUT OF ROAD TRAFFIC ACCIDENTS

CPR Part 45 Parts II–IV were introduced in October 2003 to address the problem of the costs of these often straightforward fast track personal injury claims which were perceived to be undermining the objectives of the Woolf reforms. Parts III and IV, which concern any success fee, are dealt with further on in this chapter.

Part II applies to all claims arising out of a road traffic accident occurring after 6 October 2003 that have been settled before proceedings, for less than £10,000 and more than £1,000 but where costs have not been agreed and are the subject of costs only proceedings. In these circumstances, Part II provides for fixed recoverable costs and disbursements and success fee calculated in accordance with the rules. The court has no discretion to award more costs unless there are exceptional circumstances.

WHEN COSTS ORDERS ARE DEEMED TO HAVE BEEN MADE

There are certain circumstances in which costs orders are deemed to have been made:

In favour of the claimant:

(1)   when the claimant accepts the defendant's Part 36 offer or payment; or
(2)   when the claimant's Part 36 offer is accepted by the defendant.

In favour of the defendant:

(1)   where the claim is struck out for non-payment of fees due from the claimant; or
(2)   when the claimant discontinues the claim.

In every case, a costs order will be deemed to have been made on the standard basis of assessment.

AGREEING COSTS

There is nothing to prevent parties from reaching agreement on costs in order to avoid the judge making an assessment, whether summary or detailed, and the court will only decline to endorse a consent order if the costs are obviously disproportionate. Costs payable to a child or a patient (as defined in CPR r 21.21(2)) may only be agreed if their solicitor agrees not to make any additional charge.

PAYMENTS ON ACCOUNT

Rule 44.3(8) provides that, where the court has made an order for the payment of costs to be ascertained by detailed assessment it may order the paying party to make a payment on account of the costs, even before the amount of costs has been assessed. The judge may order a payment on account of costs on his or her own initiative, but if not, you should ask for this.

ASSESSMENT OF COSTS WHERE ADDITIONAL LIABILITY

If the funding arrangements that a solicitor has with his or her client are such that he or she may claim an additional liability (see Chapter 4), the solicitor must provide information about the funding arrangement to the court and to the other parties. Section 19.4(1) of the Costs Practice Direction gives details of the information that is required, and the relevant form to use for the disclosure of this information is Form N251.

NO ASSESSMENT OF ADDITIONAL LIABILITY UNTIL THE CONCLUSION

Rule 44.3A(1) prevents the court from assessing any additional liability until the proceedings, or that part to which the funding agreement relates, have been concluded. However, the court may make an assessment of the base costs, ie the costs excluding the additional liability, on an interim application.

The reason for this is that, until the conclusion of the proceedings, the court and the other parties will not be aware of the amount of the additional liability and so it will be impossible to assess it. It would clearly be inappropriate for the other parties to know what the percentage increase was before the end of the case, as this would invariably give an indication of the view the solicitor has taken about the prospects of success and could prejudice the claimant.

SUMMARY ASSESSMENT AND ADDITIONAL LIABILITY

When a summary assessment is carried out at any stage before the conclusion of the proceedings, it is not sufficient for there to be a global figure for the base costs allowed. The court must specify separately the amounts allowed in respect of solicitors' costs, counsel's fees and disbursements.

Unless the court is satisfied that the receiving party will be entitled to at least the base costs, whatever the final outcome, the court will not make provision for payment of costs that are summarily assessed, as would otherwise be the case. For example, if the arrangement between the receiving party and his or her solicitor is 'no win, no fee', then, despite the success on the interim application, if the case is lost, the solicitor cannot make any charge to his or her client, and the operation of the indemnity principle prevents any recovery from the paying party. Some funding arrangements make provision for solicitors to recover any base costs awarded at interim hearings in any event, and, if you are acting for a client on this basis, you should have the funding arrangement available for the judge to see if you wish to obtain an order for payment of the summarily assessed costs of an interim application before the conclusion of the proceedings. An alternative is to ask the judge to make an order for payment into court or into a joint account in the names of the parties' solicitors in the sum of the summarily assessed costs, so that they are at least secured.

The boot is on the other foot when a party funded under a conditional fee agreement (CFA) has interim costs awarded against them. After-the-event costs indemnity insurance policies usually exclude paying interim costs awarded to the other side. On 12 March 1999 the Vice-Chancellor wrote to all judges suggesting that in these circumstances the judge should consider staying any order for costs until the end of the action, while the SCCO *Guide to the Summary Assessment of Costs* suggests the court should consider whether an order for payment of the costs might bring the action to an end and whether this would be just in all the circumstances.

ASSESSMENT OF ADDITIONAL LIABILITY AT THE CONCLUSION OF PROCEEDINGS

When proceedings are concluded, the base costs and any additional liability will fall to be assessed. This may be carried out by summary assessment, if appropriate, by detailed assessment, or by a combination of the two. The fact that there is a funding arrangement is not, of itself, sufficient reason for not carrying out a summary assessment of costs.

Summary assessment at the conclusion of proceedings

When assessing costs at the conclusion of proceedings, where there is a funding arrangement in favour of the receiving party, the court will first assess the base costs, separately itemising the sums allowed for solicitors' costs, counsel's fees and disbursements, and then any additional liability in respect of those costs, as well as the additional liability in respect of costs summarily assessed at any interim hearing. In order to assist the court in this, the receiving party must prepare a bundle for the judge that will include copies of the following:

(1)   all Forms N251 that have been filed for the receiving party;
(2)   all estimates and statements of costs that have been filed for the receiving party;
(3)   the risk assessment prepared at the time that the funding arrangement was entered into and on the basis of which the additional liability was agreed.

The judge may decide to assess the base costs using the summary assessment procedure and order a detailed assessment of the additional liability.

Detailed assessment at the conclusion of proceedings

The detailed assessment will follow the usual procedure. However, from the point of view of the receiving party, the paying party and the court will wish to be satisfied that the solicitor is entitled to the additional liability claimed and so all relevant documents must be served and filed. If the paying party wishes to take issue with any aspect of the additional liability, this should be detailed in the points of dispute.

ASSESSING THE ADDITIONAL LIABILITY

As we have seen from Chapter 4, Funding of Litigation, the additional liability may comprise one or more of the following:

(1)   a percentage increase (also referred to as a success fee);
(2)   an insurance premium for after-the-event (ATE) insurance;
(3)   any sum required to be paid to a membership organisation.

The fact that the receiving party may have agreed certain funding arrangements with the solicitor does not preclude the court from assessing whether what has been agreed is a reasonable amount to be paid by the paying party.

Rule 44.3B(1)(a) and (b) sets out certain limits on recovery under a funding arrangement which cannot, under any circumstances, be recovered from the paying party:

(1)   any part of the percentage increase that relates to the fact that the solicitor will have to wait until the end of the proceedings before receiving payment;
(2)   any sum required to be paid to a membership organisation that exceeds the amount that the receiving party would have had to pay for ATE insurance against the risk of having to pay the other parties' costs.

Rule 44.3B(1)(c) and (d) sets out circumstances in which the receiving party may not recover any additional liability, unless the court expressly exercises its powers under r 3.9, covering:

(1)   the additional liability for any period after issue of the proceedings in which there was a failure to provide the information required by Section 19 of PD Costs; and
(2)   the percentage increase when there has been a failure to comply with PD Costs or an order for the disclosure in assessment proceedings of the reasons for setting the percentage increase at the level provided in the funding arrangement.

FIXED-PERCENTAGE INCREASE IN ROAD TRAFFIC AND EMPLOYERS LIABILITY CLAIMS

CPR Part 45 Parts II–IV were introduced in October 2003 to address the problem of the costs of these often straightforward fast track personal injury claims which were perceived to be undermining the objectives of the Woolf reforms. Part II applies to the costs of claims arising out of a road traffic accident where there is no funding arrangement and this is dealt with earlier in this chapter.

Part III applies where there is a funding arrangement to road traffic claims to which Part II does not apply, and Part IV applies to employers liability claims.

Part III sets out the detailed rules for calculating the percentage increase or success fee that may be applied in claims arising out of a road traffic accident occurring after 6 October 2003 that is not a small claim. Part IV applies similarly to employers liability claims arising out of accident at work after 1 October 2005.

THE COURT'S DISCRETION

As well as the matters referred to in r 44.3B, which are specific to assessment of the additional liability, the court, when assessing the additional liability, will take into account the same factors as when assessing the base costs, or, indeed, a bill to which a funding arrangement does not apply.

In addition, Section 11 of PD Costs provides further guidance. In summary, this provides:

(1) that hindsight cannot be applied to the assessment of the prospects of success of a case for the purposes of deciding the percentage increase;

(2) factors relevant to whether a percentage increase is reasonable may include:
   (a) the degree of risk that costs would be payable;
   (b) whether the solicitor funds the disbursements;
   (c) whether there was an alternative means of funding;

(3) the fact that when the percentage increase is applied, the total costs may appear disproportionate is not relevant;

(4) in the case of an insurance premium, relevant factors are:
   (a) the level and extent of the cover provided;
   (b) any pre-existing insurance cover;
   (c) whether any part of the premium would be rebated on early settlement.

The exercise of the court's discretion in relation to the assessment of the additional liability was the subject of an appeal to the Court of Appeal and then to the House of Lords in the case of *Callery v Gray (Nos 1 and 2)* [2002] UKHL 28, [2002] 1 WLR 2000. In that case, the parties were involved in a road traffic accident and, after negotiations between solicitors, a compromise was reached whereby the defendant would pay an agreed figure for damages, and reasonable costs to be agreed.

The claimant's solicitors were acting under a funding arrangement which provided for a percentage increase of 60%, 20% of which related to deferment of the solicitors' charges, and the claimant took out ATE insurance at a total cost, including tax, of £367.50. Costs could not be agreed, and so the claimant's solicitors began costs-only proceedings and an order was made for a detailed assessment. There was a detailed assessment hearing before the district judge who, in assessing the costs, reduced the percentage increase to 40%, as he was bound to do in the light of r 44.3B (the 20% would, of course, have to be borne by the client under the terms of the funding arrangement) and allowed the insurance premium, inclusive of tax.

The paying party appealed on both counts to the circuit judge, and the appeal was dismissed on both counts. The paying party then applied to the Court of Appeal for permission to bring a second appeal and that application was allowed. In the Court of Appeal, the percentage increase was reduced further to 20% and the insurance premium was allowed in principle, but subject to further consideration by a costs judge of whether the amount claimed was reasonable.

Unhappy with that decision, the defendant appealed to the House of Lords, identifying 10 issues upon which the court should rule. In the event, a majority in the House of Lords took the view that the Court of Appeal was better placed to address the issues and it declined to interfere with the decision of that court. The position in relation to CFAs entered into before 1 August 2001, therefore, is that which was decided by the Court of Appeal in *Callery v Gray, Russell v Pal Pak Corrugated Limited* [2001] EWCA Civ 1117, [2001] 3 All ER 833, which is summarised below.

Percentage increase

In relation to the percentage increase, the court held that, in 'modest and straightforward' claims arising out of road traffic accidents, as was the case in *Callery v Gray*, the maximum percentage increase agreed at the outset should be 20%. Only if there was no real doubt that the prospects of success were good should this guideline be departed from.

In *Halloran v Delaney* [2002] All ER (D) 30, the court went still further and said that for CFAs entered into after 1 August 2001, after *Callery v Gray* was heard in the Court of Appeal, the appropriate success fee for simple cases settling in the protocol period should generally be 5%. The court made express reference to Lord Woolf's judgment in *Callery* which drew attention to the availability of two-stage success fees where an uplift of, say, 100% would be discounted to 5% if the claim settled before the issue of proceedings.

Some clarification of this significant shift was offered by Lord Justice Brook as a footnote in *Claims Direct Test Cases* [2003] 4 All ER 508. He said that the 5% success fee was intended to apply only to those extremely simple cases where the prospects of success were virtually 100%.

In *Callery* the court also indicated, *per curiam*, that it was always open to solicitors and their clients to agree a 'two-stage' percentage increase. This would be appropriate in cases that were unlikely to settle at an early stage. A higher percentage increase at the outset would be reasonable, but there should be provision for a rebate in the event that the case is settled sooner than anticipated. In this type of case, a percentage increase of 100% may be reasonable, but probably only if there was a mechanism for a significant rebate for early settlement.

The two-stage approach was reverted to in *KU (a child, by her mother and litigation friend PU) v Liverpool City Council* [2005] EWCA Civ 475 27 April 2005 quoting Lord Woolf's encouragement to lawyers in *Callery* to take seriously the possibility of agreeing an initial success fee of, say, 100%, on the basis that if the claim settled within the protocol period (or some other period identified by the parties to the CFA) a lower success fee would be recoverable under the CFA. At the assessment of costs, attention would then be paid to the reasonableness of the success fee which was recoverable as things turned out, and this type of arrangement would lead to a greater chance of establishing the reasonableness of a higher success fee given that the claim did not settle within the agreed period.

Costs judges should be more willing to approve what appear to be high success fees in cases which have gone a long distance towards trial if the maker of the CFA has agreed that a much lower success fee should be payable if the claim settles at an early stage.

Insurance premium

As far as the insurance premium was concerned, it was not possible to give guidance on the level of premium that may be reasonable. However, courts will take into account the market rate, as with any other form of disbursement and use this as a guideline. As to whether the claimant had taken out ATE insurance prematurely, as with the percentage fee, it was held that, in standard road-traffic cases, it is reasonable to take out ATE insurance at the outset, even before the proposed defendant has been given an opportunity to admit liability. However, in *Re Claims Direct Test Cases* [2000] All ER (D) 76, the senior costs judge held that the premium for an ATE policy taken out after the defendant had admitted liability was not recoverable.

WASTED COSTS ORDERS

In certain circumstances-the court may be asked to consider whether an order for costs should be made, not against one of the parties, but against a solicitor or counsel acting in the case. The court's power to make what are known as wasted costs orders against legal representatives derives from s 4(1) of the Courts and Legal Services Act 1990. The procedure is contained in CPR r 48.7.

An order for wasted costs will be made only where the court considers that costs have been unnecessarily incurred by a party because of improper, unreasonable or negligent conduct on the part of a legal representative and that justice requires that party to be compensated in whole or in part in respect of those costs.

The judge may consider making a wasted costs order on his or her own initiative, but it will more usually be the case that the party who has incurred the wasted costs will ask the court for an order.

Before the court may make an order for wasted costs, it must first give the legal representative an opportunity to be heard on why such an order should not be made. This will usually involve an adjournment to another hearing, but, if all parties are clear about the issues, there is no strict requirement for a two-stage procedure to be followed. The essence of the enquiry into whether a wasted costs order should be made is that the respondent to the application must be told in clear terms what it is that he or she is said to have done, or failed to do, and that he or she should be given the opportunity to deal with the allegations.

The courts have tried to stem the flow of satellite litigation arising from this provision in two cases. In *Ridehalgh v Horsefield* [1994] Ch 205, CA, the Master of the Rolls said that while judges must not reject the weapon which Parliament intended to be used for the protection of those injured by the unjustifiable conduct of the other side's lawyers, they must be astute to control what threatened to become a new and costly form of satellite litigation.

Lord Bingham reiterated this view in *Medcalf v Mardell* [2002] 3 All ER 721 saying wasted costs orders should be confined to questions which are apt for summary disposal by the court, such as failures to appear; conduct which leads to an otherwise avoidable step in the proceedings; the prolongation of a hearing by gross repetition or extreme slowness in the presentation of evidence or argument. Such matters can be dealt with summarily on agreed facts or after a brief enquiry. Any hearing to investigate the conduct of a complex action is itself likely to be expensive and time-consuming. Compensating litigating parties who have been put to unnecessary expense is only one of the public interests to be considered.

Yet another obstacle to obtaining a wasted costs order is that one cannot be made if in order to do so the judge could only come to a conclusion adverse to the lawyers if he had the opportunity of seeing legally privileged documents in the absence of waiver of that privilege by the client.

These are all matters anyone considering applying for a wasted costs order should bear in mind.

Part IX

POST-TRIAL ISSUES

Chapter 40

APPEAL

OVERVIEW

The law and procedure on appeals have been greatly simplified. Sir Jeffrey Bowman's *Review of the Court of Appeal (Civil Division)* (LCD, September 1997) ('the Bowman Report'), published some 14 months after Lord Woolf's *Access to Justice (Final) Report*, contained detailed recommendations on appeals, which were subsequently adopted. The relevant law is now contained in the AJA 1999, the Access to Justice Act 1999 (Destination of Appeals) Order 2000, SI 2000/1071, and CPR Part 52. Prior to these changes, the law and procedure were unnecessarily complex, with different rules and different time-limits scattered throughout the various procedural codes. Today, in any case, where an appeal is under consideration, your starting point is Part 52 and PD 52. Both are detailed and must be studied whenever an appeal is contemplated. However, time-limits are short and a working knowledge of appeals is a necessary part of any litigation lawyer's job. It is the function of this chapter to provide that basic working knowledge.

An aim of the CPR is that parties – and judges – should get it right first time. Gone are the days when an inadequately prepared case can automatically be taken to appeal for a second try.

The majority of civil cases do not proceed to a trial. Cases are terminated, either by compromise or by one of the other methods already considered, such as default judgment or summary judgment. It has to be accepted that, if a case does go to trial, one party is bound to be disappointed. To put it rather bluntly, half the people who come to court will lose. An unsuccessful party is bound to consider an appeal, even if only fleetingly. Judges are aware of the disappointment that the unsuccessful party will have and are, in any event, required to give reasons for their decisions (*English v Emery Reimbold and Strick Ltd* [2002] 1 WLR 2409). The European Court of Human Rights in Strasbourg has established that the right to a fair trial in ECHR, Art 6 (see HRA 1998, Sch 1) normally required a judgment to be reasoned. Often, the judge's judgment is no more than an elaborate explanation to the loser of why he or she has lost. An unsuccessful party who is contemplating an appeal has to consider very carefully whether there may be grounds for doing so. Further, the general rule is that permission to appeal is required.

Most cases settle without a trial. Most trials do not result in an appeal. Herein lies the problem, for it follows that most lawyers will have limited experience of appeals procedure, particularly to the Court of Appeal. But if you intend to go before some of the country's most senior judges (who are, of course, fully familiar with the appeal rules) you must expect as a matter of urgency to acquaint yourself with the Appeal Court's requirements and be prepared to burn the midnight oil in doing so. It is clear that the Court of Appeal has become increasingly irritated by procedural failures which detract from its main task. It may be that they have made the classic mistake of assuming that the way to get practitioners to do things that the practitioners do not want to do is to make ever more complex and increasingly prescriptive rules. Consequently, although Part 52 itself seems clear enough, PD52 is excessively long and in danger of becoming an impenetrable mess. This makes the practitioner's task more difficult not easier and the danger is that what the Court of Appeal perceives to be unacceptable will become even worse. Nevertheless, your starting point must be Part 52 and PD52.

AVENUES OF APPEAL

CPR PD 52, para 2A.1 contains the following table, which sets out the basic rule as to the court to which or judge to whom an appeal is to be made (subject to obtaining any necessary permission):

Decision of:	Appeal made to:
District judge of a county court	Circuit Judge
Master or district judge of the High Court	High Court judge
Circuit judge	High Court judge
High Court judge	Court of Appeal

It can be seen from the above table that, therefore, the basic rule is that a decision of a judge is appealed on the next highest tier. However, there are some important exceptions to this general rule, and the principal exceptions are contained in PD 52, para 2A.2. Where the decision to be appealed is a final decision in a Part 7 claim allocated to the multi-track, or made in specialist proceedings (under the Companies Acts 1985 or 1989 or to which Sections, I, II or III of Part 57 or any of Parts 58 to 63 apply), the appeal is made to the Court of Appeal (subject to obtaining any necessary permission), regardless of who made the decision.

The term 'final decision' is defined in PD 52, para 2A.3. It is a decision of a court which would finally determine the entire proceedings (subject only to any possible appeal or detailed assessment of costs), whichever way the court decided the issues before it. Thus, for example, a decision on an application for summary judgment under Part 24 is not a 'final decision' for this purpose. Obviously, if the applicant succeeds in an application under Part 24 for summary judgment, the case has been finally disposed of, but, for appeal purposes, it is not a 'final decision', for the outcome of the Part 24 application will not determine the entire proceedings 'whichever way the court decided the issues'. Accordingly, an appeal from a district judge following an application for summary judgment will be to the circuit judge, if the case is in the county court, and to the High Court judge, if it is in the High Court – it will not be to the Court of Appeal.

What if the court has ordered a split trial? This is covered in PD 52, para 2A.4. A decision of a court is to be treated as a final decision for appeal purposes where it is made at the conclusion of part of a hearing or trial which has been split into parts and would, if it had been made at the conclusion of that hearing or trial, have been a final decision. Thus, for example, where the court has ordered a split trial on the issue of liability and the trial has been conducted before a circuit judge in the county court, then the appeal is to the Court of Appeal, and not to a High Court judge pursuant to the above table.

Rule 52.14 also provides for appeals to be assigned straight to the Court of Appeal. Where the court from or to which an appeal is made, or from which permission to appeal is sought ('the relevant court'), considers that an appeal which is to be heard by a county court or the High Court would raise an important point of principle or practice, or there is some other compelling reason for the Court of Appeal to hear it, the relevant court may order the appeal to be transferred to the Court of Appeal. This is sometimes known as a 'leap-frog appeal'. In fact, orders under r 52.14 are rare. In *Clark v Perks* [2000] 1 WLR 17, the Court of Appeal suggested that these powers should be used sparingly. The reason is that AJA 1999, s 57 gives power to the Master of the Rolls to direct that the appeal should be heard in the Court of Appeal, instead of in the lower court. Accordingly, where a party invites the lower court to order a leap-frog appeal, the court is more likely to refuse the application and invite an application to the Master of the Rolls, pursuant to s 57.

Where will the appeal be heard? Both the Civil Appeals Office, which administers appeals to the Court of Appeal, and the Court of Appeal itself are based at the Royal Courts of Justice, Strand, London. Appeals to the Court of Appeal are, therefore, invariably heard in London. In county court cases, an appeal from a district judge to circuit judge is heard in the same county court if that court is a civil trial centre or, if the relevant county court is not a civil trial centre, at the civil trial centre for that county court, which will be a neighbouring county court. In the case of appeals from a circuit judge or district judge of the High Court to a High Court judge, see PD 52, para 8. The paragraph contains a table that sets out the venues for each circuit. Thus, for example, the Appeal Centres for the North-Eastern Circuit are in Leeds, Newcastle and Sheffield and appeals can be heard there or at Teesside. There are similar provisions for all six Circuits.

PERMISSION TO APPEAL

The basic rule now is that permission to appeal is required (r 52.3). However, permission is not required where the appeal is from a decision of a judge in a county court, or the High Court, against a committal order, a refusal to grant habeus corpus, or a secure accommodation order made under Children Act 1989, s 25 (r 52.3(1)).

An application for permission to appeal should be made to the lower court at the hearing at which the decision to be appealed was made. This is an application which requires tact on the part of the advocate. Nevertheless, judges know the rules and are aware of the need to make such an application. Whether permission is granted or refused, the judge will complete Form EX52, which records the decision and brief reasons for it.

Where the lower court refuses an application for permission to appeal, a further application for permission to appeal may be made to the court that will hear any appeal (r 52.3(3)).

If no application for permission to appeal is made to the lower court, it may be made in the appeal notice to the relevant court (r 52.3(2)).

In practice, an application for permission to appeal should be made immediately to the lower court. The judge is fully acquainted with the case and, indeed, may well already have decided that issues fit for appeal have been raised. An application at this stage involves no additional costs. If the party subsequently changes his or her mind and does not wish to appeal, he or she simply need not do so and nothing has been lost. Finally, if the application for permission to appeal is refused, it is still possible to make an application to the court that would hear the appeal.

An application for permission to the appeal court may well be considered without a hearing. If permission is refused, the person seeking permission may request the decision to be reconsidered at a hearing. Such requests have now become so commonplace that many judges (particularly circuit judges faced with an application for permission to appeal after a small-claims trial) do not refuse permission on paper, but order the application to be listed so that the unsuccessful proposed appellant can be told why permission is refused. In the long run, this takes less time and it should be remembered that respondents to a proposed appeal are not involved at this stage and are not, therefore, being put to any expense.

If permission to appeal is refused, that is the end of the matter – it is not possible to appeal the refusal of permission to appeal. (See AJA 1999, s 54(4) and CPR, r 52.3.)

TIME-LIMITS

An appeal is begun by an 'appellant's notice'. If the appellant has not already obtained permission to appeal (see above), it must be requested in the appellant's notice (r 52.4).

The basic time-limit for filing an appellant's notice is 14 days after the date of the decision of the lower court which the appellant wishes to appeal (r 52.4(2)). Thus, any party seeking to appeal must move quickly. However, this should not be a difficult task for the lawyers who have just been conducting the case.

The lower court has power to grant a longer period and should be invited to exercise that power in an appropriate case, for example if an imminent national holiday such as Easter or Christmas means that a 14-day period is unreasonably short. However, PD 52, para 5.19 provides that any longer period specified by the lower court 'should not normally exceed 28 days'. Where a judge in the lower court announces the result at the conclusion of the hearing, but reserves reasons until a later date, the recommended practice is that the judge should exercise the power under r 52.4(2) and fix a time-limit for filing an appellant's notice which takes that into account (PD 52, para 5.20), that is the judge should set a time-limit which runs from the date on which the reasoned judgment is made available and not the date of the decision itself.

If an extension of time is required beyond either the 14-day period prescribed in r 52.4 or any longer period granted by the lower court, the appellant must apply to the relevant appeal court. This is specifically provided by r 52.6. The rule expressly prohibits parties agreeing to extend time-limits themselves.

Somewhat oddly, a refusal of permission for an extension of time can, itself, be appealed. (See *Foenander v Bond Lewis and Co* [2001] 2 All ER 1019.) This is in contrast to the decision refusing permission to appeal, which is final. Accordingly, a judge faced with a late and unmeritorious application to appeal should, the Court of Appeal suggests, refuse permission to appeal rather than refuse to extend time for appealing, as that decision is final. We query this. Where the correct decision is to refuse to extend time to appeal, why should the High Court / circuit judge fudge this by granting an extension and then refusing permission? If the rules are not equal to their task, the Court of Appeal is in a stronger position to engineer a rule change. The High Court / circuit judge should surely base his or her decision on the merits of the case rather than on what is more convenient for the Court of Appeal.

An appeal notice must be served on each respondent as soon as is practicable and, in any event, not later than 7 days after it is filed (r 52.4(3)). A respondent's notice (see below) must be filed within such a period as may be directed by the lower court, or, if there is no such direction, within 14 days of the date in r 52.5(5).

GROUNDS OF APPEAL

As already noted, permission to appeal is required. Permission to appeal will be given only where the court considers that the appeal would have a real prospect of success or there is some other compelling reason why the appeal should be heard. An order giving permission may limit the issues to be heard and be made subject to conditions. For example, r 25.15 provides for the court to order security for costs of an appeal.

Grounds for appeal differ from grounds for permission to appeal. By r 52.11(3), the appeal court will allow an appeal where the decision of the lower court was:

'(a)   wrong, or,

(b)   unjust because of a serious procedural or other irregularity in the proceedings in the lower court.'

The appeal court may draw any inference of fact that it considers justified on the evidence. 'Wrong' in r 52.11(3) can mean either that the judge was wrong in law or wrong on the facts, or improperly exercised a discretion. Nothing need be said on the question of law and many appeals take the form of pure argument on points of law. However, an appeal court is reluctant to interfere with the lower court's exercise of a discretion, unless the decision reached was outside the generous ambit within which a reasonable disagreement is possible. As to appeals on fact, great weight is given by the appeal court to any finding made by the trial judge in the court below. That judge had the benefit of seeing and hearing the witnesses and assessing credibility at first hand. The appeal court is likely to interfere only if the trial judge misunderstood the facts, failed to take relevant matters into account, or took into account irrelevant matters, to such an extent that the decision was clearly 'wrong'.

Every appeal is limited to a review of the decision of the lower court, unless the court considers that, in the circumstances of an individual appeal, it would be in the interests of justice to hold a rehearing. The Court of Appeal has always proceeded on this basis, but, previously, appeals to a High Court judge or circuit judge often took the form of a complete rehearing – this is no longer so. An appeal court will not receive oral evidence or evidence which was not before the lower court (r 52.11(2)).

SECOND APPEALS

We have already noted the need for permission to appeal and the limited grounds of appeal (see above). There are further restrictive rules, limiting second appeals. These rules will apply, for example, where there has been an appeal from a district judge to a circuit judge or High Court judge, and one party wishes to appeal again. It should be noted that these restrictions apply whether or not the first appeal was successful. A second appeal is always to the Court of Appeal. Thus, for example, if a decision of a district judge has been appealed to a circuit judge, there is no second appeal to a High Court judge. If there is to be a second appeal at all, it will be to the Court of Appeal.

The authority to limit second appeals is derived from AJA 1999, s 55, and given effect to by CPR r 52.13. Permission is required from the Court of Appeal for any appeal to that court from a decision of a county court or the High Court which was, itself, made on appeal. The Court of Appeal will not give permission unless it considers that:

(1)   the appeal would raise an important point of principle or practice; or

(2)   there is some other compelling reason for the Court of Appeal to hear it.

The purpose of these restrictions is explained by the Court of Appeal in *Tanfern Ltd v Cameron-MacDonald (Practice Note)* [2000] 1 WLR 1311 and *Clark v Perks* [2001] 1 WLR 17. The Court of Appeal is a very senior court, staffed by Lords Justices of Appeal, and it should be troubled only on matters which really merit the attention of a court of this stature. If permission to appeal is granted, the appeal will, of course, be heard by the Court of Appeal. Applications for permission to appeal may be considered by the appeal court without a hearing. Initially, they are considered by a single Lord Justice. If permission is granted without a hearing, the parties will be notified of that decision, and the procedure in PD 52, para 6 then applies. If permission is refused without a hearing, the appellant has a right to have it reconsidered at an oral hearing (PD 52, para 4.13). A request for a decision to be reconsidered at an oral hearing must be filed at the appeal court within 7 days after service of the notice that permission has been refused. Wherever possible, the oral reconsideration will be before the same judge who refused it on paper.

If permission to appeal is refused, that is the end of the matter – there is no further appeal.

APPEALS FROM CASE MANAGEMENT DECISIONS

All that is said above regarding time-limits, permission to appeal and grounds for appeal, etc, applies to all appeals, including appeals from case-management decisions. In addition, see PD 52, para 4.4 – 'Appeals from case management decisions'. First, it defines some orders which are included within this term. Case management decisions include decisions made under r 3.1(2) and decisions about disclosure, filing of witness statements, experts' reports, directions about the timetable of the claim, adding a party to a claim and security for costs. Where the application is for permission to appeal from a case management decision, the court dealing with the application may take into account whether:

(1)   the issue is of sufficient significance to justify the costs of an appeal;
(2)   the procedural consequences of an appeal (eg loss of a trial date) outweigh the significance of the case management decision;
(3)   it would be more convenient to determine the issue at or after trial.

APPELLANT'S NOTICE

The appellant's notice should be prepared in Form N161. The procedure and forms are the same, whether the appeal is to the Court of Appeal, a High Court judge or a circuit judge. Usually, the appellant's notice is better drafted by the advocate who represented the appellant at the hearing, the result of which is being appealed.

If permission to appeal has been refused by the lower court (or no application for permission was made to that court), an application for permission must be included in the appellant's notice (r 52.4). The appeal bundle should be prepared by the appellant's solicitor and the skeleton argument should be prepared by the appellant's counsel.

Careful completion of Form N161 is, of course, required. In particular, it should clearly set out why it is said that the decision of the lower court is wrong, or that the decision of the lower court is unjust because of a serious procedural or other irregularity. PD 52, para 3.2 provides: 'The ground of appeal should set out clearly the reasons why r 52.11(3)(a) or (b) is said to apply' and specify, in respect of each ground, whether the ground raises an appeal on a point of law or is an appeal against a finding of fact. Paragraph 5.1A of PD 52 requires an appellant who is seeking to rely on any issue under the HRA 1998, or who seeks a remedy under that Act for the first time in an appeal, to include in his or her appeal notice the information required by para 15.1 of PD 15 (para 15.2 also applies as if references to a statement of case were to an appeal notice).

In the case of appeals to the circuit judge or High Court judge, the appellant's notice must be filed at the relevant court office (see above). In the case of appeals to the Court of Appeal, the document should be filed with the Civil Appeals Registry (Room E307 at the Royal Courts of Justice). The documents required in the Court of Appeal are set out in para 5.6(2) of PD 52. It provides

'(2) The appellant must file the following documents together with an appeal bundle (see paragraph 5.6A) with his appellant's notice–

  (a) two additional copies of the appellant's notice for the appeal court; and
  (b) one copy of the appellant's notice for each of the respondents;
  (c) one copy of his skeleton argument for each copy of the appellant's notice that is filed (see paragraph 5.9);
  (d) a sealed copy of the order being appealed;
  (e) a copy of any order giving or refusing permission to appeal, together with a copy of the judge's reasons for allowing or refusing permission to appeal;
  (f) any witness statements or affidavits in support of any application included in the appellant's notice.'

The 'appeal bundle', referred to above, is dealt with separately in PD 52 at para 5.6A. This paragraph lists the 13 (yes, 13) documents (some of which will be many pages long (eg the claim form, statements of case and witness statements) which have to be included. The 'appeal bundle' now has to be lodged at the initial stage when the appellant's notice is filed. Preparation of this bundle is an important task and not one to be rushed or delegated to too junior a person in the solicitor's office.

Paragraph 5.6A(1)(f) requires 'a transcript … of judgment … and … of evidence … directly relevant to any question at issue on the appeal'. Although all trials are recorded, it follows that a relevant transcript must be ordered immediately. In practice, (and this emphasises the need for a detailed note to be made by the instructing solicitor during the trial) the decision to appeal is based on notes made during the trial rather than on an analysis of a transcript obtained subsequently. However, the transcript is required for the appeal.

If it is not possible to file all the above documents with the appellant's notice (eg where a transcript of the judgment has been ordered but is not yet available), the appellant must enter, on the appellant's notice, which of the required documents have not been filed, the reasons why they are not currently available and when they are expected to be available (PD 52, para 5.7). In addition, there is, of course, the appropriate court fee to be paid.

It will be recalled that the appellant's notice and documents must be filed within 14 days after the date on which the lower court gave its decision or within such other period as the lower court has directed. The Civil Appeals Office will then issue the appellant's notice and record the day on which it was filed. It will then return a sealed copy of the appellant's notice for service on each respondent, together with a letter acknowledging that the notice has been filed, giving the Court of Appeal reference number and setting out what further steps need to be taken. The appellant's solicitor puts the Court of Appeal reference number on each sealed copy, ready for service on the respondent. Unless the Court of Appeal otherwise directs, the appeal bundle must be served on each respondent within 7 days of receiving the order giving permission to appeal (para 6.2 of PD52). The appellant's solicitor should then write to the Civil Appeals Office, confirming that service of the appellant's notice and other documents has been effected. On receipt of that confirmation, the Civil Appeals Office will send a further letter to the appellant's side, setting out what further steps must be taken. This will involve the completion of an 'appeal questionnaire'. The management of the civil appeals list is dealt with under the direction of the head of the Civil Appeals Office (who is addressed as 'Master'). The civil appeals list of the Court of Appeal is divided into seven different lists (see PD 52, para 15.8). (As to lists of authorities, see PD 52, para 15.11.)

RESPONDENT'S NOTICE

If the respondent seeks only to uphold the judgment of the court below for the reasons given by that court, then he or she is not required to serve a respondent's notice. In practice, respondents usually do file a notice. Of course, like the appellant, the respondent also needs permission to appeal. However, it is easier for the respondent to obtain permission once it has been given to an appellant. If, for example, a defendant has been given permission to appeal, challenging a finding of negligence, it would be bizarre to deny the respondent to that appeal the opportunity to challenge a finding of contributory negligence.

Respondent's notices are dealt with in r 52.5. The notice itself is in Form N162. In two instances, a respondent's notice is obligatory: first, where a respondent is seeking permission to appeal (r 52.5(2)(a)), that is where the respondent is seeking to have the order of the lower court set aside or varied in some respects, and secondly, where the respondent wishes to ask the appeal court to uphold the lower court's order for reasons different from, or additional to, those given by the lower court (r 52.5(2)(b)). Where the respondent seeks permission from the appeal court, it must be requested in the respondent's notice.

A respondent's notice must be filed within such period as may be directed by the lower court, or, where there is no such direction, 14 days after the date specified in r 52.5(5). Those dates are:

'(a)   the date the respondent is served with the appellant's notice where permission to appeal was given by the lower court or permission to appeal is not required;

(b)   the date the respondent is served with notification that the appeal court has given the appellant permission to appeal;

(c)   the date the respondent is served with notification that the application for permission to appeal and the appeal itself are to be heard together.'

Note that, unless the appellant's application for permission to appeal and the appeal itself are to be heard together, the respondent takes no part in the appellant's application for permission to appeal.

Unless the appeal court directs otherwise, a respondent's notice must be served on the appellant and any other separately represented respondent (or respondent in person) as soon as is practicable and, in any event, not later than 7 days after it was filed (r 52.5(6)). In the case of appeal to the Court of Appeal, service must always be effected by the respondent or his or her solicitor – the Civil Appeals Office does not serve documents. In the case of appeals to the county court or High Court, the court may serve the documents or give them to the respondent's solicitor to effect service.

Advocates for both parties must co-operate in providing the appeal court with relevant lists of authorities (see PD 52, para 15.11).

APPEAL COURTS' POWERS

By r 52.10, in relation to an appeal, the appeal court has all the powers of the lower court. Thus, the appeal court has power to affirm, set aside or vary any order or judgment made or given by the lower court; refer any claim or issue for determination by the lower court, order a new trial or hearing, make orders for the payment of interest, and make a costs order. The appeal court may exercise its powers in relation to the whole or part of an order of the lower court.

In an appeal from a claim tried by a jury, the Court of Appeal may, instead of ordering a new trial, make an order for damages or vary an award of damages made by the jury (r 52.10(3)).

What if the appeal is compromised after it has been filed and served? Say, for example, a claimant concedes that the trial judge has awarded too much by way of damages and negotiates a 20% reduction with the defendant/ appellant. Having reached the agreement, the better practice is to request the appeal court for an order that the appeal be dismissed (see PD 52, para 12).

Appeal courts dislike consent orders. An appeal court will not make an order allowing an appeal unless satisfied that the decision of the lower court was wrong (see PD 52, para 13). The Court of Appeal is particularly concerned not to inadvertently give a decision which will then be relied on as a precedent (which must be followed by the lower court), without having had the opportunity of full argument. This explains why it is usual to withdraw an appeal that is compromised, rather than seek a consent order. Where an appeal court is requested by all parties to allow an application or an appeal, the court may consider the request on the papers. The request should state that none of the parties is a child or patient, and set out the relevant history of the proceedings and the matters relied on as justifying the proposed order and should be accompanied by the copy of the proposed order (see PD 52, para 13.1).

SPECIAL PROVISIONS APPLYING TO THE COURT OF APPEAL

In the case of appeals to the Court of Appeal note also the provisions of PD 52, para 15, a long and detailed paragraph explaining the documents required by the Court of Appeal, filing and listing arrangements.

COSTS OF APPEAL

Costs are likely to be assessed by way of summary assessment, at the conclusion of the following appeal hearings:

(1)   contested directions hearings;
(2)   applications for permission to appeal, at which the respondent is present;
(3)   dismissal list hearings in the Court of Appeal, at which the respondent is present;
(4)   appeals from case management decisions;
(5)   appeals listed for one day or less.

Consequently, parties attending any of these hearings should be prepared to deal with summary assessment. If the costs are not summarily assessed, usually, the court will order a detailed assessment and specify what sum should immediately be paid on account.

On appeal, the court has power to deal not only with the costs of the appeal but also the costs of the lower court. In a successful appeal, the court usually orders costs 'here and below' (r 44.13). Where the court hearing an appeal dismisses the appeal, then, of course, any order for costs made by the court below will stand, and the appeal court is concerned only with the costs of the appeal itself. Such costs are usually suitable for summary assessment.

APPEAL TO THE HOUSE OF LORDS

The Administration of Justice Act 1969 contains provisions for a 'leap-frog appeal' from a High Court judge direct to the House of Lords, rather than to the Court of Appeal. (This is not to be confused with so-called leap-frog appeals under AJA 1999, s 57, which go to the Court of Appeal and are discussed above.) Appeals to the House of Lords are not dealt with in the CPR. They are governed by parliamentary standing orders and are outside the scope of this book. They will be found in Section 4A of Vol 2 of the White Book.

Chapter 41

ENFORCEMENT OF JUDGMENTS

OVERVIEW

The important topic of enforcement of judgments was outside the terms of reference of Lord Woolf's 'Access to Justice' inquiry. Thus, for the most part, enforcement is still governed by the RSC and CCR in CPR Schs 1 and 2. However, some aspects of enforcement have been made 'CPR-compliant' and are dealt with in CPR Parts 70–73. Further reform is promised, but there is a lack of consensus as to the form that any reform of the law should take. As significant changes will require legislative, rather than mere rule, changes, major change still seems some way off, although the Rule Committee can be expected to attempt some further tidying up of the old rules.

This chapter sets out all the various methods of enforcement that are available. It is necessary to know what is available before deciding which method to use. It is for the judgment creditor to decide how to enforce the judgment. To use the wrong method is just a waste of money, which is unlikely to be recoverable from the judgment debtor.

GENERAL RULES ABOUT ENFORCEMENT OF JUDGMENTS AND ORDERS

The title of this section is the same as the title to Part 70. Part 70 and the Practice Direction supplementing it should be studied first, before issuing any enforcement proceedings, together with the specific rules relevant to the method of enforcement in question.

Unfortunately, Part 70 has not incorporated all relevant rules from the old RSC and CCR and, therefore, still has to be read in conjunction with RSC Sch 1, Ord 45 and CCR Sch 2, Ord 25, both entitled 'Enforcement of judgments and orders: general'.

For the purposes of enforcement, 'judgment creditor' means a person who has obtained or is entitled to enforce a judgment or order and 'judgment debtor' means a person against whom a judgment or order was given or made.

Except where an enactment, rule or Practice Direction provides otherwise, a creditor may use any method of enforcement which is available and may use more than one method of enforcement, either at the same time or consecutively (r 70.2).

If a judgment debt or part of it is paid after the judgment creditor has issued any application or request to enforce it, but before any writ or warrant has been executed (see below), or, in any other case, the date fixed for the hearing of the application, the judgment creditor must immediately notify the court in writing, save where the judgment creditor has issued a writ of execution in the High Court (see below), in which case, he or she must immediately notify the relevant enforcement officer in writing (PD 70, para 7).

WRIT OF *FIERI FACIAS*/WARRANT OF EXECUTION

This method of enforcement is considered first, as it is the only method of enforcement which does not require a court hearing of any kind. It is also very popular and is frequently used by judgment creditors as the first-choice method. In the High Court, it is governed by CPR Sch 1, RSC Ord 46 – 'Writs of execution: general' and RSC Ord 47 – 'Writs of *fieri facias*'. In the county court, it is governed by CPR Sch 2, CCR Ord 26 – 'Warrants of execution, delivery and possession'.

Note the different terminology between the High Court and county courts. It is more than a difference of mere terminology, however. In the High Court, writs are executed by a High Court enforcement officer (who is not employed by Her Majesty's Court Service), whereas in the county court, warrants are executed by the county court's own bailiffs (who are employed by Her Majesty's Court Service). The writ/warrant gives the enforcement officer/bailiff authority to enter the judgment debtor's premises and take possession of the debtor's goods to the value of the judgment debt plus costs and expenses of enforcement. The goods so seized are then sold at public auction and the proceeds of sale (minus costs and expenses) sufficient to discharge the judgment debt are paid to the judgment creditor.

The number of writs/warrants issued every year is very large but the number of sales is very small. There are two reasons for this. First, it may well be that the debtor has goods of insufficient value to justify the cost of removal and sale (this fact illustrates that this method of enforcement may not always be the best method to choose), and, secondly, debtors often make arrangements to pay and, to this end, enter into an agreement of 'walking possession' with the enforcement officer/bailiff. Walking possession means that the goods are formally handed over to the lawful custody of the enforcement officer/bailiff, but remain in the physical possession of the judgment debtor. Once the enforcement officer/bailiff has taken possession of goods in this way, he or she can effect a forcible entry in order to gain access to them, but not otherwise (*McLeod v Butterwick* [1998] 1 WLR 1603; *Vaughan v McKenzie* [1969] 1 QB 557).

In the High Court, the judgment debtor can obtain a stay of execution pursuant to RSC Ord 47, r 1. Any application for a stay is heard by the master or district judge. Any stay usually requires payment by appropriate instalments. The equivalent rule in the county court is CCR Ord 25, r 8.

Apart from obtaining a formal stay from the court itself, judgment debtors often enter into informal arrangements with the enforcement officer/bailiff to pay by instalments. Such an arrangement is quite common where the debt can be paid relatively quickly and judgment debtors generally prefer to pay rather than have goods seized in execution.

The procedures for issuing execution differ between the High Court and county court, but are straightforward. The procedure is particularly straightforward in the county court, where all that a judgment creditor need do is file a request for a warrant of execution (Form N323) and pay the appropriate fee.

In the High Court, the relevant form is still called a *praecipe* and is in Practice Form 86 (a *praecipe* is a request to issue). In addition, a sealed copy of the judgment is required, together with two copies of the writ of *fieri facias* itself and, of course, the appropriate fee. The writ is then forwarded to the High Court enforcement officer chosen by the judgment creditor. A list of enforcement officers is available at the Royal Courts of Justice, all district registries and all county courts. (Why county courts? See below.)

Formerly, enforcement in the High Court was the responsibility of the sheriff acting through sheriff's officers. However, by Courts Act 2003, s 99 and Sch 7 the former responsibilities of the sheriff now vest in High Court enforcement officers (most of whom were formerly sheriff's officers but are now governed by the High Court Enforcement Officers Regulations 2004, SI 2004/400, and a Code of Practice). Two changes are worthy of note. Previously, a sheriff's officer had only a local jurisdiction but, although enforcement officers express a preference for which areas (defined by postcode) they wish to work in, jurisdiction is not local but covers the whole of England and Wales. Secondly, whereas formerly the under-sheriff would decide which officer would execute the writ the judgment creditor now has the choice.

By High Court and County Courts Jurisdiction Order 1991, SI 1991/724, art 8, county court judgments must be enforced in the High Court where the sum which it is sought to enforce is £5,000 or more. (Hence the need for a list of High Court enforcement officers to be available at all county courts). Judgments for less than £600 can be enforced only in the county court, but there is a choice when the debt is not less than £600 nor £5,000 or more. However, a judgment of the county court arising out of an agreement regulated by the Consumer Credit Act 1974 can be enforced only in a county court.

The general perception is that enforcement officers are more efficient in enforcing judgments than county court bailiffs. For this reason, judgment creditors, whenever they have a choice, tend to prefer to enforce in the High Court.

To enforce a county court judgment in the High Court it is first necessary to effect transfer. Form N293A should be used.

ATTACHMENT OF EARNINGS

Attachment of earnings is governed by the Attachment of Earnings Act 1971. Such orders are available only in the county court and are governed by CPR Sch 2, CCR Ord 27. It is a very effective method of enforcement where a judgment debtor is in regular employment (but not, of course, if unemployed or self-employed).

The procedure is very simple indeed: the judgment creditor completes the request in Form N337 and pays the prescribed fee. The court will do everything else. The court will obtain details of the judgment debtor's earnings from the judgment debtor (and, if necessary, the employer). Deciding on the amount to be deducted from the judgment debtor's wages always used to be the task of the district judge but it has now been delegated to court staff, who work to a prescribed formula and have an 'attachment of earnings calculator'. However, many cases are, in fact, referred to district judges by court staff, for a variety of reasons. The debtor's income may not, in fact, be sufficient to enable an order to be made after making allowance for necessary expenditure for the debtor and his or her family. Cases are always referred to district judges where the information does not come from the debtor but from the debtor's employer. Further, even where the matter has been dealt with by a member of staff, either party can ask the district judge to reconsider.

Clearly, the debtor must have enough to live on, and so the court's task is to fix the 'protected earnings rate', which is a sum which, as its name suggests, is protected and the effect of the attachment of earnings order must not be to reduce the take-home pay below the protected rate. There will then be a normal deduction rate, based on the surplus income. Thus, for example, if the court has fixed a protected earnings rate of £200 per week and a normal deduction rate of £25 per week, in any week where the debtor's take-home pay is £225 or more, the full £25 will be deducted by the employer (together with a prescribed fee for collection) and paid to the court. If, in a particular week, the judgment debtor earned, say, only £215, then there would be a shortfall that week, for the employer could not reduce the take-home pay below the protected earnings rate of £200, by virtue of the order. The creditor would thus receive only £15 that week. It follows that, in any week where the debtor earned less than the protected rate, the creditor would receive nothing.

In the first instance, particularly where the judgment debtor co-operates by giving the court all the appropriate information promptly, a suspended order is made. This means that, so long as the judgment debtor pays the appropriate sum voluntarily each week or month, as appropriate, the order is not in fact forwarded to the employer. This saves the judgment debtor not only the employer's administration fee, but also possible embarrassment. However, if default is made, then the suspension is lifted and the order is sent to the employer.

As far as collection and distribution are concerned, there is now a centralised system in operation so one office collects payments for all county courts and pays out to judgment creditors.

CHARGING ORDERS

Charging orders are governed by CPR Part 73 and by the Charging Orders Act 1979. Charging orders can be obtained on land, securities or an interest in partnership property. (The last mentioned is very rare and is not further considered; see Partnership Act 1890, s 23 and CPR Sch 1, RSC Ord 81.)

Obtaining a charging order on land is a frequently used method of enforcement but its limitations must be clearly appreciated. It does not, of itself, produce the money. A judgment creditor who obtains a charging order on the judgment debtor's interest in land becomes, in effect, a secured creditor. Broadly speaking, the judgment creditor is then in the same position as a mortgagee, subject, of course, to any prior charge. When the property is eventually sold, the judgment creditor will have his or her debt paid out of the net proceeds of sale, after prior charges and encumbrances have been paid. It is possible, having obtained a charging order, to obtain an order for sale (see r 73.10) and the knowledge that this can happen is often sufficient encouragement for the judgment debtor to enter into an agreement to pay the debt by instalments. Further, remortgaging is very common these days and, in practice, most charging orders are redeemed in this way.

CCA 1984, s 86(1) prevents the making of a charging order where a county court has made an order for the payment of the judgment debt by instalments and there is no default in the payment of instalments. Although this section does not apply in the High Court, if, in fact, the court has ordered payment by instalments, pursuant to r 40.11, then, if the debtor is up to date with his or her instalments, the court is likely, in the exercise of its discretion, to refuse to make a charging order (*Mercantile Credit Co Ltd v Ellis* (1987) *The Times*, April 1, CA). An application for a charging order is made without notice to the court which made the judgment or order in question, unless the proceedings have since been transferred to a different court, in which case, the application must be issued there (see r 73.3).

The application is made in Form N379 (land) or Form N380 (securities) and the relevant form, together with the appropriate court fee, are all that is required.

The application will be treated as urgent (for reasons of priority) and referred to the district judge. If it is in order and establishes an arguable case, the district judge will immediately make an 'interim charging order'.

There will then be a hearing before the district judge to decide whether to make a final charging order or to discharge the interim charging order and dismiss the application (r 73.8).

Copies of the interim charging order, together with the application notice (and any documents filed in support of it), must be served not less than 21 days before the hearing on the judgment debtor and such other creditors as the court directs (other creditors will have been revealed in the application notice). If any person (ie not just the judgment debtor) objects to the court's making the final charging order, he or she must file and serve on the applicant written evidence stating the ground of objection not less than 7 days before the hearing.

To ensure that the charging order is effective, it is, of course, necessary for the judgment creditor to arrange for the charge to be registered. An interim charging order is registered under Charging Orders Act 1979, s 3: in the case of land with a registered title, a notice or restriction must be entered pursuant to the Land Registration Act 2002; in the case of land with an unregistered title, an entry under the Land Charges Act 1972 is required.

Rule 73.8 provides that, at the hearing, the court may 'make a final charging order confirming that the charge imposed by the interim charging order shall continue'. Accordingly, it is submitted that a further registration of the final order is not required, for the court has simply ordered that the interim order, which you should have registered, continues in force. Failure to register does, of course, render the charging order potentially worthless: it would be defeated by a bona fide purchaser for value without notice.

If the interim charging order is made final, fixed costs will be awarded plus disbursements.

THIRD PARTY DEBT ORDERS

Third party debt orders are governed by CPR Part 72 and its supplementing Practice Direction. The procedure is a two-stage procedure, very similar to that for obtaining charging orders and, indeed, the principles are the same. If a third party owes money to the judgment debtor, it is possible for the judgment creditor to obtain a third-party debt order, requiring that third party to pay the debt to the judgment creditor, rather than to the judgment debtor, up to the value of the judgment debt. In doing so, the third party does, of course, obtain release from the debt, which he or she would otherwise have had to pay to the judgment debtor. Application is in Form N349.

An application for a third party debt order is made without notice and must be issued in the court which made the judgment or order, unless the proceedings have already been transferred to a different court, in which case, it must be issued in that court (r 72.3). An application for a third party debt order is initially dealt with by the district judge, without a hearing. The judge makes an interim third party debt order and fixes a hearing to consider whether to make it final. The interim order directs, until that hearing, that the third party must not make any payment which reduces the amount he or she owes the judgment debtor to less than the amount specified in the order. The hearing will be not less than 28 days after the interim third party debt order is made (r 72.4).

Copies of the interim third party debt order, together with the application notice and any documents filed in support, must be served on the third party not less than 21 days before the hearing, and on the judgment debtor not less than 7 days after the third party has been served and 7 days before the hearing.

A bank or building society account in credit is, of course, in law, a debt owed by that institution to its customer. Accordingly, where the judgment creditor has details of the judgment debtor's bank account, etc, a third-party debt order can be sought against the bank. Banks and building societies are well used to this and, for the special obligations imposed on them, see r 72.6. SCA 1981, s 40 and CCA 1984, s 108 greatly extended the earlier restricted position regarding attachment of deposit accounts.

It is, of course, possible that, by the effective freezing of his or her bank account under an interim third-party debt order, the judgment debtor could suffer hardship in meeting ordinary living expenses. Consequently, r 72.7 enables a judgment debtor to apply to any county court (or, in High Court proceedings, to the Royal Courts of Justice or any district registry) for a 'hardship payment order'. (See further, r 72.7.)

If either the judgment debtor or the third party objects to the court making the final order, he or she must file and serve written evidence, stating the grounds of his or her objection, not less than 3 days before the hearing (r 72.8). At the hearing, the court may make a final third-party debt order or discharge the interim third-party debt order and dismiss the application. The court also has power to decide any issues in dispute between the parties or, if necessary, direct a trial of any such issues.

COMMITTAL

Where the court makes an order of the nature of an injunction which is disobeyed, the appropriate method of enforcement is to apply for an order committing the defaulting party to prison for contempt of court. The court's powers are in the Contempt of Court Act 1981, which permits a maximum sentence of up to 2 years in prison. Civil courts sentencing to imprisonment must apply, so far as is possible, the same sentencing principles as applied in the criminal courts: see *Robinson v Murray* [2005] EWCA Civ 935 and *Hale v Tanner* [2000] 1 WLR 2377.

In the High Court, procedure is governed by CPR Sch 1, RSC Ord 52, and in the county court by CPR Sch 2, CCR Ord 29. In both courts, 'Practice Direction – Committal Applications' also applies, the Practice Direction having been made expressly to supplement RSC Ord 52 and CCR Ord 29. It is necessary to study the Practice Direction and the relevant rules because, of course, committal is a very serious step to take.

Committal applications are unique in civil procedure in that proof that the alleged contemnor has indeed been guilty of contempt of court is required beyond reasonable doubt and not on the usual civil standard of the balance of probabilities. The judge must be sure.

It will be necessary to prove that the original order, suitably endorsed with a penal notice (ie a notice warning of the consequences of not complying with the order) has been personally served on the alleged contemnor. The application is made by application notice within the proceedings, supported by written evidence, which must be in the form of an affidavit. In the county court, applications to commit are heard by the circuit judge and, in the High Court, by a High Court judge.

JUDGMENT SUMMONS

Judgment summonses are dealt with by CPR Sch 2, CCR Ord 28, but cannot be used to enforce payment of ordinary debts. Imprisonment for non-payment of ordinary debts was severely restricted long ago by the Debtors Act 1869. The procedure is now available only in certain matrimonial cases and to enforce payments of taxes and other debts due to the State. Although still contained in CPR Sch 2, CCR Ord 28 has recently been amended following a decision of the Court of Appeal that, in its original form, it was not compliant with the ECHR. Obviously, the intention of the amendments is to make the procedure compliant. However, importantly, the Court of Appeal also held (in *Mubarak v Mubarak* [2001] 1 FLR 698) that Practice Direction – Committals (supplementing RSC Ord 52 and CCR Ord 29) applies to judgment summonses.

The applicant must prove that the debtor has had the means to pay the debt and has failed to do so. Because the effect of such proof is that the court makes a committal order, proof is required beyond reasonable doubt and not on the usual civil standard of the balance of probabilities. If it is so proved at the hearing of the judgment summons, an order is made committing the debtor to prison but the order is suspended so long as specified instalments are paid.

SEQUESTRATION

Sequestration is available only in the High Court (CPR PD 70, para 1.2) and is governed by CPR Sch 1, RSC Ord 45, r 5 and Ord 46, r 5. It is a form of contempt proceedings. Sequestrators are appointed to take possession of the contemnor's property and to keep it until the contempt is purged. Permission is required to issue a writ of sequestration.

APPOINTMENT OF A RECEIVER

Appointment of a receiver (still sometimes referred to as 'equitable execution') is governed by CPR Part 69 and its supplementing Practice Direction. Part 69 and PD 69 are comprehensive as they deal with appointing a receiver in all situations where this might arise, not merely for enforcement purposes. As this method of enforcement is expensive, it should not be used where there is no impediment to legal execution.

A receiver is appointed to receive income that would otherwise go to the judgment debtor. After payment of expenses, the balance is then paid to the judgment creditor. It is quite rare in practice, but there are rare occasions where it is the appropriate method of enforcement. For example, if the judgment debtor has no assets to be seized in legal execution, has no known third parties owing him or her money and has an overdraft at the bank and is self-employed but has a sizeable rental income from various properties which he or she owns, in such a case appointing a receiver to receive the rents may, in fact, be the only appropriate method of enforcement.

WARRANT OF POSSESSION

In accordance with the provisions of CPR Part 55, nearly all possession actions are in the county court. If the court makes an order for possession and it is necessary to enforce the order, then, in the county court, the procedure is to apply for a warrant of possession. The warrant is executed by the county court bailiff. The procedure is governed by CPR Sch 2, CCR Ord 26 – Warrants of execution, delivery and possession, and the procedure is identical to that for a warrant of execution (see above). The judgment creditor files a request in Form N325 – request for warrant for possession of land – whereupon, the court issues a warrant in Form N149. Notice is given both to the judgment creditor and judgment debtor of the time and time of execution. Permission to issue the warrant is not required in the county court.

WARRANT OF DELIVERY

Warrants of delivery are also governed by CPR Sch 2, CCR Ord 26 – Warrants of execution, delivery and possession. This warrant is used to obtain delivery of specific goods which the judgment debtor has been ordered to return, but has not, in fact, returned. The most common use of this warrant in practice is to obtain the return of goods – typically a car – which the court has ordered to be returned to the judgment creditor because the judgment debtor has defaulted in payments under a hire-purchase agreement. Initially, the court usually makes a suspended order, that is the return of the goods is suspended so long as the judgment debtor makes certain payments. If, however, those payments are not made – or the debtor is not given the option of making the payment – then, once the date for return of goods has passed, the judgment creditor can apply for a warrant of delivery. The procedure is very simple. All that is required is the appropriate form of request (Form N324) and the relevant fee. The court bailiff does the rest.

STOP ORDERS AND STOP NOTICES

These are relatively rare methods of enforcement and are governed by CPR Part 73. Stop orders are dealt with in Part 73, Section II. A stop order is defined in Charging Orders Act 1979 (COA 1979), s 5. It means an order of the High Court not to take, in relation to funds in court or securities specified in the order, any of the steps listed in COA 1979, s 5(5). The stop notice is dealt with by Part 73,

Section III. A stop notice is defined in COA 1979, s 5, and means a notice issued by the court which requires a person or body not to take, in relation to securities specified in the notice, any of the steps listed in COA 1979, s 5(5) without first giving notice to the person who obtained the order.

ORDERS TO OBTAIN INFORMATION FROM JUDGMENT DEBTORS

The title of this section is the same as the title of CPR Part 71. We have listed above all available methods of enforcement and pointed out that it is for the judgment creditor to decide which method to use. Often, judgment creditors have sufficient information about the judgment debtor to make a decision without further inquiry. Where, however, the judgment creditor has no such information, or it is out of date, then the judgment creditor should consider an order under Part 71.

Part 71 deals with a procedure which used to be known as 'oral examination'. It contains rules which provide for a judgment debtor to be required to attend court to provide information for the purpose of enabling a judgment creditor to enforce a judgment or order against him or her. A judgment creditor may apply for an order requiring a judgment debtor (or, if a judgment debtor is a company or other corporation, an officer of that body) to attend court to provide information about the judgment debtor's means or any other matter about which information is needed to enforce a judgment or order.

An application is made without notice and must be issued in the court which made the judgment or order which it is sought to enforce, unless the proceedings have since been transferred to a different court, in which case, it must be issued in that court.

The application must be in the form and contain the information required by the Practice Direction which supplements Part 71. The relevant form of application is Form N316 (or Form N316A if an officer of a debtor company is to attend court for questioning).

The application is considered by a court officer, without a hearing. The order is then served and contains a notice which includes the words: 'You must obey this order. If you do not, you may be sent to prison for contempt of court' (r 71.2).

The order to attend court must be served personally on the person ordered to attend not less than 14 days before the hearing. Service of an order to attend court for questioning must be by the judgment creditor (or, more usually, a process server employed by him or her) except that, in the county court, if the judgment creditor is an individual litigant in person, the order will be served by the court bailiff (PD 71, para 3). A person so ordered to attend may, within 7 days of being served with the order, ask the judgment creditor to pay him or her a sum reasonably sufficient to cover his or her travelling expenses to and from court. The judgment creditor must pay the sum, if requested (r 71.4). Apart from this, there is no obligation to pay 'conduct money'.

The court requires proof of service of the order on the debtor and this must be in the form of an affidavit (r 71.5). At the hearing, the person ordered to attend court will be questioned on oath. The questioning will be carried out by a court officer. Only if there is a difficulty will the examination be heard by a judge.

If the questioning is by a court officer, the judgment creditor need not attend, but may do so and may ask questions in addition to those asked by the court officer. If the examination is before a judge, the judgment creditor or his or her representative must attend and conduct the questioning (r 71.6).

The hearing is in the nature of a cross-examination, bearing in mind its purpose of eliciting information to enable the judgment creditor to enforce the judgment (*Republic of Costa Rica v Strousberg* (1880) 16 Ch D 8). If the person ordered to attend does not do so, the court itself takes steps to obtain a committal order (r 71.8). (See further, CPR PD 71.)

With the information obtained at the hearing held pursuant to Part 71, the judgment creditor will now be able – at least in theory – to decide how best to enforce the judgment. As already noted, where an examination is before a court officer, it is not necessary for the judgment creditor to attend. However, in practice, it is often desirable to do so, with a view to making an arrangement with the debtor for payment or, if no such arrangement can be made, to immediately issue the appropriate enforcement process in the light of the information obtained.

INTEREST ON JUDGMENT DEBTS

High Court judgments carry interest under JA 1838, s 17. The rate of interest is fixed from time to time by statutory instrument. Since 1 April 1993 the rate has been fixed at 8% (Judgment Debts (Rate of Interest) Order 1993, SI 1993/564).

County court judgments of £5,000 or more also carry interest, under CCA 1984, s 74. Again, the rate is 8%. County court judgments under £5,000 do not carry any interest, unless the debt attracts contractual interest or statutory interest under the Late Payment of Commercial Debts (Interest) Act 1998.

By r 40.8, where interest is payable on a judgment pursuant to JA 1838, s 17 or CCA 1984, s 74, the interest shall begin to run from the date that the judgment is given, unless a rule in another Part or a Practice Direction makes different provision or the court orders otherwise. (The court also has power to order that interest begin to run from a date before the date that judgment was given.)

In the section above, entitled 'Writ of *fieri facias*/warrant of execution', it was pointed out that judgment creditors often prefer to levy execution through a High Court enforcement officer, rather the county court bailiff. Another reason for this preference is the fact that, once the judgment has been transferred to the High Court for enforcement purposes, it has now become a High Court judgment and, thus, will attract interest under JA 1838, s 17, even in the case where, had it remained in the county court, it would not have done so.

WHICH COURT?

As already noted (see 'Writ of *fieri facias*/warrant of execution' above), county court judgments for £5,000 or more must be enforced only in the High Court, where it is intended to enforce judgment by execution against goods. (This does not apply to judgments arising out of agreements regulated by the Consumer Credit Act 1974, which must be enforced in the county court.) The judgment can be enforced only in a county court when the sum is less than £600. There is a choice where the judgment is £600 or more, but less than £5,000. There are two reasons why, where it is intended to enforce by execution against goods, judgment creditors prefer the High Court and both have already been noted. The first reason is that High Court enforcement officers are perceived to have a better record of collection than county court bailiffs and, secondly, High Court judgments carry interest (see above). If it is necessary to transfer from the county court to the High Court to enforce some High Court enforcement officers will do this for you. To do it yourself use Form N293A.

Apart from the general consideration of High Court or county court, there remains the specific question of which is the relevant court for your chosen method of enforcement. This depends on the method that has been chosen and, in all cases, the relevant rule should be consulted to ascertain the relevant provision. Thus, for example, an application for an attachment of earnings order under CPR Sch 2, CCR Ord 27 must be made to the court for the district in which the debtor resides (Ord 27, r 3). On the other hand, orders to obtain information from judgment debtors under Part 71 (see r 71.2(2)), third party debt orders (see r 72.3) and charging orders (see r 73.3) must all be issued in the court which made the judgment or order which it is sought to enforce, unless the proceedings have already been transferred to a different court, in which case, the application must be issued in that court. Note that, in the case of these applications issued under CPR Parts 71–73, there is no provision for the application to be transferred to the 'defendant's home court'. This means, for example, that, where a judgment creditor has sued in his or her own local county court and obtained a default judgment there, then he or she must issue the enforcement application there. The case itself, if defended, may well have been transferred to the defendant's home court automatically, but there is no similar provision dealing with enforcement matters.

INTERPLEADER

Although not relevant solely in the context of enforcement, interpleader proceedings are considered here, as they most commonly arise in the context of enforcement proceedings.

In the High Court, interpleader is governed by CPR Sch 1, RSC Ord 17 and in the county court, by CPR Sch 2, CCR Ord 33. There are two types of interpleader, namely stakeholder's interpleader and interpleader under execution, and the latter is more common than the former.

Interpleader arises where a person finds himself in possession of goods which are claimed by two or more rival persons, in circumstances where the person in possession does not claim them for himself or herself. In the context of an interpleader under execution, this arises because the enforcement officer (or the county court bailiff) has levied execution on goods which he or she believes to be the property of the judgment debtor. However, a third person (eg the judgment debtor's spouse) now says that the item in question belongs to him or her. If the judgment creditor accepts this claim, the enforcement officer will withdraw and the goods will be handed to the third party who has claimed them. If, however, the claim is disputed, then interpleader proceedings will be necessary to resolve the issue.

In the High Court, interpleaders are dealt with by a master or district judge. However, due to an historical quirk which has not yet been addressed, the district judge cannot deal with interpleaders in the county court and, consequently, they must be dealt with by a circuit judge.

INSOLVENCY

Insolvency is mentioned but not dealt with here, as it is not strictly a method of enforcing a judgment. Winding up of companies and bankruptcy of individuals are currently covered by the Insolvency Act 1986. Where a company is insolvent, it will be wound up. Where an individual is insolvent, he or she will be declared bankrupt. The Insolvency Act 1986 prescribes a statutory scheme for the getting-in of the assets and their rateable distribution amongst creditors. They are not governed by the CPR, but by the Insolvency Rules 1986. However, Practice Direction – Insolvency Proceedings was issued after the CPR came into force, to take account of the new procedural regime. Serving a 'statutory demand' is the method by which a creditor (whether or not a judgment creditor) threatens a debtor (whether or not a judgment debtor) with bankruptcy or winding-up. There is a prescribed form of demand. It is not a court document and the court is not involved in any way at this stage. A demand gives details of the debt and demands that the debtor should pay the debt, or secure or compound it to the creditor's satisfaction. The debt must be for £750 or more. (See Insolvency Act 1986, ss 123 and 267.)

The statutory demand contains a warning that if it is not dealt with within 21 days of service, bankruptcy or winding-up proceedings can follow.

There is a procedure whereby an individual debtor can make an application to the court for the statutory demand to be set aside. Whilst there is no such procedure in the case of companies, a similar result can be achieved by applying to the court for an injunction to restrain advertisement of a winding-up petition. If the creditor knows that the debt is disputed on substantial grounds, then it is likely to be preferable to sue on the debt rather than serve a statutory demand, which the court is likely to set aside. Bankruptcy and winding up are specialist topics, beyond the scope of this work.

Part X

OTHER PROCEEDINGS

Chapter 42

RECOVERY OF LAND

Possession claims have their own procedural code, which is to be found in CPR Part 55. The rules are specific and must be strictly complied with.

A possession claim is a claim for the recovery of possession of land and those claims most commonly encountered will be those brought by a mortgagee for recovery of possession of a house when the mortgage instalments are in arrears, or by a landlord for recovery of rented property at the end of the term of the tenancy, or if there has been breach of the tenancy agreement, for example non-payment of rent.

STARTING THE CLAIM

Unlike claims under CPR Part 7, which may be commenced in any court, the general rule for possession claims is that they must be started in the county court for the district in which the relevant land is situated. Very exceptionally, claims may begin in the High Court (see CPR PD 55, paras 1.3 and 1.4).

THE CLAIM FORM

The claim form must in the prescribed Form N5. If the claim is for possession of an assured shorthold tenancy using the accelerated procedure, the correct form is Form N5B. The particulars of claim must accompany the claim form. There is no provision for the particulars of claim to be served at a later date.

CONTENTS OF THE PARTICULARS OF CLAIM

The particulars of claim must contain the information set out in CPR PD 55, para 2.1:

(1)   a description of the land to which the claim relates;
(2)   whether the claim relates to residential property;
(3)   the ground on which possession is claimed;
(4)   full details of any mortgage or tenancy; and

(5)   details of all those who the claimant knows to be in possession of the property.

ADDITIONAL INFORMATION FOR A CLAIM FOR POSSESSION BY A LANDLORD

If the claim relates to property that is let on a tenancy, and the claim includes a claim for non-payment of rent, the particulars of claim must also set out the following:

(1)   the amount of rent due when the claim was issued;
(2)   a chronological schedule showing rent due and payments made, with a running total of the arrears;
(3)   the daily rate of rent and interest;
(4)   any steps taken to recover the arrears, including details of any previous proceedings; and
(5)   any relevant information about the defendant's circumstances, in particular, whether he or she is in receipt of state benefits, and whether any benefits (eg Housing Benefit) are being paid directly to the claimant on his or her behalf.

ADDITIONAL INFORMATION FOR A CLAIM FOR POSSESSION BY A MORTGAGEE

If a claim for possession is made by a mortgagee, the particulars of claim must also set out the information prescribed by CPR PD 55, para 4:

(1)   in the case of residential property, whether any rights of occupation or other interests in the property have been registered and, if so, that the claimant will serve notice of the claim on any person registering an interest;
(2)   details of the mortgage account, including:
    (a)   the amount of the advance;
    (b)   any instalment payments;
    (c)   any interest payments that have to be made;
    (d)   the amount required to redeem the mortgage;
    (e)   in the case of a loan regulated by the Consumer Credit Act 1974, the total amount outstanding under the terms of the mortgage;
    (f)   the rate of interest payable at the start of the mortgage, immediately before any arrears accrued, and at the date of issue of the claim form;
(3)   details of any arrears, including:
    (a)   a chronological schedule showing the payments due, the payments made and a running total of the arrears;
    (b)   details of any other payments that have to be made as a term of the mortgage, for example insurance premiums, legal costs, etc, and whether any of these payments is in arrears and whether it has been included in the amount of the instalment payment;

(c)   whether the loan is regulated by the Consumer Credit Act 1974, and, if so, the date on which the default notice was served;

(d)   where appropriate, a statement that the loan agreement is not one that is regulated by the Consumer Credit Act 1974;

(e)   any relevant information about the defendant's circumstances, in particular, whether he or she is in receipt of state benefits, and whether any benefits (eg housing benefit) are being paid directly to the claimant on his or her behalf;

(f)   details of any tenancy entered into between the mortgagor and mortgagee; and

(g)   details of any steps taken to recover the arrears, including full details of any previous court proceedings.

PROCEDURE AFTER ISSUE OF THE CLAIM FORM

When the claim form is issued, the court will fix a date for the hearing. The hearing date will be no less than 28 days, and generally no more than 8 weeks, from the date of issue of the claim form. The defendant must be served with the claim form and particulars of claim not less than 21 days before the hearing date.

However, the court has power to reduce these time-limits and will usually be persuaded to do so if there is any evidence that the defendant has assaulted or threatened to assault the landlord or a member of his or her family, or another tenant; there are reasonable grounds for fearing such an assault; or the defendant or someone for whom the defendant is responsible has caused or threatened to cause serious damage to the property, or to the home or property of another resident.

An application to abridge time for the first hearing, and for service of notice of the hearing, should be made on Form N244, with a witness statement in support.

DEFENDANT'S RESPONSE TO THE CLAIM

There is a prescribed form for a defendant's response (Form N11M for a claim in respect of mortgaged property; Form N11R for a claim in respect of rented residential property). However, the Rules do not require the defendant to acknowledge service, and failure to do so does not prevent a defendant from taking part in the hearing, although it may affect the court's decision as to the costs of the hearing, for example if there had to be an adjournment.

PREPARATION FOR THE HEARING

Most possession claims are not defended and so it will be usual for the claim to be disposed of at the first hearing. This means that the evidence that either party intends to rely upon must be before the court.

All witness statements must be filed at court and served on the defendant at least 2 clear days before the hearing. Generally, the particulars of claim, endorsed with a statement of truth, will contain all the evidence upon which the claimant will rely, but there should be a witness statement from the claimant that brings the court up to date with the figure for the arrears. It is most unusual for a defendant to file evidence at this stage.

Where the claim relates to mortgaged residential property, the claimant should, not less than 14 days before the hearing, give notice of the hearing to all occupiers of the property and make sure that evidence of service of a 'notice to occupiers' is available at the hearing (see r 55.10).

Where the claim form has been served by the claimant rather than by the court, the claimant must produce a certificate of service at the hearing. The claimant must produce evidence of the loan agreement. This will usually be the original charge, but, in the case of registered land, an office copy of the charge will suffice.

THE HEARING

Although it will generally be the case that the claim will be disposed of at the first hearing, the court may adjourn the hearing in appropriate cases, or, if the claim is disputed, give case management directions, including allocation to track, rather as it would for a claim proceeding under Part 7.

In claims for possession by a mortgagee, it would be most unusual for the claimant to ask the court to make an order for costs. This is because the mortgage deed will make provision for costs to be paid on a contractual basis, and, therefore, an order of the court is not required.

RECOVERY OF LAND AGAINST TRESPASSERS

Occasionally, property will be occupied by persons who are not authorised by the owner, for example squatters. Nonetheless, a court order is required before steps can be taken to remove them.

Section III of CPR Pt 55 provides a summary procedure for the eviction of unlawful occupiers by way of an interim possession order. The procedure does not apply where there has been a lease or a licence and the tenant remains in occupation without permission beyond the term.

ACCELERATED POSSESSION PROCEDURE

This is a distinct procedure that has its own strict rules. It applies only to claims for possession of residential property let under an assured shorthold tenancy, where possession of the property is the only remedy sought. Rule 55.10 sets out further pre-conditions:

(1)   the tenancy must have been entered into after 15 January 1989 and must not have immediately followed an assured tenancy which was not an assured shorthold tenancy;

(2)   the tenancy must be in writing or must immediately follow a tenancy where there was a written agreement;

(3)   no other claim must be made, apart from a claim for possession (and costs), so, for example, the claim must not include a claim for rent arrears;

(4)   written notice of the intention to seek possession has been served on the tenant in accordance with s 21(1) or (4) of the Housing Act 1988.

THE CLAIM FORM

The claim form must be fully completed in the prescribed Form N5C and must exhibit copies of the written tenancy agreement(s), the notice seeking possession and any further evidence that the claimant wishes to have considered. It is important to note that the claim form must be signed, either by the landlord personally or by his or her solicitor, and not by a letting agent.

PROCEDURE AFTER ISSUE

On issue of the claim, the court will serve the defendant. Unlike other possession claims, the defendant must file a defence within 14 days after service of the claim form, otherwise he or she risks having a possession order made without further notice. The defence should be in the prescribed Form N11B.

On receipt of defence, or if the time for filing a defence has expired and the claimant has filed a written request for an order for possession, the claim and any defence will be referred to the district judge.

If the district judge is satisfied that the claimant has fulfilled the conditions for bringing a claim under the accelerated procedure and has complied with the procedural requirements, a possession order will be made. Possession must be ordered in 14 days, unless the claimant has indicated in the claim form that he or she will agree to a longer period, up to a maximum of 42 days. If the district judge considers that there may be exceptional hardship to the defendant, he or she must make an order for possession in 14 days, but may list a hearing before the expiry of the 14 days for postponement of the date for possession to be considered. The maximum postponement remains at 42 days from the date of the original order. The claimant has the option of indicating on the claim form if he or she is content for the district judge to consider the question of exceptional hardship without a hearing.

If the district judge is not satisfied that the claimant is entitled to a possession order, he or she will either direct a hearing or, if the claim form discloses no reasonable grounds for bringing the claim, strike it out. If the claim is struck out, reasons must be given with the order, and the claimant has the right to apply to restore the claim within 28 days being served with the order.

Chapter 43

MISCELLANEOUS PRACTICE DIRECTIONS

Under the modern rules of civil procedure, there are essentially two distinct types of Practice Direction. First, there are Practice Directions supplementing a particular Part of the CPR, and secondly, Practice Directions not related to a specific Part.

The authority to make the Civil Procedure Rules and Practice Directions derives from the Civil Procedure Act 1987. Rules themselves are made by statutory instrument, subject to the Statutory Instruments Act 1946. Practice Directions, on the other hand, are more flexible and do not need to go through a parliamentary procedure at all.

In the High Court, Practice Directions are issued by the Heads of the Division. In fact, many matters which, pre-CPR, would have been dealt with in *ad hoc* Practice Directions are now covered by a specific Practice Direction, supplementing a specific Part of the CPR.

Appendix A of this book lists not only all Parts of the CPR, but also makes it clear which Parts are supplemented by a Practice Direction (some parts have more than one) and which are not. The Practice Directions are there to expand upon and explain the Rules. Although, in the hierarchy of legislation, Rules rank above Practice Directions, just as Acts of Parliament rank above Rules, the Practice Directions are nevertheless there to be obeyed. In summary, they give useful guidance as to how to comply with the Rules themselves. Some Practice Directions are better drafted than others. In the unfortunate event of conflict between a Practice Direction and a rule, the rule will prevail, just as, in the unfortunate case of a conflict between a rule and a statute, the statute would prevail.

Practice Directions supplementing specific Parts of the CPR apply to civil litigation in the Queen's Bench Division and the Chancery Division of the High Court and to the county courts (other than family proceedings) and, where relevant, they also apply to the Court of Appeal. These Practice Directions are made by the Lord Chief Justice as Head of the Judiciary, by the new President of the Queen's Bench Division, by the Master of the Rolls for the Civil Division of the Court of Appeal, by the Vice Chancellor for the Chancery Division, and by the Lord Chancellor (or someone authorised by him – usually a Lord Justice) for the county courts. The originals of all CPR Practice Directions are, in fact, signed by these senior judges.

At least under the modern regime, Practice Directions are of universal application. Unfortunately, prior to the CPR, many county courts issued Practice Directions of local relevance only (there were over 3,000 altogether). This is no longer possible. In the county court, directions must be made only by the Lord Chancellor and CCA 1984, s 74A (as amended by the Civil Procedure Act 1997) specifically provides that Directions may not be made by any other person without the approval of the Lord Chancellor.

As mentioned, Practice Directions can be amended easily, without reference to Parliament. There has been some criticism that some topics which perhaps ought to be in the CPR themselves are, instead, governed by Practice Directions, supplementing a particular Part of the CPR. However, this is expressly authorised by the Civil Procedure Act 1997, and it is really a matter of judgment for the Civil Procedure Rule Committee itself (the Committee is constituted by Civil Procedure Act 1997, s 2).

In addition to the Practice Directions which supplement a particular Part of the CPR (which are always referred to by the specific Part which they supplement, eg PD 4, etc), there are a number of miscellaneous CPR Practice Directions of general application. These are found in Section 3 of the Brown Book and at Section B in Vol 1 of the White Book. These miscellaneous Directions are summarised below.

PRACTICE DIRECTION – PROTOCOLS

This Practice Direction deals with all pre-action protocols approved by the Head of Civil Justice and includes all those currently in force. See further, Chapter 6.

PRACTICE DIRECTION – DEVOLUTION ISSUES

The CPR apply throughout England and Wales. Other parts of the United Kingdom have their own procedural codes. This Practice Direction, therefore, supplements the provisions dealing with devolution issues under the Government of Wales Act 1998, the Northern Ireland Act 1998, and the Scotland Act 1998, but is mainly of relevance to devolution issues arising out of the Government of Wales Act 1998. Broadly, a devolution issue will involve a question of whether a devolved body has acted or proposes to act within its powers.

PRACTICE DIRECTION – DIRECTORS DISQUALIFICATION PROCEEDINGS

The Company Directors Disqualification Act 1986 (as amended) enables a court to order that a person shall not be a director of a company or in any way, whether directly or indirectly, be concerned or take part in the promotion, formation or management of a company, unless he or she has the leave of the court. This is, of course, an important topic in its own right, dealt with in specialist textbooks. The procedure is governed by the Insolvent Companies (Disqualification of Unfit

Directors) Proceedings Rules 1987 (as amended), which state that the CPR and 'the relevant practice direction' apply to disqualification applications. Appeals in disqualification matters are not dealt with by the Practice Direction, but by the disqualification rules.

PRACTICE DIRECTION – INSOLVENCY PROCEEDINGS

The provisions of the Insolvency Act 1986 have been substantially amended by the Insolvency Act 2000 and the Enterprise Act 2002. The principal rules are the Insolvency Rules 1986, which govern both company and individual insolvency proceedings in England and Wales.

Following the coming into force of the CPR, Insolvency Rules 1986, r 7.51 was amended to provide that the CPR, the practice and the procedure of the High Court and of any county court (including any Practice Direction) applied to insolvency proceedings in the High Court and county courts, as the case may be, in either case, with any necessary modifications, except so far as those inconsistent with the Insolvency Rules 1986. Practice Direction – Insolvency Proceedings came into force on 26 April 1999 (and has since been amended) and replaced all previous Practice Directions relating to insolvency proceedings. Essentially, insolvency proceedings have been adapted to bring them into line with the CPR. The most obvious change concerns costs, where the provisions of the CPR are now applied in their entirety, rather than the former rules.

PRACTICE DIRECTION – THE USE OF THE WELSH LANGUAGE IN CASES IN THE CIVIL COURTS IN WALES

The purpose of this Practice Direction is to reflect the principle of the Welsh Language Act 1993 that, in the administration of justice in Wales, the English and Welsh languages should be treated as equal.

PRACTICE DIRECTION ON THE CITATION OF AUTHORITIES

(This Practice Direction has also been reported at [2001] 1 WLR 1001.) With a view to limiting the citation of previous authority to cases that are relevant and useful to the court, this Practice Direction lays down a number of rules as to what material may be cited and the manner in which that cited material should be handled by advocates.

PRACTICE STATEMENT (SUPREME COURT: JUDGMENTS)

This Practice Direction, issued on 22 April 1998 by the then Lord Chief Justice, Lord Bingham of Cornhill, was issued with the agreement of the then Master of the Rolls, Vice-Chancellor, and President of the Family Division. It introduced new arrangements for the handing down of judgments in advance of the hearing. (It is also reported at [1998] 1WLR 825.)

PRACTICE STATEMENT (SUPREME COURT: JUDGMENTS) (NO 2)

(This Practice Direction has also been reported at [1999] 1 WLR 1.) This is a further statement, clarifying arrangements for the handing down of reserved written judgments, that was issued by the then Lord Chief Justice on 25 November 1998.

PRACTICE NOTE (RESERVED JUDGMENT: HANDING DOWN)

This further Direction, by Lord Phillips of Worth Matravers MR (also reported at [2002] 1 All ER 160), deals with the arrangements for handing down judgments in the Court of Appeal.

PRACTICE DIRECTION (JUDGMENTS: FORM AND CITATION)

This Practice Direction (also reported at [2001] 1 WLR 194) was issued by Lord Woolf CJ on 11 January 2001, changing the way in which judgments are cited in the Court of Appeal and the High Court Administrative Court. This Direction is essential reading if you are not familiar with the modern form of citation.

PRACTICE DIRECTION (JUDGMENTS: NEUTRAL CITATIONS)

This further Practice Direction (also reported at [2002] 1 WLR 346) was issued by Lord Woolf CJ, extending the neutral citation Direction of 11 January 2001 to the Chancery Division, Patents Court, Queen's Bench Division, Administrative Court, Commercial Court, Admiralty Court, Technology and Construction Court and the Family Division. It is essential reading if you are not familiar with the modern citation arrangements.

PRACTICE DIRECTION – PROCEEDS OF CRIME ACT 2002 PARTS 5 AND 8: CIVIL RECOVERY

The Proceeds of Crime Act 2002 introduced a new regime for the recovery, through the civil court, of assets held to be the proceeds of crime whether or not there have been successful criminal proceedings. This Practice Direction does not supplement any particular Part of the CPR but deals with such proceedings generally.

PRACTICE DIRECTION – COMPETITION LAW

This Practice Direction applies to any claim relating to the application of Article 81 or Article 82 of the Treaty establishing the European Community and to Chapters I and II of Part I of the Competition Act 1998.

THE QUEEN'S BENCH GUIDE

This guide has been prepared by the Senior Master of the Queen's Bench Division, acting under the authority of the Lord Chief Justice, and provides a general explanation of the working practice of the Queen's Bench Division, with particular reference to proceedings started in the Central Office (The Royal Courts of Justice). This guide is reproduced in full as Appendix C in this work.

CHANCERY GUIDE

This guide gives practical guidance on the conduct of cases in the Chancery Division. It is reproduced in full at Section 5 of the Brown Book and in Section 1 of Vol 2 to the White Book.

COMMERCIAL COURT GUIDE

This guide was brought into force by Practice Direction – Commercial Court. Practice Directions supplementing the CPR also apply to proceedings in the Commercial Court, save where otherwise provided for in the guide. The purpose of this guide is to serve the overriding objective in the specialist context of commercial cases. It is reproduced in full at Section 5 of the Brown Book and at Section 2C in Vol 2 of the White Book.

MERCANTILE COURTS GUIDE

This guide to the practice of the Mercantile Courts is issued with the approval of the Head of Civil Justice, pursuant to the Mercantile Courts and Business Lists Practice Direction, and applies to proceedings in any Mercantile Court. (See also, CPR Part 59.) The guide is to be found at Section 5 of the Brown Book and at Section 2C in Vol 2 of the White Book.

PATENTS COURT GUIDE

This guide is an explanation of the modern practice of the Patents Courts for the conduct of patent actions. (See also, CPR Part 49.) The guide is to be found at Section 5 of the Brown Book and at Section 2D in Vol 2 of the White Book.

Appendix A

QUICK GUIDE TO THE CIVIL PROCEDURE RULES 1998

PART	TITLE	SUPPLEMENTING PRACTICE DIRECTION
1	OVERRIDING OBJECTIVE – the bedrock of the CPR. Thorough knowledge of Part 1 is essential.	NO
2	APPLICATION AND INTERPRETATION OF THE RULES – includes crucial definitions. Note r 2.11: 'Time limits may be varied by parties'.	YES – Two PD 2 – Court offices PD 2B – Allocation of cases to levels of judiciary
3	THE COURT'S CASE MANAGEMENT POWERS – includes the court's general powers. Note r 3.9: 'Relief from sanctions'.	YES – Three PD 3 – Striking out a statement of case PD 3B – Sanction for non–payment of fees PD3C – Civil Restraint Orders
4	FORMS – provides for court forms to be used where applicable. Note r 4(2) – forms may be varied as required.	YES PD 4 – Forms
5	COURT DOCUMENTS – general provisions about documents used in court proceedings. Rule 5.3 provides for signature by mechanical means.	YES – Two PD 5 – Court documents PD5B – Electronic Communications and Filing of Documents

PART	TITLE	SUPPLEMENTING PRACTICE DIRECTION
6	SERVICE OF DOCUMENTS – general rules about service; special provisions about service of the claim form; special provisions about service out of the jurisdiction and service of foreign process.	YES – Two PD 6 – Service PD 6B – Service out of the jurisdiction
7	HOW TO START PROCEEDINGS – THE CLAIM FORM – includes where and how to start proceedings. Note r 7.4: particulars of claim.	YES – Five PD 7 – How to start proceedings – the claim form PD 7B – Consumer Credit Act claims PD 7C – Production centre PD 7D – Claims for the recovery of taxes PD 7E – Pilot scheme for money claims on line
8	ALTERNATIVE PROCEDURE FOR CLAIMS – sets out the situations where Part 8 can be used instead of Part 7, and the consequent variations in procedure which then follow.	YES – Two PD 8 – Alternative procedure for claims PD 8B – Part 8
9	RESPONDING TO PARTICULARS OF CLAIM – GENERAL – sets out how a defendant may respond to particulars of claim. Note r 9.1(2): defendant must respond to the particulars of claim (not the claim form as such).	NO
10	ACKNOWLEDGMENT OF SERVICE – a defendant may file an acknowledgement of service if unable to file a defence within the time specified in r 15.4 or to dispute the court's jurisdiction.	YES PD 10 – Acknowledgement of service
11	DISPUTING THE COURT'S JURISDICTION – prescribes how and when a defendant may dispute the court's jurisdiction.	NO

PART	TITLE	SUPPLEMENTING PRACTICE DIRECTION
12	DEFAULT JUDGMENT – the important procedure whereby a claimant can obtain judgment if the defendant does not respond to the proceedings.	YES PD 12 – Default judgment
13	SETTING ASIDE OR VARYING DEFAULT JUDGMENT – the procedure whereby a defendant can seek to vary or set aside a judgment obtained pursuant to Part 12.	NO
14	ADMISSIONS – the procedure for a defendant to admit the whole or part of a claim in the various types of claim. Note the claimant's right to enter judgment in r 14.1(4).	YES PD 14 – Admissions
15	DEFENCE AND REPLY – the time-limits and procedure for filing a defence (and counterclaim) and for the claimant to reply (and defend any counterclaim). Note the provision for an automatic stay of proceedings in r 15.11.	YES PD 15 – Defence and reply
16	STATEMENTS OF CASE – all the rules on pleadings including particulars of claim, defence and reply. Note r 16.3: statement of value to be included in the claim form.	YES PD 16 – Statements of case
17	AMENDMENTS TO STATEMENTS OF CASE – the procedure for amending statements of case. Note the different situations where the court's permission is or is not required, and the special rule applying to amendments after the end of the limitation period (r 17.4).	YES PD 17 – Amendments to statements of case

PART	TITLE	SUPPLEMENTING PRACTICE DIRECTION
18	FURTHER INFORMATION	YES
	– when and how to obtain further information about the opponent's case.	PD 18 – Further information
19	PARTIES AND GROUP LITIGATION	YES – Two
	– rules on addition and substitution of parties, representative parties, and group litigation.	PD 19 – Addition and substitution of parties
		PD 19B – Group litigation
20	COUNTERCLAIMS AND OTHER ADDITIONAL CLAIMS	YES
	– all the rules on the various different types of 'Part 20 Claim'. Note the details as to layout in the Practice Direction.	PD 20 – Counterclaims and other Part 20 claims
21	CHILDREN AND PATIENTS	YES
	– the special rules where either the claimant or defendant is a child (ie is under 18) or a 'patient' (see r 21.1(2)(b)). Note the requirement for a 'litigation friend' (r 21.2).	PD 21 – Children and patients
22	STATEMENTS OF TRUTH	YES
	– the important requirement for documents (ie those listed in r 22.1(1)) to be verified by a statement of truth. The relevant form of words is in the Practice Direction.	PD 22 – Statements of truth
23	GENERAL RULES ABOUT APPLICATIONS FOR COURT ORDERS	YES – Two
	– all applications for court orders in the course of proceedings are governed by Part 23.	PD 23 – Applications
		PD23B – Pilot Scheme for Telephone Hearings
24	SUMMARY JUDGMENT	YES
	– the procedure whereby either claimant or defendant may be able to apply to the court for a summary judgment, thus avoiding further expense and delay.	PD 24 – The summary disposal of claims

PART	TITLE	SUPPLEMENTING PRACTICE DIRECTION
25	INTERIM REMEDIES AND SECURITY FOR COSTS – the various orders for interim remedies including inspection of property before commencement or against a non–party, preservation of property, interim payments and interim injunctions, (including 'freezing orders' and 'search orders'). Rule 25.12 et seq deals with security for costs.	YES – Two PD 25 – Interim injunctions PD 25B – Interim payments
26	CASE MANAGEMENT – PRELIMINARY STAGE – the scope of each track is defined (r 26.6) and provisions made for allocation to the relevant track. 'Disposals' are dealt with in PD 26, para 12.8.	YES – Two PD 26 – Case Management – Preliminary Stage: Allocation and Re-allocation PD26B – Pilot Schemes for Mediation in Central London County Court
27	THE SMALL CLAIMS TRACK – the special rules applicable only to cases allocated to the small claims track.	YES PD 27 – Small Claims Track
28	THE FAST TRACK – the special rules applicable only to cases allocated in the fast track.	YES PD 28 – The Fast Track
29	THE MULTI–TRACK – provisions for cases allocated to the multi-track. Note r 29.3: case management conference and pre-trial review.	YES PD 29 – The Multi-track
30	TRANSFER – provisions for transfer from county court to High Court, within the High Court and between county courts (CCA 1984, s 40 deals with transfer from High Court to county court).	YES PD 30 – Transfer

PART	TITLE	SUPPLEMENTING PRACTICE DIRECTION
31	DISCLOSURE AND INSPECTION OF DOCUMENTS – all cases have some documents to be disclosed and inspected. Part 31 is one of the longer Parts of the CPR. Note 'standard disclosure' (r 31.6). See Annex to PD 31 for the 'Disclosure Statement'.	YES PD 31 – Disclosure and Inspection
32	EVIDENCE – important procedural rules on evidence including provisions for witness statements and the requirement to serve them (r 32.4).	YES PD 32 – Written evidence
33	MISCELLANEOUS RULES ABOUT EVIDENCE – various evidential rules, including hearsay notices and provisions for use of plans, photographs and models.	YES PD 33 – Civil Evidence Act 1995
34	DEPOSITIONS AND COURT ATTENDANCE BY WITNESSES – rarely used provisions for evidence on deposition, and frequently used provisions for witness summonses.	YES – Two PD 34 – Depositions and Court Attendance by Witnesses PD 34B – Fees for examiners of the Court
35	EXPERTS AND ASSESSORS – a very important code for obtaining and relying on expert evidence. See PD 35 for the form and content of experts reports. See also the 'Code' published by authority of the Master of the Rolls and Head of Civil Justice.	YES – One PD and one Code PD 35 – Experts and assessors Code of guidance on expert evidence
36	OFFERS TO SETTLE AND PAYMENTS INTO COURT – every party to a civil case should consider an offer to settle and/or making a payment into court. Note the costs consequences.	YES PD 36 – Offers to settle and payments into Court

PART	TITLE	SUPPLEMENTING PRACTICE DIRECTION
37	MISCELLANEOUS PROVISIONS ABOUT PAYMENTS INTO COURT – supplements Part 36 but also covers other situations such as defence of tender or payment into court under various enactments.	YES PD 37 – Miscellaneous provisions about payments into Court
38	DISCONTINUANCE – provisions for a claimant to discontinue all or part of a claim and the costs consequences of doing so.	NO
39	MISCELLANEOUS PROVISIONS RELATING TO HEARINGS – an unhelpfully titled Part which contains some very important rules on trials, including provisions for public hearings, trial timetables and trial bundles.	YES – Three PD 39 – Miscellaneous provisions relating to hearings PD 39B – Court Sittings PD 39C – Claims under the Race Relations Act 1976 (National Security)
40	JUDGMENTS, ORDERS, SALE OF LAND ETC in three parts dealing with: Judgments and orders – including drawing up and service. Note r 40.6: consent judgments and orders; and r 40.12: the 'slip rule'. Sale of land etc and conveyancing counsel. Declaratory judgments.	YES – Four PD 40 – Accounts, Inquiries etc PD 40B – Judgments and orders PD 40C – Structured settlements PD 40D – Court's powers in relation to land; Conveyancing counsel of the Court
41	PROVISIONAL DAMAGES – special rules for personal injury claims where provisional damages are sought.	YES PD 41 – Provisional damages
42	CHANGE OF SOLICITOR – includes the rule that a solicitor is considered to be acting until this Part has been compiled with (r 42.1) and the duty to give notice of change of solicitor (r 42.2).	YES PD 42 – Change of Solicitor

PART	TITLE	SUPPLEMENTING PRACTICE DIRECTION
43	SCOPE OF COST RULES AND DEFINITIONS – the basic costs definitions (see r 43.2) including summary and detailed assessment.	YES There is one Practice Direction which supplements Parts 43 to 48. It is the longest, most detailed and most complicated Practice Direction of all (Sections 1 to 6 of the Practice Direction supplement Part 43)
44	GENERAL RULES ABOUT COSTS – a long Part containing general rules about costs and entitlement to costs. Definitions in Part 43 are relevant to this Part.	YES – see Part 43 (Sections 7 to 23 of the Practice Direction supplement Part 44)
45	FIXED COSTS – sets out the amounts to be allowed as costs in various circumstances.	YES – see Part 43 (Sections 24 and 25 of the Practice Direction supplement Part 45)
46	FAST TRACK TRIAL COSTS – sets out the fixed costs in fast track cases but currently limited to trial costs only. There is no discretion to vary (save where a 'funding arrangement' applies).	YES – See Part 43 (Sections 26 and 27 of the Practice Direction supplement Part 46)
47	PROCEDURE FOR DETAILED ASSESSMENT OF COSTS AND DEFAULT PROVISIONS – a long Part in eight sections: (I) General rules about detailed assessments. (II) Costs payable by one party to another – commencement of detailed assessment proceedings. (III) Costs payable by one party to another – default provisions. (IV) Costs payable by one party to another – procedure where points of dispute are served. (V) Interim costs certificate and final costs certificate. (VI) Detailed assessment procedure for costs of a LSC funded client or an assisted	YES – see Part 43 (Sections 28 to 49 of the Practice Direction supplement Part 47)

PART	TITLE	SUPPLEMENTING PRACTICE DIRECTION
	person where costs are payable out of the Community Legal Service Fund. (VII) Costs of detailed assessment proceedings. (VIII) Appeals in detailed assessment proceedings.	
48	COSTS – SPECIAL CASES – costs payable by or to particular persons (including pre-commencement disclosure, non-parties, children and patients and litigants in person), and costs relating to solicitors and other legal representatives.	YES – Three See Part 43 (Sections 50 to 57 and the schedule supplement Part 48). PD 48B – Family Division PD Costs Pilot – Pilot Scheme for detailed assessment by the Supreme Court Costs Office of costs of civil proceedings in London county courts.
49	SPECIALIST PROCEEDINGS – special rules applicable now only to proceedings under the Companies Act 1985 and 1989.	YES PD 49 – Applications under the Companies Act 1985, and other legislation relating to companies.
50	APPLICATION OF THE SCHEDULES – the task of updating the old rules is not complete. CPR, Sch 1 retains the former RSC and CPR, Sch 2 the former CCR not yet updated and incorporated in the main body of the CPR.	NO
51	TRANSITIONAL ARRANGEMENTS AND PILOT SCHEMES – the transitional arrangements should no longer be relevant (save possibly para 19 of PD 51). As yet there is no Practice Direction authorising pilot schemes to test new practices and procedures.	YES PD 51 – Transitional Arrangements

PART	TITLE	SUPPLEMENTING PRACTICE DIRECTION
52	APPEALS – all relevant rules on appeals both final and interlocutory from all levels of judge in the county court, High Court and Court of Appeal (for appeals to the House of Lords, see the Practice Directions and Standing Orders applicable to civil appeals in the White Book, Vol 2, Section 4A).	YES PD 52 – Appeals (see centre column for House of Lords appeals).
53	DEFAMATION CLAIMS – rules about defamation claims including summary disposal under the Defamation Act 1996.	YES PD 53 – Defamation Claims
54	JUDICIAL REVIEW – all rules in claims for a judicial review as defined in r 54.1(2). The High Court has exclusive jurisdiction.	YES PD 54 – Judicial Review
55	POSSESSION CLAIMS possession claims must generally be in the county court (r 55.3). All types of possession claim – against trespassers, tenants, and mortgagors – are dealt with in this Part. In the defined limited circumstances, the accelerated possession procedure enables the court to make the order without a court hearing.	YES PD 55 – Possession Claims
56	LANDLORD AND TENANT CLAIMS AND MISCELLANEOUS PROVISIONS ABOUT LAND – applies only to 'landlord and tenant' claims as defined in r 56.1 (for possession claims, see Part 55) and various statutes listed in r 56.4.	YES PD 56 – Landlord and Tenant Claims and Miscellaneous Provisions about Land
57	PROBATE CLAIMS. RECTIFICATION OF WILLS. SUBSTITUTION AND REMOVAL OF PERSONAL REPRESENTATIVES – the title gives a clear indication of the scope of this Part.	YES PD 57 – Probate

PART	TITLE	SUPPLEMENTING PRACTICE DIRECTION
58	**COMMERCIAL COURT** – the 'Commercial Court' is part of the Queen's Bench Division and is for commercial cases in London. Part 58 modifies many general rules of the CPR.	YES PD 58 – Commercial Court
59	**MERCANTILE COURTS** – 'mercantile court' means a specialist list within the District Registries of Birmingham, Bristol, Cardiff, Chester, Leeds, Liverpool, Manchester and Newcastle and the Central London County Court (for cases which in the RCJ would be in the 'Commercial Court'). Part 59 modifies many general rules of the CPR.	YES PD 59 – Mercantile Courts
60	**TECHNOLOGY AND CONSTRUCTION COURT CLAIMS** – a Technology and Construction Court (TCC) claim includes issues or questions which are technically complex and are tried by specially nominated TCC judges (see PD 60). Such claims can be made in the High Court in London or in a District Registry or in the county courts listed in PD 60. Part 60 modifies general rules of the CPR, for example, all applications must be to a TCC judge.	YES PD 60 – Technology and Construction Court Claims
61	**ADMIRALTY CLAIMS** – an 'admiralty claim' means a claim within the Admiralty jurisdiction of the High Court. The 'Admiralty Court' is part of the Queen's Bench Division. See further r 61.1. Part 61 contains many special rules, eg r 61.3 'claims in rem'; r 61.4 'collision claims'; r 61.5 'arrest'.	YES PD 61 – Admiralty Claims
62	**ARBITRATION CLAIMS** – special rules about the Arbitration Acts 1950 to 1996.	YES PD 62 – Arbitration

PART	TITLE	SUPPLEMENTING PRACTICE DIRECTION
63	PATENTS AND OTHER INTELLECTUAL PROPERTY CLAIMS – specialist rules governing all disputes about intellectual property in the High Court and the Patents County Court. See also the Patents Court Guide.	YES Practice Direction – Patents and other intellectual property claims
64	ESTATES, TRUSTS AND CHARITIES – deals with claims relating to the administration of estates and trusts; and 'charity proceedings' under the Charities Act 1993.	YES PD 64 – Estates, Trusts and Charities PD 64B – Applications to the court for directions by trustees in relation to the administration of the trust
65	PROCEEDINGS RELATING TO ANTI-SOCIAL BEHAVIOUR AND HARASSMENT – rules governing applications for injunctions under the Housing Act 1996 and for powers of arrest: demotion claims and proceedings relating to demoted tenancies; anti-social behaviour orders under the Crime and Disorder Act 1998 and proceedings under the Protection from Harassment Act 1997.	YES PD 65 – Anti-Social Behaviour and Harassment
66	CROWN PROCEEDINGS – not yet made but imminent to replace CPR Sch 1 RSC Ord 77 and Sch 2 CCR and 42.	Not yet
67	PROCEEDINGS RELATING TO SOLICITORS Rules concerning powers under Solicitors Act 1974, Part III (remuneration of solicitors) and Sch I (intervention in a solicitor's practice).	YES PD 67 – Proceedings relating to solicitors
68	REFERENCES TO THE EUROPEAN COURT – sets out the procedure for courts to seek preliminary rulings from the Court of Justice of the	YES PD 68 – Reference to the European Court

PART	TITLE	SUPPLEMENTING PRACTICE DIRECTION
	European Communities.	
69	**COURT'S POWER TO APPOINT A RECEIVER** – sets out the court's power to appoint a receiver before proceedings have started, in existing proceedings and on or after judgment (including for enforcement purposes).	YES PD 69 – Court's power to appoint a receiver
70	**GENERAL RULES ABOUT ENFORCEMENT OF JUDGMENTS AND ORDERS** – the title is clear enough. The Practice Direction which supplements this Part is particularly well drafted and informative.	YES PD 70 – Enforcement of Judgments and Orders for the Payment of Money
71	**ORDERS TO OBTAIN INFORMATION FROM JUDGMENT DEBTORS** – consider an application under this Part before issuing enforcement proceedings.	YES PD 71 – Orders to Obtain Information from Judgment Debtors
72	**THIRD PARTY DEBT ORDERS** – the procedure to make a creditor of the judgment debtor pay the judgment creditor instead.	YES PD 72 – Third Party Debt Orders
73	**CHARGING ORDERS, STOP ORDERS AND STOP NOTICES** – charging orders are very common. Stop orders and notices are rarely used. A charging order on the judgment debtor's interest in land gives the judgment creditor security for the judgment debt.	YES PD 73 – Charging Orders, Stop Orders and Stop Notices

PART	TITLE	SUPPLEMENTING PRACTICE DIRECTION
74	ENFORCEMENT OF JUDGMENTS IN DIFFERENT JURISDICTIONS This Part deals with: 1. Enforcement in England and Wales of judgments of foreign courts. 2. Enforcement in foreign countries of judgments of the High Court and county courts. 3. Enforcement of United Kingdom judgments in other parts of the United Kingdom. 4. Enforcement in England and Wales of European Community judgments.	YES PD 74 – Enforcement of Judgments in different jurisdictions
75	TRAFFIC ENFORCEMENT – applies where traffic penalties are recoverable through the civil courts.	YES PD 75 – Traffic Enforcement
76	PREVENTION OF TERRORISM ACT 2005 – inserted to give effect to this Act. Of particular note is the role of 'special advocates'.	NO
	SCHEDULE 1 – RSC ORDERS	
RSC Ord 17	INTERPLEADER – still important. Covers both stakeholders' interpleader and interpleader under execution. A procedure whereby a person from whom two or more others claim property which he does not claim for himself. That person protects himself by requiring the rival claimants to interplead.	NO
RSC Ord 45	ENFORCEMENT OF JUDGMENTS AND ORDERS: GENERAL – to be read in conjunction with CPR Part 70.	NO

PART	TITLE	SUPPLEMENTING PRACTICE DIRECTION
RSC Ord 46	WRITS OF EXECUTION: GENERAL – an order of huge practical significance given that the most popular method of execution (ie enforcing a judgment) is the writ of *fieri facias*.	YES PD – Execution
RSC Ord 47	WRITS OF *FIERI FACIAS* – the order consists of the special rules applicable to the most popular method of execution. Note the 'Sheriff's Lodgment Centre', use of which makes it much simpler to issue the writ. Ord 47 is to be read with Ords 45 and 46.	NO
RSC Ord 52	COMMITTAL – a very important Order, widely used in practice, to enforce orders in the nature of injunctions. It requires careful study as – unusually in civil cases – the standard of proof required is 'beyond reasonable doubt' and not the usual civil standard of the 'balance of probabilities'.	YES PD – Committal Applications
RSC Ord 54	APPLICATIONS FOR WRIT OF HABEAS CORPUS – the ancient common law remedy principally used to test the validity of the commitment of a prisoner is still governed by the old Order.	YES PD – Application for Writ of Habeas Corpus
RSC Ord 64	SITTINGS, VACATIONS AND OFFICE HOURS – only r 4 survives. It deals with Divisional Court business during vacation.	NO

PART	TITLE	SUPPLEMENTING PRACTICE DIRECTION
RSC Ord 77	PROCEEDINGS BY AND AGAINST THE CROWN – these days 'the Crown' usually means a Government Department. As proceedings by and against such are common, this Order is still of importance and gives procedural effect to the Crown Proceedings Act 1947. This rule is due to be replaced by a new Part 66.	NO
RSC Ord 79	ESTREAT OF RECOGNIZANCES – only rr 8 and 9 remain and are limited to the exercise of the High Court's jurisdiction in relation to estreat of recognizances on failure to answer bail.	NO
RSC Ord 81	PARTNERS – rules governing proceedings by and against partners in the firm name. As such cases are common, these rules are important in practice.	NO
RSC Ord 93	APPLICATIONS AND APPEALS TO THE HIGH COURT UNDER VARIOUS ACTS: CHANCERY DIVISION – rules dealing with diverse statutes making provision for applications and appeals to the High Court which have to be in the Chancery Division.	NO
RSC Ord 94	APPLICATIONS AND APPEALS TO THE HIGH COURT UNDER VARIOUS ACTS: QUEEN'S BENCH DIVISION – rules dealing with diverse statutes making provision for applications and appeals to the High Court which have to be in the Queen's Bench Division.	NO

PART	TITLE	SUPPLEMENTING PRACTICE DIRECTION
RSC Ord 95	THE BILLS OF SALES ACTS 1878 AND 1882 AND THE INDUSTRIAL AND PROVIDENT SOCIETIES ACT 1967 – the most common form of bill of sale is a written instrument whereby the vendor of goods transfers possession but retains title. The purchaser thus appears to own goods which in reality belong to another. To protect third parties, the legislation and rules required such instruments to be in proper form and to be registered.	YES PD – Bills of Sale
RSC Ord 96	THE MINES (WORKING FACILITIES AND SUPPORT) ACT 1966 ETC – any proceedings under this order must be begun under CPR Part 8 in the Chancery Division.	NO
RSC Ord 109	ADMINISTRATION OF JUSTICE ACT 1960 – see, in particular, r 2 which governs appeals (by either applicant or respondent) in committal proceedings under AJA 1960, s 13.	NO
RSC Ord 110	ENVIRONMENTAL CONTROL PROCEEDINGS – rule 1 governs injunctions to prevent environmental harm.	NO
RSC Ord 112	APPLICATIONS FOR USE OF SCIENTIFIC TESTS IN DETERMINING PARENTAGE – see also CCR Ord 47, Sch 2. Provisions for 'bodily samples' (as opposed merely to 'blood tests') in the Family Law Reform Act 1987 were brought into force in 2001.	YES See Practice Note [1972] 1 WLR 353 and note also the Blood Tests (Evidence of Paternity) Regulations 1971 as amended by the Blood Tests (Evidence of Paternity) (Amendment) Regulations 2001 (S1 1976/ 1861 as amended)

PART	TITLE	SUPPLEMENTING PRACTICE DIRECTION
RSC Ord 113	SUMMARY PROCEEDINGS FOR POSSESSION OF LAND – see generally CPR Part 55. In RSC Ord 113, only r 7 – writ of possession – survives.	NO
RSC Ord 115	CONFISCATION AND FORFEITURE IN CONNECTION WITH CRIMINAL PROCEEDINGS – rules under the Drug Trafficking Act 1994, the Criminal Justice (International Co-operation) Act 1990, Criminal Justice Act 1988, Part VI, and the Terrorism Act 2000.	YES PD – Restraint Orders and Appointment of Receivers in connection with criminal proceedings and investigations
RSC Ord 116	CRIMINAL PROCEDURE AND INVESTIGATIONS ACT 1996 – detailed rules under Criminal Procedure and Investigations Act 1996, s 54.	NO
	SCHEDULE 2 – CCR ORDERS	
CCR Ord 1	CITATION, APPLICATION AND INTERPRETATION – only r 6 survives but it is important: 'where … any provision of the RSC is applied … in a county court, that provision shall have effect with the necessary modifications …'. See also CCA 1984, s 76.	NO
CCR Ord 5	CAUSES OF ACTION AND PARTIES – r 9 provides that partners may sue and be sued in Firm name and r 10 provides for a defendant carrying on business in a name other than his own.	NO
CCR Ord 16	TRANSFER OF PROCEEDINGS – only r 7 – interpleader proceedings under execution – survives.	NO

PART	TITLE	SUPPLEMENTING PRACTICE DIRECTION
CCR Ord 22	JUDGMENTS AND ORDERS – r 8: certificate of judgment; r 10: variation of payment; r 11: set-off of cross-judgments; and r 13: order of appellate court are the only four surviving but still important rules. Certificates are frequently required for enforcement purposes. Variation of orders are commonly sought both by judgment creditors and judgment debtors.	YES *Practice Direction (County Court Order: Enforcement)* [1991] 1 WLR 695 (replacing QB Masters PD No 32)
CCR Ord 24	SUMMARY PROCEEDINGS FOR RECOVERY OF LAND – r 6 deals with warrants of possession.	NO
CCR Ord 25	ENFORCEMENT OF JUDGMENTS AND ORDERS: GENERAL – to be read in conjunction with CPR Part 70 and PD 70.	NO
CCR Ord 26	WARRANTS OF EXECUTION, DELIVERY AND POSSESSION – very important provisions relating to the most common methods of enforcement.	NO
CCR Ord 27	ATTACHMENT OF EARNINGS – very important rules giving effect to the Attachment of Earnings Act 1971.	NO
CCR Ord 28	JUDGMENT SUMMONSES – important rules relating to imprisonment for debt recently amended to ensure compatibility with the ECHR.	YES PD – Committals
CCR Ord 29	COMMITTAL FOR BREACH OF ORDER AND UNDERTAKING – very important rules dealing with committal for breach of county court injunctions and undertakings.	YES PD – Committals

PART	TITLE	SUPPLEMENTING PRACTICE DIRECTION
CCR Ord 33	INTERPLEADER PROCEEDINGS – county court rules equivalent to RSC Ord 17.	NO
CCR Ord 34	PENAL AND DISCIPLINARY PROVISIONS – the procedural rules regarding the penal provisions in the CCA 1984, sections 14, 55, 92 and 124.	NO
CCR Ord 39	ADMINISTRATION ORDERS – an alternative to bankruptcy for judgment debtors owing not more than £5,000.	NO
CCR Ord 42	PROCEEDINGS BY AND AGAINST THE CROWN – these days 'The Crown' usually means a government department. As proceedings by and against such are common, this order is still of importance and gives procedural effect to the Crown Proceedings Act 1947. In High Court cases, see RSC Ord 77, Sch 1. It is about to be replaced by a new Part 66.	NO
CCR Ord 44	THE AGRICULTURAL HOLDINGS ACT 1986 – the Agricultural Holdings Act 1986 applies only to farm business tenancies created before 1 September 1995.	NO
CCR Ord 45	THE REPRESENTATION OF THE PEOPLE ACT 1983 – rules governing accounts and appeals under this Act.	NO
CCR Ord 46	THE LEGITIMACY ACT 1976 – obsolete rules (see instead the Family Proceedings Rules 1991) which ought to be repealed.	NO

PART	TITLE	SUPPLEMENTING PRACTICE DIRECTION
CCR Ord 47	DOMESTIC AND MATRIMONIAL PROCEEDINGS	NO
	– only r 5 survives and was amended in 2001 when the Family Law Reform Act 1987 amendments (substituting 'bodily samples' for 'blood tests') were brought into force.	
CCR Ord 49	MISCELLANEOUS STATUTES	NO
	Many statutes formerly within these rules now have a Part in the main CPR. The remaining rules concern injunctions to prevent environmental harm under the Town and Country Planning Act 1990 etc, and various proceedings under the Mental Health Act 1983, Postal Services Act 2000, Sex Discrimination Act 1975, Race Relations Act 1976, Disability Discrimination Act 1995, Disability Rights Commission Act 1999, Telecommunications Act 1984 and the Trade Union and Labour Relations (Consolidation) Act 1992.	

Appendix B

FORMS

Knowing which form to use is an essential element of the conduct of civil litigation. Accordingly, CPR PD 4 which lists all forms currently in use is set out here in its entirety. Bear in mind that by CPR r 4(2) a form may be varied by a party if the variation is required by the circumstances of a particular case. Thus, you are free to alter the wording or appearance of a particular form but only if it is necessary to do so. The mere fact that you think the alteration would be a sensible improvement is not enough. Moreover, nothing essential is to be omitted from a form (r 4(3)).

Unfortunately, you may be dismayed by the fact that these forms are listed in an order which may strike you as illogical. We share your dismay. It is a matter for regret that insufficient thought has been given to the order in which these forms are numbered. (For example, the prefix 'N' was introduced in 1981 when the former CCR 1981 came into force; presumably, the 'N' stood for 'New' and was inserted to distinguish the 1981 forms from their predecessors. To retain this prefix, rather than starting again with a straightforward and sensible numbering system, was misconceived.) It really is a question, therefore, of looking through PD 4 until you can ascertain the number of the form that you require.

Having ascertained the form number, where do you find the form itself? For obvious reasons of space they cannot be reproduced here. There are six main sources. First, many (but unfortunately not all) forms are available free of charge from your local county court office. Secondly, a large selection of relevant forms is available via the internet at the Court Service website, *www.hmcourts-service.gov.uk*. Forms can be accessed via the Brown Book and White Book online services. Both services also provide CD ROMS which contain a library of forms.. Finally, the White Book includes 'Civil Procedure Forms', which contains all the forms in an A4 ring-binder. The forms are designed to be easily removed and photocopied.

PRACTICE DIRECTIONS – FORMS

This Practice Direction supplements CPR Part 4 (PD4)

Scope of this practice direction:

1.1 This practice directions lists the forms to be used in civil proceedings on or after 26 April 1999, when the Civil Procedure Rules (CPR) come into force.

1.2 The forms may be modified as the circumstances require, provided that all essential information, especially information or guidance which the form gives to the recipient, is included.

1.3 This practice direction contains 3 tables –

- Table 1 lists forms required by CPR Parts 1–75

- Table 2 lists High Court forms in use before 26 April 1999 which have remained in use on or after that date (see paragraph 4 below)

- Table 3 lists county court forms in use before 26 April 1999 that will remain in use on or after that date (see paragraph 5 below)

1.4 Former prescribed forms are shown as 'No 00'. The former practice forms where they are appropriate for use in either the Chancery or Queen's Bench Division (or where no specific form is available for use in the county court, in that court also) are prefixed 'PF' followed by the number. Where the form is used mainly in the Chancery or Queen's Bench Division, the suffix CH or QB follows the form number.

Other forms:

2.1 Other forms may be authorised by practice directions. For example the forms relating to Part 61 Admiralty claims are authorised by, and annexed to, the Admiralty Claims practice direction.

TABLE 1

'N' FORMS

Contents:

3.1 This table lists the forms that are referred to and required by Rules or practice directions supplementing particular Parts of the CPR. A practice direction and its paragraphs are abbreviated by reference to the Part of the CPR which it supplements and the relevant paragraph of the practice direction, for example PD 34 1.2. For ease of reference, forms required for claims in the Commercial Court, Technology and Construction Court and for Admiralty claims and Arbitration claims, are separately listed.

Table 1	
No	**Title**
N1	Part 7 (general) claim form (PD 7 3.1)

Table 1

No	Title
N1A	Notes for claimant
N1C	Notes for defendant
N1(FD)	Notes for defendant (Consumer Credit Act cases)
N2	Claim form (probate claim) (PD 57 2.1)
N2A	Claimant's notes for guidance (probate claim)
N2B	Defendant's notes for guidance (probate claim)
N3	Acknowledgment of service (probate claim) (Rule 57.4(1))
N5	Claim form for possession of property (PD 55 1.5)
N5A	Claim form for relief against forfeiture (PD 55 1.5)
N5B	Claim form for possession of property (accelerated procedure) (assured shorthold tenancy) (PD 55 1.5)
N5C	Notes for the claimant (accelerated possession procedure)
N6	Claim form for demotion of tenancy (PD65, 5.2)
N7	Notes for defendant (mortgaged residential premises)
N7A	Notes for defendant (rented residential premises)
N7B	Notes for defendant – forfeiture of the lease (residential premises)
N7D	Notes for defendant – demotion claim
N9	Acknowledgment of service/response pack (PD 10.2)
N9A	Admission and statement of means (specified amount) (PD 14 2.1)
N9B	Defence and counterclaim (specified amount) (PD 15 1.3)
N9C	Admission and statement of means (unspecified amount and non money claims) (PD 14 2.1)
N9D	Defence and counterclaim (unspecified amount and non money claims) (PD 15 1.3)
N10	Notice that acknowledgment of service has been filed – Rule 10.4
N11	Defence form (PD 55 1.5)

Table 1

No	Title
N11B	Defence form (accelerated possession procedure) (assured shorthold tenancy) (PD 55 1.5)
N11D	Defence form (demotion of tenancy) (PD65, 5.2)
N11M	Defence form (mortgaged residential premises) (PD 55 1.5)
N11R	Defence form (rented residential premises) (PD 55 1.5)
N16	General form of injunction
N16(1)	General form of injunction (formal parts only)
N16(A)	General form of application for injunction
N17	Judgment for claimant (amount to be decided by court)
N19	Limited civil restraint order
N19A	Extended civil restraint order
N19B	General civil restraint order
N20	Witness summons (PD 34 1.2)
N21	Order for Examination of Deponent before the hearing (PD 34 4.1)
N24	Blank form of order or judgment
N26	Order for possession
N26A	Order for possession (accelerated possession procedure) (assured shorthold tenancy)
N27	Order for possession on forfeiture (for rent arrears)
N27(2)	Order for possession on forfeiture (for rent arrears) (suspended)
N28	Order for possession (rented premises) (suspended)
N30	Judgment for claimant (default HC)
N30	Judgment for claimant (default CC)
N30(1)	Judgment for claimant (acceptance HC)
N30(1)	Judgment for claimant (acceptance CC)

Table 1

No	Title
N30(2)	Judgment for claimant (after determination HC)
N30(2)	Judgment for claimant (after determination CC)
N30(3)	Judgment for claimant (after re-determination HC)
N30(3)	Judgment for claimant (after re-determination CC)
N31	Order for possession (mortgaged premises) (suspended)
N32	Judgment for return of goods
N32(1) HP/CCA	Judgment for delivery of goods
N32(2) HP/CCA	Judgment for delivery of goods (suspended)
N32(3) HP/CCA	Judgment for delivery of goods
N32(4)	Variation order (return of goods)
N32(5) HP/CCA	Order for balance of purchase price
N33	Judgment for delivery of goods
N34	Judgment for claimant (after amount decided by court HC)
N34	Judgment for claimant (after amount decided by court CC)
N37	Hardship Payment Order
N39	Order to attend court for questioning
N40A (cc)	Warrant of arrest
N40B (cc)	Warrant of committal
N40A (HC)	Warrant of arrest
N40B (HC)	Warrant of committal
N54	Notice of eviction
N79A	Suspended committal order (for disobedience)
N84	Interim Third Party debt order

Table 1

No	Title
N85	Final Third Party debt order
N86	Interim Charging order
N87	Final Charging order
N110A	Anti-social behaviour injunction – power of arrest sections 153C and 153D of the Housing Act 1996
N113	Anti-social behaviour (Order under section 1B(4) of the Crime and Disorder Act 1998)
N119	Particulars of claim for possession (rented residential premises) (PD 55 2.1)
N119A	Notes for guidance on completing particulars of claim form (rented residential premises)
N120	Particulars of claim for possession (mortgaged residential premises) (PD 55 2.1)
N121	Particulars of claim for possession (trespassers) (PD 55 2.1)
N122	Particulars of claim for demotion of tenancy (PD65, 5.2)
N130	Application for an interim possession order
N133	Witness statement of the defendant to oppose the making of an interim possession order
N134	Interim possession order
N136	Order for possession
N142	Guardianship order (Housing Act 1996, Mental Health Act 1983)
N143	Interim Hospital order (Housing Act 1996, Mental Health Act 1983)
N144	Recognizance of defendant (Housing Act 1996)
N145	Recognizance of surety (Housing Act 1996)
N146	Warrant of arrest (Housing Act 1996)
N147	Remand order (Housing Act 1996) (bail granted)
N148	Remand order (Housing Act 1996) (bail not granted)

Table 1

No	Title
N150	Allocation Questionnaire (PD 26 2.1)
N150A	Master/DJ's directions on allocation
N151	Allocation Questionnaire (amount to be decided by court)
N151A	Master/DJ's directions on allocation
N152	Notice that [defence][counterclaim] has been filed (PD 26 2.5)
N153	Notice of allocation or listing hearing (PD 26 6.2)
N154	Notice of allocation to fast track (PD 26 4.2 and 9)
N155	Notice of allocation to multi track (PD 26 4.2 and 10)
N156	Order for further information (for allocation) (PD 26 4.2(2))
N157	Notice of allocation to small claims track (PD 26 4.2 and 8)
N158	Notice of allocation to small claims track (preliminary hearing) (PD 26 4.2 and 8)
N159	Notice of allocation to small claims track (no hearing) (PD 26 4.2 and 8)
N160	Notice of allocation to small claims track (with parties consent) (PD 26 4.2 and 8)
N161	Appellant's Notice (PD 52 5.1)
N161A	Guidance notes on completing the appellant's notice
N161B	Important notes for respondents
N162	Respondent's Notice (PD 52 7.3)
N162A	Guidance notes for completing the respondent's notice
N163	Skeleton Argument (PD 52 5.9 and 7.10)
N170	Listing questionnaire (Pre-trial checklist) (PD 28 6.1)
N171	Notice of date for return of listing questionnaire (PD 26 6.1 and PD 28 8.1)
N172	Notice of trial date
N173	Notice of non-payment of fee (Rule 3.7)

Table 1

No	Title
N205A	Notice of issue (specified amount)
N205B	Notice of issue (unspecified amount)
N205C	Notice of issue (non-money claim)
N205D	Notice of issue (probate claim)
N206A	Notice of issue (accelerated possession procedure) (assured shorthold tenancy)
N206B	Notice of issue (possession claim)
N206D	Notice of issue (demotion claim)
N208	Part 8 claim form (PD 8 2.2)
N208A	Part 8 notes for claimant
N208C	Part 8 notes for defendant
N209	Part 8 notice of issue
N210	Part 8 acknowledgment of service (PD 8 3.2)
N210A	Part 8 acknowledgment of service (costs-claim only) (PD 43–48 17.9)
N211	Part 20 claim form (Rule 20.7)
N211A	Part 20 notes for claimant
N211C	Part 20 notes for defendant
N212	Part 20 notice of issue
N213	Part 20 acknowledgment of service (Rule 20.12)
N215	Certificate of service (Rule 6.10)
N216	Notice of non-service (Rule 6.11)
N217	Order for substituted service (Rule 6.8)
N218	Notice of service on a partner (PD 6 4.2)
N225	Request for judgment and reply to admission (specified amount) (PD 12 3)

Table 1

No	Title
N225A	Notice of part admission (specified amount) (Rule 14.5)
N226	Notice of admission (unspecified amount) (Rule 14.7)
N227	Request for judgment by default (amount to be decided by the court) (Rule 12.5)
N228	Notice of admission (return of goods) (PD 7 Consumer Credit Act 8.5)
N235	Certificate of suitability of litigation friend (PD 21 2.3)
N236	Notice of defence that amount claimed has been paid (Rule 15.10)
N242	Notice of payment into court (under order – Part 37)
N242A	Notice of acceptance and request for payment (Part 36)
N243A	Notice of acceptance of payment into court (PD 36 7.7)
N244	Application notice (PD 23 2.1)
N244A	Notice of hearing of application (PD 23 2.2)
N251	Notice of funding of case or claim
N252	Notice of commencement of assessment (PD 47 2.3)
N253	Notice of amount allowed on provisional assessment (PD 47 6.5)
N254	Request for default costs certificate (PD 47 3.1)
N255	Default costs certificate HC (PD 47 3.3)
N255	Default costs certificate CC (PD 47 3.3)
N256	Final costs certificate HC (PD 47 5.11)
N256	Final costs certificate CC (PD 47 5.11)
N257	Interim costs certificate (PD 47 5.11)
N258	Request for detailed assessment hearing (non-legal aid) (PD 47 4.3)
N258A	Request for detailed assessment hearing (legal aid only)
N258B	Request for detailed assessment (Costs payable out of a fund other than the Community Legal Service Fund)

Table 1

No	Title
N258C	Request for detailed assessment hearing pursuant to an order under Part III of the Solicitors Act 1974
N259	Notice of Appeal (PD 47 48.1)
N260	Statement of costs
N260	Statement of costs (summary assessment) (PD 43 3.2)
N265	List of documents (PD 31 3.1)
N266	Notice to admit facts/admission of facts (Rule 32.18)
N268	Notice to prove documents at trial (Rule 32.19)
N271	Notice of transfer of proceedings (Rule 30)
N279	Notice of discontinuance (Rule 38.3)
N292	Order on settlement on behalf of child or patient (PD 21 11.3)
N294	Claimant's application for a variation order
N316	Application for order that debtor attend court for questioning (PD 71 1.1)
N316A	Application that an officer of a company attend court for questioning (PD 71 1.1)
N322	Order for recovery of an award
N322A	Application to enforce an award (PD 70 4.1)
N322H	Request to register a High Court judgment or order for enforcement
N349	Application for third party debt order (PD 72 1.1)
N367	Notice of hearing to consider why fine should not be imposed (Rule 34.10)
N379	Application for charging order on land or property (PD 73 1.1)
N380	Application for charging order on securities (PD 73 1.1)
N434	Notice of change of solicitor (Rule 42.2)
N446	Request for re-issue of enforcement or an order to obtain information from judgment debtor (not warrant)

Table 1

No	Title
N460	Reasons for allowing or refusing permission to appeal
N461	Judicial Review claim form (Pt 54 PD)
N461 (notes)	Guidance notes on completing the Judicial Review claim form
N462	Judicial Review acknowledgment of service (Pt 54 PD)
N463	Judicial Review – application for urgent consideration
No 32	Order for examination within jurisdiction of witness before trial (Rule 34.8)
No 33	Application for issue of letter of request to judicial authority out of jurisdiction (Rule 34.13)
No 34	Order for issue of letter of request to judicial authority out of jurisdiction (Rule 34.13)
No 35	Letter of request for examination of witness out of jurisdiction (Rule 34.13)
No 37	Order for appointment of examiner to take evidence of witness out of jurisdiction (Rule 34.13(4))
No 41	Default judgment in claim relating to detention of goods (Rule 12.4(1)(c))
No 44	Part 24 Judgment for claimant
No 44A	Part 24 Judgment for defendant
No 45	Judgment after trial before judge without jury (PD 40B 14)
No 46	Judgment after trial before judge with jury (PD 40B 14)
No 47	Judgment after trial before a judge of the Technology & Construction Court or a master or district judge (PD 40B 14)
No 48	Order after trial of issue directed to be tried under rule 3.1(2)(i)
No 49	Judgment against personal representatives (PD 40B 14.3)
No 52	Notice of claim (CPR 19.8A(4)(a))
No 52A	Notice of judgment or order to an interested party
No 82	Application for appointment of a receiver

Table 1

No	Title
No 83	Order directing application for appointment of receiver and granting injunction meanwhile
No 84	Order for appointment of receiver by way of equitable execution (S 37 of Supreme Court Act 1981)
No 93	Order under the Evidence (Proceedings in Other Jurisdictions) Act 1975
No 94	Order for production of documents in marine insurance action (PD 49 7)
No 109	Order for reference to the European Court
No 111	Certificate of money provisions contained in a judgment for registration in another part of the United Kingdom (Schedule 6 to the Civil Jurisdiction and Judgments Act 1982)
No112	Certificate issued under Schedule 7 to the Civil Jurisdiction and Judgments Act 1982 in respect of non-money provisions for registration in another part of the United Kingdom
PF 1	Application for time (Rule 3.1(2)(a))
PF 2	Order for time (Rule 3.1(2)(a))
PF 3	Application for an extension of time for serving a claim form (Rule 7.6)
PF 4	Order for an extension of time for serving a claim form (Rule 7.6)
PF 6(A)	Application for permission to serve claim form out of jurisdiction (Rule 6.21)
PF 6(B)	Order for service out of the jurisdiction (Rule 6.21(4))
PF 7 QB	Request for service of document abroad (Rules 6.26(2)(a) and 6.27(2)(a))
PF 8	Standard 'unless' order (Rule 26.5(5), Part 26 PD para 2.5 and N150A)
PF 11	Application for Part 24 judgment (whole claim) (Rule 24.2)
PF 12	Application for Part 24 judgment (one or some of several claims) (Rule 24.2)
PF 13	Order under Part 24 (No 1)

Table 1

No	Title
PF 14	Order under Part 24 (No 2)
PF 15	Order under Part 24 for amount found due upon detailed assessment of solicitor's bill of costs
PF 16	Notice of court's intention to make an order of its own initiative (Rule 3.3(2) and (3))
PF 17	Order made on court's own initiative without a hearing (Rule 3.3(4) and (5))
PF19	Group Litigation Order (Rule 19.1)
PF20	Application for Part 20 directions
PF21	Order for Part 20 directions
PF 21A	Order to add person as defendant to counterclaim (Rule 20.5)
PF22	Notice claiming contribution or indemnity against another defendant (Rule 20.6)
PF43	Application for security for costs (Rule 25.12, also Companies Act 1985 s 726)
PF44	Order for security for costs (Rule 25.12, also Companies Act 1985 s 726)
PF48	Court record available for use before and at hearing
PF49	Request to parties to state convenient dates for hearing of 1st CMC
PF50	Application for directions (Part 29)
PF52	Order for case management directions in the multi-track (Part 29)
PF53	Order for separate trial of an issue (Rule 3.1(2)(i))
PF 56	Request for further information or clarification with provision for response (PD 18 1.6(2))
PF 57	Application for further information or clarification (PD 18 5)
PF 58	Order for further information or clarification (Rule 18.1)
PF63	Interim order for receiver in pending claim

Table 1

No	Title
PF67	Evidence in support of application to make order of House of Lords an order of the High Court (PD 40B 13.2)
PF68	Order making an order of the House of Lords an order of the High Court (PD 40B 13.3)
PF72	List of exhibits handed in at Trial (PD 39 7)
PF74	Order for trial of whole claim or of an issue by Master or District Judge (PD2B 4.1)
PF78 QB	Solicitor's undertaking as to expenses (re letter of request) (Rule 34.13(6)(b) and PD 34 5.3(5))
PF83	Judgment (non attendance of party) (Rule 39.3)
PF84A	Order on application arising from a failure to comply with an order (Rule 3.1(3))
PF84B	Judgment on application arising from a failure to comply with an order (Rule 3.5(1) and (4))
PF85A	Request for judgment (Rule 3.5(2))
PF85B	Judgment on Request arising from a failure to comply with an order (Rule 3.5(2))
PF113	Evidence in support of application for service by an alternative method (PD 6 9.1)
PF130	Form of advertisement (Rule 6.8)
PF147	Application for order declaring solicitor ceased to act (death etc)
PF148	Order declaring solicitor has ceased to act
PF149	Application by solicitor that he has ceased to act
PF150	Order that solicitor has ceased to act
PF152QB	Evidence in support of application for examination of witness under the Evidence (Proceedings in Other Jurisdictions) Act 1975
PF153QB	Certificate witness under the Evidence (Proceedings in Other Jurisdictions) Act 1975
PF154QB	Order for registration of foreign judgment under the Foreign Judgments (Reciprocal Enforcement) Act 1933

Table 1

No	Title
PF155	Certificates under s 10 of the Foreign Judgments (Reciprocal Enforcement) Act 1933
PF156QB	Evidence in support of application for registration of a Community judgment
PF157QB	Order for registration of a Community judgment
PF158QB	Notice of registration of a Community judgment
PF159QB	Evidence in support of application for registration of a judgment of another Contracting State or Regulation State
PF160QB	Order for registration of a judgment of another Contracting State or Regulation State
PF161QB	Notice of registration of a judgment of another Contracting State or Regulation State
PF163QB	Evidence in support of application for certified copy of a judgment for enforcement in another Contracting State or Regulation State
PF164	Evidence in support of application for certificate as to money provisions of a judgment of the High Court for registration elsewhere in the United Kingdom
PF165	Evidence in support of application for registration of a judgment of a court in another part of the United Kingdom containing non-money provisions
PF166QB	Certificate as to finality etc of Arbitration Award for enforcement abroad (Arbitration Act 1996, s 58)
PF167QB	Order to stay proceedings under s 9 of the Arbitration Act 1996 (PD 49G 6)
PF168	Order to transfer claim from the High Court to county court (County Courts Act 1984; High and County Courts Jurisdiction Order 1991; rule 30.3)
PF170(A)	Application for child or patient's settlement in personal injury or Fatal Accident Act claims before proceedings begun (Rule 21.10(2); (PD 21 6 and 7)
PF170(B)	Application for child or patient's settlement in personal injury or fatal accident claims in existing proceedings (Rule 21.10(2); PD 21 6 and 7)

Table 1

No	Title
PF172QB	Request for directions in respect of funds in court or to be brought into court (Rule 21.11)
PF197	Application for order for transfer from the Royal Courts of Justice to a district registry or vice-versa or from one district registry to another (Rule 30.2(4))
PF198	Order under PF197
PF205	Evidence in support of application for permission to execute for earlier costs of enforcement under s 15(3) and (4) of the Courts and Legal Services Act 1990
PF244	Application Notice (RCT only) (Part 23)
PF12CH	Advertisement for creditors
PF13CH	Advertisement for claimants other than creditors)
PF14CH	[Witness statement] [Affidavit] verifying list of creditors' claims
PF15CH	List of claims by persons claiming to be creditors following advertisement (Exhibit A referred to in [witness statement][affidavit] in PF14CH).
PF16CH	List of claims by persons claiming to be creditors other than those sent in following advertisement (Exhibit B referred to in [witness statement][affidavit] in PF14CH)
PF17CH	List of sums of money which may be due in respect of which no claim has been received (Exhibit C referred to in [witness statement][affidavit] in PF14CH)
PF18CH	Notice to creditor to prove claim
PF19CH	Notice to creditor or other claimant to produce documents or particulars in support of claim
PF20CH	Notice to creditor of allowance of claim
PF21CH	Notice to creditor of disallowance of claim in whole or in part
PF22CH	Order for administration: beneficiaries action reconstituted as creditors claim (Van Oppen order)
PF23CH	[Witness statement] [Affidavit] verifying list of claims other than creditors claims

Table 1

No	Title
PF24CH	List of claims not being creditors' claims sent following advertisement (Exhibit D referred to in [witness statement][affidavit] in PF23CH)
PF25CH	List of claims not being creditors' claims other than those sent in following advertisement (Exhibit E referred to in [witness statement][affidavit] in PF23CH)
PF26CH	Notice to claimant other than a creditor to prove claim
PF27CH	[Witness statement][Affidavit] verifying accounts and answering usual enquiries in administration claim (CPR Rules 32.8 and 32.16)
PF28CH	Executors (or administrators account) (account A in PF27CH)
PF29CH	Masters order stating the results of proceedings before him on the usual accounts and inquiries in an administration claim
PF30CH	Security of receiver or administrator pending determination of a probate claim (PD 44)
PF31CH	Consent to act as trustee (Rule 33.8)
PF32CH	[Witness statement][Affidavit] in support of application for appointment of new litigation friend of child claimant (Rule 21.6(4))
PF33CH	Order for distribution of a Lloyds estate
PF34CH	Order in inquiry as to title in proceedings to enforce charging order where the defendant's title is not disclosed
PF36CH	Order appointing administrator pending determination of probate claim (PD 44)
PF38CH	Order in probate claim approving compromise (PD 44)

	Commercial Court Forms (CPR Part 58)
N1(CC)	Claim form (Pt 58 PD 2.4)
N1c(CC)	Notes for defendant
N9(CC)	Acknowledgment of service (Pt 58 PD 5.1)
N208(CC)	Claim form (Part 8) (Pt 58 PD 2.4)

Table 1

No	Title
N208c(CC)	Notes for defendant
N210(CC)	Acknowledgment of service (Part 8) (Pt 58 PD 5.2)
N211(CC)	Claim form (Part 20) (Pt 58 PD 12)
N211c(CC)	Notes for defendant (Part 20)
N213(CC)	Acknowledgment of service (Part 20)
N244(CC)	Application Notice (Pt 58 PD 10.7(2))
N265(CC)	List of Documents

	Technology and Construction forms (CPR Part 60)
TCC/FCM1	Case management information sheet (Pt 60 PD 8.2)
TCC/PTR1	Pre-trial review questionnaire (Pt 60 PD 9.1)

	Admiralty forms (CPR Part 60)
ADM1	Claim form (Admiralty claim in rem) (Pt 61 PD 3.1)
ADM1A	Claim form (Admiralty claim) (Pt 61 PD 12.3)
ADM1C	Notes for defendant on replying to an in rem claim form
ADM2	Acknowledgment of service for admiralty claims in rem (Pt 61 PD 3.4)
ADM3	Collision statement of case (Pt 61 PD 4.1)
ADM4	Application and undertaking for arrest and custody (Pt 61 PD 5.1(1))
ADM5	Declaration in support of an application for warrant of arrest (Pt 61 PD 5.1(2))
ADM6	Notice to consular officer of intention to apply for warrant of arrest (Pt 61 PD 5.4)
ADM7	Request for caution against arrest (Pt 61 PD 6.2)
ADM9	Warrant of arrest (Pt 61 PD 5.5(1))

Table 1

No	Title
ADM10	Standard directions to Admiralty Marshal (Pt 61 PD 5.6)
ADM11	Request for caution against release (Pt 61 PD 7.1)
ADM12	Request for undertaking for release (Pt 61 PD 7.1)
ADM12a	Request for withdrawal and caution against release (Pt 61 PD 7.5)
ADM13	Application for judgment in default (Pt 61 PD 8.1)
ADM14	Order for sale of ship (Pt 61 PD 9.2)
ADM15	Claim form (Admiralty limitation claim) (Pt 61 PD 10.1(1))
ADM15B	Notes for defendant on replying to an Admiralty limitation claim
ADM16	Notice of admission of right of claimant to limit liability (Pt 61 PD 10.3)
ADM16a	Defence to Admiralty limitation claim
ADM16b	Acknowledgment of service (Admiralty limitation claim) (Pt 61 PD 10.4)
ADM17	Application for restricted decree (Pt 61 PD 10.5)
ADM17a	Application for general limitation decree (Pt 61 PD 10.6)
ADM18	Restricted limitation decree (Pt 61 PD 10.5)
ADM19	General limitation decree
ADM20	Defendant's claim in limitation (Pt 61 PD 10.14)
ADM21	Declaration as to liability of a defendant to file and serve statement of case under a decree of limitation (Pt 61 PD 10.16)

	Arbitration forms (CPR Part 62)
N8	Claim form (Arbitration) (Pt 62 PD 2.1)
N8A	Notes for claimant (Arbitration)
N8B	Notes for defendant (Arbitration)
N15	Acknowledgment of service (Arbitration claim)

TABLE 2

PRACTICE FORMS

Contents:

4.1 This table lists the Practice Forms that may be used under this practice direction. It contains forms that were previously –

- Prescribed Forms contained in Appendix A to the Rules of the Supreme Court 1965

- Queen's Bench masters' Practice Forms

- Chancery masters' Practice Forms

4.2 Where a rule permits, a party intending to use a witness statement as an alternative to an affidavit should amend any form in this Table to be used in connection with that rule so that 'witness statement' replaces 'affidavit' wherever it appears in the form.

4.3 The forms in this list are reproduced in an Appendix to the Chancery and Queen's Bench Guides, in practitioners' text books and on the Court Service website (*www.hmcourts-service.gov.uk*).

Table 2

No	Title
No 53	Writ of fieri facias (Sch 1 – RSC Ord 45 r 12)
No 54	Writ of fieri facias on order for costs (Sch 1 – RSC Ord 45 r 12)
No 55	Notice of seizure (Sch 1 – RSC Ord 45 r 2)
No 56	Writ of fieri facias after levy of part (Sch 1 – RSC Ord 45 r 12)
No 57	Writ of fieri facias against personal representatives (Sch 1 – RSC Ord 45 r 12)
No 58	Writ of fieri facias de bonis ecclesiasticis (Sch 1 – RSC Ord 45 r 12)
No 59	Writ of sequestrari de bonis ecclesiasticis (Sch 1 – RSC Ord 45 r 12)
No 62	Writ of fieri facias to enforce Northern Irish or Scottish judgment (Sch 1 – RSC Ord 45 r 12 and Ord 71 r 37(1) and (2))
No 63	Writ of fieri facias to enforce foreign registered judgment (Sch 1 – RSC Ord 45 r 12 and Ord 71 rr 10, 21 and 34)
No 64	Writ of delivery: delivery of goods, damages and costs (Sch 1 – RSC Ord 45 r 4)

Table 2

No	Title
No 65	Writ of delivery: delivery of goods or value, damages and costs (Sch 1 – RSC Ord 45 r 12(2))
No 66	Writ of possession (Sch 1 – RSC Ord 45 r 12(3))
No 66A	Writ of possession (Sch 1 – RSC Ord 113 r 7)
No 67	Writ of sequestration (Sch 1 – RSC Ord 45 r 12(4), Ord 46 r 5)
No 68	Writ of restitution (Sch 1 – RSC Ord 46 rr 1 and 3)
No 69	Writ of assistance (Sch 1 – RSC Ord 46 rr 1 and 3)
No 71	Notice of renewal of writ of execution (Sch 1 – RSC Ord 46 r 8)
No 85	Order of committal or other penalty upon finding of contempt of court (Sch 1 – RSC Ord 52)
No 87	Claim form for writ of habeas corpus ad subjiciendum
No 88	Notice of adjourned application for writ of habeas corpus
No 89	Writ of habeas corpus ad subjiciendum
No 90	Notice to be served with writ of habeas corpus ad subjiciendum
No 91	Writ of habeas corpus ad testificandum
No 92	Writ of habeas corpus ad respondendum
No 95	Certificate of order against the Crown (Sch 1 – RSC Ord 77 r 15 and s 25 of the Crown Proceedings Act 1947))
No 96	Certificate of order for costs against the Crown (Sch 1 – RSC Ord 77 r 15 and s 25 of the Crown Proceedings Act 1947)
No 97	Claim form to grant bail (criminal proceedings) (Sch 1 – RSC Ord 79 r 9(1))
No 97A	Claim form to vary arrangements for bail (criminal proceedings) (Sch 1 – RSC Ord 79 r 9(1))
No 98	Order to release prisoner on bail (Sch 1 – RSC Ord 79 r 9(6), (6A) and (6B))
No 98A	Order varying arrangements for bail (Sch 1 – RSC Ord 79 r 9(10))
No 99	Order of Court of Appeal to admit prisoner to bail (Sch 1 – RSC Ord 59 r 20(5))

Table 2

No	Title
No 100	Notice of bail Sch 1 – RSC Ord 79 r 9(7))
No 101	Witness summons – Crown Court
No 103	Witness summons – Crown Court
No 104	Attachment of earnings order (Attachment of Earnings Act 1971)
No 105	Notice under s 10(2) of the Attachment of Earnings Act 1971
No 110	Certificate under s 12 of the Civil Jurisdiction and Judgments Act 1982
PF23 QB	Notice by sheriff of claim to goods taken in execution (Sch 1 – RSC Ord 17 r 2(2))
PF24 QB	Notice by execution creditor of admission or dispute of title of interpleader claimant (Sch 1 – RSC Ord 17 r 2(2))
PF25 QB	Interpleader application (Sch 1 – RSC Ord 17 r 3)
PF26 QB	Interpleader application by sheriff (Sch 1 – RSC Ord 17 r 3)
PF27 QB	Evidence in support of interpleader application (Sch 1 – RSC Ord 17 r 3(4))
PF28 QB	Interpleader order (1) claim barred where Sheriff interpleads (Sch 1 – RSC Ord 17)
PF29 QB	Interpleader order (1a) Sheriff to withdraw (Sch 1 – RSC Ord 17)
PF30 QB	Interpleader order (2) interpleader claimant substituted as defendant (Sch 1 –RSC Ord 17)
PF31 QB	Interpleader order (3) trial of issue (Sch 1 – RSC Ord 17)
PF32 QB	Interpleader order (4) conditional order for Sheriff to withdraw and trial of issue (Sch 1 – RSC Ord 17)
PF34 QB	Interpleader order (6) summary disposal (Sch 1 – RSC Ord 17 r 5(2))
PF86	Praecipe for writ of fieri facias (Sch 1 – RSC Ord 45 r 12(1) and 46 r 6)
PF87	Praecipe for writ of sequestration (Sch 1 – RSC Ord 45 r 12(4) and 46 r 6)

Table 2

No	Title
PF88	Praecipe for writ of possession (Sch 1 – RSC Ord 45 r 12(3), 46 r 6 and 113 r 7)
PF89	Praecipe for writ of possession and fieri facias combined (Sch 1 – RSC Ord 45 r 12 and Ord 46 r 6)
PF90	Praecipe for writ of delivery (Sch 1 – RSC Ord 45 r 12(2) and Ord 46 r 6)
PF97 QB	Order for sale by Sheriff by private contract (Sch 1 – RSC Ord 47 r 6)
PF102	Bench warrant (Sch 1 – RSC Ord 52)
PF103	Warrant of committal (general) (Sch 1 – RSC Ord 52)
PF104	Warrant of committal (contempt in face of court) (Sch 1 – RSC Ord 52)
PF105	Warrant of committal (failure of witness to attend) (Sch 1 – RSC Ord 52)
PF106	Warrant of Committal (of prisoner) (Sch 1 – RSC Ord 52)
PF141	Witness statement/affidavit of personal service of judgment or order (Sch 1 – RSC Ord 45 r 7)
PF177	Order for written statement as to partners in firm (Sch 1 – RSC Ord 81 r 2)
PF179QB	Evidence on registration of a Bill of Sale (Bills of Sale Act 1878; Sch 1 – RSC Ord 95)
PF180QB	Evidence on registration of an Absolute Bill of Sale, Settlement and Deed of Gift (Sch 1 – RSC Ord 95)
PF181QB	Evidence in support of an application for re-registration of a Bill of Sale (s 14 Bills of Sale Act 1878; Sch 1 – RSC Ord 95)
PF182QB	Order for extension of time to register or re-register a Bill of Sale (s 14 Bills of Sale Act 1878; Sch 1 – RSC Ord 95)
PF183QB	Evidence for permission to enter a memorandum of Satisfaction on a Bill of Sale (s 15 Bills of Sale Act 1878; Sch 1 – RSC Ord 95; PD Bills of Sale para 1)
PF184QB	Claim form for entry of satisfaction on a registered Bill of Sale (s 15 Bill of Sale Act 1878; Sch 1 – RSC Ord 95 r 2; Bills of Sale PD para 3)

Table 2

No	Title
PF185QB	Order for entry of Satisfaction on a registered Bill of Sale (s 14 Bills of Sale Act 1878; Sch 1 – RSC Ord 95 r 2)
PF186QB	Evidence on registration of Assignment of Book Debts (s 344 Insolvency Act 1986; Sch 1 – RSC Ord 95 r 6(2))
PF187	Claim form for Solicitor's Charging order (s 73 Solicitors Act 1974; Sch 1 – RSC Ord 106 r 2)
PF188	Charging order: Solicitor's costs (s 73 Solicitors Act 1974; Sch 1 – RSC Ord 106 r 2)
PF6CH	Certificate on application for permission to issue execution on suspended order for possession where defendant in default of acknowledgment of service (Sch 1 – RSC Ord 46 r 2 and 4 and CPR Part 23)
PF7CH	Inquiry for persons entitled to the property of an intestate dying on or after 1 January 1926 (Sch 1 – RSC Ord 85)
PF8CH	Application notice after masters findings on kin enquiry (Benjamin order) giving permission to distribute estate upon footing (Sch 1 – RSC Ord 85)
PF9CH	Order giving leave to distribute estate upon footing (re Benjamin) (Sch 1 – RSC Ord 85)
PF10CH	Judgment in beneficiaries administration claim (Sch 1 – RSC Ord 85)
PF11CH	Judgment in creditors' administration claim (Sch 1 – RSC Ord 85)

TABLE 3

Contents:

5.1 This table lists county court forms in use before 26 April 1999 that will continue to be used on or after that date.

5.2 Where a rule permits, a party intending to use a witness statement as an alternative to an affidavit should amend any form in this Table to be used in connection with that rule so that 'witness statement' replaces 'affidavit' wherever it appears in the form.

Table 3

No	Title
N27	Judgment for claimant in Action of Forfeiture for non payment of rent
N35	Variation Order
N35A	Variation Order (determination)
N41	Order suspending judgment or Order, and/or Warrant of Execution/Committal
N41A	Order suspending warrant (determination)
N42	Warrant of Execution
N46	Warrant of Delivery and Execution for damages and Costs
N48	Warrant of Delivery, where, if goods are not returned, Levy is to be made for their value
N49	Warrant for Possession of Land
N50	Warrant of Restitution (Order 26, rule 17)
N51	Warrant of Restitution (Order 24, rule 6(1))
N52	Warrant of Possession under Order 24
N53	Warrant of Execution or Committal to District Judge of Foreign Court
N55	Notice of Application for Attachment of Earnings Order
N55A	Notice of application for attachment of earnings order (maintenance)
N56	Form for replying to an attachment of Earnings application (statement of means)
N58	Order for Defendants attendance at an adjourned Hearing of an Attachment of Earnings Application (maintenance)
N59	Warrant of Committal under section 23(1) of the Attachment of Earnings Act 1971
N60	Attachment of Earnings Order (Judgment Debt)
N61	Order for production of Statement of Means
N61A	Order to employer for production of statement of earnings

Table 3

No	Title
N62	Summons for Offence under Attachment of Earnings
N63	Notice to show Cause section 23 of the Attachment of Earnings Act 1971
N64	Suspended Attachment of Earnings Order
N64A	Suspended Attachment of Earnings Order (maintenance)
N65A	Attachment of Earnings Arrears Order
N65	Attachment of Earnings Order (Priority Maintenance)
N66	Consolidated Attachment of Earnings Order
N66A	Notice of Application for Consolidated Attachment of Earnings Order
N67	Judgment Summons under the Debtors Act 1869
N68	Certificate of Service (Judgment Summons)
N69	Order for Debtors Attendance at an Adjourned Hearing of Judgment Summons
N70	Order of Commitment under section 110 of the County Courts Act 1984
N71	Order revoking an Order of Commitment under section 110 of the County Courts Act 1984
N72	Notice to Defendant where a Committal Order made but directed to be suspended under Debtors Act
N73	New Order on Judgment Summons
N74	Warrant of Committal Judgment Summons under the Debtors Act 1869
N75	Indorsement on a warrant of Committal sent to a Foreign Court
N76	Certificate to be indorsed on duplicate Warrant of Committal issued for re-arrest of Debtor
N77	Notice as to consequences of disobedience to Court Order
N78	Notice to show good reason why an order for your committal to prison should not be made (**Family proceedings only**)

Table 3

No	Title
N79	Committal of other Order upon proof of disobedience of a court order or breach of undertaking
N80	Warrant for Committal to Prison
N81	Notice to solicitor to show cause why an undertaking should not be enforced by committal to prison
N82	Order for committal for failure by solicitor to carry out undertaking
N83	Order for discharge from custody under warrant of committal
N88	Interpleader Summons to Execution Creditor
N88(1)	Interpleader Summons to Claimant claiming goods or rent under an execution
N89	Interpleader summons to persons making adverse claims to debt
N90	Summons for assaulting an officer of the court or rescuing goods
N91	Order of Commitment and or Imposing a fine for assaulting an officer of the court or rescuing goods
N92	Request for Administration Order
N93	List of Creditors furnished under the Act of 1971
N94	Administration Order
N95	Order revoking an administration order
N95A	Order suspending or varying an administration order
N110	Power of arrest attached to injunction under section 2 Domestic Violence and Matrimonial Proceedings Act 1976
N110A	Anti social behaviour injunction – power of arrest s 152/153 HA 1996
N112	Order for Arrest under section 110 of County Courts Act 1984
N112A	Power of arrest, section 23 Attachment of Earnings Act 1971
N117	General form of undertaking
N118	Notice to Defendant where committal order made but directed to be suspended

Table 3

No	Title
N130	Application for possession including application for interim possession order (*revised with effect from 2/12/02*)
N131	Notice of application for interim possession order (*will become obsolete from 2/12/02*)
N132	Affidavit of Service of notice of application for interim possession order (*will become obsolete from 2/12/02*)
N133	Affidavit to occupier to oppose the making of an interim possession order (*revised with effect from 2/12/02*)
N134	Interim possession order (*revised with effect from 2/12/02*)
N135	Affidavit of Service of interim possession order (*will become obsolete from 2/12/02*)
N136	Order for possession (*revised with effect from 2/12/02*)
N138	Injunction order
N139	Application for warrant of arrest
N140	Warrant of arrest
N206	Notice of Issue of fixed date claim
N207	Plaint note (Adoption freeing for Adoption)
N200	Petition – **Note old number was N208**
N201	Request for entry of appeal – **Note old number was N209**
N202	Order for party to sue or defend on behalf of others having the same interest – **Note old number was N210**
N203	Notice to persons on whose behalf party has obtained leave to sue or defend – **Note old number was N211**
N204	Notice to person against whom party has obtained leave to sue or defend on behalf of others – **Note old number was N212**
N224	Request for Service out of England and Wales through the court
N245	Application for suspension of a warrant and/or variation of an instalment order
N246	Claimant's Reply to Defendant's application to vary instalment order

Table 3

No	Title
N246A	Claimant's reply to Defendant's application to suspend warrant of execution
N270	Notes for guidance (application for administration order)
N276	Notice of Hearing of Interpleader Proceedings transferred from High Court
N277	Notice of Pre Trial Review of Interpleader proceedings transferred from the High Court
N280	Order of reference of proceedings or questions for inquiry and report
N285	General form of affidavit
N288	Order to produce prisoner
N289	Judgment for Defendant
N293	Certificate or judgment or order
N293A	Combined certificate of judgment and request for writ of fi fa
N295	Order for sale of land
N296	Notice of Judgment or order to party directed to be served with notice
N297	Order for accounts and Inquiries in Creditors Administration Action
N298	Order for Administration
N299	Order for foreclosure nisi of legal mortgage of land
N300	Order for sale in action by equitable mortgagee
N302	Judgment in action for specific performance (vendors action title accepted)
N303	Order for dissolution of partnership
N304	Notice to parties to attend upon taking accounts
N305	Notice to creditor to prove his claim
N306	Notice to creditor of determination of claim
N307	District Judges order (accounts and inquiries)

Table 3

No	Title
N309	Order for foreclosure absolute
N310	Partnership order on further consideration
N311	Administrative action order on further consideration
N313	Indorsement on certificate of judgment (transfer)
N317	Bailiffs report
N317A	Bailiff's report to the claimant
N319	Notice of execution of warrant of committal
N320	Request for return of, or to, warrant
N322	Order for recovery of money awarded by tribunal
N323	Request for warrant of execution
N324	Request for warrant of goods
N325	Request for warrant for possession of land
N326	Notice of issue of warrant of execution
N327	Notice of issue of warrant of execution to enforce a judgment or order
N328	Notice of transfer of proceedings to the High Court
N329	Notes for guidance on completion of N79
N330	Notice of sale or payment under execution in respect of a judgment for a sum exceeding £500
N331	Notice of withdrawal from poss. or payment of moneys on notice of receiving or winding up order
N332	Inventory of goods removed
N333	Notice of time when and where goods will be sold
N334	Request to hold walking possession and authority to re-enter
N336	Request and result of search in the attachment of earnings index
N337	Request for attachment of earnings order

Table 3

No	Title
N338	Request for statement of earnings
N339	Discharge of attachment of earnings order
N340	Notice as to payment under attachment of earnings order made by the High Court
N341	Notice of intention to vary attachment of earnings order under section 10(2) of AE Act 1971
N342	Request for judgment summons
N343	Notice of result of hearing of a judgment summons issued on a judgment or order of the High Court
N344	Request for warrant of committal on judgment summons
N345	Certificate of payment under the Debtors Act 1869
N353	Order appointing receiver of real and personal property
N354	Order appointing receiver of partnership
N355	Interim order for appointment of receiver
N356	Order for appointment of receiver by way of equitable execution
N358	Notice of claim to goods taken in execution
N359	Notice to claimant to goods taken in execution to make deposit or give security
N360	Affidavit in support of interpleader summons other than an execution
N361	Notice of application for relief in pending action
N362	Order on interpleader summons under an execution where the claim is not established
N363	Order on interpleader summons under an execution where the claim is established
N364	Order on interpleader summons (other than execution) where there is an action
N365	Order on interpleader summons (other than execution) where there is no action

Table 3

No	Title
N366	Summons for neglect to levy execution
N368	Order fining a witness for non-attendance
N370	Order of commitment or imposing a fine for insult or misbehaviour
N372	Order for rehearing
N373	Notice of application for an administration order
N374	Notice of intention to review an administration order
N374A	Notice of intention to revoke an administration order
N375	Notice of further creditors claim
N376	Notice of hearing administration order (by direction of the court)
N377	Notice of dividend
N388	Notice to probate registry to produce documents
N390	Notice that a claim has been entered against the Crown
N391	Crown Proceedings Act affidavit in support of application directing payment by Crown to judgment creditor
N392	Crown Proceedings Act notice of application for order directing payment by the Crown to the judgment creditor
N432	Affidavit on payment into court under section 63 of the Trustee Act 1925
N436	Order for sale of land under charging order
N437	District Judges report
N438	Notice to charge holder under Matrimonial Homes Act 1983
N440	Notice of application for time order by debtor or hirer – CC Act 1974
N441	Notification of request for certificate of satisfaction or cancellation
N441A	Certificate of satisfaction or cancellation of judgment debt
N444	Details of sale under a warrant of execution
N445	Request for re-issue of warrant

Table 3

No	Title
N447	Notice to claimant of date fixed for adjourned hearing
N448	Request to defendant for employment details, attachment of earnings
N449	Notice to employer, failure to make deductions under attachment of earnings order

Appendix C

THE QUEEN'S BENCH GUIDE

A GUIDE TO THE WORKING PRACTICES OF THE QUEEN'S BENCH DIVISION WITHIN THE ROYAL COURTS OF JUSTICE

Foreword by The Rt Hon Lord Bingham of Cornhill
The Lord Chief Justice of England and Wales

We live in a new procedural world. Old landmarks have disappeared from view. New features have taken their place. And everyone seems to be speaking a different language. It is easy to become disoriented.

This Guide, prepared for those litigating in the Queen's Bench Division of the High Court, particularly in the Central Office, provides a clear and detailed road-map for those who have lost, or are not sure of, the way. The Guide draws on the unrivalled expertise and experience of the Senior Master, who takes the opportunity to give much wise advice along the route.

I am sure this Guide will prove invaluable to the many who will, I hope, use it. In preparing the Guide, the Senior Master has rendered a notable public service.

An Appreciation

With the support and encouragement of Lord Bingham of Cornhill during his tenure of office as Lord Chief Justice of England & Wales, this Guide has been prepared for the assistance of all who practice or litigate in the Queen's Bench Division.

The contributions made by the Queen's Bench masters and the staff of the Central Office have been invaluable but this Guide would not have been completed without the hard work and diligence of Bryony Young, formerly Chief Associate, to whom I am indebted.

However, all errors and omissions are mine and I would welcome any comments and suggestions from the profession and all using this Guide for its improvement.

Senior Master and
Queen's Remembrancer
18 May 2000

1 INTRODUCTION

1.1 The Guide

1.1.1 This Guide has been prepared by the Senior Master, acting under the authority of the Lord Chief Justice, and provides a general explanation of the work and practice of the Queen's Bench Division with particular regard to proceedings started in the Central Office, and is designed to make it easier for parties to use and proceed in the Queen's Bench Division.

1.1.2 The Guide must be read with the Civil Procedure Rules ('the CPR') and the supporting Practice Directions. Litigants and their advisers are responsible for acquainting themselves with the CPR; it is not the task of this Guide to summarise the CPR, nor should anyone regard it as a substitute for the CPR. It is intended to bring the Guide up to date at regular intervals as necessary.

1.1.3 The Guide does not have the force of law, but parties using the Queen's Bench Division will be expected to act in accordance with this Guide. Further guidance as to the practice of the Queen's Bench Division may be obtained from the Practice Master (see paragraph 6.1 below).

1.1.4 It is assumed throughout the Guide that the litigant intends to proceed in the Royal Courts of Justice. For all essential purposes, though, the Guide is equally applicable to the work of the district registries, which deal with the work of the Queen's Bench Division outside London, but it should be borne in mind that there are some differences.

1.1.5 The telephone numbers and room numbers quoted in the Guide are correct at the time of going to press. However, the room numbers quoted for the Clerk of the Lists and the Listing Office are effective as from 2 October 2000.

1.2 The Civil Procedure Rules

1.2.1 The Overriding Objective set out in Part 1 of the CPR is central to the new culture which enables the court to deal with cases justly. To further this aim the work is allocated to one of three tracks – the small claims track, the fast track and the multi-track – so as to dispose of the work in the most appropriate and effective way combined with active case management by the court.

1.2.2 The CPR are divided into Parts. A particular Part is referred to in the Guide as Part 7, etc, as the case may be. Any particular rule within a Part is referred to as rule 6.4(2), and so on.

1.3 The Practice Directions

1.3.1 Each Part – or almost each Part – has an accompanying practice direction or directions, and other practice directions deal with matters such as the Pre-Action Protocols and the former Rules of the Supreme Court and the County Court Rules which are scheduled to Part 50.

1.3.2 The Practice Directions are made pursuant to statute, and have the same authority as do the CPR themselves[1]. However, in case of any conflict between a rule and a practice direction, the rule will prevail[2]. Each practice direction is referred to in the Guide with the number of any Part that it supplements preceding it; for example, the Practice Direction supplementing Part 6 is referred to as the Part 6 Practice Direction. But where there is more than one practice direction supplementing a Part it will also be described either by topic, for example, Part 25 Practice Direction – Interim Payments, or where appropriate, the Part 40B Practice Direction.

1　Civil Procedure Act 1997, ss 1 and 5, and Sch 1, paras 3 and 6.
2　There is one exception: Part 8.

1.4 The forms

1.4.1 The Practice Direction supplementing Part 4 (Forms) lists the practice forms that are required by or referred to in the CPR, and also those referred to in such of the Rules of the Supreme Court and the County Court Rules as are still in force (see Part 50 of the CPR; Schedules 1 and 2).

1.4.2 Those listed in Table 1 with a number prefixed by the letter N are new forms, a number of these forms have been published with the CPR. Those listed in Table 2 are forms still in use in the High Court but altered so as to conform to the CPR. They may be used as precedents and are set out in a separate Appendix to this Guide and include:

(1)　Forms that were previously prescribed forms; these are listed under the same numbers that previously identified them.
(2)　Former practice forms common to both the Chancery and Queen's Bench Divisions; these forms have been given numbers starting with the letters PF.
(3)　Former practice forms used mainly in the Queen's Bench Division; these forms have been given numbers ending with the letters QB.
(4)　Former practice forms used mainly in the Chancery Division; these forms have been given numbers ending with the letters CH.

1.4.3 The forms may be modified as circumstances in individual cases require[3], but it is essential that a modified form contains at least as full information or guidance as would have been given if the original form had been used.

3　See rule 4.3.

1.4.4 Where the Royal Arms appears on any listed form it must appear on any modification of that form. The same format for the Royal Arms as is used on the listed forms need not be used. All that is necessary is that there is a complete Royal Arms.

1.5 The Queen's Bench Division

1.5.1 The Queen's Bench Division is one of the three divisions of the High Court, together with the Chancery Division and Family Division. The Lord Chief Justice is President of the Queen's Bench Division, and certain High Court judges and masters are assigned to it. A Lord Justice of Appeal (currently Lord Justice Kennedy) has been appointed by the Lord Chief Justice to be the Vice-President of the Division; a High Court judge is appointed as judge in charge of the Jury List (currently Mr Justice Moreland); another is appointed as judge in charge of the Trial List (currently Mr Justice Buckley).

1.5.2 Outside London, the work of the Queen's Bench Division is administered in provincial offices known as district registries. In London, the work is administered in the Central Office at the Royal Courts of Justice. The work in the Central Office of the Queen's Bench Division is the responsibility of the Senior Master, acting under the authority of the Lord Chief Justice.

1.5.3 The work of the Queen's Bench Division is (with certain exceptions) governed by the CPR. The Divisional Court, the Admiralty Court, the Commercial Court and the Technology and Construction Court are all part of the Queen's Bench Division. However, each does specialised work requiring a distinct procedure that to some extent modifies the CPR. For that reason each publishes its own Guide or practice direction, to which reference should be made by parties wishing to proceed in the specialist courts.

1.5.4 The work of the Queen's Bench Division consists mainly of claims for;

(1)   damages in respect of
        (a)   personal injury,
        (b)   negligence,
        (c)   breach of contract, and
        (d)   libel and slander (defamation),
(2)   non-payment of a debt, and
(3)   possession of land or property.

Proceedings retained to be dealt with in the Central Office of the Queen's Bench Division will almost invariably be multi-track claims.

1.5.5 In many types of claim – for example claims in respect of negligence by solicitors, accountants, etc or claims for possession of land – the claimant has a choice whether to bring the claim in the Queen's Bench Division or in the Chancery Division. However, there are certain claims that may be brought only in the Queen's Bench Division, namely:

(1)   sheriff's interpleader proceedings,
(2)   enrolment of deeds,
(3)   registration of foreign judgments under the Civil Jurisdictions and Judgments Act 1982,
(4)   applications for bail in criminal proceedings,
(5)   applications under the Administration of Justice Act 1920 and the Foreign Judgments (Reciprocal Enforcement) Act 1933,
(6)   registration and satisfaction of bills of sale,
(7)   election petitions,
(8)   obtaining evidence for foreign courts.

1.6 The Central Office

1.6.1 The information in this and the following paragraph is to be found in the Part 2 Practice Direction at paragraph 2; it is reproduced here for the convenience of litigants. The Central Office is open for business from 10 am to 4.30 pm (except during August when it is open from 10 am to 2.30 pm) on every day of the year except;

(1)   Saturdays and Sundays,
(2)   Good Friday and the day after Easter Monday,
(3)   Christmas Day and, if that day is a Friday or Saturday, then 28 December,
(4)   Bank Holidays in England and Wales (under the Banking and Financial Dealings Act 1971), and
(5)   such other days as the Lord Chancellor, with the concurrence or the Lord Chief Justice, the Master of the Rolls, the President of the Family Division and the Vice-Chancellor, may direct.

1.6.2 One of the masters of the Queen's Bench Division is present at the Central Office on every day on which the office is open for the purpose of superintending the business administered there and giving any directions that may be required on questions of practice and procedure. He is normally referred to as the 'Practice Master'. (See paragraph 6.1 below for information about the Practice Master and masters in general.)

1.6.3 The Central Office consists of the Action Department, the Masters' Secretary's Department, the Queen's Bench Associates' Department, the Clerk of the Lists, the Registry of the Technology and Construction Court and the Admiralty and Commercial Registry.

1.6.4 The Action Department deals with the issue of claims, responses to claims, admissions, undefended and summary judgments, enforcement, drawing up certain orders, public searches, provision of copies of court documents, enrolment of deeds, submission of references to the Court of Justice of the European Communities and registration of foreign judgments.

1.6.5 The Masters' Secretary's Department covers three discrete areas of work;

(1)   the Masters' Support Unit which provides support (a) to the masters, including assisting with case-management, and (b) to the Senior Master,
(2)   Foreign Process, and
(3)   Investment of Children's Funds.

1.6.6 The Queen's Bench associates sit in court with the judges during trials and certain interim hearings. The Chief Associate manages the Queen's Bench associates and also provides support to the Senior Master as the Queen's Remembrancer and as the Prescribed Officer for election petitions. The associates draw up the orders made in court at trial and those interim orders that the parties do not wish to draw up themselves.

1.6.7 The Clerk of the Lists lists all trials and matters before the judges (see paragraph 8 below).

1.6.8 The Technology and Construction Court deals with claims which involve issues or questions which are technically complex or for which a trial by a judge of that court is for any other reason desirable (see the Part 49C Practice Direction – Technology and Construction Court).

1.6.9 The Admiralty and Commercial Court deals mainly with shipping collision claims and claims concerning charters and insurance, and commercial arbitrations. See the Commercial Court Guide and the Part 49D Practice Direction – Commercial Court, the Part 49F Practice Direction – Admiralty and the Part 49G Practice Direction – Arbitrations.

1.7 The judiciary

1.7.1 The judiciary in the Queen's Bench Division consist of the High Court judges (The Honourable Mr/Mrs Justice .... and addressed in court as my Lord/my Lady) and in the Royal Courts of Justice the masters (Master ....); in the district registries the work of the masters is conducted by district judges.

1.7.2 Trial normally takes place before a High Court judge (or deputy High Court judge[4]) who may also hear pre-trial reviews and other interim applications. Wherever possible the judge before whom a trial has been fixed will hear any pre-trial review. A High Court judge will hear applications to commit for contempt of court, applications for injunctions[5] and most appeals from masters' orders. (See the Practice Direction to Part 2B Allocation of cases to levels of Judiciary, and see paragraphs 7.11 and 7.12 below for more information on hearings and applications.)

4   A deputy High Court judge may be a circuit judge or Queen's Counsel. A retired High Court judge may also sit as a High Court judge.
5   See Part 25 and the practice direction which supplements it for more information about injunctions and who may hear them, and interim remedies in general.

1.7.3 The masters deal with interim and some pre-action applications, and manage the claims so that they proceed without delay. The masters' rooms are situated in the East Block of the Royal Courts of Justice. Hearings take place in these rooms or (short hearings only) in the Bear Garden.

1.7.4 Cases are assigned on issue by a court officer in the Action Department to masters on a random basis, and that master is then known as the assigned master in relation to that case. (See paragraphs 6.2 and 6.3 below for more information about assignment and the masters' lists.)

1.7.5 General enquiries about the business dealt with by the masters should initially be made in writing to the Masters' Support Unit in Room E14.

2 GENERAL

2.1 Essential matters

2.1.1 Before bringing any proceedings, the intending claimant should think carefully about the implications of so doing. (See paragraph 3 below about steps to be taken before issuing a claim form.)

2.1.2 A litigant who is acting in person faces a heavier burden in terms of time and effort than does a litigant who is legally represented, but all litigation calls for a high level of commitment from the parties. No intending claimant should underestimate this.

2.1.3 The Overriding Objective of the CPR is to deal with cases justly, which means dealing with the claim in a way which is proportionate (amongst other things) to the amount of money involved[6]. However, in all proceedings there are winners and losers; the loser is generally ordered to pay the costs of the winner and the costs of litigation can still be large. The risk of large costs is particularly acute in cases involving expert witnesses, barristers and solicitors. Also, the costs of an interim hearing are almost always summarily assessed and made payable by the unsuccessful party usually within 14 days after the order for costs is made[7]. There may be a number of interim hearings before the trial itself is reached, so the costs must be paid as the claim progresses. (See also paragraph 2.5 Costs below.)

6   See rule 1.1.
7   See rule 44.8.

2.1.4 The intending claimant should also keep in mind that every claim must be proved, unless of course the defendant admits the allegations. There is little point in incurring the risks and expense of litigating if the claim cannot be proved. An intending claimant should therefore be taking steps to obtain statements from his prospective witnesses before starting the claim; if he delays until later, it may turn out that he is in fact unable to obtain the evidence that he needs to prove his claim. A defendant faces a similar task.

2.1.5 Any party may, if he is to succeed, need an opinion from one or more expert witnesses, such as medical practitioners, engineers, accountants, or as the case may be. However he must remember that no expert evidence may be given at trial without the permission of the court. If the claim is for compensation for personal injuries, the claimant must produce a medical report with his particulars of claim.

2.1.6 The services of such experts are in great demand, especially as in some fields of expertise there are few of them. It may take many months to obtain an opinion, and the cost may be high. (See paragraph 7.9 below for information about experts' evidence.) The claimant must remember also not to allow the time-limit for starting his claim to pass (see paragraph 2.3 below for information about time-limits).

2.1.7 Any intending claimant should also have in mind that he will usually be required to give standard disclosure of the documents on which he relies. Although rule 31.3(2) makes provision for a party not to be required to disclose documents if disclosure would be disproportionate to the value of the claim, in complex cases it may still be necessary to disclose relatively large quantities of documents, and this invariably involves much time, effort and expense. (See paragraph 7.8 below for information about disclosure.)

2.1.8 In many cases the parties will need legal assistance, whether by way of advice, drafting, representation at hearings or otherwise. It is not the function of court staff to give legal advice, however, subject to that, they will do their best to assist any litigant. Litigants in person who need assistance or funding should contact the Community Legal Service through their information points. The CLS are developing local networks of people giving legal assistance such as law centres, local solicitors or the Citizens Advice Bureaux. CLS Information Points are being set up in libraries and other public places. Litigants can telephone the CLS to find their nearest CLS Information Point on 0845 608 1122 or can log on to the CLS website at www.justask.org.uk for the CLS directory and for legal information.

2.1.9 The RCJ Advice Bureau off the Main Hall at the Royal Courts of Justice is open Monday to Friday from 10.00 am to 1.00 pm and from 2.00 pm to 5.00 pm. The Bureau is run by lawyers in conjunction with the Citizens Advice Bureau and is independent of the court. The Bureau operates on a 'first come first served' basis, or telephone advice is available on 020 7947 7604 Monday to Friday from 11.00 am to 12.00 pm and from 3.00 pm to 4.00 pm.

2.2 Inspection and copies of documents

2.2.1 Intending claimants must not expect to be able to keep the details of a claim away from public scrutiny. In addition to the right of a party to obtain copies of documents in the proceedings to which he is a party from the court record (on payment of the prescribed fee), a claim form when it has been served, and the particulars of claim where they are included in or served with the claim form, may be inspected by anyone simply on payment of the fee. Any judgment or order made in public may also be inspected on payment of the fee. Additionally, other documents may be inspected with the permission of the court[8].

8   See rule 5.4 and the practice direction supplementing Part 5.

2.2.2 Witness statements[9] used at trial are open to inspection unless the court directs otherwise[10]. Considerations of publicity are often particularly important in deciding whether to commence proceedings in respect of an alleged libel or slander; such a claim may by its attendant publicity do more damage than was ever inflicted by the original publication. In such proceedings the claimant may decide to serve his particulars of claim separately from the claim form[11].

9   See paragraph 7.10 below about evidence.
10   See rule 32.13.
11   See Part 53 and the Part 53 practice direction for matters to be included in the claim form in a defamation claim where the particulars of claim are served separately.

2.3 Time-limits

2.3.1 There are strict time-limits that apply to every claim. First, there are time-limits fixed by the Limitation Act 1980 within which proceedings must be brought. There are circumstances in which the court may extend those time-limits, but this should be regarded as exceptional. In all other cases, once the relevant time-limit has expired, it is rarely possible to start a claim.

2.3.2 Secondly, in order to try and bring the proceedings to an early trial date, a timetable will be set with which all parties must comply. Unless the CPR or a practice direction provide otherwise, or the court orders otherwise, the timetable may be varied by the written agreement of the parties[12]. However, there are certain 'milestone' events in the timetable in which the time-limits may not be varied by the parties. Examples of these are;

(1) return of the allocation questionnaire
(2) date for the case management conference
(3) return of the listing questionnaire
(4) date fixed for trial.

Where parties have extended a time-limit by agreement, the party for whom the time has been extended must advise the Masters' Support Unit in writing of the event in the proceedings for which the time has been extended and the new date by which it must be done. For example, if an extension is agreed for the filing of the defence, it is for the defendant to inform the Masters' Support Unit.

12 See rule 2.11.

2.3.3 The court has power to penalise any party who fails to comply with a time-limit. If the court considers that a prior warning should be given before a penalty is imposed, it will make an 'unless' order; in other words, the court will order that, unless that party performs his obligation by the time specified, he will be penalised in the manner set out in the order. This may involve the party in default having his claim or statement of case struck out and judgment given against him.

2.4 Legal representation

2.4.1 A party may act in person or be represented by a lawyer. A party who is acting in person may be assisted at any hearing by another person (often referred to as a McKenzie friend) subject to the discretion of the court. The McKenzie friend is allowed to help by taking notes, quietly prompting the litigant and offering advice and suggestions. The litigant however, must conduct his own case; the McKenzie friend may not represent him and may only in very exceptional circumstances be allowed to address the court on behalf of the litigant under s 27(2)(c) of the Courts and Legal Services Act 1990.

2.4.2 A written statement should be provided to the court at any hearing concerning the representation of the parties in accordance with paragraph 5.1 of the Part 39 Practice Direction.

2.4.3 At a trial, a company or corporation may be represented by an employee if the company or corporation authorise him to do so and the court gives permission. Where this is to be the case, the permission of the judge who is to hear the case may be sought informally; paragraph 5 of the Part 39 Practice Direction describes what is needed to obtain permission from the court for this purpose and mentions some of the considerations relevant to the grant or refusal of permission. A further statement concerning representation should be provided in accordance with paragraph 5.2 of the Part 39 Practice Direction.

2.4.4 The practice of allowing experienced outdoor clerks to appear before the masters will continue.

2.5 Costs

2.5.1 Costs are dealt with in Parts 43–48[13]. There are important new provisions in the costs rules, particularly with respect to;

(1)   informing the client of costs orders,
(2)   providing the court with estimates of costs,
(3)   summary assessment of costs,
(4)   interim orders for costs, and
(5)   interest on costs.

13 Rule 43.2 and sections 1 and 2 of the costs practice direction contain the definitions and
    applications used throughout Parts 43–48 and the practice direction.

2.5.2 Solicitors now have a duty under rule 44.2 to notify their client within 7 days if an order for costs is made against him in his absence. Solicitors must also notify any other person who has instructed them to act in the proceedings or who is liable to pay their fees (such as an insurer, trade union or the Legal Services Commission (LSC)). They must also inform these persons how the order came to be made (paragraphs 7.1 and 7.2 of the Costs Practice Direction).

2.5.3 The court may at any stage order any party to file an estimate of base costs (substantially in the form of Precedent H in the Schedule of Costs Precedents annexed to the Costs Practice Direction) and serve copies on all the other parties (paragraph 6.3 of the Costs Practice Direction). This will both assist the court in deciding what case management directions to make and inform the other parties as to their potential liability for payment of costs.

2.5.4 If a party seeks an order for his costs, in order to assist the court in making a summary assessment, he must prepare a written statement of the costs he intends to claim in accordance with paragraph 13.5 of the Costs Practice Direction, following as closely as possible Form N260. In addition, when an allocation questionnaire or a listing questionnaire is filed, the party filing it must file and serve an estimate of costs on all the other parties.

2.5.5 If the parties have agreed the amount of costs, they do not need to file a statement of the costs, and summary assessment is unnecessary. Or, where the parties agree a consent order without any party attending on the application, the parties should insert either an agreed figure for costs or that there should be no order for costs in the order (paragraph 13.4 of the Costs Practice Direction).

2.5.6 Unless the court decides not to order an assessment of costs where, for example, it orders costs to be 'costs in the case'[14], it may either make a summary assessment of costs or order a detailed assessment to take place[15]. The court will generally make a summary assessment of costs at any hearing which lasts for less than one day;

(1)   'summary assessment' is where the court, when making an order for costs, assesses those costs and orders payment of a sum of money in respect of them[16], and
(2)   'detailed assessment' is the procedure by which the amount of costs is decided by a costs officer at a later date in accordance with Part 47.

The provision of summary assessment means that the paying party is likely to be paying the costs at an earlier stage than he would have done under the previous rules (and see paragraph 2.5.15 below).

14 See the table in para 8.5 of the costs practice direction for some of the most common costs orders the court may make.
15 See rule 44.7 and section 12 of the costs practice direction.
16 See sections 12 and 13 of the costs practice direction.

2.5.7 The court will not make a summary assessment of the costs of a receiving party (the party to whom the costs are to be paid) where he is;

(1)   a child or patient within the meaning of Part 21 unless the solicitor acting for the child or patient has waived the right to further costs[17], or
(2)   an assisted person or a person in receipt of funded services under sections 4–11 of the Access to Justice Act 1999.

The costs payable by a party who is an assisted person or a person in receipt of funded services may be summarily assessed as the assessment is not by itself a determination of the assisted person's liability to pay those costs[18].

17 See the costs practice direction paras 13.11 and 51.1.
18 See the costs practice direction para 13.10.

2.5.8 Rule 44.3A prevents the court from assessing an additional liability in respect of a funding agreement before the conclusion of the proceedings. At an interim hearing therefore, the court will assess only the base costs. (See paragraph 14.9 of the Costs Practice Direction for assessing an additional liability and Section 19 for information about funding arrangements.)

2.5.9 Interim orders for costs; where the court decides immediately who is to pay particular costs, but does not assess the costs summarily, for example after a trial lasting more than a day, so that the final amount of costs payable has to be fixed by a detailed assessment, the court may order the paying party to pay a sum or sums on account of the ultimate liability for costs[19].

19 See rule 44.3(8).

2.5.10 Interest on costs; the court has power to award interest on costs from a date before the date of the order, so compensating the receiving party for the delay between incurring the costs and receiving payment in respect of them.

2.5.11 Parties should note that where the court makes an order which does not mention costs, no party is entitled to costs in relation to that order[20].

20 See rule 44.13(1).

2.5.12 Rule 44.3 describes the court's discretion as to costs and the circumstances to be taken into account when exercising its discretion. Rules 44.4 and 44.5 set out the basis of assessment and the factors to be taken into account in deciding the amount of costs. (See also Sections 8 and 11 of the Costs Practice Direction.)

2.5.13 The amount of costs to be paid by one party to another can be assessed on the standard basis or on the indemnity basis. The basis to be used is decided when the court decides that a party should pay the costs of another. Costs that are unreasonably incurred or are unreasonable in amount are not allowed on either basis.

2.5.14 The standard basis is the usual basis for assessment, where only costs which are proportionate to the matters in issue are allowed, and any doubt as to whether the costs were reasonably incurred or reasonable and proportionate in amount is resolved in favour of the paying party. On the indemnity basis, any such doubts are resolved in favour of the receiving party.

2.5.15 A party must normally pay summarily assessed costs awarded against him within 14 days of the assessment, but the court can extend that time, direct payment by instalments, or defer the liability to pay the costs until the end of the proceedings so that they can then be set off against any costs or judgment to which the paying party becomes entitled.

2.5.16 Fixed costs relating to default judgments, certain judgments on admissions and summary judgments etc are set out in Part 45, (see also Section 25 of the Costs Practice Direction). Part 46 relates to fast track costs.

2.5.17 Part 47 and Sections 28–49 of the Costs Practice Direction contain the procedure for detailed assessment together with the default provisions. Precedents A, B, C and D set out in the Schedule of Costs Precedents annexed to the Costs Practice Direction are model forms of bills of costs for detailed assessment. Section 43 deals with costs payable out of the Community Legal Service fund, Section 44 deals with costs payable out of a fund other than the CLS fund and Section 49 deals with costs payable by the LSC. Part 48 and Sections 50–56 of the Costs Practice Direction deal with Special Cases, in particular;

(1)   costs payable by or to a child or patient,

(2)   litigants in person, and

(3)   wasted costs orders – personal liability of the legal representative.

2.5.18 Costs-only proceedings are dealt with in rule 44.12A and Section 17 of the Costs Practice Direction. They may be brought in the High Court only where the dispute was of such a value or type that had proceedings been brought they would have been commenced in the High Court. Proceedings are brought under Part 8 by the issue of a claim form in the Supreme Court Costs Office at Clifford's Inn, Fetter Lane, London EC4A 1DQ. (See also paragraphs 4.1.16 and 6.8.13 below.)

2.6 Court fees

2.6.1 The fees payable in the High Court are set out in Schedule 1 to the Supreme Court Fees Order 1999. Fees (as amended on 25 April 2000 and 2 May 2000) relating to the Queen's Bench Division are listed in Annex 1 to the Guide.

2.6.2 In the Royal Courts of Justice fees are paid in the Fees Room E01 and are usually stamped on the document to which they relate.

2.7 Information technology

2.7.1 To support the work of the Central Office in operating the provisions of the CPR, and to facilitate effective case management, a computerised system will be introduced to provide a record of proceedings and a search facility, and to produce court forms and orders. The full system is not yet available, but an interim system has been in use since 26 April 1999.

2.7.2 A number of specific applications of information technology have been well developed in recent years; the use of fax, the provision of skeleton arguments on disk and daily transcripts on disk have become more commonplace. Short applications may be dealt with more economically by a conference telephone call, and taking evidence by video link has become more common and the available technology has improved considerably. The CPR contains certain provisions about the use of information technology, for example, Part 6 and the Part 6 Practice Direction deal with service of documents by Fax or other electronic means, the Part 23 Practice Direction refers to telephone hearings and video conferencing, rule 32.3 allows the use of evidence given by video link and the Part 5 Practice Direction refers to the filing of documents at court by Fax.

2.7.3 Parties may agree to use information technology in the preparation, management and presentation of a case, however the agreement of the judge or master should be sought before providing the court with material in electronic form. Where permission has been given, the material for use at a hearing or in support of an application can be provided on a floppy disk. The parties should check with the court which word-processing format should be used. This will normally be Word 6 for Windows or WordPerfect for DOS 5.1.

2.7.4 A protocol has been prepared as a guide to all persons who are involved in the use of video conferencing equipment in civil proceedings in the High Court. It covers its use in courtrooms where the equipment may be installed, and also the situation where the court assembles in a commercial studio or conference room containing video conferencing equipment. Copies of the Video-conferencing Protocol may be obtained from the Bar Council at a charge of £2.50 to cover expenses. A room has now been made available as an audio/video conferencing courtroom for applications to masters, as a pilot measure. More information may be obtained from the Senior Master through the Masters' Secretary's Department.

3 STEPS BEFORE ISSUE OF A CLAIM FORM

3.1 Settlement

3.1.1 So far as reasonably possible, a claimant should try to resolve his claim without litigation. The court is increasingly taking the view that litigation should be a last resort and parties may wish to consider the use of alternative dispute resolution ('ADR'). (See paragraph 6.6 below.)

3.1.2 There are codes of practice for preliminary negotiations in certain types of claim. These codes of practice are called 'Protocols' and are set out in a schedule to the Protocols Practice Direction to the CPR. At present there are protocols covering only the areas of personal injury and clinical negligence. Even if there is no protocol that applies to the claim, the parties will nonetheless be expected to comply with the spirit of the Overriding Objective[21].

21   See the Protocols practice direction paragraph 4.

3.1.3 An offer to settle a claim may be made by either party[22] whether before or after a claim is brought. The court will take account of any offer to settle made before proceedings are started when making any order as to costs after proceedings have started[23].

22   See paragraph 3.21 of the Personal Injury protocol and paragraphs 3.22 and 3.26 of the Clinical Negligence protocol.
23   See rule 36.10 and rule 44.3(4)(c).

3.2 Disclosure before proceedings are started

3.2.1 An intending claimant may need documents to which he does not yet have access. Rule 31.16 sets out the provisions for making an application for disclosure of documents before proceedings have started.

3.2.2 Essentially, the court must be satisfied that the applicant and respondent to the application are likely to be parties when proceedings are brought, that the required documents are those that the respondent would be required to disclose under rule 31.6 when proceedings are brought and that their early disclosure might dispose of or assist the disposal of anticipated proceedings or save costs.

3.3 Defamation proceedings

3.3.1 Application may be made to the court before a claim is brought for the court's assistance in accepting an offer of amends under section 3 of the Defamation Act 1996. The application is made by Part 8 claim form. For more information see paragraph 4.1.15 Part 8 procedure and paragraph 12.7 defamation below.

4 STARTING PROCEEDINGS IN THE CENTRAL OFFICE

4.1 Issuing the claim form

4.1.1 All claims must be started by issuing a claim form. The great majority of claims involve a dispute of fact, and the claim form should be issued in accordance with Part 7 of the CPR. The Part 8 procedure may be followed in the types of claim described in paragraphs 4.1.14–4.1.16 below.

4.1.2 The requirements for issuing a claim form are set out in Part 7 and the Part 7 Practice Direction, the main points of which are summarised in the following paragraphs.

4.1.3 The Practice Direction at paragraphs 2, 3 and 4 provides information as to;

(1)   where a claim should be started,
(2)   certain matters that must be included in the claim form, and
(3)   how the heading of the claim should be set out on the claim form.

In defamation cases see Part 53 and the Part 53 Practice Direction for matters that should be included in the claim form and particulars of claim. See also paragraph 12.7 below.

4.1.4 Proceedings are started when the court issues a claim form, and a claim form is issued on the date entered on the claim form by the court[24]. However, where a claim form is received in the court office on an earlier date than the date of issue, then, for the purposes of the Limitation Act 1980, the claim is brought on the earlier date (see paragraphs 5.1–5.4 of the Part 7 Practice Direction).

24 See rule 7.2.

4.1.5 To start proceedings in the Central Office, a claimant must use form N1 or form N208 for a Part 8 claim (or a form suitably modified as permitted by Part 4), and should take or send the claim form to Room E17, Action Department, Central Office, Royal Courts of Justice, Strand, London WC2A 2LL. If the court is to serve the claim form, the claimant must provide sufficient copies for each defendant. A claimant who wishes to retain for his file a copy of the claim form as issued should provide a further copy of the claim form which the court will seal and return it to him marked 'claimant's copy'. This copy will bear any amendments which have been made to the court's copy and the copies for service. Copies of practice forms relevant to the work of the Action Department (including the claim form and response pack) are available from that office. Alternatively, claimants may produce their own forms, which may be modified as the circumstances require, provided that all essential information, especially any information or guidance that the form gives to the recipient, is included. (See Part 4 Forms.)

4.1.6 On issuing the claim form, the court will give or send the claimant a notice of issue endorsed with the date of issue of the claim form. If the claimant requires the court to serve the claim form, the date of posting and deemed date of service will also be endorsed on the notice of issue. Claimants, especially solicitors who have been accustomed to using the Action Department, are encouraged to continue to serve their own documents but must inform the court when service has been effected (see paragraph 4.2.4 in relation to service by the claimant and the certificate of service). For certain types of claims, the notice of issue contains the request for judgment. (See paragraph 5 below for information about default judgments.)

4.1.7 A claim form must be served within 4 months after the date of issue (rule 7.5) unless it is to be served out of the jurisdiction, when the period is 6 months; and rule 7.6 and paragraph 7 of the Practice Direction set out how an extension of time for service of the claim form may be sought. (See paragraph 4.2 below about service.)

4.1.8 The particulars of claim may be;

(1)   included in the claim form,
(2)   in a separate document served with the claim form, or
(3)   in a separate document served within 14 days of service of the claim form provided that the particulars of claim are served within the latest time for serving the claim form[25].

25 See rule 7.4.

4.1.9 A claim form that does not include particulars of claim must nonetheless contain a concise statement of the nature of the claim[26]. Any claim form that;

(1)   does not comply with the requirements of rule 16.2, or
(2)   is garbled or abusive,

will be referred to a master and is likely to be struck out by the court[27].

26 See rule 16.2(1), and paragraph 8 of the Part 16 practice direction in respect of defamation claims.
27 See rule 3.2.

4.1.10 Where the particulars of claim are neither included in or served with the claim form;

(1)   the claim form must contain a statement that particulars of claim will follow, and

(2)   the particulars of claim must be served by the claimant[28].

However, where a claim form is to be served out of the jurisdiction[29], the particulars of claim must accompany the claim form. (See paragraph 4.2.13 below.)

28   See rule 7.4(1)(b).
29   See rule 2.3 for the definition of 'jurisdiction'.

4.1.11 Certain forms must accompany the particulars of claim when they are served on the defendant. These forms are listed in rule 7.8 and are included in a response pack, which is available from the Action Department.

4.1.12 A party who has entered into a funding arrangement and who wishes to claim an additional liability must give the court and any other party information about that claim if he is to recover the additional liability. Where the funding arrangement has been entered into before proceedings are commenced, the claimant should file a notice of funding in form N251 when the claim form is issued[30].

30   See rule 44.15 and section 19 of the costs practice direction.

4.1.13 Part 22 requires the particulars of claim, and where they are not included in the claim form itself, the claim form to be verified by a statement of truth; see paragraph 6 of the Part 7 Practice Direction, and the Part 22 Practice Direction.

4.1.14 Part 16 and the Part 16 Practice Direction deal with statements of case, and in particular the contents of the claim form and the particulars of claim. Part 16 does not apply to claims in respect of which the Part 8 alternative procedure for claims is being used. See paragraph 5.6 below for more about statements of case.

4.1.15 A claimant may use the Part 8 procedure where;

(1)   he seeks the court's decision on a question that is unlikely to involve a substantial dispute of fact, or
(2)   a rule or practice direction requires or permits the use of the Part 8 procedure[31],

however, the court may at any stage order the claim to continue as if the claimant had not used the Part 8 procedure[32].

31   See rule 8.1.
32   See rule 8.1(3).

4.1.16 Certain matters that must be included on the claim form when the Part 8 procedure is being used are set out in rule 8.2. The types of claim for which the Part 8 procedure may be used include[33];

(1)   a claim by or against a child or patient that has been settled before the commencement of proceedings, the sole purpose of the claim being to obtain the approval of the court to the settlement,

(2)   provided there is unlikely to be a substantial dispute of fact, a claim for a summary order for possession against named or unnamed defendants occupying land or premises without the licence or consent of the person claiming possession (Schedule 1 – RSC Ord 113),

(3)   a claim for provisional damages that has been settled before the commencement of proceedings, the sole purpose of the claim being to obtain a judgment by consent,

(4)   a claim under s 3 of the Defamation Act 1996 (made other than in existing proceedings), and

(5)   a claim under rule 44.12A where the parties have agreed all issues before the commencement of proceedings except the amount of costs and an order for costs is required.

33   See paragraph 1.4 of the Part 8 practice direction.

4.1.17 In addition to the provisions of rule 8.1, attention is drawn also to the Part 8(B) Practice Direction which deals with proceedings brought under 'the Schedule Rules'[34].

See Paragraph 6.7 below for more information regarding the Part 8 procedure.

34   See paragraph 1.1 of the Part 8B practice direction.

4.2 Service

4.2.1 Service of documents is dealt with in Part 6; Section I (rules 6.1–6.11) contains provisions relating to service generally and Section II (rules 6.12–6.16) contains special provisions relating to service of the claim form. Section III (rules 6.17–6.31) deals with service out of the jurisdiction. Some of the more important provisions are described below.

WITHIN THE JURISDICTION

4.2.2 The methods by which a document may be served are to be found in rule 6.2. The court will serve a document that it has issued or prepared unless;

(1)   the party on whose behalf it is to be served notifies the court that he wishes to serve it himself,

(2)   the court orders otherwise, or

(3)   a rule or practice direction provides otherwise[35].

It is anticipated that practitioners familiar with Central Office procedures will wish to continue to serve their own documents.

35   See rule 6.3.

4.2.3 Where a party has entered into a funding agreement the notice of funding (form N251) must be served on all the other parties. If a claimant files his notice of funding when his claim form is issued, the court will serve it on the other parties provided sufficient copies are provided. Otherwise the claimant must serve the notice of funding with the claim form[36]. A defendant should file his notice of funding with his first document, ie his defence or acknowledgment of service etc. Sufficient copies of the notice should be provided for the court to serve.

36 See rule 44.15 and section 19 of the costs practice direction.

4.2.4 In all other circumstances a party must serve a notice of funding within 7 days of entering into the funding agreement[37].

37 See para 19.2 of the costs practice direction.

4.2.5 Where the court has tried to serve a document but has been unable to serve it, the court will send a notice of non-service to the party on whose behalf it was to be served stating the method attempted[38]. On receipt of this notice, the party should take steps to serve the document himself, as the court is under no further duty to effect service. The method of service used by the court will normally be first-class post.

38 See rule 6.11.

4.2.6 Where a claimant has served a claim form, he must file a certificate of service that complies with the provisions of rule 6.10. The certificate of service must be filed within 7 days of service of the claim form, and the claimant may not obtain judgment in default if it has not been filed[39].

39 See rule 6.14(2)(b).

4.2.7 Information as to how personal service is to be effected and as to service by electronic means is to be found in the Part 6 Practice Direction. Rule 6.6 deals with service on a child or patient.

4.2.8 A party must give an address for service within the jurisdiction. Rule 6.5 contains information as to the address for service.

4.2.9 A party may make an application for permission to serve a document by an alternative method[40] to those set out in rule 6.2. The application may be made without notice, and paragraph 9.1 of the Practice Direction sets out the evidence that will be required in support of the application. (Paragraph 7.12 below contains information in relation to applications.)

40 See rule 6.8.

OUT OF THE JURISDICTION

4.2.10 The provisions for service out of the jurisdiction are contained in rules 6.17–6.31. Rule 6.19 sets out the provisions whereby a claim form may be served out of the jurisdiction without the permission of the court, and rule 6.20 sets out the circumstances where the court's permission is required. Parties should also see the Practice Direction on service out of the jurisdiction.

4.2.11 A claimant may issue a claim form against defendants, one or some of whom appear to be out of the jurisdiction, without first having obtained permission for service out of the jurisdiction, provided that where the claim form is not one which may be served without the permission of the court under rule 6.19, the claim form is endorsed by the court that it is 'not for service out of jurisdiction'.

4.2.12 Where a claim form is to be served in accordance with rule 6.19 it must contain a statement of the grounds on which the claimant is entitled to serve it out of the jurisdiction. The statement should be as follows;

(1) 'I, (*name*) state that the High Court of England and Wales has power under the Civil Jurisdiction and Judgments Act 1982 to hear this claim and that no proceedings are pending between the parties in Scotland, Northern Ireland or another Convention territory of any contracting state as defined by section 1(3) of the Act.', or

(2) where the proceedings are those to which Article 16 of Schedule 1, 3C or 4 to the Act refers,
'I, (*name*) state that the High Court of England and Wales has power under the Civil Jurisdiction and Judgments Act 1982, the claim having as its object rights in rem in immovable property or tenancies in immovable property (or otherwise in accordance with the provisions of Article 16 of Schedule 1, 3C or 4 to that Act) to which Article 16 of Schedule 1, 3C or 4 to that Act applies, to hear the claim and that no proceedings are pending between the parties in Scotland, Northern Ireland or another Convention territory of any contracting state as defined by section 1(3) of the Act.', or

(3) where the defendant is party to an agreement conferring jurisdiction to which Article 17 of Schedule 1, 3C or 4 to that Act applies,
'I, (*name*) state that the High Court of England and Wales has power under the Civil Jurisdiction and Judgments Act 1982, the defendant being a party to an agreement conferring jurisdiction to which Article 17 of Schedule 1, 3C or 4 to that Act applies, to hear the claim and that no proceedings are pending between the parties in Scotland, Northern Ireland or another Convention territory of any contracting state as defined by section 1(3) of the Act.'.

4.2.13 The above statement should be signed and have set out the full name of the signatory. If a claim form as specified in paragraph 4.2.10 above does not bear the above statement, the claim form will be endorsed 'not for service out of the jurisdiction'.

4.2.14 An application for an order for permission to issue a claim form for service out of the jurisdiction or to serve the claim form out of the jurisdiction should be made in accordance with Part 23 (form PF6(A) may be used). The application must be supported by written evidence, and may be made without notice. The written evidence should state the requirements set out in rule 6.21(1) and (2).

4.2.15 An order giving permission for service out of the jurisdiction will be drawn up by the court (in form PF6(B)), unless a party wishes to do so, and will;

(1)   specify the country in which, or place at which, service is to be effected, and
(2)   specify the number of days within which the defendant may either
        (a)   file an acknowledgment of service,
        (b)   file or serve an admission, or
        (c)   file a defence to
        the claim, and where an acknowledgment of service is filed, specify a further 14 days within which the defendant may file a defence.

4.2.16 Where service is to be effected in a country which requires a translation of the documents to be served[41], it is the claimant's responsibility to provide the translation of all the documents for each defendant. In every case, it is the claimant's duty to ensure that the response pack clearly states the appropriate period for responding to the claim form, and form N9, form N1C and other relevant forms must be modified accordingly. Every translation must be accompanied by a statement by the person making it;

(1)   that it is a correct translation, and
(2)   including the person's name, address and qualifications for making the translation[42].

41   See rule 6.28.
42   Rule 6.28(3).

4.2.17 The periods for acknowledging service of a claim form served out of the jurisdiction are set out in rule 6.22 and in the Table contained in the Part 6 Section III Practice Direction, and the periods for serving a defence to a claim form served out of the jurisdiction are set out in rule 6.23 and in the Table in the Practice Direction. Rule 6.24 describes the methods of service.

4.2.18 Where the claim form is to be served through;

(1)   the judicial authorities of the country where the claim form is to be served,
(2)   a British Consular authority in that country,
(3)   the authority designated under the Hague Convention in respect of that country, or
(4)   the government of that country, or
(5)   where the court permits service on a State, the Foreign and Commonwealth Office,

the claimant should provide the Senior Master with the following documents by forwarding them to the Foreign Process section, Room E 02;

        (a)   a request for service by the chosen method (in form PF7),
        (b)   a sealed copy and a duplicate copy of the claim form,
        (c)   the response pack as referred to in paragraph 4.2.14,

(d)   a translation in duplicate, and the statement referred to in paragraph 4.2.13, and

(e)   any other relevant documents.

4.2.19 Where service has been requested in accordance with paragraph 4.2.16, the particulars of claim, if not included in the claim form, must accompany the claim form (in duplicate). Where the claimant is effecting service of the claim form direct (and not as in paragraph 4.2.16) and the claim form states that particulars of claim are to follow, the permission of the court is not required to serve the particulars of claim out of the jurisdiction.

4.2.20 Where an official certificate of service[43] is received in a foreign language, it is the responsibility of the claimant to obtain a translation of the certificate. Where a defendant served out of the jurisdiction fails to attend a hearing, the official certificate of service is evidence of service. Otherwise the claimant may take no further steps against the defendant until written evidence showing that the claim form has been duly served is filed[44].

43 See rules 6.26(5) and 6.27(4).
44 See rule 6.31.

4.2.21 Further advice on service out of the jurisdiction may be obtained from the Foreign Process section, Room E 02.

5 RESPONSE TO A PART 7 CLAIM

5.1 General

5.1.1 Responding to particulars of claim is dealt with in Part 9. A defendant may respond to the service of particulars of claim by[45]:

(1)   filing or serving an admission in accordance with Part 14,
(2)   filing a defence in accordance with Part 15,
(3)   doing both if part only of the claim is admitted, or
(4)   filing an acknowledgment of service in accordance with Part 10.

45 See rule 9.2.

5.1.2 Where a defendant receives a claim form that states that particulars of claim are to follow, he need not respond to the claim until the particulars of claim have been served on him[46].

46 See rule 9.1(2).

5.1.3 If a defendant fails to:

(1)   file an acknowledgment of service within the time specified in rule 10.3, and
(2)   file a defence within the time specified in rule 15.4, or
(3)   file or serve an admission in accordance with Part 14

the claimant may obtain default judgment if Part 12 allows it[47]. (See paragraph 5.5 below for information about default judgments.)

47 See rule 10.2.

5.2 Acknowledgment of service

5.2.1 Acknowledgments of service are dealt with in Part 10. A defendant may file an acknowledgment of service if;

(1)   he is unable to file a defence within the period specified in rule 15.4, or
(2)   he wishes to dispute the court's jurisdiction[48].

Filing an acknowledgment of service extends the time for filing the defence by 14 days.

48 See rule 10.1(3).

5.2.2 A defendant who wishes to acknowledge service of a claim form should do so by using form N9. Rule 10.5 states that the acknowledgment of service must;

(1)   be signed by the defendant or his legal representative, and
(2)   include the defendant's address for service.

The Part 10 Practice Direction contains information relating to the acknowledgment of service and how it may be signed.

5.3 Admissions

5.3.1 The manner in which a defendant may make an admission of a claim or part of a claim is set out in rules 14.1 and 14.2, and rules 14.3–14.7 set out how judgment may be obtained on a written admission.

5.3.2 Included in the response pack that will accompany the particulars of claim when they are served on the defendant is an admission form (form N9A for a specified amount and form N9C for an unspecified amount). If the defendant makes an admission and requests time to pay, he should complete as fully as possible the statement of means contained in the admission form, or otherwise give in writing the same details of his means as could have been given in the admission form.

5.3.3   Where the defendant has;

(1)   made an admission in respect of a specified sum and requested time to pay, or
(2)   made an admission in respect of an unspecified sum, offered a sum in satisfaction (which is accepted) and requested time to pay,

and the claimant has not accepted the request for time to pay, on receipt of the claimant's notice the court will enter judgment for the amount admitted or offered (less any payments made) to be paid at the time and rate of payment determined by the court[49].

49 See rule 14.10(4).

5.3.4 Where the defendant has;

(1)   made an admission for an unspecified amount, or
(2)   made an admission for an unspecified amount and offered in satisfaction a sum that the claimant has not accepted,

on receipt of the claimant's request for judgment the court will enter judgment for an amount to be decided by the court and costs[50].

50 See rules 14.6(7) and 14.7(10).

5.3.5 The matters that the court will take into account when determining the time and rate of payment are set out in paragraph 5.1 of the Part 14 Practice Direction.

5.3.6 The court may determine the time and rate of payment with or without a hearing, but, where a hearing is to take place, the proceedings must, where the provisions of rule 14.12(2) apply, be transferred to the defendant's home court. Where the claim form was issued in the Royal Courts of Justice the defendant's home court will be the district registry for the district in which the defendant's address given in the admission form is situated. If there is no such district registry the proceedings will remain in the Royal Courts of Justice[51].

51 Derived from rule 2.3.

5.3.7 The procedure for an application for re-determination of a decision determining the time and rate of payment is to be found in rule 14.13 and paragraphs 5.3–5.6 of the Practice Direction.

5.3.8 Where judgment has been entered for an amount to be decided by the court and costs, the court will give any directions that it considers appropriate, which may include allocating the case to a track[52]. (See paragraph 6.5 below about allocation.)

52 See rule 14.8.

5.3.9 Judgment will not be entered on an admission where;

(1)   the defendant is a child or patient, or
(2)   the claimant is a child or patient and the admission is made in respect of
        (a)   a specified amount of money, or
        (b)   a sum offered in satisfaction of a claim for an unspecified amount of money.

See Part 21 and the Part 21 Practice Direction, and in particular rule 21.10 which provides that, where a claim is made by or on behalf of a child or patient or against a child or patient, no settlement, compromise or payment shall be valid, so far as it relates to that person's claim, without the approval of the court.

5.4 Defence

5.4.1 A defendant who wishes to defend all or part of a claim must file a defence, and if he fails to do so, the claimant may obtain default judgment if Part 12 allows it[53]. The time for filing a defence is set out in rule 15.4.

53 See rules 15.2 and 15.3.

5.4.2 A form for defending the claim[54] is included in the response pack. The form for defending the claim also contains provision for making a counterclaim[55]. Part 22 requires a defence to be verified by a statement of truth (see the Part 15 Practice Direction, paragraph 2; and see also Part 22 and the Part 22 Practice Direction).

54 Forms N9B and N9D.
55 See Part 20.

5.4.3 The parties may, by agreement, extend the period specified in rule 15.4 for filing a defence by up to 28 days[56]. If the parties do so, the defendant must notify the court in writing of the date by which the defence must be filed.

56 See rule 15.5.

5.5 Default judgment

5.5.1 A party may obtain default judgment under Part 12 except in the circumstances set out in rule 12.2 and paragraphs 1.2 and 1.3 of the Part 12 Practice Direction, which list the circumstances where default judgment may not be obtained.

5.5.2 To obtain default judgment under the circumstances set out in rules 12.4(1) and 12.9(1), a party may do so by filing a request[57]. A request is dealt with by a court officer and provided he is satisfied that the provisions of paragraph 4.1 of the Part 12 Practice Direction have been complied with, he will enter the default judgment.

57 Forms N205A, N255, N255B or N227.

5.5.3 Default judgment in respect of claims specified in rules 12.4(2)(a), 12.9 and 12.10 must be obtained by making an application to a master. The following are some of the types of claim which require an application for default judgment;

(1)   against children and patients,
(2)   for costs (other than fixed costs) only,
(3)   by one spouse against the other on a claim in tort,
(4)   for delivery up of goods where the defendant is not allowed the alternative of paying their value,
(5)   against the Crown, and

(6) against persons or organisations who enjoy immunity from civil jurisdiction under the provisions of the International Organisations Acts 1968 and 1981.

Paragraph 4 of the Practice Direction provides information about the evidence required in support of an application for default judgment.

5.5.4 Where default judgment has been obtained for an amount to be decided by the court, the matter will be referred to a master for directions to be given concerning the management of the case and any date to be fixed for a hearing.

Statements of case

5.6.1 Statements of case comprise the particulars of claim and defence in the main proceedings and also in any Part 20 proceedings, and are dealt with in Part 16. (Part 16 does not apply to claims proceeding under Part 8.)

5.6.2 The particulars of claim, whether contained in the claim form or served separately, should set out the claimant's claim clearly and fully. The same principle applies to the defence.

5.6.3 Part 16 sets out certain matters which must be included in a statement of case. Paragraphs 8 and 9 of the Part 16 Practice Direction contain matters which should be included in the particulars of claim in specific types of claim, and paragraph 10 lists matters which must be set out in the particulars of claim if relied on. In addition to the matters listed in paragraph 10, full particulars of any allegation of dishonesty or malice and, where any inference of fraud or dishonesty is alleged, the basis on which the inference is alleged should also be included. Points of law may be set out in any statement of case. For information in respect of statements of case in defamation claims see the Part 53 Practice Direction.

5.6.4 In addition to the information contained in Part 16 and the Part 16 Practice Direction, the following guidelines on preparing a statement of case should be followed;

(1) a statement of case must be as brief and concise as possible,
(2) a statement of case should be set out in separate consecutively numbered paragraphs and sub-paragraphs,
(3) so far as possible each paragraph or sub-paragraph should contain no more than one allegation,
(4) the facts and other matters alleged should be set out as far as reasonably possible in chronological order,
(5) the statement of case should deal with the claim on a point by point basis, to allow a point by point response,
(6) where a party is required to give reasons[58], the allegation should be stated first and then the reasons listed one by one in separate numbered sub-paragraphs,
(7) a party wishing to advance a positive claim must identify that claim in the statement of case,

(8)   any matter which if not stated might take another party by surprise should be stated,

(9)   where they will assist, headings, abbreviations and definitions should be used and a glossary annexed; contentious headings, abbreviations, paraphrasing and definitions should not be used and every effort should be made to ensure that they are in a form acceptable to the other parties,

(10)   particulars of primary allegations should be stated as particulars and not as primary allegations,

(11)   schedules or appendices should be used if this would be helpful, for example where lengthy particulars are necessary, and any response should also be stated in a schedule or appendix,

(12)   any lengthy extracts from documents should be placed in a schedule.

58   See rule 16.5(2).

5.6.5 A statement of case should be verified by a statement of truth[59]. If a party fails to verify his statement of case, it will remain effective unless struck out, but that party may not rely on the statement of case as evidence of any of the matters contained in it[60]. Any party may apply to the court for an order to strike out a statement of case which has not been verified[61].

59   See rule 22.1.
60   See rule 22.2(1).
61   See rule 22.2(2) and (3).

6 PRELIMINARY CASE MANAGEMENT

6.1 The Practice Master

6.1.1 On every working day, the Practice Master is available from 10.30 am to 1.00 pm and from 2.00 pm to 4.30 pm to answer questions about the practice of the Queen's Bench Division. Usually, one master takes the Morning Practice, and another master takes the Afternoon Practice. This will be shown on the case-lists for the day and on the notice boards in the masters' corridors. Also, a board is placed on the door of the master who is sitting as Practice Master.

6.1.2 The Practice Master cannot give advice, whether about a given case or about the law generally. He is there simply to answer general questions about the CPR and practice governing the work of the Queen's Bench Division, and can deal with any consent order, notwithstanding that the claim in which it is to be made has been assigned to another master. The Practice Master may grant stays of execution and deal with urgent applications which do not require notice to be given to the respondent. It is unnecessary to make an appointment to see the Practice Master, litigants are generally seen in order of arrival.

6.2 Assignment to masters

6.2.1 A claim issued in the Central Office will normally be assigned at the issue stage to a particular master as the procedural judge responsible for managing the claim. The Action Department will endorse the name of the assigned master on the claim form. However, assignment may be triggered at an earlier stage, for example, by one of the following events;

(1)   an application for pre-action disclosure under rule 31.16,

(2)   an application for an interim remedy before the commencement of a claim or where there is no relevant claim (Part 25).

It occasionally happens that a claim is assigned to a master who may have an 'interest' in the claim. In such cases the Senior Master will re-assign the claim to another master.

6.2.2 Where either an application notice or Part 8 claim form is issued which requires a hearing date to be given immediately, the Masters' Support Unit will give a hearing date and assign it to the master who has the next available date for the hearing. The Masters' Support Unit will endorse the name of that master on the application notice or Part 8 claim form at the time of entering it in the list for hearing.

6.2.3 The Senior Master may assign a particular master to a class/group of claims or may re-assign work generally. At present clinical negligence claims are assigned to Master Murray and Master Ungley. In the event of an assigned master being on leave or for any other reason temporarily absent from the Royal Courts of Justice then the Masters' Support Unit may endorse on the appropriate document the name of another master.

6.2.4 A court file will normally be opened when a defence is filed, provided that the claim is not one that will automatically be transferred (see paragraph 6.4 below). The court file will be endorsed with the name of the assigned master. Any application notice in an assigned claim for hearing before a master should have the name of the assigned master entered on it by the solicitors making the application.

6.3 Listing before masters

6.3.1 The masters' lists consist of;

(1)   the ordinary list – short applications in Rooms E102 and E110 ('the Bear Garden lists'),

(2)   the Floating list,

(3)   private room appointments[62], and

(4)   the sheriff's first return applications.

---

62 A private room appointment is given where the hearing will be more than 20 minutes and takes place in the master's private room rather than a Bear Garden room. The appointment must be made by the master personally.

6.3.2 Parties attending on all applications before the masters are requested to complete the court record sheet (form PF48) which will be used to record details of the claim, representation and the nature of the application, and will be used by the master for his notes. Copies of this form may be found in the writing desks in the masters' corridors and the Bear Garden.

6.3.3 Masters will sit each day at 10.30 am in the Bear Garden to hear applications in the Bear Garden lists. Applications of up to 20 minutes duration are listed at 10.30 am, 11.00 am, 11.30 am and 12 noon. Solicitors and Counsel may attend any application in these lists although the costs of being represented by Counsel may be disallowed if not fully justified. If an application is estimated to take longer than 20 minutes the applicant must request a private room appointment. To do so the applicant must complete the PRA form giving details of the parties' availability as fully as possible. Failure to do so may result in the request form being returned for further information thereby delaying the hearing date.

6.3.4 Hearing dates for the Bear Garden lists are given by the Masters' Support Unit. Hearing dates for private room appointments are given by the assigned master personally. The parties or their legal representatives must inform the Masters' Support Unit of any settlements as soon as possible. All time estimates must be updated as necessary.

6.3.5 Applications in the Bear Garden list may, by agreement or where the application notice has not been served, be transferred (in the case of a 10 minute application) to the next available 12 noon list or (in either case) for a private room appointment on a date to be specified by the master. In all other cases an application for a postponement of the hearing date must be made to the master to whom the claim has been assigned. An application may be re-listed in the Bear Garden list without permission of a master if for any reason the application has not been heard or has not been fully disposed of.

6.3.6 When an application in the Bear Garden list is adjourned by a master he will specify the date to which it is adjourned. An application for the adjournment of a private room appointment must be made to the master who gave the appointment unless the application is by agreement of all parties and the master approves. The master will usually require details of parties' availability. Any adjournment will normally now be to a new hearing date.

6.3.7 Where an application for which a master has given a private room appointment has been settled, it is the duty of the parties or their legal representatives, particularly those who obtained that appointment, to notify the master immediately.

6.3.8 If the master hearing an application considers that the result might affect the date fixed for a trial, he may refer the application to the judge in charge of the list. This possibility should be considered when making an application and a request should be included in the application notice asking the master to refer the application to the judge.

6.3.9 If the master considers that an application should more properly be heard by a judge, he may either during the hearing or before it takes place refer the application to the Interim Applications judge. Among the circumstances that may make this appropriate are;

(1)   that the time required for the hearing is longer than a master could ordinarily make available,

(2)   that, whatever the master's decision on the application, an appeal to the judge is considered inevitable,

(3)   that the application raises issues of unusual difficulty or importance, etc or

(4)   that the outcome is likely to affect the trial date or window.

However, it is emphasised that no single factor or combination of factors is necessarily decisive, and the master has a complete discretion.

6.3.10 The sheriff's first return applications are interpleader applications (under RSC Ord 17 as set out in Schedule 1 to the CPR) and are listed at monthly intervals.

6.3.11 The Floating List is run by the Masters' Support Unit. Applications in this list will usually have a time estimate of not more than 30 minutes and are released by the assigned master, if he considers them suitable, when the request for a private room appointment is made. Dates and times of hearings are allocated by staff in Room E14. The parties should assemble at Room E14 well before the appointed time in order to facilitate the allocation of the application to a master or deputy who is free.

6.4 Automatic transfer

6.4.1 Part 26 requires certain claims to be transferred automatically[63]. Where;

(1)   the claim is for a specified amount of money,

(2)   the claim has not been issued in a specialist list[64],

(3)   the defendant, or one of the defendants is an individual,

(4)   the claim has not been issued in the individual defendant's home court, and

(5)   the claim has not already been transferred to another individual defendant's home court,

the claim will, on receipt of the defence, be transferred to the individual defendant's home court.

63   See rules 26.1 and 2.
64   See Part 49.

6.4.2 Where the claim form was issued in the Royal Courts of Justice the defendant's home court will be the district registry for the district in which the defendant's address for service as shown on the defence is situated. If there is no such district registry the proceedings will remain in the Royal Courts of Justice[65]. If the claim is against more than one individual defendant, the claim will be transferred to the home court of the defendant who first files his defence. (See paragraph 6.9 below about transfer following an order.)

65   See rule 2.3(1)(b).

6.5 Allocation

6.5.1 When a defence to a claim is received in the Central Office from all the defendants, or from one or more of the defendants and the time for filing a defence has expired, the Action Department Registry will send an allocation questionnaire to those defendants who have filed a defence[66], unless it has been dispensed with.

66   See Part 26 and the Part 26 practice direction.

6.5.2 The allocation questionnaire to be used in accordance with Part 26 is form N150. The allocation questionnaire will state the time within which it must be filed, which will normally be at least 14 days after the day on which it is deemed served. Where proceedings are automatically transferred to a defendant's home court, notwithstanding that the issuing court will send out the allocation questionnaire before transfer, the allocation questionnaire should nevertheless be returned to the receiving court.

6.5.3 Each party should state in his allocation questionnaire if there is any reason why the claim should be managed and tried at a court other than the Royal Courts of Justice or the trial centre for a particular district registry. Paragraph 2.6 of the Part 29 Practice Direction sets out certain types of claim which are suitable for trial in the Royal Courts of Justice. Form PF49 will be sent out to parties with the allocation questionnaire requesting the parties to state convenient dates for a case management conference, if one should be ordered, or for other hearings. Parties are encouraged to agree directions for the management of the claim.

6.5.4 Where a party fails to file his allocation questionnaire within the specified time the court officer will refer the proceedings to the master for his directions. The master's directions may include 'the standard unless order', that is that unless the defaulting party files his allocation questionnaire within 3 days, his statement of case will be struck out[67].

67   See paragraph 2.5 of the Part 26 practice direction.

6.5.5 Where one but not all of the parties has filed an allocation questionnaire the master may allocate the claim to the multi-track where he considers that he has sufficient information to do so. Alternatively, the master may order that an allocation hearing take place and that all or any particular parties must attend. The court officer will then send out a Notice of Allocation Hearing (form N153) giving reasons for the hearing and any other directions.

6.5.6 Parties requesting a stay to settle the proceedings should do so in their allocation questionnaire or otherwise in writing. The court encourages parties to consider the use of ADR (see paragraph 6.6 below). The master will normally direct the proceedings to be stayed for one month, but parties may by agreement seek an extension of the stay. Paragraph 3 of the Part 26 Practice Direction sets out the procedure for seeking an extension.

6.5.7 Parties are reminded that an estimate of costs must be filed and served when the allocation questionnaire is filed (paragraph 6.4 of the Costs Practice Direction).

6.5.8 On receipt of the allocation questionnaires or on an allocation hearing the master will allocate the claim to the multi-track or transfer the claim to the appropriate county court[68]. Rule 26.6 sets out the scope of each track. Claims proceeding in the Royal Courts of Justice must be allocated to the multi-track.

68 County Courts Act 1984, ss 40–42 and Part 30.

6.6 Alternative dispute resolution ('ADR')

6.6.1 Parties are encouraged to use ADR (such as, but not confined to, mediation and conciliation) to try to resolve their disputes or particular issues. Legal representatives should consider with their clients and the other parties the possibility of attempting to resolve the dispute or particular issues by ADR and they should ensure that their clients are fully informed as to the most cost effective means of resolving their dispute.

6.6.2 The settlement of disputes by ADR can;

(1)   significantly reduce parties' costs,
(2)   save parties the delay of litigation in resolving their disputes,
(3)   assist parties to preserve their existing commercial relationships while resolving their disputes, and
(4)   provide a wider range of remedies than those available through litigation.

The master will in an appropriate case invite the parties to consider whether their dispute, or particular issues in it, could be resolved by ADR. The master may also either adjourn proceedings for a specified period of time or extend the time for compliance with an order, a rule or practice direction to encourage and enable the parties to use ADR. Parties may apply for directions seeking a stay for ADR at any time.

6.6.3 Information concerning ADR may be obtained from the Admiralty and Commercial Court registry.

6.7 Part 8 – alternative procedure for claims

6.7.1 Paragraphs 4.1.14–4.1.16 above deal with issuing a Part 8 claim form. The alternative procedure set out in Part 8 ('the Part 8 procedure') may not be used if a practice direction disapplies it in respect of a particular type of claim. A practice direction may require or permit the Part 8 procedure and may disapply or modify any of the rules contained in Part 8. The Part 8B Practice Direction deals with commencement of proceedings under the Rules of the Supreme Court and the County Court Rules the provisions of which remain in force in Schedules 1 and 2 to the CPR ('the Schedule rules'). The Schedule rules and the practice directions supporting them may require certain proceedings to be commenced by the issue of a Part 8 claim form with appropriate modifications to the Part 8 procedure.

6.7.2 The main features of the Part 8 procedure are;

(1)   Part 16 (statements of case) does not apply,

(2)   Part 15 (defence and reply) does not apply,

(3)   judgment in default may not be obtained (rule 12.2),

(4)   Rules 14.4–14.7 (judgment by request on an admission) do not apply,

(5)   a Part 8 claim shall be treated as being allocated to the multi-track[69]

69   Rule 8.9.

6.7.3 A master may give directions for managing the claim as soon as the Part 8 claim form is issued. In certain circumstances this may include fixing a hearing date. Where a hearing date is fixed, notice of the hearing date must be served with the claim form[70]. Where the master does not fix a hearing date when the claim form is issued he will give directions for the disposal of the claim as soon as practicable after the receipt of the acknowledgment of service or as the case may be, the expiry of the period for acknowledging service.

70   See paragraph 4 of the Part 8 practice direction (alternative procedure) about managing the claim.

6.7.4 Where a Part 8 claim form has been issued for the purpose of giving effect to a consent order for an award of damages to a child or patient or an award of provisional damages as in paragraph 4.1.15 (1) and (2) above, a draft of the order sought should be attached to the claim form. For more information see paragraphs 6.8.1–6.8.8 and 9.3.8–9.3.10 below about children and patients, and paragraphs 6.8.12, 9.3.11 and 9.3.12 below about provisional damages.

6.7.5 A defendant who wishes to respond to a Part 8 claim form should acknowledge service of it and may do so either by using form N210 or otherwise in writing giving the following information;

(1)   whether he contests the claim, and

(2)   where he is seeking a different remedy from that set out in the claim form, what that remedy is.

If a defendant does not acknowledge service of the claim form within the specified time, he may attend the hearing of the claim but may not take part in the hearing unless the court gives permission[71].

71   See rule 8.4.

6.7.6 Rules 8.5 and 8.6 and paragraph 5 of the Part 8 Practice Direction (alternative procedure) deal with evidence to be relied on in Part 8 proceedings; the claimant's evidence must be filed and served with the claim form, and the defendant's evidence (if any) must be filed with his acknowledgment of service. If the defendant files written evidence he must at the same time serve it on the other parties. It is helpful to the court if, where the defendant does not intend to rely on written evidence, he notifies the court in writing to that effect.

6.7.7 Where a defendant contends that the Part 8 procedure should not be used, he should state the reasons for his contention on his acknowledgment of service. On receipt of the acknowledgment of service, the master will give appropriate directions for the future management of the claim.

6.8 Specific matters which may be dealt with under the Part 8 procedure

SETTLEMENTS ON BEHALF OF CHILDREN AND PATIENTS

6.8.1 Part 21 and the Part 21 Practice Direction set out the requirements for litigation by or against children and patients. References in Part 21, the Part 21 Practice Direction and in this guide to;

(1)   'child' means a person under 18, and
(2)   'patient' means a person who by reason of mental disorder within the meaning of the Mental Health Act 1983 is incapable of managing and administering his own affairs[72].

No settlement or compromise of a claim by or against a child or patient will be binding unless and until it has been approved by the court. In addition, a party may not obtain a default judgment against a child or patient without the permission of the court, and may not enter judgment on an admission against a child or patient.

72   See rule 21.1(2).

6.8.2 A patient must have a litigation friend to conduct proceedings on his behalf, and so must a child unless the court makes an order permitting the child to act on his own behalf. A litigation friend is someone who can fairly and competently conduct proceedings on behalf of the child or patient. He must have no interest in the proceedings adverse to that of the child or patient, and all steps he takes in the proceedings must be taken for the benefit of the child or patient. Rules 21.5–21.8 and paragraphs 2 and 3 of the Practice Direction set out how a person may become a litigation friend.

6.8.3 Applications for the approval of settlements or compromises of claims by or against a child or patient proceeding in the Central Office are heard by a master. If the purpose of starting the claim is for the approval of a settlement, a Part 8 claim form should be issued in accordance with form PF170(A) which must contain a request for approval of the settlement (or compromise) and, in addition to the details of the claim, must set out the terms of the settlement (or compromise) or must have attached to it a draft consent order. The draft consent order should be in form N292. See paragraph 6 of the Practice Direction for further information which the master will require.

6.8.4 Where parties reach a settlement (or compromise) in proceedings started by the issue of a Part 7 claim form (where the trial has not started) an application may be made to the master in accordance with Part 23 for the approval of the settlement. The application notice should be in form PF170(B) and should have attached to it a draft consent order in form N292. The application notice should be filed in Room E16. (See paragraph 7.12 below for information about applications.)

However, where the trial hearing has been listed, the application notice should be filed in Room WG5. If the trial has started, oral application may be made to the trial judge. Applications for approval of a settlement on behalf of a child or patient will normally be heard in public unless the judge or master orders otherwise[73]. If a settlement is approved in private, the terms of settlement can be announced in public.

73 See rule 39.2.

6.8.5 Paragraph 8 of the Practice Direction gives information about control of money recovered by or on behalf of a child or patient. Paragraph 10 deals with investment of money on behalf of a child and paragraph 11 deals with investment on behalf of a patient. Enquiries concerning investment for a child are dealt with in Room E13.

6.8.6 In respect of investment on behalf of a child, the litigation friend or his legal representative should provide the master with form PF172 (request for investment) for completion by the master. The child's birth certificate should also be provided. The PF172 will then be forwarded to the Court Funds Office for their investment managers to make the appropriate investment. The Court of Protection is responsible for the administration of patients' funds (unless they are small). Paragraph 11 of the Practice Direction gives full information about procedure for investment by the Court of Protection. These procedures may also be used for investment of money on behalf of a child or patient following an award of damages at trial.

6.8.7 Damages may also be paid to a child or patient by way of a structured settlement. A structured settlement on behalf of a child or patient must be approved by a judge or master. A structured settlement on behalf of a patient must also be approved by the Court of Protection. (For more information about structured settlements see the Part 40C Practice Direction – Structured Settlements.)

6.8.8 Control of a child's fund, provided he is not also a patient, passes to him when he reaches the age of 18 (see paragraph 12.2 of the Practice Direction).

SUMMARY ORDER FOR POSSESSION

6.8.9 Where there is unlikely to be a substantial dispute of fact, a claim for a summary order for possession against named or unnamed defendants occupying land or premises without the licence or consent of the person claiming possession under RSC Ord 113 (Schedule 1 to the CPR) may be started by the issue of a Part 8 claim form.

6.8.10 When the claim form has been issued in the Action Department it will be passed to the Masters' Support Unit who will assign a master to the claim and fix a hearing date. Parties should check that they have sufficient time for service.

6.8.11 At the hearing the master may make the order sought or such other order as appropriate including directions for the management of the claim.

SETTLEMENT OF A PROVISIONAL DAMAGES CLAIM

6.8.12 A claim for provisional damages may proceed under Part 8 where the claim form is issued solely for the purpose of obtaining a consent judgment[74]. The claimant must state in his claim form in addition to the matters set out in paragraph 4.4 of the Part 16 Practice Direction that the parties have reached agreement and request a consent judgment. A draft order in accordance with paragraph 4.2 of the Part 41 Practice Direction should be attached to the claim form. The claimant or his legal representative must lodge the case file documents (set out in the draft order) in Room E14 for the case file to be compiled and preserved by the court. For more information about provisional damages claims and orders see Part 41 and the Part 41 Practice Direction, and paragraph 9.3 below.

74 See paragraph 1.4(2) of the Part 8 practice direction.

COSTS-ONLY PROCEEDINGS

6.8.13 Proceedings may be brought under Part 8 where the parties to a dispute have reached a written agreement before proceedings have been started but have been unable to agree an amount of costs. The costs-only proceedings may be started by the issue of a claim form in the Supreme Court Costs Office at Clifford's Inn, Fetter Lane, London EC4A 1DQ. The Costs Practice Direction at Section 17 sets out in detail the provisions for issue and proceeding with the claim.

6.9 Transfer

6.9.1 Part 30 and the Part 30 Practice Direction deal with transfer of proceedings, within the High Court, and between county courts. The jurisdiction of the High Court to transfer proceedings to the county courts is contained in s 40 of the County Courts Act 1984 as substituted by s 2(1) of the Courts and Legal Services Act 1990. Under that section the court has jurisdiction in certain circumstances to strike out claims which should have been started in a county court.

6.9.2 Rule 30.2 sets out the provisions for the transfer of proceedings between;

(1)   county courts,
(2)   the Royal Courts of Justice and a district registry of the High Court, and
(3)   between district registries.

Rule 30.3 sets out the criteria to which the court will have regard when making an order for transfer. The High Court may order proceedings in any Division of the High Court to be transferred to another Division or to or from a specialist list. An application for the transfer of proceedings to or from a specialist list must be made to a judge dealing with claims in that list[75]. (See paragraph 6.4 above about automatic transfer.)

75 See rule 30.5.

6.9.3 A claim with an estimated value of less than £50,000 will generally be transferred to a county court, if the county court has jurisdiction, unless it is to proceed in the High Court under an enactment or in a specialist list.

6.9.4 An order for transfer takes effect from the date it is made[76]. When an order for transfer is made the court officer will immediately send notice of the transfer to the receiving court. The notice will contain the title of the proceedings and the claim number. At the same time, the court officer will also notify all parties of the transfer.

76 See paragraph 3 of the Part 30 practice direction.

6.9.5 Paragraph 5 of the Practice Direction sets out the procedure for appealing an order for transfer. Where an order for transfer is made in the absence of a party, that party may apply to the court which made the order to have it set aside[77]. The transferring court will normally retain the court file until the time for appealing the order or applying to set it aside has expired, whereupon the court officer will send the court file to the court manager of the receiving court. If, at the time an order for transfer is made a court file has not been compiled, the court officer will send to the receiving court those documents which have been filed at that time.

77 See paragraph 6 of the practice direction.

6.9.6 Where money has been paid into court before an order for transfer is made, the court may direct transfer of the money to the control of the receiving court.

6.10 Part 20 proceedings

6.10.1 Part 20 deals with (a) counterclaims and (b) other additional claims, being claims for contribution or indemnity and what were formerly called 'third party' claims. A Part 20 claim is treated as a claim for the purpose of the CPR with certain exceptions, for which see rule 20.3.

6.10.2 A defendant may make a counterclaim by completing the defence and counterclaim form provided in the response pack. If the counterclaim is not filed with the defence, the permission of the court is required[78]. Where a counterclaim brings in a new party, the defendant (Part 20 claimant) must apply to the court for an order in form PF21A adding the new party as defendant[79].

78 Rule 20.4.
79 Rule 20.5.

6.10.3 A defendant claiming contribution or indemnity from another defendant may do so by filing a notice, in form PF22, containing a statement of the nature and grounds of his claim and serving the notice on the other defendant[80].

80 Rule 20.6.

6.10.4 Any other additional claim may be brought by the issue of a Part 20 claim form, N211. If the Part 20 claim form is issued at a time other than when the defence is filed, the permission of the court is required. Rule 20.8 deals with service of a Part 20 claim form and rule 20.12 sets out the forms which must accompany the Part 20 claim form.

6.11 Summary judgment

6.11.1 The court may give summary judgment under Part 24 against a claimant or defendant;

(1)   if it considers that (a) the claimant has no real prospect of succeeding on the claim or issue, or (b) the defendant has no real prospect of successfully defending the claim, and

(2)   there is no other reason why the claim or issue should be disposed of at a trial.

6.11.2 The court may give summary judgment against a claimant in any type of proceedings, and against a defendant in any type of proceedings except (a) proceedings for possession of residential premises against a mortgagor, or a tenant or person holding over after the end of his tenancy where occupancy is protected within the meaning of the Rent Act 1977 or the Housing Act 1988, (b) proceedings for an Admiralty claim in Rem, and (c) contentious probate proceedings[81]. For information about summary disposal of defamation claims see Part 53, the Part 53 Practice Direction and paragraph 12.7 below.

81   See rule 24.3 but see also Schedule 1 RSC Ord 77, r 7(1).

6.11.3 An application for summary judgment should be made in accordance with Part 23 and the application notice should contain the information set out in paragraph 2 of the Part 24 Practice Direction (parties may use forms PF11 and PF12 as precedents). The application notice should be filed and served on the respondent giving at least 14 days notice of the date fixed for the hearing and the issues to be decided at the hearing. Unless the application notice contains all the evidence on which the applicant relies, the application notice should identify that evidence. In claims which include a claim for;

(1)   specific performance of an agreement,

(2)   rescission of such an agreement, or

(3)   forfeiture or return of a deposit made under such an agreement,

the application notice and any evidence in support must be served on the defendant not less than 4 days before the hearing[82].

82   See the Part 24 practice direction paragraph 7.

6.11.4 The application will normally be listed before a master unless for example, an injunction is also sought. In that case the application notice should state that the application is intended to be made to a judge.

6.11.5 Where an order made on an application for summary judgment does not dispose of the claim or issue, the court will give case management directions in respect of the claim or issue.

6.12 Offers to settle and payments into and out of court

6.12.1 A party may offer to settle a claim at any time. Part 36 deals with offers to settle and payments into court. An offer to settle made in accordance with Part 36 will have the costs and other consequences specified in that Part and may be made at any time after proceedings have started. Paragraph 1 of the Part 36 Practice Direction defines an offer made in accordance with Part 36. See also paragraph 5 of the Part 36 Practice Direction which contains general provisions concerning Part 36 offers and Part 36 payments.

6.12.2 A Part 36 offer may be made by any party, but to comply with Part 36 a defendant who makes an offer to settle for a specified sum must do so by way of a Part 36 payment into court. Paragraph 4.1(2) of the Part 36 Practice Direction sets out the requirements for making a Part 36 payment in respect of a claim proceeding in the Royal Courts of Justice. If a defendant has made a pre-action offer to settle and proceedings are then started, in order for the court to take account of his offer he must make a Part 36 payment of not less than the amount offered within 14 days of service of the claim form. See also paragraph 10 of the Part 36 Practice Direction which deals with compensation recovery in respect of Part 36 payments.

6.12.3 The times for accepting a Part 36 offer or Part 36 payment are set out in rules 36.11 and 36.12; the general rule is that a Part 36 offer or Part 36 payment made more than 21 days before the start of the trial may be accepted without the permission of the court, within 21 days after it was made. Otherwise, the permission of the court must be obtained. A Part 36 offer is made when received by the offeree. A Part 36 payment is made when the Part 36 payment notice (form N242A) is served on the claimant.

6.12.4 A party may accept a Part 36 offer or Part 36 payment by serving on the offeror a notice of acceptance (form N243 may be used to accept a Part 36 payment) within the times set out in rules 36.11 and 36.12. When a Part 36 offer or Part 36 payment is accepted within those times, the general rule is that the claimant will be entitled to his costs up to the date of service of the notice of acceptance.

6.12.5 To obtain money out of court on acceptance of a Part 36 payment, the claimant should file a request for payment (form N243) in the Action Department of the Central Office, and file a completed Court Funds Office form 201 in the Court Funds Office. See paragraph 8 of the Part 36 Practice Direction for more information about obtaining payment out of court.

6.12.6 The court's permission is required for acceptance of a Part 36 offer or Part 36 payment;

(1)   which is not made or accepted within the times set out in rules 36.11 and 36.12,

(2)   where acceptance is by or on behalf of a child or patient[83], or

(3)   where a defence of tender has been put forward, or

(4)   otherwise as mentioned in rule 36.17.

83   See rule 21.10.

6.12.7 Where a Part 36 offer or Part 36 payment is not accepted and a trial of the claim takes place, rule 36.20 sets out the costs consequences where a claimant fails to do better than the Part 36 offer or Part 36 payment, and rule 36.21 sets out the costs and other consequences where a claimant does better than he proposed in his Part 36 offer.

7 CASE MANAGEMENT AND INTERIM REMEDIES

7.1 Case management – general

7.1.1 The CPR require the court to provide a high degree of case management. Case management includes; identifying disputed issues at an early stage; fixing timetables; dealing with as many aspects of the claim as possible on the same occasion; controlling costs; disposing of proceedings summarily where appropriate; dealing with the applications without a hearing where appropriate; and giving directions to ensure that the trial of a claim proceeds quickly and efficiently. The court will expect the parties to co-operate with each other, and where appropriate, will encourage the parties to use ADR or otherwise help them settle the case.

7.1.2 Parties and their legal representatives will be expected to do all that they can to agree proposals for the management of the claim in accordance with rule 29.4 and paragraphs 4.6–4.8 of the Part 29 Practice Direction. There is provision in the allocation questionnaire for proposing certain directions to be made, otherwise parties may use form PF50 for making the application (attaching to it the draft form of order in form PF52) and file it for the master's approval. If the master approves the proposals he will give directions accordingly.

7.1.3 Parties should consider whether a case summary would assist the master in dealing with the issues before him. Paragraph 5.7 of the Part 29 Practice Direction sets out the provisions for preparation of a case summary.

7.2 The case management conference

7.2.1 Parties who are unable to agree proposals for the management of the case, should notify the court of the matters which they are unable to agree.

7.2.2 Where;

(1)   the parties proposed directions are not approved, or

(2)   parties are unable to agree proposed directions, or

(3)   the master wishes to make further directions,

the master will generally either consult the parties or direct that a case management conference be held.

7.2.3 In relatively straightforward claims, the court will give directions without holding a case management conference.

7.2.4 Any party who considers that a case management conference should be held before any directions are given should so state in his allocation questionnaire, (or in a Part 8 claim should notify the master in writing), giving his reasons and supplying a realistic time estimate for the case management conference, with a list of any dates or times convenient to all parties, or most of them, in form PF49.

7.2.5 Where a case management conference has been fixed, parties should ensure that any other applications are listed or made at that hearing. A party applying for directions at the case management conference should use form PF50 for making their application and attach to it the draft order for directions (form PF52).

7.2.6 The advocates instructed or expected to be instructed to appear at the trial should attend any hearing at which case management directions are likely to be given. In any event, the legal representatives who attend the case management conference must be familiar with the case and have sufficient authority to deal with any issues which may arise. Where necessary, the court may order the attendance of a party[84].

84 See rule 3.1(c).

7.3 Preliminary issues

7.3.1 Costs can sometimes be saved by identifying decisive issues, or potentially decisive issues, and by the court ordering that they be tried first. The decision of one issue, although not necessarily itself decisive of the claim as a whole, may enable the parties to settle the remainder of the dispute. In such a case, the trial of a preliminary issue may be appropriate.

7.3.2 At the allocation stage, at any case management conference and again at any pre-trial review, the court will consider whether the trial of a preliminary issue may be helpful. Where such an order is made, the parties and the court should consider whether the costs of the issue should be in the issue or in the claim as a whole.

7.3.3 Where there is an application for summary judgment, and issues of law or construction may be determined in the respondent's favour, it will usually be in the interests of the parties for such issues to be determined conclusively, rather than that the application should simply be dismissed.

7.4 Trial timetable

7.4.1 To assist the court to set a trial timetable[85], a draft timetable should be prepared by the claimant's advocate(s) after consulting the other parties advocates.

If there are differing views, those differences should be clearly indicated in the timetable. The draft timetable should be filed with the trial bundle.

85 See rules 29.8 and 39.4.

7.4.2 The trial timetable will normally include times for giving evidence (whether of fact or opinion) and for oral submissions during the trial.

7.4.3 The trial timetable may be fixed at the case management conference, at any pre-trial review or at the beginning of the trial itself.

7.5 Listing questionnaire

7.5.1 The court may send out a listing questionnaire (N170) to all parties for completion, specifying the date by which it must be returned. The master will then fix the trial date or period ('the trial window'). It is likely however, that the master will already have sufficient information to enable him to fix a trial window, and will dispense with the need for a listing questionnaire subject to any requirement of the Clerk of the Lists for one to be filed. Instead, the master will direct the parties within a specified time to attend before the Clerk of the Lists to fix a trial date within that window.

7.5.2 Paragraph 6.4 of the Costs Practice Direction requires an estimate of costs to be filed and served with the listing questionnaire. If the filing of a listing questionnaire has been dispensed with, the estimate of costs should be filed on attendance before the Clerk of the Lists.

7.6 Pre-trial review

7.6.1 Where the trial of a claim is estimated to last more than 10 days, or where the circumstances require it, the master may direct that a pre-trial review ('PTR') should be held[86]. The PTR may be heard by a master, but more usually is heard by a judge.

86 See rule 29.7.

7.6.2 Application should normally be made to the Clerk of the Lists for the PTR to be heard by the trial judge (if known), and the applicant should do all that he can to ensure that it is heard between 8 and 4 weeks before the trial date, and in any event long enough before the trial date to allow a realistic time in which to complete any outstanding matters.

7.6.3 The PTR should be attended by the advocates who are to represent the parties at the trial.

7.6.4 At least 7 days before the date fixed for the PTR, the applicant must serve the other parties with a list of matters to be considered at the PTR, and those other parties must serve their responses at least 2 days before the PTR. Account must be taken of the answers in any listing questionnaires filed. Realistic proposals must be put forward and if possible agreed as to the time likely to be required for each stage of the trial and as to the order in which witnesses are to be called.

7.6.5 The applicant should lodge a properly indexed bundle containing the listing questionnaires (if directed to be filed) and the lists of matters and the proposals, together with the results of discussions between the parties, and any other relevant material, in the Listing Office, Room WG5, by no later than 10.00 am on the day before the day fixed for the hearing of the PTR. If the PTR is to take place before a master and he asks for the bundle in advance, it should be lodged in the Masters' Support Unit, Room E14. Otherwise it should be lodged at the hearing.

7.6.6 At the PTR, the court will review the parties' state of preparation, deal with any outstanding matters, and give any directions or further directions that may be necessary.

7.7 Requests for further information

7.7.1 A party seeking further information or clarification under Part 18 should serve a written request on the party from whom the information is sought before making an application to the court. Paragraph 1 of the Part 18 Practice Direction deals with how the request should be made, and paragraph 2 deals with the response. A response should be verified by a statement of truth[87]. Parties may use form PF56 for a combined request and reply, if they so wish.

87 See Part 22.

7.7.2 If a party who has been asked to provide further information or clarification objects or is unable to do so, he must notify the party making the request in writing[88].

88 See paragraph 4 of the Part 18 practice direction.

7.7.3 Where it is necessary to apply for an order for further information or clarification the party making the application should set out in or have attached to his application notice;

(1)   the text of the order sought specifying the matters on which further information or clarification is sought, and
(2)   whether a request has been made and, if so, the result of that request[89].

Applicants may use form PF57 for their application notice.

89 See paragraph 5 of the Part 18 practice direction.

7.8 Disclosure

7.8.1 Under Part 31, there is no longer any general duty to disclose documents. Instead, a party is prevented from relying on any document that he has not disclosed, and is required to give inspection of any document to which he refers in his statement of case or in any witness statement, etc[90]. The intention is that disclosure should be proportionate to the value of the claim.

90 Rules 31.14 and 31.21.

7.8.2 If an order for disclosure is made, unless the contrary is stated, the court will order standard disclosure, namely disclosure of only;

(1)   the documents on which a party relies,
(2)   the documents that adversely affect his own or another party's case,
(3)   the documents that support another party's case, and
(4)   the documents required to be disclosed by a relevant practice direction.

Parties should give standard disclosure by completing form N265 but may also list documents by category[91].

91 See paragraph 3.2 of the Part 31 practice direction.

7.8.3 The court may either limit or dispense with disclosure (and the parties may agree to do likewise). The court may also order disclosure of specified documents or specified classes of documents. In deciding whether to make any such order for specific disclosure, the court will want to be satisfied that the disclosure is necessary, that the cost of disclosure will not outweigh the benefits of disclosure and that a party's ability to continue the litigation would not be impaired by any such order.

7.8.4 The court will therefore seek to ensure that any specific disclosure ordered is appropriate to the particular case, taking into account the financial position of the parties, the importance of the case and the complexity of the issues.

7.8.5 If specific disclosure is sought, a separate application for specific disclosure should be made in accordance with Part 23; it is not a matter that would be routinely dealt with at the CMC. The parties should give careful thought to ways of limiting the burdens of such disclosure, whether by giving disclosure in stages, by dispensing with the need to produce copies of the same document, by requiring disclosure of documents sufficient merely for a limited purpose, or otherwise. They should also consider whether the need for disclosure could be reduced or eliminated by a request for further information.

7.8.6 A party who has the right to inspect a document[92] should give written notice of his wish to inspect to the party disclosing the document. That party must permit inspection not more than 7 days after receipt of the notice.

92 See rules 31.3 and 31.15.

7.9 Experts and assessors

7.9.1 The parties in a claim must bear in mind that under Part 35 no party may call an expert or put in evidence an expert's report without the court's express permission, and the court is under a duty to restrict such evidence to what is reasonably required.

7.9.2 The duty of an expert called to give evidence is to assist the court. This duty overrides any obligation to the party instructing him or by whom he is being paid (see the Part 35 Practice Direction). In fulfilment of this duty, an expert must for instance make it clear if a particular question or issue falls outside his expertise or if he considers that insufficient information is available on which to express an opinion.

7.9.3 Before the master gives permission, he must be told the field of expertise of the expert on whose evidence a party wishes to rely and where practicable the identity of the expert. Even then, he may, before giving permission, impose a limit on the extent to which the cost of such evidence may be recovered from the other parties in the claim[93].

93 Rule 35.4.

7.9.4 Parties should always consider whether a single expert could be appointed in a particular claim or to deal with a particular issue. Before giving permission for the parties to call separate experts, the master will always consider whether a single joint expert ought to be used, whether in relation to the issues as a whole or to a particular issue[94].

94 Rule 35.7.

7.9.5 In very many cases it is possible for the question of expert evidence to be dealt with by a single expert. Single experts are, for example, often appropriate to deal with questions of quantum in cases where primary issues are as to liability. Likewise, where expert evidence is required in order to acquaint the court with matters of expert fact, as opposed to opinion, a single expert will usually be appropriate. There remain, however, a body of cases where liability will turn upon expert opinion evidence and where it will be appropriate for the parties to instruct their own experts. For example, in cases where the issue for determination is as to whether a party acted in accordance with proper professional standards, it will often be of value to the court to hear the opinions of more than one expert as to the proper standard in order that the court becomes acquainted with a range of views existing upon the question and in order that the evidence can be tested in cross-examination.

7.9.6 It will not be a sufficient ground for objecting to an order for a single joint expert that the parties have already chosen their own experts. An order for a single joint expert does not prevent a party from having his own expert to advise him, though that is likely to be at his own cost, regardless of the outcome.

7.9.7 When the use of a single joint expert is being considered, the master will expect the parties to co-operate in agreeing terms of reference for the expert. In most cases, such terms of reference will include a statement of what the expert is asked to do, will identify any documents that he will be asked to consider and will specify any assumptions that he is asked to make.

7.9.8 The court will generally also order that experts in the same field confer on a 'without prejudice' basis, and then report in writing to the parties and the court on the extent of any agreement, giving reasons at least in summary for any continuing disagreement. A direction to 'confer' gives the experts the choice of discussing the matter by telephone or in any other convenient way, as an alternative to attending an actual meeting. Any material change of view of an expert should be communicated in writing to the other parties through their legal representatives, and when appropriate, to the court.

7.9.9 Written questions may be put to an expert within 28 days after service of his report, but are for purposes of clarification of the expert's report when the other party does not understand it. Questions going beyond this can only be put with the agreement of the parties or the master's permission. The procedure of putting written questions to experts is not intended to interfere with the procedure for an exchange of professional opinion in discussions between experts or to inhibit that exchange of professional opinion. If questions that are oppressive in number or content are put without permission for any purpose other than clarification of the expert's report, the court is likely to disallow the questions and make an appropriate order for costs against the party putting them. (See paragraph 4.3 of the Part 35 Practice Direction with respect to payment of an expert's fees for answering questions under rule 35.6.)

7.9.10 An expert may file with the court a written request for directions to assist him in carrying out his function as an expert[95]. The expert should guard against accidentally informing the court about, or about matters connected with, communications or potential communications between the parties that are without prejudice or privileged. The expert may properly be asked to be privy to the content of these communications because he has been asked to assist the party instructing him to evaluate them.

95 See rule 35.14.

7.9.11 Under rule 35.15 the court may appoint an assessor to assist it in relation to any matter in which the assessor has skill and experience. The report of the assessor is made available to the parties. The remuneration of the assessor is decided by the court and forms part of the costs of the proceedings.

7.10 Evidence

7.10.1 Evidence is dealt with in the CPR in Parts 32, 33 and 34.

7.10.2 The most common form of written evidence is a witness statement. The Part 32 Practice Direction at paragraphs 17, 18 and 19 contains information about the heading, body (what it must contain) and format of a witness statement. The witness must sign a statement of truth to verify the witness statement; the wording of the statement of truth is set out in paragraph 20.2 of the Practice Direction.

7.10.3 A witness statement may be used as evidence in support of an interim application and, where it has been served on any other party to a claim, it may be relied on as a statement of the oral evidence of the witness at the trial. Part 33 contains provisions relating to the use of hearsay evidence in a witness statement.

7.10.4 In addition to the information and provisions for making a witness statement mentioned in paragraph 7.10.2, the following matters should be borne in mind;

(1) a witness statement must contain the truth, the whole truth and nothing but the truth on the issues it covers,

(2) those issues should consist only of the issues on which the party serving the witness statement wishes that witness to give evidence in chief and should not include commentary on the trial bundle or other matters which may arise during the trial,

(3) a witness statement should be as concise as the circumstances allow, inadmissible or irrelevant material should not be included,

(4) the cost of preparation of an over-elaborate witness statement may not be allowed,

(5) Rule 32.14 states that proceedings for contempt of court may be brought against a person if he makes, or causes to be made, a false statement in a document verified by a statement of truth without an honest belief in its truth,

(6) if a party discovers that a witness statement which they have served is incorrect they must inform the other parties immediately.

7.10.5 Evidence may also be given by affidavit[96] but unless an affidavit is specifically required either in compliance with a court order, a rule or practice direction, or an enactment, the party putting forward the affidavit may not recover from another party the cost of making an affidavit unless the court so orders[97].

96 See rule 32.15(2).
97 See rule 32.15(1) and (2).

7.10.6 The Part 32 Practice Direction at paragraphs 3–6 contains information about the heading, body, jurat (the sworn statement which authenticates the affidavit) and the format of an affidavit. The court will normally give directions as to whether a witness statement or, where appropriate, an affidavit is to be filed[98].

98 See rule 32.4(3)(b).

7.10.7 A statement of case which has been verified by a statement of truth and an application notice containing facts which have been verified by a statement of truth may also stand as evidence other than at the trial.

7.10.8 Evidence by deposition is dealt with in Part 34. A party may apply to a master for an order for a person to be examined before a hearing takes place (rule 34.8). Evidence obtained on an examination under that rule is referred to as a deposition. The master may order the person to be examined before either a judge, an examiner of the court or such other person as the court appoints. The Part 34 Practice Direction at paragraph 4 sets out in detail how the examination should take place.

7.10.9 Provisions relating to applications for evidence by deposition to be taken either;

(1)   in this country for use in a foreign court[99], or
(2)   abroad for use in proceedings within the jurisdiction[100]

are set out in detail in the Part 34 Practice Direction at paragraphs 5 and 6.

99 See RSC Ord 70 (Schedule 1 to Part 50).
100 See rule 34.13.

7.10.10 The procedure for issuing a witness summons is also dealt with in Part 34 and the Practice Direction. A witness summons may require a witness to;

(1)   attend court,
(2)   produce documents to the court, or
(3)   both,

on either a date fixed for the hearing or another date as the court may direct[101] (but see also rule 31.17 which may be used when there are areas of contention).

101 See rule 34.2(4).

7.10.11 The court may also issue a witness summons in aid of a court or tribunal which does not have the power to issue a witness summons in relation to the proceedings before it (and see the Part 34 Practice Direction at paragraphs 1, 2 and 3).

7.10.12 To issue a witness summons, two copies should be filed in the Action Department, Room E14 for sealing; one copy will be retained on the court file.

7.11 Hearings

HEARINGS GENERALLY

7.11.1 All hearings are in principle open to the public, even though in practice most of the hearings until the trial itself will be attended only by the parties and their representatives. However, in an appropriate case the court may decide to hold a hearing in private. Rule 39.2 lists the circumstances where it may be appropriate to hold a hearing in private. In addition, paragraph 1.5 of the Part 39 Practice Direction sets out certain types of hearings which may be listed in private.

7.11.2 The court also has the power under section 11 of the Contempt of Court Act 1981 to make an order forbidding publication of any details that might identify one or more of the parties. Such orders are granted only in exceptional cases.

7.11.3 References in the CPR and Practice Directions to hearings being in public or private do not restrict any existing rights of audience or confer any new rights of audience in respect of applications or proceedings which under the rules previously in force would have been heard in court or chambers respectively[102]. Advocates (and judges) do not wear robes at interim hearings before High Court judges, including appeals from masters, district judges and the county courts. Robes are worn for trials and certain other proceedings such as preliminary issues, committals etc. It is not intended that the new routes of appeal should restrict the advocate's right of audience, in that a solicitor who appeared in a county court matter which is the subject of an appeal to a High Court judge would normally be allowed to appear at the appeal hearing.

102 See paragraph 1.14 of the Part 39 practice direction.

7.11.4 Parties are reminded that they are expected to act with courtesy and respect for the other parties present and for the proceedings of the court. Punctuality is particularly important; being late for hearings is unfair to the other parties and other court users, as well as being discourteous to them and to the court.

PREPARATION FOR HEARINGS

7.11.5 To ensure court time is used efficiently there must be adequate preparation prior to the hearing. This includes the preparation and exchange of skeleton arguments, the compilation of bundles of documents and giving realistic time estimates. Where estimates prove inaccurate, a hearing may have to be adjourned to a later date, and the party responsible for the adjournment is likely to be ordered to pay the costs thrown away.

7.11.6 The parties should use their best endeavours to agree beforehand the issues, or main issues between them, and must co-operate with the court and each other to enable the court to deal with claims justly; parties may expect to be penalised for failing to do so.

7.11.7 A bundle of documents must be compiled for the court's use at the trial, and also for hearings before the Interim Applications judge or a master where the documents to be referred to total 25 pages or more. The party lodging a trial bundle should supply identical bundles to all parties and for the use of witnesses. The efficient preparation of bundles is very important. Where bundles have been properly prepared, the claim will be easier to understand and present, and time and costs are likely to be saved. Where documents are copied unnecessarily or bundled incompetently, the costs may be disallowed. Paragraph 3 of the Part 39 Practice Direction sets out in full the requirements for compiling bundles of documents for hearings or trial.

7.11.8 The trial bundle must be filed not more than 7 and not less than 3 days before the start of the trial. Bundles for a master's hearing should be brought to the hearing unless the master directs otherwise. The contents of the trial bundle should be agreed where possible, and it should be made clear whether in addition, they are agreeing that the documents in the bundle are authentic even if not previously disclosed and are evidence of the facts stated in them even if a notice under the Civil Evidence Act 1995 has not been served.

7.11.9 Lists of authorities for use at trial or at substantial hearings before a judge should be provided to the usher by 9.00 am on the first day of the hearing. For other applications before a judge, or applications before a master, copies of the authorities should be included in the bundle.

7.11.10 For trial and most hearings before a judge, and substantial hearings before a master, a chronology, a list of the persons involved and a list of the issues should be prepared and filed with the skeleton argument. A chronology should be non-contentious and agreed with the other parties if possible. If there is a material dispute about any event stated in the chronology, that should be stated.

7.11.11 Skeleton arguments should be prepared and filed;

(1)   for trials, not less than 2 days before the trial in the Listing Office, and
(2)   for substantial applications or appeals, not later than 1 day before the hearing in the Listing Office and, where the master has requested papers in advance of the hearing, in the Masters' Support Unit Room E16.

7.11.12 A skeleton argument should;

(1)   concisely summarise the party's submissions in relation to each of the issues,
(2)   cite the main authorities relied on, which may be attached,
(3)   contain a reading list and an estimate of the time it will take the judge to read,
(4)   be as brief as the issues allow and not normally be longer than 20 pages of double-spaced A4 paper,
(5)   be divided into numbered paragraphs and paged consecutively,
(6)   avoid formality and use understandable abbreviations, and
(7)   identify any core documents which it would be helpful to read beforehand.

7.11.13 Where a party decides not to call a witness whose witness statement has been served, to give oral evidence at trial, prompt notice of this decision should be given to all other parties. The party should also indicate whether he proposes to put, or seek to put, the witness statement in as hearsay evidence. If he does not, any other party may do so[103].

103 Rule 32.5(5).

RECORDING OF PROCEEDINGS

7.11.14 At any hearing, including the trial, any oral evidence, the judgment or decision (including reasons) and any summing up to a jury will be recorded. At hearings before masters, it is not normally practicable to record anything other than oral evidence and any judgment, but these will be recorded. A party to the proceedings may obtain a transcript of the proceedings on payment of the appropriate charge, from the Mechanical Recording Department, Room WG5. A person who is not a party to the proceedings may not obtain a transcript of a hearing which took place in private without the permission of the court.

7.11.15 No person or party may use unofficial recording equipment at a hearing without the permission of the court; to do so constitutes a contempt of court[104].

104 Section 9, Contempt of Court Act 1981.

7.12 Applications

7.12.1 Applications for court orders are governed by Part 23 and the Part 23 Practice Direction. Rule 23.6 and paragraph 2 of the Part 23 Practice Direction set out the matters an application notice must include. The Part 23 Practice Direction states that form N244 may be used, however, parties may prefer to use form PF244 which is available for use in the Royal Courts of Justice only. To make an application the applicant must file an application notice unless a rule or practice direction permits otherwise or the court dispenses with the requirement for an application notice[105]. Except in cases of extreme urgency, or where giving notice might frustrate the order (as with a search order), an application notice must be served on every party unless a rule or practice direction or a court order dispenses with service[106] (see paragraph 7.12.3 below).

105 See rule 23.3.
106 See rule 23.4.

7.12.2 Applications for remedies which a master has jurisdiction to grant should ordinarily be made to a master. The Part 2 Practice Direction (Allocation of cases to levels of Judiciary) contains information about the types of applications which may be dealt with by masters and judges. An application notice for hearing by;

(1)   a judge should be issued in the Listing Office, Room WG5, and
(2)   a master should be issued in the Masters' Support Unit, Room E16,

and wherever possible should be accompanied by a draft in double spacing of the order sought.

7.12.3 The following are examples of applications which may be heard by a master where service of the application notice is not required;

(1)   service by an alternative method (rule 6.8),
(2)   service of a claim form out of the jurisdiction (section III of Part 6),
(3)   default judgment under rule 12.11(4) or (5),
(4)   substituting a party under rule 19.1(4),
(5)   permission to issue a witness summons under rule 34.3(2),
(6)   deposition for use in a foreign court (Schedule 1 to the CPR – RSC Ord 70),
(7)   charging order to show cause (Schedule 1 to the CPR – RSC Ord 50, r 1(2)), and

(8)   garnishee order to show cause (Schedule 1 to the CPR – RSC Ord 49, r 2(1).

7.12.4 Paragraph 3 of the Part 23 Practice Direction states in addition that an application may be made without serving an application notice;

(1)   where there is exceptional urgency,
(2)   where the overriding objective is best furthered by doing so,
(3)   by consent of all parties, and
(4)   where a date for a hearing has been fixed and a party wishes to make an application at that hearing but does not have sufficient time to serve an application notice[107].

With the court's permission an application may also be made without serving an application notice where secrecy is essential.

107 See paragraph 2.10 of the Part 23 practice direction.

7.12.5 Where an application is heard in the absence of one or more of the parties, it is the duty of the party attending to disclose fully all matters relevant to the application, even those matters adverse to the applicant. Failure to do so may result in the order being set aside. Any party who does not attend a hearing may apply to have the order set aside[108].

108 See rule 23.11.

7.12.6 Where notice of an application is to be given, the application notice should be served as soon as practicable after issue and, if there is to be a hearing, at least 3 clear days before the hearing date[109]. Where there is insufficient time to serve an application notice, informal notice of the application should be given unless the circumstances of the application require secrecy.

109 See rule 23.7(1)(b).

7.12.7 The court may deal with an application without a hearing if;

(1)   the parties agree the terms of the order sought,
(2)   the parties agree that the application should be dealt with without a hearing, or
(3)   the court does not consider that a hearing would be appropriate[110].

110 See rule 23.8.

7.12.8 The court may deal with an application or part of an application by telephone where it is convenient to do so or in matters of extreme urgency. See paragraph 6 of the Part 23 Practice Direction and paragraph 4.5 of the Part 25 Practice Direction (Interim Injunctions).

7.12.9 Applications of extreme urgency may be made out of hours and will be dealt with by the duty judge. An explanation will be required as to why it was not made or could not be made during normal court hours.

7.12.10 Initial contact should be made through the Security Office on 020 7947 6260 who will require the applicants phone number. The clerk to the duty judge will then contact the applicant and will require the following information;

(1)   the name of the party on whose behalf the application is to be made,
(2)   the name and status of the person making the application,
(3)   the nature of the application,
(4)   the degree of urgency, and
(5)   the contact telephone number(s).

7.12.11 The duty judge will indicate to his clerk if he thinks it appropriate for the application to be dealt with by telephone or in court. The clerk will inform the applicant and make the necessary arrangements. Where the duty judge decides to deal with the application by telephone, and the facility is available, it is likely that the judge will require a draft order to be faxed to him. An application for an injunction will be dealt with by telephone only where the applicant is represented by counsel or solicitors.

7.12.12 It is not normally possible to seal an order out of hours. The judge is likely to order the applicant to file the application notice and evidence in support on the same or next working day, together with two copies of the order for sealing.

7.13 Interim remedies

7.13.1 Interim remedies which the court may grant are listed in rule 25.1. An order for an interim remedy may be made at any time including before proceedings are started and after judgment has been given[111]. Some of the most commonly sought remedies are injunctions, most of which are heard by the Interim Applications judge.

111 See rule 25.2(1).

7.13.2 An application notice for an injunction should be filed in the Listing Office, Room WG5, and may be made without giving notice to the other parties in the first instance. This is most likely to be appropriate in applications for search orders and freezing injunctions which may also be heard in private if the judge thinks it appropriate to do so. Where the injunction is granted without the other party being present it will normally be for a limited period, seldom more than 7 days. The Part 25 (Interim Injunctions) Practice Direction at paragraph 4 deals fully with making urgent applications and those without notice, and paragraphs 6, 7 and 8 deal specifically with search orders and freezing injunctions, examples of which are annexed to the Practice Direction.

7.13.3 Applications for interim payments are heard by a master. The application notice should be filed in the Masters' Support Unit, Room E14. The requirements for obtaining an order for an interim payment are fully dealt with in the Part 25 (Interim Payments) Practice Direction.

8 LISTING BEFORE JUDGES

8.1 Responsibility for listing

8.1.1 The Clerk of the Lists (Room WG3, Royal Courts of Justice) is in general responsible for listing. All applications relating to listing should in the first instance be made to him. Any party dissatisfied with any decision of the Clerk of the Lists may, on one day's notice to all other parties, apply to the judge in charge of the list.

8.1.2 The application should be made within 7 days of the decision of the Clerk of the Lists and should be arranged through the Queen's Bench Listing Office, Room WG5.

8.2 The lists

8.2 There are three lists, namely;

(1)   the Jury List
(2)   the Trial List, and
(3)   the Interim Hearings List.

The lists are described below.

8.3 The Jury List

8.3.1 Claims for damages for libel and slander (defamation), fraud, malicious prosecution and false imprisonment will be tried by a judge and jury unless the court orders trial by a judge alone.

8.3.2 Where a claim is being tried by a judge and jury it is vitally important that the jury should not suffer hardship and inconvenience by having been misled by an incorrect time estimate. It is therefore essential that time estimates given to the court are accurate and realistic.

8.3.3 Dates for the trial of substantial claims will be fixed by the Listing Office after consideration of the parties' views. In such cases the Listing Office may, in addition, impose an alternative reserve date several weeks or months in advance of the trial date, in an endeavour to dispose of claims more quickly and to fill gaps in the list created by frequent settlements. When a reserve date is so allocated a 'cut off' date will be stated by the Clerk of the Lists again, after consideration of any views expressed by the parties and having regard to the complexity of the claim and the commitments of counsel and expert witnesses. On the cut off date a decision will be made by the Clerk of the Lists to break or confirm the reserved date for trial.

8.3.4 If a party considers that he will suffer significant prejudice as the result of the decision of the Clerk of the Lists relating to either a reserved date or the cut off date he may apply to the judge in charge of the Jury List for reversal or variation of the decision, as set out in paragraph 8.1.1 above.

8.3.5 Jury applications will enter the Interim Warned List not less than two weeks from the date the application notice is filed. Parties may 'offer' a date for hearing the application within the week for which they are warned. Subject to court availability, the application will be listed on the offered date. Any application not reached on the offered date will return to the current Warned List and will be taken from that list as and when required.

8.3.6 Applications in defamation claims in respect of 'meaning' (for an explanation of 'meaning' see paragraph 4.1 of the Part 53 Practice Direction) may be listed in private on a specific day allocated for such matters.

8.3.7 Jury applications of length and/or complexity may be fixed by the same manner as set out in paragraph 8.3.6 above. (See the section below on the Trial List for general information about fixing trials).

8.3.8 Applications for directions and other applications within the master's jurisdiction should firstly be made to a master unless;

(1)   a direction has been given for the arranging of a trial date, or
(2)   a date has been fixed or a window given for the trial.

Interim applications made after (1) or (2) above should be made to the judge. The master will use his discretion to refer a matter to the judge if he thinks it right to do so.

8.3.9 If a party believes that the master is very likely to refer the application to the judge, for example where there is a substantial application to strike out, the matter should first be referred to the master or Practice Master on notice to the other parties without waiting for a private room appointment. The master will then decide whether the application should be referred to the judge.

8.4 The Trial List

8.4.1 This list consists of trials (other than Jury trials), preliminary questions or issues ordered to be tried and proceedings to commit for contempt of court.

8.4.2 The Royal Courts of Justice presents unique problems in terms of fixing trial dates. The number of judges and masters involved and their geographical location has caused, for the time being at least, a different approach to the fixing of trials in the Chancery and Queen's Bench Divisions.

8.4.3 The requirement of judges to go on circuit, sit in the Criminal Division of the Court of Appeal, deal with cases in the Crown Office and other lists make it difficult to fix dates for trials before particular judges. Accordingly the following will only apply to the Listing Offices in the Royal Courts of Justice.

8.4.4 At as early an interim stage as practicable, the court will give directions with a view to fixing the trial date, week, or other short period within which the trial is to begin (the trial window).

8.4.5 For that purpose the court may;

(1)   direct that the trial do not begin earlier than a specified date calculated to provide enough time for the parties to complete any necessary preparations for trial, and/or
(2)   direct that the trial date be within a specified period, and/or
(3)   specify the trial date or window.

8.4.6 If directions under 8.4.5(1) or (2) are given the court will direct the parties to attend upon the Clerk of the Lists in Room WG5 in order to fix the trial date or trial window.

8.4.7 The claimant must, unless some other party agrees to do so, take out an appointment with the Clerk of the Lists within 7 days of obtaining the direction in paragraph 8.4.6 above. If an appointment is not taken out within the 7 days, the Listing Office will appoint a date for a listing hearing and give notice of the date to all parties.

8.4.8 At the listing hearing the Clerk of the Lists will take account, in so far as it is practical to do so, of any difficulties the parties may have as to availability of counsel, experts and witnesses. The Clerk of the Lists will, nevertheless, try to ensure the speedy disposal of the trial by arranging a firm trial date as soon as possible within the trial period or, as the case may be, after the 'not before' date directed by the court under paragraph 8.4.5 above. If exceptionally it appears to the Clerk of the Lists at the listing hearing that a trial date cannot be provided within a trial window, he may fix the trial date outside the trial period at the first available date. (If a case summary has been prepared (see the Part 29 Practice Direction The Multi-track, paragraphs 5.6 and 5.7) the claimant must produce a copy at the listing hearing together with a copy of particulars of claim and any orders relevant to the fixing of the trial date.)

8.4.9 The Listing Office will notify the Masters' Support Unit of any trial date or trial window given. In accordance with rule 29.2(3) notice will also be given to all the parties.

8.4.10 A party who wishes to appeal a date or window allocated by the Listing Officer must, within 7 days of the notification, make an application to the judge nominated by each Division to hear such applications. The application notice should be filed in the Listing Office and served, giving one days notice, on the other parties.

8.5 The Interim Hearings List

8.5.1 This list consists of interim applications, appeals and applications for judgment.

8.5.2 On each Thursday of Term and on such other days as may be appropriate, the Clerk of the Lists will publish a Warned List showing the matters in the Interim Hearings List that are liable to be heard in the following week. Any matters for which no date has been arranged will be liable to appear in the list for hearing with no warning save that given by the Cause List for the following day, posted each afternoon outside Room WG5.

8.5.3 Fixtures will only be given in exceptional circumstances. The parties may by agreement 'offer' preferred dates for their matter to be heard, to be taken from the list on designated days, within the week following entry into the Warned List in accordance with Listing Office practice. Matters lasting less than a day are usually offered for two preferred consecutive days and matters lasting more than a day are usually offered for three preferred consecutive days.

8.6 General

8.6.1 In addition to the matters listed to be heard by individual judges, the Daily Cause List for each day may list 'unassigned cases'. These are matters from the two lists to be heard that day but not assigned to a particular judge. If on any day a matter assigned to a particular judge proves to be ineffective, he will hear an unassigned case. It is hoped that the great majority of unassigned cases will be heard on the day that they are listed but this cannot be absolutely guaranteed. Parties engaged in matters listed as unassigned should attend outside the court where the matter is listed. The Clerk of the Lists will notify them as soon as possible which judge is to hear the matter. It is not the practice to list cases as unassigned unless the parties consent and there are no witnesses.

8.6.2 Appeals from masters' decisions will appear in the Interim Hearings List. The appeal notice (stamped with the appropriate fee) must be filed in Room WG7. On filing the appeal notice the solicitors should inform the Clerk of the Lists whether they intend to instruct counsel and, if so, the names of counsel.

8.7 Listing before the Interim Applications judge

8.7.1 All interim applications on notice to the Interim Applications judge will initially be entered in a list for hearing. They will be listed for hearing in Room E101 or some other nominated venue on any day of the week. Any matter which cannot be disposed of with within one hour will not be taken on the date given for the listed hearing.

8.7.2 If the parties agree that a matter cannot be disposed of within one hour, the applicant/appellant;

(1)   may, on filing the application notice/notice of appeal, seek to have the matter placed directly into the Interim Hearings Warned List, or

(2)   must as soon as practicable and in any event not later than 24 hours before the hearing date transfer the matter into the Interim Hearings List.

If the parties do not so agree, or agree less than 24 hours before the hearing date, the parties must attend on that date.

8.7.3 Matters in the Interim Hearings List will be listed by the Clerk of the Lists in Room WG3, and the parties will be notified by the Listing Office (Room WG5) of the date on which the matter will enter the Warned List. Matters in the Warned List may be listed for hearing at any time on or after that date.

8.7.4 In order to ensure that a complete set of papers in proper order is available for the judge to read before the hearing, the parties must in advance of the hearing lodge in room WG4 a bundle, properly paginated in date order, and indexed, containing copies of the following documents;

(1)   the application notice or notice of appeal,

(2)   any statements of case,

(3)   copies of all written evidence (together with copy exhibits) on which any party intends to rely, and

(4)   any relevant order made in the proceedings.

8.7.5 The bundle should be agreed if possible. In all but simple cases a skeleton argument and, where that would be helpful, a chronology should also be lodged. (See paragraph 8.9.1 and 8.9.2 below in respect of skeleton arguments.)

8.7.6 Where a date for the hearing has been arranged the bundle must be lodged not later than 3 clear days before the fixed date. For application or appeals where there is no fixed date for hearing, the bundle must be lodged not later than 48 hours after the parties have been notified that the matter is to appear in the Warned List. (For information concerning trial bundles see the Part 39 Practice Direction.)

8.7.7 Except with the permission of the judge no document may be used in evidence or relied on unless a copy of it has been included in the bundle referred to in paragraph 8.7.6 above. If any party seeks to rely on written evidence which has not been included in the bundle, that party should lodge the original (with copy exhibits) in Room WG5 in advance of the hearing, or otherwise with the court associate before the hearing commences.

8.7.8 In appeals from circuit and district judges the provisions of paragraphs 8.7.4, 8.7.5, 8.7.6 and 8.7.7 should be complied with. In addition, the notes (if any) of reasons given by the circuit judge or district judge, prepared by the judge, counsel or solicitors should be lodged.

8.7.9 Subject to the discretion of the judge, any application or appeal normally made to the Interim Applications judge may be made in the month of September.

In the month of August, except with the permission of a judge, only appeals in respect of orders;

(1)   to set aside a claim form, or service of a claim form,
(2)   to set aside judgment,
(3)   for stay of execution,
(4)   for any order by consent,
(4)   for permission to enter judgment,
(5)   for approval of settlements or for interim payment,
(6)   for relief from forfeiture,
(7)   for a charging order,
(8)   for a garnishee order,
(9)   for appointment or discharge of a receiver,
(10)   for relief by way of sheriff's interpleader,
(11)   for transfer to a county court or for trial by master, or
(12)   for time where time is running in the month of August,

may be heard, and only applications of real urgency will be dealt with, for example, urgent applications in respect of injunctions, or for possession (under RSC Ord 113 in Schedule 1 to Part 50).

8.7.10 It is desirable, where this is practical, that application notices or appeal notices are submitted to the Practice Master or a judge prior to the hearing of the application or appeal so that they can be marked 'fit for August' or 'fit for vacation'. If they are so marked, then normally the judge will be prepared to hear the application or appeal in August, if marked 'fit for August' or in September if marked 'fit for vacation'. The application to a judge to have the papers so marked should normally be made in writing, the application shortly setting out the nature of the application or appeal and the reasons why it should be dealt with in August or in September, as the case may be.

8.8 The lists generally

8.8.1 Where a fixed date has been given it is the duty of the parties to keep the Clerk of the Lists fully informed as to the current position of the matter with regard to negotiations for settlement, whether all aspects of the claim are being proceeded with, an estimate of the length of the hearing, and so on.

8.8.2 Applications for adjournments will not be granted except for the most cogent reasons. If an application is made because solicitors were unaware of the state of the list they may be ordered personally to pay the costs of the application.

8.8.3 A party who seeks to have a hearing before a judge adjourned must inform the Clerk of the Lists of his application as soon as possible. Applications for an adjournment immediately before a hearing begins should be avoided as they take up valuable time which could be used for dealing with effective matters and, if successful, may result in court time being wasted.

8.8.4 If the application is made by agreement, the parties should, in writing, apply to the Clerk of the Lists who will consult the judge nominated to deal with such matters. The judge may grant the application on conditions which may include giving directions for a new hearing date.

8.8.5 If the application is opposed the applicant should apply to either the nominated judge or the judge to whom the matter has been allocated. A hearing should then be arranged through the Clerk of the Lists. A short summary of the reasons for the adjournment should be lodged with the Listing Office where possible by 10.30 am on the day before the application is to be made. Formal written evidence is not normally required.

8.8.6 The applicant will be expected to show that he has conducted his own case diligently. Any party should take all reasonable steps;

(1)   to ensure his case is adequately prepared in sufficient time to enable the hearing to proceed, and
(2)   to prepare and serve any document (including any evidence) required to be served on any other party in sufficient time to enable that party also to be prepared.

8.8.7 If a party or his solicitor's failure to take reasonable steps necessitates an adjournment, the court may dismiss the application or make any other order including an order penalising the defaulting party in costs.

8.9 Listing Office – general matters

8.9.1 To facilitate the efficient listing of proceedings, parties are reminded that skeleton arguments concisely summarising each party's submissions must be prepared and filed with the Listing Office;

(1)   for trials, not less than 3 days before the trial, and
(2)   for substantial applications or appeals, not later than 1 day before the hearing.

8.9.2 If it is anticipated that a skeleton argument will be filed late, a letter of explanation should accompany it which will be shown to the judge before whom the trial or hearing is to take place.

8.9.3 For parties' information, the following targets for the disposal of matters in the lists have been agreed as set out below:

Interim Hearings Warned List	within 4 weeks
From date of fixing;	
Trials under 5 days	within 4 months
Trials over 5 but under 10 days	within 6 months
Trials over 10 but under 20 days	within 9 months
Trials over 20 days	within 12 months.

9 TRIAL, JUDGMENTS AND ORDERS

9.1 General

9.1.1 The trial of a claim in the Royal Courts of Justice normally takes place before a High Court judge or a deputy sitting as a High Court judge. A master may assess the damages or sum due to a party under a judgment and, subject to any practice direction, may try a claim which is

(1) treated as being allocated to the multi-track because it is proceeding under Part 8, or

(2) with the consent of the parties, allocated to the multi-track under Part 26[112].

112 See paragraph 4 of the Part 2B practice direction.

9.1.2 Claims for defamation, malicious prosecution or false imprisonment will be tried by a judge sitting with a Jury unless the court orders otherwise.

9.2 The trial

9.2.1 See paragraphs 2.4.2 and 2.4.3 above about representation at the trial, and paragraphs 7.11.14 and 7.11.15 above about recording of proceedings.

9.2.2 Rule 39.3 sets out the consequences of a party's failure to attend the trial and see also paragraph 2 of the Part 39 Practice Direction.

9.2.3 The judge may fix a timetable for evidence and submissions if it has not already been fixed. The claimant's advocate will normally begin the trial with a short opening speech, and the judge may then allow the other party to make a short speech. Each party should provide written summaries of their opening speeches if the points are not covered in their skeleton arguments.

9.2.4 It is normally convenient for any outstanding procedural matters or applications to be dealt with in the course of, or immediately after, the opening speech. In a jury trial such matters would normally be dealt with before the jury is sworn in.

9.2.5 Unless the court orders otherwise, a witness statement will stand as the evidence in chief of the witness, provided he is called to give oral evidence. With the court's permission, a witness may amplify his witness statement or give evidence in relation to new matters which have arisen since the witness statement was served on the other parties[113].

113 Rule 32.5.

9.2.6 The court associate will be responsible for any exhibits produced as evidence during the trial. After the trial, the exhibits are the responsibility of the party who produced them. Where a number of physical exhibits are involved, it is desirable, if possible, for the parties to agree a system of labelling and the manner of display, beforehand. The associate will normally draw the judgment or order made at the trial.

9.2.7 At a jury trial, it is the parties' responsibility to provide sufficient bundles of documents for the use of the jury.

9.2.8 Facilities are available to assist parties or witnesses with special needs. The Listing Office should be notified of any needs or requirements prior to the trial.

9.3 Judgments and orders

9.3.1 Part 40 deals with judgments and orders. Rule 40.2 contains the standard requirements of a judgment or order and rule 40.3 contains provisions about drawing them up, see also paragraph 1 of the Part 40B Practice Direction for more information.

9.3.2 Provisions concerning consent orders are contained in rule 40.6 which sets out in paragraph (3) the types of consent judgments and orders that may be sealed and entered by a court officer, provided;

(1)   that none of the parties is a litigant in person, and
(2)   the approval of the court is not required by a rule, a practice direction or an enactment.

Other types of consent order require an application to be made to a master or judge for approval. It is common for a respondent to a consent order not to attend the hearing but to provide a written consent. The consent may either be written on the document or contained in a letter, and must be signed by the respondent, or where there are solicitors on record as acting for him, by his solicitors. Paragraph 3 of the Part 40B Practice Direction contains further information about consent orders.

9.3.3 Rule 40.11 sets out the time for complying with a judgment or order, which is 14 days unless the judgment or order specifies otherwise (for example by instalments), or a rule specifies a different time, or the judgment or proceedings have been stayed.

9.3.4 The Part 40B Practice Direction contains further information about the effect of non-compliance with a judgment or order (and sets out the penal notice), adjustment of the final judgment sum in respect of interim payments and compensation recovery, and refers to various precedents for types of judgments and orders. See also;

(1)   the Part 40 Practice Direction – Accounts and Enquiries, and
(2)   the Part 40C Practice Direction – Structured Settlements which sets out the procedure to be followed both on settlement and after trial. Precedents for structured settlement orders, Parts 1 and 2, are annexed to the Practice Direction.

9.3.5 Where judgment is reserved, the judge may deliver his judgment by handing down the written text without reading it out in open court. Where this is the case, the advocates will be supplied with the full text of the judgment in advance of delivery. The advocates should then familiarise themselves with the contents and be ready to deal with any points which may arise when the judgment is delivered. Any direction or requirement as to confidentiality must be complied with.

9.3.6 The judgment does not take effect until formally delivered in court. If the judgment is to be handed down in writing copies will then be made available to the parties and, if requested and so far as practicable, to the law reporters and the press.

9.3.7 The judge will usually direct that the written judgment may be used for all purposes as the text of the judgment, and that no transcript need be made. Where such a direction is made, a copy will be provided to the Mechanical Recording Department from where further copies may be obtained (and see paragraph 7.11.14 above).

JUDGMENT OR ORDER FOR PAYMENT OF MONEY ON BEHALF OF A CHILD OR PATIENT

9.3.8 The usual order made at trial will make provision for any immediate payment to the litigation friend or his legal representative and for the balance of the award to be placed to a special investment account pending application to a master or district judge (in the case of a child) or the Court of Protection (in the case of a patient) for investment directions. The order will specify the time within which the application should be made.

9.3.9 The litigation friend or his legal representative should then write to or make an appointment with;

(1)   in the case of a child, the master or district judge in accordance with paragraph 6.8.6 above and the Part 21 Practice Direction, or

(2)   in the case of a patient, the Court of Protection in accordance with paragraph 11 of the Part 21 Practice Direction.

9.3.10 Where after trial the judge has found in favour of a child or patient, instead of judgment being given, the proposed award of damages may be paid by way of a structured settlement. The structure must be approved by the judge, and in the case of a patient must also be approved by the Court of Protection. (See also the Part 40C Practice Direction – Structured Settlements.)

PROVISIONAL DAMAGES

9.3.11 Rule 41.1 defines an award of provisional damages. Where there is a chance that a claimant may in the future develop a particular disease or deterioration as a result of the event giving rise to the claim, he can seek an award of damages for personal injury on the assumption that he will not develop the disease or deterioration, with provision for him to make a further application within the time specified in the order, if he does so develop the disease or deterioration.

9.3.12 The Part 41 Practice Direction gives further information about provisional damages awards and, in particular, about the preservation of the case file for the time specified in the order for making a further application, and the documents to be included in the case file. A precedent for a provisional damages judgment is annexed to the Practice Direction.

10 APPEALS

10.1 General

10.1.1 Appeals are governed by Part 52 and the Part 52 Practice Direction. The contents of Part 52 are divided into two sections; General rules about Appeals and Special Provisions applying to the Court of Appeal. The Practice Direction is divided into three sections; General Provisions about Appeals, General Provisions about Statutory Appeals and Appeals by way of Case Stated, and Provisions about Specific Appeals. The following paragraphs apply to orders made after 2 May 2000 and are intended only to draw parties' attention to the basic provisions for making an appeal in or from the Queen's Bench Division. For further information about these procedures and about other specific types of appeal, parties should refer to the Part 52 Practice Direction and the Civil Appeals Guide.

10.1.2 In the Queen's Bench Division an appeal from a master will lie to a High Court judge unless it is a final decision in a claim allocated to the multi-track or in specialist proceedings referred to in Part 49 in which case the appeal will lie to the Court of Appeal. An appeal from a High Court judge will lie to the Court of Appeal.

10.1.3 Unless the lower court or the appeal court orders otherwise, an appeal does not operate as a stay of any order or decision of the lower court.

10.2 Permission to appeal

10.2.1 Permission is required to appeal from a decision of a judge in a county court or the High Court, except where the appeal is in respect of;

(1)   a committal order,
(2)   a refusal to grant habeas corpus,
(3)   certain insolvency appeals, and
(4)   certain statutory appeals.

For the purposes of Part 52 and the Part 52 Practice Direction, the term 'judge' includes a master or district judge.

(For more information see rule 52.3).

10.2.2 Permission should be sought at the hearing at which the decision to be appealed against is made. If it is not, or if it is sought and refused, permission should be sought from the court appealed to ('the appeal court'). Where permission is sought from the appeal court it must be requested in the appellant's notice. Permission may be granted, or refused, or granted in part (whether as to a part of the order, a ground of appeal or an issue) and refused as to the rest. Paragraphs 4.1–4.12 of the Practice Direction deal with permission to appeal including the matters to be stated in the notice and the documents to be filed with it.

10.2.3 An application to the appeal court for permission may be dealt with without a hearing, but if refused without a hearing the applicant may request that it be reconsidered at a hearing; the court need not require that notice of the hearing be given to the respondent.

10.3 Notices

10.3.1 Rule 52.4 and paragraph 5 of the Practice Direction deal with the appellant's notice. The appellant must file his notice at the appeal court either within a period specified by the court appealed from ('the lower court') or, if no such period is specified, within 14 days of the date of the decision appealed from. The notice must be served on each respondent as soon as practicable and in any event not later than 7 days after it is filed.

10.3.2 A respondent must file a notice where;

(1)   he also wishes to appeal the lower court's decision,
(2)   he wishes to uphold the decision of the lower court for different or additional reasons to those given by the lower court, or
(3)   he is seeking permission to appeal from the appeal court.

10.3.3 The respondent's notice must be filed either within a period specified by the lower court or, if no such period is specified, within 14 days of;

(1)   the date the respondent is served with the appellant's notice where
        (a)   permission to appeal was given by the lower court or
        (b)   permission to appeal is not required,
(2)   the date the respondent is served with notification that the appeal court has given the appellant permission to appeal, or
(3)   the date the respondent is served with notification that the application for permission to appeal and the appeal itself are to be heard together.

(Paragraph 7 of the Practice Direction deals with the respondent's notice of appeal.)

10.3.4 The notices to be used are as follows;

(1)   the Appellant's Notice is form N161, and
(2)   the Respondent's Notice is form N162.

There is a leaflet available from the Listing Office, Room WG5 entitled 'I want to appeal', which provides information about appealing other than to the Court of Appeal.

10.4 Appeals in cases of contempt of court

10.4.1 Appellant's notices which by paragraph 21.4 of the Part 52 Practice Direction are required to be served on 'the court from whose order or decision the appeal is brought' may be served, in the case of appeals from the Queen's Bench Division, on the Senior Master of the Queen's Bench Division; service may be effected by leaving a copy of the notice of appeal with the Clerk of the Lists in Room WG5, Royal Courts of Justice, Strand, London WC2A 2LL.

11 ENFORCEMENT

11.1 General

11.1.1 Enforcement in the High Court is still governed by RSC Orders 17, 45–52 and 71 as in Schedule 1 to the CPR.

11.1.2 RSC Ord 45 deals with enforcement generally. A judgment or order for payment of money (other than into court) may be enforced by a writ of fieri facias, garnishee proceedings, a charging order or the appointment of a receiver[114]. A judgment or order to do or abstain from doing an act may be enforced by a writ of sequestration (with the permission of the court) or an order of committal[115]. A judgment or order for possession of land may be enforced by a writ of possession[116], and a judgment or order for delivery of goods without the alternative of paying their value by a writ of specific delivery[117]. In each case, where RSC Ord 45, r 5 applies enforcement may also be by a writ of sequestration or an order of committal.

114 RSC Ord 45, r 1.
115 RSC Ord 45, r 5.
116 RSC Ord 45, r 3.
117 RSC Ord 45, r 4.

11.2 Writs of execution

11.2.1 RSC Ord 46 deals with writs of execution generally. Rules 2 and 3 set out the circumstances when permission to issue a writ is necessary[118]. Rule 4 contains provisions for making an application for permission. Rule 5 deals with applications for permission to issue a writ of sequestration. RSC Ord 47 contains provisions concerning writs of fieri facias. Forms of writs of execution may be used as follows:

(1)   writs of fieri facias in form Nos 53–63,
(2)   writs of delivery in form Nos 64 and 65,
(3)   writs of possession in form Nos 66 and 66A,
(4)   writ of sequestration in form No 67,

(5)   writ of restitution in form No 68,

(6)   writ of assistance in form No 69.

118 See also RSC Ord 45, r 3.

11.2.2 With certain exceptions, writs of execution issued in the Royal Courts of Justice are executed by the sheriff of the county in which the debtor has assets, or his officer. RSC Ord 46, r 6 sets out the provisions for issue of writs of execution. In the Queen's Bench Division writs of execution are issued in the Central Office in Room E17. Before the Writ can be sealed for issue, a signed praecipe for its issue must be filed[119] in one of forms PF86–90, as appropriate, stamped with the appropriate fee. A copy of the judgment or order requiring enforcement should also be provided.

119 RSC Ord 46, r 6(3).

11.2.3 On an application for permission to issue a writ of possession under RSC Ord 45, r 3(2), if the property consists of a house of which various parts are sublet to, or in the occupation of, different persons, the evidence in support should show the nature and length of the notice which has been given to the various occupiers. Where the defendant or any other persons are in actual possession of the premises of which possession is sought, the evidence must contain the following information:

(1)   whether the premises or any part of it is residential,

(2)   if so,

    (a)   what is the rateable value of the residential premises, and

    (b)   whether it is let furnished or unfurnished and, if furnished, the amount of furniture it contains, and

(3)   any other matters that will assist the master in deciding whether any occupier is protected by the Rent Acts.

11.2.4 Where a party wishes to enforce a judgment or order expressed in a foreign currency by the issue of a writ of fieri facias, the praecipe must be endorsed with the following certificate:

> 'I/We certify that the rate current in London for the purchase of (*state the unit of foreign currency in which the judgment is expressed*) at the close of business on (*state the nearest preceding date to the date of issue of the writ of fieri facias*) was (   ) to the £ sterling and at this rate the sum of (*state amount of the judgment debt in the foreign currency*) amounts to £   .'

The schedule to the writ of fieri facias should be amended;

(1)   showing the amount of the judgment or order in the foreign currency at paragraph 1.

(2)   inserting a new paragraph 2 as follows:

    '2 Amount of the sterling equivalent as appears from the certificate endorsed on the praecipe for issue of the writ £   '

(3)   renumbering the remaining paragraphs accordingly.

11.2.5 County court judgments or orders to which Article 8(1) of the High Court and County Courts Jurisdiction Order 1991 applies may be enforced in the High Court, and since 26 April 1999, any county court judgment for over £600 may be transferred to the High Court sheriff for enforcement (except where it is a judgment arising from a regulated agreement under the Consumer Credit Act).

11.2.6 The party seeking enforcement should obtain from the appropriate county court a certificate of judgment of the county court in compliance with CCR Ord 22, r 8(1A) (in Schedule 2 to the CPR), setting out details of the judgment or order to be enforced, sealed with the seal of that court and dated and signed by an officer of that court and stating on its face that it is granted for the purpose of enforcing the judgment or order by execution against goods in the High Court. Form N293A is a 'Combined Certificate of Judgment and Request for Writ of Fieri Facias' and should be used.

11.2.7 A correctly completed form N293A together with a copy should be filed in Room E17 where the court officer will;

(1)   allocate a reference number,
(2)   date seal the certificate and copy, returning the original to the party and retaining the copy, and
(3)   enter the proceedings in a register kept for that purpose.
The certificate shall be treated for enforcement purposes as a High Court judgment and interest at the appropriate rate shall run from the date of the certificate.

11.2.8 The title of all subsequent documents shall be set out as follows:

'
                                        QUEEN'S BENCH DIVISION
                                        IN THE HIGH COURT OF
                                        JUSTICE
                                        High Court Claim No
                                        County Court Claim No

(Sent from the [   ] County Court by certificate dated (*date*))

Claimant

Defendant   '

When the writ of fieri facias is issued, the certificate of judgment retained by the party shall be date sealed by the court officer on the bottom left hand corner and endorsed with the designation of the Sheriff to whom the writ is directed.

11.2.9 The Sheriffs Lodgment Centre at 2 Serjeant's Inn, Fleet Street, London EC4Y 1NX provides a service for arranging transfer up of county court judgments, and will complete the required forms and take all the above steps on behalf of the judgment creditor. (A helpline is provided on 020 7353 3640.)

11.2.10 It is important to remember in these cases that although any application for a stay of execution may be made to a master in the High Court by application notice filed in accordance with Part 23, all other applications for enforcement or other relief must be made to the issuing county court. This practice is followed in the district registries with such variations as circumstances require.

11.2.11 When a writ of execution has been issued in the Royal Courts of Justice it may then be delivered to the Sheriffs Lodgment Centre. Value Added Tax is payable in addition to the sheriff's fee on the services for which the fee is payable, and must be paid at the time of delivery. If the goods, chattels and property to be seized in execution are not within Greater London, the sheriff will direct the writ to the sheriff of the appropriate county. Goods which may not be seized in execution of a writ are set out in s 138(3A) of the Supreme Court Act 1981 as follows:

(1)   such tools, books, vehicles and other items of equipment as are necessary to that person for use personally by him in his employment, business or vocation,

(2)   such clothing, bedding, furniture, household equipment and provisions as are necessary for satisfying the basic domestic needs of that person and his family,

(3)   any money, bank notes, bills of exchange, promissory notes, bonds, specialties or securities for money belonging to that person.

11.2.12 When first executing a writ of fieri facias the sheriff will deliver to the debtor or leave at each place where execution is levied a notice of seizure in form No 55[120]. This is commonly known as 'walking possession' and the notice explains to the debtor the situation with regard to the goods seized and what he then has to do.

120 RSC Ord 45, r 2.

11.2.13 After execution of a writ of execution, the sheriff will endorse on the writ a statement of the manner in which he has executed it and will send a copy of the statement to the party issuing the writ.

11.3 Interpleader proceedings (RSC Ord 17)

11.3.1 Where a person is under liability in respect of a debt or property and has been, or expects to be claimed against by two or more persons claiming the same debt or property, if the person under liability does not dispute the debt or claim the property, he may apply to the court for relief by way of interpleader, ie for the entitlement of the persons claiming the same debt or property to be established in separate proceedings between them.

11.3.2 Where the sheriff has seized goods in execution and a person other than the person against whom the writ of execution was issued wishes to claim the goods seized, he must give notice of his claim to the sheriff, including in his notice a statement of his address which will be his address for service. The sheriff will then give notice of that claim to the claimant on whose behalf the goods were seized, in form PF23. The notice requires the claimant to state whether he admits or disputes the claim. The claimant must do so within 7 days of receipt of the sheriff's notice and may use form PF24 to do so.

11.3.3 Where the claimant admits the claim, the sheriff will withdraw from possession of the goods and may apply under RSC Ord 17, r 2(4) for an order to restrain a claim being brought against him for having taken possession of the goods. Where the claimant disputes the claim, the sheriff may apply for interpleader relief. An application for interpleader relief if made in existing proceedings is made by an application in accordance with Part 23, otherwise it is made by the issue of a Part 8 claim form.

11.3.4 The master may deal with the claims summarily, or may direct an issue to be tried between the parties in dispute (see RSC Ord 17, r 5) or make such other order as is appropriate.

11.4 Examination of judgment debtor (RSC Ord 48)

11.4.1 Where a person ('the judgment creditor') has obtained a judgment or order for payment of a sum of money against a person ('the judgment debtor'), the judgment creditor may apply for an order requiring the judgment debtor to attend to be orally examined concerning his assets and means[121]. If the judgment debtor is a company or corporation, the court will order an officer of the company or corporation to attend for examination. In the case of a judgment or order which is not for payment of a sum of money, the court may make an order for the attendance of the party liable for his examination on such questions as may be specified in the order.

121 RSC Ord 48, r 1.

11.4.2 An application for an order under RSC Ord 48, r 1 should be made in accordance with Part 23 without notice to any other party. The application must be supported by evidence giving details of the judgment or order, including the amount still owing, and showing that the judgment creditor is entitled to enforce the judgment or order. Where the judgment debtor is a company or corporation the evidence must give details of the officer to be examined. Form PF98 may be used as a precedent for the evidence in support. Where a judgment creditor has obtained judgments in several different proceedings against the same judgment debtor, only one application need be made, setting out in the body of the application details of all the judgments on which examination is sought.

11.4.3 The examination will take place before a master, registrar, district judge or nominated officer, as may be ordered, and will normally be at the court where the least expense will be incurred, usually the county court for the area where the judgment debtor lives. If a different court is requested the reason why should be given.

11.4.4 The application notice/evidence should be filed in the Masters' Support Unit Room E16 for consideration by a master who will, if satisfied, make the order sought. Where the examination is to take place in a county court, the judgment creditor should lodge a copy of the order with the county court and obtain an appointment for the examination. If the examination is to take place in the Royal Courts of Justice, the order should be taken to Room E17 where the appointment will be endorsed on the order. In the Central Office the nominated officer is nominated at the discretion of the Senior Master and their names may be obtained from Room E17.

11.4.5 The order (endorsed with the penal notice as set out in paragraph 9.1 of the Part 40B Practice Direction) together with details of the appointment must be served personally on the judgment debtor or on the officer of the judgment debtor company or corporation to be examined. A judgment debtor should be offered his conduct money, ie expenses of travelling to and from the examination and of attending to give evidence.

11.4.6 The officer conducting the examination will take down, or arrange to have taken down in writing the judgment debtor's statement. The officer will read the statement to the judgment debtor and will ask him to sign it. If he refuses to do so the officer will sign the statement. If the judgment debtor refuses to answer any question or if any other difficulties arise, the matter will be referred to the Senior Master or the Practice Master who will give such direction as he thinks fit.

11.5 Garnishee proceedings (RSC Ord 49)

11.5.1 Where a judgment creditor has obtained a judgment or order for payment of a sum of money of at least £50 against a judgment debtor, and another person ('the garnishee') is indebted to the judgment debtor, the judgment creditor may apply to the master for an order that the garnishee pays to the judgment creditor the amount of the debt due to the judgment debtor, or sufficient of it to satisfy the judgment debt.

11.5.2 The application should be made in accordance with Part 23 but the application notice need not be served on the judgment debtor. The application will normally be dealt with without a hearing and must be supported by evidence as set out in RSC Ord 49, r 2. Parties may use form PF100 for their evidence in support. If the master is satisfied that such an order is appropriate, he will make an order in form No 72 specifying the debt attached and appointing a time for the garnishee to attend and show cause why the order should not be made absolute.

11.5.3 The garnishee order to show cause must be served personally on the garnishee, and served on the judgment debtor, in accordance with RSC Ord 49, r 3. Where the garnishee fails to attend the hearing or attends but does not dispute the debt, the master may make a garnishee order absolute against the garnishee under RSC Ord 49, r 1. The order absolute may be enforced in the same manner as any other order for the payment of money[122]. Where the garnishee disputes the debt, the master may dispose of the matter as set out in RSC Ord 49, r 5.

---

122 RSC Ord 49, r 4(2).

11.5.4 Where the judgment creditor seeks to enforce a judgment expressed in a foreign currency by garnishee proceedings, the evidence in support of the application must contain words to the following effect:

> 'The rate current in London for the purchase of (*state the unit of foreign currency in which the judgment is expressed*) at the close of business on (*state the nearest preceding date to the date of verifying the evidence*) was (   ) to the £ sterling, and at this rate the sum of (*state the amount of the judgment debt in the foreign currency*) amounts to £   . I have obtained this information from (*state source*) and believe it to be true.'

11.6 Charging Orders (RSC Ord 50)

11.6.1 A judgment creditor may apply for a charging order on the property or assets of the judgment debtor, which will have the effect of providing him with security over the property of the judgment debtor. The High Court has jurisdiction to impose a charging order in the following cases:

(1)   where the property is a fund lodged in the High Court,

(2)   where the order to be enforced is a maintenance order[123] of the High Court, and

(3)   where the judgment or order is made in the High Court and exceeds £5000[124].

The property and assets of the judgment debtor on which a charge may be imposed by a charging order are specified by s 2 of the Charging Orders Act 1979.

123 See s 2(a) Attachment of Earnings Act 1971.
124 In the case of subparas (2) and (3) the county court also has jurisdiction.

11.6.2 A charging order to show cause imposing a charge on land will be drawn in respect of the judgment debtors interest in the land and not the land itself, unless the court orders otherwise. If a charging order to show cause is made on stocks or shares in more than one company, a separate order must be drawn in respect of each company. If the judgment debt is expressed in a foreign currency, the evidence in support of any application for a charging order should contain a similar provision to that set out in paragraph 11.5.4 above.

11.6.3 The application for a charging order is made to a master and should be made in accordance with Part 23 but the application is made without being served on the judgment debtor. The application will normally be dealt with without a hearing and must be supported by evidence as set out in RSC Ord 50, r 3. Parties may use form PF101 for their evidence in support. If the master is satisfied that such an order is appropriate, he will make an order in form No 75 appointing a time for the judgment debtor to attend and show cause why the order should not be made absolute.

11.6.4 The order to show cause and the evidence in support should be served in accordance with RSC Ord 50, r 2, or otherwise as directed by the master. After further consideration at the hearing the master will either make the order absolute (with or without modifications) as in form No 76, or discharge it. Where the order is discharged, the order of discharge must be served in accordance with RSC Ord 50, r 7.

11.6.5 See RSC Ord 50, r 4 for provisions concerning imposing a charge on an interest held by a trustee. RSC Ord 50, r 5 deals with the effects of a charging order in relation to securities out of court, and RSC Ord 50, r 6 with funds in court. Proceedings for the enforcement of a charging order by sale of the property charged must be begun by a Part 8[125] claim form issued out of Chancery Chambers or a Chancery district registry (RSC Ord 50, r 9A).

125 See Table 1, Part 8B practice direction.

11.7 Receivers; equitable execution (RSC Ord 51)

11.7.1 Equitable execution is a process which enables a judgment creditor to obtain payment of the judgment debt where the interest of the judgment debtor in property cannot be reached by ordinary execution.

11.7.2 An application for appointment of a receiver by way of equitable execution may be made to a master, who also has jurisdiction to grant an injunction if, and only so far as, the injunction is ancillary or incidental to the order. The procedure follows that set out in RSC Ord 30, rr 1–6, and the application should be made in accordance with Part 23 and the Part 23 Practice Direction as described in the following paragraphs.

11.7.3 If the judgment creditor seeks an injunction (as in 11.7.2 above) he should file his application notice based on form No 82 but setting out in addition the injunction sought, together with a witness statement or affidavit in support stating:

(1)   the date and particulars of the judgment, and that it remains wholly unsatisfied, or to what extent it remains unsatisfied,

(2)   the particulars and result of any execution which has been issued, and the nature of the sheriff's return (if any),

(3)   that the judgment debtor has no property which can be taken by the ordinary process of execution, (*if he has, give reasons showing that legal execution would be futile*),

(4)   particulars of the property in respect of which it is proposed to appoint a receiver,

(5)   the name and address of the receiver proposed to be appointed, and that in the deponent's judgment he is a fit and proper person to be appointed receiver, and

(6)   that the judgment debtor is in financial difficulties [that the immediate appointment of a receiver without the delay of giving security is of great importance] and that the deponent believes that the judgment debtor may assign or dispose of his estate or interest in (*give details of property*) unless restrained from doing so by the order and injunction of the court.

11.7.4 The judgment creditor need not give notice of this application which will normally be dealt with without a hearing. If the master is satisfied with the evidence he will make an order in form No 83 for a hearing to take place in respect of the application for the appointment of the receiver and granting an injunction meanwhile.

11.7.5 If the judgment creditor does not seek an injunction, the application notice should be filed and served together with the evidence in support (as in paragraph 11.7.3 above but without paragraph (6)).

11.7.6 At the hearing of the application to appoint the receiver, the master will, if he thinks fit, make an order in form No 84. A copy of the order appointing the receiver shall be served by the judgment creditor on the receiver and all other parties to the proceedings[126].

126 RSC Ord 30, r 4.

11.7.7 Where a receiver has been ordered to give security under RSC Ord 30, r 2, the judgment creditor should obtain an appointment before the master who made the order appointing the receiver, to settle the form and amount of the security. Unless otherwise ordered, the security will be in the form of a guarantee. The judgment creditor should have prepared a draft form of guarantee for the master to approve at the appointment. Form PF30CH may be used as a precedent for the guarantee.

11.7.8 RSC Ord 30, r 3 deals with the remuneration of the receiver which may either be assessed by the master or referred to a costs judge. RSC Ord 30, r 5 contains the provisions for submitting the receiver's accounts.

11.8 Committals, etc (RSC Ord 52)

11.8.1 The court has power to punish contempt of court by an order of committal to prison or by other means. These may be by ordering the payment of a fine, by the issue of a writ of sequestration, or by making a hospital or guardianship order under certain provisions of the Mental Health Act 1983. Committal applications under RSC Ord 52, r 4 are always dealt with by a High Court judge. The following provisions apply to applications made under RSC Ord 52, r 4.

11.8.2 The application should be made in existing proceedings by filing an application notice. If not in existing proceedings, a Part 8 claim form should be issued[127] (see paragraphs 2.1 and 2.2 of the Practice Direction – Committal Applications). Evidence in support of a committal application must be by affidavit [128]and, together with the Part 8 claim form or application notice, must be served personally on the person sought to be committed. A date for the hearing must be obtained from the Listing Office, Room WG5 and endorsed on or served with the claim form or application notice.

127 See the Part 8B practice direction, Table 1.
128 RSC Ord 52, r 4(2).

11.8.3 Paragraphs 2.5, 2.6 and 3.1–3.4 of the Practice Direction deal with the content of the evidence, and serving and filing, and paragraph 4 deals with the hearing date and management of the proceedings.

11.8.4 Committal proceedings will normally be heard in public, but see RSC Ord 52, r 6 which sets out certain types of cases which may be heard in private, and see paragraph 9 of the Practice Direction.

11.8.5 Where the court makes a finding of contempt, details of the contempt and of the order or undertaking breached (where appropriate) must be set out in the order. The term of any period of committal must be stated in the order and must not exceed 2 years[129]. A fine must be expressed as payable to Her Majesty the Queen and the order must state the amount of the fine and the date and time within which it must be paid. A contemnor and his solicitors will be notified separately as to how the fine should be paid. A precedent of the order is in form No 85 and will normally be drawn by the court.

129 Contempt of Court Act 1981, s 14.

11.8.6 When an order for committal to prison is made, the court will issue a warrant to the Tipstaff authorising him to convey the contemnor to the appropriate prison. A copy of the order should be served on the prison governor. RSC Ord 52, r 8 deals with the discharge of a person committed.

11.9 Execution against property of foreign or Commonwealth States

11.9.1 In cases where judgment has been obtained against a foreign or Commonwealth State and it is sought to execute the judgment by a writ of fieri facias, a charging order or a garnishee order, the following provisions apply:

(1)   Before the writ of fieri facias is issued, the master must be informed in writing and his direction sought. In cases where an application is to be made for a charging order to show cause or a garnishee order to show cause, the evidence in support of the application must include a statement that the execution sought is against a foreign or Commonwealth State.

(2)   The master, having been so informed will, as soon as practicable, inform the Foreign and Commonwealth Office ('FCO') of the application and will not permit the issue of a writ of fieri facias, nor grant an order to show cause until the FCO has been so informed. The Privileges and Immunities Section of the Protocol Department of the FCO may be contacted by telephone on 020 7210 4053 or by Fax on 020 7270 4126.

(3)   Having regard to all the circumstances of the case, the master may postpone the decision whether to issue the writ or grant the order to show cause for so long as he considers reasonable for the purpose of enabling the FCO to furnish further information relevant to his decision, but not for longer than 3 days from the time of his contacting the FCO. In the event that no further information is received from the FCO within 24 hours of its being informed, then the writ of fieri facias may be issued or the order to show cause may be sealed without further delay.

11.10 Recovery of enforcement costs

11.10.1 Subsection (3) of section 15 of the Courts and Legal Services Act 1990 enables a person taking steps to enforce a money judgment in the High Court to recover the costs of any previous attempt to enforce that judgment. Subsection (4) of section 15 excludes costs that the court considers to have been unreasonably incurred.

11.10.2 The application for an enforcement costs order is made to a master and should be made in accordance with Part 23 but the application notice need not be served on the judgment debtor. The application will normally be dealt with without a hearing and must be supported by evidence substantially as set out in form PF205. The deponent should exhibit sufficient vouchers, receipts or other documents as are reasonably necessary to verify the amount of the costs of previous attempts to enforce the judgment.

11.10.3 If the master is satisfied that such an order is appropriate, he will make an order for payment of the amount of such costs as he considers may be recoverable under subsection (3) of section 15. If the amount of such costs is less than that claimed by the judgment creditor, the master may either disallow the balance or give directions for a detailed assessment or other determination of the balance. If after assessment or other determination it appears that the judgment creditor is entitled to further costs beyond those originally allowed, he may issue a further writ of fieri facias or take other lawful steps to enforce those costs. Interest on the costs runs either from the date the master made the enforcement costs order or from the date of the costs certificate.

11.11 Enforcement of magistrates' courts' orders

11.11.1 The Magistrates' Courts Act 1980, s 87 provides that payment of a sum ordered to be paid on a conviction of a magistrates' court may be enforced by the High Court or a county court (otherwise than by the issue of a writ of fieri facias or other process against goods or by imprisonment or attachment of earnings) as if the sum were due to the clerk of the magistrates' court under a judgment of the High Court or county court, as the case may be.

11.11.2 In the Central Office, the application is made to a master and should be made in accordance with Part 23. Where enforcement is sought by a garnishee or charging order to show cause, the application will normally be dealt with without a hearing. Otherwise the application notice and evidence in support should be served on the defendant.

11.11.3 The application must be supported by a witness statement or affidavit in a form appropriate to the type of execution sought and must have exhibited to it the authority of the magistrates' court to take the proceedings which will recite the conviction, the amount outstanding and the nature of the proceedings authorised to be taken (Magistrates Courts Forms Rules 1981, Form 63).

11.11.4 The application notice and evidence in support together with an additional copy of the exhibit should be filed in Room E15 where it will be assigned a reference number from the register kept for that purpose. The matter will then be dealt with by the master according to the type of enforcement sought.

11.11.5 This practice will also be followed in the district registries with such variations as circumstances may render necessary.

11.12 Reciprocal enforcement of judgments and enforcement of European Community judgments and recommendations etc under the Merchant Shipping (Liner Conferences) Act 1982 (RSC Ord 71)

RECIPROCAL ENFORCEMENT; THE ADMINISTRATION OF JUSTICE ACT 1920 AND THE FOREIGN JUDGMENTS (RECIPROCAL ENFORCEMENT) ACT 1933

11.12.1 RSC Ord 71, r 2 sets out how an application under s 9 of the Act of 1920 or under s 2 of the Act of 1933 for registration of a foreign judgment in the High Court may be made. The application should be made without notice being served on any other party, but the master may direct that a Part 8 claim form should be issued and served.

11.12.2 RSC Ord 71, r 3 sets out what the evidence in support of the application should contain or have exhibited to it. The title of the witness statement or affidavit should;

(1)   expressly state whether it is made 'In the matter of the Administration of Justice Act 1920' or 'In the matter of the Foreign Judgments (Reciprocal Enforcement) Act 1933', and
(2)   identify the judgment by reference to the court in which it was obtained and the date it was given.

The foreign judgment will be registered in the foreign currency in which it is expressed and must not be converted into Sterling in the evidence in support. When it comes to enforcing the foreign judgment, the amount should then be converted in accordance with the instructions set out above in paragraph 11 in respect of the type of enforcement sought.

11.12.3 The order giving permission to register the judgment must be drawn up by, or on behalf of the judgment creditor (Form PF154 may be used as a precedent) and will be entered in the Register of Judgments kept in the Central Office for that purpose[130]. The order will usually contain a direction that the costs of and caused by the application and the registration be assessed and added to the judgment as registered. Notice of registration of the judgment must state the matters set out in RSC Ord 71, r 7(3) including the right of the judgment debtor to apply, and the time within he may do so, to have the registration set aside. The notice must be served on the judgment debtor in accordance with RSC Ord 71, r 7(1).

130 RSC Ord 71, rr 5 and 6.

11.12.4 An application to set aside the registration of a judgment under RSC Ord 71, r 9 must be made in accordance with Part 23 and be supported by a witness statement or affidavit.

11.12.5 An application for a certified copy of a judgment entered in the High Court must be made without notice by witness statement or affidavit in accordance with RSC Ord 71, r 13. The certified copy will be endorsed with a certificate signed by the master in accordance with RSC Ord 71, r 13(4). Where the application was made under s 10 of the Act of 1933, an additional certificate will be issued and signed by the master as in form PF155. Judgment creditors who intend to seek enforcement abroad should ensure that their judgment is endorsed as follows:

> 'This judgment carries interest from (*date*) at the rate of 8% per annum in accordance with the provisions of the Judgments Act 1838.'.

ENFORCEMENT OF EUROPEAN COMMUNITY JUDGMENTS

11.12.6 RSC Ord 71, rr 15–24 contains provisions concerning applications for enforcement of Community judgments and Euratom inspection orders under the European Communities (Enforcement of Community Judgments) Order 1972 and for their enforcement. The application for registration may be made without notice being served on any other party and must be supported by a witness statement or affidavit containing or having exhibited to it the matters referred to in RSC Ord 71, r 18. Form PF156 may be used as a precedent.

11.12.7 The order for registration (form PF157) will be entered in the register of the Community judgments and Euratom inspection orders kept in the Central Office for that purpose. The court will serve notice of the registration in form PF158 in accordance with RSC Ord 71, r 20.

11.12.8 An application to vary or cancel a registration under the provisions of RSC Ord 71, r 22 shall be made by application notice in accordance with Part 23, supported by a witness statement or an affidavit.

RECIPROCAL ENFORCEMENT; THE CIVIL JURISDICTION AND JUDGMENTS ACT 1982

APPLICATIONS UNDER S 4 OF THE ACT OF 1982

11.12.9 The provisions concerning applications for registration of judgments of another Contracting State under s 4 of the Act of 1982 are set out in RSC Ord 71, rr 25–35. The application is made without notice being served on any other party and must be supported by evidence as set out in RSC Ord 71, r 28. Form PF159 may be used as a precedent.

11.12.10 The order for registration (form PF160) will be entered in the register of judgments ordered to be registered under s 4 of the Act of 1982 kept in the Central

Office for that purpose. The notice of registration in form PF161 should be served in accordance with RSC Ord 71, r 32.

11.12.11 An appeal against registration must be made to a judge under the provisions of RSC Ord 71, r 33(2) by application notice in accordance with Part 23, and should be served in accordance with RSC Ord 71, r 33(2)(a) and (b).

APPLICATIONS UNDER S 12 OF THE ACT OF 1982

11.12.12 RSC Ord 71, r 36 deals with applications for enforcement of High Court judgments in other Contracting States under s 12 of the Act of 1982. The application for a certified copy of the judgment entered in the High Court must be made without notice being served on any other party and must be supported by evidence as set out in RSC Ord 71, r 36(2). Form PF163 may be used as a precedent.

11.12.13 The court will issue a certified copy of the judgment together with a certificate in form PF110 signed by the master, and having annexed to it a copy of the claim form by which the proceedings were begun.

APPLICATIONS UNDER S 18 OF THE ACT OF 1982; JUDGMENT CONTAINING MONEY PROVISIONS

11.12.14 RSC Ord 71, r 37 deals with applications for registration in the High Court of a certificate in respect of any money provisions contained in a judgment given in another part of the United Kingdom. The certificate may be obtained by filing a draft certificate in form No 111 together with a witness statement or affidavit in accordance with RSC Ord 71, r 37(3). Form PF164 may be used as a precedent.

11.12.15 The certificate must be filed for registration in Room E13 in the Central Office within 6 months from the date of its issue. Under paragraph 9 of schedule 6 to the Act of 1982 an application may be made to stay the enforcement of the certificate. The application may be made without notice being served on any other party supported by a witness statement or affidavit stating that the applicant is entitled and intends to apply to the judgment court to set aside or stay the judgment.

APPLICATIONS UNDER S 18 OF THE ACT OF 1982; JUDGMENT CONTAINING NON-MONEY PROVISIONS

11.12.16 RSC Ord 71, r 38 deals with applications for registration in the High Court of a judgment which contains non-money provisions, given in another part of the United Kingdom. The application should be made broadly in accordance with paragraphs 11.12.11 and 11.12.12 above, without notice being served on any other party, but the master may direct that a Part 8 claim form should be issued and served.

11.12.17 The application should be accompanied by a draft certificate in form No 112 and must be supported by a witness statement or affidavit in accordance with

RSC Ord 71, r 37(3) (with the necessary modifications). Form PF165 may be used as a precedent. An application to set aside registration of a judgment under schedule 7 to the Act of 1982 may be made in accordance with RSC Ord 71, r 9 (1) and (2).

11.12.18 The certificates will be entered in the register of certificates in respect of judgments ordered to be registered under Schedules 6 or 7 of the Act of 1982 kept in the Central Office for that purpose.

ENFORCEMENT OF RECOMMENDATIONS ETC UNDER THE MERCHANT SHIPPING (LINER CONFERENCES) ACT 1982

11.12.19 Applications under s 9 of the Act of 1982 for registration of a recommendation, determination or award, are dealt with by a commercial judge and shall be made by the issue of a Part 8 claim form[131]. The application should be supported by evidence in accordance with RSC Ord 71, r 42.

131 RSC Ord 71, r 41 and the Part 8B practice direction, Table 1.

11.12.20 The order giving permission to register the recommendation, determination or award must be drawn up by or on behalf of the party making the application, and entered in the register of the recommendations, determinations and awards ordered to be registered under s 9 of the Act of 1982, directed by the Senior Master to be kept in the Admiralty and Commercial Registry.

12 MISCELLANEOUS

12.1 Service of foreign process (RSC Ord 69)

12.1.1 RSC Ord 69 applies to the service on a person in England or Wales of any process in connection with civil or commercial proceedings in a foreign court or tribunal. A request for service is made to the Senior Master from either Her Majesty's Principal Secretary of State for Foreign and Commonwealth Affairs, or where the foreign court or tribunal is in a convention country[132], from a consular or other authority of that country.

132 For definition of 'convention country' see RSC Ord 69, r 1.

12.1.2 Where the foreign court or tribunal certifies that the person to be served understands the language of the process, it is not necessary to provide a translation. RSC Ord 69, r 3 deals with the manner of service; the process may be served through the machinery of the county court and the usual practice is for the Senior Master to provide a certificate for the bailiff or county court officer to use. The Senior Master may make an order for service by an alternative method based on the bailiff's certificate.

12.1.3 When service has been effected, the Senior Master will send a certificate, together with a copy of the process served, to the authority who requested service, stating how service was effected, or why service could not be effected. There is a discretion to charge for the costs of service or attempted service, but recovery is usually sought only where the country requesting service does not provide a reciprocal free service.

12.2 Rectification of register of deeds of arrangement (RSC Ord 94, r 4)

12.2.1 Deeds of arrangement must be registered[133]. The registration office is at the Department of Trade.

133 Deeds of Arrangement Act 1914, as amended by the Administration of Justice Act 1925, s 22.

12.2.2 An application for an order as set out in RSC Ord 94, r 4(1)(a) or (b) must be made to a master of the Queen's Bench Division. Notice need not be served on any other party and the application must be supported by a witness statement or affidavit as described in rule 4(2).

12.3 Exercise of jurisdiction under the Representation of the People Acts (RSC Ord 94, r 5)

12.3.1 RSC Ord 94, r 5 describes the jurisdiction of the High Court under the above Acts. The practice is governed by the Election Petition Rules 1960 (as amended).

12.3.2 Under Part III of the Representation of the People Act 1983, the result of a parliamentary or local government election may be questioned on the grounds of some irregularity either before or during the election. The provisions of Part III have also been applied to European Parliamentary elections.

12.3.3 The challenge is made by the issue of an election petition

(a)   in respect of a Parliamentary election by one or more electors or
(b)   in respect of a local government election by four or more electors,

or by an unsuccessful or alleged candidate. The member/councillor whose election is complained of is a respondent to the petition as is the returning officer if his conduct is complained of. The petition is issued in the Election Petitions Office, Room E218, normally within 21 days of the election, although this may be extended in certain circumstances.

12.3.4 The petition is tried by two High Court judges of the Queen's Bench Division in respect of parliamentary elections or by a Commissioner in respect of local government elections. The Commissioner must be a lawyer of not less than 10 years standing who neither resides nor practices in the area concerned. The trial usually takes place in the constituency/local government area although preliminary matters are dealt with at the Royal Courts of Justice.

12.3.5 The election court may confirm the result of the election, or substitute another candidate as the member/councillor, or may order the election to be re-run.

12.3.6 Applications for remedies under various sections of the Representation of the People Act 1983 are also issued in the Election Petitions Office, and are usually heard by an Election Rota judge.

12.3.7 Outside the court offices' opening times, but while the building is still open to the public, election petitions and applications may be left in the letter box fixed to the door of Room E218. When the building is closed, election petitions and applications may be left with Security at the Main Entrance, up until midnight.

12.4 Bills of Sale Acts 1878 and 1882 and the Industrial and Provident Societies Act 1967 (RSC Ord 95)

12.4.1 Every bill of sale and absolute bill of sale to which the Act of 1878 applies must be registered under s 8 of that Act, within 7 clear days of its making, and, under s 11 of the Act of 1878, the registration of a bill of sale must be renewed at least once every 5 years. The register for the purpose of the Bills of Sale Acts contains the particulars of registered bills of sale and an alphabetical index of the names of the grantors, and is kept in the Action Department in Room E10.

12.4.2 An application to register a bill of sale which is made within the prescribed time should be made by filing in Room E17 the original bill of sale and any document annexed to it together with a witness statement or affidavit in form PF179 or PF180. An application to re-register a bill of sale which is made within the prescribed time should be made by filing in Room E17 a witness statement or affidavit in form PF181.

12.4.3 An application to rectify;

(1)   an omission to register, by extending the time for registration, or
(2)   an omission or mis-statement of the name, residence or occupation of a person in the register, by correcting the registration,

must be made by witness statement or affidavit to a master of the Queen's Bench Division. In addition to the matters set out in forms PF179 or PF180, the evidence in support must also set out the particulars of the omission and state the grounds on which the application is made.

12.4.4 Where the residence of the grantor of the bill of sale or the person against whom the process is issued is outside the London bankruptcy district, or where the bill of sale describes the goods as being in a place outside that district, the Central Office will send copies of the bill of sale to the appropriate county court district judge[134].

134 Section 11, Bills of Sale Act 1882 and the Bills of Sale (Local Registration) Rules 1960.

12.4.5 The master, on being satisfied that the omission or mis-statement of name, residence or occupation of a person in the register was accidental or due to inadvertence, may order the omission or mis-statement to be rectified by the insertion in the register of the correct name, residence or occupation of the person.

12.4.6 Where the master is satisfied that the omission to register a bill of sale or a witness statement or affidavit of renewal within the prescribed time was accidental or due to inadvertence, he may extend the time for registration on such terms as he thinks fit. In order to protect any creditors who have accrued rights of property in the assets in respect of which the bill of sale was granted between the date of the bill and its actual registration, any order to extend the time for registration will normally be made 'without prejudice' to those creditors. The order will be drawn up in form PF182.

12.4.7 An application for an order that a memorandum of satisfaction be written on a registered copy of a bill of sale, made without the consent of the person entitled to the benefit of the bill of sale, must be made by the issue of a Part 8 claim form. Where the consent of the person entitled to the benefit of the bill of sale has been obtained, the application may be made by a witness statement or affidavit[135] containing that consent and verifying the signature on it. Form PF183 contains precedents for the evidence and forms of consent. Where the application is made with consent, the evidence need not be served on any other person. If the master is satisfied on the evidence, he will endorse his approval on the witness statement or affidavit (an order is not normally drawn up) and send it to Room E17 for satisfaction to be entered. If a copy of the bill of sale has been sent to a county court district judge, a notice of satisfaction will be sent to that district judge.

135 See the practice direction – Bills of Sale.

12.4.8 Where the consent has not been obtained, the claim form must be served on the person entitled to the benefit of the bill of sale and must be supported by evidence that the debt (if any) for which the bill of sale was made has been satisfied or discharged.

12.4.9 An application to restrain removal on sale of goods seized in accordance with RSC Ord 95, r 3 and under the proviso to s 7 of the Bills of Sale Act (1878) Amendment Act 1882 must be made by the issue of a Part 8 claim form for hearing before the Interim Applications judge.

12.4.10 Under the Industrial and Provident Societies Act 1967 an application to record an instrument creating a fixed or floating charge on the assets of a registered society or to rectify any omission or mis-statement in it must be made within 14 days beginning with the date of its execution.

12.4.11 Under RSC Ord 95, r 5 and in accordance with s 1(5) of the Act of 1967 the court may order;

(1)   that the period for making an application for recording a charge be extended, or
(2)   an omission or mis-statement in such an application be rectified.

The procedure for obtaining an order as in (1) or (2) above is similar to that under s 14 of the Bills of Sale Act 1878 and must be made by witness statement or affidavit to a master of the Queen's Bench Division as in paragraph 12.4.3 above and must exhibit a copy of the instrument duly authenticated in the prescribed manner together with any other particulars relating to the charge.

12.4.12 RSC Ord 95, r 3 refers to the assignment of book debts; the register of assignments of book debts is kept in Room E10 in the Central Office. An application for registration under s 344 of the Insolvency Act 1986 should be made in accordance with RSC Ord 95, r 6(2). Parties may use form PF186 for their evidence in support. It is helpful if the original assignment is also produced.

12.5 Enrolment of deeds and other documents

12.5.1 Any deed or document which by virtue of any enactment is required or authorised to be enrolled in the Supreme Court may be enrolled in the Central Office. See the Part 5 Practice Direction at paragraph 6 which fully sets out the procedure for enrolment and contains in an appendix the Enrolment of Deeds (Change of Name) Regulations 1994.

12.6 Bail (RSC Ord 79, r 9)

12.6.1 Under the provisions of subsections (1) and (2) of section 22 of the Criminal Justice Act 1967 (as amended by Schedule 2 to the Bail Act 1976) the High Court may grant bail in criminal proceedings to a defendant in custody who has been refused bail, or vary the arrangements for bail of an inferior court.

12.6.2 The application must be made to the Interim Applications judge by the issue of a Part 8 claim form in form No 97 or 97A, and supported by a witness statement or affidavit in accordance with RSC Ord 79, r 9 (1) to (3). The claim form should be issued in the Listing Office, Room WG5, and will be given a bail number from the register kept there for recording bail applications.

12.6.3 If a defendant wishing to apply for bail is unable to instruct a solicitor to act for him through lack of means, he may write to the Interim Applications judge to that effect and requesting that the Official Solicitor act for him. The letter should be addressed to the Listing Office, Room WG5, marked for the attention of the Interim Applications judge. Where the judge assigns the Official Solicitor to act for the defendant, he may dispense with the issue of a claim form and a witness statement or affidavit in support.

12.6.4 Where the judge grants bail, the order will be drawn up in form No 98 which provides for the conditions to be complied with both before release, including the provision of sureties, and after release. An order varying the arrangements for bail will be drawn up in form No 98A. Copies of those orders must be sent to the appropriate officer of the Crown Court or of the court which committed the defendant.

12.7 Defamation

12.7.1 Defamation claims are governed by Part 53 and the Part 53 Practice Direction. Paragraph 2 of the Practice Direction sets out the information which should be included in a statement of case.

OFFER TO MAKE AMENDS

12.7.2 Under section 2 of the Defamation Act 1996 a person who has published a statement alleged to be defamatory of another may offer to make amends ('a section 2 offer'). The section 2 offer must;

(1)　be in writing,
(2)　be expressed to be an offer to make amends under section 2 of the Act, and
(3)　state whether it is a qualified offer, and if so, set out the defamatory meaning in relation to which it is made.

A section 2 offer is an offer;

(1)　to make a suitable correction of the statement complained of and sufficient apology,
(2)　to publish the correction and apology in a manner that is reasonable and practicable in the circumstances, and
(3)　to pay to the aggrieved party compensation (if any) and costs as may be agreed or determined to be payable.

12.7.3 Where a section 2 offer is accepted by an aggrieved person he may not bring or continue defamation proceedings against the person making the offer, but he may apply to the court under section 3 of the Act for an order that the other party fulfil his offer by taking the agreed steps. If the parties are unable to agree the amount of compensation or costs, the aggrieved party may apply to the court for the amount to be decided.

12.7.4 In the event that the parties are unable to agree on the steps to be taken, the person making the offer may take such steps as he thinks appropriate, including making an application for the court's approval of the terms of a statement to be read in court containing a correction and apology. He may also give an undertaking to the court as to the manner of their publication.

12.7.5 In existing proceedings the above applications may be made in accordance with Part 23, otherwise a Part 8 claim form should be issued. The application or claim must be supported by written evidence as set out in the Part 53 Practice Direction at paragraph 3.3, and should be made to a master. If the application or claim involves the court's approval for a statement to be read in court, it should be made to the Senior Master. The claim form or application notice should be issued or filed in the Masters' Support Unit, Room E17.

RULING ON MEANING

12.7.6 An application for an order determining whether or not a statement complained of is capable of;

(1)   having any meaning or meanings attributed to it in a statement of case,
(2)   being defamatory of the claimant, or
(3)   bearing any other meaning defamatory of the claimant,

should be made in accordance with Part 23 and may be made at any time after service of the particulars of claim. Paragraphs 4.3 and 4.4 or the Practice Direction state the information which must be included in the application notice and evidence in support.

12.7.7 The application notice should be filed in the Listing Office, Room WG5, for hearing by the judge in charge of the Jury list, or another designated judge.

SUMMARY DISPOSAL

12.7.8 Section 8 of the Act gives the court power to dispose summarily of the claimant's claim. The court may;

(1)   dismiss the claim if it appears that it has no realistic prospect of success and there is no reason why it should be tried, or
(2)   give judgment for the claimant and grant him summary relief.

12.7.9 Summary relief includes the following;

(1)   a declaration that the statement was false and defamatory of the claimant,
(2)   an order that the defendant publish or cause to be published a suitable correction and apology,
(3)   damages not exceeding £10,000,
(4)   an order restraining the defendant from publishing or further publishing the matter complained of.

12.7.10 Applications for summary disposal are dealt with in rule 53.2 and paragraphs 5.1–5.3 of the Part 53 Practice Direction. Substantial claims and those involving the police authorities or the media or those seeking an order restraining publication will be dealt with by the judge in charge of the Jury list or another designated judge, and the application notice should be filed in the Listing Office, Room WG5. Applications for summary disposal in other defamation claims may be made at first instance to a master.

12.7.11 An application notice for summary disposal must state;

(1)   that it is an application for summary disposal made in accordance with section 8 of the Act,
(2)   the matters set out in paragraph 2(3) of the Part 24 Practice Direction, and
(3)   whether or not the defendant has made an offer to make amends under section 2 of the Act, and whether or not it has been withdrawn.

The application may be made at any time after service of the particulars of claim and the provisions of rule 24.4(1)(a) and (b) do not apply.

12.7.12 Where the court has made an order for summary relief as in 12.7.9(2) above (specifying the date by which the parties should agree the content, time, manner, form and place of publication of the correction and apology) and the parties are unable to comply within the specified time, the claimant must prepare a summary of the court's judgment and serve it on the other parties within 3 days following the date specified in the order for the content to be agreed by the parties[136].

136 Paragraph 5.3 of the Part 53 practice direction.

12.7.13 If the parties are unable to agree the summary, they must within 3 days of its receipt, apply to the court by;

(1)   filing an application notice, and
(2)   filing and serving on all the other parties a copy of the summary showing the revisions they wish to make to it.

The court (normally the judge who delivered the judgment) will then settle the summary.

STATEMENTS READ IN COURT

12.7.14 Paragraph 6 of the Practice Direction only applies where a party wishes to accept a Part 36 offer, Part 36 payment or other offer of settlement.

12.7.15 An application for permission to make the statement before a judge in court may be made before or after acceptance of the Part 36 offer, Part 36 payment or other offer to settle, and should be made in accordance with Part 23 to the Senior Master, or if he is not available, to the Practice Master. The application notice, together with a copy of the statement, should be filed in the Masters' Support Unit, Room E17.

12.7.16 Where permission has been given, the parties may take a copy of the order to the Listing Office, Room WG5 for the matter will be listed before the judge in charge of the Jury List for mention. Otherwise, the Action Department will send the court file to the Listing Office for the matter to be listed.

12.8 References to the Court of Justice of the European Communities

12.8.1 A party wishing to apply for an order[137] under RSC Ord 114 (Schedule 1 to the CPR) may do so by application before or at the trial or hearing. An application made before the trial or hearing should be made in accordance with Part 23.

137 An 'order' means an order referring a question to the European Court for a preliminary ruling under article 234 (formerly article 177) of the Treaty establishing the European Community, article 150 of the Treaty establishing the European Atomic Energy Community or article 41 of the Treaty

establishing the European Coal and Steel Community, or for a ruling on the interpretation of any of the Brussels Conventions (within the meaning of s 1(1) of the Civil Jurisdiction and Judgments Act 1982) or any of the instruments referred to in s 1 of the Contracts (Applicable Law) Act 1990.

12.8.2 Before making an order for reference, the court will pay close attention to the terms of the appropriate article, to RSC Ord 114, to form PF109 and to the 'Guidance of the Court of Justice of the European Communities on References by National Courts for Preliminary Rulings' which may be found in the Practice Direction (ECJ References: Procedure) (1999) 1 WLR 260.

12.8.3 It is the responsibility of the court, rather than the parties, to settle the terms of the reference. This should identify as clearly, succinctly and simply as the nature of the case permits the question to which the British court seeks an answer and it is very desirable that language should be used which lends itself readily to translation.

12.8.4 The referring court should, in a single document scheduled to the order (in form PF109);

(1)   identify the parties and summarise the nature and history of the proceedings,
(2)   summarise the salient facts, indicating whether these are proved or admitted or assumed,
(3)   make reference to the rules of national law (substantive and procedural) relevant to the dispute,
(4)   summarise the contentions of the parties as far as relevant,
(5)   explain why a ruling of the European Court is sought, identifying the EC provisions whose effect is in issue, and
(6)   formulate, without avoidable complexity, the question(s) to which an answer is requested.

12.8.5 Where the document is in the form of a judgment, passages which are not relevant to the reference should be omitted from the text scheduled to the order. Incorporation of appendices, annexes or enclosures as part of the document should be avoided, unless the relevant passages lend themselves readily to translation and are clearly identified.

12.8.6 When the order of reference has been approved by the judge and sealed by the court, the order, together with any other necessary documents should be promptly passed to Room E.13 for the attention of the Senior Master of the Queen's Bench Division, for transmission to Luxembourg without avoidable delay.

12.9 Group litigation orders 'GLOs'

12.9.1 Section III of Part 19 and the Practice Direction – Group Litigation deal with claims where multiple parties are claimants.

12.9.2 When considering applying for a GLO, the applicant should contact the Law Society at 113 Chancery Lane, London WC2A 1PL, who may be able to assist in putting the applicant in contact with other parties who may also be interested in applying for a GLO in the same matter.

12.9.3 The consent of either the Lord Chief Justice or the Vice-Chancellor to the GLO is required. In the Queen's Bench Division the application should be made to the Senior Master in accordance with Part 23. If the Senior Master is minded to make the GLO he will forward a copy of the application notice and any written evidence to the Lord Chief Justice. The application notice should include the information set out in paragraph 3.2 of the Practice Direction.

12.9.4 A group register will be set up and maintained in the court of all the parties to the group of claims to be managed under the GLO. In order to publicise the GLO when it has been made, a copy should be supplied to the Law Society and to the Senior Master. A record of each GLO made will be maintained in the Central Office.

12.9.5 The Practice Direction sets out how the group litigation will be managed. In particular, a managing judge will be appointed. The case management directions are likely to direct;

(1) that a 'group particulars of claim' containing the various claims of the claimants on the group register are served,
(2) that one claim proceed as a 'test' claim, and
(3) a cut-off date after which no additions may be made to the group register.

****

ANNEX 2

The following is a list of the abbreviations commonly used by masters on endorsements of orders, though there may be some variation as between individual masters.

ADR	Alternative dispute resolution
Aff	Affidavit
AM-T	Allocate to multi-track
AN	Appointment Notice
App	Application
AQ	Allocation questionnaire
AS	Assessed summarily
BNLT	By no later than
CC	County court
CIA	Costs in the application
CIAE	Costs in any event
CIC	Costs in the case
Cl	Claimant
Col	Certificate for counsel
CMC	Case management conference

COA	Charging order absolute
COCB	Costs of and caused by
COSC	Charging order to show cause
CR	Costs reserved
CTR	Costs of today reserved
D/Def	Defendant/Defence
DAI/NA	Detailed assessment if not agreed
Disc	Disclosure
Dism	Dismissed
Disp C/S	Dispense with requirement of certificate of service
FC	Fixed costs
FI	Further information
FO	Further order
FOD	First open date
GOA	Garnishee order absolute
GOSC	Garnishee order to show cause
IAE	In any event
IB	Indemnity basis
Insp	Inspection
J	Judgment (as in Part 24 applications)
LA	Legal aid
LAA	Legal aid assessment
LQ	Listing questionnaire
O	Order
On CServ	On producing certificate of service
O Exam	Oral examination
P/C	Particulars of claim
PD	Practice direction
Pm	Permission
Pm A	Permission to apply
Pm R	Permission to restore
Pm RFD	Permission to restore for further directions
Pt	Part
PRA	Private room appointment
R	Rule
SA	Set aside/Special allowance
SOJ	Service out of the jurisdiction
S/C	Statement of case
SB	Standard basis
S/T	Statement of truth
Tfr	Transfer
WN	Without notice
WCO	Wasted costs order
WS	Witness statement

Appendix D

PROTOCOL FOR THE INSTRUCTION OF EXPERTS TO GIVE EVIDENCE IN CIVIL CLAIMS

1. INTRODUCTION

Expert witnesses perform a vital role in civil litigation. It is essential that both those who instruct experts and experts themselves are given clear guidance as to what they are expected to do in civil proceedings. The purpose of this Protocol is to provide such guidance. It has been drafted by the Civil Justice Council and reflects the rules and practice directions current [in June 2005], replacing the Code of Guidance on Expert Evidence. The authors of the Protocol wish to acknowledge the valuable assistance they obtained by drawing on earlier documents produced by the Academy of Experts and the Expert Witness Institute, as well as suggestions made by the Clinical Dispute Forum. The Protocol has been approved by the Master of the Rolls.

2. AIMS OF PROTOCOL

2.1 This Protocol offers guidance to experts and to those instructing them in the interpretation of and compliance with Part 35 of the Civil Procedure Rules (CPR 35) and its associated Practice Direction (PD 35) and to further the objectives of the Civil Procedure Rules in general. It is intended to assist in the interpretation of those provisions in the interests of good practice but it does not replace them. It sets out standards for the use of experts and the conduct of experts and those who instruct them. The existence of this Protocol does not remove the need for experts and those who instruct them to be familiar with CPR35 and PD35.

2.2 Experts and those who instruct them should also bear in mind para 1.4 of the Practice Direction on Protocols which contains the following objectives, namely to:

(a)   encourage the exchange of early and full information about the expert issues involved in a prospective legal claim;

(b)   enable the parties to avoid or reduce the scope of litigation by agreeing the whole or part of an expert issue before commencement of proceedings; and

(c)   support the efficient management of proceedings where litigation cannot be avoided.

3.   APPLICATION

3.1   This Protocol applies to any steps taken for the purpose of civil proceedings by experts or those who instruct them on or after 5th September 2005.

3.2   It applies to all experts who are, or who may be, governed by CPR Part 35 and to those who instruct them. Experts are governed by Part 35 if they are or have been instructed to give or prepare evidence for the purpose of civil proceedings in a court in England and Wales (CPR 35.2).

3.3   Experts, and those instructing them, should be aware that some cases may be 'specialist proceedings' (CPR 49) where there are modifications to the Civil Procedure Rules. Proceedings may also be governed by other Protocols. Further, some courts have published their own Guides which supplement the Civil Procedure Rules for proceedings in those courts. They contain provisions affecting expert evidence. Expert witnesses and those instructing them should be familiar with them when they are relevant.

3.4   Courts may take into account any failure to comply with this Protocol when making orders in relation to costs, interest, time limits, the stay of proceedings and whether to order a party to pay a sum of money into court.

Limitation

3.5   If, as a result of complying with any part of this Protocol, claims would or might be time barred under any provision in the Limitation Act 1980, or any other legislation that imposes a time limit for the bringing an action, claimants may commence proceedings without complying with this Protocol. In such circumstances, claimants who commence proceedings without complying with all, or any part, of this Protocol must apply, giving notice to all other parties, to the court for directions as to the timetable and form of procedure to be adopted, at the same time as they request the court to issue proceedings. The court may consider whether to order a stay of the whole or part of the proceedings pending compliance with this Protocol and may make orders in relation to costs.

4.   DUTIES OF EXPERTS

4.1   Experts always owe a duty to exercise reasonable skill and care to those instructing them, and to comply with any relevant professional code of ethics. However when they are instructed to give or prepare evidence for the purpose of civil proceedings in England and Wales they have an overriding duty to help the court on matters within their expertise (CPR 35.3). This duty overrides any obligation to the person instructing or paying them. Experts must not serve the exclusive interest of those who retain them.

4.2   Experts should be aware of the overriding objective that courts deal with cases justly. This includes dealing with cases proportionately, expeditiously and fairly (CPR 1.1). Experts are under an obligation to assist the court so as to enable them to deal with cases in accordance with the overriding objective. However the overriding objective does not impose on experts any duty to act as mediators between the parties or require them to trespass on the role of the court in deciding facts.

4.3   Experts should provide opinions which are independent, regardless of the pressures of litigation. In this context, a useful test of 'independence' is that the expert would express the same opinion if given the same instructions by an opposing party. Experts should not take it upon themselves to promote the point of view of the party instructing them or engage in the role of advocates.

4.4   Experts should confine their opinions to matters which are material to the disputes between the parties and provide opinions only in relation to matters which lie within their expertise. Experts should indicate without delay where particular questions or issues fall outside their expertise.

4.5   Experts should take into account all material facts before them at the time that they give their opinion. Their reports should set out those facts and any literature or any other material on which they have relied in forming their opinions. They should indicate if an opinion is provisional, or qualified, or where they consider that further information is required or if, for any other reason, they are not satisfied that an opinion can be expressed finally and without qualification.

4.6   Experts should inform those instructing them without delay of any change in their opinions on any material matter and the reason for it.

4.7   Experts should be aware that any failure by them to comply with the Civil Procedure Rules or court orders or any excessive delay for which they are responsible may result in the parties who instructed them being penalised in costs and even, in extreme cases, being debarred from placing the experts' evidence before the court. In[1] *Phillips v Symes* Peter Smith J held that courts may also make orders for costs (under section 51 of the Supreme Court Act 1981) directly against expert witnesses who by their evidence cause significant expense to be incurred, and do so in flagrant and reckless disregard of their duties to the Court.

5.   CONDUCT OF EXPERTS INSTRUCTED ONLY TO ADVISE

5.1   Part 35 only applies where experts are instructed to give opinions which are relied on for the purposes of court proceedings. Advice which the parties do not

---

[1] *Phillips v Symes* [2004] EWHC 2330 (Ch)

intend to adduce in litigation is likely to be confidential; the Protocol does not apply in these circumstances [1] [2].

5.2   The same applies where, after the commencement of proceedings, experts are instructed only to advise (e.g. to comment upon a single joint expert's report) and not to give or prepare evidence for use in the proceedings.

5.3   However this Protocol does apply if experts who were formerly instructed only to advise are later instructed to give or prepare evidence for the purpose of civil proceedings.

6.   THE NEED FOR EXPERTS

6.1   Those intending to instruct experts to give or prepare evidence for the purpose of civil proceedings should consider whether expert evidence is appropriate, taking account of the principles set out in CPR Parts 1 and 35, and in particular whether:

(a)   it is relevant to a matter which is in dispute between the parties.
(b)   it is reasonably required to resolve the proceedings (CPR 35.1);
(c)   the expert has expertise relevant to the issue on which an opinion is sought;
(d)   the expert has the experience, expertise and training appropriate to the value, complexity and importance of the case; and whether
(e)   these objects can be achieved by the appointment of a single joint expert (see section 17 below).

6.2   Although the court's permission is not generally required to instruct an expert, the court's permission is required before experts can be called to give evidence or their evidence can be put in (CPR 35.4).

7.   THE APPOINTMENT OF EXPERTS

7.1   Before experts are formally instructed or the court's permission to appoint named experts is sought, the following should be established:

(a)   that they have the appropriate expertise and experience;
(b)   that they are familiar with the general duties of an expert;
(c)   that they can produce a report, deal with questions and have discussions with other experts within a reasonable time and at a cost proportionate to the matters in issue;
(d)   a description of the work required;
(e)   whether they are available to attend the trial, if attendance is required; and
(f)   there is no potential conflict of interest.

---

[1] *Carlson v Townsend* [2001] 1 WLR 2415
[2] *Jackson v Marley Davenport* [2004] 1 WLR 2926

7.2   Terms of appointment should be agreed at the outset and should normally include:

(a)   the capacity in which the expert is to be appointed (e.g. party appointed expert, single joint expert or expert advisor);

(b)   the services required of the expert (e.g. provision of expert's report, answering questions in writing, attendance at meetings and attendance at court);

(c)   time for delivery of the report;

(d)   the basis of the expert's charges (either daily or hourly rates and an estimate of the time likely to be required, or a total fee for the services);

(e)   travelling expenses and disbursements;

(f)   cancellation charges;

(g)   any fees for attending court;

(h)   time for making the payment; and

(i)   whether fees are to be paid by a third party.

(j)   if a party is publicly funded, whether or not the expert's charges will be subject to assessment by a costs officer.

7.3   As to the appointment of single joint experts, see section 17 below.

7.4   When necessary, arrangements should be made for dealing with questions to experts and discussions between experts, including any directions given by the court, and provision should be made for the cost of this work.

7.5   Experts should be informed regularly about deadlines for all matters concerning them. Those instructing experts should promptly send them copies of all court orders and directions which may affect the preparation of their reports or any other matters concerning their obligations.

Conditional and Contingency Fees

7.6   Payments contingent upon the nature of the expert evidence given in legal proceedings, or upon the outcome of a case, must not be offered or accepted. To do so would contravene experts' overriding duty to the court and compromise their duty of independence.

7.7   Agreement to delay payment of experts' fees until after the conclusion of cases is permissible as long as the amount of the fee does not depend on the outcome of the case.

8.   INSTRUCTIONS

8.1   Those instructing experts should ensure that they give clear instructions, including the following:

(a)   basic information, such as names, addresses, telephone numbers, dates of birth and dates of incidents;

(b)   the nature and extent of the expertise which is called for;

(c)   the purpose of requesting the advice or report, a description of the matter(s) to be investigated, the principal known issues and the identity of all parties;

(d)   the statement(s) of case (if any), those documents which form part of standard disclosure and witness statements which are relevant to the advice or report;

(e)   where proceedings have not been started, whether proceedings are being contemplated and, if so, whether the expert is asked only for advice;

(f)   an outline programme, consistent with good case management and the expert's availability, for the completion and delivery of each stage of the expert's work; and

(g)   where proceedings have been started, the dates of any hearings (including any Case Management Conferences and/or Pre-Trial Reviews), the name of the court, the claim number and the track to which the claim has been allocated.

8.2   Experts who do not receive clear instructions should request clarification and may indicate that they are not prepared to act unless and until such clear instructions are received.

8.3   As to the instruction of single joint experts, see section 17 below.

9.   EXPERTS' ACCEPTANCE OF INSTRUCTIONS

9.1   Experts should confirm without delay whether or not they accept instructions. They should also inform those instructing them (whether on initial instruction or at any later stage) without delay if:

(a)   instructions are not acceptable because, for example, they require work that falls outside their expertise, impose unrealistic deadlines, or are insufficiently clear;

(b)   they consider that instructions are or have become insufficient to complete the work;

(c)   they become aware that they may not be able to fulfil any of the terms of appointment;

(d)   the instructions and/or work have, for any reason, placed them in conflict with their duties as an expert; or

(e)   they are not satisfied that they can comply with any orders that have been made.

9.2   Experts must neither express an opinion outside the scope of their field of expertise, nor accept any instructions to do so.

10.   WITHDRAWAL

10.1   Where experts' instructions remain incompatible with their duties, whether through incompleteness, a conflict between their duty to the court and their instructions, or for any other substantial and significant reason, they may consider withdrawing from the case. However, experts should not withdraw without first discussing the position fully with those who instruct them and considering carefully whether it would be more appropriate to make a written request for directions from the court. If experts do withdraw, they must give formal written notice to those instructing them.

11.   EXPERTS' RIGHT TO ASK COURT FOR DIRECTIONS

11.1   Experts may request directions from the court to assist them in carrying out their functions as experts. Experts should normally discuss such matters with those who instruct them before making any such request. Unless the court otherwise orders, any proposed request for directions should be copied to the party instructing the expert at least seven days before filing any request to the court, and to all other parties at least four days before filing it. (CPR 35.14).

11.2   Requests to the court for directions should be made by letter, containing.

(a)   the title of the claim;
(b)   the claim number of the case;
(c)   the name of the expert;
(d)   full details of why directions are sought; and
(e)   copies of any relevant documentation.

12.   POWER OF THE COURT TO DIRECT A PARTY TO PROVIDE INFORMATION

12.1   If experts consider that those instructing them have not provided information which they require, they may, after discussion with those instructing them and giving notice, write to the court to seek directions (CPR 35.14).

12.2   Experts and those who instruct them should also be aware of CPR 35.9. This provides that where one party has access to information which is not readily available to the other party, the court may direct the party who has access to the information to prepare, file and copy to the other party a document recording the information. If experts require such information which has not been disclosed, they should discuss the position with those instructing them without delay, so that a request for the information can be made, and, if not forthcoming, an application can be made to the court. Unless a document appears to be essential, experts should assess the cost and time involved in the production of a document and whether its provision would be proportionate in the context of the case.

13.   CONTENTS OF EXPERTS' REPORTS

13.1   The content and extent of experts' reports should be governed by the scope of their instructions and general obligations, the contents of CPR 35 and PD35 and their overriding duty to the court.

13.2   In preparing reports, experts should maintain professional objectivity and impartiality at all times.

13.3   PD 35, para 2 provides that experts' reports should be addressed to the court and gives detailed directions about the form and content of such reports. All experts and those who instruct them should ensure that they are familiar with these requirements.

13.4   Model forms of Experts' Reports are available from bodies such as the Academy of Experts or the Expert Witness Institute.

13.5   Experts' reports must contain statements that they understand their duty to the court and have complied and will continue to comply with that duty (PD35 para 2.2(9)). They must also be verified by a statement of truth. The form of the statement of truth is as follows:

> 'I confirm that insofar as the facts stated in my report are within my own knowledge I have made clear which they are and I believe them to be true, and that the opinions I have expressed represent my true and complete professional opinion.'

This wording is mandatory and must not be modified.

Qualifications

13.6   The details of experts' qualifications to be given in reports should be commensurate with the nature and complexity of the case. It may be sufficient merely to state academic and professional qualifications. However, where highly specialised expertise is called for, experts should include the detail of particular training and/or experience that qualifies them to provide that highly specialised evidence.

Tests

13.7   Where tests of a scientific or technical nature have been carried out, experts should state:

(a)   the methodology used; and
(b)   by whom the tests were undertaken and under whose supervision, summarising their respective qualifications and experience.

Reliance on the work of others

13.8 Where experts rely in their reports on literature or other material and cite the opinions of others without having verified them, they must give details of those opinions relied on. It is likely to assist the court if the qualifications of the originator(s) are also stated.

Facts

13.9   When addressing questions of fact and opinion, experts should keep the two separate and discrete.

13.10 Experts must state those facts (whether assumed or otherwise) upon which their opinions are based. They must distinguish clearly between those facts which experts know to be true and those facts which they assume.

13.11 Where there are material facts in dispute experts should express separate opinions on each hypothesis put forward. They should not express a view in favour of one or other disputed version of the facts unless, as a result of particular expertise and experience, they consider one set of facts as being improbable or less probable, in which case they may express that view, and should give reasons for holding it.

Range of opinion

13.12 If the mandatory summary of the range of opinion is based on published sources, experts should explain those sources and, where appropriate, state the qualifications of the originator(s) of the opinions from which they differ, particularly if such opinions represent a well-established school of thought.

13.13 Where there is no available source for the range of opinion, experts may need to express opinions on what they believe to be the range which other experts would arrive at if asked. In those circumstances, experts should make it clear that the range that they summarise is based on their own judgement and explain the basis of that judgement.

Conclusions

13.14 A summary of conclusions is mandatory. The summary should be at the end of the report after all the reasoning. There may be cases, however, where the benefit to the court is heightened by placing a short summary at the beginning of the report whilst giving the full conclusions at the end. For example, it can assist with the comprehension of the analysis and with the absorption of the detailed facts if the court is told at the outset of the direction in which the report's logic will flow in cases involving highly complex matters which fall outside the general knowledge of the court.

Basis of report: material instructions

13.15 The mandatory statement of the substance of all material instructions should not be incomplete or otherwise tend to mislead. The imperative is transparency. The term 'instructions' includes all material which solicitors place in front of experts in order to gain advice. The omission from the statement of 'off-the-record' oral instructions is not permitted. Courts may allow cross-examination about the instructions if there are reasonable grounds to consider that the statement may be inaccurate or incomplete.

14.   AFTER RECEIPT OF EXPERTS' REPORTS

14.1 Following the receipt of experts' reports, those instructing them should advise the experts as soon as reasonably practicable whether, and if so when, the report will be disclosed to other parties; and, if so disclosed, the date of actual disclosure.

14.2 If experts' reports are to be relied upon, and if experts are to give oral evidence, those instructing them should give the experts the opportunity to consider and comment upon other reports within their area of expertise and which deal with relevant issues at the earliest opportunity.

14.3 Those instructing experts should keep experts informed of the progress of cases, including amendments to statements of case relevant to experts' opinion.

14.4 If those instructing experts become aware of material changes in circumstances or that relevant information within their control was not previously provided to experts, they should without delay instruct experts to review, and if necessary, update the contents of their reports.

15.   AMENDMENT OF REPORTS

15.1 It may become necessary for experts to amend their reports:

(a)   as a result of an exchange of questions and answers;
(b)   following agreements reached at meetings between experts; or
(c)   where further evidence or documentation is disclosed.

15.2 Experts should not be asked to, and should not, amend, expand or alter any parts of reports in a manner which distorts their true opinion, but may be invited to amend or expand reports to ensure accuracy, internal consistency, completeness and relevance to the issues and clarity. Although experts should generally follow the recommendations of solicitors with regard to the form of reports, they should form their own independent views as to the opinions and contents expressed in their reports and exclude any suggestions which do not accord with their views.

15.3   Where experts change their opinion following a meeting of experts, a simple signed and dated addendum or memorandum to that effect is generally sufficient. In some cases, however, the benefit to the court of having an amended report may justify the cost of making the amendment.

15.4   Where experts significantly alter their opinion, as a result of new evidence or because evidence on which they relied has become unreliable, or for any other reason, they should amend their reports to reflect that fact. Amended reports should include reasons for amendments. In such circumstances those instructing experts should inform other parties as soon as possible of any change of opinion.

15.5   When experts intend to amend their reports, they should inform those instructing them without delay and give reasons. They should provide the amended version (or an addendum or memorandum) clearly marked as such as quickly as possible.

16.   WRITTEN QUESTIONS TO EXPERTS

16.1   The procedure for putting written questions to experts (CPR 35.6) is intended to facilitate the clarification of opinions and issues after experts' reports have been served. Experts have a duty to provide answers to questions properly put. Where they fail to do so, the court may impose sanctions against the party instructing the expert, and, if, there is continued non-compliance, debar a party from relying on the report. Experts should copy their answers to those instructing them.

16.2   Experts' answers to questions automatically become part of their reports. They are covered by the statement of truth and form part of the expert evidence.

16.3   Where experts believe that questions put are not properly directed to the clarification of the report, or are disproportionate, or have been asked out of time, they should discuss the questions with those instructing them and, if appropriate, those asking the questions. Attempts should be made to resolve such problems without the need for an application to the court for directions.

Written requests for directions in relation to questions

16.4   If those instructing experts do not apply to the court in respect of questions, but experts still believe that questions are improper or out of time, experts may file written requests with the court for directions to assist in carrying out their functions as experts (CPR 35.14). See Section 11 above.

17.   SINGLE JOINT EXPERTS

17.1   CPR 35 and PD35 deal extensively with the instruction and use of joint experts by the parties and the powers of the court to order their use (see CPR 35.7 and 35.8, PD35, para 5).

17.2   The Civil Procedure Rules encourage the use of joint experts. Wherever possible a joint report should be obtained. Consideration should therefore be given by all parties to the appointment of single joint experts in all cases where a court might direct such an appointment. Single joint experts are the norm in cases allocated to the small claims track and the fast track.

17.3   Where, in the early stages of a dispute, examinations, investigations, tests, site inspections, experiments, preparation of photographs, plans or other similar preliminary expert tasks are necessary, consideration should be given to the instruction of a single joint expert, especially where such matters are not, at that stage, expected to be contentious as between the parties. The objective of such an appointment should be to agree or to narrow issues.

17.5   Experts who have previously advised a party (whether in the same case or otherwise) should only be proposed as single joint experts if other parties are given all relevant information about the previous involvement.

17.6   The appointment of a single joint expert does not prevent parties from instructing their own experts to advise (but the costs of such expert advisers may not be recoverable in the case).

Joint instructions

17.7   The parties should try to agree joint instructions to single joint experts, but, in default of agreement, each party may give instructions. In particular, all parties should try to agree what documents should be included with instructions and what assumptions single joint experts should make.

17.8   Where the parties fail to agree joint instructions, they should try to agree where the areas of disagreement lie and their instructions should make this clear. If separate instructions are given, they should be copied at the same time to the other instructing parties.

17.9   Where experts are instructed by two or more parties, the terms of appointment should, unless the court has directed otherwise, or the parties have agreed otherwise, include:

(a)   a statement that all the instructing parties are jointly and severally liable to pay the experts' fees and, accordingly, that experts' invoices should be sent simultaneously to all instructing parties or their solicitors (as appropriate); and

(b)   a statement as to whether any order has been made limiting the amount of experts' fees and expenses (CPR 35.8(4)(a)).

17.10 Where instructions have not been received by the expert from one or more of the instructing parties the expert should give notice (normally at least 7 days) of a deadline to all instructing parties for the receipt by the expert of such instructions. Unless the instructions are received within the deadline the expert may begin work. In the event that instructions are received after the deadline but before the signing off of the report the expert should consider whether it is practicable to comply with those instructions without adversely affecting the timetable set for delivery of the report and in such a manner as to comply with the proportionality principle. An expert who decides to issue a report without taking into account instructions received after the deadline should inform the parties who may apply to the court for directions. In either event the report must show clearly that the expert did not receive instructions within the deadline, or, as the case may be, at all.

Conduct of the single joint expert

17.11 Single joint experts should keep all instructing parties informed of any material steps that they may be taking by, for example, copying all correspondence to those instructing them.

17.12 Single joint experts are Part 35 experts and so have an overriding duty to the court. They are the parties' appointed experts and therefore owe an equal duty to all parties. They should maintain independence, impartiality and transparency at all times.

17.13 Single joint experts should not attend any meeting or conference which is not a joint one, unless all the parties have agreed in writing or the court has directed that such a meeting may be held [1] and who is to pay the experts' fees for the meeting.

17.14 Single joint experts may request directions from the court – see Section 11 above.

17.15 Single joint experts should serve their reports simultaneously on all instructing parties. They should provide a single report even though they may have received instructions which contain areas of conflicting fact or allegation. If conflicting instructions lead to different opinions (for example, because the instructions require experts to make different assumptions of fact), reports may need to contain more than one set of opinions on any issue. It is for the court to determine the facts.

Cross-examination

17.16 Single joint experts do not normally give oral evidence at trial but if they do, all parties may cross-examine them. In general written questions (CPR 35.6) should be put to single joint experts before requests are made for them to attend court for the purpose of cross-examination [2].

---

[1] *Peet v Mid Kent Area Healthcare NHS Trust* [2002] 1 WLR 210
[2] *Daniels v Walker* [2000] 1 WLR 1382

18. DISCUSSIONS BETWEEN EXPERTS

18.1   The court has powers to direct discussions between experts for the purposes set out in the Rules (CPR 35.12). Parties may also agree that discussions take place between their experts.

18.2   Where single joint experts have been instructed but parties have, with the permission of the court, instructed their own additional Part 35 experts, there may, if the court so orders or the parties agree, be discussions between the single joint experts and the additional Part 35 experts. Such discussions should be confined to those matters within the remit of the additional Part 35 experts or as ordered by the court.

18.3   The purpose of discussions between experts should be, wherever possible, to:

(a)   identify and discuss the expert issues in the proceedings;
(b)   reach agreed opinions on those issues, and, if that is not possible, to narrow the issues in the case;
(c)   identify those issues on which they agree and disagree and summarise their reasons for disagreement on any issue; and
(d)   identify what action, if any, may be taken to resolve any of the outstanding issues between the parties.

Arrangements for discussions between experts

18.4   Arrangements for discussions between experts should be proportionate to the value of cases. In small claims and fast-track cases there should not normally be meetings between experts. Where discussion is justified in such cases, telephone discussion or an exchange of letters should, in the interests of proportionality, usually suffice. In multi-track cases, discussion may be face to face, but the practicalities or the proportionality principle may require discussions to be by telephone or video conference.

18.5   The parties, their lawyers and experts should co-operate to produce the agenda for any discussion between experts, although primary responsibility for preparation of the agenda should normally lie with the parties' solicitors.

18.6   The agenda should indicate what matters have been agreed and summarise concisely those which are in issue. It is often helpful for it to include questions to be answered by the experts. If agreement cannot be reached promptly or a party is unrepresented, the court may give directions for the drawing up of the agenda. The agenda should be circulated to experts and those instructing them to allow sufficient time for the experts to prepare for the discussion.

18.7   Those instructing experts must not instruct experts to avoid reaching agreement (or to defer doing so) on any matter within the experts' competence. Experts are not permitted to accept such instructions.

18.8   The parties' lawyers may only be present at discussions between experts if all the parties agree or the court so orders. If lawyers do attend, they should not normally intervene except to answer questions put to them by the experts or to advise about the law [1].

18.9   The content of discussions between experts should not be referred to at trial unless the parties agree (CPR 35.12(4)). It is good practice for any such agreement to be in writing.

18.10 At the conclusion of any discussion between experts, a statement should be prepared setting out:

(a)   a list of issues that have been agreed, including, in each instance, the basis of agreement;
(b)   a list of issues that have not been agreed, including, in each instance, the basis of disagreement;
(c)   a list of any further issues that have arisen that were not included in the original agenda for discussion;
(d)   a record of further action, if any, to be taken or recommended, including as appropriate the holding of further discussions between experts.

18.11 The statement should be agreed and signed by all the parties to the discussion as soon as may be practicable.

18.12 Agreements between experts during discussions do not bind the parties unless the parties expressly agree to be bound by the agreement (CPR 35.12(5)). However, in view of the overriding objective, parties should give careful consideration before refusing to be bound by such an agreement and be able to explain their refusal should it become relevant to the issue of costs.

19.   ATTENDANCE OF EXPERTS AT COURT

19.1   Experts instructed in cases have an obligation to attend court if called upon to do so and accordingly should ensure that those instructing them are always aware of their dates to be avoided and take all reasonable steps to be available.

19.2   Those instructing experts should:

(a)   ascertain the availability of experts before trial dates are fixed;
(b)   keep experts updated with timetables (including the dates and times experts are to attend) and the location of the court;
(c)   give consideration, where appropriate, to experts giving evidence via a video-link.
(d)   inform experts immediately if trial dates are vacated.

---

[1] *Hubbard v Lambeth, Southwark and Lewisham HA* [2001] EWCA 1455.

19.3   Experts should normally attend court without the need for the service of witness summonses, but on occasion they may be served to require attendance (CPR 34). The use of witness summonses does not affect the contractual or other obligations of the parties to pay experts' fees.

Index